DAVID BARROWS

CRIMINOLOGY

CRIMINOLOGY

Gresham M. Sykes
University of Virginia

Under the General Editorship of
Robert K. Merton
Columbia University

HARCOURT BRACE JOVANOVICH, PUBLISHERS
San Diego   New York   Chicago   Atlanta   Washington, D.C.
London   Sydney   Toronto

Cover: Original collage by Gresham M. Sykes

ISBN: 0-15-516120-2
Library of Congress Catalog Card Number: 77-92248
Printed in the United States of America

Preface

In the last several decades crime has emerged as one of the most important areas of study in the social sciences. In part, this has been due to the great increase in public concern with criminal behavior as rates of murder, robbery, rape, assault, burglary, and larceny have shot upward. Of no less importance, however, is the fact that the meaning of crime—and the meaning of reactions to crime—has changed.

Crime often used to be seen as a pathological form of behavior rooted in such pathological social conditions as the slum, poverty, or the broken family. As for reactions to crime, interest was likely to center on finding the most effective means of controlling crime, within the framework of the existing laws of criminal procedure, or of rehabilitating the individual offender. This viewpoint persists and continues to influence much of the research in criminology, as well as the formation of public policy. But there are now many social scientists who question what precisely is meant by crime as a form of pathology, even while recognizing that much of society finds many forms of crime undesirable. Crime, it is pointed out, is found throughout the stratification system and is not the exclusive product of poverty and its attendant deprivations. Reactions to crime may be no less important a political and social issue than the problem of the crime that is to be controlled. Much behavior is labeled crime by the law without a clear rationale, and enforcement of the criminal law can be used as a means of political suppression.

The study of crime, in other words, has grown more complex and the subject matter has become of greater interest to a greater number of people. In addition to the concern with crime as a pressing social problem, there is now a concern with crime as a political issue of profound importance for a democratic society. Furthermore, many social scientists are interested in crime as a form of deviance that is to be fitted into a comprehensive theory of social behavior.

These diverse views of criminology have made it increasingly difficult to achieve the objectivity that is implied by the term *social science* and that is supposed to distinguish sociology from other approaches to social behavior—the judgments of the moral philosopher or the social reformer, let us say, or the imaginative creations of the novelist. There are, of course, many sociologists today who say that objectivity is impossible in the examination of society, that value judgments are inevitable in such an enterprise, and that the teacher must take a stand on issues arising in the formation of public policy. These questions are not to be resolved here, although I would agree that value judgments permeate almost all aspects of the social sciences. (But I also think that much of the insistence in recent years that values cannot be divorced from sociology and that social scientists must declare their political beliefs turns out to be a kind of moral posturing in which the writer claims virtue by loudly announcing a commitment to *liberté, égalité, et fraternité.*) I believe that the task of criminology—and that of the teacher of criminology—is to try to develop a reasoned analysis of social reality and not to impose *ex cathedra* preferences for one particular social policy rather than another. When the person engages in social action, that is another matter, for then a great variety of moral and political decisions must come to the fore.

The growth of criminology in the last several decades, in terms of articles and books published, research projects undertaken, and symposia held, has carried another problem in its train—the increasing difficulty of keeping up with the field. There are some writers, I think, who would argue that it cannot be done, that the day of the comprehensive treatise by a single author is past. This is probably true in some sense, but the attempt continues to offer a stimulating challenge. Only by continuing to search for a coherent, unified perspective can we understand the significance of the parts. In any event, I have tried to present here a broad, balanced picture of criminology—one that is fair both to the many intellectual orientations of those who study crime and to the great variety of the subject matter, and one that is relatively free of sociological jargon, since I think that sociology, along with other social sciences, is beginning to choke to death on its own language.

The book is divided into five parts. Part 1, "The Content of Criminology," deals with the history of the discipline, the reasons for studying crime, and how crime is defined. My purpose is to show how criminology is bound by the limitations of time and place and to convey the fascination exerted by the study of crime as an effort to solve a persistent puzzle in social behavior. The chapter on the nature of crime is concerned with various explanations of why the state declares certain forms of behavior criminal and with the extent to which the criminal law can be viewed as an instrument of exploitation rather than as an expression of a shared morality. In this area there is much argument at present, and political commitments are no less important than scientific judgments.

Part 2, "Breaking the Law," includes analyses of property rights and wrongs, crimes of violence, sexual offenses, the illegal use of drugs, gambling (along with a discussion of whether the Mafia is a myth), and political crime. Governmental lawlessness has received more and more attention in criminology since the middle of the 1960s, and my intention is to show why it is important to the field and why accurate judgments in this area are difficult.

Part 3, "The Causes of Crime," covers both sociological and social psychological theories. Some writers today think the search for the causes of crime is a waste of time. I think they are mistaken, although it is true that we still know very little about why crime occurs. In any event, this section of the text attempts to bring many diverse ideas about crime causation together in a coherent fashion in order to show how they have changed and developed. Two important themes are apparent. First, the criminal is increasingly seen to be much like the noncriminal in terms of values, attitudes, and so on. Second, any true understanding of criminal behavior must depend on many disciplines—on the viewpoints of psychology and anthropology, for example, as well as sociology. We may be able to discover the causes of crime, but I think it is now clear that they will not take the form of a mechanical determinism.

Part 4, "The State Versus the Accused," is concerned with criminal procedure, the police, and the criminal court. The central issue here is how the protection of society can and should be balanced against the protection of the suspected offender's legal rights, in an urban, industrial society in which the flood of cases threatens to overwhelm the legal system. I have tried to show that fear of the oppressive state has long been a part of American political traditions; the problem emerges clearly as we examine how the law is supposed to separate the guilty from the innocent and what happens in reality.

Part 5, "Social Reactions to Criminal Behavior," considers how society reacts to those people labeled criminal—and here, perhaps more than in any other section, the tragedy and waste of crime for the criminal as well as for the victim come to the fore. The chapter on crime and punishment traces the history of punishment from early English society to the present and examines the various rationales and justifications for punishment that have been offered. The aim is to make clear how the ideal of rehabilitation, which a short time ago was thought to represent an enlightened alternative to retribution and deterrence, is now in disarray. The whole question of the proper relationship between crime and punishment is, in fact, being reexamined. The chapter on prisons is concerned with those curious worlds that come into existence when human beings are confined en masse under conditions of great deprivation. Recent research—particularly on prisons for women and on the development of political movements within custodial institutions—has greatly enlarged our understanding of prison life and has raised important questions about the meaning of imprisonment today. The chapter on probation, parole, and the Therapeutic State examines correctional efforts in the community, pointing out that most convicted offenders are now in the community rather than behind walls. In this area, too, a demonstrated effectiveness in terms of rehabilitation is lacking, and one result has been a growing interest in new techniques for reforming the offender, such as chemotherapy and operant conditioning. These techniques, which can be seen as part of what has been called the Therapeutic State, appear to hold as much threat as promise. The final chapter looks at current trends in society's reactions to crime, including stricter enforcement of the criminal law, decriminalization and diversion, and programs of prevention; it concludes with a brief discussion of the future of crime in the United States.

This book, then, is more or less customary in form. Its special contribution, I hope, lies in its content. I think a textbook should be clear, fair, coherent, comprehensive, and stimulating. The judgment of whether this book succeeds in achieving these qualities is best left to the reader.

Writing this textbook has given me the opportunity to thank the many people who have helped me to understand something of the nature of crime and its place in society. My instructors at Princeton and Northwestern universities who later became colleagues and friends—Paul Hatt, Melvin Tumin, Harry Bredemeier, Ed Devereux, Wilbert Moore, Bob Winch, and Kimball Young—were particularly helpful. Other colleagues to whom I owe thanks are Tom Shaffer, Karl Schuessler, Don Cressey, Lloyd McCorkle, Aaron Cicourel, John Kitsuse, Arnold Sagalyn, Sol Tannenbaum, Bob Yegge, Leonard Davies, Bob Sulnick, Jackson Toby, Lloyd Ohlin, Larry Tiffany, Dick Means, Lyle Shannon, and John Stratton.

In addition, I would like to express my appreciation for the time and effort of many who helped in bringing this book to completion. Albert J. Cohen, Gary T. Marx, Albert J. Reiss, Jr., Richard D. Schwartz, James F. Short, Jr., and Marvin E. Wolfgang all provided invaluable criticisms of the manuscript, and I will always be grateful to Charles Murdter, Ann Stein, Lorraine Cote, and Joycelyn Smith at the University of Virginia for their work. Helen Faye, Judith Greissman, Elizabeth Holland, Susan Joseph, Nancy Kirsh, Lois Paster, Kenzi Sugihara, and Abigail Winograd at Harcourt Brace Jovanovich provided unfailing support and assistance.

I have saved for last the names of two whose criticisms, comments, and suggestions were so helpful that I have come to a new appreciation of the word *colleague*. Sheldon L. Messinger was generous beyond measure with his knowledge of criminology, and he continually helped to keep me aware of the ideological nuances of the issues in the field. Robert K. Merton, in his enthusiasm for the enterprise, served as a constant source of encouragement. He was of the greatest possible help in spotting logical pratfalls and infelicities of phrasing in the manuscript and in urging me to come to grips with the theoretical implications of the material. I owe these people much, and I welcome this opportunity to express my indebtedness.

Gresham M. Sykes

Contents

CRIMINOLOGY

Part 1

The Content
of Criminology

FAMILY OF SIX MURDERED

Bank Loss Set at $1 Million— Robbers Escape

Youth Convicted on Marijuana Charge—
One-Tenth of an Ounce Found in Pocket

1500 PROSTITUTES ARRESTED IN CONVENTION CLEANUP

Price Fixers Indicted

Rapist Caught in Subway

EMBEZZLEMENT IN STATE FUNDS

Skid-Row Alcoholics: A Growing Problem

Boys 12 and 14 Held after Mugging of 103-year-old Brooklyn Woman

Headlines like these give daily expression to people's concern with criminal behavior. In trying to understand such behavior, we need to start with the fact that crimes are acts prohibited and punished by the state. Why does the state intervene with regard to some acts but not to others? The attempt to answer this question provides much of the content of modern criminology, along with the study of the causes of crime, the administration of criminal law, and the prevention of criminal behavior.

The designation of murder, rape, robbery, burglary, assault, and larceny as crimes is undoubtedly accepted by most people in American society. A great variety of other forms of behavior, however, may also be declared crimes by the state, including gambling, prostitution, the use of drugs, public drunkenness, homosexuality, and sedition—and their criminal status is a matter of intense debate.

Some legal commentators see the criminal law as an instrument—admittedly flawed—for the maintenance of a shared vision of order. Other writers, far more skeptical about the rightfulness of the present form of American society, are inclined to view the criminal law as an instrument of oppression to make the many conform to the rules of the few. These opposing perspectives on the criminal law have been part of criminology since the beginning of the discipline in the eighteenth century. In the 1960s, however, the two viewpoints began to be advanced with a special vehemence, and the argument between them promises to pervade criminology for many years to come. The debate transcends questions of scientific fact, for values are frequently involved in fundamental disagreements such as those about the nature of society, the role of law, and the place of the social sciences. Because the controversy influences much of the research and theorizing in criminology today, we must keep the two positions in mind if we are to understand current approaches to the study of crime.

Chapter 1
The Study of Crime

Modern criminology is the study of the social origins of criminal law, the administration of criminal justice, the causes of criminal behavior, and the prevention and control of crime, including individual rehabilitation and modification of the social environment.

This diverse subject matter means that criminology must draw on many disciplines for theory and data. In the United States criminology is generally encountered as a specialty in the field of sociology, yet criminology has depended upon psychology, criminal jurisprudence, political science, public administration, history, and anthropology for much of its substance. The variety of contributions is a source of both strength and weakness. An interdisciplinary viewpoint gives breadth to an understanding of the subject—as it does to that of any major segment of human activity—but the mixture of many disparate elements has made it difficult to develop a unified approach to the study of crime.

Criminology, like other areas of academic study, has changed and developed over the years, for reasons that go beyond the accumulation of empirical evidence and the construction of logically consistent theory. Historical events, social problems, and general intellectual climates have also helped to shape the field. Criminology, in other words, is not an autonomous body of thought, growing in a vacuum or moving along some line of scientific progress under the sway of pure reason. Changes in the understanding of crime are linked to changes in the society in which the study of crime is embedded.

Social change influences an academic enterprise like criminology in a number of ways. The choice of new lines of inquiry is often a product of pressing social concerns. The sudden interest in political crime in the 1960s and 1970s, for example, reflects a period of intense political conflict and government scandals. The people drawn to a field of study, bringing with them distinctive interests and modes of interpretation, are likely to be motivated in part by their involvement in the social problems of the age. The resources society is willing to allot to a particular avenue of study—and resources play a large part in shaping the type and amount of knowledge in a particular area—are greatly influenced by what those in positions of power see as the immediate needs of public policy. (This textbook will sometimes speak of society, criminology, and similar abstractions as if they were persons, with attitudes, sentiments, and the like. The usage is convenient, for it often helps to avoid a cumbersome phrasing, but such reifications can be misleading if we forget they are simply a figure of speech.) The funding of research on rehabilitation in the community, for example, has been tied closely to the increasing use of probation and parole rather than imprisonment. Finally, the way in which knowledge is used by society also leaves its mark, for theory must be modified as application reveals new gaps in the framework of knowledge. For these reasons an understanding of criminology requires more than a grasp of abstract principles and a body of empirical data. We must also be aware of the changing social context that helps to determine theoretical explanations, the major lines of investigation, and what is believed to be possible in controlling human behavior. In studying crime we must realize that scientific findings, commonly perceived as impersonal and objective, must always carry the stamp of their time and place.[1]

In this chapter, we will be concerned with the changes in criminology and its social context over the years (particularly in the last decade or so), the reasons for studying criminology, and the relationships between criminology and the allied disciplines of psychiatry and criminal jurisprudence, which are sometimes viewed as having a special claim on the interpretation of crime.

The History of Criminology

Tracing the development of criminology is more than a matter of historical interest. Some ideas from the past continue to provide the framework for current thinking in the field. Some ideas, long since rejected by criminologists, still influence popular thought. Bits and pieces of older theories continue to float to the surface, like debris from a sunken ship; and some formulations, now abandoned, warrant reexamination. Moreover, an awareness of how ideas grow, come to dominate a field, and then decay helps to keep us skeptical of current theoretical explanations as the final word. In other areas of sociological thought, such as those concerning social class, community life, the social roles of men and women, and economic progress, we have come to realize that we need to

---

[1] See Robert K. Merton, *Social Theory and Social Structure* (New York: The Free Press, 1968), Chapter XIV.

understand how existing theories developed if we are to assess the conventional wisdom. The need is no less acute in the field of criminology.

The Eighteenth Century

Although discussions about crime can be traced far into the past, the origins of criminology as a coherent body of thought are usually assigned to the eighteenth century. In a number of European countries during the 1700s, the harsh and oppressive system of justice (much of it a remnant of a feudal social order) was subjected to the rational analysis of the men of the philosophical movement known as the Enlightenment. The common use of the death penalty for trivial offenses began to be questioned; and, for the first time, the nature of the criminal law, the causes of crime, and the treatment of the criminal were examined systematically and at length. The spirit of reform crossed the Atlantic to the American colonies, where so many men and women were seeking justice as well as a means of livelihood.

One of the Enlightenment thinkers was Cesare Beccaria (1738–1794), a young Italian aristocrat who had allied himself with the Milanese intelligentsia. His brief essay, *On Crimes and Punishments,* published in 1764, aroused immediate excitement, acclaim, and controversy. To understand this high-pitched reception, notes Elio Monachesi, we must look into the condition of the criminal law at that time.[2]

In the eighteenth century, says Monachesi, the criminal law reflected an archaic social order and was "repressive, uncertain, and barbaric. Its administration permitted and encouraged incredibly arbitrary and abusive practices. The agents of the criminal law, prosecutors and judges, were allowed tremendous latitude in dealing with persons accused and convicted of crime, and corruption was rampant throughout continental Europe."[3] Torture to extract confessions was commonplace, sentences were wildly inconsistent, and equality before the law existed neither in principle nor in practice.

In the eyes of Cesare Beccaria, the system was savage, stupid, and ineffective; and other men of the Enlightenment, looking for a rational form of society to suit a mankind viewed as rational by nature, were quick to agree. It was a time of ethical ferment, preparing the way for the French Revolution (1789) that would topple the *ancien régime,* and Beccaria's hurriedly written tract (it was completed in less than eight months with the aid of a band of like-minded iconoclasts) found an appreciative audience.[4] "It was soon realized," notes one historian, "that Beccaria

[2] See Monachesi, "Cesare Beccaria," in Hermann Mannheim, ed., *Pioneers in Criminology* (Montclair, N.J.: Patterson Smith, 1972), pp. 36–50.

[3] Ibid., p. 38.

[4] Beccaria's treatise was quoted by John Adams as early as 1770 in defense of the British soldiers implicated in the Boston Massacre. See David J. Rothman, *The Discovery of the Asylum* (Boston: Little, Brown, 1971), p. 59.

had really wished to respond not only to the need to humanize and improve the law, but that his thought was directed at the very center of society."[5] Equality before the law, the control of governmental actions, the right of a people to shape their institutions by deliberate, rational choice rather than by passively accepting tradition—these ideas interested Beccaria no less than the humane and rational treatment of the convicted felon.

Although there were writers who did not like the style of the essay (Giuseppe Baretti, a literary critic and friend of Samuel Johnson's, described it as a "wretched little thing, bastardly written"), the needed reforms were set forth succinctly:

The criminal law should be clear, so that all could know and understand it.

Torture to obtain confessions should be abolished.

Judges should be impartial, and the sovereign who makes the law should not determine guilt or innocence.

The accused should be allotted the time and resources necessary for his defense.

The death penalty should be abolished.

Secret accusations and royal warrants for the imprisonment of people without trial should be done away with.

Punishment should be quick, certain, and commensurate with the crime.

The true measure of crime should be the harm done to the rights and liberties of individuals in society, rather than vague standards of moral virtue.

In conclusion, said Beccaria, "from what has thus been demonstrated one may deduce a general theorem of considerable utility, though hardly conformable with custom, the usual legislator of nations; it is this: *In order for punishment not to be, in every instance, an act of violence of one or many against a private citizen, it must be essentially public, prompt, necessary, the least possible in the given circumstances, proportionate to the crime, dictated by laws.*"[6] If today the conclusion seems obvious to us, we must recognize that Cesare Beccaria first opened people's eyes.

Beccaria's ideas form the core of what is called the classical school in criminology, and legal philosophers and social reformers such as Jeremy

---

[5] Franco Venturi, *Utopia and Reform in the Enlightenment* (Cambridge, England: Cambridge University Press, 1971), p. 106.

[6] Cesare Beccaria, *On Crimes and Punishments,* trans. Henry Paolucci (New York: Bobbs-Merrill, 1963), p. 99.

Bentham (1748–1832) and Sir Samuel Romilly (1757–1818) played a major part in developing these ideas and forcing them upon the attention of the English legal system, which in turn helped to shape the criminal law in emerging American society. All human motivation, said Bentham, can be reduced to a simple formula: the pursuit of pleasure and the avoidance of pain. The purpose of the criminal law is to make sure that if an individual contemplates a criminal act, he will be convinced that the pain will outweigh the pleasure and avoid such a bad bargain. Punishments involving great brutality are unsatisfactory, said Bentham, because they produce more pain than is necessary; we should never use a preventive means of a nature to do more evil than the offense to be prevented.[7] Romilly, less dedicated to fine logical distinctions, devoted himself to fighting for reform in Parliament. He managed to secure the abolition of the death penalty for stealing and for traveling without a pass in the case of soldiers and sailors.[8]

The picture of human motivation that provided much of the rationale for the classical school in criminology now seems much too simple to social scientists. People do not methodically add and subtract conveniently quantified pains and pleasures to arrive at precise sums that determine their actions; plainly other forces are at work. But eighteenth-century thought concerning crime is not therefore to be dismissed altogether. The classical school had, and continues to have, a marked influence on the criminal law. The ideal of a humane, just, and effective legal system that controls crime with the aid of reason still beckons us along the path of legal reform.

The Nineteenth Century   In the last quarter of the 1700s many thoughtful observers were convinced that a harsh and capricious system of criminal law was a potent source of popular resentment, which in turn served as a major cause of crime. During the next fifty years, after penal codes in a number of countries had been purged of some of their more brutal aspects, crime still flourished, and the argument that bad laws made bad people seemed much less conclusive. What, then, caused crime?[9]

---

[7] Gilbert Geis, "Jeremy Bentham," in Mannheim, *Pioneers in Criminology*, pp. 51–68.

[8] Such an achievement may not seem very great, note Arthur Wood and John Waite, "considering that at the time of Romilly's death in 1818, and for years after, there remained in English statutes nearly two hundred offenses for which the death penalty was inflicted. However, by 1840 they were reduced to fourteen, and since 1861 only four crimes have been capital in England, namely, treason, murder, piracy, and setting fire to arsenals." See *Crime and Its Treatment* (New York: American Book Company, 1940), p. 458.

[9] In the United States, according to David Rothman, during the twenty years after Washington's inauguration, "Americans expected that a rational system of correction, which made punishment certain but humane, would dissuade all but a few offenders from a life of crime. . . . By the 1820's, however, these ideas had lost persuasiveness. The focus shifted to the deviant and the penitentiary, away from the legal system. Men intently scrutinized

The classical school, it was now felt, had been too concerned with laws, too beguiled by the idea of free will, too absorbed in armchair speculations. And as the Enlightenment's rather uncomplicated view of Rational Man began to fade, the nineteenth century's search for an explanation of crime took a variety of forms. Some of these efforts, as we now realize with the advantages of hindsight, were little more than bizarre fads. Phrenology, for example, tried to detect the shape of the personality in the shape of the skull. Different portions of the brain, it was argued, controlled some thirty-five traits of human behavior such as combativeness, love of children, and acquisitiveness. The strong development of particular portions would be indicated by the cranial configuration, and an expert could thus diagnose character. These speculative doctrines were widely presented to credulous audiences.[10] (Phrenology is not likely to experience a revival, but the idea that specific areas of the brain control specific types of behavior may appear again in criminology in the form of psychosurgery, which will be discussed in Chapter 14.) Other studies, standing on the threshold of modern psychology, started on the long task of analyzing the relationship between mind and behavior. In the United States, Isaac Ray (1807–1881) began his investigations in forensic psychiatry, launching a series of attacks on legal conceptions of insanity and making recommendations for the treatment of the mentally ill. Still other writers in England, France, Germany, and Belgium laid the groundwork for a sociological approach to crime. Quetelet (1796–1874), Guerry (1802–1866), and Tarde (1843–1904) were among those who developed concepts, theories, and research methods that provided a valuable first step in looking at the relationship between crime and the social environment.[11]

The publication of Darwin's *Origin of Species* in 1859 and *Descent of Man* in 1871, however, helped turn the scientific thinking of the time in quite a different direction. Evolutionary interpretations of human behavior rocketed into prominence, and in 1876 the first edition of *Delinquent Man,* by Cesare Lombroso (1836–1909), appeared. The criminal, he argued, was a throwback to a more primitive form of human being—a spectre, as it were, from the evolutionary past, marked by atavistic characteristics such as a large jaw, facial asymmetry, and ears of unusual size. These were the stigmata that branded the born criminal. With the aid of Enrico Ferri (1856–1928), Lombroso founded the positive school of crimi-

the life history of the criminal and methodically arranged the institution to house him" (*The Discovery of the Asylum,* pp. 61–62).

[10] See John D. Davies, *Phrenology: Fad and Science* (New Haven: Yale University Press, 1955).

[11] For an excellent summary of this early, much neglected body of work, see Alfred Lindesmith and Yale Levin, "The Lombrosian Myth of Criminology," *American Journal of Sociology* (July 1936–May 1937), pp. 653–71.

nology, so named because of its alleged empirical rather than speculative method; and textbooks have traditionally accorded Lombroso the title of father of criminology.

His contemporaries in other countries, however, quickly set about making a hash of his ideas and evidence. Lombroso had failed to examine noncriminals for the purpose of comparison, they said; and he had no evidence of primitive people's supposed characteristics. Lombroso modified and added to his theories in four more editions of his work, but to no avail; and in 1913 Charles Goring delivered what is generally regarded as the finishing stroke with the publication of *The English Convict*. Goring's study made a careful comparison between some 3000 English convicts and a large number of noncriminal Englishmen.[12] "We have," said Goring, "exhaustively compared, with regard to many physical characters, different kinds of criminals with each other, and criminals, as a class, with the law-abiding. . . . Our results nowhere confirm the evidence [of a physical criminal type], nor justify the allegations of criminal anthropology."[13]

Because the theories of Lombroso have been completely discredited, observe Lindesmith and Levin, it is something of a mystery that he is so often portrayed as the dominant figure in nineteenth-century criminology and that so little attention is paid to the valuable work done by others just before him who stressed the social environment as a causal factor. The explanation, they suggest, is that doctors and psychiatrists "appropriated" the field at the turn of the century, found Lombroso's general approach congenial to their intellectual background, and managed to convey a misleading impression of Lombroso's significance.[14]

This argument is not entirely convincing. Lombroso did establish a world-wide reputation during his lifetime in his attempts to place the explanation of crime on a scientific footing—even though his theories later proved to be in error. In any event, by the early years of the twentieth century the idea of physical degeneracy as a cause of crime had generally fallen from favor. The stage was now set for further developments in psychology and sociology.

[12] *The English Convict: A Statistical Study* (London: His Majesty's Stationery Office, 1913).

[13] Quoted in George B. Vold, *Theoretical Criminology* (New York: Oxford University Press, 1958), p. 58, who gives a lucid, brief summary of the debate.

[14] Lindesmith and Levin, "The Lombrosian Myth of Criminology." For a contrary viewpoint, see Thorsten Sellin's comment on "The Lombrosian Myth in Criminology," *American Journal of Sociology* 42 (May 1937), pp. 897–99. See also Marvin Wolfgang, "Cesare Lombroso," in Mannheim, ed., *Pioneers in Criminology*, pp. 168–227. "The 'spirit of Lombroso' is very much alive in some European contemporary research, especially in Italy, while in America generally Lombroso has been used as a straw man for attacks on biological analyses of criminal behavior" (p. 168).

The period immediately before and after World War I saw a flurry of interest in the relationship between intelligence and crime. The idea, in a way, was a residue from the Age of Enlightenment, for it was argued that the dull-witted simply could comprehend neither the punishments attached to illegal behavior nor the rewards linked to conformity. With the development of scales to measure intelligence (the work of Alfred Binet and Theodore Simon in 1905), it was possible to put the idea to some sort of test. An I.Q. of 75 had been set as the dividing line between normal intelligence and feeble-mindedness (on the basis of a rather dubious set of assumptions), and a number of studies indicated that by this standard a substantial proportion of imprisoned criminals were mentally deficient. However, extensive intelligence testing by the Army Psychological Corps revealed that by this standard almost one-third of the recruits for the draft were feeble-minded, a finding that made many people understandably suspicious of the definitions and procedures of the intelligence testers. In addition, more careful comparisons between prisoners and nonprisoners showed little difference between the two populations. Theories about the causal role of mental deficiency diminished in popularity.[15]

During the 1920s and 1930s, modern criminology began to emerge, showing two main currents. One explanation of criminal behavior was based, to a large extent, on the influential theories of Sigmund Freud, with crime generally interpreted as the symbolic expression of tensions and conflicts existing within the psyche of the individual. The other explanation stemmed from the work of sociologists who saw crime mainly as the result of the social environment in which the individual lived.

These two viewpoints still dominate the field today. As an academic discipline, however, American criminology has developed primarily within the domain of sociologists in most colleges and universities, and a sociological perspective has tended to crowd out other explanatory schemes; at the same time, a substantial amount of therapy and rehabilitative work in the community and in correctional institutions has remained in the hands of those with a psychiatric orientation.

The sociological and psychiatric views of crime contradict each other at a number of crucial points, and we shall return to this issue in the last part of the chapter. For the moment, however, the important point is that after World War II the bulk of research and theoretical writing in criminology was carried out by sociologists who continued to ascribe the causes of crime to the social milieu, either the one in which the individual was socialized or the one in which he or she was currently functioning. The structure of the family, the influence of delinquent peer groups,

---

[15] See Vold, *Theoretical Criminology,* Chapter 5.

the impact of the slum, the role of cultural values conducive to criminal behavior, the organization of professional criminals—these and similar topics provided the main lines of inquiry.

In summary, the development of criminology over a period of more than 200 years has not been an even, stately procession—and in this respect criminology is like any other field that calls itself a science. Its basic ideas about human nature have changed and changed again; theories have sometimes been accepted on flimsy evidence; and interdisciplinary jealousies have often bred a studied indifference to relevant data and alternative perspectives. Nonetheless, our understanding of crime has greatly increased, and we have moved far beyond the simple formulations of the past that were only a step away from folklore. Criminology has accumulated a wealth of empirical studies that are often models of acute and objective observation; and it has repeatedly challenged the conventional connections between crime and punishment that so often represent society's unthinking reaction to the deviant in its midst.

The Rise of
Critical
Criminology

Somewhere near the beginning of the 1960s—it is difficult to date such things precisely—criminology in the United States witnessed the start of an effort to transform some of its fundamental assumptions concerning criminal behavior. The theory, methods, and application of criminology have been exposed to a new scrutiny, and there seems to be little doubt that the field will be involved in an intricate controversy for some years to come. It is that controversy, its nature and its roots, with which we are now concerned.

The controversy was set into motion during the social turbulence of the 1960s, when sociology was subjected to a barrage of criticisms from a variety of sources. The attack centered on the claim—set forth in almost every introductory sociology textbook—that the discipline had largely freed itself of subjective evaluations. Heretofore, if the status of sociology as a science had not been exactly clear, few doubts had been expressed about its dedication to scientific methods and objectivity.[16] It was generally accepted that sociology did not—or should not—make value judgments. These assumptions now began to be contested.

The critics argued that sociology's claim to the cool neutrality of science—particularly in the area of sociological theory—was a sham. Sociology, they said, was still contaminated by the bias and subjectivity of particular interest groups. The interpretation of social institutions was based on false premises. The social order was not determined by consensus, as many sociologists had argued, but represented the will of a small portion of society imposed on the whole. People in positions of power

[16] See Allan Mazur, "The Littlest Science," *The American Sociologist* 3 (1968), pp. 195–200.

The New Criminology
Views the Old

One problem with conventional criminology is the general absence of historical insights in its theories. The student of criminology is presented with a history of sorts that upon scrutiny proves to be misleading, at best. Historical studies that can be found in early American criminology were written primarily by persons who were intimately concerned with the control of crime. This tradition of history written by persons whom Platt calls "scholar-technicians" is dominated by managers and spokesmen for the criminal justice system. The picture presented is of a steady march of enlightenment and reform. Almost never is this history related to sociopolitical events occurring at the time. Historical accounts of the development of social control agencies are usually descriptive, with little or no emphasis placed upon analysis and theory building. . . .

We have learned from the studies cited above that the Progressive era (roughly 1880–1920) was a critical period in that most of what we think of as the modern criminal justice system was created during this time. We are led to conclude that most of the reforms developed in this period were designed to restore social order for a wealthy white establishment that felt threatened by labor strife, urban disorder, and the possibility of its own extinction. The reform effort was designed to strengthen the existing social structure through the introduction of rational and scientific means of controlling the

"dangerous classes." From this historical perspective, the oppression of blacks, women, children, and political activists by the criminal justice system in modern America can be understood and analyzed. But serious gaps remain in our knowledge of the history of crime and social control. We still know relatively little about the development of the police. We have no accurate accounts of the treatment of blacks in Southern prison systems, nor do we as yet have a thorough understanding of the political, social, and economic factors that gave rise to social-control strategies and institutions.

Critics of the "Old" Criminology have commented on how that field has prostituted itself in serving law enforcement and criminal justice agencies. Criminological theory has fostered and disseminated the hegemonic concepts of the ruling class, and empirical criminological studies have often supplied the technology of social control that has been employed in both domestic and foreign spheres. Millions of dollars poured into criminological research by the Safe Streets and Omnibus Crime Control Act of 1967 through the LEAA have created an army of researchers who are attempting to introduce more "sophisticated" statistical techniques into court management, offender information systems, and predictions of delinquency, as well as mathematical models of riot control. Some criminologists have merged their role of researcher with the role of government consultant. And as Marvin Wolfgang has observed, when the criminologist is asked to join the "societal therapy team," he is likely to promote theories consistent with the views of those in power.

From Barry Krisberg, *Crime and Privilege: Toward a New Criminology*, © 1975, pp. 14–16. Reprinted by permission of Prentice-Hall, Inc., Englewood Cliffs, New Jersey.

were not motivated by rational decisions concerning the public good but by self-interest. Social problems did not flow from individual pathologies—an argument that helped to maintain the status quo—but from faults in the social system itself. Finally, real social change did not come about by small steps but required radical leaps.

These issues had been discussed in sociology since the turn of the century, but in the 1960s they became the focus of debates that were bitter, shot through with a variety of antagonisms (including a conflict between generations), and heavily influenced by political considerations. The debates involved a great many of the specialized fields of sociology, but they were nowhere more evident than in criminology. It became clear that a new strain of thought had entered American criminology, challenging many of its basic ideas.

Some sociologists have called this new approach radical criminology, but the term is misleading because it suggests a particular ideological underpinning that probably does not exist. Critical criminology is perhaps a better term, as long as we keep in mind that all such summary phrases can obscure as well as illuminate.[17]

Departures from standard assumptions Whatever we call the new orientation, the themes involved can be summarized roughly as follows:

First, there is a profound skepticism accorded any individualistic theory of crime causation. Not only are biological and psychological theories of personality maladjustment to be abandoned; sociological theories dependent on notions of individual defects due to inadequate socialization or peer-group pressures are also viewed with great suspicion. The question for a number of criminologists, as indicated earlier, has become why some persons and not others are stigmatized with the label of criminal, rather than what objectively determined characteristics separate the criminal from the noncriminal. "If preconceptions are to be avoided," wrote Austin Turk, "a criminal is most accurately defined as any individual who is identified as such."[18] Some writers in criminology, indeed, have pushed the idea to within a hairline of the claim that the only important reality is the act of labeling—and not because labeling overrides the difference between criminals and noncriminals, but because we all have committed criminal acts at one time or another.

Second, critical criminology is marked by a profound shift in the interpretation of motives behind the actions of the public officials dealing with crime. Many criminologists, of course, had long pointed out that

[17] See Geoff Pearson, "Misfit Sociology and the Politics of Socialization," in Ian Taylor, Paul Walton, and Jock Young, eds., *Critical Criminology* (London: Routledge & Kegan Paul, 1975), pp. 147–66.

[18] *Criminality and the Legal Order* (Chicago: Rand McNally, 1969), p. 18.

the "criminal-processing system" was often unfair—and, specifically, that the poor and members of minority groups suffered from an acute disadvantage.[19] Few criminologists, however, were willing to go so far as to claim that the system was inherently unjust. Rather, the usual explanation was that legal agencies—the police, courts, and correctional institutions—were frequently defective because of lack of funds, unenlightened policies, individual stupidity, prejudice, and corruption. The critical criminology perspective takes a different view. It interprets the operation of legal agencies either as the deliberate use of the law to maintain the status quo for those who hold the power in society, or as an activity aimed at maintaining organizations' self-interests, with "careerism" of the agency's personnel being used as both the carrot and the stick. If the system is unjust, then, it is not due to relatively minor structural flaws or random individual faults. It is because the criminal law and its enforcement are largely instruments deliberately designed for the control of one social class by another.[20]

The third theme concerns the rightfulness of the criminal law. This aspect of the law had been questioned infrequently by American criminologists, even if they were willing to admit that the application might leave something to be desired. A few areas—such as the insanity plea, the definition of juvenile delinquency, the death sentence, and the prohibition of gambling—were open to vigorous critical scrutiny, but the great bulk of the criminal law was taken as expressing a widely shared set of values. And, in any event, the rightfulness of the law was not a suitable question for the social sciences. According to the emerging critical criminology, however, the criminal law should not be viewed as the collective moral judgments of society promulgated by a government defined as legitimate by almost all people. Instead, our society is best seen as a *Gebietsverband*—a territorial group living under a regime imposed by a ruling few in the manner of a conquered province. The argument is not that murder, rape, and robbery are acceptable, but that popular attitudes toward the sanctity of property, the sanctity of the physical person, and the rather puritanical morality embedded in the law are far less uniform than American criminology has been willing to admit. In many cases the

---

[19] See Jerome H. Skolnick, *Justice Without Trial* (New York: John Wiley, 1966); see also Charles Reasons and Jack L. Kuykendall, eds., *Race, Crime, and Justice* (Pacific Palisades, Calif.: Goodyear Publishing, 1972).

[20] See for example, Jack Douglas, ed., *Crime and Justice in American Society* (New York: Bobbs-Merrill, 1971). "If there were no groups trying to control the activities of other groups," he notes in his introduction, "and capable of exercising sufficient power to try to enforce their wills upon those other groups through the legislative processes, there would be no laws making some activities 'crimes' and there could, consequently, be no 'criminals.' . . . Criminal laws are specifically enacted by the middle and upper classes to place the poorer classes under the more direct control of the police" (p. xviii).

law clearly reflects the wishes or the interests of only a portion of society.

Fourth, critical criminology questions the use of, and the assumptions about, official crime statistics. American criminologists have long been skeptical of the accuracy of these statistics, which they nonetheless accepted, reluctantly, as a major source of data for their field. The *Uniform Crime Reports* of the Federal Bureau of Investigation were, after all, the only national figures available on criminal behavior. If the use of other official statistics obtained from cities, states, and particular legal agencies were almost always coupled with disclaimers—well, they were still used.

The inaccuracy of statistics, however, was apt to be treated in a rather desultory fashion, in terms of developing a theory about the relationship between crime and society, or simply noted as one more difficulty placed in the path of securing precise data. The essential task was to get better data, either by seeing to it that official statistics became more accurate or by finding other ways to gather information about the true incidence of criminal behavior, such as sociological surveys using the reports of victims and self-reporting methods in which people are asked about their own criminal behavior. Critical criminological thought, however, does not dismiss the problem as unfortunate error. It sees the collection and dissemination of official information about the incidence of crime as an important theoretical variable in its own right. The crime rate, writes Peter Manning, is "simply a construction of police activities," and the actual amount of crime is unknown and probably unknowable.[21] Just as the legitimacy of the rules expressed in the criminal law can no longer be taken for granted, neither can the credibility of the government reporting on their violation. The most fruitful line of inquiry with regard to the causes of inaccuracy is not chance error. Instead, we are urged to look for a systematic distortion that is part of the machinery for social control.[22]

Crime and the maintenance of the status quo Critical criminology might be viewed as merely a matter of emphasis, its major themes no more than bits and pieces of the conventional wisdom of the field. The set of ideas, however, form a coherent whole that is sufficiently different from much of American criminology immediately before and after World War II to warrant the term "new." At the heart of this orientation lies the perspective of a stratified society in which the criminal law is used by those in power to control the poor and members of minority groups. According to

[21]"The Police: Mandate, Strategies, and Appearance," in Richard Quinney, ed., *Criminal Justice in America* (Boston: Little, Brown, 1974), pp. 170–200.

[22]For an excellent discussion of the problem, see Albert D. Biderman and Albert J. Reiss, Jr., "On Exploring the 'Dark Figure' of Crime," *The Annals of the American Academy of Political and Social Science* 374 (November 1967), pp. 1–15. See also Yale Kamisar, "How to Use, Abuse—And Fight Back With—Crime Statistics," *Oklahoma Law Review* 25 (May 1972), pp. 239–58.

this view, the legal apparatus enables the upper strata of society to impose their particular morality and standards of good behavior on the entire society; to protect their property and physical safety from the depredations of the have-nots, even though the cost may be high in terms of the legal rights of those perceived as a threat; and to extend the definition of illegal or criminal behavior, as needed, to encompass those who may threaten the status quo. The middle classes or the lower-middle classes are drawn into this pattern of domination, it is said, either because they are led to believe that they too have a stake in maintaining the status quo, or because they are made a part of the agencies of social control, with the rewards of organizational careers providing the inducements for keeping the poor in their place.

The coercive aspects of this arrangement are hidden, at least in part, the argument continues, by labeling those who challenge the system as "deviants" or "criminals" and thus associating them in the public mind with social pathology, psychiatric illness, or the like. If these interpretative schemes are insufficient to arouse widespread distaste for the rule breaker as bad or tainted, official statistics can serve to create a sense of a more direct and personal danger in the form of an alleged crime wave that will convince any people (including many of the people in the lower classes) that draconian measures are justified.

The poor, according to this viewpoint, may or may not break the legal rules more often than others—although they will certainly be arrested more often and treated more harshly, in order to prevent more extensive nonconformity. In any event, the poor are seen as more likely to be driven in the direction of crime because, first, the rules imposed upon them from above have little relationship to the normative prescriptions of their own subcultures; second, in a consumer society where the fruits of affluence are widely publicized, the material frustrations of the lower classes prove almost unbearable; and third, there is generated among the lower classes a deep hostility to a social order in which they are not allowed to participate fully and which they have had so little hand in shaping.

This perspective of society would seem to fit well with an ideological position on the left side of the political spectrum. While political associations may possibly account for the attention the perspective has received from criminology writers with a jaundiced view of the capitalist-industrial social order, it seems doubtful that the emergence of critical criminology can be linked neatly to a particular political stance. At the same time, it does not appear that a flood of new data has burst upon the field, requiring a new interpretation. Nor can the rise of this viewpoint be attributed to the birth of a totally new theory about crime and its causes, since the ideas involved have long been part of the discipline. But the emphasis is new, the synthesis is new, and there is a new audience. It seems likely that the emergence of critical criminology has been part of the intellectual ferment that has taken place in sociology in general and that the reception given the new perspective is an outgrowth, in part, of the social-historical forces at work in the sixties.

The impact of the 1960s Among the many social changes that have been involved, at least three appear to have had a major influence on criminological thought. The first is the Vietnam War. Although its impact on American society has yet to be assessed fully, the events of the war clearly contributed to the rise of a widespread cynicism concerning the institutions of government, the motives of those in power, and the credibility of official pronouncements. The authority of the state—including the authority of the state made manifest in law—was called into question. The good intentions—indeed, the good sense—of those running the apparatus of the state became suspect for many. And the truth of official statements, whether they be body counts or crime counts, was no longer easily accepted among many segments of the population. Revelations of clandestine military operations, misrepresentations of events, unrealistic predictions of impending victories, and questions about the legitimacy of the war itself all shook the confidence of many citizens in the American system. The notion of a social contract as the basis of government may have been long recognized as a metaphor expressing a faith in government by consent. In the 1960s, many people (including many in the social sciences) felt that the metaphor was coming apart. Government was more apt to be seen, at least by some, as manipulation and coercion, as part of a social order imposed by a ruling elite.

Second, the growth of a counterculture in the United States, the significance of which is also not yet clear, unquestionably produced a shift in values and ideas. One important theme concerned the use of drugs—particularly marijuana. The arguments for and against drugs have been repeated so often that the subject has taken on the appearance of a litany; nonetheless, it did happen that millions of people engaged in behavior they regarded as harmless but that was defined by society as a crime— and not a minor or relatively harmless breach of the law, according to the authorities, but a dangerous offense. We may not be able to identify the exact changes in popular attitudes toward the law and law enforcement agencies, but we do know that the drug issue made criminologists take a long, skeptical look at traditional ideas about the nature of the criminal and the causes of criminal behavior.

In addition, as a consumer-oriented middle class wedded to establishment values emerged as one of the counterculture's favorite targets in its analysis of what was wrong with American life, evidence of middle-class crime took on a new prominence. Far from being a form of behavior largely confined to those at the bottom of the social structure, crime was everywhere. "If you are a typical American citizen," says Erik Olin Wright, in the opening sentence of his book *The Politics of Punishment*, "chances are that in your life you have committed some crime for which you could have been sent to jail or prison."[23] If this was true, and yet the people caught up and punished by the system of criminal justice were so largely drawn from the lower classes, then the machinery of the criminal law must be far from impartial. Being labeled a criminal must involve something more than criminal behavior.

The third influential social change of the 1960s was the rise of, and reactions to, political protest. It took a variety of forms—from civil rights sit-ins at Southern lunch counters and antiwar teach-ins at Eastern universities to bloody "Black Power" confrontations in the streets. And it became clear to even the most dispassionate observer that in a number of instances the police power of the state had been used to suppress political dissent. The criminal law was seen by many as becoming more than a device for controlling run-of-the-mill criminality. It was becoming an arm of Leviathan, not as a matter of abstract theory, but as something directly experienced or immediately observed.

The intellectual climate produced by these and similar social and historical events, it can be argued, played as crucial a part in the rise of critical criminology as any forces at work within the field of traditional criminology itself. The new perspective is touched by ideology but not determined by it, incorporates points made before but builds something different, and offers a new interpretation of crime rather than a vast quantity of new data.

This discussion, of course, leaves untouched the issue of the validity of the critical perspective for the study of crime and society. There are, unfortunately, some signs that the viewpoint is occasionally accepted too easily—too uncritically—and is in danger of becoming another fad. The historical roots of many of the central ideas are often ignored. Flat declarations are frequently substituted for reasoned analysis supported by fact, and a number of crucial assertions are little more than polemics dressed up to look like scientific statements. Peter Manning, in discussing the recent studies in deviance that have been so influential in shaping critical criminology, has pointed to the "vulgarization and politicization of ideas," the "declining degree of originality and precision of conceptualization," the tendency "to cast us 'good guys' in defense of politically weak groups against the 'bad guys' lurking behind badges and guns, sinisterly wielding the establishment's power."[24] But we cannot understand criminology today unless we take this perspective

---

[23] *The Politics of Punishment* (New York: Harper & Row, 1973), p. 3.

[24] See "On Deviance," *Contemporary Sociology: A Journal of Reviews* 2 (March 1973), pp. 123–28.

into account and realize that theories about crime and society cannot be divorced from their intellectual and social context.

Why Study Crime?

Crime as Drama Some students, if asked why they wanted to study crime, might simply answer that they expected to find the subject intriguing. It is true that accounts of crime often contain dramatic elements that can hardly fail to capture attention. The excitement of violence, the thrill of the chase, the tense confrontation between accuser and accused, the horror of executions, and the plight of the prisoner: all cater to an apparently endless appetite for vivid and expressive action in which character and situation meet. The persistent popularity of the detective story, the countless portrayals of crime in the movies and on television, and the time and space devoted to crime in the news media attest to widespread interest in wrongdoing in a world where most men and women must conform.[25] And beyond these presentations in the mass culture are the many serious efforts dealing with crime that we number among the highest achievements in literature, such as the Greek tragedies, Shakespeare's *Macbeth*, and Dostoevski's *Crime and Punishment*. The sheer drama of wrongdoing draws a student to the academic study of the matter, and cannot be ignored.

Nonetheless, a number of social scientists—particularly psychologists—view the widespread interest in crime with a wary eye. The popularity of accounts of crime, it is argued, indicates that our society is suffused with repressed criminal impulses seeking an outlet, vicarious or otherwise. And once an individual had broken the law, fulfilling our unconscious desires for aggression, the lawbeaker can be made to shoulder the guilt we refuse to accept for ourselves. "Crime is everybody's temptation," notes the psychiatrist Karl Menninger, and we label our fellow citizens criminals because "in this way we exculpate ourselves from the guilt we feel and tell ourselves that we do it to 'correct' the 'criminal' and make us all safe from crime."[26]

There may be some truth in these assertions. But there is another reason to be wary of the popular interest in crime. Much crime is far more mundane than the mass media would suggest, and our understanding of the subject is distorted by theatrical constructions. The in-

[25] For an excellent discussion of the possible connections between depersonalized mass society and a widespread taste for vicarious violence, see George Orwell, "Raffles and Miss Blandish," in *A Collection of Essays* (Garden City, N.Y.: Doubleday, 1957), pp. 139–54.

[26] *The Crime of Punishment* (New York: Viking Press, 1968), pp. 6–9. See also A. A. Brill, ed., *The Basic Writings of Sigmund Freud* (New York: Modern Library, 1938), p. 862.

cidence of different kinds of crime in the headlines of newspapers or the pages of novels bears little relationship to the incidence of different kinds of crime in reality, as we shall see in the following chapters. The causes of crime are rarely revealed by flamboyant accounts of desperadoes. The depiction of trials on television bears little resemblance to the squalid proceedings that mark so many courtrooms.[27] And only occasionally does the portrayal of the police or the prison make clear the real nature of those special worlds.

The point is not that the dramatic presentation of crime and the criminal is under an obligation to achieve verisimilitude; it is rather that the plethora of material catering to a popular interest in crime as drama is frequently misleading.

Many people are interested in studying crime because it is commonly perceived as a social problem demanding a solution. Crime poses an immediate threat to a great many persons—even if at times the perception of the threat may be somewhat mistaken—and there is a constant demand that "something be done."

Crime as a Social Problem

The harm caused by crime seems clear enough, at first glance. There is the financial loss of the man or woman whose money is stolen, of the consumer who is swindled, of the householder who comes home to find the house looted, and of the business executive whose profits are diminished by the thievery of employees. There is the physical hurt of the person who is assaulted in a quarrel, of the woman who is raped, and of the pedestrian who is struck down by a drunken driver. When we try to measure the harm attributable to crime, however, we find that the task is extremely difficult, even if we confine ourselves to trying to estimate the costs in dollars.

The figures in this area can be no more than estimates, based on limited facts and numerous assumptions that are soon outdated, but the best available data are provided by the President's Commission on Law Enforcement and Administration of Justice. Table 1 presents a list of selected offenses and the amounts of money, in 1967 dollars, they drain from the legitimate economy each year, giving rough orders of magnitude rather than precise sums.[28] The economic loss due to willful homicide looms large because it is measured by the future earning capacity of the victim at time of death, which also accounts for much of the loss due

[27]See Stephen Arons and Ethan Katsh, "How TV Cops Flout the Law," *Saturday Review* (March 3, 1977).

[28]President's Commission on Law Enforcement and Administration of Justice, *Task Force Report: Assessment of Crime* (Washington, D.C.: Government Printing Office, 1967). A number of these estimates are based on *net* losses, taking into account the amount of property recovered by the police, the amount of money won by bettors in the case of gambling, and so on.

The daring robbery, the chase, the tense confrontation between accuser and accused, the dreary life of prison—these aspects of crime capture the interest of the public. But there are important reasons for studying crime that transcend the inherent drama of the subject.

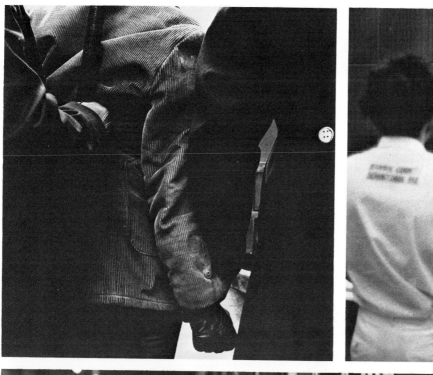

to the crime of driving an automobile under the influence of alcohol. Of the six crimes in Table 1 with greatest economic impact (in descending order, gambling, drunken driving, unreported business theft, fraud, willful homicide, and burglary), only willful homicide and larceny (including business thefts) are included in the list used by the FBI for their index of serious offenses. The provision of illegal goods and services by organized crime takes nearly twice as much money fom the legitimate economy as do all other kinds of criminal activity combined, yet this fact receives little recognition in many discussions of "the crime problem," which are apt to center on offenses such as robbery and burglary.[29] Besides these costs of crime, large sums of public money must be spent on prevention and control. In 1965, expenditures for police, courts, and corrections were estimated to be approximately $4 billion—more than double similar expenditures in 1955—with the great bulk of the money being spent on local police work.[30] The Law Enforcement Assistance Adminis-

---

Table 1. Types of Crime and Estimated Dollar Cost

Type of Crime	Estimated Cost Per Year in Dollars (Millions)
Crimes of Violence	
Willful homicide	750
Assault	65
Crimes Against Property	
Arson	100
Vandalism	210
Burglary	450
Larceny	196
Embezzlement	200
Unreported business theft (retail trade)	1300
Auto theft	140
Fraud	1300
Forgery	64
Robbery	60
Illegal Goods and Services	
Gambling	7000
Narcotics	350
Loansharking	350
Prostitution	225
Illicit alcohol	150
Other	
Tax fraud	100
Driving under the influence of alcohol	1800

SOURCE: President's Commission on Law Enforcement and Administration of Justice, *Task Force Report: Assessment of Crime* (Washington, D.C.: Government Printing Office, 1967).

---

[29] Ibid., p. 43.
[30] Ibid., pp. 53–56.

tration (LEAA)—a federal program established in 1968 to combat crime—had spent nearly $4.5 billion by 1976. Today, the annual expenditures of federal, state, and local governments on the effort to control crime probably exceeds $14 billion.[31] Furthermore, there are substantial private expenditures for protection against crime, such as those for private police and detective services, burglar alarms, locking devices, bank vaults, insurance, bullet-proof glass, special photographic equipment, special lighting, and accounting systems to forestall embezzlement. For particular categories of crimes, estimates of costs are not much more than a stab in the dark. For the total amount of such costs, it is probably best not to hazard any estimate at all.

An economist may be bothered by calculations of the costs of crime such as these, for although crime entails an economic loss to some individuals, it can be argued that for some crimes there is little or no economic loss to society as a whole. For example, stolen goods are not destroyed but are transferred (illegally, to be sure) from the victim to the thief, although they may lose some monetary value by passing into an underworld market. Similarly, it can be claimed that much of the money flowing into the hands of a gambling czar is not a loss to society, in a strict economic sense, nor is the money paid for illegal liquor, the services of a prostitute, and prohibited drugs. Instead, the money represents a fee charged for providing goods and services that some people want and are willing to pay for. The use of phrases such as "economic loss to society" may obscure such economic realities.[32]

In the perception of crime as a social problem, however, emotional costs are even more important to people than financial losses. These costs cannot easily be quantified, let alone reduced to a monetary accounting.[33] There is the shock and pain of the individual victim and of those with whom he or she is bound by social ties. There is the more general sense of insecurity, such as apprehension felt about one's person and possessions or about venturing into public places at night. Beyond these, even more vague and elusive, there is the diminished sense of trust in social interaction, the disquieting suspicion of a widespread moral duplicity, and a fear of a readiness for violence covered with a fragile veneer.

[31] See Arthur Rosett and Donald R. Cressey, *Justice by Consent* (Philadelphia: J. B. Lippincott, 1976), p. x.

[32] Systematic attempts to apply economic theory to the phenomenon of crime are fairly recent, despite much talk of costs. See, however, E. R. Hawkins and Willard Waller, "Critical Notes on the Cost of Crime," *Journal of Criminal Law and Criminology* 26 (April–May 1936), pp. 679–94. For a more up-to-date look at the problem, see A. J. Rogers III, *The Economics of Crime* (Hinsdale, Ill.: Dryden Press, 1973).

[33] In civil suits involving claims for damages based on mental suffering, attempts are made to construct a scale of money equivalence. These efforts, however, appear to be more a matter of establishing a metaphor than creating a true measure.

These fears may be needlessly inflated by sensational stories in the mass media; and those people who speak most vociferously about the problem of crime are often the ones who are least likely to be victimized in actuality. As a number of studies have indicated, poor persons living in the deteriorating center city are much more apt to be the target of the criminal than the suburban middle class, particularly with regard to the predatory street crimes that arouse the greatest indignation in the press. The worry expressed about the problem of "crime in the streets," it has been suggested, frequently disguises middle-class racial prejudice and class antagonisms.[34] Nonetheless, a feeling of insecurity and distrust let loose in the public at large must be accounted a major cost of crime, for it tears at the fabric of a civilized society.[35]

There is one more issue about which we must be careful in discussing crime as a social problem. In the literature of sociology, a social problem is commonly defined as "a condition affecting a significant number of people in ways considered undesirable, about which it is felt something can be done through collective action."[36] The definition should alert us to the fact that what some people consider a social problem is not necessarily regarded in the same way by others. This is particularly true in the case of crime, for major segments of popular opinion concerning the harmfulness of certain offenses (such as the illegal use of drugs, white-collar crime, abortions, gambling, and homosexuality) may differ from the judgments embedded in the legal system and supported by many. Furthermore, our society exhibits deep disagreements about the best course of collective action in a range of areas—from the role of the police to the utility of punishment. These disagreements do not turn on merely technical questions of efficiency; instead, they involve the most profound questions about the proper power of the state and the rights of conflicting moralities to co-exist. When we talk about crime as a social problem, then, we must remember to stay attuned to the complexities underlying the summary phrase.

Crime and Sociological Theories

The study of crime is also important for the contribution it can make to our general understanding of human behavior. Students with an interest in sociology must come to grips with theories of both conformity and deviance. Much of human behavior—perhaps most of it—involves conformity—that is, adherence to the rules of the society in which one lives

[34] James Q. Wilson, "Crime and the Liberal Audience," *Commentary* (January 1971), pp. 71–78; see also Irving Howe, "The Cities' Secret: Heading Toward Apartheid," *The New Republic* (January 22, 1977).

[35] See Robert LeJeune and Nicholas Alex, "On Being Mugged: The Event and Its Aftermath," in *Urban Life and Culture* 2 (1973), pp. 259–87.

[36] See Paul Horton and Gerald Leslie, *The Sociology of Social Problems* (New York: Appleton-Century-Crofts, 1965), p. 4.

or of the social groups to which one belongs. A large part of the work of the social sciences, in fact, has centered on the way in which these norms or rules are learned and incorporated into the individual's system of values. But the members of society frequently violate the norms as well as conform to them; and until we understand how and why this is so, our theories of human behavior are far from complete. Until fairly recently, the theoretical interest of sociologists in the field of criminology has concentated to a large extent on causal explanations of crime, which has been viewed as one of the most important and troublesome forms of deviant behavior.[37]

Much valuable work in criminology has been done with this general orientation in mind. As we shall see in later chapters, studies have been made of the presumed sources of illegal behavior, such as the breakdown of the family, conflicting moral demands, and the lack of economic opportunity. The person who violates the law has committed a wrong; and, as is so often the case, it has seemed reasonable enough to pursue the hypothesis that something must be amiss with either the wrongdoer or the social environment in which he or she functions.[38]

In the last several decades, however, the theoretical interpretation of crime as deviant behavior has changed markedly, and the overriding concern with the problem of crime causation has been displaced in part by other issues. There are several reasons for this shift. First, it is now clear that much behavior defined as deviant by large segments of society is not defined as criminal by the law; and, perhaps more important, many acts prohibited by the criminal law are not accepted as deviant by much of the population.[39]

In 1933, Michael Adler argued that "most of the people in any community would probably agree that most of the behavior proscribed by their criminal law is socially undesirable," and most criminologists would probably have agreed.[40] Today, however, a good deal of attention is paid to the idea that the criminal law does not *necessarily* represent a set of rules accepted by all or almost all members of society. Furthermore, violations of the law may not involve *normless* behavior but adherence to an *alternative* body of rules or norms. In important areas of social life, there

[37] See Vold, *Theoretical Criminology*, p. 13.

[38] See, for example, Ely Chinoy, *Society* (New York: Random House, 1961), Chapter 19.

[39] See Simon Dinitz, Russell R. Dynes, and Alfred C. Clarke, *Deviance: Studies in the Process of Stigmatization and Societal Reactions* (New York: Oxford University Press, 1969), pp. 3–22; see also Hermann Mannheim, *Criminal Justice and Social Reconstruction* (New York: Oxford University Press, 1946). A penetrating examination of the problem of the criminal law incorporating normative prohibitions about which there is widespread disagreement is provided by John Kaplan, *Marijuana: The New Prohibition* (New York: World Publishing, 1970).

[40] Quoted in Richard Quinney, *The Problem of Crime* (New York: Dodd, Mead, 1970), p. 29.

may be not one normative system but several. The idea of an alternative body of norms has been a part of criminological thought for some time, it is true, particularly in terms of criminal subcultures such as those of delinquent gangs or groups of professional thieves; but these were apt to be seen as small, peculiar islands of contrary normative structure in a great sea of social agreement.[41] Today, however, criminology is much more inclined to see widespread normative conflict than in the past and to examine the problem of crime in terms of possible allegiance to a competing set of rules.

Second, as indicated in the discussion of critical criminology, a strong interest has emerged in what is called the labeling perspective. This view argues that an important social reality needing examination is not why some people commit deviant acts while others do not, but how and why society attaches the label of deviant to particular individuals.[42] Deviance, it is claimed, is in the eye of the beholder. "For deviance to become a social fact," assert Earl Rubington and Martin Weinburg, "somebody must perceive an act, person, situation, or event as a departure from social norms, must categorize that perception to others, must get them to accept this definition of the situation, and must obtain a response that conforms to this definition. Unless all these requirements are met, deviance as a social fact does not come into being."[43] And since there is reason to believe that violations of the criminal law are to be found in all segments of society, the fact that officially recorded crime and delinquency are so heavily concentrated among the poor, the members of minority groups, and the politically powerless gives rise to the suspicion that the stigma of being labeled a criminal may be due in large measure to factors such as prejudice and the organizational interests of law enforcement agencies.

The search, then, for characteristics that distinguish criminals from noncriminals and cause the difference in their behavior is regarded by some criminologists as the search for a chimera—the monster in Greek mythology represented as vomiting flames, having the head of a lion, the body of a goat, and the tail of a dragon, and unlikely to be encountered in reality.[44] Many criminologists—probably most—would not take such

[41] The idea of deviant behavior as an expression of alternative norms can be found in the writings of Charles Cooley at the turn of the century, as Robert Merton has pointed out. The conception of crime as normatively guided behavior, however, was often pushed to one side in favor of theories about inadequate socialization, personality maladjustments, and so on. See Merton, *Social Theory and Social Structure*, pp. 411–22.

[42] For an excellent discussion of the development of this viewpoint and its place in sociological theory, see Edwin M. Schur, *Labeling Deviant Behavior: Its Sociological Implications* (New York: Harper & Row, 1971).

[43] *Deviance: The Interactionist Perspective* (New York: Macmillan, 1968), p. v.

[44] See Norval Morris and Gordon Hawkins, *The Honest Politician's Guide to Crime Control* (Chicago: University of Chicago Press, 1970). "The search for the causes of crime is illu-

an extreme position, but in recent years criminology has shifted much of its attention from the dynamics of the criminal act to the dynamics of the social institutions that touch on the prevention and control of crime. (The prison, of course, has been of long-standing interest to criminology, but even there we can see a change in the focus of concern.) Because of the extensive interest in the labeling process—and a growing conviction that the alleged criminal behavior of the person who is labeled is often only a small part of the process—the structure and functioning of the organizations determining the assignment of the criminal label have moved into a position of greater theoretical prominence. In addition, many sociologists working in the field of criminology have come to emphasize the broader implications of their investigations, for it is now evident that a variety of issues central to sociological theory—such as the nature of power, bureaucracies, the social role of professional occupations, and the forms of decision making—are illuminated by the study of the administration of criminal law.[45]

In summary, in the last twenty years or so, the relationship between criminology and sociological theory has become less and less confined to a rather naive attempt to find the individual and social pathologies driving people into crime, on the assumption that crime is a clear-cut, scientific category of human behavior.[46] The concept of crime, it is now realized, is far more complex, the appropriate model of causation more difficult to discover, and the range of questions to be asked much greater than was commonly assumed in the past. If some of the present theoretical formulations in the field are marked by a polemical tone—and we must be careful to distinguish persuasive statements from proof—modern criminology at least holds out the promise of giving us a better view of the relationship between society and criminal behavior.

One of the most important contributions that criminology can make to the student's understanding of society involves the social role of legal institutions. In the long development of the administration of criminal law, society has sounded its most fundamental themes about the relationship between the individual and the state. When crimes have been committed, the state is hungry to find the offenders, prove them guilty, and punish them for their wrongdoing. Unfortunately, it is a process in

Crime and Democratic Institutions

---

sory," the authors state flatly in Chapter 2. "Though recommended in some otherwise respectable criminological texts and pursued by many expensively outfitted criminological safaris . . . we are convinced that attempts to fit all the phenomena of crime into a Procrustean cause/effect framework are fundamentally misconceived."

[45]See Stanton Wheeler, "The Social Sources of Criminology," *Sociological Inquiry* 32 (Spring 1962), pp. 139–59.

[46]See Clarence Ray Jeffery, "The Historical Development of Criminology," in Mannheim, *Pioneers in Criminology*, pp. 458–98.

which the innocent may suffer along with the guilty; and the Anglo-American legal system—along with others—has carefully tried to prevent such injustice. The right to confront one's accusers, the right to a speedy trial in the public view before an impartial tribunal, the right not to be tried twice for the same offense, the right to place the burden of proof on the prosecution, the right to protection from laws declaring behavior criminal after the behavior has occurred, and the right to an orderly process of appeal have all emerged during centuries of struggle between the government and the accused. We have come to regard such rights as crucial components of a democratic social order.

These protections for the suspected offender did not grow out of any special fondness for the cutthroat or the thief, however; they were largely secured in the attempts of law-abiding people of substance to protect themselves and their interest from the oppressive power of a despotic monarch.[47] But when one argues for justice on the basis of general principles, it is difficult to make exceptions: the most disreputable member of society must be afforded the law's protection no less than the ordinary citizen. We moved toward our modern conception of the rights of the accused by making the outlaw our kin.

An interest in crime, then, may flow from something more than a fascination with crime as drama, a desire to solve a social problem of wide concern, or a scientific interest in norm violation. It may arise from a concern with the legal rights of individuals and how they are achieved in various forms of political structure.

Knowledge of the law and its administration is often missing from the intellectual background of people, even those who may be considered well versed in the workings of society. As Max Radin has pointed out, an educated person feels he or she should know at least something about history, science, art, literature, politics, and economics. When it comes to the law, the ordinary citizen is likely not only to be ignorant but to boast about it, treating the law as something mysterious, irrational, and unnecessary.[48] Yet the law provides one of the foundation stones of society, for it underlies major social institutions such as the system of stratification, the family, and the production and distribution of goods and services. Our concepts of private property, marriage, commercial relationships, and corporate organization take effective form as legal rules. And the criminal law, in particular, plays a basic role in one of the most important issues of our age: namely, the place of the individual in mass society. We may no longer fear despotic monarchs, but powerful bureaucracies can trample us underfoot without even being aware of it. If a

[47] See T. H. Marshall, *Citizenship and Social Class* (Cambridge, England: Cambridge University Press, 1950).
[48] *The Law and You* (New York: New American Library, 1948).

study of crime can lead us to a better understanding of the legitimate scope of governmental powers, it will have served a larger purpose than the illumination of its particular subject matter.

Criminology and the Criminal Law

In tracing the development of criminology, this chapter has pointed to the influence of biology, psychology, and sociology. Legal scholars in the field of criminal law might have been expected to play a more important role, but this has not been the case. Only recently has criminology in the United States begun to devote substantial attention to the legal aspects of its subject matter. In Europe and in Latin America, criminology and the study of criminal law have been intertwined to a much greater extent; but, as Stanton Wheeler has indicated, "one of the features of American criminology that is likely to confound a European visitor is the lack of concern for criminology within the law schools. Most criminologists have not been trained in law, nor have the law schools given much emphasis to criminology."[49]

This mutual neglect has existed for some time, despite repeated efforts by a handful of scholars to cultivate cross-disciplinary work, and reflects a larger indifference separating the social sciences and law in general. Efforts on the legal side—the writings of Oliver Wendell Holmes, Jr., in the late nineteenth century; the programs at Yale, Johns Hopkins, and Columbia in the 1920s and 1930s—failed to generate a widespread response. And although Karl Marx, Max Weber, and Emile Durkheim had an interest in legal institutions, later theorists in the social sciences seemed reluctant to follow their lead.[50] Criminal law became a subject matter for lawyers and law schools; criminology turned up in the liberal arts curriculum as a specialty of sociologists.

In some ways, this might appear to be a reasonable division of labor. A knowledge of the criminal law is, after all, part of a lawyer's professional skills, even if the practice of criminal law tends to lack the prestige attached to other areas of law that are financially more rewarding. But the lawyer's interest in the criminal law is apt to center on the nature of the legal rules and their interpretation by the courts; any concern with why people break the rules and what happens to the accused after they leave the courtroom is likely to be fleeting. These questions, however, fall easily into the theoretical and conceptual framework of the sociologist.

[49] "The Social Sources of Criminology," p. 146.
[50] See Lawrence M. Friedman and Stewart Macaulay, *Law and the Behavioral Sciences* (New York: Bobbs-Merrill, 1969), Chapter 1.

Intellectual style, as well as a special taste in subject matter, lie behind the mutual neglect exhibited by criminologists and scholars of criminal law. The study of law, it has been said, is organized for action, while the social sciences are organized for the accumulation of knowledge; and this has been particularly true in the United States, where professional education is so heavily geared to legal practice. As Robert Merton has indicated, sociologists have generally been guided in their work by the scientific ethos, not an interest in application. The search for knowledge is to be undertaken in a spirit of neutrality; scientists, it is expected, will have the same passion for proving their hypotheses wrong as for proving them right. The validity of ideas is to be established by impersonal standards of proof, and learned authority must stand on an equal footing with the brashest newcomer in the empirical testing of facts. Scientific knowledge should be shared with one's colleagues, and no information should be kept secret because it might bring an advantage or might be disturbing. And, finally, the scientist is supposed to be under the sway of an organized skepticism that accepts no conclusion as final, no fact as forever proven. Every issue can be reopened and reexamined.[51]

These norms have not always been followed by social scientists (and recent interest in applied science echoes concern with social reform at the turn of the century), but in a rough way they have guided much scientific behavior, including the behavior of sociologists. The settling of legal disputes, however, is apt to follow a different pattern. Lawyers are typically involved as partisans with a far-from-disinterested concern in the outcome of a case. In law, much is made of the weight of authority and the binding force of tradition. The discrediting of arguments by appeals to prejudice rather than to reason is a familiar occurrence. Information may be withheld on the grounds of privileged communication or of its potential for distorting the reasoning of a lay jury. And there is a strong impulse to settle cases quickly and not to reopen old disputes—a sort of self-imposed statute of limitations.

Differences in the intellectual styles of sociologists and lawyers appear to have increased the difficulty of an exchange of ideas between the two fields and to have reinforced their separate development. In any event, the fact that criminal law and criminology tended to remain in separate academic compartments led to a number of unfortunate consequences. Much of the criminal law, its sources, and its functions remained outside the purview of criminologists, who concentrated instead on questions of crime causation and corrections. The concept of crime was apt to remain singularly crude as the social scientist pursued the goal of building an

[51] See Merton, *The Sociology of Science* (Chicago: University of Chicago Press, 1973), Part IV. See also David Riesman, *Abundance for What?* (Garden City, N.Y.: Doubleday, 1964), pp. 454–92.

explanatory scheme for criminal behavior. A great variety of criminal acts were frequently lumped together under such headings as "norm violation," "delinquency," or "criminality" in the interest of developing large-scale generalizations, and the careful distinctions of legal thought were shoved to one side. Many of the distinctions were irrelevant, it is true, from the viewpoint of the social sciences, for they were based on the attempt to justify punishment, an outmoded concept of human beings as hedonistic calculators, and arbitrary categories such as felonies and misdemeanors. But the law at least recognized that crime was not a homogeneous form of behavior, while criminology exhibited a disquieting tendency to speak of crime and the criminal in general. A greater interplay between the two fields might have stimulated efforts to build useful typologies that would have paid more attention to the variety of behavior. Finally, the lack of contact between the two fields meant that many of the findings emerging from criminology received a less than sympathetic hearing from those more closely tied to the criminal law. Serious doubts about the efficacy of juvenile services, prisons, probation, and so on were expressed by criminologists, but their voices seldom seemed to carry into the halls of the law schools, let alone beyond the groves of academe.

The mutual indifference of criminology and the study of the criminal law appears to be lessening; the sporadic attempts to join the two fields are beginning to produce an alliance that may endure. Sociologists, as we have seen, are becoming more attuned to questions of criminal procedure, the formation of criminal law, and the operation of law enforcement agencies—and they are taking a keen interest in the legal issues involved. Legal scholars, on the other hand, are showing an increased concern with such sociological issues as the roots of crime, the play of conflicting perspectives, and the realities of imprisonment. Greater attention is being paid to the work of individual writers—such as Paul Tappan and Jerome Hall—who had long been trying to unite the two disciplines. The Law and Society Association, founded in 1965, has provided a framework for the expression of joint interests. A variety of programs, institutes, and research projects, such as those supported by the Russell Sage Foundation at Harvard, Yale, the University of California at Berkeley, Northwestern, the University of Wisconsin, and the University of Denver, are attempting to blend legal and sociological approaches to the study of crime. American criminology, in short, now shows signs of a broadening perspective; and if the difference in intellectual styles between law and the social sciences is still a barrier, the current impulse is to overcome it rather than accept it as insurmountable.

Some portion of this rapprochement can probably be traced to the

Cooperative Ventures

growth of social activism in both fields. In the past several decades, the law has been seen less as a rigid, conservative force wedded to the status quo and more as a potent weapon for social change. The philosophy we mentioned before—that the law is organized for action whereas the social sciences are organized for the accumulation of knowledge—no longer provides an acceptable summary; and people in both fields, with a shared interest in the reform of society, have found that law and the social sciences can work effectively in tandem.[52]

Aside from any question of social activism, however, American criminology appears to have realized that without greater attention to the law, its framework for the study of crime is simply too restricted to handle the realities of an industrial, urbanized society riven by a variety of cleavages. The creation of law (that is, the process by which behavior becomes defined as criminal by the state and thus susceptible to state-inflicted sanctions); the inequalities in law enforcement and in the processing of suspected offenders; the limits of the law in imposing a particular morality—these and similar issues are no longer viewed as peripheral, safely left to other disciplines, but as central to the field of criminology. And these are issues that require some familiarity with legal concepts.

Criminology and Psychiatry

In trying to understand nonconforming behavior, we can look inward at the individual's mind and emotions, and we can look outward at the society in which he or she lives. Some scholars claim we must do one or the other. One side argues that only psychiatry can explain deviance; the other, that social determinism—behavior as a product of culture and social structure—provides the key.

Although only a few writers have taken such extreme positions, the tension between the two viewpoints is evident in many of the struggles to lay claim to a valid interpretation of norm-violating actions. In the field of criminology, it has taken the form of asserting, on the one hand, that criminal behavior is largely caused by psychological abnormalities,

[52] The best known instance is probably in the area of school desegregation, in *Brown v. Board of Education*, 347 U.S. 483. There are many other examples of joint effort, such as those involving the discriminatory use of the death penalty and jury selection. See, for example, Michael O. Finklestein, "The Application of Statistical Decision Theory to the Jury Discrimination Cases," *Harvard Law Review* 80 (December 1966), pp. 338–76; Marvin E. Wolfgang, Arlene Kelly, and Hans C. Nolde, "Comparison of the Executed and the Commuted Among Admissions to Death Row," *The Journal of Criminal Law, Criminology, and Police Science* 53 (September 1962), pp. 301–11; Michael Meltsner, *Cruel and Unusual—The Supreme Court and Capital Punishment* (New York: Random House, 1973).

such as emotional disturbances, psychosis, personality defects that drive the individual into violent behavior, attempts to escape from reality in a variety of addictions, and a lack of affect with regard to the rights of others. On the other hand, it is claimed that criminal behavior is caused in the main by a social environment that pushes a normal person into violations of the law, due to inadequate socialization in the past or social pressures acting on the individual in the present. The psychiatric perspective does not argue that the social environment is irrelevant, nor does the sociological perspective argue that the psychological functioning of the individual plays no part. But the two viewpoints do differ, and differ significantly, with regard to psychological abnormality as a factor in the causation of crime.

At one level, the resolution of this dispute comes close to being what Ralf Dahrendorf has called a "meta-theoretical" decision that determines the direction of theory and research rather than a proposition that can be tested objectively.[53] When David Abrahamsen, for example, argues that "since much of the criminal's behavior expresses his aggressions and since mind and behavior are intimately connected, it is obvious that the psychoanalyst or psychiatrist, whose profession brings him into daily contact with the personality and behavior of man, must play a major part in solving the enigma of crime," we seem to be confronted with the chauvinism of a discipline rather than a scientific statement.[54] At another level, however, the matter of psychological abnormality is an empirical question—even if the practical problems of research are formidable—in so far as we are talking about psychological abnormality as a general explanatory variable.

According to many criminologists in the United States today, most of the available evidence suggests that while a small proportion of criminal behavior is due to psychiatric disturbances, there is in general very little difference between criminals and noncriminals. Those who break the law, it is argued, tend to show a distribution of psychological abnormality similar to that of their law-abiding fellows.

The studies in this area, it must be admitted, are inconsistent, seldom use comparable measures, often differ in their definitions of criminality and psychological abnormality, and generally fail to employ random samples of the populations in question. For these reasons, the conclusions in this area must be tentative, and the vehemence of some writers speaking on one side or the other of the controversy should not be confused with scientific proof. Frank Tannebaum, for example, in one of the earliest statements of the labeling position, has said that he "rejects all

[53] See *Class and Class Conflict in Industrial Society* (Stanford, Calif.: Stanford University Press, 1959), pp. 112–13.

[54] *The Psychology of Crime* (New York: John Wiley, 1960), pp. 12–13.

assumptions that would impute crime to the individual in the sense that a personal shortcoming of the offender is the cause of the unsocial behavior. The assumption that crime is caused by any sort of inferiority, physiological or psychological, is . . . completely and unequivocally repudiated."[55] But this seems to be a stronger position than is warranted by the available data; and we are perhaps better off, in theorizing about the mental abnormality of the criminal, to hold to the provisional judgment that in light of the existing evidence mental abnormality cannot be used as a general explanation of crime. This at least has been the position taken by most sociologists working in the field of criminology. While allowing for the possibility that some crime is rooted in psychological disturbances or inadequacies and that there may be some psychological differences between criminals and noncriminals, the great mass of criminal behavior has been viewed as the activity of normal individuals.

Criminology and psychiatry, then, look at crime in quite a different way, and it seems likely that they will continue to do so. The disagreement between the two fields is more than a matter of emphasis and goes beyond a quarrel over the relative weights to be attached to different kinds of causal factors. It involves a fundamental difference in opinion about the nature of nonconformity. While this book stresses the sociological viewpoint, the reader should be aware that there is an opposing body of thought.

This is not to say, however, that psychology of the normal individual has no part to play in the understanding of crime; and, in fact, social psychology (or a particular brand of it) has long provided a vital element in criminological theories. Social psychology, says Stanton Wheeler, has supplied "a kind of half-way house for those sociologists interested in matters of mind, consciousness, and psychological processes," and has been much influenced by the writings of George Herbert Mead, John Dewey, and W. I. Thomas.[56] Here too, however, there has been an important shift in recent years. Where earlier writers were apt to describe the individual exposed to crime-producing social forces in rather passive terms, the tendency now is to see the criminal as "striving, achieving, wanting, struggling, failing"—the vision of criminal behavior that Wheeler felt had been lacking in the social-psychological perspective.[57]

The tendency of social thinkers to view the individual as a mere bit of matter being pushed about by external social forces can be traced to the eighteenth century; it was, in fact, a viewpoint sardonically lampooned

---

[55] *Crime and the Community* (New York: Columbia University Press, 1938), p. 22. For a contrary viewpoint, see Samuel Yochelson and Stanton E. Samenow, *The Criminal Personality* (New York: Jason Aronson, 1976).

[56] Wheeler, "The Social Sources of Criminology," pp. 144–45.

[57] Ibid., p. 145.

by Thorstein Veblen in an attack on Bentham. "The hedonistic conception of man," said Veblen, "is that of a lightning calculator of pleasures and pains, who oscillates like a homogeneous globule of desire of happiness under the stimuli that shift him about the area, but leave him intact. . . . Self-imposed in elemental space, he spins symmetrically about his own spiritual axis until the parallelogram of forces bears down upon him, whereupon he follows the line of the resultant."[58] The view persisted in American sociology—and criminology—and the lawbreaker was commonly portrayed as more acted upon than acting, as passive, ineffectual, stigmatized.[59] The deviant, said David Matza, in discussing the work of the prominent criminologist Edwin H. Sutherland, was treated as a captive of the milieu, as an inanimate object or an unthinking creature.[60] Now, however, more and more writers in criminology are trying to build a theory in which the criminal is a person who chooses and, even more important, deliberately allies himself with a collective response to the frustrations and problems of his particular social environment. We shall return to this point later, for it is an important one; for the moment, it is enough to point out that the psychology of the individual—the actor—is a crucial part of criminological thought, although the issue is handled in terms of the normal rather than the pathological.

Conclusions

In this chapter we have examined briefly the nature of criminology and its development as a field of study. Clearly, the subject matter is diverse. The history of the discipline has been marked by sudden shifts in attention and by professional clashes linked to the changing social context; and ideology, as well as logic and empirical observations, continue to shape our understanding of the relationship between crime and society. The confrontation between opposing theories about important issues accounts for much of the vitality evident in the field today. In addition, the persistent interest in criminology springs from its capacity to help us understand the most profound questions about the social order.

At the present time, criminology appears to be at one of those turning points that have marked its path so often in the past. In a sense, the discipline seems to have circled back to the mood of Beccaria that attended its birth and to be caught up in a new enlightenment that chal-

[58] Thorstein Veblen, "Why is Economics Not an Evolutionary Science?" *The Place of Science in Modern Civilization* (New York: Viking, 1942), p. 73.

[59] Ian Taylor, Paul Walton, and Jock Young, *The New Criminology* (London: Routledge & Kegan Paul, 1973), p. 47.

[60] Matza, *Becoming Deviant* (New York: Prentice-Hall, 1969), p. 107.

lenges fundamental concepts about the criminal and the criminal law. The issues involved in the study of crime, of course, are apt to emerge in passionate and clangorous debate in times of social and political upheaval, and our age of uncertainty is no exception. But there is a familiar ring in the controversy over the proper police powers of the state, the legitimacy and utility of punishment, and the nature of human behavior. Once again we are urged to see the individual as a rational being striving to come to grips with a restrictive social and political order. Once again we are called on to find a reasonable basis for the law's prohibitions, to bring Leviathan to heel. And most important, once again we are urged to examine the criminal law and its operation from the vantage point of justice. Criminology, by grappling with these ideas, cannot fail to lay a claim on the attention of the serious student of human behavior.

Recommended Readings

To understand criminology as an intellectual discipline that has changed and developed over the years, it is important to see the works of earlier writers in their social and historical contexts. Along with the writings of outstanding figures in the field, such as Cesare Beccaria, *On Crimes and Punishment,* trans. Henry Paolucci (New York: Bobbs-Merrill, 1963; first published in 1764); Cesare Lombroso, *Crime: Its Causes and Remedies* (Boston: Little, Brown, 1911; first published as *L'uomo delinquente* in 1876); Willem Bonger, *Criminality and Economic Conditions* (Bloomington: Indiana University Press, 1969; first published in 1916); Thorsten Sellin, *Culture Conflict and Crime* (New York: Social Science Research Council, 1938); and Albert Cohen, Alfred Lindesmith, and Karl Schuessler, eds., *The Sutherland Papers* (Bloomington: Indiana University Press, 1956), the reader will find it useful to consult Hermann Mannheim, ed., *Pioneers in Criminology* (Montclair, N.J.: Patterson Smith, 1972) for a set of interpretative essays. George B. Vold, *Theoretical Criminology* (New York: Oxford University Press, 1958) provides an excellent comprehensive view of the field before the 1960s, with an emphasis on schools of thought rather than individual theorists. For some of the recent developments in criminology, the reader should see Richard Quinney, ed., *Criminal Justice in America* (Boston: Little, Brown, 1974); Ian Taylor, Paul Walton, and Jock Young, eds., *Critical Criminology* (London: Routledge & Kegan Paul, 1975); and James Q. Wilson, *Thinking About Crime* (New York: Basic Books, 1975).

The reader will also find it useful to review *The Journal of Criminal Law, Criminology, and Police Science.* This journal provides an excellent illustration of the way in which criminology has shifted its areas of concern and its underlying assumptions in response to changes in society.

Chapter 2
The Nature of Crime

When we ask "What is a crime?" we encounter an ancient and persistent puzzle, as Morris Cohen has warned us, and there is no simple, clear-cut answer.[1] Many writers in a variety of fields have hoped to identify forms of behavior that would always be called crime regardless of time and place; and scholars have variously argued that one must look to Divine Law or an intuitive sense of right and wrong or the need to protect the well-being of society to find a universal definition of criminal wrongdoing. Such arguments, however, are not very satisfactory. The dictates of God, as presented in a variety of religious doctrines, are apt to be inconsistent and lacking in detail. A supposedly constant intuitive morality varies greatly in the definition of criminality. And the well-being of society, as a baseline from which criminal behavior could be measured, is a vague concept that invites shifting opinion.[2]

Like the definition of so many other aspects of society, the definition of crime apparently cannot be freed from the flux of human values and changing social conditions. *Nullum crimen sine lege, nulla poene sine lege,* says the law, fond of cloaking its ideas in Latin: "No crime or punishment without law."[3] This means that for wrongdoing to be defined and treated as crime, it must be declared illegal and assigned a penalty by those in government. Most criminologists are likely to agree, looking for a boundary line to fix the limit of their subject matter.[4]

The law, however, does not define all illegal wrongdoing as crime.

[1] Morris Cohen, *Reason and Law* (New York: Collier Books, 1961).

[2] Paul W. Tappan, "Who is the Criminal?" *American Sociological Review* 12, No. 1 (February 1947), pp. 96–102.

[3] See Wayne R. LaFave and Austin W. Scott, Jr., *Handbook of Criminal Law* (St. Paul, Minn.: West, 1972), pp. 5–6.

[4] Some writers, it should be pointed out, find this viewpoint unduly restrictive and continue to argue for a definition of crime free of the criminal law. See Herman and Julia Schwendinger, "Defenders of Order or Guardians of Human Rights?" in Ian Taylor, Paul Walton, and Jock Young, eds., *Critical Criminology* (London: Routledge & Kegan Paul, 1975), pp. 113–46.

Some illegal acts are defined as civil wrongs, as we shall see later in this chapter. Furthermore, in declaring a particular form of behavior a crime, the law looks at the intent of the actor as well as at the act; it also attempts to distinguish between serious and minor offenses. Despite the apparent simplicity, then, of defining crime as whatever the criminal law says it is, the nature of crime remains complex and difficult to grasp.

The Normative System of the Law

The rules of society are commonly referred to as social norms and make up what is called the social order or the normative system. In all modern industrial societies, a significant portion of the normative system takes the form of law—that is, social rules enunciated and enforced by the state. These legal rules differ from other social norms in four important ways.

First, laws are usually specific, setting forth in explicit terms what is expected of the individual. Vague admonitions and ambiguous prohibitions are avoided, at least in theory. The laws are supposed to be exact and, accordingly, are hammered out in carefully worded statements such as judicial decisions, constitutions, and legislative acts. Second, the basis of the laws' authority is formally presented for public inspection. Unlike other norms that usually rely on unspoken custom to give them weight, the laws are rooted in express grants of governmental power. Frequently this takes the form of a close regard for the procedures by which the state is entitled to enunciate legal rules, such as the deliberations of a legislative body. Third, legal rules are relatively stable. If the law changes too quickly, a disturbing element of uncertainty is introduced into social life. The desire to avoid such uncertainty also leads many legal systems to avoid retroactive rules—that is, rules declaring behavior illegal after the behavior has occurred. Finally, laws are under strong pressure to achieve logical consistency. The principles, concepts, and terms of the legal rules are expected to remain more or less the same from one portion of the law to another, and the law is not supposed to require *and* prohibit the same act under the same circumstances. Without such consistency the legal rules become arbitrary, whimsical, and once again disturbingly uncertain.[5]

These characteristics, which can be labeled specificity, formal legitimacy, stability, and consistency, are matters of degree; and the laws of

Characteristics of the Law

[5] See Edwin M. Schur, *Law and Society: A Sociological View* (New York: Random House, 1968). See also Harry C. Bredemeier, "Law as an Integrative Mechanism," in Vilhem Aubert, ed., *Sociology of Law* (Harmondsworth, England: Penguin Books, 1975) pp. 52–67.

the United States exhibit them imperfectly, as do the laws in all legal systems. Nonetheless, the fact that laws are expected to exhibit these characteristics distinguishes them from other types of social norms. The laws, after all, are enforced with all the power of the state, and not by informal means of ridicule, ostracism, and expressions of moral indignation, as is the case with social norms such as folkways and mores. The need to keep the laws of the state free of oppressive, illogical caprice is a recurring problem—and one we will constantly return to in the following chapters.

The Forms of Law In the United States today, laws are to be found in the form of judicial decisions, legislation, state and federal constitutions, and administrative regulations. This body of legal rules has been pieced together over the centuries and often wears the patina of time. Many basic legal concepts, in fact, are rooted in English law stretching back for more than two thousand years to pre-Roman Britain and influenced by Greek, Semitic, Assyrian, and Egyptian thought, as well as by the English temper.[6] During the growth of the American colonies, much of this legal system was transported to the New World and further modified; and the present law in the United States, still growing and slowly changing, bears the stamp of this complex legal history. Although American and English law have developed independently since 1775, they are still marked by a fundamental unity and continual exchange of legal ideas. Both systems stand in contrast to continental jurisprudence, which is based on the Napoleonic Codes.[7]

To understand the present legal system in America, it is important to remember that a large portion of the legal rules is based on what is called the *common law*. The phrase originally referred to a rudimentary compendium made up of the laws and customs of different parts of Britain and declared the law of the land by King Edward the Confessor (c. 1003–1066). Much of this law remained unwritten. "It was mainly preserved," says one writer, "in the breasts and closets of the clergy, who, as a rule, were the only persons educated in the law; in the knowledge and recollection of the thanes [barons] and the landowners whose lands and whose persons were governed by it; and in the traditions handed down from fathers to sons."[8] After the conquest of England by the Normans, in 1066, however, the king's judges set about the task of translating this largely unwritten, customary law of the society into explicit, authoritative rules, in the course of judicial proceedings. As the judges

[6]See Theodore F. T. Plucknett, *A Concise History of the Common Law* (London: Butterworth, 1948) and Alan Harding, *A Social History of the English Law* (New York: Penguin Books, 1966).

[7]See W. Friedmann, *Legal Theory* (London: Stevens & Sons, 1953), Chapter 24. See also Lawrence M. Friedman, *A History of American Law* (New York: Simon and Schuster, 1973).

[8]See F. A. Inderwick, *The King's Peace* (London: Swan Sonnenschein, 1895), p. 3.

reached their decisions in the parade of cases appearing in the king's courts, there developed a body of maxims and principles derived in theory from custom—a set of legal rules taking the form not of legislative statutes but of judicial decisions that provided precedents for the resolution of future disputes. It was this body of decisions, modified over time, that became the usual referrent for the term *common law* and was given the force of governmental decree. *Stare decisis*—let the decision stand—became a basic doctrine of the Anglo-American legal system.[9]

Over the centuries, judicial decisions continued to provide the various branches of the law, including the criminal law, with much of their substance. Indeed, the criminal law would be a mere skeleton without the common law to flesh it out, and it is important to recognize that a large share of the law has been created by judges who have claimed to look to custom for a guide. But legislative bodies have also defined crimes—new crimes undreamed of by custom—and penal codes created by legislative bodies have gradually incorporated much of the common law and taken its place.

The process of codification continues to the present day. In 1923 the American Law Institute was organized in the United States by judges, lawyers, and law teachers with the objective of clarifying and improving the law. The criminal law was given immediate attention.[10] Some forty years and many drafts later, a proposed official version of a model penal code was accepted by the institute and presented to state legislatures for possible adoption. Portions of the Model Penal Code have been used for the legislative modification of the criminal law in a number of states, but both the common law and laws established by statute set forth definitions of criminal behavior at the present time and will probably continue to do so long into the future. As more and more states adopt comprehensive criminal codes in place of a collection of uncoordinated statutes, predict LaFave and Scott, common-law crimes will be absorbed into statutory law. But the process will take a long time, and the definition of crimes in common law form will continue for many years.[11]

In addition to common-law crimes and crimes defined by statute, a portion of the criminal law in the United States (such as the law dealing with treason) is to be found in state and federal constitutions, although most of the criminal law in this form is concerned with matters of procedure, such as the right to trial, rather than substantive issues, such as the

[9] It has long been pointed out that relying on precedents from the past seems to give the legal system a great rigidity, but the system is more flexible than it appears. *Stare decisis* is more a matter of general policy than an inviolable rule. See Benjamin N. Cardozo, *The Nature of the Judicial Process* (New Haven: Yale University Press, 1921.)

[10] See Herbert Wechsler, "Codification of the Criminal Law in the United States: The Model Penal Code," *Columbia Law Review* 68 (December 1968), pp. 1424–56.

[11] LaFave and Scott, *Handbook of Criminal Law*, p. 69.

definition of murder or robbery. Beyond this, however, the Constitution of the United States gives the federal government the power to prohibit and penalize conduct deemed criminal in federal territory and in the territory of the states, under the constitutional provisions of the commerce clause, the taxation clause, and the war power clause. Finally, a substantial amount of criminal law—much neglected by criminology—is to be found in regulations created by authority delegated to administrative agencies such as the Department of Agriculture and state food boards.[12]

The criminal law in the United States, in short, is a mixture of precedents, legislation, constitutional provisions, and administrative rules accumulated over the years and differing, sometimes significantly, among the fifty-one different jurisdictions of the states and the federal government. The move toward codification of the common law has achieved some uniformity among the states, and a number of inconsistencies have been eliminated; but the definition of crime still varies with geographical location. It is within this body of legal rules that are part of the normative system of society that we must look for the nature of crime.

Public and Private Wrongs

The law of modern society is divided into two main parts—criminal law and civil law. A large part of the civil law is concerned with what are called *torts*—private wrongs, or wrongs against the individual. (The word *tort* comes from the Latin *tortus*—twisted or crooked—and refers to such illegal acts as the selling of defective goods, the invasion of privacy, defamation, trespass, assault, and negligence.)[13] Criminal law is concerned with public wrongs, or wrongs against society, and covers a wide range of offenses frequently classified into three broad categories. In the first category are acts involving physical violence, such as murder and rape. In the second are acts that infringe on property rights, such as theft, fraud, and burglary. The third category—an extremely heterogeneous grouping often labeled crimes against health, morals, and public safety—includes acts involving prostitution, gambling, the use of drugs, public drunkenness, homosexuality, and sedition.[14]

The acts prohibited by the criminal law often resemble the illegal acts called torts, but crimes and torts are relatively easy to tell apart by the way legal proceedings are conducted. Criminal cases begin with an arrest

[12] With a few notable exceptions, criminology has paid little attention to crime defined by administrative rules. See, however, Marshall Clinard, *The Black Market* (New York: Rinehart, 1952).

[13] See Bernard F. Cataldo et al., *Introduction to the Law and the Legal Process* (New York: John Wiley & Sons, 1965), Chapter 18.

[14] See LaFave and Scott, *Handbook of Criminal Law*, p. 9.

by the police and lead to an indictment or information (to be discussed in Chapter 9), at least where more serious offenses are concerned. The state initiates the action and has the power to carry the proceedings forward regardless of the wishes of the person who has been wronged.[15] Civil cases begin with an action taken by a private citizen and lead to a summons to appear in a civil court. If the parties to the dispute can reach an agreement, they are at liberty to do so and the state will not interfere. In criminal cases which carry the possibility of penal sanctions, the rules of evidence are more strict than in civil cases; the state must show the defendant guilty "beyond a reasonable doubt." In civil cases, however, the party bringing the suit need only establish a claim by a "preponderance of the evidence." In criminal proceedings, the decision of the court results in conviction or acquittal; in civil proceedings, the law speaks of a finding or a judgment. Finally—and this is the crucial difference—crimes are supposed to involve criminal intent, or *mens rea* (guilty mind), on the part of the lawbreaker, with the proceedings resulting in the punishment of offenders. In civil wrongs, the emphasis is not on the punishment of the wrongdoer but on compensation for the victim or an adjustment of the conflicting interests of the parties. The aim is restitution for the victim rather than sanctions imposed on the lawbreaker— although sometimes punitive damages are imposed on an individual who has violated the civil law by willful and malicious conduct.

Where the line between torts and crimes is to be drawn is not a mere legal quibble; it is a social decision of far-reaching importance, for it sets a limit on the police power of the state. Torts are acts that the state has declared illegal but that call for a large measure of private initiative in finding a remedy. The state establishes the rules governing the rights of parties to the dispute, provides a judge to hear the case, and insures that the decision of the court is enforced. The individuals involved, however, must hire their own lawyers, initiate the proceedings, collect the necessary evidence, and are often expected to reach a settlement out of court if at all possible. The role of the state is largely that of referee. In the case of crimes, on the other hand, the state is assigned a far more significant part. The judge still serves as an umpire, but the state provides police for the detection and apprehension of the alleged lawbreaker, supplies a lawyer for the prosecution (and a lawyer for the defense, if the accused is indigent), gathers evidence against the accused, and imprisons the convicted lawbreaker in the name of punishment, deterrence, or rehabilitation.

Although the procedural difference between torts and crimes is clear, the reason why particular acts are assigned to one category or the other is

[15] In some cases, though, the victim may refuse to testify, thus bringing the case to a close for lack of evidence.

not as simple as it might seem. Some legal scholars claim that civil wrongs are distinguished from crimes by the fact that the former involve harm done to an individual, but this is obviously true for a great many crimes as well. Moreover, a number of illegal acts are defined by the law as both a crime *and* a tort. An assault, for example, or an automobile accident caused by a drunken driver, may be brought into court as either a criminal or a civil matter—or both, in different proceedings. Perhaps most important, in legal theory crime is viewed as a special form of misconduct that warrants punishment because the wrongdoing is "harmful to society." As pointed out before, however, what constitutes a harm to society's well-being is not easily ascertained. The law, presumably, is pointing to something more than a mass of individual harms, but the meaning of the phrase is ambiguous.

In short, there is a difference in terms of legal proceedings between crimes and other forms of behavior prohibited by the law, but there is still the perplexing question of *why* certain illegal acts are categorized as crime and handled in criminal proceedings ending in punishment, while other illegal acts are labeled civil wrongs and end in restitution. Some writers have stated that the difference between crimes and civil wrongs cannot be pinned down in an objective fashion. "It is sometimes asserted," says Morris Cohen, "that the civil law protects the private interests of individuals while the criminal law protects the interests of the state or community. But this contrast is of little value. . . . Positivistic sociologists and jurists as well as moralists often identify crime with acts which are contrary to the social interests or endanger social existence. But the most obvious reflection shows that this begs the question. Acts are criminal not because they *are* harmful, but because they are *deemed* harmful by those who make or interpret the law." [16]

Other legal philosophers, perhaps more anxious to justify the ways of the law, have attempted to determine how society is protected when certain patterns of behavior are treated as crime. Their findings flow in three main directions. First, crimes are said to be violations of the fundamental morality underlying a particular society, and violations must be punished if the morality—and the society—is to survive. "Societies disintegrate from within more frequently than they are broken by external pressures," claims Patrick Devlin. "There is disintegration where no common morality is observed and history shows that the loosening of moral bonds is often the first stage of disintegration, so that society is

---

[16]Cohen, *Reason and Law,* p. 17. The problem of scientifically determining what harms society is similar to that of identifying what helps or hinders the survival of society. As Robert Merton has indicated, however, "this remains one of the cloudiest and empirically most debatable concepts in functional theory." See Merton, *Social Theory and Social Structure* (New York: The Free Press, 1968), p. 106.

justified in taking the same steps to preserve its moral code as it does to preserve its government and other essential institutions."[17] We treat certain behavior as crime, punishing it to underline our condemnation, not primarily because of the crime's tangible and specific harm but because punishment symbolizes a reaffirmation of moral imperatives that have been violated. The norms do not thrive without replenishment and we feed them with ritual. The trial of the criminal offender, it has been said, is the Passion play of a secular society.

Second, crimes are said to be acts deeply repugnant to the members of a society, arousing vengeance or a demand for expiation through punishment. But if private citizens were to seek to inflict punishment on the offenders, grave public disorders would occur and incite countervengeance. Such disruptive legal self-help is avoided by state intervention, which provides a neutral third party to establish guilt and inflict appropriate penalties. The concept of crime as an act that is prohibited and penalized by the state is a device to maintain a social order threatened not so much by the original wrong as by the inevitable retaliation. "The criminal law," said Sir James Stephen, "stands to the passion of revenge in the same relation as marriage to the sexual appetite."[18]

Third, what can be called the commonsense viewpoint of the law argues that the formal punishment administered by the state is simply an authoritative and effective deterrent to wrongdoing that cannot be controlled in any other way. In this argument, the concept of state intervention is based on the need to curb wrongdoing. The moral condemnation of the offense is taken for granted and the desire for revenge is largely ignored. The important point is that the state intervenes, in the form of the criminal law, to deter the offender from repeating the act and to deter others who might contemplate such behavior; widespread violations are thus prevented—and "widespread violations" are equated with "harm to society."

These three explanations have a certain air of plausibility about them, but they do not carry us far enough. The morality that is supposed to underlie society remains obscure, and the moral threat posed by particular illegal acts is largely conjectural. The desire for revenge unquestionably exists, sometimes taking the form of lynch mobs or vigilante movements, but whether the state should intervene in the vast array of acts called crimes (which includes many minor offenses like public drunkenness, removing the serial number of a motor vehicle, and advertising a lottery)

[17] *The Enforcement of Morals* (London: Oxford University Press, 1965), p. 3. For a discussion of this issue, see Gilbert Geis, *Not the Law's Business?* (Washington, D.C.: Government Printing Office, 1972).

[18] Quoted in Oliver Wendell Holmes, Jr., *The Common Law* (Boston: Little, Brown, 1881), p. 41.

in order to forestall an impassioned citizenry is open to doubt. A large number of "traditional" crimes—robbery, murder, rape, and arson—are undoubtedly offensive to a great majority of people in society, can be counted as individual injuries, and may require state intervention for their control. However, the assertion that misconduct of this sort causes "harm to society" does not increase our understanding of its nature. We have merely given individual injuries a new name. In order to talk about harm to society meaningfully, one would need to be a good deal more specific about what the word *society* denotes and how the behavior in question is likely to harm it. All this leaves to one side, of course, the question of whether the intervention of the state is in fact a deterrent.

Consensus and Conflict

The various arguments claiming the criminal law to be an instrument for the protection of society are united by an implicit assumption—that there is an agreed-upon social order to be shielded from harm. Society, from this viewpoint, is a structure based on a shared commitment, a commonly accepted way of doing things; and although disagreements obviously exist, they are seen as disputes within an overarching consensus. The designation of certain acts as crimes and the assignment of penalties express a unity of values.

One intellectual tradition, however, holds a contrary view of the matter. Society, according to this view, is based not on consensus but on conflict, and competing interest groups constantly struggle to impose their will on one another. Social order is a result of coercion rather than consent, and the history of societies is a record of the victories and losses of particular factions. Your law is merely the will of your class, erected into legislation, said Marx and Engels describing the bourgeoisie in *The Communist Manifesto;* and thus the form of society reflects the wishes of the few rather than of the many.

These opposing views of the law are only one aspect of a larger opposition between two perspectives of society whose advocates are apt to caricature each other's viewpoints. The one, under the banner "consensus," stresses the relative continuity of social institutions, the consistency of the elements making up society, the contribution each part makes to the maintenance of the whole, and the shared values of society's members. The other, under the banner "conflict," emphasizes social change, inconsistencies and struggle, the factors contributing to the emergence of new social institutions, and the constraints imposed on one part of society by another.[19] And behind these contrasting views of society lie whole ar-

[19] See Ralf Dahrendorf, "Toward a Theory of Social Conflict," *Journal of Conflict Resolution* 2 (June 1958), pp. 170–83.

mies of arguments on such matters as the nature of humankind, the quality of freedom, the meaning of social causation, and appropriate research methods.[20]

The controversy between these positions may be impossible to resolve, at least to the extent of showing that one side is wholly right and the other wholly wrong; as Ralf Dahrendorf has indicated, conflict and consensus are in fact characteristics of every society. The adherents of the conflict perspective, nonetheless, are convinced that their viewpoint is the more accurate explanation of the true nature of crime—and critical criminology, discussed in Chapter 1, has proved to be one of the most illuminating expressions of the conflict perspective in the sociological literature. The value-consensus model of society, argue William Chambliss and Robert Seidman, "is not only incapable of accounting for the shape and character of the legal system, but it even fails to raise the most fundamental and sociologically relevant questions about the law. The conflict model, by contrast, while having many shortcomings and not providing a complete answer to the questions raised by the study of law, is nonetheless much more useful as a heuristic model for analyzing the legal system."[21]

The conflict perspective on crime has its roots in a long history of social thought, but in recent years the work of George Vold, Richard Quinney, Austin Turk, and Chambliss and Seidman must be accorded a central place in the effort to state the position in a concise and coherent fashion for criminology.[22] In brief, their argument is based on the idea that society is broken into a variety of social segments. These are seen variously as hierarchically arranged social classes, as the rulers and the ruled in bureaucratic structures, or—at a very abstract level of generalization—as the inevitable fragmentation of large-scale industrial societies into a variety of cultural traditions. However the lines are drawn, the social groups that make up society are seen as having different values, goals, and normative standards and as being in conflict with one another. Each strives to maximize its interests and impose its view of the proper form of social life on the society as a whole. In the process, it is argued, the apparatus of the state becomes a vital bastion, for those who control the state directly or indirectly can legitimize their particular val-

---

[20]See John Horton, "Order and Conflict Theories of Social Problems as Competing Ideologies," *The American Journal of Sociology* 71 (May 1966), pp. 701–13.

[21]*Law, Order, and Power* (Reading, Mass.: Addison-Wesley, 1971), p. 19; see also William Chambliss and Milton Mankoff, eds., *Whose Law? What Order?* (New York: John Wiley & Sons, 1976), pp. 1–28.

[22]See George Vold, *Theoretical Criminology* (New York: Oxford University Press, 1958); Richard Quinney, *The Social Reality of Crime* (New York: Little, Brown, 1970); Austin Turk, *Criminality and Legal Order* (Chicago: Rand McNally & Company, 1972); and Chambliss and Seidman, *Law, Order, and Power.*

Judges in Vermont law court, about 1890.

Your law is merely the will of your class, erected into legislation, said Marx and Engels describing the bourgeoisie in The Communist Manifesto. *From this viewpoint, the dignity of the court is violence disguised, and the maintenance of law and order is simply the maintenance of the status quo.*

The Whiskey Rebellion, 1794.

Massachusetts State Police
and Harvard Square rioters.

ues, goals, and norms, as well as decide how rules will be translated into reality.

The definition of what is right or wrong, then, both in theory and in practice, becomes the prerogative of those in power. They declare criminal whatever is opposed to their interests and to their conception of proper behavior, for the stigma of criminality is a potent weapon. "Criminalization" is a form of legitimate coercion; it declares that those in opposition are not simply mistaken—they are tainted with bad motives as well. People who fight the law, it can then be argued, do so not because of an honest difference of opinion but because they are driven by evil minds. In short, according to this viewpoint, the nature of crime is determined by the ruling elite in such a way as to advance their material interests and their conception of morality.

On the face of it, this portrayal of the way in which behavior comes to be defined as crime has a persuasive if somewhat banal look. "In a democracy, theoretically, people make the laws," say Lawrence Friedman and Stewart Macaulay. "But no one has ever been so naive as to believe that it is all the people who make all the laws. The very structure of American government presupposes narrower groups representing narrower interests."[23] We would suppose, without much elaborate theorizing, that those who manage to play an influential role in making the law and setting the conditions for its enforcement are anxious to see their interests and their ideas of the good society advanced rather than the interests and ideas of those with whom they disagree.

Other sociologists, however, have been less inclined to view the conflict theory of the criminal law as being true but obvious. They have questioned whether the interests of those who make the law are in fact generally at odds with the interests of other social groups who are not in power. Many acts defined as crimes, such as murder, theft, robbery, rape, and inciting to riot, seem to run counter to common ideas about right behavior. In what sense are these definitions the exclusive expression of special-interest groups that have managed to capture the apparatus of the state? Presumably, no law is supported by everyone. At the very least, some of those who violate a law would wish to see it otherwise. If the conflict perspective is to lead us beyond this conclusion, it must specify the extent to which the objectives of the few allegedly controlling the state actually are opposed to the objectives of the many; the perspective must not merely rest on the observation that 100 percent agreement does not exist. Furthermore, there is a serious question whether any single, clear-cut interest group has the power to make the legal rules and determine the way in which they will be enforced. While

---

[23] *Law and the Behavioral Sciences* (New York: Bobbs-Merrill, 1969), p. 575.

it may be true that the few make laws for the many, even in a democratic society, it may not be the same few who make all the laws.[24]

As the authors of *The New Criminology* have pointed out, the challenges offered to the consensual viewpoint by the new conflict theorists "appear to have been prompted not so much by a re-examination of the classical social theorists, but rather by events in the real world which have thrown the assumptions of 'consensus' into doubt."[25] The social turmoil of the 1960s, in the United States and in Europe, pitted many segments of the population against governmental authority on a host of issues. Conflicts concerning the status of minority groups, the use of drugs, and the expression of political dissent were merely the most visible elements of a wave of discontent that continues to encounter a variety of legal prohibitions. In this situation, it is relatively easy to see the criminal law being used on numerous occasions to prohibit and punish behavior about which there is widespread disagreement. In fact, according to a number of social scientists, we are faced with a crisis of "over-criminalization"—the criminal law has been extended far beyond its customary task of protecting persons, property, and the state, and now includes forms of behavior posing a trivial threat or none at all.[26] It has also become all too plain that the criminal law is frequently enforced in a discriminatory fashion; and the powerless, as usual, come off badly. These observations are valid enough, but the theoretical assertion that all or most of the criminal law is deliberately erected and administered by a powerful few in the exclusive interests of the few is another matter.

The empirical basis for the conflict perspective of crime is, unfortunately, limited. True, a number of excellent studies clearly demonstrate the way in which the criminal law can be made to conform to the interests of small groups with access to power.[27] Such studies, however, have tended to focus on a relatively small area of the criminal law, primarily offenses against health and morals, rather than covering the full range of crimes. The prohibition against abortion, the sale of liquor, and the possession and sale of drugs—these and similar offenses have received a good deal of attention, but the crimes of murder, robbery, assault, and

[24] See Arnold Rose, *The Power Structure* (New York: Oxford University Press, 1967).

[25] Ian Taylor, Paul Walton, and Jock Young, *The New Criminology* (London: Routledge & Kegan Paul, 1973), p. 237.

[26] See Sanford H. Kadish, "The Crisis of Overcriminalization," *The Annals of the American Academy of Political and Social Science* 374 (November 1967), pp. 157–70.

[27] See, for example, William J. Chambliss, "A Sociological Analysis of the Law of Vagrancy," *Social Problems* 12 (Summer 1964), pp. 67–77; Alfred R. Lindesmith, *The Addict and the Law* (Bloomington: Indiana University Press, 1965); Edwin H. Sutherland, "The Sexual Psychopath Laws," *Journal of Criminal Law, Criminology, and Police Science* 40 (January–February 1950), pp. 543–54; Anthony Platt, *The Child Savers: The Invention of Delinquency* (Chicago: University of Chicago Press, 1969); and Andrew Sinclair, *Era of Excess: A Social History of the Prohibition Movement* (New York: Harper & Row, 1964).

rape have not yet been analyzed adequately from a conflict perspective. Crimes against property have received surprisingly little attention, although the extent to which business interests can influence the law in their favor, both in terms of formulation and administration, would appear to offer a fruitful line of inquiry.[28] Impressive studies of law enforcement in recent years leave little room for doubt that the poor, the young, and members of minority groups are frequently hard pressed to get justice from those who run the legal machinery.[29] Nonetheless, there has not yet been sufficient exploration of the idea that law enforcement is deliberately chosen as a weapon by those in power for the maintenance of the status quo. The administration of the criminal law frequently works to the disadvantage of the powerless, but it is often assumed—with little concrete evidence—that this is the intended and recognized goal of those administering the criminal law. Sociological analysis, however, requires more than a superficial imputation of motives.

The conflict perspective on criminology, in short, purports to offer a comprehensive theory of how misconduct comes to be prohibited and penalized by the criminal law; but the empirical base for the argument is relatively restricted, and major components of the theory are still undeveloped. At the same time, the exponents of the conflict perspective have made it clear that the criminal law does not represent a crystallization of the mores of society, a simple reflection of widely accepted judgments about what is right and wrong. The definition of a crime can and often does represent the imposition of morality and the pursuit of narrow interests; and the enforcement of the criminal law can be and often is wedded to the objectives of those who do the enforcing rather than to impartial standards of justice. The conflict perspective has greatly increased the theoretical significance of criminology as a field of study, opened invaluable lines of inquiry, and helped to demolish the easy assertion that the definition of crime is inevitably to be found in the need to protect society as a whole. The future task of the discipline will be to determine precisely how interest groups do or do not gain control of the criminal law, the process by which competing interest groups reach a compromise, the relationship between the objectives of interest groups and the sentiments of various segments of society, and the extent to

[28] See Gilbert Geis, "Deterring Corporate Crime," in Ralph Nader and Mark Green, eds., *Corporate Power in America* (New York: Grossman, 1973), pp. 182–97.

[29] See, for example, Jerome H. Skolnick, *Justice Without Trial* (New York: John Wiley & Sons, 1966) and David Sudnow, "Normal Crimes: Sociological Features of the Penal Code in a Public Defender Office," *Social Problems* 12 (Winter 1965), pp. 255–75; James Q. Wilson, *Varieties of Police Behavior* (New York: Atheneum, 1971); Peter K. Manning, "The Police: Mandates, Strategies, and Appearances," in Jack D. Douglas, ed., *Crime and Justice in American Society* (New York: Bobbs-Merrill, 1971); Abraham S. Blumberg, *Criminal Justice* (Chicago: Quadrangle Books, 1967).

which the actual operations of the legal machinery are part of a conscious design rather than an unanticipated or unwanted result. If future research can increase our understanding of these issues, the nature of crime—the central variable requiring understanding in criminology—will take on a new clarity.

Criminal Intent

In discussing the nature of crime, our attention has centered on the question of why certain *acts* are prohibited and punished by the state. As we have seen, however, illegality alone does not make an act a crime. In the eyes of the law, the illegal act must be accompanied by *mens rea,* or the guilty mind, commonly referred to as criminal intent. Indeed, the concept of criminal intent is so fundamental to the law's definition of crime that it pervades every aspect of the administration of criminal justice, and we must now examine the subject in greater detail.

In the distant past of the English legal tradition, as custom was molded into law, persons could be punished for an injury they caused even though the harm was accidental. The social reaction to injury was predominantly one of vengeance, and little attention was paid to the motives or intentions of the individual who caused the harm.[30]

From Vengeance to Deterrence

Animals and inanimate objects could also be made to suffer for the injury they caused. Oliver Wendell Holmes, Jr., in his book *The Common Law*, describes a number of examples from ancient records: an ox stoned to death for goring a human being and a tree chopped to pieces after falling on a man and killing him. The demand for vengeance in such cases might seem irrational to the modern reader, but Justice Holmes gently reminds us that we have all undoubtedly felt hatred for an inanimate object that has harmed us—an emotion, he notes, that "leads even civilized man to kick a door when it pinches his finger."[31]

Over time, the intent to harm came to take a place in the thinking of the law where once harm alone had ruled. By 1600 the concept of crime contained two indispensible elements: an act prohibited by law and the mental state of the person who committed the act. Neither one alone con-

[30] If a man's sword wounded someone while it was being sharpened by a swordsmith, for example, the owner could be held guilty for the injury. The instruments of an injury were frequently forfeited by their owners as a *deodand,* or gift to God. See James Marshall, *Intention—In Law and Society* (New York: Funk & Wagnalls, 1968), Chapter 1.

[31] See Oliver Wendell Holmes, Jr., *The Common Law* (Boston: Little, Brown, 1881), p. 11. The punishment of animals for their misdeeds forms a curious chapter in the history of penology. See E. P. Evans, *The Criminal Prosecution and Capital Punishment of Animals* (London: Heinemann, 1906).

Criminal Intent

The contention that an injury can amount to a crime only when inflicted by intention is no provincial or transient notion. It is as universal and persistent in mature systems of law as belief in freedom of the human will and a consequent ability and duty of the normal individual to choose between good and evil. A relation between some mental element and punishment for a harmful act is almost as instinctive as the child's familiar exculpatory "But I didn't mean to," and has afforded the rational basis for a tardy and unfinished substitution of deterrence and reformation in place of retaliation and vengeance as the motivation for public prosecution. Unqualified acceptance of this doctrine by English common law in the Eighteenth Century was indicated by Blackstone's sweeping statement that to constitute any crime there must first be a "vicious will." Common-law commentators of the Nineteenth Century early pronounced the same principle, although a few exceptions not relevant to our present problem came to be recognized.

Crime, as a compound concept, generally constituted only from concurrence of an evil-meaning mind with an evil-doing hand, was congenial to an intense individualism and took deep and early root in American soil. As the states codified the common law of crimes, even if their enactments were silent on the subject, their courts assumed that the omission did not signify disapproval of the principle but merely recognized that intent was so inherent in the idea of the offense that it required no statutory affirmation. Courts, with little hesitation or division, found an implication of the requirement as to offenses that were taken over from the common law. The unanimity with which they have adhered to the central thought that wrong-doing must be conscious to be criminal is emphasized by the variety, disparity and confusion of their definitions of the requisite but elusive mental element. However, courts of various jurisdictions, and for the purposes of different offenses, have devised working formulae, if not scientific ones, for the instruction of juries around such terms as "felonious intent," "criminal intent," "malice aforethought," "guilty knowledge," "fraudulent intent," "willfulness," "*scienter*," to denote guilty knowledge, or "*mens rea*," to signify an evil purpose or mental culpability. By use or combination of these various tokens, they have sought to protect those who were not blameworthy in mind from conviction of infamous common-law crimes.

From *Morissette v. United States,* 342 U.S. 246 (1952), 11.

stituted a crime, a viewpoint expressed in the law by yet another Latin maxim: *Actus non facit reum nisi mens sit rea* ("An act does not make one guilty unless his mind is guilty").

Punishing a person for an act for which he or she is not responsible becomes a disturbing event, it may be supposed, in societies that place a growing emphasis on individualism and self-determination. Such punishment introduces an eccentric element into the moral equations linking personal virtue with reward and individual sin with suffering. In English society, in any event, the idea came to be accepted that the moral world is kept in balance by reserving punishment for those who have deliberately violated the rules. The decision of the judge in the case of *Duncan v. State* in America in 1873 sums up the sentiment in an often-quoted form: "It is a sacred principle of criminal jurisprudence that the intention to commit a crime is the essence of a crime, and to hold that a man shall be held criminally responsible for an offense, of the commission of which he was ignorant at the time, would be intolerable tyranny."[32]

The "sacred principle" is concerned with the idea of *fairness*—at least in part—and is based on the implicit model of an individual freely choosing conformity to or deviation from the norm. If a person does not freely choose behavior, it does not "belong" to the individual and neither does the praise or blame that may result from the behavior. And, in the view of the Anglo-American legal tradition, the individual is seen as freely choosing acts when the acts are performed with a conscious purpose and the results are foreseen. Criminal intent, then, refers to the purpose and knowledge that join the individual to his or her actions, and without these punishment is unfair or unjust. Without purpose and knowledge there is, in fact, no crime at all.[33]

It is not simply a commitment to fairness, however, that underlies the concern with criminal intent. The emphasis on *mens rea* appears to have developed hand-in-hand with a changing understanding of the purpose of punishment. Whereas a desire for vengeance had dominated the social response to crime in the earliest phases of the Anglo-Saxon legal system, a concern with deterrence was present and slowly emerged into prominence, becoming a matter for much explicit discussion in the eighteenth century. As the prevention of crime—the discouragement of potential offenders—began to assume an importance equal to or greater than the desire for retribution, the mental state of the wrongdoer took on evergreater relevance. This is not to say that the desire for vengeance disappeared, for the wrongdoer was often treated with a savagery that far transcended any possible calculation of controlling crime. (In fact, the an-

[32]See Albert J. Klein, *Criminal Law in New Jersey* (New Brunswick: Rutgers University Press, 1953), p. 26.
[33]LaFave and Scott, *Handbook of Criminal Law*, pp. 191–203.

cient desire to exact vengeance continues to shape much of today's thinking about the criminal.) But a concern with deterring future crime rather than punishing past derelictions became an official rationale for punishment, serving to justify the penalties inflicted by the state.

The argument for the deterrent function of the criminal law was developed by the classical school in the writings of men such as Beccaria and Bentham, and it can be summarized briefly:

Some human actions are willed or intended and can be said to be voluntary. The individual can choose to engage in them or not. Other acts, however, are outside the scope of human control and must be viewed as unintended or involuntary.

When a person has a free choice between alternative courses of action, he or she mentally weighs their consequences. Since people are rational beings, they pursue a course of behavior in which the positive consequences or pleasures outweigh the negative consequences or pains.

The threat of state-inflicted penalties helps to make the possible painful consequences outweigh the possible pleasurable consequences of criminal behavior and thus serves as a deterrent to crime.

Therefore, an individual should not be held guilty of a crime and liable to punishment when the criminal act is involuntary or beyond his or her control. If an act is not caused by criminal intent, the person should be absolved of responsibility.[34]

The effectiveness of state-imposed punishment as a means of controlling criminal behavior will concern us in Part IV. The important point for the moment is that an interest in both fairness and deterrence leads the criminal law to view the mental state of the individual as an indispensible element in its concept of crime. To be categorized as a criminal, a person must be seen not only as having set his hand against the laws of society but—in the language of another era—as having hardened his heart as well.

Interpreting Criminal Intent This view of crime poses certain problems for the legal system, since there are cases in which the criminal intent seems to be lacking and yet the law is reluctant to say that no crime has been committed. A, for example, shoots B with the intent to kill, but misses B and kills C instead. There was no intention of killing C, according to A, and C's death was accidental. There are similar cases in which the type of harm is unintended or the degree of harm is claimed to be a matter of bad luck. Furthermore, in some situations the individual intends no harm to anyone, but acts in such a careless manner that others are injured nonetheless. By

[34] See Gresham M. Sykes, *Crime and Society* (New York: Random House, 1967), pp. 29–30.

and large, the law has found ways to deal with such instances. A variety of legal fictions, such as *constructive intent,* argue that the individual intends not only the immediate outcome of the action but also its "natural and inevitable consequences." Similarly, the law has employed the idea of *transferred intent,* in which it is claimed that if an individual intends to harm one person but actually harms another, the intention to do harm has been transferred from one victim to another. The law has developed the concepts of *recklessness* and *negligence,* along with *purpose* and *knowledge,* arguing that these too, under certain conditions, constitute a state of mind that can be labeled *mens rea.* An individual may be held guilty of a crime when he harms others in situations that a reasonable person, acting with due care, would have avoided. The concept of criminal intent, in other words, is pulled and stretched by the law to cover a number of situations in which an individual causes injury to others without specifically meaning to do so. The law holds the person responsible in such cases—and punishes him not because his mind was filled with malice but because he was careless, and the law wishes to make him and others more careful in the future.

In some cases involving recklessness and negligence, the law would seem to ignore the principle of fairness and aim only at deterrence. The individual may be quite unaware of the risks attached to certain actions and yet still be held guilty of a crime. Thus, in the case of *Commonwealth v. Welansky,* the owner of a nightclub was convicted of manslaughter when a large number of people died in a fire and the prosecution proved that the owner had failed to provide adequate fire escapes. Even if a particular defendant was so stupid or heedless, said the court, that he did not realize the danger he had created, he was still guilty of a crime "if an ordinary, normal man under the same circumstances would have realized the gravity of the danger."[35]

It is possible, of course, to deter people from violating the rules by punishing the innocent along with the guilty, as is illustrated by the ancient Roman practice of *decimation,* in which the members of a legion that exhibited cowardice in battle were discouraged from future cowardice by the execution of every tenth man regardless of his conduct. In the not too distant past, similar tactics were used by the Nazis in the random execution of civilians to combat resistance fighters in occupied Europe. The modern criminal law generally rejects such arbitrary measures, but on occasion legislatures have created a number of offenses—referred to as *strict-liability* crimes—in which the idea of criminal intent is eliminated. Liquor and narcotics laws, pure food laws, and traffic laws may impose liability without reference to the mental state of the individual. The

[35] *Commonwealth v. Welansky,* 316 Mass. 383, 398, 55N.E. 2nd 902, 910 (1944).

rationale usually given for the classification of strict-liability crimes is the difficulty in obtaining convictions if fault must be proved. Most legal commentators, however, claim Wayne LaFave and Austin Scott, "are of the view that this is not an adequate justification. The better view is that strict liability should never be relied upon to impose a sentence of imprisonment and moral condemnation which goes with it, but many examples of serious strict-liability crimes are to be found in existing law."[36] The area stands much in need of sociological research.

Outside of these exceptions, proof of criminal intent saturates the law's approach to crime, and wrongdoing is generally viewed as having a dual nature. Over two hundred years ago, the English jurist Sir William Blackstone (1723–1780) indicated in his famous commentaries on the law that "to make a complete crime cognizable by human laws, there must be both a will and an act. . . . And, as a vicious will without a vicious act is not civil crime, so, on the other hand, an unwarrantable act without a vicious will is no crime at all."[37] Today, both a vicious will and an unwarrantable act continue as necessary elements in the legal definition of criminal behavior.

Defenses to Crimes

The criminal law recognizes a number of situations in which criminal intent is lacking. If one of these can be shown to exist in the case of an individual charged with a crime, the individual is held not responsible for the criminal act and is absolved of wrongdoing. Such *defenses to crimes* are important not only in the day-to-day operation of the criminal law but in revealing the assumptions about the nature of crime and human behavior that are incorporated in the legal system.

Accident The undesigned, chance events that are commonly referred to as accidents provide one obvious basis for the claim that criminal intent is absent. "There are many acts which are innocent if committed accidentally," notes one legal writer, "but which if done intentionally would constitute a crime."[38] The criminal law, however, does not allow all accidental wrongdoing to escape punishment. The general rule is that the wrongdoing will not be viewed as a crime *if* it occurred while the individual was engaged in a lawful act and exercising due care.[39] Thus, if

---

[36] *Handbook of Criminal Law*, p. 218.

[37] William Blackstone, *Commentaries on the Laws of England* (Philadelphia: Robert Bell, 1772).

[38] Klein, *Criminal Law in New Jersey*, p. 38.

[39] Ibid., p. 38.

someone is handling a hatchet in a lawful manner and the head flies off and kills a bystander, the death is regarded as a chance misfortune and the hatchet user is held not punishable. If, however, a person is speeding recklessly and illegally in an automobile and accidentally kills a pedestrian, the driver can be convicted of criminal homicide. The law is obviously concerned with making sure that people maintain reasonable care for the lives and persons of others—and is willing to limit the meaning of accident to accomplish this end.

The criminal law does not allow ignorance of the law as a defense. Every person, it is said, is presumed to know the law. Even foreigners who violate the law by an act not defined as a crime in their own country and who may never have heard of the legal rule they have broken are not excused.[40] The presumption of the law, however, is not a statement about reality but an imperative: every person is "bound to know the law," or is "charged with knowing the law," or "must know what law is and act at his peril." If a defendant, said a California court, "could shield himself behind the defense that he was ignorant of the law which he violated, immunity from punishment would in most cases result. . . . The plea would lead to interminable questions incapable of solution."[41] Because, in fact, everyone does not know the law, injustice may result; but its occurrence is far outweighed, in the viewpoint of the criminal law, by the social good attained.

Mistake of Fact

A mistake of fact, however, can be used as a defense. This applies to cases in which it can be shown that the individual committed the illegal act because of an honest and reasonable mistake and that his behavior would have been lawful if the facts of the situation had been what he thought they were. If a person mistakenly believes he has been insulted, for example, and violently attacks the supposed slanderer, he can be held guilty of a crime. Even if he had actually been insulted, his assault would be a violation of the law. If, however, a person defends himself against someone whom he honestly and reasonably believes to be threatening his life, he may be declared guiltless, even though his supposed assailant turns out to be an innocent stranger who had no harm in mind.

Distinguishing between honest and pretended mistakes of fact is not always easy for the criminal law. Still more difficult to determine, however—and more important for an understanding of how the law defines a crime—is whether the mistake is a *reasonable* one. We have encountered the idea of the reasonable man before and we will encounter it again in following chapters, for the law often uses this hypothetical fig-

[40] See Rollin M. Perkins, *Criminal Law* (Brooklyn, N.Y.: The Foundation Press, 1957), p. 808.
[41] Ibid., pp. 809–12.

ure as a standard to judge whether individuals are acting with adequate care and good sense.

In the uncertain flow of human activity, with its many opportunities for misunderstandings and unexpected consequences, the law demands that people act with prudence to minimize risk. People are to pattern themselves on a reasonable man who is cautious, always looks before he leaps, and often decides it is better not to leap at all (the law speaks of reasonable doubt concerning a conviction of guilty, reasonable grounds for an arrest, and so on, as we shall see). Such a paragon of care may be rare, but the law insists that members of society make every effort to conform to the model in their daily affairs, and it penalizes people when they fail.[42]

According to the law, however, what is reasonable can never be precisely spelled out in advance. A reasonable doubt, for example, is defined by *Black's Law Dictionary* as "such a doubt as would cause a reasonable and prudent man in the grave and more important affairs of life to pause and hesitate to act upon the truth of the matter charged."[43] Such a circular definition may well make a reasonable man uneasy, but the indeterminate quality of one of the law's most important concepts flows from the fact that no system can make rules for behavior in explicit enough detail to provide guidance in all future situations. The crucial point for the present discussion is that when key words in the legal rules are not fully defined, those administering the law become partially free to use local standards of behavior and the changing moral standards of society to determine whether a crime has been committed. Ambiguity, in other words, creates flexibility. When the behavior of an individual from one social class is being judged by the members of another—as when, let us say, a predominantly middle-class jury is trying to decide whether a lower-class defendant had reasonable grounds to fear for his life in a quarrel—such flexibility may produce an unfair severity. On the other hand, a certain vagueness of important legal concepts may allow extenuating circumstances unrecognized by the law to be taken into account. Community opinion can thus influence the results. In short, the law is not as fixed as it is supposed to be, and the application of the criminal law is not a mechanical process.

Self-Defense The claim that one acted in self-defense is perhaps one of the better-known defenses to crime. "If while defending oneself one commits an act which in itself is a crime," it has been pointed out, "the act, under certain limitations, is justified and such justification will be available as a

---

[42] For a discussion of the reasonable man in legal thought, see Max Gluckman, *The Judicial Process Among the Barotse of Northern Rhodesia* (Glencoe, Ill.: The Free Press, 1955), Chapter III.

[43] Henry C. Black, *Black's Law Dictionary* (St. Paul, Minn.: West, 1951), p. 580.

defense to criminal responsibility."[44] Again, as in accepting the claim of accident, the criminal law attempts to hedge the defense with qualifications to arrive at a principle that is thought to be both fair and workable. The person claiming self-defense must, in general, be free of fault—he cannot, for example, start a fight, kill his opponent, and then claim he was forced to save himself. The apprehension of imminent danger must be reasonable—as a mistake of fact has to be—and threatening words alone are not enough. The amount of force used to defend one's self must be commensurate with the attack; and if the individual uses more force than is reasonably necessary, he becomes the aggressor and makes himself liable for criminal violence.[45]

Duress or Compulsion

The claim of duress or compulsion is similar to the claim of self-defense, for in both defenses an individual argues that he has been forced, against his will, to commit a criminal act. In the case of duress as a defense to crime, however, the individual directs his wrongdoing against an innocent third party rather than against someone who threatens him. Thus, for example, an employee of a store opens the safe of her employer and removes the contents under the threat of a pistol pointed at her head by an armed robber. The employee argues that she should not be held criminally responsible, and the law is likely to agree. "It is well settled that one is exempted from criminal responsibility for doing a criminal act where one is forced to do the act against one's will," declares Albert Klein. "The act performed under duress is deemed to be the act of another. The criminal intent is also that of another, and the law absolves the doer from liability."[46]

Under certain circumstances, the command of a person in a position of authority has been accepted by the law as a form of duress or compulsion that relieves the individual of responsibility for an illegal act. For example, the common law held that a married woman compelled by her husband to engage in criminal conduct was held blameless. This doctrine, notes Rollin Perkins, has been attributed to the reasoning of early legal decisions that spoke of the legal identity of husband and wife, the position of the wife as no more than a servant to the husband, and the wife's role of a "marionette moved at will by the husband."[47] In actuality, Perkins argues, this special use of the defense of compulsion was probably due in large part to the courts' unwillingness to inflict the death penalty on women when many crimes were punishable by death.[48] The trend today is toward the abolition of this defense in the case of wives,

[44] Klein, *Criminal Law in New Jersey*, p. 44.
[45] Ibid., pp. 44–45.
[46] Ibid., p. 38.
[47] Perkins, *Criminal Law*, pp. 796–97.
[48] Ibid., pp. 798–805. See also LaFave and Scott, *Handbook of Criminal Law*, Chapter 5.

but the issue of orders or commands as a form of compulsion remains to plague the law.

At the Nuremburg trials for war criminals after World War II, a number of defendants claimed that they should not be held responsible for the crimes with which they were charged, on the grounds that they were acting under the orders of superior authority. Their arguments were rejected. Civilian courts, military courts, and the Nuremburg tribunal agreed that although the order of a superior might absolve a wrong-doer from responsibility under some circumstances, such would not be the case if the action the subordinate was ordered to perform was clearly unlawful. It was the soldier's duty—and legal responsibility—to disobey in such circumstances. The claim of acting under orders formed a crucial part of Lieutenant Calley's defense for his part in the Mai Lai massacre in the Vietnam War, but his claim was also rejected on the same grounds.[49] Yet when a number of soldiers in the United States armed forces during the Vietnam War refused to participate in bombing missions, they were court-martialed; and the court refused to recognize their argument that their conscience declared the war to be either illegal or immoral.

The idea that subordinates in a hierarchy of authority must weigh the lawfulness of the orders flowing down from above is obviously filled with complexities. The legal system demands, in effect, that individuals decide whether they should conform to the biddings of those in authority, but at the same time it is highly intolerant of private moralities that generate actions at variance with the law. Stanley Milgram, a social psychologist, designed a series of controversial experiments in which he found that most people would inflict a supposedly painful electric shock on others if they were told to do so by a person in authority.[50] Some critics were quick to see this as evidence of how close American society had come to Nazi Germany and how unwilling Americans were to challenge those in power, but one reviewer argued that the most important implication lay elsewhere. According to R. J. Herrenstein, the findings of Milgram's experiments were of interest because they pointed to the conflict between the inescapable need for loyalty and obedience that help to hold society together and the high value placed on individual conscience and autonomy in American culture. The solution is to be found, said Herrenstein, not in trying to create a higher percentage of insubordinates—which he thought an unlikely event—but in gaining greater control over those in authority.[51] The argument is debatable, but it is clear that the dilemma of the person faced with directives he or she believes to

[49] See Joseph Goldstein, Burke Marshall, and Jack Schwartz, *The My Lai Massacre and Its Cover-up: Beyond the Reach of the Law?* (New York: The Free Press, 1976).

[50] Stanley Milgram, *Obedience to Authority* (New York: Harper & Row, 1974).

[51] See "Measuring Evil," a review of Milgram's book by R. J. Herrenstein, *Commentary* (June 1974), pp. 82–88.

be illegitimate poses great difficulties for both the individual and the law. The defense of compulsion in the form of a command will undoubtedly continue to be tested in the courts—as it was in the case of the Watergate defendants who sought to be excused on the grounds that they were acting under orders.

Immaturity can also serve as a defense to crime, for the criminal law accepts the idea that children below a certain age are incapable of possessing a deliberate, malicious intention to harm others. The precise age, however, at which innocence ends and the possibility of harboring criminal intent begins has changed over the years, reflecting changing social conditions of childhood. **Immaturity**

In the common law, children under the age of seven were assumed to be incapable of formulating a criminal intent, and no evidence would be accepted that attempted to show otherwise; children between seven and fourteen were presumed incapable, but if the prosecution could prove the contrary, the child could be held guilty; after the age of fourteen (when, in an earlier era, children often left home to serve as apprentices), children were viewed as being no less capable of malice than were adults and thus equally capable of committing a crime.

In the nineteenth and twentieth centuries, increased schooling and delayed entry into the labor force began to prolong the period of dependency, and the line set by the law for the onset of possible criminal responsibility began to drift upward. With the passage of the first juvenile court act in Illinois, in 1899, a statutory distinction between adult crime and juvenile delinquency was created. The latter was not crime, from the viewpoint of the law, for criminal intent was considered to be lacking, and the illegal acts of juveniles were to be handled in juvenile court, with reform rather than punishment as the goal. In many jurisdictions, in recent times, the dividing line between delinquency and crime has come to stand at about sixteen or seventeen years of age.

The special regard of the criminal law for the youthful offender has often generated criticism, however, particularly in the past few years. Some critics view the juvenile court as too harsh, depriving youthful offenders of many of their legal rights. Others believe that the juvenile court is far too lenient. "For decades," notes a story in *The New York Times*, "authorities have dealt with juvenile delinquents as troubled individuals, rather than as criminals. The deliquents have been offered help, but have seldom been punished. But now, with a tougher, more dangerous delinquent emerging, committing more violent crime than ever before, it is clear that the old approach is not working."[52] A liberal assemblyman from the Bronx, reports *The New York Times*, has felt it nec-

[52] "Juvenile Criminals an Increasing Problem," *The New York Times* (May 23, 1976).

essary to introduce a bill that would send fourteen- and fifteen-year-olds to the adult criminal court. The use of immaturity as a defense to crime, then, is accepted in principle by the criminal law, but society often exhibits uneasiness about the matter; and there is little question that the distinction between juvenile delinquency and adult crime will continue to be a matter of dispute as long as the concept of childhood remains mutable.

Insanity There is one additional defense to crime—the insanity plea—that is most important not for the frequency of its use but for the light it throws on the criminal law's view of the causes of crime.

As pointed out earlier, much of the criminal law in the United States has its roots in English history. This is particularly evident in the case of the plea of insanity, which has long been governed by the *M'Naghten Rules*. In 1843 Daniel M'Naghten was brought to trial for murder, having shot and killed the secretary of Sir Robert Peel, the prime minister of England. M'Naghten suffered from the delusion that he was pursued by deadly enemies, including Peel, and in attempting to assassinate him he killed Peel's secretary by mistake. M'Naghten was found "not guilty, on the ground of insanity."[53] A few years earlier, a man named Oxford had been charged with treason for firing a pistol at Queen Victoria and been acquitted because of "mental derangement." The M'Naghten decision created an uproar—dangerous criminals, it appeared, were being set free on flimsy reasoning—and the queen asked the House of Lords to debate the issue of insanity as a defense to crime. The House of Lords turned to the judges of the Common Law Courts and requested their opinion on the matter. The result was the M'Naghten Rules, which continue as a subject of noisy controversy to the present day.

An individual "is punishable according to the nature of crime committed, if he knew at the time of committing such crime that he was acting contrary to the law," declared the advisory opinion of the judges. To establish a defense on the ground of insanity, they continued, "it must be clearly proved that, at the time of the committing of the act, the party accused was laboring under such a defect of reason, from disease of the mind, as not to know the nature and quality of the act he was doing; or if he did know it, that he did not know that he was doing what was wrong."[54]

The M'Naghten Rules were quickly adopted in the United States (except in New Hampshire) and continue to provide much of the basis for the plea of insanity as a defense to crime. About half the states have

---

[53] See John Biggs, Jr., *The Guilty Mind* (New York: Harcourt, Brace & World, 1955); Hans Toch, ed., *Legal and Criminal Psychology* (New York: Holt, Rinehart, and Winston, 1961); and David Abrahamsen, *The Psychology of Crime* (John Wiley & Sons, 1960).

[54] Abrahamsen, *The Psychology of Crime*, p. 247.

added the doctrine of *irresistible impulse*, which requires a verdict of not guilty by reason of insanity if it is found that the defendant suffered from a mental aberration that prevented him from controlling his behavior. In 1954 another concept of insanity was established by Judge Bazelon's decision in the Durham case in the District of Columbia Circuit Court of Appeals, in which it was asserted that "an accused is not criminally responsible if his unlawful act was the product of mental disease or mental defect."[55] The preoccupation with the distinction between right and wrong was no longer central in the Durham decision, but despite the fact that the decision was hailed as a great step forward by a number of psychiatrists and legal commentators, the decision's reasoning has seldom been adopted outside of Judge Bazelon's court.

Although the M'Naghten Rules are supposed to govern much of the substance of the insanity plea, the law is by no means the whole story. A number of legal scholars have indicated that when the M'Naghten Rules are used, trial evidence (including the testimony of psychiatrists) is seldom limited to the defendant's ability to distinguish right from wrong. Juries, in fact, often take the law's concept of the insanity plea as little more than a rough guideline in deciding whether a mental aberration should excuse the defendant of responsibility for his criminal act.[56]

Nevertheless, psychiatrists continue to attack the law's concept of insanity as a defense to crime, arguing that the legal rules have little to do with the realities of mental illness. (The law's definition of insanity appears in a variety of legal issues, including the grounds for divorce, the ability to make a will and to enter into a contract, the ability to serve on a jury and to stand trial, and the competence to undergo execution.[57] These definitions are inconsistent and differ from the law's view of mental illness used in the plea of insanity in criminal cases, but only the last concerns us here.) Equating insanity with a defect of reason, it is argued, ignores a wide variety of mental disorders that go beyond the inability to tell right from wrong. Such an ability is a doubtful concept in any case. The human mind, psychiatrists claim, cannot be divided into compartments labeled the intellectual and the emotional. The human personality forms a psychic unity that cannot be so easily dissected, and the criminal law errs in trying to pin down a supposedly defective rational faculty.

As far as the law's concept of irresistible impulse is concerned, say the critics, mental illness does not necessarily find expression as a sudden, impulsive act but may take behavioral form after a long period of brooding and reflection. The idea that impulses are irresistible is also flawed if

[55] *Durham v. United States,* 94 U.S. App. D.C. 228, 214 F. 2d 862 (1954).

[56] See LaFave and Scott, *Handbook of Criminal Law,* Chapter 4.

[57] The law says that a person must know that he is being killed for his crime—otherwise the punishment is wrong (isn't fair, is useless, etc.). Thus a person can be held "incompetent" to be executed.

it is taken to mean that volitional capacity is totally impaired. "Most exhibitionists, for example," it has been pointed out, "have enough control not to yield to their impulse in the presence of a policeman. . . . Nevertheless, these individuals are the victims of urges so strong that most persons could not resist them under most circumstances."[58]

At first glance, these criticisms seem telling, but some legal commentators have found the position of the psychiatrists less than convincing. A precise definition of mental illness is impossible to obtain, it is claimed, even from psychiatrists, and the law at least offers a rough guide. Other critics of the psychiatric position have been less kind. Psychiatric testimony about the mental health of those accused of crime, argues Thomas Szasz, is little more than a commodity that can be bought by those who can pay the price. "I am bitterly opposed to forensic psychiatry," he has declared in a discussion of the conflicting psychiatric testimony in the Patty Hearst case, "not merely because it is a fraud, but because it is so profoundly inimical to the loftiest moral principles of Anglo-American law. Those principles, summed up by the phrase 'The Rule of Law,' are, simply put, to acquit the innocent and to convict and punish the guilty, giving the defendant the benefit of doubt, and the prosecution the burden of proving guilt. This sounds simple enough, and it would be without psychiatry." Forensic psychiatrists masquerading as doctors, Szasz declares, do nothing more than offer "contrived speculations" that confuse rather than clarify.[59]

Such criticisms may be overblown, but there seems to be little question that wealthy defendants are most likely to secure a convincing array of psychiatric testimony; that a plea of insanity in a criminal trial is a clumsy and inadequate device for determining the influence of mental illness in criminal behavior; and that the various legal definitions of insanity used in different jurisdictions have little scientific value.

These conclusions do not dispose of the controversy; and in several ways the conflict between law and psychiatry transcends the debate concerning the plea of insanity and cannot be resolved by a mere appeal to evidence. First, the debate has reflected a battle between two professions, each laying claim to the right to interpret the actions of an individual who is supposed to be both a criminal and mentally ill. In addition, the controversy is an outgrowth of the disagreement between those who fear that a psychiatric viewpoint may serve to absolve people who should be punished and those who fear that a legal viewpoint may lead to the punishment of people who do not deserve it. Most important, perhaps, the debate about the insanity plea raises a number of issues that go beyond the question of mental illness and criminal responsibility and threaten the entire edifice of *mens rea* so carefully constructed by the law.

[58] LaFave and Scott, *Handbook of Criminal Law*, p. 285.
[59] Thomas Szasz, "Mercenary Psychiatry," *The New Republic* (March 13, 1976).

If the criminal law were to accept the idea that the plea of insanity is to be shaped largely by the views of psychiatry with regard to *internal* forces influencing human conduct, it might find itself forced to reexamine its ideas about *external* forces as well—not just physical events or physical coercion, which are now recognized, but the forces of the socio-cultural environment as well. If it could be shown that such factors as the patterns of family life, the conditions of ghetto life, and socioeconomic status act as determinants beyond the individual's choice or control, then it might be necessary to modify the law's conceptions about defenses to crimes in general. Defenses to crime might no longer be a matter of legal definitions and common sense, as is now so largely the case, but an empirical question subject to the findings of the social sciences. That might prove to be far more disruptive of the law's concept of criminal responsibility than merely modifying the categories of mental illness.

Defenses to crime are designed to exculpate individuals who have committed an illegal act if they lack the *mens rea* necessary for crime. Only in this way, according to the criminal law, can the principle of fairness be maintained and the penal sanctions of the state be reserved for those who are marked by the guilty mind that justifies the use of punishment for retribution or deterrence. Before accepting this argument, however, it must be recognized that individuals lacking criminal intent may be convicted and punished on occasion in the name of public policy. When ignorance of the law, for example, is prohibited as a defense to crime, on the grounds that to do otherwise would be too inefficient, the idea of punishing only those knowingly or intentionally breaking the law may be violated. Limiting the plea of insanity to the law's view of mental illness may prevent responsible individuals from going scot-free and maintain an effective threat of punishment for those who may be strongly tempted to break the law precisely because they do suffer from a mental illness; yet it may also result in the punishment of individuals who are in fact unable to control their actions.[60] The concept of defenses to crime, in short, may be based on a passion for justice and a concern to avoid pointless suffering, but the quests for fairness and deterrence may sometimes be in conflict; and both, on occasion, may be sacrificed to the ancient desire for retribution.

Major and Minor Crimes

The criminal law makes an effort to classify breaches of the law according to their seriousness by dividing them into two categories—*felonies*, or

[60] See Herbert Wechsler, "The Criteria of Criminal Responsibility," *University of Chicago Law Review* 22 (Winter 1955), pp. 367–76.

major crimes; and *misdemeanors,* or minor crimes. This effort, as we shall see, is not very successful. Nevertheless, the division affects every aspect of the operation of the criminal law, from arrest to trial to sentencing to place of confinement.

The common law of England divided crimes into four groups: high treason, petit treason, felonies, and misdemeanors. The first consisted in killing the king, levying war against him, supporting his enemies, or lending his enemies aid and comfort. Petit treason involved the killing of a husband by a wife, a master or mistress by a servant, or a prelate by a clergyman—a breach of allegiance, in short, in a superior–subordinate relationship other than king and subject. Felonies were defined as crimes other than treason that caused great moral indignation or did serious harm and were punishable by death and the forfeiture of land and goods. Misdemeanors consisted of offenses that were considered minor and were punishable with lesser penalties, such as whipping and branding.

The law continues to make these distinctions to the present day, with the exception of petit treason, which was abolished by statute in 1828. The harshness of penalties has been greatly reduced, and high treason occupies the attention of society only on occasion; but in the Anglo-American legal system crimes are still categorized as felonies or misdemeanors, with punishments of greater and lesser severity. In general, those offenses calling for the death penalty (or which once did so) or imprisonment for more than a year are labeled felonies. All other offenses are lumped under the heading of misdemeanors.

The criteria distinguishing between more and less serious crime presumably involve the amount of injury or harm done and the degree of moral outrage that is elicited. However, the lack of any explicit and objective standard in the law for measuring harm or moral outrage means that crimes are often defined as felonies and misdemeanors in an inconsistent fashion.

The classification of crimes differs from one state to another, so that particular offenses may vary in imputed seriousness with geographical location. Within a state, property offenses may change abruptly from misdemeanors to felonies when the value of the stolen object rises above a certain figure, say $50. In a number of states, an offense that is a misdemeanor the first time it is committed becomes a felony when it is repeated.[61] "There is no single classification of crimes or of penalties that are identical and uniform in all jurisdictions," notes Donald Newman. "Only by reference to specific statutory provisions in each jurisdiction

---

[61] See Hazel B. Kerper, *Introduction to the Criminal Justice System* (St. Paul, Minn.: West, 1972), p. 329.

can it be determined whether an offense is a felony or misdemeanor, or its ranking or degree of seriousness be measured."[62]

If the distinction between misdemeanors and felonies is inconsistent and often seems to be based on tradition rather than on reasoned analysis, it nevertheless has far-reaching importance. First, the definition of a crime is sometimes contingent on the classification of another; burglary, for example, is defined as breaking and entering a dwelling at night with intent to commit a felony rather than a misdemeanor. Second, in some jurisdictions conviction of a felony disqualifies the individual from holding public office, voting, and serving on a jury. Conviction for a misdemeanor does not carry such consequences. Third—and this is particularly important for the administration of the criminal law—the fact that felonies and misdemeanors differ in their punishments provides the basis for *plea bargaining*. The charge against a defendant may be reduced from a felony to a misdemeanor in return for a plea of guilty, thus saving the state the time and expense of a trial. As we shall see in Chapter 11 in more detail, the courts assert that without such bargains to reduce their overcrowded calendars, the legal system in the United States would founder.

The classification of crimes as felonies and misdemeanors, or as more and less serious, represents a normative judgment of society that is important not only in the day-to-day administration of the criminal law, but in the modification of the penal code, the allocation of resources for the control of crime, and the understanding of the causes of crime. It is surprising, then, that measuring public attitudes toward the seriousness of crimes received relatively little attention in criminology until the last several decades and that so many crucial questions still remain unanswered.

The pioneering work of Thorsten Sellin and Marvin Wolfgang (1964) examined the ratings of 141 offenses, using groups of college students, police, and judges to make evaluations of seriousness. The offenses ranged from murder to obscene phone calls, and in general the three rating groups tended to agree about the relative degree of seriousness of the various crimes.[63] Offenses involving physical injuries were apt to be ranked as more serious than those involving the loss of property, as might be expected, and intimidation with a weapon increased the seriousness of an offense in the eyes of the evaluators. Subsequent studies by other researchers have obtained similar results, tending to confirm

[62] Donald J. Newman, *Introduction to Criminal Justice* (Philadelphia: J. B. Lippincott, 1975), p. 22.
[63] Thorsten Sellin and Marvin E. Wolfgang, *The Measurement of Delinquency* (New York: John Wiley & Sons, 1964). Crimes and delinquent acts are treated by the authors as virtually identical; the emphasis is on the illegal act, not the age of the offender.

the relative weights attached by Sellin and Wolfgang to such aspects of crimes as number of victims; value of property stolen, damaged, or destroyed; and bodily harm.[64]

A study of community attitudes toward the seriousness of crimes, conducted in Baltimore in 1972, attempted to use a cross-section of the population to do the judging and focused more sharply on the question of consensus.[65] Again, much agreement was found, with the planned killing of a policeman scoring as most serious and being drunk in a public place appearing at the bottom of the list.

Studies of popular attitudes toward the seriousness of various crimes are apt to be flawed, however, on a number of points. First, seriousness is seldom defined for the respondents. The person being interviewed may be thinking of the amount of harm done or the degree of moral indignation that is aroused, or both, or neither. Since these two common meanings of seriousness are not necessarily correlated (incest may be viewed as morally offensive, for example, but not destructive of others, while shoplifting may be regarded as morally trivial but economically damaging), the results can be confusing. Second, the crimes to be rated are usually described in brief, abstract terms, but the ranking of crimes is likely to depend on a host of factors such as the age, sex, race, and social class of the offender and the victim; their prior relationship; the motives of the offender and possible provocation on the part of the victim; the type of physical injury and its extent; the type of monetary loss and its amount; and the psychological suffering that may be involved. Unless these are made explicit, an individual's ranking of a crime is likely to depend on the unknown picture of the crime the person happens to have in his or her mind. Third, the search for general patterns in the ranking of crimes by their relative seriousness is apt to neglect particular anomalies. General agreement about most crimes does not preclude a conflict of opinions about specific offenses or types of offenses, and the latter is sometimes the crucial fact rather than the tendency to agree. Furthermore, general agreement that certain crimes are *not* serious may be quite at variance with the punishments embedded in the criminal law.

As Sellin and Wolfgang have pointed out, attempting to come to grips with the problem of measuring the seriousness of different offenses is essential, whether it be a matter of designing a rational sentencing system

[64] See D. D. Akman, A. Normandeau, and S. Turner, "The Measurement of Delinquency in Canada," *The Journal of Criminal Law, Criminology, and Police Science* 58 (September 1967), pp. 330–37. See also Angel Velez-Draz and Edwin I. Megargee, "An Investigation of Differences in Value Judgments Between Youthful Offenders and Non-offenders in Puerto Rico," *The Journal of Criminal Law, Criminology, and Police Science* 61 (December 1970), pp. 549–53.

[65] Peter H. Rossi, Emily Waite, Christine E. Bose, and Richard E. Berk, "The Seriousness of Crimes: Normative Structure and Individual Differences," *American Sociological Review* 39 (April 1974), pp. 224–37.

or building a theory of the relationship between crime and social structure.[66] The understanding of crime will be greatly increased when public attitudes toward the degree of wrongdoing involved in different offenses can be discerned more precisely.

Crime and Official Figures

Much of what people know about crime is based on the official records of governmental agencies. The incidence of particular types of crime reported to the police, the characteristics of suspected offenders who have been arrested, and estimates of monetary costs are typical examples of the kind of data that are presented to the American public on a regular basis, often with fanfare in the press and lengthy editorial comment, and that undoubtedly help to shape public opinion about the nature of crime and its meaning for society.

Such official reports are also used by social scientists in their effort to understand the relationship between crime and society. As indicated in Chapter 1, however, official figures suffer from a number of defects as a measure of crime, and their use requires considerable caution.

The *Uniform Crime Reports* of the Federal Bureau of Investigation are the major source of national crime statistics collected on a continuing basis, and they have provided data for American criminology for many years. First published in 1930, the *Reports* now supply information on crimes known to the police, arrests, the disposition of persons charged, and other related matters from approximately 11,000 law enforcement agencies covering 93 percent of the population of the United States.

The FBI's reliance on data obtained from local law enforcement agencies introduces serious problems. Local agencies vary in their procedures for gathering information, the legal definitions employed, and the care taken in keeping records; and the FBI admits that it cannot vouch for the accuracy of the figures appearing in its annual publications. Local police agencies may record fewer crimes than have been reported to them to hide a disturbing rise in crime rates. Or they may inflate the figures to win public support for a fight against a crime wave that does not exist. It was this last accusation, in fact, that was often leveled against J. Edgar Hoover and the FBI by critics on the left side of the political fence. We will return to this issue, but it is clear that the data of the FBI have often been presented in a form that has tended to exaggerate the increase in crime over the years.[67]

Far more important as a source of error, however, is the fact that only a

[66] *The Measurement of Delinquency,* Chapter 20.
[67] See Marvin E. Wolfgang, "Uniform Crime Reports: A Critical Appraisal," *University of Pennsylvania Law Review* 111 (April 1963), pp. 708–38.

fraction of all crimes come to the attention of the police. There is a so-called dark figure of crime, a great mass of offenses that are never discovered or, if discovered, never reported.[68] And of those crimes that are reported to the police, only a small fraction (some 21 percent in 1976) are "cleared by arrest"—that is, result in the detection and apprehension of a suspected culprit. Crimes known to the police, then, give a poor indication of the actual amount of criminal behavior occurring in society in any given year, and information concerning suspected offenders who have been arrested gives a distorted picture of all criminals. The problem of accurate crime statistics is made still more difficult by the fact that for some types of crime—such as murder—the data are probably fairly reliable, but with other crimes—such as fraud—the data are almost worthless.

The work of the Commission on Law Enforcement and Administration of Justice appointed by President Johnson in the 1960s represented a major inquiry into the nature and extent of crime in American society. As might be expected, the commission depended heavily on information about the incidence of crime provided by the FBI, but it was quite aware of the need to take into consideration the mass of unreported crime as well. As a consequence, the commission had a number of special studies prepared, most notably a national survey of 10,000 randomly selected households conducted by the National Opinion Research Center at the University of Chicago (NORC) and more detailed surveys in Chicago, Boston, and Washington.[69] As had been suspected, the amount of crime revealed by these surveys, in which people reported whether they had been victimized, was far greater than the amount of crime reported by the police. The number of forcible rapes and burglaries was more than three times greater than the official figures indicated. The number of larcenies and assaults was more than twice as large as the official figure, and the number of robberies was 50 percent greater.[70]

In the NORC survey, victims who said they had not notified the police were asked why. The reason most frequently cited was the belief that the police could not do anything. This might have been a rationalization for their failure to report, but in view of the small proportion of reported crimes that are cleared by arrest, the respondents' assessment is undoubtedly correct in many instances. The second most frequent reason given for not reporting was that the crime was a private matter or the victim did not want to harm the offender.[71] The survey technique of

[68] See Albert D. Biderman and Albert J. Reiss, Jr., "On Exploring the 'Dark Figure' of Crime," *The Annals of the American Academy of Political and Social Science* 347 (November 1967), pp. 1–15.

[69] President's Commission on Law Enforcement and Administration of Justice, *Task Force Report: Crime and Its Impact—An Assessment* (Washington, D.C.: Government Printing Office, 1967), p. 17.

[70] Ibid., p. 17.

[71] See Philip H. Ennis, "Criminal Victimization in the United States: A Report of a Na-

measuring criminal activity by using a random sample of households has some obvious advantages, and the Law Enforcement Assistance Administration (LEAA) continues to publish reports of this kind. Law enforcement agencies dealing with crime on a day-to-day basis, however, will probably continue as the major source of data.[72]

The FBI divides reported crimes into Part I (more serious) offenses and Part II (less serious) offenses, as shown in Table 1. The FBI finds the states' classification of felonies or misdemeanors too inconsistent to be relied on, but it provides no clear explanation for its own classification.[73] Part I offenses are nearly identical to the offenses forming the FBI's so-called Crime Index—which is not an index at all in the usual sense, but simply consists of those crimes described by the FBI as "serious" or "the most common local problem."[74] Aside from this vague clue, there is no rationale offered for the division of crimes into two groups, and it is apparently based on an assumed consensus. Even if the basis for the distinction between Part I and Part II offenses is unclear, however, the distinction itself has important consequences. Most significant, perhaps, is the fact that the Crime Index of the FBI provides the data for the summary tables and dramatic graphs reported each year in the *Uniform Crime Reports* and has a major influence on the public's view of current criminal activity.

The number of crimes known to the police is reported for Part I offenses, but the only figure provided for Part II offenses is the number of persons arrested. The reason for this is not entirely clear, but Part II offenses do not always come readily to the attention of the police and their definition is likely to vary greatly among the states. For Part II offenses, then, the number of persons arrested may be viewed by the FBI as the best possible estimate.[75] It is to be remembered, however, that persons arrested are suspected offenders rather than proven culprits. The *Uniform Crime Reports* indicate that in many instances persons arrested are not charged with the crime for which they were arrested or are not convicted

---

tional Survey," *Field Survey II, President's Commission on Law Enforcement and Administration of Justice* (Washington, D.C.: Government Printing Office, 1967). The causes that lie behind victims' failure to report crimes are complex. Nonreporting has been found to be linked to home ownership, family structure, and education. See Albert D. Biderman, "Surveys of Population Samples for Estimating Crime Incidence," *The Annals of the American Academy of Political and Social Science* 374 (November 1967), pp. 16–33.

[72]*Criminal Victimization in the United States: A Comparison of 1973 and 1974 Findings* (Washington, D.C.: Government Printing Office, 1976). For an evaluation of the crime surveys of the Law Enforcement Assistance Administration, see Betty K. Eidson Penick and Maurice E. B. Owens III, eds., *Surveying Crime* (Washington, D.C.: National Academy of Sciences, 1976).

[73]*Uniform Crime Reports—1976* (Washington, D.C.: Government Printing Office, 1977), p. 1.

[74]Ibid., p. 302. The Crime Index excludes manslaughter by negligence, which is included in Part I offenses.

[75]See Wolfgang, "Uniform Crime Reports: A Critical Appraisal," p. 709.

Table 1. Classification of Offenses by the Federal Bureau of Investigation

PART I OFFENSES

Criminal homicide. (1) Murder and nonnegligent manslaughter: All willful felonious homicides as distinguished from deaths caused by negligence. Excludes attempts to kill, assaults to kill, suicides, accidental deaths, or justifiable homicides. Justifiable homicides are limited to: (a) the killing of a person by a peace officer in line of duty; (b) the killing of a person in the act of committing a felony by a private citizen. (2) Manslaughter by negligence: Any death which the police investigation established was primarily attributable to gross negligence of some individual other than the victim.

Forcible rape. Rape by force, assault to rape, and attempted rape. Excludes statutory offenses (no force used—victim under age of consent).

Robbery. Stealing or taking anything of value from the care or control of a person by force or violence or by putting in fear, such as strong-arm robbery, stickups, armed robbery, assaults to rob, and attempts to rob.

Aggravated assault. Assault with intent to kill or for the purpose of inflicting severe bodily injury by shooting, cutting, stabbing, maiming, poisoning, scalding, or by the use of acids, explosives, or other means. Excludes simple assaults.

Burglary. breaking or entering—Burglary, housebreaking, safecracking, or any breaking or unlawful entry of a structure with the intent to commit a felony or a theft. Includes attempted forcible entry.

Larceny–theft. The unlawful taking, carrying, leading, or riding away of property from the possession of another (except auto theft). Thefts of bicycles, automobile accessories, shoplifting, pickpocketing, or any stealing of property or article which is not taken by force and violence or by fraud. Excludes embezzlement, "con" games, forgery, worthless checks, etc.

Auto theft. Unlawful taking or stealing of a motor vehicle.

PART II OFFENSES

Other assaults. Assaults which are not of an aggravated nature.

Arson. Willful or malicious burning with or without intent to defraud. Includes attempts.

Forgery and counterfeiting. Making, altering, uttering, or possessing, with intent to defraud, anything false which is made to appear true. Includes attempts.

if they are charged. Clearly, measuring the amount of criminal behavior in society is an imperfect process. Data are lost at each step in the administration of justice, and the greater the distance from the commission of the criminal act the more imperfect are the data.

In summary, the *Uniform Crime Reports* can provide a crude picture of the volume of crime in American society. Although they are based on the records of enforcement agencies at work in a great variety of jurisdictions rather than on scientific research, if used with care they furnish data in a field where, due to the covert nature of crime, information is in short supply.

Conclusions

Some scholars have found little rationality in much of the criminal law. "We are always passing laws in America," said sociologist Robert E. Park. "We might as well get up and dance. The laws are largely to relieve emotions, and the legislators are quite aware of that fact."[76] But this

Fraud. Fraudulent conversion and obtaining money or property by false pretenses. Includes bad checks except forgeries and counterfeiting. Also includes larceny by bailee.

Embezzlement. Misappropriation or misapplication of money or property entrusted to one's care, custody, or control.

Stolen property, buying, receiving, possessing. Buying, receiving, and possessing stolen property and attempts.

Vandalism. Willful or malicious destruction, injury, disfigurement, or defacement of property without consent of the owner or person having custody or control.

Weapons: carrying, possessing, etc. All violations of regulations or statutes controlling the carrying, using, possessing, furnishing, and manufacturing of deadly weapons or silencers. Includes attempts.

Prostitution and commercialized vice. Sex offenses of a commercialized nature and attempts such as prostitution, keeping a bawdy house, procuring or transporting women for immoral purposes.

Sex offenses (except forcible rape, prostitution, and commercialized vice). Statutory rape, offenses against chastity, common decency, morals, and the like. Includes attempts.

Narcotic drug laws. Offenses relating to narcotic drugs, such as unlawful possession, sale, use, growing, manufacturing, and making of narcotic drugs.

Gambling. Promoting, permitting, or engaging in gambling.

Offenses against the family and children. Nonsupport, neglect, desertion, or abuse of family and children.

Driving under the influence. Driving or operating any motor vehicle or common carrier while drunk and under the influence of liquor or narcotics.

Liquor laws. State or local liquor law violations, except "drunkenness" and "driving under the influence." Excludes federal violations.

Drunkenness. Drunkenness or intoxication.

Disorderly conduct. Breach of the peace.

Vagrancy. Vagabondage, begging, loitering, etc.

All other offenses. All other violations of state or local laws, except traffic.

Suspicion. Arrests for no specific offense and released without formal charges being placed.

Curfew and loitering laws (juveniles). Offenses relating to violation of local curfew or loitering ordinances where such laws exist.

Runaway (juveniles). Limited to juveniles taken into protective custody under provisions of local statutes as runaways.

SOURCE: *Uniform Crime Reports—1976* (Washington, D.C.: Government Printing Office, 1977), Appendix II.

---

viewpoint is too simple to capture reality, for it ignores the mix of elements that determine the nature of crime in our society.

A portion of the criminal law prohibits behavior that a large majority of people probably finds repugnant and wants to see eliminated or at least much diminished. The behavior includes many forms of personal violence and the familiar forms of property offenses such as theft, burglary, and robbery. The precise definitions of these crimes have varied with time, depending on concepts of private property, the intricacies of ownership, and ideas about the sanctity of the body, but the underlying values appear to be both durable and fairly clear. Another portion of the criminal law prohibits behavior that violates the precepts of the Judeo-Christian system of morals, particularly in the area of sexuality. While it is doubtful that these prohibitions represent a morality imposed by an

[76]Quoted in E. H. Sutherland and Donald R. Cressey, *Criminology* (Philadelphia: J. B. Lippincott, 1970), p. 10.

elite contrary to the ethical judgments of the masses, the public is clearly not unanimous on a number of the issues involved.

Beyond these prohibitions, the criminal law has swept into its catalogue of banned behavior a great variety of acts that seem to have little connection with the collective conscience of society. The rules concerning some of these acts are based not on ethical judgments but on matters of convenience, such as the decision that people should drive on one side of the road rather than on the other. The public accepts these rules, but it is expediency rather than moral content that provides legitimacy. Other rules, such as those dealing with drugs, have been made a part of the criminal law and are invested with a great deal of moral content by some people but not by others. The criminal status of the behavior in question is sometimes sharply contested, introducing into the system a great deal of conflict that is likely to flow into areas that have long been taken for granted. Still other portions of the criminal law are largely beyond the public ken; they are either buried in forgotten codes and rarely if ever enforced, or they involve matters such as building regulations and business transactions that are not of widespread public concern.[77] Finally, parts of the criminal law—and the *lack* of criminal law as well—reflect the interests of particular social groups that have managed to shape the legal system to fit their needs.

This sprawling mass of prohibitions has accumulated over a long period of time, and the social forces that shaped the definition of a particular crime may have long since disappeared. The search for the nature of crime, therefore, must often take a historical turn. This is particularly true when we ask why society employs the criminal law—rather than tort law, for example, or administrative regulations—to deal with a particular type of unwanted behavior.

In part, state intervention—in the form of prohibitions and punishment—can be seen as a continuation of the ancient desire for retaliation. A faith in the deterrent effect of punishment, however, has also been at work over the centuries. Society has defined as crimes acts that are said to be socially harmful and thought to be preventable by the use of penal sanctions. The meaning of the term *socially harmful* is elusive, and we may suspect that it is often used as an unexamined substitute for unwanted behavior, but the effort to control crime is clear enough. Society has proceeded on the assumptions that people weigh the future as they contemplate alternative actions and that the state can influence their choices. Crime becomes those unwanted forms of behavior which can

[77] The Penal Code of California, for example, authorizes criminal convictions for the failure of a school principal to use required textbooks, the provision of private commercial performances by a state-supported band, and the waste of an artesian well by a landowner. See Kadish, "The Crisis of Overcriminalization," p. 158.

best be prevented, it is thought, by the intervention of the state—because only the state has the resources to undertake the task, because no one else will undertake it, or, perhaps, because deterrence by the state is believed to curb further disturbances where private action might touch off more conflict.

The assumption about deterrence may be wrong, as we shall see. But the criminal law has made the intentional choice of criminal behavior one half the meaning of crime, on the grounds that only those persons who make a choice can be deterred and that the punishment of others is unfair. If that choice is lacking, if no criminal intent is present, deterrence is said to be impossible and punishment serves no justifiable purpose. In a long series of judicial decisions and legislative codes, the criminal law has spelled out in detail those situations that are accepted as indicating the absence of *mens rea*.

The nature of crime as defined by law, in short, is intricate and changing; and normative proscriptions are fused with theories, usually implicit, about human nature and the causes of human behavior. Probably no single explanation of why certain acts come to be designated as crimes can be adequate, and the nature of crime will continue to be enigmatic. It is within this framework of uncertainty that criminology must seek to establish its conclusions about the relationships between crime and society.

Recommended Readings

The legal view of the nature of crime—which criminology has more or less accepted—can be found in such textbooks of criminal law as Wayne R. LaFave and Austin W. Scott, Jr., *Criminal Law* (St. Paul, Minn.: West, 1972). This viewpoint needs to be examined in a broader context of the nature of law in general and its relationship to society—a need that is well met by a book like Lawrence M. Friedman and Stewart Macaulay, *Law and the Behavioral Sciences* (New York: Bobbs-Merrill, 1977). The reader will also find it worthwhile to consult William Chambliss and Robert Seidman, *Law, Order, and Power* (Reading, Mass.: Addison-Wesley, 1971) and Edwin M. Schur, *Law and Society: A Sociological View* (New York: Random House, 1968) for alternative approaches. For the nature of criminal law in primitive societies, the reader should see E. Adamson Hoebel, *The Law of Primitive Man* (Cambridge, Mass.: Harvard University Press, 1954). Discussions of the problem of consensus concerning the criminal law in modern society can be found in William Chambliss and Milton Mankoff, eds., *Whose Law? What Order?* (New York: John Wiley & Sons, 1976).

For the reader without training in legal research, legal references often appear mysterious. "Appendix A: How to Find and Cite the Law," in Hazel B. Kerper, *Introduction to the Criminal Justice System* (St. Paul, Minn.: West, 1972), provides a clear, brief guide.

Part 2

Breaking the Law

From a legal viewpoint, crimes are to be analyzed in terms of the wrong that has been committed, the right that has been invaded. Sociological analysis requires a broader perspective.

In examining particular crimes, we must pay attention to a number of variables that allow us to place the offense in its full social context: the age, sex, and socioeconomic background of the offender; motivations other than criminal intent; the relationship between criminal and victim; the public attitude toward the offense; the extent to which the crime is part of the offender's occupational role; and informal peer-group support for the behavior. Crime is not to be seen simply as an isolated, individual act; rather, it is best viewed as a multifaceted aspect of social behavior, interlocked with society in a diffuse body of causes and consequences. In trying to understand the meaning of crime, then, we must examine not only the legal definition of particular offenses but their structure, the rate at which they occur, and the social situations in which they arise.

We will look first at crimes against property, which form by far the largest share of all crimes committed in the United States each year. Next we will examine crimes of violence, which, despite their relatively low incidence, often excite the greatest public concern. We will then turn to a great grab bag of offenses conventionally lumped together under the heading of crimes against health, morals, and public safety—and we will look at the ways in which society continues to cater to the so-called vices by means of organized crime in spite of sporadic attempts to root out gambling, prostitution, and drug addiction. Finally, we will examine political crime, which involves both the malfeasance of public officials and illegal attacks on the political order.

Chapter 3
Property Rights and Wrongs

In terms of numbers, the "crime problem" in the United States today is primarily a problem of crimes against property. Such crimes constitute the overwhelming majority of all violations of the criminal law reported to the police. Of the 11 million major crimes known to the police in 1976, according to the *Uniform Crime Reports* of the Federal Bureau of Investigation, approximately 91 percent were crimes against property, and the preponderance of such crimes has been a feature of official criminal statistics since their inception.[1]

Crimes against property take many different forms, ranging from embezzlement to confidence games, but the property offenses that preoccupy the police are *larceny, burglary, auto theft,* and *robbery.*[2] These can be considered the "conventional" property offenses (the police call them "real" crimes), because they are familiar, easily identified, and what most people have in mind when they think of the separation of property from its owner. Social scientists, however, have long been aware that there are other crimes against property, probably far more numerous and certainly far more costly, that seldom come to the attention of law enforcement officials. These are crimes perpetrated by businesses and business employees, and they fall into two categories. *White-collar crime* consists of criminal violations of property committed for the benefit of a business or corporation by persons of high social status in the course of their work.[3] Crimes *by white-collar workers* are committed for personal gain and consist of such illegal acts as bribery and embezzlement.

In the first decades of this century, the American sociologist and economist Thorstein Veblen attacked the "captains of industry," whom he

[1] *Uniform Crime Reports—1976* (Washington, D.C.: Government Printing Office, 1977).

[2] The *Uniform Crime Reports* classify robbery as a crime of violence rather than as a property crime, but, in line with the usual legal classification of offenses, it is treated in this book as belonging in the latter category.

[3] Edwin H. Sutherland, *White Collar Crime* (New York: Holt, Rinehart and Winston, 1949).

disparaged as stock manipulators, shady bankers, and assorted economic predators who had gained money and power after the Civil War by violating the law.[4] The muckrakers enthusiastically exposed numerous business scandals, with Lincoln Steffens, Ida M. Tarbell, and Upton Sinclair using popularly priced magazines to reach mass audiences. In 1907 the sociologist Edward Ross published a scathing analysis of the *criminaloid*—"The adulterator, the rebater, the commerical freebooter, the fraud promoter, the humbug dealer, the law-defying monopolist" who conducted business dealings on the edge of the law and often stepped outside it.[5] After World War I, with the onset of the prosperous twenties, the attacks on business leaders and industrialists who violated the law for economic gain became less sharp; but with the coming of the Great Depression, social commentators returned to the theme. In 1934 Matthew Josephson's book *The Robber Barons* was published, and in 1939 Edwin Sutherland delivered his presidential address to the American Sociological Society on the subject of "white-collar criminality." Whatever the ambiguities of Sutherland's term—and there are many, as we shall see in this chapter—American criminology would no longer think of the property offender exclusively in terms of the holdup man, the burglar, and the sneak thief. The business executive could also be a criminal and often was.

That fact, for a variety of reasons, is still not reflected in official crime statistics. The public at large has not incorporated the idea of white-collar criminality into its thinking about crime to any great extent, despite frequent exposés, and criminology has been slow to explore the issue.[6] Since the late 1960s, however, with the increasing suspicion of the military–industrial complex, the marked growth of giant corporations beyond the limits of national control, the rise of the consumer-protection movement, and the threat of ever more dangerous forms of pollution, the study of white-collar crime has taken on a new urgency. Now, as criminology continues its examination of the crimes of business and business executives, and not simply the property offenses of persons from the lower class, it is clear that crimes against property are not only the result of individual characteristics such as poverty or minority status. Property crimes—as Sutherland's pioneering work suggested—are also rooted in the structure of society.

This chapter begins with the illegal forms of taking property—larceny,

[4] See David Riesman, "The Relevance of Thorstein Veblen," in *Abundance for What?* (Garden City, N.Y.: Doubleday, 1964), pp. 388–401.

[5] See Edward Alsworth Ross, "The Criminaloid," reprinted in Gilbert Geis and Robert F. Meier, eds., *White-Collar Crime* (New York: The Free Press, 1977), pp. 29–37.

[6] See, however, Geis and Meier, *White-Collar Crime*. This book of readings brings together much of the academic discussion of white-collar crime published in the four decades after Sutherland's presidential address.

burglary, and robbery—that occupy so much of the attention of the public and the police. We will then turn our attention to Sutherland's concept of white-collar crime and to the allied category with which it is sometimes confused—property offenses by white-collar workers. Violations of the criminal law as a means of earning a living—a form of criminality that includes the professional thief, the burglar, and the fence, as well as the confidence man—will be our third concern. Finally, we will consider the meaning of property in modern society and the implicit assumptions that play a large role in determing whether property rights will be turned into property wrongs.

Forms of Theft

Criminal laws dealing with the theft of property were relatively simple in England before the eighteenth century, reflecting forms of economic organization and property relationships that had not yet grown complex. The dominant concepts were those of larceny, burglary, and robbery. *Larceny* referred to an act of trespass in which property was taken out of the owner's possession with intent to steal it. *Burglary* was more specific and emphasized intention rather than the act of theft: it was defined as breaking into and entering a dwelling place with the intention of committing a felony. *Robbery* concerned the taking of property with the use of force rather than stealth.

Social definitions of crime tend to change, however, with changes in the patterns of social organization. With the growth of manufacturing and trade, England moved away from a largely agricultural, feudal social order; and earlier definitions of property crimes could no longer cover the kinds of offenses coming into being. The growing complexities of commercial relationships, impersonal business dealings, and large financial enterprises provided opportunities for new forms of theft and led to the demand for more elaborate definitions of larceny for the protection of property.[7]

The judges of the English courts in the eighteenth century refused to take on this task—perhaps because larceny carried the death penalty with it, and the judges, reflecting a growing public revulsion against capital punishment for minor offenses, did not wish to see the definition of larceny expanded. If the judges were reluctant to extend the concept of larceny, however, the English Parliament felt no such hesitation. Two new crimes involving theft were designated by legislative action—em-

[7] See Jerome Hall, *Theft, Law, and Society* (Boston: Little, Brown, 1935) and Douglas Hay, "Property, Authority, and the Criminal Law," in Douglas Hay et al., *Albion's Fatal Tree: Crime and Society in Eighteenth-Century England* (London: Allen Lane, 1975), pp. 17–63.

bezzlement and obtaining property by false pretenses. The crime of embezzlement was established to cover those situations in which an employee, a business agent, and others in similar roles stole property not by trespass but by violating a position of trust. The crime of obtaining property by false pretenses was defined by statute to include those cases—growing increasingly troublesome—in which the owner knowingly parted company with his property but was defrauded in the process.

The United States adopted the legal concepts of larceny, embezzlement, and false pretenses, although the distinctions among the three types of theft have often proven difficult to apply. But if the definitions of these property offenses sometimes appear to involve excessive legal refinements, the distinctions are nevertheless important. Different types of crimes against property vary greatly in the frequency with which they are committed, and in the economic and social burden they place on the members of society. Moreover, crimes against property differ in the nature of the social relationship between the criminal and the victim. As Peter Letkemann has indicated, property offenses often include surreptitious acts in which the victim remains unknown and unseen; and in these situations the offender avoids direct confrontations, the threat of violence and the necessity for manipulative skills.[8] This variation in the nature of the criminal act has a profound effect on the extent to which norms protecting private property come into play and is related to the class background of offenders engaging in different types of property crimes and public attitudes toward the wrongfulness of the behavior involved.

Slightly more than half of the crimes against property reported to the police each year are classified as larcenies. Some of these are the well-planned work of professional thieves, and others are the impulsive acts of middle-class shoplifters; some are thefts by employees from commercial establishments—although these are far less likely to be reported to the police than are larcenies from individuals and households—and still others are the acts of employers misappropriating company property. But probably the great mass of reported larcenies are petty acts of pilfering committed by people from the lower portion of the socioeconomic structure who believe they are acting out of immediate economic need. The relative frequency of the different types of larceny reported by the *Uniform Crime Reports* remains fairly constant from one year to the next. In 1976 about half of them involved the theft of bicycles, auto accessories, and other articles taken from cars. (See Table 1.) Slightly less than half

Larceny

[8] See Peter Letkemann, *Crime as Work* (Englewood Cliffs, N.J.: Prentice-Hall, 1973), Chapter 3.

Table 1. Percent Distribution of Larcenies Known to the Police, 1976

Type of Larceny	Percent
Pickpocketing	1
Purse-snatching	2
Shoplifting	10
From motor vehicles	20
Motor vehicle accessories	22
Bicycles	10
From buildings	15
From coin-operated machines	1
Other	18

SOURCE: *Uniform Crime Reports—1976* (Washington, D.C.: Government Printing Office, 1977), p. 29.

of the larcenies reported in recent years have involved goods valued at $50 or less, and about 43 percent of those arrested were eighteen years of age or under.[9]

Small losses are not necessarily unimportant to the victims, and teenage thefts are not necessarily mere pranks. Many larcenies entail an economic blow for those who can ill afford it, and thefts committed by adolescents are sometimes the prelude to criminal careers. Furthermore, according to a study conducted in Detroit in the early 1970s, many "revenue-producing crimes" such as larceny are closely tied to the use of heroin, and the volume of larcenies is apt to fluctuate with the price of the drug.[10] Nevertheless, it is important to remember that most crimes known to the police in the United States are crimes against property rather than crimes of violence, the majority of the crimes against property are larcenies, most of these larcenies involve relatively small monetary losses, and a large share of individuals arrested for these offenses are not yet out of their teens. These facts, as limited and ambiguous as they are, may help to keep the officially recognized "crime problem" in perspective.

Auto theft is accorded a separate category in police records, for although it can be legally viewed as a subdivision of larceny, the value of stolen automobiles exceeds the loss due to all other reported larcenies combined. In 1976, for example, there were about one million auto thefts (compared to about six million other larcenies), but the stolen au-

[9]*Uniform Crime Reports—1976.* In 1973, the FBI stopped distinguishing among larcenies on the basis of the value of the goods stolen, as far as the Crime Index is concerned. All larcenies, regardless of value, are now classified as Part I, or serious, offenses.

[10] See *The New York Times*, "Heroin Crackdown May Not Cut Crime" (April 25, 1976).

tomobiles were listed as being worth one and one-half times all other stolen property.[11]

Auto theft, even more than other larcenies, is primarily a crime of youth, at least as far as arrests are concerned. Of all the individuals apprehended and charged with auto thefts in 1976, 64 percent ended up in the juvenile court. The clearance rate for this crime (14 percent) is somewhat lower than that for larceny (19 percent), but the value of the recovered stolen property is far greater. A large proportion of the automobiles recorded as stolen in the FBI's National Crime Information Center are recovered each year. Some of these thefts can be attributed to the work of organized car thieves—sometimes stealing particular makes and models of automobiles to fit the demands of specific customers—but evidence suggests that the purpose of most auto thefts is joy riding. Many stolen cars—sometimes badly damaged—are simply abandoned.[12] Studies by William Wattenberg and James Balistrieri, Leonard Savitz, Erwin Schepses, Don Gibbons, and others indicate that car thieves intent on joy riding are generally young, male, and middle class. They are usually motivated by a desire to do something exciting and daring, to show off, and to assert their masculinity. Particularly important, as Gibbons has pointed out, is the fact that these youths typically view themselves as "tough" or "cool" but not as criminal. Like a number of adults who break the law, they fail to attach a clear sense of wrongdoing to their actions. Their victim often remains unknown or unseen—or even nonexistent in the eyes of the offenders, since they can claim they merely intended to borrow the car, not to steal it.[13]

The English common law, which developed in a crude society in which **Burglary** the isolated householder was in frequent danger of roving bands of brigands, established the crime of burglary early in its history. As indicated earlier, burglary was originally defined as breaking into and entering the dwelling house of another during the night with the intent to commit a felony, but over the years these elements of burglary have been greatly modified by statute and have become much less restrictive. Today, in many states, no forcible entry is required, all kinds of structures are defined as "dwelling houses" (including cars, ships, and air-

[11] *Uniform Crime Reports—1976* pp. 31–33.
[12] See David Barry et al., *Preliminary Study of the Effectiveness of Auto Anti-Theft Devices* (Washington, D.C.: Government Printing Office, 1975).
[13] See William W. Wattenberg and James Balistrieri, "Automobile Theft: A Favored-Group Delinquency," *American Journal of Sociology* 58 (May 1952), pp. 575–79; Leonard D. Savitz, "Automobile Theft," *Journal of Criminal Law, Criminology, and Police Science* 50 (July–August 1959), pp. 132–43; Erwin Schepses, "Boys Who Steal Cars," *Federal Probation* 25 (March 1961), pp. 56–62; and Don C. Gibbons, *Society, Crime, and Criminal Careers* (Englewood Cliffs, N.J.: Prentice-Hall, 1973), pp. 312–20.

planes), and the time of day is ignored. The modern concept of burglary has little in common with its common-law ancestor except for the name. In fact, it has been said, burglary is really a type of "attempt" law, as all the required elements merely comprise a step taken toward the commission of some other offense.[14]

There were about 3 million burglaries in 1976 known to the police, according to the *Uniform Crime Reports*. About 63 percent of these involved residences, and more than half of residential burglaries occurred during the day. The total money loss to the victims was reported to be $1.4 billion, approximately the same amount that was placed on the value of stolen cars. In the case of burglary, however, unlike auto theft, only a small proportion of the stolen goods is recovered, and the average economic loss to the owner ($449 in 1976) is fairly high.[15] Clues are usually lacking; but if there are clues, they can seldom be followed up because of lack of police personnel. This is one of the reasons, in fact, why burglaries are often not reported to the police; in the NORC survey described on page 76, more than 60 percent of the respondents who failed to notify the authorities after a burglary said they thought the police would not be effective or would not want to be bothered.[16]

The threat of burglary has undoubtedly played a large part in creating a sense of living in a beleaguered fortress for many of today's urban citizens. The barrred windows, the chains, and the bolts may sometimes be discussed with wry humor, but the fear is often real—and appears to have spread to suburban and rural areas, where the burglary rate is rising. The measures taken by people to defend themselves against the threat of burglary are indicative of the public mood. The NORC survey revealed that 82 percent of the respondents always locked their doors at night, 28 percent kept their doors locked even in the daytime when other members of the family were at home, 28 percent kept watchdogs, and 37 percent had firearms.[17] The reported fear of crime was greater among nonwhites than among whites, and this could possibly be explained by the fact that nonwhites—so often crowded into deteriorating, crime-ridden sections of the community—are more frequently the victims of crimes like larceny, burglary, and robbery than are whites. The reported fear of crime, however, was also greater among females than among males; and since there is no evidence that females are the victims of

[14] Wayne R. LaFave and Austin W. Scott, Jr., *Criminal Law* (St. Paul, Minn.: West, 1972), pp. 715–16. Legal distinctions can carry far-reaching consequences. In Illinois, the stealing of a car is punishable by no more than ten years in prison, but reaching through a window to steal an article inside the car can bring conviction of burglary and life imprisonment.

[15] *Uniform Crime Reports—1976*, p. 23.

[16] President's Commission on Law Enforcement and Administration of Justice, *Task Force Report: Assessment of Crime*, (Washington, D.C.: Government Printing Office, 1967), p. 18.

[17] Ibid., p. 88.

these property offenses more often than are males, it would appear that the fear of crime cannot be treated as a direct reflection of the chances of being victimized. Terror feeds on rumor, newspaper stories, official pronouncements, and a sense of one's vulnerability, as well as on direct experience with crime—and the last may often prove to be of secondary importance.[18]

Burglary, like larceny and auto theft, represents a mix of professional and nonprofessional criminality. (Later in the chapter we will examine the distinction between professional and nonprofessional crime more closely.) Isolated acts of burglary, such as children breaking into an abandoned factory or teenagers seizing an oppportunity to steal from an empty house, must be set against the work of the professional thieves, such as safecrackers or organized gangs of youths looting offices. No official figures give the proportions of professional and amateur burglaries, but other data drawn from criminological studies, case histories, and personal accounts suggest that many juveniles engage in sporadic thefts, including burglaries, and then abandon this pattern of behavior as they move into the adult world of marriage and work. As in the case of larceny and auto theft, the victim of burglary is often an impersonal abstraction, and the wrong that is done is diminished in the eyes of the wrongdoer by the lack of any direct encounter.

In these property crimes, then, the criminal often does not intend to use violence or manipulate other persons. The target is a storeroom, a deserted office, an empty house, or a parked automobile. For property offenders who make their living by crime and for whom crime is habitual rather than occasional, the fact that the victim is an absent owner has great practical consequence—the chances of detection and apprehension are much diminished, although the returns may be less than in the case of robbery.[19] The lack of interaction between the criminal and the victim has, however, additional significance. If the social norms are viewed as a set of restraints, behavior contrary to the norms can be expected to occur when the norms are absent or ineffective. The ability of norms to control behavior depends in large measure on the extent to which the norms have been internalized—that is, made a part of the individual's conscience in the process of socialization. The likelihood of acting in a prohibited way is decreased by the threat of self-disapproval or sense of guilt. But the social norms operating within the individual do not come automatically into play; they must be evoked, and this depends on the

---

[18] The fear of crime has increased in recent years, according to a number of surveys, but has maintained much the same pattern with regard to sex and race. See *Sourcebook of Criminal Justice Statistics—1974* (Washington, D.C.: Government Printing Office, 1975), pp. 171–76.

[19] See Letkemann, *Crime as Work,* Chapter 3.

external circumstances. If material possessions are obtained by the use or threat of violence, an awareness of the victim and the victim's loss cannot be avoided. If the possessions of another are obtained by stealth, however, the meaning of the criminal behavior is more easily repressed or ignored. The sense of a "real" harm is weakened, and the internal mechanisms of guilt or self-disapproval are brought into play with a greatly reduced force.[20]

It can be argued, then, that the likelihood of activating norms governing private property is reduced when the injury is inflicted on an unknown or absent figure. Such crimes as larceny, auto theft, and burglary are frequently constructed around the lack of confrontation, thus easing the path to law violation for the amateur or the occasional offender who is not committed to a criminal way of life. The preference for a lack of confrontation, for "quiet work," is expressed in an interview with a burglar reported by Letkemann:

> You said something about working where it's noisy and where it's quiet? Well, there's a lot of people like noise—action. They want action. They go into a firm—they'll probably go there in the daytime and they go in there and they'll have a ball. They get a kick out of that—they do it in public. I like a place where it's empty, there's no noise. There's nobody in there, nobody to molest, or anything like that. And take it and leave quietly, and that's it.[21]

Robbery The crime of robbery is sometimes described as "larceny plus," for it involves the theft of property and the use or the threat of violence as a means. In view of the foregoing discussion, the fact that robbery is the least frequent crime against property reported to the police should not be surprising. The 420,000 robberies known to the police in 1976, down from 465,000 in 1975, were less than 5 percent of all property crimes.[22] Half of these robberies occurred in the street, with the remainder scattered among gas stations, chain stores, residences, and other public and private facilities. Holding up banks, which looms so large in the public imagination, accounted for less than 1 percent of all robberies.

Approximately two-thirds of the robbers were armed, according to police records, and the average loss for those who were robbed was $338. The chance of someone being apprehended for these crimes is the highest among all the property offenses discussed. Approximately 27 percent of the robberies known to the police were cleared by arrest. (See Table 2.)

---

[20] See Gresham M. Sykes, *Crime and Society* (New York: Random House, 1967), p. 58.
[21] Letkemann, *Crime as Work*, p. 50.
[22] *Uniform Crime Reports—1976*, pp. 19–21.

Table 2. Percentage of Property Offenses Cleared by Arrest, 1976

Offenses	Percentage Cleared by Arrest
Robbery	27
Larceny	19
Burglary	17
Auto Theft	14

SOURCE: *Uniform Crime Reports—1976* (Washington, D.C.: Government Printing Office, 1977), p. 161.

Of the persons arrested for robbery, 34 percent were under the age of eighteen.[23]

In the eyes of the police, adults who commit robberies are apt to be viewed as hardened criminals and particularly dangerous. Juveniles who engage in robberies are likely to be seen as thoroughly alienated from society and well on their way to a life of crime. The general public is prone to share these attitudes, and robbery is one of the so-called street, or predatory, crimes most likely to arouse public fear and outrage.[24] Robbery combines two harms—property loss and personal violence—but even more important, apparently, is the perception of the robber as a stranger armed with a gun or a knife and ruthless enough to use violence if necessary.[25] For much of the public, the robber is a vicious individual, the epitome of the enemy of society.

The personal accounts of professional criminals give a different picture. The robber is seen as belonging to the so-called heavy rackets—that is, those forms of crime that depend on force. But it is not a taste for brutality that is said to distinguish him; rather, he is characterized by self-confidence, an ability to manage other people in moments of stress, the possession of "guts" or fearlessness.[26] Such accounts frequently appear to be romanticized visions of the outlaw life (in contrast, let us say, to a film like *Dog Day Afternoon*, which showed the criminal as confused, frightened, and inept), but it is possible that the different images of the

---

[23] Ibid., p. 21.

[24] See John Conklin, *Robbery and the Criminal Justice System* (Philadelphia: J. B. Lippincott, 1972); see also Morton Hunt, *The Mugging* (New York: Atheneum, 1972).

[25] See Philip H. Ennis, "Criminal Victimization in the United States: A Report of a National Survey," *Field Survey II, President's Commission on Law Enforcement and Administration of Justice* (Washington, D.C.: Government Printing Office, 1967).

[26] See, for example, Peter Letkemann, *Crime as Work*, Chapter 4. See also Everett DeBaum, "The Heist: The Theory and Practice of Armed Robbery," *Harper's Magazine* (February 1950), pp. 69–77.

robber are partial reflections of a complex reality. The available evidence suggests that the behavior covered by the term *robbery* is surprisingly diverse. As in the case of larceny, burglary, and auto theft, there are full-time experts and inept tyros. Some robberies are the thoughtless, casual acts of teenagers that accidentally end in murder.[27] Some are the well-planned efforts of experienced gunmen who have no wish to turn the threat of violence into an actuality unless they are—according to their own accounts—left with no choice. Some robberies are sadistic attacks in Lovers Lane, and some are the desperate acts of inexperienced criminals willing to take a chance for minimal gain. And the activities of "Jones"—the pseudonym of a professional mugger interviewed at great length by James Willwerth—show to what extent stereotypes can miss the mark. Jones earns $15,000 a year by mugging and never has any money. He is a ghetto dweller, a registered Republican, and has a police lock on his door to ward off burglars.[28] If robbery stands somewhat apart from other crimes against property, in the sense that in some cases the willingness to confront a victim with the threat of violence involves a greater likelihood that the offender sees himself as clearly violating the norms of society, the varied nature of robbery should make us cautious about stereotyping the robber.

White-Collar Crime

The idea that most crimes are committed by persons from the lower classes emerged with explicit clarity in the nineteenth century and continues to dominate much of the thinking about criminality at the present time.[29] The overwhelming majority of the persons arrested and convicted of these property offenses coming to the attention of the police have been and continue to be from the lower portion of the socioeconomic ladder. Furthermore, it has been evident from the beginnings of the cartographic school of criminology (which explored the relationship between crime rates and the characteristics of geographical areas in the nineteenth century), that poor areas, as measured by such factors as the proportion of families on relief, unemployment, and inadequate housing, had the highest rates of crime and delinquency.[30] The work of Clifford Shaw and Henry McKay in Chicago strongly reinforced the idea that crime and poverty-stricken portions of the community went hand in hand; and if

[27] See, for example, Morton Hunt, *The Mugging*.
[28] James Willwerth, *Jones: Portrait of a Mugger* (New York: M. Evans, 1974).
[29] The nineteenth-century perspective on crime is well presented in Kellow Chesney, *The Victorian Underworld* (New York: Schocken Books, 1972).
[30] See Terence Morris, *The Criminal Area* (London: Routledge, 1957).

such "ecological" correlations needed to be interpreted with some caution, as William Robinson made clear, the close association between crime and economic want seemed well established.[31]

With the stock market crash of 1929 and the Depression that followed, a new viewpoint emerged. It involved a vast reconsideration of American values and beliefs and a profound shift in the social roles accorded respect and reprobation. The business executive, long considered a model of sagacity, was now frequently cast in the role of the fool; and in 1939, in his presidential address to the American Sociological Society, Edward Sutherland drew the attention of criminology to the idea that many people engaged in business were crooks as well.[32]

If we looked more closely at the idea that crime was largely a result of living in economic want, said Sutherland, clarifying his argument in a book published a decade later, we would find the notion plainly erroneous. More specifically, he argued, we would find that respectable well-to-do business leaders were guilty of numerous violations of the criminal law in the course of their daily work. He was not talking about such crimes as murder and adultery, but about crimes against property that were more or less accepted as a part of occupational activities.[33]

"Ideological cleavage has clear expression in Sutherland's denunciation of the failure of conventional crime statistics to reflect white-collar crime," argue Albert Biderman and Albert Reiss. "In prevalence and in economic and social effects, Sutherland sought to show, law violations by a person of the 'upper socioeconomic class in the course of his occupational activities' were more consequential than the typically lower-class crimes that comprised the index of the *Uniform Crime Reports*."[34] Sutherland's criticisms of conventional crime statistics may not have been as ideologically motivated as this quotation suggests, but there is no question that, in his view, the prevalence of white-collar crime destroyed the notion of criminality as an exclusively lower-class phenomenon. Using the records of courts and administrative commissions, he showed that the executives of the seventy largest manufacturing, mining, and mercantile corporations in America had violated the law on numerous occasions with regard to restraint of trade, misrepresentation in advertising, infringement of patent rights, and other prohibited activities. There were 980 decisions holding that the law had been violated

---

[31] Clifford R. Shaw and Henry D. McKay, *Juvenile Delinquency and Urban Areas* (Chicago: University of Chicago Press, 1942) and William S. Robinson, "Ecological Correlations and the Behavior of Individuals," *American Sociological Review* 15 (June 1950), pp. 351–56.

[32] See Geis and Meier, *White-Collar Crime*, pp. 23–27.

[33] Sutherland, *White Collar Crime*.

[34] Albert D. Biderman and Albert J. Reiss, "On Exploring the 'Dark Figure' of Crime," *The Annals of the American Academy of Political and Social Science* 374 (November 1967), p. 9.

Table 3. Decisions by Courts and Commissions Against 70
Large Corporations, by Types of Law Violated

Violations	Number
Restraint of trade	307
Misrepresentation in advertising	97
Infringement of patent rights	222
Unfair labor practices	158
Rebates	66
Other	130
Total	980

SOURCE: From *White Collar Crime* by Edwin H. Sutherland. Copyright © 1949 by Holt, Rinehart and Winston.
Adapted by permission of Holt, Rinehart and Winston.

during the lifetime of the corporations, with an average of 14 violations
for each corporation. (See Table 3.)

After analyzing the available data, Sutherland concluded that (1) large
corporations were violating the law with great frequency; (2) personal
and social pathologies were of little use as an explanation of such offenses; (3) business executives learn to engage in illegal behavior in associating with their colleagues; (4) financial loss from white-collar
crime—however great—is less important than the fact that the crimes
create a distrust that may lower social morale and produce social disorganization; and (5) theories about criminal behavior were misleading and
incomplete, because they tended to ignore crimes committed by persons
of high social status.

Sutherland argued that variation in the rate of white-collar crime is not
related to the age or the size of the corporation but to the industrial category to which the corporation belongs. Manufacturing and mining corporations are most likely to violate the antitrust laws; retail
establishments are inclined to commit offenses involving misrepresentation in advertising; and violations of the National Labor Relations
Law are encountered most often among firms in which the greatest out-
lays are for labor and in which increased labor costs cannot be passed on
to the consumer.[35] White-collar crime is primarily a matter of opportunity, and corporate executives are motivated by the competitive nature of
American business to seize the opportunity. The source of white-collar
criminality is to be found in the struggle of rival firms to maximize
profits.

Corporate managers, said Sutherland, learn to engage in crime in the
same way that other people do. Associating with executives who seek to

[35] Sutherland, *White Collar Crime*, p. 9.

protect themselves from the effects of competition (regardless of their public devotion to free enterprise) and insulated from criticism of sharp business dealing, they are led to violate the law and rationalize their wrongdoing.[36] And a crucial factor in the ability of business executives to avoid labeling themselves criminals is the public attitude toward white-collar crime. Such offenses are frequently diffuse in their harm, a collection of small wrongs that become serious only in the aggregate. Criminals and victims do not face each other, and, often enough, the victims do not even realize that they have suffered a loss. The offender is a person of respectability and conformity, an admired figure in the community, whose violations of the law are commonly treated with great restraint by the police, the court, and the press; and penalties, when they are imposed, are likely to be mild and in the form of a fine or probation rather than a stigmatizing period of imprisonment.

Sutherland's concept of white-collar crime has had a significant though confusing impact on American criminology. One difficulty lies in the fact that Sutherland, in a portion of his discussion, included both offenses committed for personal gain (such as embezzlement) and offenses committed for the benefit of the corporation (such as price fixing) under the label of white-collar crime. But it is clear that in Sutherland's view these two types of crime differed greatly, and his theories about the causes and consequences of white-collar crime were concerned almost entirely with corporate criminality. Furthermore, Sutherland placed violations of administrative regulations in the category of white-collar crime as well as violations of the criminal law, thus blurring the distinction between crime and other forms of illegal behavior. Even more troublesome, however, is the fact that later writers often used the term *white-collar crime* to condemn any behavior of the business community that they viewed as reprehensible, even though the behavior might in fact be legal. The concept of white-collar crime "has spread into vacuity, wide and handsome," said Paul Tappan, writing a few years after the appearance of Sutherland's theory in the *American Sociological Review,* and the concept is used even more loosely today.[37]

Conceptual precision is certainly desirable, but arguments about whether white-collar crime really is crime absorbed so much time and energy that the study of the behavior of business executives and their relationship to the law tended to be neglected. Despite the frequent mention of white-collar crime in the literature of criminology, careful empiri-

[36] See, for example, John G. Fuller, *The Gentlemen Conspirators: The Story of the Price-Fixers in the Electrical Industry* (New York: Grove Press, 1962).
[37] See Paul W. Tappan, "Who Is the Criminal?" *American Sociological Review* 12 (February 1947), pp. 96–102. For an excellent review of the concept of white-collar crime, see George B. Vold, *Theoretical Criminology* (New York: Oxford University Press, 1958), Chapter 13.

cal studies undertaken with a sociological perspective and systematic theorizing remained in short supply for many years after Sutherland's initial statement.[38] When business groups turned their attention to the problem, white-collar crime was often treated as a matter of individual executives plundering the corporation rather than as a pattern of behavior condoned or initiated by the highest levels of management.[39]

Changing Attitudes Toward Corporate Crime

The question that arises is why Sutherland's ideas failed to generate the extensive body of work in criminology that might have been expected. Writing in the field is still surprisingly sparse, with only a few notable studies, such as those conducted by Clinard, Hartung, Cressey, Ball, and Quinney.[40] "Even the monumental report of the President's Crime Commission—*The Challenge of Crime in a Free Society*—devoted only two pages to the entire subject of 'white-collar offenders and business crimes,'" notes one writer, "with but a seven-page systematic discussion tucked away in one of the nine lengthy task-force reports on various aspects of crime problems in America."[41]

This neglect might be attributed to the forbidding complexity of a subject that sometimes appears to call for the combined skills of a social scientist, lawyer, accountant, and investigative reporter. The ease with which white-collar crime is construed as something else may have sidetracked those working in criminology no less than the general public. Possibly more important, however, is the fact that the structure of economic activity in the United States changed markedly after World War II, and concern with the nature of business enterprise changed as well.

Prior to the Second World War, the power of business appeared threatening in two main areas. First, there was the danger of monopolies that could raise prices at will, extracting wealth from the buyer and resulting in a smaller output of goods than if prices were set competitively. ("In the English language," says John Kenneth Galbraith, speaking of monopoly, "only a few words—fraud, defalcation, subversion and sodomy—have a greater connotation of nonviolent wickedness."[42]) In 1890, the Sherman Antitrust Act declared the monopolistic restraint of trade a crime, and for some fifty years thereafter much of the American public viewed such behavior as the exemplar of corporate illegality. Second, the power of business was seen, at least among liberal reformers, as a threat to the rights of organized labor. Other dangers were recognized, it is

[38] See Geis and Meier, *White-Collar Crime*, "Introduction."

[39] See *White Collar Crime* (Washington, D.C.: Chamber of Commerce of the United States, 1974).

[40] See Geis and Meier, *White-Collar Crime*, "Introduction."

[41] See Stuart L. Hills, *Crime, Power, and Morality* (Scranton, Pa.: Chandler, 1971), p. 187.

[42] John Kenneth Galbraith, *The New Industrial State* (New York: New American Library, 1967), p. 190.

true, such as the adulteration of food and the close control of a company town, but price rigging and the harshness of corporate labor relations were apt to appear at the top of the list.[43]

These elements played a major role in the formation of Sutherland's concept of white-collar crime, but after World War II the dangers posed by Big Business came to be seen in a new light. Labor developed its own structures of power, and what used to be seen as an uneven struggle between the corporation and the workers began to appear to many as a standoff, or possibly a coalition of forces threatening the consuming public. As far as monopolies were concerned, Heilbroner argues, the average citizen became "far less incensed with the problem of big-business pricing than with the exactions of local labor monopolists such as the local TV repair man or the only plumber in town."[44] Between 1947 and the latter part of the 1960s, real income in the United States increased each year, lending corporate America a benevolent mien. Many economists, too, began to look at the corporate threat of monopoly in a different fashion. The regulation of prices was necessary, it was argued, if the economy was to function smoothly. Monopolies might be illegal, but the same end was achieved legally by *oligopolies*—that is, a few large firms controlling most of the market.[45] A number of economists disagreed violently, declaring that the lack of competition did serious economic harm. Estimates of unnecessary costs borne by the public ranged between $16 billion and $160 billion a year.[46] Two facts, however, were clear. First, a great concentration of economic power after the Second World War had led to a situation in which many industries in America were effectively monopolized.[47] Second, the antitrust laws were seldom evoked and were of little consequence in any event. The control of the market by a few large firms was regarded benignly by the law, and these firms found it unnecessary to resort to price fixing. "Price leadership,"—one firm setting prices which would benefit all—worked just as well.

Whether the attacks on the monopolistic practices of American business tended to lose their fervor after World War II because such practices came to be regarded as inevitable, as beneficial, or simply as the price to

[43] See Robert L. Heilbroner et al., *In the Name of Profit* (Garden City, N.Y.: Doubleday, 1972), Part Two.

[44] Ibid., p. 230.

[45] Galbraith, *The New Industrial State*, pp. 189–207.

[46] See Charles E. Mueller, "Monopoly," in Ralph Nader, ed., *The Consumer and Corporate Accountability* (New York: Harcourt Brace Jovanovich, 1973), pp. 314–24.

[47] A commonly accepted definition of a monopolistic industry is one in which the four largest firms control 50 percent or more of the market. By the 1970s, nearly 50 percent of all manufacturing activity in the United States took place in industries in which the four-firm share was 70 percent or more (Mueller, "Monopoly," p. 319).

A Slap on the Wrist

. . . Since 1890, when the Sherman Antitrust Act was passed, only 54 persons have gone to prison for price-fixing and other pure antitrust violations. Their sentences have added up to just 76 months, Justice Department statistics show. Assistant Attorney General Baker figures that persons who illegally hunt game birds are more apt to go to prison than are price-fixers.

Mr. Baker, for one, wants judges to stop treating price-fixers so kindly. Most price-fixers should get prison sentences of at least 18 months, he believes, and he's begun to campaign for such stiff sanctions. Just last month, after a personal plea from Mr. Baker, federal Judge James B. Parsons sentenced 15 paperboard-box company executives—who had pleaded no contest to charges of fixing prices—to serve prison terms of five to 60 days. . . .

There isn't much question that price-fixers get off lightly. Statistics from the administrative office of the U.S. courts show that last year, individuals convicted of securities fraud or transporting forged securities received an average prison sentence of just under 46 months, bank embezzlers got an average sentence of 22.6 months, and income-tax evaders got an average sentence of 15.4 months. But only two of the 75 defendants convicted of antitrust misdemeanors actually went to prison—for a total of 75 days.

Federal Judge Charles B. Renfrew of San Francisco suggests one reason mild sentences are imposed against price-fixers is that judges generally don't understand the impact price-fixing has had on U.S. society.

"It hasn't really been forcibly brought home to many judges," says Mr. Renfrew. "You are talking about conduct that essentially is unlawful only in this country. You shouldn't rob a bank in Pakistan, you shouldn't rob a bank in England, and the U.S. is no different. But businessmen getting together and discussing the prices at which they are currently selling their goods to a customer, that's done all over the world without any fear of criminal sanctions."

Another reason for mild sentences, contends Judge Renfrew, is that many price-fixers haven't been aware fully of what they were doing. That factor persuaded Mr. Renfrew two years ago to suspend prison sentences imposed against eight corporate officers who pleaded no contest to price-fixing charges. Instead, he required them to give 12 speeches about price-fixing to business and civic groups.

"I was persuaded that many of the individuals here had no idea that what they were doing constituted a criminal act," says Judge Renfrew. "They thought maybe they shouldn't be talking about prices or doing price verification with a competitor, but they really had no idea it was criminal conduct."

be paid for American economic growth, the zeal for trustbusting showed a decline. And Sutherland's conception of white-collar crime, first presented in 1939 with a heavy emphasis on illegal restraint of trade, somehow failed to elicit that important indication of scholarly enthusiasm it appeared to deserve—namely, a large number of derivative investigations. Not until the latter part of the 1960s and the beginning of the 1970s did the public expression of antibusiness sentiment in the United States equal that of the Depression years—and when it surfaced once again, it was not illegal behavior in the areas of labor relations and restraint of trade that captured the most attention. Rather, it was the rape of the environment, the arrogance of the impenetrable corporate bureaucracy, the involvement in political corruption, the shoddy goods passed off to the consumer, and the influence of business on American foreign policy.[48]

Criminology has only begun to explore these patterns of corporate behavior and to see what they can add to our knowledge of white-collar crime. Only some of these patterns are illegal (the bribery of foreign officials, for example, is not a violation of the law), and of those that are illegal only some are criminal—the same issue that occupied so much attention when Sutherland first introduced his concept of white-collar crime. It would be unfortunate, however, if criminology failed to devote a large share of its scholarly efforts to a study of the behavior of the corporation, for there is little doubt that corporate crimes against property (such as defrauding the consumer) far outweigh more conventional property offenses. Of particular importance is the question of the ways in which corporate power can shape the law to fit its interest, for an understanding of white-collar crime must include a knowledge of the social processes that powerful interests can use to avoid the label of crime altogether.

Criminals in White Collars

Sutherland's theories about white-collar crime centered mainly on crimes committed for the economic benefit of the business enterprise in which the offender is employed, with the implicit or explicit approval of management. A large number of crimes, however, are committed by white-collar workers for their personal gain, in the course of their work and without the knowledge of their employers. Indeed, many of these crimes are directed against their employers and overlap with property offenses discussed previously, such as larceny. There are also property offenses not mentioned before, such as kickbacks, bribes, padded expense ac-

[48]See Heilbroner et al., *In the Name of Profit*, pp. 233–36. See also Ralph Nader and Mark J. Green, eds., *Corporate Power in America* (New York: Grossman, 1973).

counts, and embezzlements involving the falsification of time cards, production records, and inventory accounts. Unlike some property offenders, these "criminals in white collars" do not think of themselves as committed to a criminal way of life; unlike "white-collar criminals," they do not think that breaking the law is expected of them in the name of corporate goals. Instead, these middle-class offenders fall into a great limbo of criminality in which theft for one's personal gain is a commonplace part of one's job but is rationalized as something else.

The average economic loss involved in these offenses may be small, but the aggregate loss is probably large. "According to insurance company figures," said Norman Jaspan, "white-collar employees, rank and file, supervisory and executive, are stealing about four million dollars in cash and property from their employers each working day." And, he added, "in 1960 an estimated five billion dollars will probably change hands in kickbacks, payoffs, and bribes."[49] In 1967 the President's Commission on Law Enforcement and Administration of Justice hazarded a guess, based on data supplied by the Supermarket Institute, that in the grocery industry the percentage of loss due to employee theft and shoplifting is about the same as the industry's net profit after taxes.[50] In 1974 the United States Chamber of Commerce arrived at an estimate of a $40 billion annual loss due to theft by white-collar workers.[51]

This type of crime apparently accounts for a substantial part of the increase in the criminality of women that has taken place since the end of World War II. Official records have long indicated that men have been arrested for the great majority of crimes, including crimes against property, and this pattern continues at the present time. In the 1950s, however, the percentage of women among those arrested began to grow, and the increase was particularly marked after the middle of the sixties. The increase was greater for serious crimes than for all crimes, involving crimes against property rather than crimes of violence; and within the area of serious property offenses, larceny led the list.[52] Rita Simon notes the hazards of using arrest statistics but concludes that women are increasingly responsible for crimes against property and that the explanation is to be sought in the fact that as women increase their participation

[49] Norman Jaspan, *The Thief in the White Collar* (Philadelphia: J. B. Lippincott, 1960), pp. 11–12.

[50] President's Commission on Law Enforcement and Administration of Justice, *Task Force Report: Assessment of Crime*, p. 49. Losses due to shoplifting are thought to form only a small proportion of the total loss.

[51] *White Collar Crime* (Chamber of Commerce of the United States), p. 5.

[52] See Rita James Simon, *The Contemporary Woman and Crime* (Washington, D.C.: National Institute of Mental Health, 1975), Chapter 4. See also Freda Adler, *Sisters in Crime: The Rise of the New Female Criminal* (New York: McGraw-Hill, 1975) and Dale Hoffman-Bustamente, "The Nature of Female Criminality," *Issues in Criminology* 8 (1973), pp. 117–36.

in the labor force their opportunity to commit certain types of crimes also increases—and it is an opportunity that is seized. "This explanation," she points out, "assumes that women have no greater store of morality than do men. Their propensities to commit crimes do not differ, but, in the past, their opportunities have been much more limited. As women's opportunities to commit crime increase, so will their deviant behavior and the types of crimes they commit will much more closely resemble those committed by men." [53]

The crime of embezzlement, as indicated earlier, was not a common-law **Embezzlement** crime but was created by statute in England at the end of the eighteenth century and then adopted in the United States as a defense against the growing problem of theft committed by employees. Like many other crimes committed by white-collar workers, embezzlement often elicits mild public reaction. The offense is frequently not reported to the police because the victim is willing to forego prosecution in an attempt to get the money returned or because the victim is afraid that public disclosure may harm the reputation of the business.[54] (Embezzlement, it has been said, is often viewed by business people as a social disease of the corporation—and the less said about it the better.) As a consequence, the economic losses involved can only be estimated crudely. In 1967 the President's Commission on Law Enforcement drew on a variety of sources to arrive at an estimated loss of $200 million in 1964—an amount greater than the loss attributed to larcenies in that year—and these embezzlements are almost certainly no more than the tip of the iceberg.[55]

Donald Cressey, in one of the best-known studies of embezzlement, has concluded that employees are likely to steal funds entrusted to them when they have knowledge of specific techniques necessary for embezzlement and financial problems they cannot share with others. Even more important, however, is acceptance of a set of rationalizations for their criminal conduct that allows them to see themselves as trusted, law-abiding citizens whose actions are morally justified.[56] The claim that they have been underpaid for many years or that their employers have consistently taken advantage of them serves as an excuse for what they view as fair retaliation. Seeing themselves as more sinned against than sinning, thieves in white collars break the law and yet manage to avoid the full meaning of their actions.

In recent years, the opportunities for embezzlement have been much

[53] Simon, "The Contemporary Woman and Crime," p. 48.

[54] President's Commission on Law Enforcement and Administration of Justice, *Task Force Report: Assessment of Crime,* p. 47.

[55] Ibid., p. 47. See also Don C. Gibbons, *Society, Crime, and Criminal Careers,* pp. 341–42.

[56] Donald Cressey, *Other People's Money* (New York: The Free Press, 1953).

increased with the use of the computer. (The largest business crime ever prosecuted in the United States—the $2 billion Equity Funding Corporation fraud—involved a heavy reliance on computer technology.[57]) Disbursement records, payrolls, inventory accounts, shipping documents—all can be manipulated with the aid of electronic data processing systems, and detection is often difficult. "Once you've built a window into the system," says one writer, "it's there permanently, and large amounts or small amounts of money can pass through that window over a period of time without any change in risk. . . . Business has probably never been so vulnerable to theft."[58]

Computer technology makes possible many small fraudulent entries that provide worthwhile booty when added together. Thus, for example, a corporation executive combining the duties of accountant and electronic data processing manager altered a computer program so that a few pennies were added to the cost of many purchased items. The altered program "enabled him to keep a double set of records (the actual costs and the inflated costs), a technique that permitted him to steal amounts that did not overly distort the reported results. Without the computer it would have been impossible to make the thousands of cost changes. . . . Over a period of five years or so, the accountant siphoned off about $1 million."[59] Even more important, however, electronic data processing provides the criminal in the white collar with access to a wide range of company activity, often by the use of remote terminals or other means not easily controlled or detectable. A teller using a remote terminal in a branch of a major New York bank was able to steal a million and a half dollars from the central office. An employee in the welfare department of a large city entered fraudulent data into the payroll system and stole $2.75 million over a nine-month period. In this case, a fictitious work force identified by fake social security numbers was created and processed weekly through the payroll routine. The computer automatically printed a check for each bogus worker, and the employee—with a number of accomplices—intercepted the checks, endorsed them, and cashed them.[60] In another instance, "a fifteen-year-old schoolboy completely cracked the security system of a major London computer time-sharing service. . . . Gaining access to the most secret files stored on the computer by other users, he was able to read and change them at will without anyone noticing. He used no special technical gadgets and started with no special knowledge of the computer's inner workings—in-

---

[57] See "The Increasing Binary Nature of Crime," *The New York Times* (July 11, 1976).
[58] *White Collar Crime* (Chamber of Commerce of the United States), p. 20.
[59] Ibid., p. 21.
[60] See Brandt Allen, "Embezzler's Guide to the Computer," *Harvard Business Review* 53 (July–August 1975), pp. 79–89.

stead he relied only on ingenuity and a teletype terminal in his school."[61] The schoolboy may not have had criminal intentions, but his escapade illustrates the vulnerability of the company that entrusts its records to electronic data processing. Vulnerability to crime by computer is enhanced, it has been pointed out, by management's failure to recognize the dangers posed by the new technology, the inability to penetrate the mystique of the computer and its technical staff, and naive assumptions about the computer's invincibility.[62]

Much of the illegal activity of criminals in white collars is probably less lucrative than these large-scale embezzlements, less immediately recognizable as a violation of the law, or less reprehensible by common standards of morality. In the ordinary course of the business executive's day, many occasions for criminal acts arise, and business people—respected members of the middle class—casually violate the criminal law for their own convenience or economic advantage. The following hypothetical account undoubtedly closely parallels reality:

A Business Day

> Take an active, if concentrated, day in the life of a reputable New York State businessman. . . . As he walks to his downtown office after leaving his car resting snugly in a No-Parking zone, he warmly greets the veteran cop on the beat, who thanks him for his recent annual present, a case of good blended whiskey (penalty for attempting to influence a police officer with a gift: $5000 fine and/or 10 years in jail). After a few routine desk chores the businessman has a profitable late morning session with his personal income tax consultant, who has found a happy device for distorting repair and depreciation costs on some rental property he owns (penalty for filing a fraudulent income tax return: $10,000 fine and/or five years in jail). By this time he has worked up an appetite for a good expense account meal, so he entertains his wife and two close friends at a lavish lunch, all on the company tab (a misdemeanor, Section 665 of the State Penal Law, subject to a $500 fine and/or one year in jail). Back in his office, he reminds one of his assistants to "take care of" the building inspector with jurisdiction over the new plant site, thus getting as much red tape out of the way as possible (penalty for bribing a public officer: $5000 and/or 10 years in jail). He then dictates a letter to an executive of a small concern with whom he has just signed a contract, thanking him for his thoughtful gift of a new model portable TV set (penalty for secretly accepting a gift in return for corporate favors: $500 fine and/or one year in jail).

[61] Ibid., p. 89.
[62] White Collar Crime (Chamber of Commerce of the United States), p. 20.

At a late afternoon conference he congratulates the controller on a new bookkeeping device that handily pads a few of the firm's more controversial assets (penalty for concurring in a bookkeeping fraud: $500 fine and/or one year in jail). He later tells the head of his company's advertising agency to disregard a recent Federal Trade Commission cease-and-desist order about misleading TV commercials, at least until after the fall sales drive (this ultimately puts the company in line for an embarrassing and costly federal court action). As the day closes, he asks his secretary to wrap up one of the new company desk sets, which will be just the thing for his den at home (penalty for appropriating company property to one's personal use: $500 fine and/or one year in jail). Safe at home, he advises his wife not to worry about the maid's social security payments because she is leaving soon anyway (penalty for willful nonpayment of employer's social security contribution: $10,000 fine and/or five years in jail). Laying aside the cares of the day, he settles down to watch the news on his souvenir TV set—and fulminates about the dishonesty of the "union racketeers" he sees on the screen.[63]

There is, perhaps, an echo of a populist cry in this exposé of the hypocritical Eastern businessman, a distrust of anyone who does not work with his hands—and we need to be skeptical about the idea that the middle and upper classes are composed of criminals hiding behind a facade of respectability or that the nature of modern business life is such that it inevitably corrupts. But if some business executives and white-collar workers are scrupulous about matching their behavior to the law, many are not. And if some of the violations would be considered petty by most people, a large number of them would probably be viewed as serious offenses. Most important is the fact that the stereotype of the property offender as a member of the lower class is a gross error. Not only do corporation executives violate the criminal law in the pursuit of greater profits for the organization, as Sutherland contended; in addition, white-collar personnel at a variety of levels within the organization commit crimes against property for their individual benefit—and these crimes, the evidence suggests, are both numerous and costly. Any theory of crime causation must take these facts into account, as must any program that is seriously concerned with the just and effective enforcement of the law.

[63] Excerpted from "The Crooks In White Collars," by Frank Gibney, *Life,* © 1957 Time Inc. Used with permission.

There is little agreement among scholars in criminology about the exact meaning of the term professional crime. Some writers are inclined to stress the application of esoteric knowledge and skills as a defining characteristic and to direct their attention to the trained safecracker, pickpocket, and second-story man. The police sometimes speak of "classy" crime and professional crime as if they were the same thing, referring not to an arcane expertise but to shrewdness and disciplined planning that result in a "big sting," or large financial windfall.[64] For many police, style, as much as anything else, sets professional and nonprofessional crime apart. Other writers emphasize the idea that the distinction between professional and nonprofessional crime is akin to that made between professional and amateur sport or pursuit of the arts, the one being a means of earning a living, the other an activity engaged in by dilettantes.[65]

It is, perhaps, an explicit, conscious commitment to criminal activity as a means of earning some portion of one's livelihood that is most useful in drawing a line between professional and nonprofessional offenders.[66] The professional criminal, that is to say, may or may not be highly skilled in special techniques, may or may not devote all working hours to illegal activities, may or may not show shrewdness and an ability to obtain large sums by illegal means. He or she makes no bones about the nature of the activity involved, however, and engages in crime not simply on impulse or as a one-time fling, but as a regular source of income.

Criminals themselves appear to prefer the term *rounder* or *true criminal* rather than *professional*, but the thought seems to be much the same. Rounders distinguish themselves from other types of offenders like bums, young punks, alkies, and dope fiends. *Bums* are would-be thieves, misfits, nuisances, who are somehow not really "in the life." *Young punks* are criminals who have not acquired the maturity or experience to be classified as professionals, unless it is obvious that they are "serious" or "mean business." *Alkies* are alcoholics who may be chronic thieves but who fail to be accorded rounder status because they lack the necessary commitment. *Dope fiends* are drug addicts who are simply too undependable, too likely "to sell their soul for a cap," to be labeled

[64] See Sheldon L. Messinger, "Some Reflections on 'Professional Crime' in West City." This unpublished paper, based on the work of Messinger and Egon Bittner for the President's Commission on Law Enforcement, provides a brief but incisive examination of important aspects of modern professional crime.

[65] For an excellent discussion of the difficulties encountered in the use of the concept of professional crime, see Theodore M. Becker, review essay on the criminal craft in *Contemporary Sociology* 5 (September 1976), pp. 567–70.

[66] See Letkemann, *Crime as Work*, p. 20.

"Conventional" crimes, like robbery and burglary, absorb much of the law's efforts to control crimes against property. "Unconventional" crimes, such as tax fraud and thievery by employees, are far more costly but receive relatively little attention from either the police or the public.

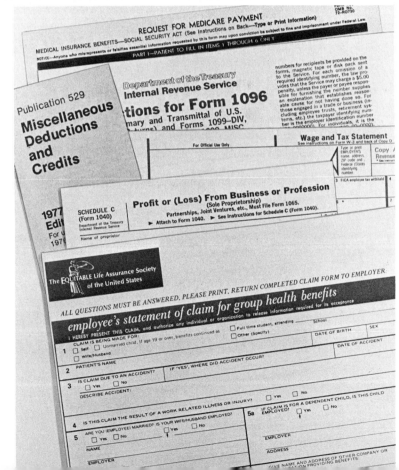

rounders.[67] At the heart of the professional criminal's orientation toward the world is what has been called the "exploitative perspective"—a viewpoint based on the aim of making as much money as possible, illegally, with maximum speed and safety. The similarity of this perspective to that of the small business entrepreneur embroiled in cutthroat competition is obvious, Messinger points out, and has often been mentioned in the criminological literature.[68] It is also a perspective, however, that is not unknown in more respectable-appearing form in the large corporate enterprise.

Accounts of professional crime go back to the fifteenth and sixteenth centuries, when war and economic change forced many peasants off the land. Masterless and penniless, they were joined by jugglers, minstrels, gypsies, robbers, poachers, and bandits to form a criminal subculture that gradually shifted to the newly emerging cities. Tracts, pamphlets, and ballads described the life of rogues, vagabonds, thieves, and sharpers in the Elizabethan era.[69] The popularity of Henry Mayhew's explorations of the London underworld in the nineteenth century testified to the perennial fascination exerted by people who make crime a way of life.[70] The social reformers and moralists of the time read his books about swindlers and professional beggars with an avid interest in which guilt and anxiety were mingled, for a criminal class in the urban slums was both a reproach to Victorian England and a source of alarm. In the twentieth century, numerous accounts of confidence games, pickpocketing, robbery and burglary, receiving stolen goods, shoplifting, forgery, and passing bad checks have continued to probe the nature of professional crime and its relationship to society.[71]

The Professional Thief These reports on professional crime have the virtue of describing criminal behavior not as an isolated act or a mere datum for the calculation of crime rates but as part of a larger social pattern. The publication of Suth-

[67] Ibid., pp. 23–26.

[68] Messinger, "Some Reflections on 'Professional Crcme.' " p. 21.

[69] James A. Inciardi, *Careers in Crime* (Chicago: Rand McNally, 1975). See also Eric Hobsbawm, *Bandits* (New York: Delacorte Press, 1969).

[70] See Peter Quennel, *London's Underworld: Being Selections from "Those That Will Not Work," The Fourth Volume of: London Labor and the London Poor by Henry Mayhew* (London: William Kimber, 1950).

[71] See, for example, Edwin H. Sutherland, *The Professional Thief* (Chicago: University of Chicago Press, 1937); J. B. Martin, *My Life in Crime* (New York: Harper Brothers, 1952); David Maurer, *Whiz Mob* (Gainesville: American Dialect Society, University of Florida, 1955); Mary Owen Cameron, *The Booster and the Snitch* (New York: The Free Press of Glencoe, 1964); Irving Spengal, *Racketville, Slumtown, Haulburg* (Chicago: University of Chicago Press, 1964); Bruce Jackson, *Outside the Law: A Thief 's Primer* (New Brunswick, N.J.: Transaction Books, 1972); Harry King, *Box Man*, ed. William Chambliss (New York: Harper & Row, 1972); and Carl B. Klockars, *The Professional Fence* (New York: The Free Press, 1974).

erland's *The Professional Thief*, in 1937 was particularly influential, for it provided a systematic analysis of the values, attitudes, and social organization of those who made theft a business. Sutherland's book—based on the recollections of Chic Conwell, a professional thief born in Philadelphia in the latter part of the nineteenth century—argued that the way of life of the professional thief was marked by a number of distinctive features:

> The professional thief devotes all his working time and energy to his illegal occupation and does not allow himself to be drawn into the legitimate world of Square Johns. He may steal three hundred and sixty-five days a year.

> The crimes of the professional thief are carefully planned. The selection of a target, the criminal act, the disposing of stolen property—all are thought out in advance and are not left to the vagaries of impulse and chance.

> The professional thief possesses technical skills of a high order which he must learn from others. The professional criminal has specialized, trained ability in which he takes great pride.

> Those who engage in professional theft share cultural values emphasizing loyalty and mutual aid among thieves and scorn for the straight world. The argot of the underworld binds them together and symbolizes their style of life as distinct from the conventional ways of the law-abiding.

In short, said Sutherland, those who explicitly accept a criminal role based on the rational pursuit of money using the specialized skills of the pickpocket, the shoplifter, and the confidence man have nothing in common with the casual property offender or the person who commits crimes of violence. The professional criminal, no less than other professionals, is a disciplined and dedicated individual who takes pleasure in seeing a difficult job accomplished with finesse.[72]

Sutherland's depiction of the professional thief has dominated the criminological literature concerning professional crime for many decades; it has been supported by other studies that have described similar patterns of behavior. In recent years, however, a number of writers have suggested that the type of professional criminal portrayed by Sutherland is growing increasingly rare and is being replaced by criminals who are committed to crime as a means of earning money but whose behavior is cut on another pattern. Messinger, for example, indicates that in interviews with both criminals and law enforcement officials, the idea that "old-time professionals are a dying breed" appeared again and again.

[72] Sutherland, *The Professional Thief*, Chapter I.

The passing of the specialist ("Nowadays, everybody chippys a little bit at everything"), the disappearance of the expert ("Nobody knows how to take a safe anymore except a few oldtimers, and they aren't teaching anyone else"), the weakening of loyalty to other criminals ("You know what they say in Los Angeles—it's a question of who gets his story down first, he gets off lightest")—all point to a decline in professionalism, in Sutherland's sense, among those who engage in crime to make money.[73] Instead of being a full-time occupation, part of a life style set off sharply from the law-abiding world, much criminal activity appears to be a form of moonlighting, in which crime is used to supplement the income from legitimate but low-paying work. There are self-taught professional thieves and professional criminals who stay aloof from all others.[74] And for many of those today who do concentrate on crime, illegal activities often take on the form not of highly skilled, well-planned attacks on property but of hustling: "For the small-time professional criminal, hustling means moving around bars and being seen; it means asking 'what's up.' It means 'connecting' in the morning with two others who have a burglary set up for the evening, calling a man you know to see if he wants to buy 10 stolen alpaca sweaters at $5 each, and scouting the streets for an easy victim. It means being versatile; passing checks, burglarizing a store. It's a planless kind of existence, but with a purpose—to make as much money as can be made each day, no holds barred."[75] This seedy, hand-to-mouth existence is perhaps the growing reality of professional crime, rather than the activities of a well-organized, mutually supportive group of highly skilled criminals.

Problems of definition and lack of solid data make it difficult to reach a conclusion about the present nature of professional crime. It seems reasonable to suppose, however, that those who use crimes against property as a means of livelihood have changed as has the society that nourished them in the past. Fewer safes contain anything worth taking, Messinger has suggested, as checks and the use of credit cards replace cash; and improvements in the design of safes and burglar alarms make safes an increasingly difficult target.[76] Mass education and the decline of immigration have probably reduced the ranks of the gullible, who served as victims of the confidence game—although, as P. T. Barnum has told us and as the newspapers daily affirm, a sucker is born every minute. The sophistication of communications techniques among law enforcement

[73] "Some Reflections on 'Professional Crime,' " pp. 17–18. See also Inciardi, *Careers in Crime*, Chapter 10.

[74] See Jackson, *Outside the Law*, "Introduction." See also Werner J. Einstadter, "The Social Organization of Armed Robbery," *Social Problems* 17 (Summer 1969), pp. 64–83.

[75] President's Commission on Law Enforcement and Administration of Justice, *Task Force Report: Assessment of Crime*, p. 97.

[76] Messinger, "Some Reflections on 'Professional Crime,' " p. 18.

agencies has sharply increased the hazards incurred by criminals who engage in an habitual form of crime and have a recognizable style.[77]

Possibly most important is what Messinger has called the "latent criminal potential" of society—that is, the existence of situations that can be exploited for illegal gain. A large and increasing proportion of the criminal labor force, he argues, "is being sustained by certain kinds of quasi-legitimate business enterprises. We have in mind, particularly, those enterprises where the possibilities of consumer manipulation are large, where the 'hard sell' is routine, where the quasi-legitimate, the legitimate, and the illegitimate blend into each other with no gaps. The used car business is apparently such; contracting; real estate sales; all kinds of repair businesses; and others."[78] If the criminal professionalism analyzed by Sutherland has diminished over the years, it is due perhaps not to a decline in the number of persons with a talent for and an interest in crime as a means of livelihood, but to an increase in the range of more or less legal economic enterprises that can use their abilities.

The laws defining the crimes of larceny by trick and false pretenses are **Fraud** varied and complex. Most of these offenses, however, can be lumped under the heading of *fraud*, generally described as obtaining property by the deliberate use of false representation.

Fraud is possibly the most common of all crimes.[79] It may also be the most costly. Those most frequently reported by the FBI—which represent only a tiny fraction of all the frauds committed each year—are the passing of bad checks; other areas of fraud include crimes involving the use of the mail, the sale of securities, the claims of medical and food products, home repairs and improvements, the sale of new and used cars, and solicitations for charities. In the area of taxes it was estimated, on the basis of a survey in 1962, that unreported taxable income amounted to some $24 billion and that a large share represented deliberate omissions for the purpose of nonpayment of taxes.[80] Although current estimates are not available, the evidence strongly suggests that the losses due to the various forms of fraud—committed to a large extent by people in the middle and upper classes—far outweigh the cost of "conventional" property crimes such as burglary and robbery.

A few forms of fraud have been studied in some detail. Edwin Lemert's investigations of check forgery, for example, indicate that offenders are likely to be native white males; and compared to other

---

[77] See Inciardi, *Careers in Crime*, Chapter 7.

[78] Messinger, "Some Reflections on 'Professional Crime,' " pp. 18–19.

[79] President's Commission on Law Enforcement and Administration of Justice, *Task Force Report: Assessment of Crime*, p. 49.

[80] Ibid., p. 51.

confined criminals, they are older when they commit their first offense (somewhere in their late twenties or early thirties), more intelligent and from higher socioeconomic backgrounds.[81] They differ substantially among themselves, however, in terms of their patterns of involvement. "Some forgers pass worthless checks only once and quit," says Lemert. "Others, casual offenders, intersperse periods of stable employment with check writing sorties quickly followed by arrest. Some people imprisoned for bad checks are alcoholics who have unwisely passed worthless checks during a drinking spree, drug addicts 'supporting a habit,' or gamblers desperately trying to cover losses."[82]

The behavior of those who habitually pass worthless checks appears to be based on pseudonymity (rather than anonymity), geographical mobility, and lack of intimate social interaction with either criminals or noncriminals. They commit their crimes against property less to earn a living, Lemert argues, than to live fast and well; the money flowing into their hands is spent freely on clothes, food, drink, travel, and entertainment. But it is a way of life that carries the seeds of its own destruction. A long history of false identities is apt to leave the offender totally unable to define himself in relation to others. The self becomes amorphous, apathy replaces motivation, and arrest for forgery often follows.[83]

Such individuals do not fit neatly into the category of professional criminal, but there are others who engage in fraud—in the form of the confidence game—who certainly appear to do so. The confidence game, according to August Vollmer, is based on the same psychological principles found in legitimate forms of economic exchange; but if a confidence game is to be successful, the confidence man (or woman) must find the right victim to swindle: "An honest man will not allow himself to be a party to any scheme in order to gain sudden riches. A man must have larceny in his mind to become a perfect victim."[84] It is possible that Vollmer accepted too easily the rationalization so often offered by confidence men to justify their behavior. In any event, we find, in the confidence game, criminal and victim joined in a caricature of American business, in a long list of swindles with names like the "Pigeon-drop" and the "Italian Major Bunco." The victim, expecting economic gain, is taken advantage of by the confidence man, who knows precisely how to awaken the victim's cupidity. Although the details of some confidence games have changed over the years—perhaps in response to a growing

[81] Edwin M. Lemert, *Human Deviance, Social Problems, and Social Control* (Englewood Cliffs, N.J.: Prentice-Hall, 1972), Chapter 9.

[82] Ibid., p. 165.

[83] Ibid., pp. 180–81.

[84] August Vollmer, "Introduction," in John C. R. MacDonald, *Crime Is a Business: Buncos, Rackets, and Confidence Schemes* (Stanford, Calif.: Stanford University Press, 1939), p. 2.

sophistication among the population, as suggested earlier—the various swindles persist and continue to be effective.[85]

Interest in the confidence game is undoubtedly based in part on the provocative image of the criminal as one who lives by his wits on the edges of society and preys on victims only slightly more reputable than himself. But if the confidence man is sometimes overly admired as a clever rogue, the confidence game does involve psychological manipulation that is illuminating for an understanding of social interaction in many other realms of behavior.

The criminal argot used by confidence men caught the attention of David Maurer; approaching the study of the confidence game from the viewpoint of linguistics, he wrote what proved to be a classic analysis of the patterns of behavior of people who steal with words by instilling confidence in a scheme designed to cheat the victim.[86]

The following steps, involved in a swindle in which the victim is led to believe that he is being given an opportunity to bet on a rigged horse race, reveal a typical pattern that underlies many of the more elaborate confidence games:[87]

1. Locating and investigating a well-to-do victim. (*Putting the mark up.*)

2. Gaining the victim's confidence. (*Playing the con for him.*)

3. Steering him to meet the insideman. (*Roping the mark.*)

4. Permitting the insideman to show him how he can make a large amount of money dishonestly. (*Telling him the tale.*)

5. Allowing the victim to make a substantial profit. (*Giving him the convincer.*)

6. Determining exactly how much he will invest. (*Giving him the breakdown.*)

7. Sending him home for this amount of money. (*Putting him on the send.*)

8. Playing him against a big store and fleecing him. (*Taking off the touch.*)

9. Getting him out of the way as quickly as possible. (*Blowing him off.*)

10. Forestalling action by the law. (*Putting in the fix.*)

---

[85] See Jay Robert Nash, *Hustlers and Con Men* (New York: M. Evans, 1976).

[86] David W. Maurer, *The American Confidence Man* (Springfield, Ill.: Charles C. Thomas, 1974). See also Maurer's *Whiz Mob* for a further analysis of criminal argot.

[87] Maurer, *The American Confidence Man*, p. 6. Reprinted by permission of Charles C. Thomas, Publishers, and David W. Maurer.

The last step clearly requires skillful maneuvering. One device is to persuade the mark that he has become an accessory to a murder. The confidence man engages in a sham quarrel with the inside man, angrily blaming him for their alleged loss, and finally pretends to shoot him. A concealed bag spurts chicken blood, the inside man falls to the floor apparently dead, the mark is terrified—and his future silence is assured as the confidence man promises to keep them both out of trouble by getting rid of the "corpse."

The problem of preventing people from giving vent to noisy, troublesome complaints when they feel they have been wronged often occurs in normal social life, Erving Goffman has argued. The rejected suitor, the dissatisfied customer in a restaurant, the discharged worker—all are likely to feel acutely disgruntled, and somehow their anger must be controlled. They too need "cooling out," and Goffman suggests that the confidence man's techniques of manipulating the mark—such as making the victim feel culpable—often have their counterparts in everyday life.[88] In a similar vein, Burton Clark has analyzed the problem of students who are anxious to obtain a college degree but lack the necessary ability. In America, he points out, the aspirations of the masses for higher education are encouraged by the less than rigorous admissions policies of many publicly supported universities. An insistence that those who do attend college must maintain academic standards means, however, that many will fail. The necessity of handling the inevitable, *structured* disappointment is avoided, at least in part, by sidetracking unpromising students to two-year, public junior colleges. For students who would like to transfer from a junior college to a state university but whose grades are inadequate, a variety of devices are used to lessen the frustration: students are encouraged to shift to a vocational program; counselors "lay out the facts of life"; through probation lingering hopes are slowly killed off. Thus, argues Clark, the cooling-out process in higher education "is one whereby systematic discrepancy between aspiration and avenue is covered over and stress for the individual and the system is minimized. . . . Society can continue to encourage maximum effort without major disturbance from unfilled promises and expectations."[89]

As interesting as the analysis of the confidence game may be, however, it must be recognized that most of the frauds perpetrated against the public fail to reach such a degree of elaboration. Misleading advertising, "bait-and-switch" selling tactics, deceptive packaging—these and similar practices arising in the daily course of business life are both

[88] Erving Goffman, "On Cooling the Mark Out: Some Aspects of Adaptation to Failure," *Psychiatry* 15 (November 1952), pp. 451–63.

[89] Burton R. Clark, "The 'Cooling-Out' Function in Higher Education," *The American Journal of Sociology* 65 (May 1960), pp. 569–576.

simpler and more common. If these ordinary events have not exerted the same fascination as some of the more flamboyant examples of the confidence game, their impact on property rights is certainly of equal or greater importance. It has been estimated, for example, that short-weighting alone may cost the American consumer as much as $10 billion a year.[90]

The Meaning of Property in Modern Society

Crimes against property obviously do not constitute a simple phenomenon easily explained by stereotypical ideas about the nature of theft. There are many different kinds of behavior involved, varying greatly in their social and economic impact, and the underlying social situations and motivational patterns are still only dimly understood.

Clearly, however, an impressive number of crimes against property are committed in the United States each year, even if we confine ourselves to reported offenses. It would be interesting to know if the United States has a higher incidence of crimes against property than do other countries. The problems in comparing criminal statistics on an international basis are formidable, as Hermann Mannheim has indicated, involving differences in criminal law, criminal procedures, reporting methods, and so on.[91] The limited evidence available, however, does suggest that crime rates for property offenses are higher in the United States than in Canada, England, and Denmark, at least as far as burglary and robbery are concerned; and it seems likely that the rates for other forms of property offenses are higher as well.[92]

The incidence of property offenses in the United States is almost certainly influenced by the sheer abundance of possessions. Cars, radios, television sets, clothing, boats, household furnishings, jewelry—all are part of that flood of material goods that has been the pride of the American economic system. Furthermore, this great quantity of personal property is widely distributed in millions upon millions of offices, shops, stores, factories, warehouses, and homes.

As a consequence, the opportunity for crimes against property is great indeed, at least in the sense that there are many situations in which

[90] See Ralph Nader, ed., *The Consumer and Corporate Accountability* (New York: Harcourt Brace Jovanovich, 1973), p. 6. The possibility of fraud appears to be greatly enhanced by an increasingly complex technology. See, for example, Kenneth Sonenclar, "Bogus Transistors for Defense," *The New York Times* (October 24, 1976).

[91] Hermann Mannheim, *Comparative Criminology* (Boston: Houghton Mifflin, 1965), pp. 118–22.

[92] See Leon Radzinowicz and Marvin E. Wolfgang, eds., *The Criminal in Society* (New York: Basic Books, 1971), pp. 225–40.

stealing is feasible. Automobiles offer a striking example; in few societies are so many objects of value left unguarded on the street. (According to the FBI, in 42 percent of all cars stolen the key has been left in the ignition.)[93] And, in general, a great deal of property in American society is handled with a singular lack of attention paid to its protection. The security measures taken by banks, for example, particularly in rural areas, are often minimal. Material in transit—in trains, trucks, ships, and planes—is frequently plundered with ease. Some commentators may credit the absence of precaution to a pervasive trust in one's fellows; others may call it carelessness or indifference instilled by the accessibility of insurance.[94] In any case, although empirical research on the matter is lacking, it does seem likely that personal property in America represents a vast hoard of vulnerable objects, an invitation to theft as it were. (In recent years—as we shall see in Chapter 15—there has been a growing interest in new ways to make property more secure, ranging from the surveillance of shopping centers by closed-circuit television to sensor devices installed in private homes.)

Once goods are stolen they are often disposed of without great difficulty, partly because the business of receiving stolen goods is apparently well organized and partly because much of what is stolen is mass-produced, and therefore articles are hard to identify or trace. There have been few investigations of the illegal marketing of property, but scattered evidence suggests that it is an established enterprise.[95] The New York City police, for example, claim that one month after an increase in the city cigarette tax had been imposed, "an entire system for distributing bootlegged cigarettes had been set up and was operating smoothly. The out-of-state suppliers, the truckers, and both the wholesale and retail distributors had been organized, and the system was operating on a scale capable of handling full truckloads of untaxed cigarettes shipped in from the South."[96] Much stolen property, however, is probably sold to friends and neighbors rather than passed through the hands of a fence.

If the "opportunity structure" of personal property in the United States is an important element in the problem of crimes against property, the changes that have taken place in the forms of ownership are no less crucial. Modern economic developments have done much to destroy the respect for property by placing so much wealth in the hands of imper-

[93] See Norval Morris and Gordon Hawkins, *The Honest Politician's Guide to Crime Control* (Chicago: University of Chicago Press, 1970), p. 102.

[94] For a discussion of the impact of insurance on precautions against property crimes, see R. L. Carter, *Theft in the Market* (London: Institute of Economic Affairs, 1974).

[95] Klockars, *The Professional Fence.*

[96] President's Commission on Law Enforcement and Administration of Justice, *Task Force Report: Assessment of Crime*, p. 99.

sonal agencies, both private and public. In America—as in most other capitalist societies—a great deal of property is now held by large, impersonal corporations, and thus the sense of an owner as a person linked to his or her possessions by inviolable bonds is diminished. The ordinary person's respect for the property of others, argues Mannheim, is closely tied to the existence of a specific, identifiable owner.[97] And there has been a vast increase in intangible property, particularly in the form of wealth dispensed by government authority, such as money payments, benefits, services, contracts, franchises, and licenses.[98]

The concept of private property is so deeply embedded in American society that it is apt to be taken for granted. When we call on the law to protect our possessions, we easily assume that the legal rules reflect a shared set of values and that the threatened rights are cherished by all. Roscoe Pound, for example, in setting forth a list of "jural postulates" containing what he believed to be basic social values expressed in the law, declared that "in a civilized society men must be able to assume that they may control for beneficial purposes what they have discovered or appropriated to their own use, what they have created with their own labor, and what they have acquired under the existing social and economic order."[99] Civilization and private property are thus necessarily joined, and the law protects their union.

The question of private property is, however, a good deal more complex than this. In particular there is the problem of the extent to which the sanctity of private property is actually accepted by the members of society and incorporated into the norms and attitudes that help guide behavior. We cannot understand property wrongs, that is to say, until we understand property rights, and the evidence suggests that the latter are not viewed with unanimity. This is not to suggest that many people in the United States today would reject generalized normative statements supporting private property. Even thieves do not like to see their stolen possessions stolen. Norms governing private property as an operative morality are, however, another matter.

"Property," according to Max Lerner, "is not a simple or single right. It has become a property complex—a tangle of ideas, emotions, and attitudes, as well as of legal and economic practices. As such it has been drastically transformed in the era of Big Technology and the corporate empires."[100] In the nineteenth century, he argues, Americans were inclined to believe that "a man had a right to the things with which he had

[97] See Hermann Mannheim, *Criminal Justice and Social Reconstruction* (New York: Oxford University Press, 1946), p. 100.
[98] See Charles A. Reich, "The New Property," *The Yale Law Journal* 73 (1964), pp. 733–87.
[99] Roscoe Pound, *Jurisprudence* (St. Paul, Minn.: West, 1959), pp. 367–456.
[100] Max Lerner, *America as a Civilization* (New York: Simon & Schuster, 1957), p. 297.

mixed his sweat, that his property was linked with his craft and job and therefore with his personality. . . ."[101] This view of private property helped to throw a protective screen around one's possessions, in the sense that the legal rules concerning property were endowed with a moral force that many people could recognize and accept. To the extent that property had been *earned,* it belonged to its owner by virtue of past effort. Inherited property was brought into this scheme of things, somewhat uneasily, through the idea that parents had both the right and the duty to confer the fruits of their labor on their children, who extended the "self" into the future.

This vindication of private property—suitable enough, perhaps, for a nation of farmers, artisans, and owners of small businesses—began to seem less compelling as economic enterprises increased enormously in size and the "owner" became a vague abstraction. It is difficult to think of General Motors, Standard Oil of Illinois, U.S. Steel, or American Telephone and Telegraph as incorporating their sweat in their property; dispersed stockholders are no less "disembodied"; and today the large-scale bureaucracy is frequently seen as an impersonal entity that one can steal from without feeling much compunction. Erwin Smigel found, for example, that in a random sample of 212 adults, 102 selected a large business as the type of organization they would steal from if in need; 53 chose government, and 10 said they would pick a small business. (Of the remaining people in the sample, 9 regarded large business and government as equally suitable targets, 5 did not differentiate at all, 30 refused to steal under any conditions, and 3 would not answer the question.)[102] The reasons for selecting large business are complex, as Smigel's study indicated, varying with sex, religion, and socioeconomic status, and mixing a calculation of risk with ideas about victims who deserve what happens to them; but a regard for the sanctity of property—when it comes to corporate ownership—is evidently rather meager. The lack of a clearly defined, deserving personal owner renders offenses against property less damaging in the eyes of potential wrongdoers.

Donald Horning, in a study of blue-collar workers in an industrial plant, found similar attitudes. A variety of company property was apt to be viewed as being of uncertain ownership—particularly small, plentiful, and inexpensive materials, components, and tools; pilfering such property was often regarded not as stealing but as "taking things from the plant" and would not arouse feelings of guilt.[103]

---

[101] Ibid.

[102] Erwin O. Smigel and H. Lawrence Ross, *Crimes Against Bureaucracy* (New York: Van Nostrand Reinhold, 1970), p. 20.

[103] Donald Horning, "Blue Collar Theft," in Smigel and Ross, *Crimes Against Bureaucracy,* pp. 46–64.

It could be argued, of course, that the tendency to see corporate enterprises as exploitative bureaucracies that do not deserve their wealth is simply a rationalization, a justification for theft erected after the act. But this overlooks the extent to which rationalizations—verbalizations making behavior intelligible and excusable to oneself and to others—pave the way for action as well as follow it.[104] They are motives as well as apologies, and many people today jeer at claims of legitimacy of private property in the hands of business corporations. The big corporation cheats the public, it is said, and exploits employees; people are entitled to cheat and exploit it in return. This sort of cynicism is not confined to those at the bottom of the social order, who might be expected to view the inequalities of this world with a disenchanted eye. Many middle-class citizens are, apparently, quite ready on occasion to view the large commercial enterprise as an appropriate victim. It has been reported, for example, that the purloining of "souvenirs" from hotels and motels throughout the country has reached "staggering" proportions, with an estimated loss of $500 million in 1974. Many guests satisfy themselves with the ubiquitous ashtray, but others carry off towels, sheets, bedspreads, flatware, Bibles, lamps, television sets, and suites of furniture. "Most guests," reports one writer, "who go home with free mementos of their stay do not regard their actions as stealing—and they have some curious ways of rationalizing their behavior, one being that room rates are so high that only by adding to their own possessions at a hotel's expense can they get their money's worth."[105]

The new forms of wealth bestowed by governmental authority also appear to have diluted traditional concepts of the sanctity of property. In recent decades, as Reich has indicated, there has been a vast expansion of property rights in the form of claims on goods and services furnished through federal, state, and local political structures. "The valuables which derive from relationships to government are of many kinds," he points out. "Some primarily concern individuals; others flow to businesses and organizations. Some are obvious forms of wealth, such as direct payments of money, while others, like licenses and franchises, are indirectly valuable."[106] In this vast amount of intangible property— claims to monetary benefits flowing from the government or government-protected rights to earn such benefits—the concept of an "owner" has almost vanished altogether. The falsification of records to qualify for

[104] See Donald R. Cressey, "The Violators' Vocabularies of Adjustment," in Smigel and Ross, *Crimes Against Bureaucracy*, pp. 65–85; see also Gresham M. Sykes and David Matza, "Techniques of Neutralization," *American Sociological Review* 22 (December 1957), pp. 664–670.

[105] See Michael S. Lasky, "One in 3 Hotel Guests Is a Towel Thief, Bible Pincher, or Worse," *The New York Times* (January 27, 1974), Section 10, p. 1.

[106] Reich, "The New Property," p. 734.

welfare payments or unemployment compensation, the bribery of public officials to secure a franchise, and the winning of government contracts in return for political contributions have a long history in America, but they are now part of what well may be a greatly enlarged field of illegal activity that has economic gain as its goal. Wealth becomes governmental largesse, and stealing becomes an abstract act without the sense of any real victim. Unfortunately, criminology has not yet directed much attention to such forms of property offenses.

When we examine crimes against property, then, we must realize that many of the existing ideas about the misappropriation of property are based on implicit notions of possessions lodged in the hands of particular individuals who have somehow earned them, thus justifying the law's protection. This viewpoint—a comforting one to most property owners—is no longer so easily accepted, however. The nature of the owner and the basis of property rights are frequently elusive in the case of large corporate enterprises, and the picture has been clouded further by new forms of property in which wealth is disassociated from any owner at all. When these changes in property relationships in American society are coupled with the vulnerability of so many personal possessions, the vast number of attacks on property seems less than surprising.

Conclusions

The protection of property has long been one of the primary functions of the criminal law, and in the United States today property offenses make up the largest share of the crimes commonly classified as serious or important and that are known to the police. Most of these crimes against property—consisting of burglary, auto theft, robbery, and larceny—are likely to be committed by persons in the lower socioeconomic levels of society; and taken together, these crimes extract a substantial economic toll from property owners each year.

There is a vast number of crimes against property, however, that do not receive official recognition. Some of these offenses are similar to the offenses that are reported, in terms of the criminal, the victim, and the nature of the criminal act; but people fail to bring them to the attention of the police, frequently because they believe it would be useless or they consider the crime a private matter. Many unreported crimes against property, however, are of a different order. Some are white-collar crimes, which are committed by business firms and include monopolistic practices, patent infringements, consumer fraud, and illegal political donations. Other frequently unreported crimes against property are committed by white-collar employees. It seems likely that the economic loss due to unreported crimes by corporations and their employees far exceeds the loss due to the property offenses that are reported to the police, and that the socioeconomic background of the offenders would be generally characterized as middle or upper class.

It would appear, then, that the public attention paid to different kinds of property offenses distorts the reality of the problem. The "conventional" crimes, like robbery and burglary, receive a large share of the public's concern and absorb much of the law's efforts to control crimes against property. "Unconventional" crimes, such as consumer fraud and theft from commercial establishments by employees, are far more costly but receive relatively little attention from either the public or law enforcement agencies. If the aim of public policy is to reduce the economic toll of crimes against property, our present priorities would appear to be somewhat misplaced. It is true, of course, that the problem of crime cannot be reduced to a dollars-and-cents accounting, even when we are dealing with crimes against property. Nonetheless, the failure to devote more attention to the problem of white-collar crime and crimes committed by "thieves in white collars" must be accounted a severe case of social myopia.

Beyond this, there is the question of whether criminology has provided a balanced picture of crimes against property. And it must be admitted that despite Sutherland's plea for a broader view of property crimes to include illegal activities of business corporations, the discipline has moved only slowly toward a comprehensive examination of property offenses. Criminology's ideas about the causes of crimes against property are not so much wrong as unduly restricted. An academic discipline, of course, does not necessarily shape itself to fit a frequency distribution of the events with which it concerns itself. The availability of data, the funding of research, and the emergence of problems of broad theoretical interest also serve to determine the pattern of growth. But if criminology is to provide a firm understanding of crimes against property and effective means for their control, the image of lower-class theft must give way to a less reassuring view of property offenses as a diversified form of behavior that is found at all class levels.

Recommended Readings

The historical development of the laws concerning crimes against property is examined in Jerome Hall, *Theft, Law, and Society* (Boston: Little, Brown, 1935). Crimes against property as a means of earning a living—however precarious—are analyzed by Peter Letkemann in *Crime as Work* (Englewood Cliffs, N.J.:

Prentice-Hall, 1973). Amateur and professional theft are both presented in Mary Owen Cameron, *The Booster and the Snitch* (New York: The Free Press of Glencoe, 1964). It is professional theft, however, that has occupied most of the attention in criminology, and Edwin H. Sutherland, *The Professional Thief* (Chicago: University of Chicago Press, 1937) remains the classic work. For an up-to-date analysis of how the stolen property is disposed of, the reader should see Carl B. Klockars, *The Professional Fence* (New York: The Free Press, 1974).

Gilbert Geis and Robert F. Meier, eds., *White-Collar Crime* (New York: The Free Press, 1977) provides a comprehensive picture of the studies that have been made of crime against property committed by business people in the course of their work. The violation of financial trust for personal gain is analyzed in Donald Cressey, *Other People's Money* (New York: The Free Press, 1953). For an admittedly speculative estimate of the cost of all forms of crime against property, the reader should consult the President's Commission on Law Enforcement and Administration of Justice, *Task Force Report: Assessment of Crime* (Washington, D.C.: Government Printing Office, 1967).

Chapter 4
Crimes of Violence

Crimes of physical violence directed against the person are undoubtedly the offenses most uniformly abhorred in our society. "To millions of Americans," it has been declared, "few things are more pervasive, more frightening, more real today than violent crime and the fear of being assaulted, mugged, robbed, or raped."[1] The heaviest penalties are reserved for such offenses, and a brutal murder or a vicious sexual attack can touch off a public clamor for punishment.

One reason that crimes of violence are so commonly condemned is the almost universal fear of physical suffering and the finality of death. But a widespread agreement that murder, assault, and rape should be punished by the state exists not simply because of personal apprehensions. This fear for oneself makes the anguish of others who are victims of violent crime readily understandable—especially in a society that concerns itself with the rights and feelings of all its people. As Alexis de Tocqueville observed, the egalitarianism of a democratic society widens the area within which human compassion can operate. In a rigidly stratified society, the notion of personal suffering is apt to be reserved for people of quality.[2] If a variety of social cleavages in the United States limit the reach of our empathy and indignation for some kinds of crimes, there is also a belief in a common humanity helping to support a general agreement that inflicting bodily harm is one of the most heinous of offenses.[3]

In recent years, questions about the nature and extent of crimes of vio-

[1] National Commission on the Causes and Prevention of Violence, Staff Report, vol. 12, *Crimes of Violence* (Washington, D.C.: Government Printing Office, 1969), p. xxvii. Another study, based on the responses of college students, suggests that while attitudes toward crime have become more heterogeneous over a forty-year span, crimes against the person are now judged to be a more serious problem than it was in the past, whereas crimes against property are judged to be a less serious one. See Clyde H. Coombs, "Thurstone's Measurement of Social Values Revisited Forty Years Later," *Journal of Personality and Social Psychology* 6 (May–August 1967), pp. 85–91. See also Monica D. Blumenthal et al., *Justifying Violence: Attitudes of American Men* (Ann Arbor: Institute for Social Research, University of Michigan, 1972).

[2] See Robert K. Merton and Robert A. Nisbet, eds., *Contemporary Social Problems* (New York: Harcourt, Brace & World, 1966), pp. 8–9.

[3] "If you prick us, do we not bleed? If you poison us, do we not die?" asks Shylock in *The Merchant of Venice*, suggesting that common suffering gives evidence of a common humanity.

lence have taken on a special force. Beginning in the early 1960s, the rate of violent crime reported by the FBI began to increase with a speed that many people found alarming. Political assassinations; urban riots; bizarre multiple killings; kidnappings; numerous stories of rapes, assaults, muggings, and murders—all helped to create a picture of a rapidly rising tide of violence threatening to engulf society.[4] And for some people the sources of this apparently growing lawlessness have been easy to identify. They have named, as the causes of our ills, permissiveness in raising children, a spate of Supreme Court decisions that "coddle criminals," ethnic militancy that has become willing to seize on any means to achieve its ends, and a counterculture that glorifies drugs and violence.

Many criminologists, however, have considered such explanations grossly misleading. The increase in violent crimes such as murder, assault, and rape, has been greatly exaggerated, it is argued; people are simply reporting crime more frequently than they did in the past, and the mass media distort reality in their search for sensational news. Demographic changes, such as increased urbanization and alterations in the age structure of American society, account for much of whatever growth in violent crime has actually occurred; and poverty and discrimination, rather than any supposed erosion of traditional American values, continue to be among the most potent sources of criminality.

A portion of this debate is colored by ideological considerations; as long as the poor and members of minority groups are heavily overrepresented in official crime statistics, the political left and right are likely to be entangled in arguments in which the assignment of blame takes precedence over the discovery of cause.[5] A "politicized" view of the world became particularly influential in the 1960s, Gary Marx has pointed out, as ghetto riots and confrontations in the streets led to a profound reexamination of the meaning of violence in American life.

For the pioneering theorists of collective behavior in the late nineteenth and early twentieth centuries, the actions of crowds had been viewed as wildly destructive; such thinkers as G. LeBon and E. A. Ross wrote of "herd instincts," "the group mind," the "atavistic vulnerability of civilized men," and the "dangerous classes."[6] Riotous crowds were

[4] For an excellent account of the accelerating concern with the problem of violent crime, see Fred P. Graham, "A Contemporary History of American Crime," in Hugh Davis Graham and Ted Robert Gurr, eds., *The History of Violence in America* (New York: Bantam Books, 1969), pp. 485–504. See also Morton Hunt, *The Mugging* (New York: Atheneum, 1972). By 1968, according to the public opinion polls, crime was viewed as the most serious problem confronting the nation; see Gwynn Nettler, *Explaining Crime* (New York: McGraw-Hill, 1974), pp. 3–4.

[5] See James Q. Wilson, "Crime and the Liberal Audience," *Commentary* (January 1971), pp. 71–78.

[6] See Gary T. Marx, "Issueless Riots," *The Annals of the American Academy of Political and Social Science* 391 (September 1970), pp. 21–33.

thought to be irrational, made up of social misfits giving vent to emotion rather than pursuing a goal. In the 1960s the work of such writers as Neil Smelser, Carl Couch, and Jerome Skolnick helped to change this stereotype.[7] Crowd behavior came to be interpreted in a far more favorable light, observes Gary Marx, as many social scientists found themselves in sympathy with the political and social dissent in which it was rooted: "In direct contrast to certain early conservative theorists such as LeBon," he writes, "most American sociologists studying collective behavior hold liberal-to-left political perspectives. . . . Their analysis and ideology lead them to see black, student, and 'third world' collective violence as intricately tied to injustice and strain, and often to imbue all crowd participants with ideological ends and a disinterested morality."[8]

There is reason to believe, then, that the study of violence in America reflects a variety of personal convictions and ideological positions, thus complicating the attempt to understand the nature and extent of crimes against the person and the changes that have taken place over time. But whether we agree with H. Rap Brown's mordant declaration that violence is as American as cherry pie, or with the assertion that we are experiencing an unprecedented wave of crimes of violence, we must examine the empirical evidence available.

In this chapter we will be concerned with the nature of individual crimes such as murder, assault, and rape, which occupy much of the public's attention in the area of violence, and with the large increase in the number of such crimes in recent years. In addition we will examine collective violence, with particular reference to the riots that swept over the United States in the 1960s. The analysis of such events has done much to alter the interpretation of violent behavior and its place in society.

Individual Violence

Of the seven major crimes classified as Part I offenses in the *Uniform Crime Reports* of the FBI (see p. 78), criminal homicide, forcible rape, and aggravated assault involve crimes against the person and make up approximately 5 percent of all the major crimes known to the police; if robbery is included as a crime against the person, the figure is about 9 percent. (See Table 1.) These can be called the "conventional" crimes of violence, just as we have called larceny, burglary, robbery, and auto theft

[7] See Neil Smelser, *Theory of Collective Behavior* (Englewood Cliffs, N.J.: Prentice-Hall, 1963); Carl Couch, "Collective Behavior: An Examination of Some Stereotypes," *Social Problems* 15 (Winter 1968), pp. 310–22; and Jerome H. Skolnick, *The Politics of Protest* (New York: Ballantine Books, 1969).

[8] Gary T. Marx, "Issueless Riots," p. 23.

Table 1. Offenses Known to the Police, 1975

Type of Crime	Number	Percent
Criminal homicide	18,780	.17
Forcible rape	56,730	.50
Aggravated assault	490,850	4.34
Robbery	420,210	3.72
Burglary	3,089,800	27.33
Larceny	6,270,800	55.47
Auto Theft	957,600	8.47
Total:	11,304,800	100.

SOURCE: *Uniform Crime Reports—1976* (Washington, D.C.: Government Printing Office, 1977), p. 35.

the "conventional" crimes against property. They are the offenses that come most immediately to mind when people speak of illegal bodily harm, receive the most detailed recognition in official records, and occupy much of the attention of the police.

The unlawful killing of one person by another is very likely one of the first crimes to be recognized in the development of human society, but what constitutes an unlawful killing varies from one society to another and changes with the passage of time.[9]

Criminal Homicide

In the history of the English common law, a distinction between innocent and criminal homicide has long been recognized, with the former including both justifiable homicide (in which the killing is commanded or authorized by law, such as an execution) and excusable homicide (in which the killing is the result of an accident or a reasonable mistake of fact.)[10] Only in the last several hundred years, however, did the common law divide criminal homicide into the two crimes of murder and manslaughter. Murder was originally defined as the unlawful killing of another with "malice aforethought," without which it was considered manslaughter, but as the boundaries of murder came to be fixed by judicial decisions, the literal meaning of the phrase gradually disappeared. Hatred, spite, or ill will became unnecessary for a conviction of murder, and the killing did not need to be planned in advance. Instead, murder came to be seen as taking four forms that are still recognized in most jurisdictions in the United States today:

[9] See, for example, E. Adamson Hoebel, *The Law of Primitive Man* (Cambridge, Mass.: Harvard University Press, 1954), with regard to the legitimacy of killing the sick and the aged in various cultures.
[10] Rollin M. Perkins, *Criminal Law* (Brooklyn, N.Y.: The Foundation Press, 1957), pp. 28–29.

1. "Intent-to-kill murder," in which the individual desires to kill another and acts accordingly; or the individual knows that the death of another is very likely to result from his actions, whatever may be his desire concerning the matter.

2. "Intent-to-do-serious-bodily-harm murder," in which the individual wishes to seriously injure another, short of causing death, but where death is the result nonetheless.

3. "Depraved-heart murder," in which the individual acts in a manner so negligent that another dies because of the perpetrator's actions, although there is no intent to kill or to do serious bodily injury.

4. "Felony murder," in which the individual, in the commission of a felony dangerous to life, causes the death of another. Originally, any felony would do, but as the number of felonies grew to include a great number of minor offenses, the harshness of the felony-murder rule was lessened by restricting it to the commission of those felonies that could be considered dangerous, such as rape, burglary, robbery, and arson.[11]

The concept of murder, then, as unlawful killing with malice aforethought, was gradually extended to cover a number of circumstances where neither malice nor forethought existed. The original concept of murder—based essentially on the idea of a villain lying in wait to kill a victim—would no longer suffice for a variety of criminal homicides occurring in a society building a more precise body of criminal law. It remained for the United States to divide murder into degrees, however; this step had never been taken by England. In most states, intent-to-kill murder and felony murder are classified as murder in the first degree and have carried the death penalty. Depraved-heart murder and intent-to-do-bodily-harm murder are categorized as second-degree murder and carry a lesser penalty, generally life imprisonment.

There remain a number of killings that the law has viewed as less serious or less blameworthy than murder and yet not to be dismissed as justifiable or excusable homicide. "It is not the purpose of the law to unbridle the passions of men," argues Rollin Perkins, setting forth the legal viewpoint. "On the contrary, one very important aim of the criminal law is to induce men to keep their passions under proper control. At the same time the law does not ignore the weaknesses of human nature. Hence, as a matter of common law, an unlawful killing may be intentional and yet of a lower degree than murder."[12]

The "weaknesses of human nature" taken into account by the law consist mainly of (1) an intense emotion, such as rage or fear, induced by

[11] Wayne R. LaFave and Austin W. Scott, Jr., *Criminal Law* (St. Paul, Minn.: West, 1972), pp. 528–61.
[12] Perkins, *Criminal Law*, p. 42.

what the law is willing to recognize as adequate provocation; and (2) a degree of recklessness below what is called for by the notion of "depraved-heart murder," but still involving unreasonable risk. The first constitutes *voluntary manslaughter;* the second is labeled *involuntary manslaughter,* carries lesser penalties, and includes many of the traffic-accident deaths in which criminal negligence is involved.

This classification of criminal homicides, worked out with such care over the years, is based largely on an effort to distinguish degrees of moral blame. An intent-to-kill murder is more reprehensible in the eyes of the law than an intent-to-do-bodily-harm murder, and murder is more blameworthy than manslaughter, though both result in death. The criminal law, having determined the degree of moral blame, can then assign the appropriate amount of retribution. Those legal theorists who reject retribution as the purpose of the criminal law have tried to justify the various penalties attached to different kinds of criminal homicide on the basis of deterrence.[13] Their arguments, however, are not very satisfactory; and the lines drawn between degrees of murder and between murder and manslaughter appear to be based largely on an effort to establish punishment that corresponds to the wrongfulness of an act rather than on an attempt to construct a rational schedule of penalties to deter the potential wrongdoer.[14]

In the *Uniform Crime Reports,* murder and nonnegligent (voluntary) manslaughter are listed as a single category. There were approximately 19,000 such offenses known to the police in 1976, a drop of some 8 percent from 1975.[15] Three out of four victims were male and about half of the victims were white. Handguns were used in 51 percent of the cases; knives or cutting instruments were the other weapons most frequently involved (18 percent).[16]

Clearly, many different motives can lie behind the intentional killing of another human being. There are acts of political terrorism, cold-

[13] See Herbert Wechsler and Jerome Michael, "A Rationale of the Law of Homicide," *Columbia Law Review* 37 (May 1937), pp. 701–61; (December 1937), pp. 1261–1325.

[14] The classification of unlawful killing constructed by the criminal law is often difficult to apply to factual situations in which lay juries must struggle with the fine points of legal reasoning. The distinction between murder in the first and second degrees, for example, is, according to Judge Cardozo, "so obscure that no jury hearing it for the first time can fairly be expected to assimilate and understand it. I am not at all sure that I understand it myself after trying to apply it for many years and after diligent study of what has been written in the books" (Benjamin Cardozo, *Law and Literature and Other Essays* [New York: Harcourt Brace, 1931], pp. 99–100).

[15] *Uniform Crime Reports—1976* (Washington, D.C.: Government Printing Office, 1977), p. 7. As the FBI points out, the classification of offenses is based on police investigations rather than on the determination of a court, medical examiner, coroner, jury, or other judicial body. The problem of accurately classifying offenses from a legal viewpoint is a constant one.

[16] Ibid., p. 10.

blooded murders for economic gain, expressions of paranoid fantasies, gangland slayings, sadistic sexual attacks. Evidence from a variety of sources, however, indicates that most killings are based on far more ordinary motivations. "Homicide," it has been noted, "often appears to reflect the dynamic interplay between two persons caught up in a life drama where their relationship plays a role in explaining why such a flagrant violation of conduct norms has occurred. This should really not be very surprising. Everyone is within easy striking distance of intimates for a large part of the time. Although friends, lovers, spouses, and the like are a main source of pleasure in one's life, they are equally a main source of frustration and hurt. Few others can anger one so much."[17]

This jaundiced view of intimacy is probably correct, and a large share of homicides committed each year in the United States can be attributed to quarrels arising within the family or circle of close friends and relations.[18]

That it is not strangers or people from different segments of society who are most likely to slaughter one another, but intimates flaring into a deadly quarrel, helps explain why the murderer and victim are so often of the same race and socioeconomic background and live in the same area. For example, in a survey of seventeen large cities it was found that of the criminal homicides for which data were available, 24 percent involved whites killing whites and 66 percent involved blacks killing blacks. Only 10 percent of the homicides revealed an interracial relationship.[19] The concept of motive as used in official records is rudimentary and too imprecise to reveal the social and psychological causes of criminal behavior, as we shall see in Chapter 8, but the data collected by the police strongly suggest that many homicides spring from relationships established prior to the crime. Taken together, family quarrels (7.7 percent), jealousy (4.4 percent), revenge (2.5 percent), and altercation (35.7 percent) provided the motive for approximately one half of the criminal homicides examined in the survey cited above; if the categories are fuzzy and probably overlapping, they at least point to tensions arising among people who are bound by intimate ties.

The social relationship that so often exists between the murderer and the victim also helps to explain the fact that alleged offenders are

[17] National Commission on the Causes and Prevention of Violence, Staff Report, vol. 11, *Crimes of Violence* (1969), p. 218.

[18] Beginning in 1974, the number of so-called stranger murders began to increase sharply in New York City, but whether that pattern will spread to other parts of the country remains unknown. See "New York Is First in 'Stranger Murders,' " *The New York Times* (March 23, 1975).

[19] National Commission on the Causes and Prevention of Violence, Staff Report, vol. 11, *Crimes of Violence*, Chapter 5. See also Marvin E. Wolfgang, *Patterns in Criminal Homicide* (Philadelphia: University of Pennsylvania Press, 1958).

frequently found with ease. Homicides are cleared by arrests (79 percent in 1976) more often than any other crime included among Part I offenses by the FBI.[20] In ordinary life, it has been pointed out, as contrasted to the crime novel, "when the homicide squad encounters a crime of violence there is no murder mystery at all. Several people already know who was the criminal. If not, some patient questioning of close friends, lovers, or spouse reveals who the culprit was."[21] Moreover, criminal homicide appears to be reported to the police more frequently than most other offenses. There generally is, after all, a corpse that requires some sort of explanation; and the crime is neither likely to go unnoticed nor easily ignored. The homicide rate revealed by the survey of households conducted by the National Opinion Research Center and the homicide rate presented in the *Uniform Crime Reports* do not differ markedly. Although the relative infrequency of homicide and the size of the sample in the survey mean that the comparison is not very useful for this form of criminal behavior, the "dark figure" for murder is apparently a good deal smaller than that for most other offenses.[22]

Only a small proportion of violent arguments and quarrels, fortunately, end in homicide—and the proportion has been reduced by improvements in medicine and medical services. For lesser injuries and attempts to commit bodily harm, the law has established the categories of assault and battery. The expression "assault and battery" is commonly used to refer to a single offense—the infliction of a physical harm—but in the eyes of the criminal law, two separate offenses are involved. *Assault* is the attempt to injure someone, whereas *battery* is the actual wounding or hurting of the victim; battery includes, as well, what the law terms "offensive touching," such as kissing a woman against her will or spitting into another's face. All jurisdictions in the United States recognize the difference between more and less serious attack, labeling the former *aggravated assault and battery* and treating them as felonies.

Assault and Battery

According to the *Uniform Crime Reports,* there were some 491,000 crimes of aggravated assault known to the police in 1976 (see Table 1, p. 131). The FBI, however, includes attempted homicides, aggravated assault, and aggravated battery in the general category of *aggravated assault,* and there is no way of distinguishing these various offenses in the official figures. Furthermore, the instructions given to the police for sep-

---

[20] *Uniform Crime Reports—1976,* p. 10.

[21] National Commission on the Causes and Prevention of Violence, Staff Report, vol. 13, *Crimes of Violence,* p. 941.

[22] See Philip H. Ennis, "Criminal Victimization in the United States: A Report of a National Survey," *Field Survey II, President's Commission on Law Enforcement and Administration of Justice* (1967), Chapter II.

arating aggravated assault and battery from less serious attacks are far from precise, and the latter may at times be included in the former.[23] Thus the figures must be read with caution, as was pointed out before—and there is, once again, the problem of underreporting. The NORC survey suggests that twice as many crimes of aggravated assault are committed each year as are known to the police.[24] As in the case of homicide, many of these crimes occur within the family and the offender's circle of friends, although a slightly larger proportion of other social relationships are involved in aggravated assault than in murder and voluntary manslaughter.[25] Most assaults are committed by males, and the rate for blacks far exceeds the rate for whites. A number of studies have indicated that approximately one half of the assaults known to the police occur in the home and other inside locations; most of the rest occur in the street. The offender and the victim are generally similar in terms of race, age, social class, and residential location.[26]

Homicide and aggravated assault differ markedly, however, in the type of weapon used. According to the FBI, firearms are employed in about two thirds of the cases of murder, but in only one quarter of the cases of aggravated assault.[27] This can be interpreted two ways. On the one hand, it can be argued that homicide and assault are similar crimes, in that they are generated by the same social and psychological circumstances. That one ends in death and the other does not may be explained largely by the fact—unfortunate and perhaps accidental—that homicide offenders happen to have access to deadlier weapons at the moment of an emotional outburst. On the other hand, it can be argued that the homicide offender is more determined to kill than the person who commits an assault and deliberately selects a weapon capable of achieving that end.[28] The weight of the evidence, it is claimed, favors the first explanation, since homicide and aggravated assault appear to be so much alike in terms of the age, sex, and race of the offender; the nature of the relationships involved; and the types of motives ascribed by police investigations.[29] The evidence is not conclusive, but the logic is per-

[23] The National Commission on the Causes and Prevention of Violence cites as an example a case in which two boys decided to give another boy a hot foot. The prospective victim, however, was not wearing shoes—so a match was applied to his back, raising a blister. The incident was recorded by the police as aggravated assault. See Staff Report, vol. 11, *Crimes of Violence,* p. 25.

[24] Ibid., p. 20.

[25] Ibid., p. 217.

[26] Ibid., Chapter 5.

[27] *Uniform Crime Reports—1976,* pp. 9–13.

[28] See National Commission on the Causes and Prevention of Violence, Staff Report, vol. 11, *Crimes of Violence,* p. 236.

[29] Ibid., pp. 229–37.

suasive. Common sense alone suggests that a gun at hand during an argument raises the risk of murder or manslaughter.[30]

Of the aggravated assaults coming to the attention of the police, approximately two thirds are cleared by arrests. The relatively high clearance rate can be traced to the same factors lying behind a similar rate for criminal homicide. Of those arrested for aggravated assault, about 68 percent are prosecuted; and of those prosecuted approximately 40 percent are convicted. "Law enforcement agencies have difficulty in obtaining convictions on the original charge in the aggravated assault category," notes the FBI. "The close family or other relationship which exists between victims and assailants in this category accounts for the victim's frequent unwillingness to testify for the prosecution."[31] It is, in fact, these primary ties that often make police intervention in violent altercations so hazardous. The quarreling husband and wife may suddenly unite to face the intruder from officialdom, or the police officer may find himself serving as substitute target for one spouse or the other. In 1976, responding to "disturbance calls"—usually domestic quarrels—led to 32 percent of all assaults on law enforcement officers.[32]

The crime of *forcible rape* consists of unlawful sexual intercourse with a woman without her consent; and, like homicide and aggravated assault, rape has been regarded as a serious offense throughout recorded history.[33] The precise definition of rape has varied, and in some primitive societies the occurrence of rape is said to be virtually unknown.[34] In general, however, the wrongfulness of rape appears to have been widely recognized, along with the view that rape is a crime justifying severe penalties.

From the viewpoint of the criminal law, such circumstances as intoxication, idiocy, and fraud may give rise to *lack of consent*, the element central to the definition of rape. But forcing a woman to submit to sexual

Forcible Rape

---

[30] See Joseph D. Alviani and William R. Drake, *Handgun Control* (Washington, D.C.: Conference of Mayors, 1975). As Franklin E. Zimring has pointed out, "Guns are not just another weapon used in crime. Serious assault with a gun is five times as likely to cause death as a similar attack with a knife, the next most dangerous weapon, and gun robberies are four times as likely to result in the death of a victim as are other kinds of robberies" ("Getting Serious About Guns," *The Nation* [April 10, 1972], p. 457). See also Robert Sherrill, *The Saturday Night Special* (New York: Charterhouse, 1973).

[31] *Uniform Crime Reports—1972*, p. 12.

[32] *Uniform Crime Reports—1976*, p. 282. See also Morton Bard and Joseph Zacker, *The Police and Interpersonal Conflict* (Washington, D.C.: The Police Foundation, 1976).

[33] In the Anglo-American legal tradition, the concept of rape applies only to unlawful sexual intercourse; since sexual intercourse between husband and wife is lawful, a husband cannot be held guilty of raping his wife even if she fails to give her consent.

[34] See Margaret Mead, *Sex and Temperament in Three Primitive Societies* (New York: New American Library, 1950), pp. 80–81.

intercourse by means of physical violence is the form of rape most commonly recognized, and the prevalence of the prohibition against rape is attributable in part to the general condemnation of physical violence as an element in social interaction. In addition, the widespread designation of rape as a crime would appear to be partially based on an interpretation of rape as an act of sexual defilement or an attack on chastity. Sexual intercourse with a female below a specified age, for example, is also categorized as rape—so-called *statutory rape*—but the issue of consent or the use of force is declared to be irrelevant. It is the violation of sexual innocence that is declared a crime, not forcible sexual intercourse.

When forcible rape is involved and the female is above the age of consent, the law's concern with the violation of sexual purity is still apparent. There is no legal requirement of chastity on the part of the victim in order to secure a conviction of rape, it is true, but legal practice is another matter. "To speak of sexual intercourse with a prostitute without her consent as an 'outrage to her person and feeling' is in the nature of a mockery," commented the author of a textbook on the criminal law in 1957, showing an obtuseness that was notable even then, before the rise of the women's liberation movement. "Her unlawful career has not placed her beyond the protection of the law . . . but when her only grievance is that she was taken without being paid, the law of assault and battery would seem more appropriate than to include such an act within the scope of one of the greatest felonies [rape] which is still a capital crime in a number of states. Fortunately the character of the woman as to chastity or unchastity is admissible in evidence because of its probative value in judging whether she did or did not consent to the act in question."[35]

What this means in effect is that the rape victim who is not a prostitute may find herself treated as if she were, particularly by a defense attorney who will probe into her past sexual experiences in the hope of proving her "promiscuous," thereby discrediting her testimony.[36]

The concern over violence and sexual innocence is only part of society's conception of rape as a crime. There is also the fact that women have long been treated as a form of property, and rape has been regarded as a violation of the owner's property rights. Kingsley Davis analyzed this perspective some forty years ago in a classic paper on the subject, ar-

[35] Perkins, *Criminal Law* p. 117.

[36] The police, as well as lawyers for the defense, often treat allegations of rape with a good deal of suspicion. "Rape is the only crime where the victim is put in the position of having to prove her innocence," State Senator Minnette Doderer of Iowa has argued. "If someone reports a stereo stolen, the police don't treat them as if they dreamed up the crime. But with rape, the police seem to assume the victim is lying until she can prove differently" (*Des Moines Sunday Register* [April 7, 1974]). Iowa and California have now passed laws barring defense lawyers from inquiring into a woman's past sexual conduct.

The Price of Rape

It was about 1 o'clock on a Saturday afternoon last October. The captain of the Reasonable Women, an intramural basketball team at Catholic University law school in Washington, D.C., was early when she headed into the gym for practice. The women's locker room looked deserted. It was not. As the woman slipped into her togs, a young black man stepped into view. Frightened, she asked him to leave and made a break for the door. He grabbed her, choked her and raped her. When he heard other voices approaching, he escaped.

The victim, 24, sued the university. She argued that the assault was a direct result of the school's failure to provide proper security at the gym. After a five-day trial, a D.C. jury agreed and awarded the student $20,000 in compensatory damages. "A very bad precedent," Catholic University Counsel Denver Graham calls it. "A university cannot be the insurer of everyone who comes onto the campus." The precedent, however, rests on well-established principles applied more and more across the U.S. Juries are penalizing slack security against rape attacks and are likely to make those they find negligent pay large damages.

Last year, for instance, a Maryland jury awarded $13 million (later cut to $1.9 million in an out-of-court settlement) to the family of a woman who had been raped and beaten to death in a bloody 45-minute battle in her apartment. The rapist-killer, on parole for armed robbery, had been allowed into the building to move furniture in a next-door apartment, even though he was clearly drunk. Worse, a fellow workman noticed his absence when he heard the woman screaming. Instead of rushing to the rescue, he phoned his boss. The jury found the murderer's employers and the landlord liable. The company had not checked out the man's background, while the landlord did not provide adequate screening measures for visitors.

Similarly, in July a Brooklyn jury hit Howard Johnson's Motor Lodges, Inc. with a $2.5 million damage award to Singer Connie Francis, who was raped at knife point in a company motel on Long Island. The six-man panel found that the motel had failed to put the singer in a "safe and secure room."

Armed Camps. What is secure? It is a troubling question for apartment-building owners, motel operators and universities nervous about being hauled into court to face staggering damage judgments. "I can't believe the law says you have to provide a bodyguard for every female student," says Graham. While the law does not demand turning campuses and buildings into armed camps, landlords are being pressed to become more security conscious. Owners, say the courts, have long been liable to a tenant injured by a negligently maintained elevator; they will now have to pay for exposing people to an "unreasonable" risk of criminal attack. "What is reasonable?" asks Attorney George Shadoan, who represented the family of the Maryland victim. "A TV camera system, guards—that's reasonable."

It is also costly. Catholic U.'s annual security budget has jumped nearly 500% since 1970, up to $350,000. Since the rape, the school has beefed up security in the 64 buildings on its 190-acre campus. "I don't want a state-of-siege campus," says University President Clarence Walton, "but the courts are holding universities responsible for an amount of security higher than that demanded in the public domain."

What is next? "Are we headed in the direction where a woman can sue the police department if she is raped, screams and no one comes?" asks Walton. Shadoan thinks the trend in tort law—toward no-fault auto, product liability and medical malpractice insurance—may block that next step. He points to Great Britain, where "if you get raped, you get medical care and a government payment. Damage suits will soon be a relic of the past." Many lawyers are betting it will never happen.

guing that the emphasis on the defense of chastity found in so many cultures may be traced to the definition of women as private sexual property and to a concern with lines of descent based on biological parenthood that must be kept clear and unambiguous at any cost.[37] Rape, from this viewpoint, is not merely a sexual assault on the female victim; it is a violation of the sexual rights of her husband or father and a threat to the family unit bound by consanguine ties (blood relationship). In fourteenth-century England, for example, high treason included the violation of the king's consort, his eldest unmarried daughter, or the wife of his eldest son or heir. In recent years, the conception of rape as an attack on the property rights of the male has been developed and expanded by writers such as Susan Brownmiller, who has shown how rape can function as an act of conquest, an expression of power and domination in which the sexual impulse plays an ancillary part. Rape, particularly in wartime, often serves as a further means of humiliating the vanquished enemy, and sex become equated with sadistic acts of violence.[38]

There is no question that public attitudes toward rape spring from a profound psychic level that is laden with emotion for both men and women. This is particularly marked in the case of interracial rape. The image of a black man raping a white woman can touch off an explosion of fear and rage in the white community. Six of the states have never executed any but a Negro for rape, note Herbert Bloch and Gilbert Geis. "Since 1908, for instance, when Virginia got its electric chair, forty-one persons have been executed for rape, thirteen for attempted rape, one for rape and robbery, and one for attempted rape and robbery. All were Negroes, despite the fact that Negroes make up only twenty-five percent of the state's population and despite the fact that whites have been convicted of 44 percent of the rapes in that state."[39] The idea of a white man raping a black woman is no less enraging to the black community, although the chances that the wrongdoer will be punished are far less.

There were about 57,000 cases of forcible rape known to the police in 1976. These cases comprise less than 1 percent of the FBI's Crime Index and approximately 10 percent of the major crimes of violence, if robbery is excluded.[40] The "dark figure" for forcible rape, however, appears to be extremely large. Actual cases of forcible rape may be three-and-one-half times the number reported, and it has been suggested that the gap be-

[37] See "Jealousy and Sexual Property," *Social Forces* 14 (March 1936), pp. 345–405.

[38] See *Against Our Will: Men, Woman and Rape* (New York: Simon and Schuster, 1975).

[39] Herbert A. Bloch and Gilbert Geis, *Man, Crime, and Society* (New York: Random House, 1970), p. 252.

[40] *Uniform Crime Reports—1976*, p. 35. Before 1958, the FBI's category of rape included both statutory and forcible rape; at the present time, only the latter is classified as a Part I offense.

tween actual and reported offenses is greater for this crime than for any other major crime of violence.[41]

The evidence indicates that a large proportion of rapes are not reported because of the victim's fear or embarrassment; Edwin Sutherland claimed that the FBI hesitated for some time before including rape as one of the crimes on which official statistics should be collected, on the grounds that the figures would be excessively unreliable.[42] The problem of estimating the number of rapes that occur in the United States each year is further complicated by the fact that judges and juries apparently find it difficult to distinguish terrorized acquiescence from consent. The use of force may be questioned, or a prior relationship between the victim and the offender may raise doubts about the existence of coercion. Approximately 19 percent of all forcible rapes reported to the police are considered by them to be unfounded; and of those individuals arrested and prosecuted for the crime, almost 50 percent are acquitted of the charge.[43]

A male bias is certainly operating in this matter—a tendency, that is, to be overly suspicious of an allegation of rape, to readily believe that women will often engage voluntarily in sexual intercourse and then cry "Rape!" for the purpose of blackmail or the protection of their reputations. And even a criminologist as astute as Sutherland accepted the statement that forcible rape is practically impossible unless the woman has been rendered nearly unconscious by drugs or injury[44]—a viewpoint that ignores both the fact that women can be physically overpowered and the role of intimidation in forcible rape. Menachem Amir's sociological study of forcible rape in Philadelphia indicates that in 43 percent of the cases examined during two years (1958 and 1960), the victim was raped by two or more persons. The literature on sexual offenses has seldom discussed group rape—a reticence that is explainable, Amir suggests, by the fact that "the literature is dominated by the clinical approach and the survey method, which deals with the individual offender or (rarely) the victim, rather than with the act of rape as a social and group event."[45]

In about one fourth of the cases of rape reported, the offender and the victim were acquainted with each other prior to the crime.[46] The significance of a prior relationship, however, is largely conjectural, for no

[41] National Commission on the Causes and Prevention of Violence, Staff Report, vol. 11, *Crimes of Violence*, p. 59.

[42] Albert Cohen, Alfred Lindesmith, and Karl Schuessler, eds., *The Sutherland Papers* (Bloomington: Indiana University Press, 1956), p. 187.

[43] See *Uniform Crime Reports—1976*, pp. 16–17.

[44] Cohen, Lindesmith, and Schuessler, *The Sutherland Papers*, p. 187.

[45] *Patterns in Forcible Rape* (Chicago: University of Chicago Press, 1971), pp. 199–200.

[46] See *Sourcebook of Criminal Justice Statistics—1974* (Washington, D.C.: Government Printing Office, 1975), p. 239.

longer can it be casually assumed—as it so often was in the past—that rapes are provoked by the victim's behavior or that when a woman is raped "she's really asking for it."[47] Such myths persist, but the women's liberation movement has done much to change the way society regards the crime of rape. Women have become far more willing to report rapes to the police, as women's groups have brought the problem into the realm of public discussion and put pressure on the police to provide more sympathetic handling. The criminal law has been modified, reducing the demands for corroborative testimony and providing women with greater protection from public humiliation on the witness stand.[48] There is an increasing awareness that rape cannot be explained simply by reference to psychological abnormality—that is, rapists are probably no more or less "disturbed" than nonrapists, and the causes of rape are likely to be found not in a sick psyche but in a complex of accepted cultural values in which masculinity, violence, and aggressive sexuality are entwined.[49] In spite of these changes, however, the criminal law's definition of rape and the handling of rape cases by law enforcement officials continue to be marked by a male bias that is quick to shift the burden of guilt from the criminal to the victim.

Official statistics indicate that in cases of rape, as in homicide and aggravated assault, the arrest rate is much higher for blacks than for whites, for the young than for the old, and for the poor than for the well-off. Rape, then, appears to be one element in a pattern of violence that is found, with a persistently disproportionate frequency—as far as official statistics are concerned—in a particular segment of society. It will be our task in Chapter 7 to see what theoretical interpretation can best be attached to the imperfect evidence of a link between violence and demographic characteristics, but now we must turn our attention to the changes that have taken place in the officially recorded patterns of violence in recent years.

Trends in Violent Crimes

In the 1960s, the data published by the FBI indicated that the United States was experiencing an increase in the crime rate, particularly with

[47] See particularly William J. Goode, "Violence Among Intimates," in National Commission on the Causes and Prevention of Violence, Staff Report, vol. 13, *Crimes of Violence*, Appendix 19.

[48] *Note*, "Recent Developments in the Definition of Forcible Rape," *Virginia Law Review* 61 (June 1975), pp. 1500–43.

[49] See LeRoy G. Schultz, ed., *Rape Victimology* (Springfield, Ill.: Charles C. Thomas, 1975). See also Nancy Gager and Cathleen Schurr, *Sexual Assault: Confronting Rape in America* (New York: Grosset & Dunlap, 1976).

regard to crimes of violence. America had long been marked by a high rate of crime against the person, compared to most other Western industrial societies, but it now appeared that homicides, assaults, rapes, and robberies (which the FBI classified as a crime of personal violence) were increasing far more rapidly than the population. Between 1958 and 1968, the *Uniform Crime Reports* showed a 52 percent increase in the homicide rate; the rate for aggravated assault went up 82 percent; robbery increased 143 percent; and rape went up 71 percent.[50] Statistics have a great appeal in the fact-minded culture of America, and the official figures of the FBI were widely accepted as clear evidence that the nation was entering a period of lawlessness.[51] "Crime in the streets" became a new political phrase expressing a widespread fear that the social order was in danger of disintegration.

Academic criminologists, however, were not convinced that the FBI statistics showed a profound shift in the underlying pattern of criminality. There were four main reasons for their skepticism.

First, the baby boom after the Second World War resulted in a large increase in the size of the younger age groups. As these cohorts entered the period of greatest criminality—roughly fourteen to twenty-five years of age—an increase in the amount of crime was inevitable. Even if the crime rate for each age group remained unchanged, the crime rate for the United States as a whole was bound to go up, since the age groups with the highest rates now formed a larger proportion of the population.[52]

Second, the population of the United States was becoming more urbanized; from 1960 to 1967 the population living in standard metropolitan statistical areas increased by 19 percent.[53] Since crime rates in large cities were higher than in small cities and rural areas, the growing concentration of the population in large urban areas could also be expected to result in a higher crime rate. The two factors—an increase in the size of the younger age groups and in the proportion of the population living in cities—were estimated to account for some 30 percent of the increase in all crime between 1950 and 1965 in the United States.[54]

Third, it was argued that crimes were being reported that had pre-

[50] National Commission on the Causes and Prevention of Violence, Staff Report, vol. 11, *Crimes of Violence*, p. xxvi.

[51] Yale Kamisar, "How to Use, Abuse, and Fight Back with Crime Statistics," *Oklahoma Law Review* 25 (May 1972), p. 239.

[52] For an illuminating analysis of the impact of the age structure on crime, see Roland Chilton and Adele Spielberger, "Is Delinquency Increasing? Age Structure and the Crime Rate," *Social Forces* 49 (March 1971), pp. 487–93.

[53] National Commission on the Causes and Prevention of Violence, Staff Report, vol. 11, *Crimes of Violence*, p. 60.

[54] Ibid., pp. 145–52.

viously gone unrecognized. Americans were becoming far more willing, it was said, to report crimes to the police than they had been in the past. The poor and members of minority groups in particular were showing an increased readiness to go to the police and to demand more adequate protection, partly as a result of the civil rights movement.[55] In addition (and perhaps more important), it appeared that police forces throughout the country had improved their recording procedures and transmission of data to the FBI. In recent years, "there have been efforts to professionalize the reporting process in many urban police departments. As a result, reported levels of crime have increased so rapidly that a more thorough reporting of crime seems to be the only logical explanation."[56] In New York, for example, the reporting of complaints by precinct was replaced in 1950 by a centralized system, with the result that the volume of reported robberies increased 400 percent in ten years. In Chicago, the volume of reported robberies almost doubled between 1959 and 1961, after a central complaint system was installed in 1960.[57] The "dark figure" of crime, according to this argument, was coming into the light, and the result was a spectacular leap in the crime rate.

Finally, the time period in which trends in the crime rate were being analyzed was much too brief, it was said, to provide an accurate picture. Crime rates are subject to fluctuation, and if we extended our perspective back several decades, we would find that we had mistaken a momentary upsurge in crime for a persistent pattern of growth. The data for those years were admittedly poor, and the *Uniform Crime Reports* did not publish figures on murder and nonnegligent manslaughter until 1949; but the rate of those crimes in 1949 was 5.2 per 100,000, in 1957, and 6.1 in 1968. Analyzing unpublished data from the FBI, the Pesident's Commission on Law Enforcement and Administration of Justice concluded that the murder rate had decreased to about 70 percent of its high in 1933. "Looking further back to the 1870s and the late 1890s," noted Norval Morris and Gordon Hawkins, "it seemed clear that rates of murder, nonnegligent homicide, rape, and assault have all appreciably declined with the passage of time."[58]

For many criminologists, then, the talk of a crime wave was an exaggeration or a distortion based on inadequate information and likely to give rise to unnecessary fears. Some writers came close to saying that the reports of increasing violence were little more than a sham. "The 'rising

[55] President's Commission on Law Enforcement and Administration of Justice, *Task Force Report: Assessment of Crime* (Washington, D.C.: Government Printing Office, 1967), p. 22.

[56] National Commission on the Causes and Prevention of Violence, Staff Report, vol. 11, *Crimes of Violence*, p. 22.

[57] Ibid., p. 22.

[58] *The Honest Politician's Guide to Crime Control* (Chicago: University of Chicago Press, 1970), p. 56.

tide of violence,' " noted one commentator, "is almost certainly a fabrication of newspaper excitement, moralistic preaching, and changes in police reporting."[59] Others, more cautious, were willing to admit that the rate of violent crime had probably increased but discounted the importance of the change. The Department of Justice, however—along with political contestants campaigning in 1968 who found it a potent theme—was apparently convinced that the problem of violent crime had reached emergency proportions. The crime index of the *Uniform Crime Reports* lay at the heart of the controversy. "While the general public tended erroneously to accept the crime index as gospel," it was argued, "the sophisticated reader who delved far enough into news articles to find the scholars' comments was usually persuaded that the statistical proof of rapidly increasing crime was almost certainly wrong. Most of the academic experts did not intend to go that far—but the most respected ones agreed, at least until 1967 or 1968, that the FBI had not proved its case."[60]

By the 1970s, however, it began to seem likely that the FBI had been right after all, even if its arguments had rested on shaky foundations. Between 1969 and 1974, the rate of violent crime increased by 47 percent. Between 1960 and 1974, the rate for murder almost doubled; assault increased by 150 percent, rape by 175 percent, and the robbery rate went up 248 percent.[61] Between 1974 and 1975, the rate of crimes against the person continued to increase, with the exception of murder, which showed a slight decline. It seemed possible that, rather than being a momentary or random fluctuation, the rise in the violent-crime rate was a reflection of a profound alteration in the social structure transcending shifts in the age distribution of the population, the growth of urbanization, and modifications in reporting procedures. Violent crimes might not be increasing as rapidly as had been reported in the 1960s, but it still seemed possible that the United States had experienced an upsurge in criminal violence that needed to be examined.

Several theories could be offered to explain both the increase in the rate of violent crime in the last fifteen years or so and the similar increase in the rate of property offenses. A pervasive sense of alienation, a distrust of authority, the growth of a counterculture that spread beyond the ranks of the young, a revolution of expectations that resulted in increasing frustration in an economic system that would not or could not change—all might be crucial factors, along with shifts in the age structure, the reporting of crimes, and the degree of urbanization. No systematic theories buttressed by empirical evidence are yet available, however,

[59] National Commission on the Causes and Prevention of Violence, Staff Report, vol. 13, *Crimes of Violence*, p. 947.
[60] Fred Graham, "A Contemporary History of American Crime," pp. 487–88.
[61] *Uniform Crime Reports—1974*, p. 11.

For some people the explosion of civil strife in recent years has been without precedence. But collective violence is no stranger to America. It has often arisen as social groups struggled to achieve their goals, and the question is what meaning to attach to it.

Washington, D.C., riots after the assassination of Martin Luther King, Jr., 1968.

Antibusing riot in Louisville, Kentucky.

Anti–Vietnam War protesters and construction workers, New York City, 1970.

and such explanations must remain, for the moment at least, largely speculative. Recent increases in crime in the United States are a problem awaiting a solution, rather than a mystery that has been solved, and it is not yet clear whether the rate of violent crime will continue on an upward course, stabilize, or begin to turn down.

The Distribution of Crimes of Violence

Regional Patterns The idea that America is a violent society has often been thought to find fullest expression in the Southern states. In folklore and in novels, in dramas and in personal reminiscences, the image of the violent Southerner has emerged as the exemplar of the American who settles quarrels with gun, knife, or fists.

The empirical data of the social sciences analyzed by H. C. Brearley, Stuart Lottier, Austin Porterfield, and others have tended to support this view. Brearley, for example, describing the South as "that part of the United States lying below the Smith and Wesson line," found that in a five-year period, from 1920 to 1924, the homicide rate of the Southern states was more than twice that of the rest of the United States.[62] Lottier, some ten years later, reported much the same pattern: homicide and assault rates in the southeastern United States were much higher than in any other part of the nation.[63] When Porterfield examined homicide rates in a selected group of cities in the United States, for the ten-year period between 1936 and 1945, the data showed that of the forty-nine Southern cities only four had a homicide rate as low as 12 per 100,000 population; none of the sixty-two non-Southern cities had a rate as high as 12 and only four reached 10.[64] Lyle W. Shannon, reexamining the regional distribution of crime and using the *Uniform Crime Reports* from 1946 to 1952, found once again that the South was marked by a relatively high rate of violent crime. Virginia, Mississippi, Florida, North Carolina, Texas, Tennessee, Alabama, and Georgia had the highest rates of murder and non-negligent manslaughter. The homicide rate in Georgia—21.35 per 100,000 population—headed the list and was 61 times as great as the lowest homicide rate, 0.35, found in North Dakota. The pattern for aggravated assault was similar.[65]

[62] "The Pattern of Violence," in W. T. Couch, ed., *Culture in the South* (Chapel Hill: University of North Carolina Press, 1935), pp. 678–92.

[63] "Distribution of Criminal Offenses in Sectional Regions," *Journal of Criminal Law and Criminology* 29 (September–October, 1938), pp. 329–44.

[64] "Indices of Suicide and Homicide by States and Cities: Some Southern–Non-Southern Contrasts with Implications for Research," *American Sociological Review* 14 (August 1949), pp. 481–90.

[65] "The Spatial Distribution of Criminal Offenses by States," *The Journal of Criminal Law, Criminology, and Police Science* 45 (September–October 1954), pp. 264–73.

Table 2. Crimes Against the Person in the United States by Region, 1976. (Rate per 100,000 population.)

Offense	Northeastern States	North-Central States	Southern States	Western States
Murder	7.0	7.4	11.3	8.5
Forcible rape	20.4	23.4	26.3	38.9
Aggravated assault	208.1	175.1	251.7	294.1
Robbery	288.1	175.8	139.9	206.8

SOURCE: *Uniform Crime Reports—1976* (Washington, D.C.: Government Printing Office, 1977), p. 34.

Fifteen years after Shannon's study, the Commission on the Causes and Prevention of Violence indicated that the homicide rates in the South continued to outstrip those of other regions. The rate for the South as a whole was 9 per 100,000 population, compared to 5 in the north-central states, the West, and the Northeast.[66] On the other hand, the rate for forcible rape was highest in the West, and the South ranked lowest in robbery. Although the *Uniform Crime Reports* showed the South to be highest in the rate for aggravated assault, the difference was small; and the figures of the victim survey of the National Opinion Research Center suggested that the assault rate was actually highest in the Western states.[67] But in criminal homicide, the South was still clearly in the lead; in 1975 the pattern persisted (see Table 2).

According to a number of social scientists, the relatively high homicide rate in the South is attributable to a predisposition to violence rooted in a culture that developed well before the Civil War. Sheldon Hackney, for example, noted an extensive scholarly literature in which "the image of the violent South confronts the historian at every turn: dueling gentlemen and masters whipping slaves, flatboatmen indulging in a rough-and-tumble fight, lynching mobs, country folk at a bear baiting or a gander pulling, romantic adventures on Caribbean filibusters, brutal police, panic-sticken communities harshly suppressing real and imagined slave revolts, robed night riders engaged in systematic terrorism, unknown assassins, church burners, and other less physical expressions of a South whose mode of action is frequently extreme."[68] These patterns, Hackney suggested, were part of a long-standing cultural tradition in which violence was a familiar aspect of social life and flowered easily into criminal homicide. Raymond D. Gastil, pursuing a similar argument, claimed that, over the centuries, a specifically Southern culture

[66] Staff Report, vol. 11, *Crimes of Violence*, p. 69.
[67] Ibid., pp. 69–80.
[68] "Southern Violence," in Graham and Gurr, *The History of Violence in America*, p. 505.

had developed which supported violence both directly and indirectly and was a major factor in explaining regional variation in the rate of criminal homicide.[69] The continued institutionalization of dueling, long after it had been given up in the North; the deep interest in military training and display; the widespread practice of carrying guns or knives; the concern with personal honor—all, suggested Gastil, were aspects of a distinctive southern taste for violence.

Both Hackney and Gastil attempted to provide evidence for their arguments by showing that other possible explanations for the relatively high rates of homicide in the South were inadequate—that there remained a "southernness" factor that must be classified as a cultural tradition playing a major causal role.[70] Gastil, using multiple-correlation analysis, measured the relationship between state homicide rates and such variables as median income, median number of school years completed, percent of the population that was black, and percent of the population in the twenty-to-thirty-four age bracket, since other studies had provided convincing evidence that these factors were related to the homicide rate. He concluded that after the influence of such variables was taken into account, a high correlation between an index of "southernness" and homicide remained that could best be interpreted as expressing the effect of a regional tradition of violence.

Loftin and Hill, in a carefully reasoned analysis of these findings, remain unconvinced. Based on such factors as infant mortality rates, percent of the population illiterate, and percent of families with incomes under $1000 a year, their data show that poverty is the most powerful predictor of homicide rates and that the effect of region is statistically insignificant.[71] Noting that there are serious conceptual problems in treating culture as something distinct from situational and social factors, such as income and ethnic background, they argue that the apparent consensus concerning the predominantly cultural basis of regional variation in homicide rates is based on an uncritical acceptance of research and that a more definite assessment of the role of cultural and situational-structural variables on interpersonal violence will require the specification of an explicit theoretical model.[72]

The debate over this issue turns on a number of complex points involving theory, conceptual distinctions, and techniques of statistical analysis. On the whole, however, it would appear that Loftin and Hill

[69] "Homicide and a Regional Culture of Violence," *American Sociological Review* 36 (June 1971), pp. 412–27.

[70] See Colin Loftin and Robert H. Hill," Regional Subculture and Homicide: An Examination of the Gastil-Hackney Thesis," *American Sociological Review* 39 (October 1974), pp. 714–24.

[71] Ibid., pp. 14–17.

[72] Ibid., pp. 19–21.

are correct and that the influence of a Southern culture of violence on the incidence of criminal homicide has not been clearly demonstrated. The relatively greater frequency of homicide in the Southern states is fairly well established, and a distinctive Southern tradition certainly seems to exist; but an empirically grounded explanation firmly linking the two patterns is still far from complete.[73]

Somewhat the same problem confronts us when we attempt to come to grips with the relationship between homicide rates and city size. The fact that larger cities tend to show higher crime rates than smaller cities and towns has been observed since the founding of criminology.[74] Such covariation with regard to crimes of violence can be seen in the United States today, but the reasons lying behind this phenomenon are still not clear (see Table 4). In 1976 the combined crime rate for murder, rape, robbery, and assault in cities with more than one million inhabitants was approximately six times greater than in cities with a population of less than 10,000; six cities with one million or more inhabitants—comprising approximately 10 percent of the total population—contributed about one third of all major crimes of violence.[75] In the 1960s the rate of crimes of violence increased in cities of all sizes, but it went up most sharply in cities with a population of 250,000 or more. Comparisons over time, however, can be misleading unless the data are used with care, since many cities in the United States have experienced

Urban Patterns

Table 4. City Size and Rate of Violent Crime

City Size	Number of Violent Crimes per 100,000 Inhabitants
Over 1,000,000	1,365.0
500,000 to 1,000,000	920.8
250,000 to 500,000	865.2
100,000 to 250,000	572.7
50,000 to 100,000	415.9
25,000 to 50,000	337.9
10,000 to 25,000	254.1
Under 10,000	215.5

SOURCE: *Uniform Crime Reports—1976* (Washington, D.C.: Government Printing Office, 1977), pp. 153–54.

[73] See Keith D. Harries, *The Geography of Crime and Justice* (New York: McGraw-Hill, 1974). We will examine culture as an explanatory factor at greater length in Chapter 7, when we analyze theories of crime causation.

[74] See Judith A. Wilks, "Ecological Correlates of Crime and Delinquency," in President's Commission on Law Enforcement and Administration of Justice, *Task Force Report: Assessment of Crime*, pp. 138–56.

[75] *Uniform Crime Reports—1976*, pp. 153–54.

The Fear of Crime

Ask virtually any American city-dweller today what crime he most fears, and feels he is most apt to be the victim of some day; in all likelihood he will answer: a mugging.

Yet vaster and far more dreadful crimes exist all around him: the savage acts and relentless extortions of Mafia "families" seeking and maintaining control over businesses, unions, and even political clubs; the white-collar crimes, so destructive of the moral premises on which our society is built, that are daily practiced by businessmen, politicians, and office employees; the widespread trafficking in heroin by dealers and pushers, actively aided by some of the very police assigned to narcotics control; and the bombing, arson, sniping, and other revolutionary acts by means of which urban guerrillas are turning parts of our major cities into battlefields.

But despite the magnitude and seriousness of these forms of crime, what most alarms us and most gravely damages our faith in our society is the ever present threat of some sudden, unpredictable, savage assault upon our own body by a stranger—a faceless, nameless, fleet-footed figure who leaps from the shadows, strikes at us with his fists, an iron pipe, or a switchblade knife, and then vanishes into an alley with our wallet or purse, leaving us broken and bleeding on the sidewalk. Headlines are made by riots, rapes, dope-smuggling, embezzlement, and kidnapping, while the mugging—moronically simple in execution and trifling in yield—is relegated to inside pages or ignored altogether; yet it is this, rather than the more complex and newsworthy crimes, that is responsible for the flight of millions of Americans to the suburbs, the nightly self-imprisonment of other millions behind locked doors and barred windows, and the mounting attacks of law-and-order advocates upon constitutionally guaranteed rights that are fundamental to our concept of democracy.

Crimes of violence against the person—homicide, rape, robbery, and aggravated assault—have grown steadily more common for the past several decades until they have changed much of the tenor and character of daily life in America. At a conservative estimate, such crimes are three times as common today, per 100,000 population, as they were thirty years ago; in consequence, our feelings about our fellow men have sadly deteriorated and our freedom to do what we wish and to go where we like has radically diminished. This is truest in our great cities, for there the growing cancer of violent crime has metastasized, spreading wildly throughout the vitals of the urban organism: in cities of over 250,000 persons, the rate of violent crime has more than tripled in just the last ten years, profoundly disorganizing the patterns of everyday living developed by generations of city-dwellers.

major changes during the last several decades. Sometimes boundaries have shifted as new areas have been annexed, and sometimes portions of the population have moved away and been replaced by inhabitants with different social backgrounds. In a number of cities the affluent have fled to the suburbs, taking their relatively low crime rates with them; the poor with their higher crime rates have stayed behind. In such cases, the city crime rate has gone up dramatically, although the crime rate for the metropolitan area, which includes the suburbs, has remained relatively unchanged.[76]

The quest for an explanation of why big cities seem to breed more crimes against the person has ranged over such factors as the anonymity, depersonalization, and social disorganization presumed to attend city life; the adverse effects of migration; the frustrations and resentments bred by urban poverty; and variation in the crime-reporting procedures of local police.[77] Many criminologists, however, would agree that the development of tested theory to explain variation in the rate of violent crime by city size has lagged behind description and that a good deal of research will be needed before systematic knowledge can replace speculation.[78]

Collective Violence

As the social and political tensions of American society in the 1960s erupted in riots and angry confrontations, it became obvious that conventional crimes against the person—murder, assault, and rape—were only one part of the problem of violence in the United States. Unfortunately, as Lewis Coser has pointed out, social scientists had been remiss in examining the problem of violence in all its guises, and their theories were apt to be inadequate for an understanding of violence in collective social action.[79] For Coser, the failure to explore the full meaning of violence could be traced to an excessive commitment on the part of American social science to models of society based on the notion of social harmony. Such a commitment fits well with the widespread revulsion

[76] See President's Commission on Law Enforcement and Administration of Justice, *Task Force Report: Assessment of Crime,* p. 37. This pattern was particularly marked in Washington, D.C.; Cleveland, Ohio; and Houston, Texas.

[77] See, for example, J. J. Tobias, *Crime and Industrial Society in the 19th Century* (New York: Schocken Books, 1972). For some contrary evidence, see Abdul Qaiyum Lodhi and Charles Tilly, "Urbanization, Crime, and Collective Violence in 19th Century France," *American Journal of Sociology* 79 (September 1973), pp. 296–317.

[78] See Wilks, "Ecological Correlates of Crime and Delinquency," pp. 138–43.

[79] "Some Social Functions of Violence," *The Annals of the American Academy of Political and Social Science* 364 (March 1966), pp. 8–18.

against violence that was noted at the beginning of the chapter. (One of the functions of a moral denunciation of violence, as Marvin Wolfgang, going back to the arguments of George Sorel, has indicated, "is to deter direct attacks against the Establishment, to prevent the dethroned and the weak from using violent methods like revolution to usurp positions of power."[80]) But whatever the reasons for such a restricted view of the subject, violence had in fact long been defined largely in terms of criminal acts in which physical force directed against another was an expression of individual rage or an illegitimate means to secure a highly personal or selfish end.[81]

In the latter part of the 1960s, however, a major shift in perspective became apparent. In 1967 President Johnson appointed the National Commission on Civil Disorders to investigate urban riots; in 1968, following the assassination of Martin Luther King, Jr., fresh disturbances broke out in scores of cities, and in Washington smoke from burning stores filled the air while federal troops guarded the White House. To many people the nation appeared close to the point of disintegration.[82] President Johnson established the National Commission on the Causes and Prevention of Violence, instructing the commission members "to go as far as man's knowledge takes them" in probing the causes and control of violence; and the staff, made up of lawyers, public officials, physicians, sociologists, psychiatrists, psychologists, political scientists, historians, biologists, and anthropologists, extended the concept of violence—and the interpretation of its causes—far beyond the conventional boundaries.

The commission, for example, reported that traffic accidents took some 53,000 lives in 1967; many of these deaths (perhaps 12 percent) are to be classified as negligent manslaughter, and yet they are not included in the Crime Index of the *Uniform Crime Reports*.[83] Suicide, once categorized as a felony by the English common law, is no longer considered a crime in the United States; but suicide nonetheless represents physical violence directed against the person, and the loss of life from suicide—consistently greater than the loss of life from criminal homicide—is considerable. The commission, in fact, ranged over a great many different kinds of behavior, including child abuse, vandalism, arson, and political assas-

[80] Wolfgang, "A Preface to Violence," *The Annals of the American Academy of Political and Social Science* 364 (1966), p. 3; see also Georges Sorel, *Reflections on Violence* (Glencoe, Ill.: The Free Press, 1950).

[81] There were a few writers who claimed a positive, creative role for violence. Frantz Fanon saw the violent struggles of colonial peoples as a cleansing force, a means of restoring self-respect. See Fanon, *The Wretched of the Earth*, trans. Constance Farrington (New York: Grove Press, 1963). But such ideas were viewed as largely inapplicable to early-1960s America.

[82] See Graham and Gurr, *The History of Violence in America*, p. xiv.

[83] See Staff Report, vol. 11, *Crimes of Violence*, pp. 7, 96–97.

sination. But in an effort to examine violence from a comprehensive viewpoint—to go beyond the conventional crimes of violence that had long been regarded as fixing the boundaries of the subject—the commission devoted the lion's share of its work to an investigation of collective violence. Riots, mass protests, social groups engaging in violent acts against members of other social groups—these were the forms of behavior perceived as urgently needing analysis.[84]

Racial conflict formed a crucial part of the issue. More than 200 race riots occurred in the mid-1960s.[85] In 1963 serious disorders erupted in several Southern cities—Cambridge, Maryland; Birmingham; and Savannah; in some of the large Northern cities—Chicago, Philadelphia, New York and Rochester; and in Jersey City, Elizabeth, and Paterson, New Jersey.[86] In 1965 the roster of unhappy cities exhibiting collective violence lengthened. Selma, Alabama, and Bogalusa, Louisiana, experienced murders and beatings, and in the latter city blacks formed a group for self-defense called the "Deacons for Defense of Justice." In August, in the Watts section of Los Angeles, rioting, burning, shooting, beatings, and looting broke out after a highway patrolman struck a bystander with his nightstick during the arrest of a young black for speeding, and a young black woman—accused of spitting on the police—was roughly handled by law enforcement officers.[87] During the ensuing riot, some 4,000 people were arrested, 34 were killed, and hundreds were injured. Property damage was estimated at $35 million. By 1966, noted the *Report* of the National Commission on Civil Disorders, such riots had apparently become part of the American scene. There was a new flare-up in Los Angeles and riots in Chicago, Cleveland, and Baltimore. The year 1967 saw even more intense violence, in Detroit, Nashville, Tampa, Cincinnati, Atlanta, and Jackson, Mississippi; and in Newark, Plainfield, and New Brunswick, New Jersey. During the Detroit riot more than 7200 persons were arrested, 43 persons were killed, and property damage was estimated at $50 million.[88]

Running roughly parallel to these disorders, and no less disturbing to many people, was a wave of antiwar protests. A number of wars in

[84] The definition of *collective violence* remained hazy, but in most discussions of the topic attention was focused on the violent behavior of masses of individuals acting as members of a social group or collectivity and motivated by shared feelings of hostility toward other groups. See Allen D. Grimshaw, "Interpreting Collective Violence: An Argument for the Importance of Social Structure," *The Annals of the American Academy of Political and Social Science* 391 (September 1970), pp. 9–20.

[85] August Meier and Elliott Rudwick, "Black Violence in the 20th Century: A Study in Rhetoric and Retaliation," in Graham and Gurr, *The History of Violence in America*, p. 400.

[86] National Advisory Commission on Civil Disorders, *Report* (Washington, D.C.: Government Printing Office, 1968), Chapter 1.

[87] Ibid., Chapter 1.

[88] Ibid., pp. 60–61.

United States history had been unpopular among some sections of the American public—the War of 1812, the Mexican War, and the Spanish-American War—but the Vietnam War created a level of dissension that the nation had not seen before. The antiwar movement—loosely organized, scattered across the country, and taking a variety of forms ranging from teach-ins to demonstrations in the streets—moved erratically toward violent confrontations.[89] The first protests against the war often involved behavior that was illegal (such as trespass) but not violent.[90] But over time, in a process that still remains incompletely analyzed, demonstrations against the Vietnam War were increasingly tinged with violence, both on the part of those who opposed the war and those who viewed opposition as a step removed from treason.[91] Protests against the war found their fullest expression on university campuses, where the antiwar movement became a fundamental part of the student protest movement. The latter, springing from a variety of sources that transcended the particular conflicts of American society (similar protest movements could be found in many other nations), was, like the antiwar movement, marked by growing bitterness and increasing violence.[92]

Estimates of the extent of collective violence in the United States are inevitably imprecise, because many different kinds of events are involved, and no mechanism exists for collecting systematic data on a national basis. Much of the violence in the 1960s involved the destruction of property; and when violence against the person did occur, a large share of it was the work of law enforcement officials. Using information from a variety of sources, Ted Robert Gurr has suggested that between 1963 and 1968 there were more than one thousand instances of violent disorder, involving more than two million participants, nine thousand casualties, and fifty thousand arrests.[93] But whatever the exact level of collective violence—it was probably greater than these figures indicate—

[89] See Robin Brooks, "Domestic Violence and America's Wars: An Historical Interpretation," in Graham and Gurr, The History of Violence in America, pp. 529–50.

[90] For the legal status of various forms of protest activity, see M. Cherif Bassiouni, The Law of Dissent and Riots (Springfield, Ill.: Charles C. Thomas, 1971).

[91] See Jerome H. Skolnick, The Politics of Protest (New York: Ballantine Books, 1969).

[92] Ibid., Chapter III. Student protest, noted Hannah Arendt, "has been blamed on all kinds of social and psychological factors—on too much permissiveness in their upbringing in America and on an explosive reaction to too much authority in Germany and Japan, on the lack of freedom in Eastern Europe and too much freedom in the West, on the disastrous lack of jobs for sociology students in France and the superabundance of careers in nearly all fields in the United States—all of which appear locally plausible enough but are clearly contradicted by the fact that the student rebellion is a global phenomenon. A social common denominator of the movement seems out of the question" (On Violence [New York: Harcourt, Brace & World, 1970], p. 15).

[93] "A Comparative Study of Civil Strife," in Graham and Gurr, The History of Violence in America, pp. 576–77.

the emergence in the 1960s of widespread group violence was plain enough. The question was the meaning to be attached to it.

For some people the explosion of civil strife seemed to be without precedent. The scholars preparing the staff reports for the National Commission on Violence, however, took pains to point out that collective violence had long been an element in American society. "Americans," it was said, "have always been given to a kind of historical amnesia that masks much of their turbulent past. Probably all nations share this tendency to sweeten memories of their past through collective repression, but Americans have probably magnified this process of selective recollection, owing to our historic version of ourselves as a latter-day chosen people, a new Jerusalem."[94]

What had most notably been repressed, it was argued, was the amount of collective violence that managed to cloak itself in the mantle of legitimacy. We are quick to decry "negative" violence, argued Richard Maxwell Brown, referring to conventional crimes against the person undertaken for individual ends. But we overlook "positive" violence, undertaken on a mass basis for allegedly worthwhile purposes.[95] Violence, he claimed, "has formed a seamless web with some of the noblest and most constructive chapters in American history. The birth of the nation (Revolutionary violence), the freeing of the slaves and the preservation of the Union (Civil-War violence), the occupation of the land (Indian Wars), the stabilization of frontier society (vigilante violence), the elevation of the farmer and the laborer (agrarian and labor violence), and the preservation of law and order (police violence)."[96]

Such arguments, rising into prominence at the end of the 1960s, were often indifferent to the distinction between the legal and the illegal use of force. And phrases such as "positive" violence sometimes appeared to suggest—for those writers anxious to provide civil protest with a sympathetic hearing—that if violence were employed in a cause considered good, the means itself became virtuous as well.[97] But even more impor-

---

[94] Graham and Gurr, *The History of Violence in America*, p. xiv.

[95] See "Historical Patterns of Violence in America," in Graham and Gurr, *The History of Violence in America*, pp. 45–46. See also Arthur I. Waskow, *From Race Riot to Sit-In* (Garden City, N.Y.: Doubleday, 1966).

[96] Ibid., p. 75.

[97] Cobbs and Grier, for example, writing a foreword to *The Politics of Protest,* asserted that "we take the position that the growth of this country has occurred around a series of violent upheavals and that each one has thrust the nation forward. The Boston Tea Party was an attempt by a few to alter an oppressive system of taxation without representation. The validation of these men rested on their attempts to effect needed social change. If the Boston Tea Party is viewed historically as a legitimate method of producing such change, then present-day militancy, whether by blacks or students, can claim a similar legitimacy" (Skolnick, *The Politics of Protest,* p. xi). This appeal to the patriotic past, however, leaves obscure the meaning of "validation," "needed social change," and "legitimacy."

tant is the question of whether the sociological view of the collective violence of the 1960s—particularly the riots involving racial conflict—is valid.

As black urban riots exploded in the United States, two conflicting explanations quickly appeared. One argument, presented in documents like the report of the McCone Commission, claimed that rioting was to be attributed to riffraff, to individuals coming from the ranks of the unemployed and the uneducated and representing the bottom of the black community.[98] Such individuals, it was said, frequently were recent immigrants from the rural South to the urban North and constituted fringe members of the black ghetto. The other explanation asserted that rioting was to be traced largely to the activity of "the new urban blacks," individuals who were Northern-born or Northern-socialized, educated, well employed, impatient with racial injustice, and committed to social change.[99] The latter viewpoint was the one accepted by black leaders and liberal intellectuals, indicate Abraham Miller and his associates, and soon came to dominate not only the sociological literature but the arguments for a public policy that would move in the direction not of brutal repression but of accommodation.

The urge to interpret the urban riots as the work of "the new urban black" is understandable, it is claimed, since the criminal behavior involved can then be encrusted with political meaning and taken as a measure of the depth of the alienation and affliction of the black community.[100] A number of empirical studies, indeed, appear to confirm this viewpoint, including the influential report of the National Advisory Commission on Civil Disorders. A reanalysis of some of the basic data, however, suggests that such conclusions were based on methodological errors and (possibly) the liberal biases of the original researchers. "If there is some lesson in the philosophy of science to be imparted from our analysis," say Miller, Bolce, and Halligan, "it is that even in the throes of the most heated controversy, in the most far-reaching policy implications, there is no substitute for dispassionate, objective, data-guided analysis."[101] The empirical findings, they conclude, support the idea that rioters were most likely to be unemployed, from a broken home, unmarried, and relatively uneducated, although there is no evidence that new immigrants from the South were prominently involved. There is indeed

[98] California. Governor's Commission on the Los Angeles Riots. *Violence in the City—An End or a Beginning?* Report prepared by John A. McCone and others (Sacramento, 1965).

[99] See Abraham H. Miller, Louis H. Bolce, and Mark R. Halligan, "The New Urban Blacks," *Ethnicity* 3 (December 1976), pp. 338–67.

[100] Ibid., pp. 339–40.

[101] Ibid., p. 341. See also H. Edward Ransford, "Isolation, Powerlessness, and Violence: A Study of Attitudes and Participation in the Watts Riot," *The American Journal of Sociology* 73 (1968), pp. 581–91.

a new urban black—educated, holding a good job, and militantly in support of rights for blacks—but he or she engages in nonviolent protest rather than rioting in the streets.[102]

These findings illuminate but do not settle the question about the nature of collective violence in the form of black urban riots. It is probable that a sense of political purpose was frequently involved, even though the rioters, expressing their anger and frustration, may have been from the lower echelons of the social hierarchy rather than somewhere in the middle. "We won," said one unemployed black youth after the Watts riot in 1965, "because we made the whole world pay attention to us. The police chief never came here before; the mayor always stayed uptown. We made them come."[103] The crucial issue, however, is that collective violence is not a stranger to America; it has often arisen as social groups struggled to achieve collective rather than individual goals. If we are to understand this form of social behavior, we will need a more sophisticated conceptual scheme and further research to show how individual and collective goals are intermeshed with the need to express emotion in violent behavior; how political perceptions arise and are transformed at a variety of socioeconomic levels in the course of events such as riots; and how effective collective violence is as a means of political action.

Conclusions

Although violent crimes like murder, manslaughter, assault, and rape form only a small proportion of all the violations of the criminal law committed in the United States each year, these offenses dominate much of the public's concern with the problem of illegal behavior. Presumably, this is because such crimes rank high on society's scale of wrongdoing and because violence is widely feared as an inexplicable attack coming like a bolt out of the blue.

Violence from a stranger is, of course, by no means uncommon, but it is important to recognize that many—perhaps most—crimes against the person arise out of a preexisting social relationship. Crimes of violence must often be seen as part of a process of social interaction, and our understanding of many violent acts is not complete until we understand the social patterns in which they are rooted.

While the data are far from adequate, the empirical evidence strongly suggests that the incidence of crimes of violence correlates highly with age, sex, socioeconomic status, ethnic background, region, and city size.

[102] Ibid., pp. 362–63.
[103] Quoted in Bayard Rustin, "The Watts 'Manifesto' and the McCone Report," *Commentary* (March 1966), pp. 29–35.

The interpretation of these facts must await an examination of theories of crime causation, but one important point seems fairly clear when we compare crimes against property and crimes against the person. It is evident that property offenses known to the police—such as burglaries, larcenies, and robberies—are concentrated in the lower segments of society. At the same time, there is good reason to believe that large numbers of crimes against property fail to come to official attention and that many of these offenses (such as restraint of trade, embezzlement, business fraud, and employee thefts) are committed by individuals well up on the socioeconomic ladder. The image of crimes against property as a lower-class phenomenon, then, is a distortion of reality. In the case of crimes against the person, however, the picture is different. Once again we find that a very large proportion of crimes known to the police is concentrated in the lower classes. It is also true that many crimes of violence are not reported to the police, although the percentage appears to be smaller in the case of crimes against the person than in the case of crimes against property. But the most important fact is that there is little reason to believe that unreported crimes of violence occur with great frequency in the middle and upper classes. The picture is modified to some extent by instances of police brutality, child abuse, negligent manslaughter, and other acts of violence, and such crimes as murder and assault are committed at all class levels. Nonetheless, it seems safe to say that violent crimes are linked to socioeconomic position far more tightly than are crimes against property.[104] Any attempt to explain criminal behavior must take into account the fact that two great classes of crime—crimes against the person and crimes against property—appear to stand in a different relationship to the social order.

Collective violence further complicates the effort to deal with the problem of crimes against the person, for it appears likely that the patterns of motivation underlying collective violence differ greatly from those that lie behind the conventional individual crimes of violence. The ideological character of collective violence may have been exaggerated or distorted in recent years, as criminologists engaged themselves in the study of riots in black ghettoes and confrontations between the police and students protesting the Vietnam War. Nonetheless, there is enough evidence at hand to indicate that individual acts of violence and collective violence cannot be crammed into the same theoretical framework, and criminology is no longer content to view violent behavior as simply the product of individual frustration, emotional tension, and social friction. Instead, there is a growing interest in acts of violence other than murder, assault, and rape, and an awareness that criminology's understanding of

[104] See Suzanne K. Steinmetz and Murray A. Straus, eds., *Violence in the Family* (New York: Dodd, Mead, 1974), pp. 3–25.

violent behavior has been much restricted by the conventional assumption that violence is always abnormal, perverse, and pathological.[105]

Recommended Readings

The National Commission on the Causes and Prevention of Violence, *Crimes of Violence* (Washington, D.C.: Government Printing Office, 1969) stands as one of the most comprehensive attempts to understand the nature of violence and its causes. Excellent studies of different types of violence, more limited in scope, are to be found in Marvin E. Wolfgang, *Patterns in Criminal Homicide* (Philadelphia: University of Pennsylvania Press, 1958) and Nancy Gager and Cathleen Schurr, *Sexual Assault: Confronting Rape in America* (New York: Grosset & Dunlap, 1976). A useful discussion of gun control—a theme that usually crops up in any treatment of violence in America—is found in Joseph D. Alviani and William R. Drake, *Handgun Control* (Washington, D.C.: U.S. Conference of Mayors, 1975) and Robert Sherrill, *The Saturday Night Special* (New York: Charterhouse, 1973).

Morton Hunt, *The Mugging* (New York: Atheneum, 1972) provides an extremely readable account of how a robbery committed by juveniles turned into murder, seen within the larger context of how the criminal law is administered in the United States today. For a valuable examination of collective violence, see Arthur I. Waskow, *From Race Riot to Sit-In* (Garden City, N.Y.: Doubleday, 1966). The reader should also see the issue on violence in *The Annals of the American Academy of Political and Social Science* 364 (March 1966) and Jerome H. Skolnick, *The Politics of Protest* (New York: Ballatine Books, 1969).

[105] See, for example, Albert Cohen's comments on the uses and meaning of violence, in Albert K. Cohen, George F. Cole, and Robert G. Bailey, eds., *Prison Violence* (Lexington, Mass.: Lexington Books, 1976), pp. 3–21.

Chapter 5
The Enforcement
of Morals

The protection of life and property is usually viewed as the major objective of the criminal law, but the legal system has also long been involved in suppressing a variety of acts entailing less tangible benefits. Heresy, sacrilege, sedition, incest, bigamy, homosexuality, fornication, gambling, public drunkenness, the use of drugs—all of these and more have been outlawed by the state and subjected to penal sanctions. These diverse offenses, conventionally grouped under the heading of crimes against morals, health, and public safety, form one of the most debated areas of the criminal law; their analysis poses complex problems of values, empirical evidence, and theoretical interpretation.

Many of these crimes (particularly gambling, the performing of abortions, public drunkenness, prostitution, and the illegal use of drugs) have come to be called, in the literature of criminology, *crimes without victims*. In such crimes, it is said, the individual who violates the law inflicts no harm or injury on another person; instead, society's judgment of wrongdoing is based either on the harm the individual does to herself or himself or on the failure of the individual to conform to a standard of moral behavior erected by society.[1]

Many people today are quick to argue that the criminal law has no business concerning itself with acts that do not harm others; they claim that attempts to "legislate morality" are an intolerable intrusion by the state on individual privacy. If those trying to justify the criminal law assert that the state reaches into such areas to prevent harm that one may do to oneself, the argument is much the same: the only justification for state-imposed penal sanctions is the prevention of harm that goes

---

[1] See Edwin M. Schur, *Crimes Without Victims* (Englewood Cliffs, N.J.: Prentice-Hall, 1965), pp. 169–79. In Schur's important work, crimes without victims are defined as those offenses in which an illegal service or commodity is provided in an exchange transaction and no apparent harm is done to others. Making exchange a necessary part of the definition is, however, a somewhat arbitrary limitation on the concept of victimless crimes, as Schur himself points out.

beyond the individual; and if people harm themselves, that is their affair. "The only purpose for which power can rightfully be exercised over any member of a civilized community against his will is to prevent harm to others," said John Stuart Mill in the nineteenth century. "His own good, either physical or moral, is not a warrant." A man, he asserted, "cannot rightfully be compelled to do or forebear because it will be better for him to do so, because it will make him happier, because in the opinion of others, to do so would be wise, or even right. There are good reasons for remonstrating with him, or reasoning with him, or persuading him, or entreating him, but not for compelling him, or visiting him with any evil in case he does otherwise."[2] Many writers in the United States today—both popular and academic—are happy to echo such sentiments, convinced that the criminal law is inclined to be a puritanical busybody. "We must strip off the moralistic excrescences on our criminal justice system," assert Norval Morris and Gordon Hawkins, "so that it may concentrate on the essential. The primary function of the criminal law is to protect our persons and our property; these purposes are now engulfed in a mass of other distracting, inefficiently performed legislative duties. . . . For the criminal law at least, man has an inalienable right to go to hell in his own fashion, provided he does not directly injure the person or property of another on the way. The criminal law is an inefficient instrument for imposing the good life on others."[3]

The need to place private forms of behavior beyond the reach of the criminal law is underscored, the argument continues, by the amount of money and time that law enforcement agencies devote to these relatively trivial offenses. "Almost half of all arrests are on charges of drunkenness, disorderly conduct, vagrancy, gambling, and minor sexual deviations," notes the President's Commission on Law Enforcement and Administration of Justice[4]; and the "decriminalization" of such behavior would free the resources of the police for much more crucial tasks. Still more important is the fact that although the use of drugs, gambling, and prostitution have been declared illegal, there is a strong and continuing public demand for the services or commodities involved. The passion for embedding moral judgments in the criminal law sets the stage for the rise of organized crime that diverts vast sums of money into illegal channels, corrupts law enforcement agencies and the political process, and sets an example of tolerated criminal activity that undermines the entire legal system.

[2] *On Liberty* (London: Longmans, Green, 1892), p. 6.
[3] *The Honest Politician's Guide to Crime Control* (Chicago: University of Chicago Press, 1970), p. 2.
[4] *Task Force Report: Assessment of Crime* (Washington, D.C.: Government Printing Office, 1967), p. 16.

The criminal law, then, from this point of view, has overreached its legitimate grasp in the area of crimes without victims and the following program offered by Morris and Hawkins is accepted by many criminologists as a sensible, necessary goal of legal reform:

Drunkenness. Public drunkenness shall cease to be a criminal offense.

Narcotics and drug abuse. Neither the acquisition, purchase, possession, nor the use of any drug will be a criminal offense. The sale of some drugs other than by a licensed chemist (druggist) and on prescription will be criminally proscribed; proof of possession of excessive quantities may be evidence of a sale or of intent to sell.

Gambling. No form of gambling shall be prohibited by the criminal law; certain fraudulent and cheating gambling practices will remain criminal.

Disorderly conduct and vagrancy. Disorderly conduct and vagrancy laws will be replaced by laws precisely stipulating the conduct proscribed and defining the circumstances in which the police should intervene.

Abortion. Abortion performed by a qualified medical practitioner in a registered hospital shall cease to be a criminal offense.

Sexual behavior. Sexual activities between consenting adults in private will not be subject to the criminal law. Adultery, fornication, illicit cohabitation, statutory rape and carnal knowledge, bigamy, incest, sodomy, bestiality, homosexuality, prostitution, pornography, and obscenity, in all of these the role of the criminal law is excessive.[5]

The argument, at first glance, is fairly persuasive, with its stress on individual liberty, the rational allocation of police effort, and the need to avoid the corrosive effects of illicit enterprise. When we examine the argument more closely, however, unresolved issues become apparent. First, the claim that the criminal law pertaining to victimless crimes is somehow uniquely and wrongly involved in making moral judgments is not convincing, since much of the criminal law is a matter of moral judgments. The decision to protect private property or the physical safety of the individual is based on societal considerations of what is right and wrong in human conduct, and here too the law is constantly "legislating morality." Second, the assertion that in victimless crimes no harm is done to others frequently represents the arbitrary shutting off of extensive debate. Gilbert Geis, for example, has pointed out that many people view abortion as the murder of an unborn child.[6] And the writer of a letter to a liberal magazine argued as follows:

---

[5] Morris and Hawkins, *The Honest Politician's Guide to Crime Control*, p. 3.
[6] *Not the Law's Business?* (Washington, D.C.: Government Printing Office, 1972), p. 3.

The Catholics and others who oppose abortion are desperate to shake America loose of its obsession with materialism. Doctors and nurses and others trained in the care of life here, as in Nazi Germany, are now working, and at great profit, toward the destruction of life at its very beginning. . . . Since the Supreme Court decision was handed down, over a million babies have been killed through legal abortions.[7]

Others disagree, but the phrase "victimless crime" obscures the dispute. Similar difficulties are encountered in considering possible harm done to one's self in crimes such as prostitution, gambling, and the illegal use of drugs. The fact that an act is voluntary does not necessarily render it harmless to the actor. There can be the economic exploitation of the prostitute, for example, or the regretted losses of the compulsive gambler; and the idea that the state has no right or obligation to protect persons from self-inflicted harm cannot be said to be a settled argument.[8] The handling of crimes without victims in the literature of criminology is apt to prejudge the issue, to assume too readily that the argument of John Stuart Mill has already won the day and to dismiss the social forces that continue to support prohibitions against victimless crimes as no more than irrational prejudice.[9]

Resolved or not, the issue of victimless crimes is an important one, for the criminal law focuses a major portion of its attention on demands that individuals conform to specified standards of behavior, and in these demands the possible harm done to the self or others is generally less tangible—and more debatable—than in the case of crimes against property or crimes against persons. The law imposes an obligation to fit one's acts within a permissible range of sexual and political behavior, to conform to certain rules of public decorum, to meet certain requirements of health and safety; and it justifies its concern on the grounds that to do otherwise is to open the door to harm to the self and to others. The law's rationale may be much contested, but the use of state-inflicted sanctions to enforce conformity to the behavioral codes of society is neither new nor unusual.

---

[7] Letter to *The New Republic* (June 8, 1974), p. 33. In 1977 arguments over the issue of abortion broke out anew in the wake of the Supreme Court's decision holding that states participating in Medicaid programs are not required to provide abortions.

[8] In some states, for example, it is a criminal offense for a person to ride a motorcycle without a helmet; such laws, however, have been declared unconstitutional in other states. See Geis, *Not the Law's Business?* pp. 9–10.

[9] See Edwin M. Schur and Hugo Adam Bedau, *Victimless Crimes: Two Sides of a Controversy* (Englewood Cliffs, N.J.: Prentice-Hall, 1974).

The laws concerning sexual behavior attempt to regulate four major aspects of sexual relationships.[10] First, there are legal rules governing the *degree of consent,* which was mentioned before in the discussion of forcible rape. Second, there are laws concerning the *nature of the sexual partner,* with most states restricting legitimate sexual partners to humans of the opposite sex over a specified age and with a certain distance in terms of kinship. In general, in most jurisdictions, the only legitimate sexual partner is one's spouse. Sodomy, bestiality, homosexuality, prostitution, statutory rape, indecent liberties or child molestation, incest, fornication, and adultery are all thus prohibited. Third, legal restrictions are placed on the *nature of the sexual act,* with legitimate sexual relationships largely confined to heterosexual intercourse and excluding practices such as oral-genital contact and digital manipulation. Finally, the *setting in which the act occurs* is limited by the law. Sexual relationships deemed wrongful by the law may be prohibited when they occur in public or are conducted in such a manner that the public can easily become aware of them. "States that do not punish single or even repetitive acts of fornication or adultery," notes Wheeler, "may do so if there is evidence of 'notorious' show of public indecency. Public solicitation statutes as well as indecent exposure laws are likewise oriented to control the setting, rather than the act itself."[11]

The origin of many of the laws concerning sexual relationships can be traced to the influence of the canon law of the Christian church. As a body of rules governing the organization of the church and the discipline of its members in ecclesiastical matters, the canon law began to shape the character of English life well before the Norman Conquest.[12] The power of the ecclesiastical tribunals to establish the laws concerning marriage, testaments, the nature of sacrilege, the proper forms of sexual behavior, and similar issues subject to religious doctrine rose and fell over the centuries as the English kings struggled with the authority of the Catholic church. At the end of the reign of Henry VIII, the secular courts had clearly won the right to regulate these matters, but much of the content of the canon law had been absorbed into the larger body of English law. The legal regulation of sexual behavior had come to bear the stamp of theological dogma.

It has been argued that the ideals of sexual behavior developed by the canon law and incorporated in the so-called penitential books were much

[10] The classification is derived from Stanton Wheeler, "Sex Offenses: A Sociological Critique," *Law and Contemporary Problems* 25 (Spring 1960), pp. 258–78.

[11] Ibid., p. 259.

[12] See Helen Cam, *England Before Elizabeth* (London: Hutchinson's University Press, 1950) and R. C. Mortimer, *Western Canon Law* (Berkeley: University of California Press, 1953).

at variance with the rather easygoing sexual mores of the Anglo-Saxon people—and, indeed, had little support in the biblical injunctions of either the Old or the New Testament.[13] In any event, the rules governing sexual conduct, gradually shaping the secular legal tradition, stressed an ascetic view of sexual behavior that continues to influence the criminal law to the present day. The major components of this medieval viewpoint, according to G. Rattray Taylor, were as follows: (1) complete celibacy was held forth as an ideal for all and an obligation for those with priestly functions; (2) an absolute ban was placed on all forms of sexual activity other than intercourse between married persons carried out with the object of procreation; (3) the sexual act performed within the marital relationship must be subjected to extensive limitation and control, including such details as the position of the partners and the days of the week when sexual intercourse is to be permitted. "The Christian code," says Taylor, "was based, quite simply, upon the conviction that the sexual act was to be avoided like the plague, except for the bare minimum necessary to keep the race in existence. Even when performed for this purpose it remained a regrettable necessity. Those who could were exhorted to avoid it entirely, even if married. For those incapable of such heroic self-denial there was a great spider's web of regulations whose overriding purpose was to make the sexual act as joyless as possible. . . .

"It was not actually the sexual act which was damnable," he adds, "but the pleasure derived from it—and this pleasure remained damnable even when the act was performed for the purpose of procreation, a notion which reached its crudest expression with the invention of the *chemise cagoule,* a sort of heavy nightshirt, with a suitably placed hole, through which a husband could impregnate his wife while avoiding any other contact."[14]

The repudiation of sexual pleasure expressed by the early Christian church has undergone great alterations over time, and many people in the United States today would find such sentiments little more than the expression of neurotic fears and obsessions. Nonetheless, the striking fact is that despite the liberalization of sexual attitudes, the criminal law continues to prohibit all but a small segment of sexual behavior occurring within marriage—an example of "legal inertia" that has not received the attention it deserves from the social sciences and that still awaits sociological analysis. "Although laws do vary from state to state," Fred Rodell points out, "throughout most of the nation the only kinds of sexual gratification that are not subject to police interference . . . are three: petting or necking short of intercourse; solitary masturbation in private;

[13] See G. Rattray Taylor, *Sex in History* (New York: Harper & Row, 1970), Chapter III.
[14] Ibid., p. 51.

and intercourse (in the orthodox manner) between husband and wife." [15]

The extent to which public attitudes toward sexual behavior differ from the standards set forth by the criminal law is not an easy matter to establish, since systematic research in this area is of fairly recent origin. "Review of objective data on social norms and sexual conduct reveals above all else the paucity of useful information," wrote Stanton Wheeler in 1960. "Aside from an occasional item in an opinion poll, a handful of studies of college students, and one or two anthroplogical accounts, there is nothing that even makes for intelligent speculation as to the sources and types of community reactions to sexual deviations between consenting adults." [16] Recent studies of sexual norms and sexual behavior, such as those conducted by the Institute of Sex Research at Indiana University, may have modified this picture to some degree, and an increasing frankness about sexual matters has helped to dispel some of the ignorance that has long marked our society in this basic aspect of human behavior; but the lack of empirical data means that the government, presumably acting as an agent for a portion of the public, proceeds with little knowledge about the causes of the conduct in question, its incidence, or its consequences for the self and others.

Recommendations to liberalize the criminal law in this area frequently have as little scientific support as recommendations that our existing sexual prohibitions must be maintained at any cost. Anthony F. C. Wallace, for example, who served as a member of the National Institute of Mental Health Task Force on Homosexuality, declared: "I have no problem endorsing the two policy recommendations in themselves (i.e., that a homosexual act should not be regarded in and of itself as either a crime or cause for refusing employment). But I do so on the basis of personal moral conviction and *not* as a result of the extremely, nay woefully, inadequate evidence. . . . The matter appears important to me because it is becoming increasingly common for legislative, judicial, and administrative bodies to call upon the evidence of psychology, sociology, etc., to give the authority of 'science' to expressions of social values. This procedure is in the long run destructive of the credibility of science itself because it requires the scientist to claim that his findings are far more conclusive than in fact they are. My complaint about the Task Force Report is that it implies that scientific research somehow backs up the policy statement when in fact all that really backs it up is moral conviction." [17]

---

[15] "Our Unlovable Sex Laws," in John H. Gagnon and William Simon eds., *The Sexual Scene* (Chicago: Aldine, 1970), pp. 81–82.

[16] Wheeler, "Sex Offenses: A Sociological Critique," p. 276.

[17] See John M. Livingood, ed., *National Institute of Mental Health Task Force on Homosexuality: Final Report and Background Papers* (Washington, D.C.: Government Printing Office, 1972), pp. 71–72.

The substitution of opinion for fact as a basis of policy is apparent in the sexual-psychopath laws passed by a number of states. These laws, created in an effort to protect the public from "sexual psychopaths" or "persons with criminal propensities to the commission of sex offenses" by authorizing commitment to a mental institution, are based on an implicit set of ideas that are simply erroneous, according to Paul Tappan, Edwin Sutherland, and other criminologists. It is assumed that tens of thousands of homicidal sex fiends stalk the land, that sex offenders are usually recidivists, that they move in a steady progression from less serious to more serious crimes, that psychiatric testing makes it possible to predict the future criminal behavior of sexual offenders, and that reasonably effective treatment is available to deal with the problem.[18] In reality, homicidal sexual offenders are relatively rare. The recidivism rate of sexual offenders is lower than that of most other groups of violators, at least according to official records of criminal behavior. There is no evidence that sexual offenders move along a clear-cut path of crime leading to ever more serious violations of the law. However useful various psychiatric tests may be (such as the Rorschach or Thematic Apperception tests) for the purposes of clinical diagnosis, their ability to predict future criminal behavior is negligible. And whatever the success of psychiatric treatment in dealing with behavioral disorders, deviant sexual behavior—particularly homosexuality—appears to be resistant to such modes of therapy. The attempt, then, to respond to public fears about sexual crimes by committing offenders to indeterminate sentences in a mental hospital is based on a series of fallacies. The sexual-psychopath laws are vague; the legal rights of offenders are frequently violated in the process of adjudication and in prolonged, indefinite confinement; and the problem of sexual crime remains largely untouched.

We have seen that estimates of the number of rapes committed in the United States each year are extremely unreliable, and the same may be said of other forms of sexual behavior declared to be criminal. Many of these acts are committed in private and often involve consenting partners who share an abhorrence for the watchful eyes of the state. A large number of such offenses as voyeurism and exhibitionism may not be reported to the police because of embarrassment or the belief that it is useless; and accusations of minor sexual offenses often disappear in the plea-bargaining process, to be replaced by more innocuous-sounding charges, thus distorting the official records.[19]

[18] See Paul W. Tappan, "Some Myths About the Sex Offender," *Federal Probation* 19 (June 1955), pp. 7–12; Edwin H. Sutherland, "The Sexual Psychopath Laws," *The Journal of Criminal Law and Criminology* 40 (January–February 1950), pp. 543–54; and Nicholas N. Kittrie, *The Right to Be Different* (Baltimore: Penguin Books, 1973), pp. 193–97.

[19] See David Sudnow, "Normal Crimes: Sociological Features of the Penal Code in a Public Defender Office," *Social Problems* 12 (Winter 1965), pp. 255–76.

Fornication and adultery probably make up the most frequent forms of sexual crime but are almost totally ignored by law enforcement agencies. Such offenses are defined wholly by statutory enactment, since they were a development of the ecclesiastical courts rather than the common law, and as a result their definition varies widely from state to state. In some jurisdictions, proof of "notorious illicit cohabitation" is required, while in others this element is unnecessary.[20] The discrepancy between law and law enforcement is, perhaps, nowhere else more striking, and it offers a clear illustration of Thurman Arnold's observation that such laws "are uninforced because we want to continue our conduct, and unrepealed because we want to preserve our morals."[21] Prostitution and homosexuality receive far more attention from the police, but here too the actual incidence of behavior labeled criminal is greatly in excess of the amount that is accorded official recognition.

Prostitution Prostitution has been defined by the law as "the practice of a female in offering her body to an indiscriminate intercourse with men for money or its equivalent,"[22] and is associated with a number of other illegal activities deemed criminal, such as maintaining a bawdy house, pandering, and solicitation. The President's Commission on Law Enforcement and Administration of Justice reports that there were 37,000 arrests for prostitution and commercialized vice in 1965 and makes the assumption that about 45,000 persons were engaged in such activity, with a yearly income of $225 million.[23] Charles Winick and Paul M. Kinsie, however, have claimed that prostitution involves 100,000 to 500,000 women in the United States and that the profession grosses more than a billion dollars a year.[24] The vast difference in the estimates does not reflect a difference in date but is instead an indication of our ignorance. Similar differences of opinion exist with regard to changes in the practice of prostitution in recent decades, with some writers asserting that the alleged sexual revolution in the United States has curtailed commercialized vice, and others claiming that it has been little affected.[25] It is clear in any case that prostitution has changed its form to some extent. "The business of prostitution," notes one newspaper, "embracing modern marketing techniques and skirting the law, is branching out from its downtown closet into Middle America. Like its cousin the blue movie, today's brothel is likely to be around the corner—in the form of a mas-

---

[20] Rollin M. Perkins, *Criminal Law* (Brooklyn: The Foundation Press, 1957), pp. 328–30.

[21] *Symbols of Government* (New Haven: Yale University Press, 1936), p. 160.

[22] *Ferguson v. Superior Court*, 26 Cal. App. 554, 558, 147 p. 603, 605 (1915).

[23] *Task Force Report: Crime and Its Impact* (Washington, D.C.: Government Printing Office, 1967), p. 53.

[24] *The Lively Commerce: Prostitution in the United States* (Chicago: Quandrangle, 1971).

[25] See Geis, *Not the Law's Business?* Chapter V.

sage parlor, lotion studio, nude photo club, sexual intercourse school, escort service, dial-a-massage, sauna bath house or some other thinly disguised supermarket for sexual services."[26] But the motives of the prostitute's client appear to remain much the same—the craving for sexual variety, perverse gratification, and intercourse free of entangling cares.[27] And for the prostitue herself, the evidence suggests that now as in the past her activity is predominantly voluntary, representing, for some, "a considerable range of vocational advantages, including flexible hours of work, contact with diverse kinds of persons, a heightened sense of activity, and the opportunity to make substantial sums of money"; for others it is a dangerous enterprise with beatings, ugly copulations, and small financial rewards.[28]

The attention devoted to prostitution by criminologists, journalists, ministers, social reformers, and others may appear somewhat puzzling. "The world's literature contains hundreds of volumes whose authors have attempted to assay the social significance of prostitution," notes Alfred Kinsey. "For an activity which contributes no more than this does to the sexual outlet of the male population, it is amazing that it should have been given such widespread consideration."[29] As Geis points out, however, it is frequently the quality of behavior rather than the quantity that engages public concern, and prostitution represents a fundamental challenge to conventional ideas about the proper form of sexual relationship, as well as evoking sexual fantasies. Sexual intimacy, at least in theory, is supposed to be founded on love, within the bonds of marriage, and is not to be tainted by the commercial considerations of the marketplace. This may be no more than an ideal, and the sexual intimacy of marriage itself may often be no more than an economic transaction, as some exponents of the women's liberation movement have claimed. The criminal law, with its prohibition against prostitution, may be an ill-designed instrument to move human behavior in the desired direction.[30] The idea of exchanging sexual favors for cash is, however, intolerable to many people, and the criminal law gives verbal expression to such distaste.

[26] The New York Times (June 9, 1974). Increases in unemployment rates, however, are likely to lead to an increase in old-fashioned streetwalking.

[27] See Kingsley Davis, "Sexual Behavior," in Robert K. Merton and Robert A. Nisbet, eds., Contemporary Social Problems, 2nd ed. (New York: Harcourt Brace Jovanovich, 1976), pp. 245–52.

[28] Geis, Not the Law's Business? p. 208.

[29] Alfred Kinsey, Wardell B. Pomeroy, and Clyde E. Martin, Sexual Behavior in the Human Male (Philadelphia: Saunders, 1948), n. 94, p. 605, quoted in Geis, Not the Law's Business?, p. 217.

[30] For a discussion of whether prostitution should be regarded as a criminal offense, see United Nations Secretariat, "Prostitution in Selected Countries of Asia and the Far East," International Review of Criminal Policy 13 (October 1958); see also Great Britain. Committee on Homosexual Offences and Prostitution, Report (New York: Stein and Day, 1963).

Homosexuality Male homosexual behavior is prohibited by the criminal law in all states except Illinois and Connecticut. It is called by a variety of names: "sodomy," "buggery," "fellatio," a "crime against nature," and "unnatural carnal copulation" and is usually defined as a felony. The penalties assigned by the law are severe, but many arrests of alleged homosexuals are made on other charges, such as lewd and lascivious behavior or loitering, to facilitate arrests by the police. The realities of law enforcement can sometimes make discussions of the need for change in statutory provisions somewhat irrelevant.

Estimates of the extent of homosexual behavior in the United States are almost completely meaningless; we are, once again, speaking of behavior that, by and large, involves the private acts of consenting individuals. Patterns of law enforcement are highly selective and frequently involve either the periodic harassment, by the police, of gay bars or the entrapment in public lavatories of suspected offenders.[31] The figures on the number of homosexuals are perhaps more useful, although they are based on nonrepresentative samples. Kinsey and his associates have claimed that, after the onset of adolescence, 4 percent of American white males are exclusively homosexual throughout their lives, and that 30 to 45 percent of American males have experienced some overt homosexual contact to the point of orgasm.[32] As in the case of fornication, adultery, and prostitution, the amount of criminal behavior in this area reaching official attention bears little relationship to the amount that actually occurs.[33]

It has been argued that public reactions to homosexuality are changing in the United States and that we are witnessing a trend toward a more enlightened, dispassionate perspective.[34] The frankness with which homosexuality is now handled in the mass media, the willingness of many homosexuals to declare themselves publicly, the rise of gay liberation as an organized political movement, the pronouncement by the American Psychiatric Association that homosexuality is not an expression of mental illness—all might be taken as indications that the contempt long directed at the homosexual is lessening. In Great Britain, in 1966, Parliament finally implemented the recommendations of the Wolfenden Committee

[31] For an excellent analysis of the role of the gay bar in the homosexual community, see Evelyn Hooker, *Perspectives in Psychopathology* (New York: Oxford University Press, 1951). See also Maurice Leznoff and William A. Westley, "The Homosexual Community"; Albert J. Reiss, Jr., "The Social Integration of Queers and Peers"; and Nancy Achilles, "The Development of the Homosexual Bar as an Institution," all in John Gagnon and William Simon, eds., *Sexual Deviance* (New York: Harper & Row, 1967), pp. 167–244.

[32] Kinsey, Pomeroy, and Martin, *Sexual Behavior in the Human Male,* pp. 650–51.

[33] The category "sex offenses" is listed by the FBI as a Part II offense, and excludes forcible rape, prostitution, and commercialized vice. There were 63,000 arrests reported in this category in 1976. See *Uniform Crime Reports—1976* (Washington, D.C.: Government Printing Office, 1977), p. 173.

[34] See Wheeler, "Sex Offenses: A Sociological Critique."

that private, consensual homosexual behavior between adults should no longer be defined as a criminal offense. Many social commentators in the United States have urged that we follow the same course. Homosexuality does not pose a social harm, it is said; it is a sexual preference, a matter of individual choice, and should be of no concern to the criminal law. Other observers have argued that homosexuality is best viewed not as a preference but as a compulsion; yet they still agree that such behavior is not to be subjected to penal sanctions.[35] It seems unlikely, however, that homosexuality will be "decriminalized" in the United States for some time to come, despite the strength of the arguments to do so, for the great majority of the public appears to find homosexuality abhorrent and somehow feels that that not to condemn such behavior by means of the criminal law is to lend it approval.

The Illegal Use of Drugs

Of all the aspects of the criminal law that have been subjected to critical examination in the last several decades, probably none has received more attention than efforts to control the use of heroin, marijuana, LSD, amphetamenes, and barbiturates. The issue, for many people, has come to symbolize the entire question of the proper limits of the power of the state; and the pros and cons of the decriminalization of drug use are often argued with a fervor that make an analysis of the problem difficult. The prohibitions on drugs have, in fact, become an ideological and political matter, and objective statements of fact form only one portion of the debate.

The prohibitions against drugs in the United States are of fairly recent origin. It is said that addiction to morphine became a problem because the drug was used to treat the wounded during the Civil War—a claim that David Musto views with some skepticism, since relatively few cases of addiction occurred in France, Germany, Great Britain, Russia, and Italy, where morphine was also used as a wartime painkiller in the latter half of the nineteenth century.[36] In any event, opium and its various derivatives were apparently widely used in the United States in the late nineteenth and early twentieth centuries, frequently in the form of patent medicines that could be purchased over the counter in drugstores or general stores or ordered through the mails.[37] A growing awareness of the dangers of addiction led to a spate of antimorphine laws at the state level in the 1890s (although patent medicine manufacturers continued to obtain exceptions for quantities of narcotics in their products), and the

---

[35] See Albert Ellis, "Sexual Manifestations of Emotionally Disturbed Behavior," *The Annals of the American Academy of Political and Social Science* 376 (March 1968), pp. 96–105.

[36] David F. Musto, *The American Disease* (New Haven: Yale University Press, 1973), Chapter I.

[37] See Geis, *Not the Law's Business?* p. 109.

"I Started Cutting Dope at 13"

When she was 15 years old, Janet P. was arrested for selling drugs on the streets of Harlem. At the time, she had $900 and three glassine envelopes of heroin.

Janet, one of four children in a family that tried unsuccessfully to get off welfare, said she "took to the streets" to help make things easier at home.

Today she is 20 and a high-school dropout, and she dreams only of opening her own carpentry shop. She works when and wherever she can. In a park across from the Lower East Side apartment she occupies, Janet talked about her former life as an adolescent drug dealer.

"I started cutting dope on the kitchen table of my family's apartment when I was 13. I was getting $150 a day, so I stopped going to school. The same man who had me cutting dope for him asked if I'd like to work the streets. In no time I was making $500 to $600 a day selling dope. If your stuff is good, the junkies will follow you home to get it. This guy I was working for liked the way I was dealing, so he made me a lieutenant. I was 14. I had to give out a consignment to five or six other kids who reported directly to me with the money. And I gave it to the man.

"Was it dangerous? Yeah. The biggest danger was being taken off by some junkie. They had

some guys coming from Jersey stealing our stuff. That's when my man gave me a .38-caliber revolver to protect myself.

"I remember one time this junkie tried to take me off and I had my stash hidden under some peppermint balls in a paper bag. This guy looked in the bag, saw peppermint candy and says, 'I thought you had some dope.'

"I was spending my money to help my family. Mom didn't care if I ever went back to school, so long as I brought in the money. I got her a washing machine, bought clothes for my sisters and brothers. But I had to be in by 1 A.M. so I worked all day.

"The turning point was when I got busted. I had just bought myself a whole new outfit and had a heavy date. Cops followed me into this bar, searched me, found the dope and the money and took me down to the 23d Precinct. They made me strip off all my clothes. This black cop kept saying he hoped they locked me up forever. But this white cop said he would get me off since it was a first offense.

"I sat on a wooden block in a cell and cried all night. I promised the Lord that if I got off this time, I'd never go back to selling dope again."

She kept that promise. After the police officer got her off, she recalled, he asked her for $100 to pay the District Attorney and $50 for himself.

"He could have had the whole $900 for all I cared. I was so happy to be out of there."

"I Started Cutting Dope at 13," by Lena Williams. © 1977 by The New York Times Company. Reprinted by permission.

first significant federal legislation appeared in 1914 with the passage of the Harrison Act.[38]

The original purpose of the Harrison Act, at least in theory, was to make the distribution of drugs within the country a matter of record, with a nominal excise tax being imposed when persons or firms handling drugs were registered. There was no indication of a legislative intent, Alfred Lindesmith has claimed, to deny addicts access to drugs or to stop doctors from supplying drugs to patients in the course of their professional practice.[39] A series of Supreme Court decisions, however, and the policies developed by the Federal Bureau of Narcotics—charged with the administration of the Harrison Act—soon made it clear that the law viewed the illegal use of opiates as dangerous behavior to be suppressed by harsh sanctions. Drug addiction quickly ceased to be a medical problem handled in a physician–patient relationship, and became instead a criminal problem involving the police and the offender. "Public attitudes," noted John O'Donnell, "which before had regarded addiction as a mildly deviant behavior, harmful to the individual and his family, now regarded it as one of the worst of evils, and as a threat to the community. Achieving abstinence was regarded as requiring only an act of will, so that when addicts relapsed after treatment they were perceived as hopeless weaklings, or as having chosen evil in place of good."[40]

The realities of drug use, however, are a good deal more complex than such public perceptions suggest. The opiate drugs can be eaten, smoked, or injected, and they act chiefly on the central and autonomic nervous systems. In general, their effect is to produce *analgesia* (relief of pain), *sedation* (freedom from anxiety, relaxation of tension, and decreased activity), *hypnosis* (drowsiness or lethargy), and *euphoria* (sense of well-being and contentment).[41] The precise process by which addiction occurs is still unknown, but a tolerance for the opiate drugs is quickly established. It takes larger and larger quantities to produce the same effect; and when the use of the drugs is discontinued, the physical reactions can be both varied and violent. Yawning, sneezing, crying, running nose, goose flesh, rapid pulse, sexual orgasm, increased blood pressure, dilated pupils, hot and cold flushes, nausea, vomiting, diarrhea, muscular spasms—all may strike the addict, in so-called withdrawal symptoms, with a painfulness that one user has described as the worst possible toothache in every inch of the body.[42] The withdrawal symptoms are

[38] See Alfred R. Lindesmith, *The Addict and the Law* (Bloomington: Indiana University Press, 1965), Chapter I.

[39] Ibid., p. 304.

[40] "The Rise and Decline of a Subculture," *Social Problems* 15 (Summer 1967), p. 80, quoted in Geis, *Not the Law's Business?* p. 110.

[41] See David P. Ausubel, *Drug Addiction* (New York: Random House, 1958), Chapter 2.

[42] Alfred R. Lindesmith, *Opiate Addiction* (Bloomington, Ind.: Principia Press, 1947).

self-limiting and usually disappear in about ten days to two weeks, although some physiological variables may not return to normal for up to six months if the individual has become accustomed to a relatively high dosage.

Once a person is hooked, it is claimed, the kick which the drug provides is of minor importance in explaining continued use. The addict must stay on the drug simply to feel normal.[43] This viewpoint, however, has been severely criticized by Ausubel and others, who raise a number of pertinent questions.[44] First, it is asked whether withdrawal symptoms are indeed as painful as drug addicts say they are. Ausubel argues:

> The popular misconception that addicted individuals deprived of the drug suffer the tortures of the damned, and that once caught in the grip of physiological dependence the average person is powerless to help himself, are beliefs that have been touted on a credulous public by misinformed journalists and by addicts themselves.[45]

Ausubel may strike the reader as being somewhat insensitive, dismissing too easily a pain that he has not endured. Nonetheless, the agony of withdrawal may have been exaggerated.[46] Second, there is a question of why the amount of drugs taken by addicts is frequently two to five times the amount required to stave off withdrawal symptoms. If the addict is simply trying to achieve a normal state, the surplus dosage is an inexplicable luxury, considering the high price of heroin. Third, withdrawal symptoms can be adequately relieved by subcutaneous injections. Why, then, do many addicts come to prefer "mainlining," or injecting the drug in a vein, which increases the kick? Fourth, the recidivism rate among addicts is extremely high, running 75 to 85 percent or higher. Why, after passing through the withdrawal period, do so many addicts get hooked again?

The literature on opiate addition is both voluminous and, unfortunately, inconclusive, and we cannot yet answer these questions with much certainty. But whatever the causes of addiction may be and however intense the pains of withdrawal, it seems fairly clear that the continued use of opiate drugs is not itself physiologically damaging. "One of the most interesting medical facts about heroin and the other narcotics," notes Erich Goode, "is that aside from the danger of over-dosing

[43] Ibid.

[44] See Ausubel, *Drug Addiction*, and I. Chein et al., *The Road to H* (New York: Basic Books, 1964).

[45] Ausubel, *Drug Addiction*, p. 26.

[46] A. Wilker has pointed out that under experimental conditions addicts are willing to undergo severe withdrawal reactions for relatively minor rewards. See Wilker, "On the Nature of Addiction and Habituation," *British Journal of Addiction* 57 (July 1961), pp. 73–79.

they are relatively nontoxic drugs."[47] American physicians, for example, have an addiction rate far higher than that of the general population, with doctors who are addicts numbering about 3,000 to 4,000. The physicians, however, rarely suffer any of the negative physical consequences that are found among street junkies, because their dosage is standardized, their needles and other equipment are sterile, they compensate for nutritional deficiencies when narcotics depress their appetite, and they do not suffer the hazards of street addicts searching for money and drugs.[48] "Opiate effects per se must be differentiated from the medical complications associated with the hectic way of life pursued by youthful heroin addicts," argue John C. Ball and John C. Urbaites. "While there is ample evidence that the aberrant way of life followed by most heroin abusers has both acute and chronic medical consequences . . . there is insufficient scientific basis for maintaining that the long-term use of opiates—in and of itself—is related to any major medical condition."[49]

This does not mean, of course, that the use of opiate drugs does not result in hepatitis and tetanus from infected needles, deaths from overdoses and contaminated drugs, numerous property crimes to secure money to buy drugs, and other ill effects. Quite the contrary. Narcotic overdosing, for example, mainly involving the use of heroin, is the major cause of death in New York City in the fifteen-to-thirty-five age group, with approximately 70 percent of such deaths occurring among those twenty-three years of age or younger.[50] Instead, the argument is that many of the problems arising from the use of opiate drugs are due to their illegality. The criminal monopolies of organized crime that drive up the price, the uncertain dosages provided by street sellers, the clandestine and disorganized life of the addict—these, it is said, are the important sources of the difficulties with opiate drug use, not the specific properties or effects of the drugs themselves.

Much the same argument is made with regard to marijuana. Public sentiment against the use of marijuana emerged at a later date than in the case of the opiate drugs, but by 1937—the year of the Federal Marijuana Tax Act—every state had enacted some form of legislation prohibiting the sale or possession of the drug.[51] Today, as Geis has pointed

[47] *Drugs in American Society* (New York: Alfred A. Knopf, 1972), p. 164.
[48] Ibid., p. 164.
[49] "Absence of Major Medical Complications Among Chronic Opiate Addicts," in John C. Ball and Carl D. Chambers, eds., *The Epidemiology of Opiate Addiction in the United States* (Springfield, Ill.: Charles C. Thomas, 1970), pp. 305–06.
[50] Geis, *Not the Law's Business?* p. 132.
[51] Most of the laws dealing with the illegal use of drugs are based on the criminality of sale or possession. Since 1962, the Supreme Court has declared that statutes making addiction to narcotics a criminal offense violated constitutional principles. Drug addiction is an illness, declared the Court, comparable to leprosy, insanity, and the common cold, and criminal punishment for such an illness is prohibited by the Eighth Amendment. See *Robinson v. California*, 370 U.S. 660, 666–667 (1962).

out, "the nationwide pattern of laws relating to marijuana is something of a 'crazy quilt,' with maximum sentences ranging from 7 days in jail in Nebraska to life imprisonment in Texas for the possession of marijuana. Typical of the newer laws is the one in Arizona that allows the judge to decide whether the first-time defendant charged with possession should be convicted of a felony or a misdemeanor. Equally typical of the kinds of situations which occur under present laws was the conviction in Minnesota of a man for the possession of $1/2800$th of an ounce of marijuana, which was recovered when the lining of his jacket was vacuumed and the sample was identified under a microscope." [52]

But all penalties for the use of marijuana are ridiculous, it is argued, since there is little or no evidence that the drug has any deleterious effects. Research in this area is admittedly inadequate for a number of reasons, including legal impediments, disinterest in the topic among most scientists until recently, and the lack of correlation between the effects of marijuana in animals and in people. [53] The data do suggest, however, that the short-term subjective effects of marijuana are likely to be variable; that the short-term physical effects are minor and largely limited to a rise in the heartbeat, a reddening of the membrane covering the whites of the eyes, and a dryness in the throat and mouth; and that the long-term physical effects are largely conjectural, although there is no convincing evidence that they are harmful. The claim that the prolonged use of marijuana leads to an "amotivational syndrome," a kind of lethargy, remains no more than a speculation. [54] In short, the supposed injurious effects of marijuana have very little empirical evidence; the development of the tolerance and addiction that is associated with the opiate drugs is lacking; and, in the eyes of many, the reaction of much of society to the use of the drug borders on the hysterical. The argument that the use of marijuana leads to the use of more dangerous drugs such as heroin has repeatedly been shown to be spurious. "All told," concludes Geis, "the evidence seems to indicate that marijuana does not represent any serious threat to the well-being of the American society." [55]

As was indicated before, however, clear proof of harm to the self or others is not necessarily the only basis of the prohibitions of the criminal law—although the criminal law usually claims that such harms exist and many legal philosophers insist that such harms can be the only justification for the interference of the state. But that is a statement of what

[52] *Not the Law's Business?* p. 151.
[53] John Kaplan, *Marijuana—The New Prohibition* (New York: World, 1970), Chapter III.
[54] See National Commission on Marijuana and Drug Abuse, *Marijuana: A Signal of Misunderstanding* (New York: New American Library, 1972); see also Edward M. Brecher, "Marijuana: The Health Question," *Consumer Reports* (March 1975), pp. 143–49.
[55] *Not the Law's Business?* p. 161.

should be rather than what is, and in fact the state employs the criminal law to interfere in the lives of its citizens for a variety of reasons. In the case of drugs, the harsh reactions of the criminal law must be understood partly in terms of diffuse symbolic meanings. Whatever their physical or social hazards, heroin and marijuana have tended to become associated in much of the public mind with the provision of pleasure without effort, the impairment of vocational commitment, and the avoidance of reality. As such, they are apt to be feared and despised. No less important, the use of such drugs is often viewed as being part of a drug culture, as a gesture of alienation or repudiation of many of America's most cherished values. Moreover, since the use of drugs is likely to be concentrated in certain segments of society, social reactions are apt to be influenced by the characteristics of the user. While addiction to opiate drugs was once found in both men and women at all class levels, after the disappearance of opiate-saturated patent medicines the number of female addicts declined, and the use of drugs gradually became concentrated in the lower socioeconomic classes.[56] Today, the use of heroin, in particular, appears most likely to be found among blacks and Puerto Ricans living in slum areas in large cities. Public attitudes about the "drug problem" are undoubtedly influenced by more general attitudes concerning the "deplorable" habits of the poor. The use of marijuana, in earlier years, was associated with the Mexican-American community and was strongly condemned; and the identification of marijuana with the youthful protest movements of the 1960s has surely strengthened public sentiment concerning the dangers of indiscriminate drug use. "American concern with narcotics is more than a medical or a legal problem," notes Musto. ". . . The energy that has given impetus to drug control and prohibition came from profound tensions among socio-economic groups, ethnic minorities, and generations—as well as the psychological attraction of certain drugs."[57] If certain forms of conduct, in short, are prohibited and punished by the state, it is wise to take into account the social location of the conduct.

Estimates of the amount of illegal drug use in the United States are highly dubious at best, since the figures are thoroughly contaminated by the needs and interests of the law enforcement agencies that have a stake in the size of the drug problem as it is presented to the American public (that is, the bigger the problem, the more the public will support law enforcement). Standardized reporting procedures do not exist, definitions of illegal drug use are inconsistent, and police activity—in the form of arrests, for example—are apt to be hopelessly confused with the criminal

[56] Ibid., pp. 109–10.
[57] The American Disease, p. 244.

behavior that the police are attempting to control. "A great many statistical compilations are presented to the public and the lawmakers," it has been pointed out, "but very little of it can be relied upon for understanding drug abuse problems. . . . Many of the supposed reports showing narcotics activity are in reality compiled from statistical records showing *police* activity. A report showing the number of arrests made by a narcotics squad is a necessary and helpful document to a police commissioner, but 1,000 arrests may represent 200 offenders or even fewer. To add to the confusion, terminology may vary greatly. Arrest may mean the act of bringing an individual to the police station, or it may mean placing charges against a suspect. Comparison requires extensive background study if any valid conclusions are to be drawn."[58]

Nowhere is the problem of compiling accurate data made clearer than in Lindesmith's analysis of the reports of the Federal Bureau of Narcotics.[59] Over the years, according to bureau officials, a policy of vigorous law enforcement has led to a drastic drop in the number of addicts in the United States. From a total of approximately 200,000 at the time the Harrison Act was passed (1914), the number of addicts declined to some 60,000 during World War II and has since increased only slightly. Lindesmith argues that these figures represent little more than fantasy. The estimation of the number of addicts in 1914 was based on a limited survey made in Michigan in 1878. The calculation of trends in addiction is based on questionable assumptions, such as the claim that illegally obtained narcotics were not a significant factor in supplying addicts in the period after World War I and that legal sales alone provided a sound basis for estimating extent of use. The current census of addicts compiled by the Federal Bureau of Narcotics is based on the voluntary reporting of local agencies and incorporates doubtful procedures, such as the elimination of names from the list of known addicts who have not come to the attention of the police in a five-year period. Addicts in prison are not included in the figures, nor are those obtaining legal drugs from doctors. And no attempt is made to arrive at an objectively based estimate of the number of addicts who have never been officially identified.[60] Thus the figures for both past and present drug addiction are unreliable and prob-

[58] White House Conference on Narcotic and Drug Abuse, *Proceedings* (Washington, D.C.: Government Printing Office, 1962), pp. 139–40. See also Lois B. DeFleur, "Biasing Influences on Drug Arrests Records: Implications for Deviance Research," *American Sociological Review* 40 (February 1975), pp. 88–102.

[59] *The Addict and the Law,* Chapter 4.

[60] John Clausen, in examining the inadequacy of the statistics of the Federal Bureau of Narcotics, has pointed out, for example, that in 1962 California listed 13,620 known narcotic addicts and users within the state while the federal bureau reported only 7412. See John A. Clausen, "Drug Addiction," in Robert K. Merton and Robert A. Nisbet, eds., *Contemporary Social Problems* (New York: Harcourt, Brace & World, 1966), p. 205.

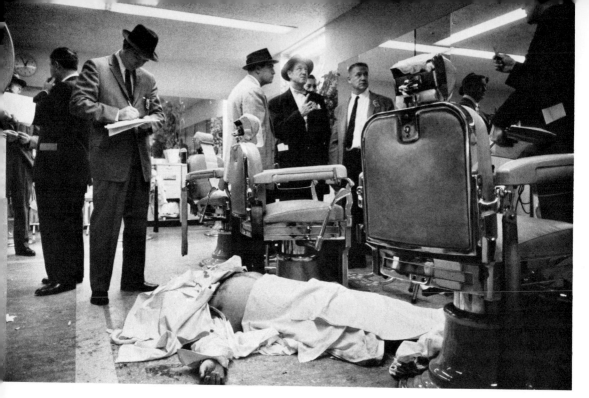

The murder of Albert Anastasia, 1957.

Organized crime has long fascinated the American public, and innumerable movies and books have explored the nature of the racketeer. The reality of organized crime in the United States has been no less persistent.

Al Capone relaxing in Florida.

Edward G. Robinson
in *Little Caesar*.

Marlon Brando in *The Godfather*.

ably inestimable, concludes Lindesmith, and federal narcotic officials have consistently underreported the problem.[61]

Attempts to gauge the extent of marijuana use in the United States are almost as unrewarding, although the lower degree of social opprobrium attached to marijuana probably makes self-reported use a more helpful source of information. The data suggest that prior to World War II the use of marijuana was relatively restricted and that even in the beginning of the 1960s middle-class adolescents and college youths had barely begun to experiment with the drug. After 1967 veterans returning from Vietnam introduced the drug into a great variety of social settings, and today the majority of young people have probably had at least some experience with marijuana. The level of use among different segments of the population remains largely unknown. "It would be embarrassing for a student to admit that he hadn't at least tried pot," it has been asserted, "just as it would be embarrassing to admit that he was a virgin."[62] While the statement was probably an exaggeration when it was made in the early 1960s, it is more apt to be true today. In 1975 it was reported that 29 million Americans have tried marijuana and 12 million smoke it regularly.[63]

Should the illegal use of drugs be decriminalized? Should opiate addiction be defined once more as a medical problem and returned to the physician for treatment and possible cure? Should marijuana be viewed in the same manner as alcohol, and, with some state regulation perhaps, its use left largely to individual discretion? The pros and cons have been thoroughly discussed in the last ten to fifteen years, and it is probably fair to say that the weight of informed opinion is heavily in favor of decriminalization in some form or another, as suggested by the program presented by Morris and Hawkins (see p. 165).[64] "Although, like many Americans of my generation," says Kaplan, reflecting the opinion of many lawyers, "I cannot escape the feeling that drug use, aside from any harm it does, is somehow wrong, I am deeply moved by the consequences of our present marijuana policy. As a lawyer and a teacher of law, I regard it as a matter of desperate urgency to repair the damaged integrity, credibility, and effectiveness of our criminal law."[65] And the

[61] *The Addict and the Law,* p. 122.

[62] William H. McGlothlin and Sidney Cohen, "The Use of Hallucinogenic Drugs Among College Students," *American Journal of Psychiatry* 122 (November 1965), pp. 572–74, quoted in Stanley E. Grupp, ed., *Marijuana* (Columbus, Ohio: Charles E. Merrill, 1971).

[63] See "Newsline," *Psychology Today* (April 1975), pp. 39–40. See also William H. McGlothlin, *Marijuana: An Analysis of Use, Distribution, and Control* (Washington, D.C.: Department of Justice, 1971) and James R. Henley and Larry D. Adams, "Marijuana Use in Post-Collegiate Cohorts: Correlates of Use, Prevalence Patterns and Factors Associated with Cessation," *Social Problems* 20 (Spring 1973), pp. 514–20.

[64] For an excellent review of the arguments see Geis, *Not the Law's Business?* Chapter IV, and Kaplan, *Marijuana—The New Prohibition.*

[65] *Marijuana—The New Prohibition,* p. x.

only sensible course of action, it is argued, is a liberalization of the drug laws to avoid reliance on penal sanction.

"Informed opinion," however, is not the same as public opinion, and many social scientists doubt that there will be a substantial change in the laws governing the use of drugs in the immediate future. The political hazards of advocating easier access to drugs are sure to impede the path of legislative reform. Nonetheless, a growing awareness of the social and economic costs of present drug policies, more accurate information concerning drugs, and widespread experimentation with such drugs as marijuana may all set the stage for changes in the law that would have appeared impossible a short time ago.

It must be emphasized again that the presence or absence of harmful effects, whether real or imagined, is not the sole determinant of society's reaction to a particular drug, as is evident in its attitude toward ethyl, or beverage, alcohol. Although in 1919 its manufacture and sale was prohibited by the Eighteenth Amendment to the Constitution—after more than half a century of agitation—ethyl alcohol was accepted once again less than fifteen years later within a variety of legal limitations such as the time and place of sale and the age of the purchaser.[66] While the deleterious effects of alcohol resulting from sporadic or chronic intoxication are widely recognized, our society has chosen to incorporate the use of alcohol into the normative framework and handle the problem of abuse as best it can.

Alcohol Abuse

For some people, this is simply hypocrisy. Both marijuana and alcohol are intoxicants that are used for relaxation and pleasure, and marijuana is certainly no more damaging than liquor either in its physical or behavioral effects. The counterarguments are held to be unconvincing, and the double standard is viewed as the work of a generation of drinkers inveighing against a younger generation that finds its pleasure in pot and seeks its legalization. But while the law does regard consistency as a virtue, as Kaplan has indicated, it is under no compulsion to achieve an absolute symmetry. Although the law licenses the sale of alcohol, it need not do the same with marijuana. If substantiating facts could be found, Kaplan notes, "we might rationally acknowledge that Prohibition was repealed because alcohol was too firmly established in our culture, but as to marijuana we may still strangle the baby monster in its cradle."[67] The important issues for our present discussion, however, are that the use of alcohol is legally accepted by society, that a good deal of both sporadic and chronic intoxication occurs, and that the criminal law's main efforts

---

[66] Robert Straus, "Alcohol," in Merton and Nisbet, *Contemporary Social Problems,* pp. 236–80.

[67] *Marijuana—The New Prohibition,* p. 289.

to deal with the problem take the form of prohibitions against public drunkenness.

Public intoxication is punishable under a number of different laws, including prohibitions against being "drunk in a public place," "committing a breach of the peace," and "loud and profane discourse." Maximum jail sentences ranging from five days to six months are provided in most states, the most common one being thirty days. In some states a two-year sentence in prison is imposed on a conviction of "habitual drunkenness."[68] In 1976 there were about two and three-quarter million arrests for public drunkenness, driving under the influence of alcohol, and disorderly behavior—about 30 percent of all arrests—and it is evident that dealing with the problem of public drunkenness absorbs a large share of the attention of the police in many jurisdictions.[69] In the District of Columbia, for example, even the uniformed tactical police force—a special unit used "to combat serious crime"—devotes much of its efforts to handling drunks. Of 14,542 arrests made by the tactical force in a nine-month period, 6,363 were for drunkenness.[70]

The present procedure for handling public drunkenness is an expensive one, for it has been estimated that each arrest costs the criminal justice system $50—with an aggregate cost to the nation of no less than $100 million a year. But it is also a procedure that is unanimously regarded as a failure. "The criminal justice system appears ineffective to deter drunkenness or to meet the problems of the chronic alcoholic offenders," it has been said. "What the system usually does accomplish is to remove the drunk from public view, detoxify him, and provide him with food, shelter, emergency medical service, and a brief period of forced sobriety."[71]

Largely ineffective, then, costly in terms of money and police resources, and frequently involving the abuse of the defendant's legal rights, the present method of handling public drunkenness is understandably viewed as needing serious modification. It is generally agreed that there should be a routine medical examination of all suspected offenders and the establishment of sobering-up stations, outpatient clinics, community homes, and social centers.[72] But even more important is the widespread recognition that the criminal law is not the proper instrument for handling the problem of alcohol abuse. Those arrested for public intoxication include a variety of offenders, from the blue-collar

[68] See President's Commission on Law Enforcement and Administration of Justice, *Task Force Report: Drunkenness* (Washington, D.C.: Government Printing Office, 1967), p. 1.

[69] *Uniform Crime Reports—1976* (Washington, D.C.: Government Printing Office, 1977), p. 173.

[70] *Task Force Report: Drunkenness*, p. 4, and Appendix F.

[71] Ibid., p. 3.

[72] Ibid., pp. 17–22.

worker on a weekend spree, to the college youth drinking with friends, to the middle-class partygoer who has gotten out of hand on the way home. But the great majority of arrests involve chronic offenders living in rundown hotels and flophouses, penniless and plagued by personal problems. The most complete study of these offenders has been made by David J. Pittman and C. W. Gordon, and their data indicate that those arrested are mainly male; single, divorced, separated, or widowed; poorly educated; and semi- or unskilled. Blacks, who are disproportionately represented, are largely from a rural or small-town Southern background and have had severe difficulties in adjusting to a Northern urban setting. White offenders, who tend to be concentrated in the older age groups, are primarily of English or Irish extraction and, like the blacks, are apt to be poor.[73] These chronic offenders apparently have little control over their drinking and are unaffected by an appearance in court and a period of imprisonment; hundreds of arrests for an individual are not uncommon and many chronic drunks have spent much of their lives in jail.

The criminal law, however, is willing to exclude only some of these habitual offenders from the endlessly revolving door of arrest, confinement, release, and re-arrest. In 1966, in the cases of *Driver v. Hinnant* and *Easter v. District of Columbia*, federal appellate courts held that an alcoholic cannot be found guilty of the crime of public intoxication. Alcoholism is a disease, it was said, which destroys the individual's will to resist the constant, excessive consumption of alcohol. The public drunkenness of such a person is not a volitional act but a compulsive one, and the stigmatization of him as a criminal is cruel and unusual punishment. "It is unlikely that any state at this moment in history," argued the court in the *Driver* case, quoting an earlier legal decision, "would attempt to make it a criminal offense for a person to be mentally ill, or a leper, or to be afflicted with a venereal disease. A state might determine that the general health and welfare require that the victims of these and other human afflictions be dealt with by compulsory treatment, involving quarantine, confinement, or sequestration. But in the light of contemporary knowledge, a law which made a criminal offense of such a disease would doubtless be universally thought to be an infliction of cruel and unusual punishment in violation of the Eighth and Fourteenth Amendments."[74] The alcoholic, in short, lacks criminal intent for his unfortunate behavior,

---

[73] *Revolving Door: A Study of the Chronic Police Case Inebriate* (Glencoe, Ill.: The Free Press, 1958). See also Howard M. Bahr and Theodore Caplow, *Old Men Drunk and Sober* (New York: New York University Press, 1974).

[74] See *Driver v. Hinnant*, 356 F. 2d 761 (4th Cir. 1966), reviewing 243 F. Supp. 95 (E.D.N.C. 1965); and *Easter v. District of Columbia*, 361 F 2d 50 (D.C. Cn. 1966) (en banc), reviewing 209 A. 2d 625 (D.C. Ct. App. 1965).

and punishment can serve no useful purpose. Samuel Butler's savage attack on the harsh system of criminal law in Victorian England, which he depicted as being so senseless that it inflicted the death penalty on those suffering from pulmonary consumption, had at long last found recognition in the legal thought of the United States.[75]

While the two decisions might seem to mark a notable advance in society's methods of dealing with the problem of the public drunk, the consequent realities have not been encouraging. In the first place, the decisions of the *Driver* and *Easter* cases excluded only the alcoholic from the sanctions of the criminal law. While some legal writers have argued that most of those arrested for public intoxication *are* alcoholics—that is, persons suffering from a disease that makes it impossible for them to control their drinking—other writers (and judges) have insisted that the definition of alcoholism is vague and slippery and that many of those arrested for public drunkenness must bear the responsibility for their actions. It is well within the state's power and right to deter and punish public drunkenness, said the court in the *Driver* case—unless it can be proved that the offender was publicly succumbing to the disease of alcoholism. In many cases of public drunkenness, in any event, alcoholism is not used as a defense; or, if it is, can be rejected because the decisions of federal appellate courts are held not binding on state courts until adopted by the United States Supreme Court.[76]

The second problem arising from the *Driver* and *Easter* decisions is that in those jurisdictions in which alcoholism has been used successfully as a defense to the charge of public drunkenness, communities have quickly discovered that facilities for treating the alcoholic are completely inadequate. In the District of Columbia, for example, in the first eight months after the *Easter* decision 3400 persons were adjudged alcoholics and declared to be suffering from a disease that needed to be cured rather than exhibiting criminal behavior that demanded punishment. But there were no suitable diagnostic or treatment facilities that could handle them. Many were assigned to an outpatient program of the Alcoholic Rehabilitation Clinic in the area, which was incapable of coping with the new workload. "Since *Easter* there has been, in fact, a marked deterioration in the health of the city's derelict alcoholics," notes one writer, "a condition which goes unheeded only by a callous disregard for human life."[77] The problem of dealing with public intoxication may indeed best be taken out of the hands of the criminal law, as so many have urged; but if adequate alternative services are not provided, the lot

[75] See Samuel Butler, *Erewhon and Erewhon Revisited* (New York: Modern Library, 1927). *Erewhon* was first published in 1872.
[76] *Task Force Report: Drunkenness,* Appendix H.
[77] Ibid., p. 75.

of the alcoholic may remain unchanged. Between 1960 and 1976, arrests for public drunkenness (but not including driving under the influence of alcohol and disorderly conduct) dropped sharply, from 38 percent of all arrests to 13 percent.[78] The social problem of excessive alcohol use has not been solved, and it seems doubtful that the amount of public drunkenness has declined. It is possible, however, that it will be increasingly ignored, at least by the police, as long as it does not pose an obvious danger.

When the state erects laws to protect health, morals, and the public safety, it sometimes appears that society is more unified in these matters than is actually the case. The law speaks with an authoritative voice, its prescriptions are surrounded with the symbols of tradition, and it is easy to assume that the members of society are in accord. The dictates of the law, however, often obscure profound conflicts and ambivalent feelings in society, and they do so particularly in the case of gambling. The criminal law attempts to interdict betting on games of chance in a variety of ways, including prohibitions against gambling houses, bookmaking, and the enforcement of gambling debts. Yet many Americans do not believe that gambling is harmful or that it needs to be suppressed by the state.

Gambling

The laws against gambling in the United States are largely a matter of statutory enactment and do not have deep roots in the common law. According to the English common law, Morris Ploscowe has pointed out, "any game of chance played by a group of individuals in a private house was not a criminal offense if the gambling was not accompanied by a breach of the peace, or by corruption of the public morals, or by a general invitation to the public to come to play, or by cheating."[79] But if the common law took a permissive view of gambling, early English statutes were not so tolerant; and from the time of Henry VIII various enactments were used to try to curb the English passion for gaming. In fact, it was not merely betting which the government viewed as an evil to be restrained. Games themselves were frequently thought to be an unwholesome diversion even when no wagering was involved. Dicing, backgammon, cards—all were thought to compete with military training, to draw laborers and servants from work to play, to interfere with the proper observation of the Sabbath; and they were duly assigned criminal sanctions.[80]

It is sometimes claimed that antigambling legislation in the United

[78] *Uniform Crime Reports—1976*, p. 173.

[79] "The Law of Gambling," *The Annals of the American Academy of Political and Social Science* 269 (May 1950), p. 1.

[80] See "Gaming and Wagering," *The Encyclopaedia Britannica*, 11th ed. (1910), pp. 446–50.

States can be traced to the Puritan tradition. The claim, however, is without historical foundation. "It was during the early period in our national life, when the Puritan influence was strongest," notes Virgil W. Peterson, "that the United States had its longest experience with legalized gambling. Lotteries have been commonplace during colonial times."[81] After considerable experimentation with legalized gambling in the eighteenth century, however, the legal acceptance of gambling began to decline, and today every state except Nevada places prohibitions, of one form or another, on gambling.[82]

Antigambling statutes vary widely in scope among the different states, but most of the prohibitions apply to five main areas: (1) the running of a gambling house; (2) gambling in places such as taverns, bowling alleys, and restaurants; (3) the activities of the professional gambler, gamekeeper, or bookmaker; (4) the possession, maintenance, rental, or sale of gambling equipment such as slot machines; and (5) the activities of touts and shills.[83] Many states, however, permit a wide variety of other forms of gambling, such as on-track betting, beano, and slot machines allowed on a local-option basis. The gambling activity that is prohibited is commonly defined as a misdemeanor, although some offenses, such as the maintenance of a gambling house, are classified as felonies.

The amount of gambling that takes place in the United States each year is unknown, but various estimates suggest that both the number of people and the total sum of money involved are very large indeed. The number of arrests reported by the FBI—79,000 in 1976—is clearly no more than the most fragmentary indicator.[84] The NORC national survey of households confined itself to the question of how many people bet on the horses (both legally and illegally) and how much money they wagered. The President's Commission on Law Enforcement and Administration of Justice concluded that "the total number of horse bettors could be estimated at about 4½ million. The median amount of betting reported was about $15 a bet or about $3.3 billion annually. Since legal betting on horses totals more than $4.5 billion and the survey covered legal as well as illegal gambling, it is clear that the amount is underestimated."[85] Using other sources, the commission hazarded a guess that

---

[81] "Obstacles to Enforcement of Gambling Law," *The Annals of the American Academy of Political and Social Science* 269 (May 1950), p. 15.

[82] After the Civil War a number of Southern states used lotteries as a source of revenue, but the device was soon abandoned.

[83] See Ploscowe, "The Law of Gambling," pp. 1–8. A *tout* is a person who sells tips on racehorses; a *shill* is the confederate of a gambler, who pretends to buy, bet, or bid in order to lure onlookers into participating.

[84] *Uniform Crime Reports—1976*, p. 173.

[85] *Task Force Report: Assessment of Crime* (Washington, D.C.: Government Printing Office, 1967), p. 52. A number of problems, such as the respondent's inability to remember how much was bet and lack of knowledge of the betting habits of other members of the household, helped to obscure the results.

at least $20 billion a year was spent on illegal gambling in the United States, with $6 to $7 billion going as profits to organized crime. The great bulk of the money (an estimated $10 billion) went to bookmakers, with the remainder being distributed among the numbers game, lotteries, punchboards, illegal dice games, illegal card games, and illegal coin machines.[86]

The double truth, then, is that a multitude of laws against gambling exist in America and a multitude of people break them repeatedly. "The public press sporadically inveighs against gambling and its attendant evils," note Morris Ploscowe and Edwin J. Lukas, "yet facilitates it by publishing the data essential to gambling in many forms. Churches condemn gambling, yet profit from raffles and lotteries. Legislatures enact anti-gambling statutes, yet make it possible for states to participate in moneys wagered at race tracks. Flurries of strict enforcement of gambling statutes alternate with long periods of quasi-official tolerance. The citizen who becomes outraged at revelations of police corruption in connection with gambling nevertheless patronizes the neighborhood bookmaker or the 'one-armed bandit.' "[87]

Some people might mark this down as another case of the hypocrisy that uses the law as a mere public show of virtue, while others see the prevalent impulse to gamble as a sickness. One psychiatrist, for example, analyzing the problem from a Freudian viewpoint, regards all gambling as "a regression to the anal level of libidinous development," a substitute for masturbation and a symptom of a deep-seated illness.[88] It is a clinical notion of dubious validity. (Theodor Reik, a pupil and colleague of Freud's, described gambling in a more poetic vein as a kind of question addressed to destiny.) Much of the gambling in America, however, taking the form of off-track betting and the numbers game, is probably best interpreted within a simpler framework.[89] The small daily or weekly bets made by so many of the urban poor offer a touch of excitement, a brief but interesting contact with a larger world of money and action.

[86] Ibid., pp. 82–83.

[87] "Foreword," *The Annals of the American Academy of Political and Social Science* 269 (May 1950), p. vii. In 1976, *Time* magazine, drawing on a variety of sources, including a nationwide study conducted by the Survey Research Center of the University of Michigan, estimated that some 60 percent of the American population aged eighteen and older identified themselves as bettors and possibly wagered as much as $75 billion a year in legal and illegal gambling. See "Gambling Goes Legit," *Time* (December 6, 1976).

[88] See Robert M. Lindner, "The Psychodynamics of Gambling," *The Annals of the American Academy of Political and Social Science* 269 (May 1950), pp. 93–107.

[89] The numbers game, or "policy," is a lottery with the winning number taken from any easily verified set of public figures, such as the payoff on parimutuel tickets or the transactions of a stock exchange. A three-digit number pays off at approximately 500 to 1, with the odds varying by locality. The world *policy* is said to come from the Italian *polizza*, tickets used in lotteries conducted among early Italian immigrants. See Oswald Jacoby, "The Forms of Gambling," *The Annals of the American Academy of Political and Social Science* 269 (May 1950), pp. 39–54.

They provide a basis for gossip, for tales and daydreams of lucky wins. Comfortable habit rather than unconscious compulsion is likely to be behind much of the wagering engaged in by so many people.[90]

Those who support the prohibition of gambling are not, however, inclined toward such a benign view of the matter. Gambling, it is held, ruins the character and impoverishes the player. The following statement, made in 1935, typifies an attitude that is still current: "The Federal Council of Churches reaffirms its vigorous opposition to gambling which we regard as an insidious menace to personal character and morality. By encouraging the idea of getting something for nothing, of getting a financial return without rendering any service, gambling tends to undermine the basic idea of public welfare."[91]

The condemnation of "getting something for nothing" appears to be an important element in understanding society's use of the criminal law for the enforcement of morals. Just as drugs are thought to provide unearned pleasure, prostitution to provide sexual intimacy unearned by love, and alcoholic intoxication to provide an undeserved escape from reality, so too is gambling often regarded as providing the hope of money without work. The activities declared a crime violate one of the most cherished moral tenets of American society—namely, that the desired things in this world do not come free, they must be earned. While there may be no victim other than the self, the fact remains that a fundamental norm is being challenged, and many people believe that such challenges must be answered with the sanctions of the criminal law.

Many others, of course, disagree. In the matter of gambling, as in other crimes discussed in this chapter, it is claimed that the individual does not harm others; the individual does not harm himself; and even if it can be shown that the individual is harmed by his behavior, that is his concern and no business of the state. And once again, as in the case of marijuana, it is argued that the social and economic costs of trying to control gambling by means of the criminal law far outweigh any possible good that is achieved. The illegal gambling profits that flow to organized crime provide a major basis for police corruption. Gambling, it is said, should be legalized and run by the state or by licensed private enterprises.

Other people arguing in favor of legalized gambling say that gambling is an irrepressible human weakness—it has always been with us and always will be—and that the state should bow to the inevitable. The argument is spurious, however; murder and rape are also persistent forms of behavior, but few would suggest that they should therefore be legalized.

[90] See Erving Goffman, *Interaction Ritual* (Chicago: Aldine, 1967), pp. 149–270.
[91] Quoted in Paul S. Deland, "The Facilitation of Gambling," *The Annals of the American Academy of Political and Social Science* 269 (May 1950), p. 24.

Social scientists have expressed doubts about legalization, not on the grounds of morality or a commitment to earning one's way, but because the existing illegality of gambling in the numbers game is economically advantageous to the poor.[92] As St. Clair Drake and Horace Cayton pointed out more than two decades ago, the numbers game in the Black Belt of Chicago has provided an important source of capital for legitimate black business enterprises.[93] In addition, gambling has long provided jobs as numbers operators for people living in the ghetto and in that way plays a vital part in the black community's economy.[94] However, whatever may be the merits of maintaining the status quo from the viewpoint of ghetto residents, many cities and states have found themselves forced to consider the legalization of gambling in the desperate search for new sources of revenue. Connecticut, Delaware, Illinois, Maine, Maryland, Massachusetts, Michigan, Nebraska, New Hampshire, New Jersey, New York, Ohio, Pennsylvania, and Rhode Island have all approved the operation of a state lottery in the hope that it would provide a relatively painless way of raising money; and New York has created the Off-Track Betting Corporation (OTB). "Start a new morning routine," says an OTB advertisement. "Coffee and doughnuts and the daily double."[95]

Thus there is likely to be continuing pressure for the decriminalization of gambling. It will not gather its strength from theoretical arguments but from the economic needs of the states, which covet the profits that now flow into illegal channels.

The current phase of experimentation with legalized gambling has been too brief for a full and accurate assessment. Three important questions remain to be answered. First, a great deal of the illegal gambling that now takes place involves small bets, of 50 cents or less, placed with a local, familiar numbers man. State lotteries and legal off-track betting may find it difficult to compete with such a system.[96] Second, there is the possibility that racketeers will infiltrate state-run gambling operations. It

[92] See Geis, *Not the Law's Business?* Chapter VI.

[93] *Black Metropolis: A Study of Negro Life in a Northern City* (New York: Harcourt, Brace, 1945), pp. 493–94.

[94] One writer has claimed that some 60 percent of Harlem's economic life depends on the numbers game. See Fred J. Cook, "The Black Mafia Moves into the Numbers Racket," *New York Times Magazine* (April 4, 1971), pp. 24–27ff. Other writers, however, have been extremely skeptical about the alleged economic benefits, since most of the profits are said to be drained out of the black community into the hands of organized crime, which remains largely white. See Geis, *Not the Law's Business?* pp. 226–31.

[95] "City Betting Agency Sets March 29 Goal," *The New York Times* (March 3, 1971), quoted in Geis, *Not the Law's Business?* p. 234. The move toward the legalization of gambling began with New York City mayor William O'Dwyer's request to the New York State Legislature, in 1950, for a change in the law. See "Legalized Gambling in New York?" *The Annals of the American Academy of Political and Social Science* 269 (May 1950), pp. 35–38.

[96] There is, of course, the additional fact that state-sanctioned gambling exposes winnings to taxation. See "Bettors Up in Arms Over New OTB Tax," *The New York Times* (June 30, 1974).

is frequently alleged, for example, that organized criminals manage to skim off large sums of money from the gambling establishments in Las Vegas and Reno. Third, the impact of widespread, legally recognized gambling on the quality of community life is unknown. Many people continue to argue that if gambling is given the backing of the state, an unacceptable increase in economic losses to the poor and a general lowering of ethical standards are likely to result.[97]

These problems may turn out to be relatively insignificant, and gambling may become one more form of social behavior—like miscegenation and blasphemy—that has successfully made the transition from criminal to noncriminal. In the meantime, it is difficult to disagree with the balanced judgment of Gilbert Geis on the subject: "Gambling is one of the less serious vices in regard to its direct harm to the individual. It has no physical consequences except by indirection. It is not apt to be particularly time-consuming. It may engender a philosophy rather unrealistic in terms of mundane existence, but it is arguable whether such a philosophy is more detrimental than enabling to an individual. That some individuals who do not now gamble will become inextricably involved in its operation if it were made legal, to the point that they will be defined as 'problem' gamblers, seems inevitable. . . . Society might care to discover techniques to handle the situation that are a good deal more effective than those hit-and-miss, haphazard approaches now in fashion when gambling flourishes undercover."[98]

Organized Crime

The existence of a strong and persistent demand for such illegal goods and services as illicit sex, drugs, and gambling presents an opportunity to make enormous profits. The cost of providing such goods and services is low, and the price can be set high by those able and willing to circumvent the law in the creation of a monopoly based on the intimidation of small operators and competitors.[99] It is this situation that allows organized crime to flourish in the United States in an illegal parody of American business enterprise.[100]

[97] That large numbers of people in society can become infused with a feverish desire for gambling—with disastrous results—is undeniable. See Charles MacKay, *Extraordinary Popular Delusions and the Madness of Crowds* (Boston: L. C. Page, 1962).

[98] *Not the Law's Business?* p. 245.

[99] See Thomas C. Schelling, "Economic Analysis and Organized Crime," in John E. Conklin, ed., *The Crime Establishment* (Englewood Cliffs, N.J.: Prentice-Hall, 1973), pp. 75–103.

[100] The term *organized crime* is somewhat ambiguous, since it is used to refer to gangs of professional thieves, extortion rings, and other enduring groups of criminals, as well as to gangs supplying illicit goods and services. It is the last, however, that is the focus of our present discussion.

Organized crime has long fascinated the American public, as is evidenced by the innumerable books, movies, and newspaper articles exploring the nature of the racketeer.[101] Violence, the themes of loyalty and betrayal, and the role of the ethnic community all undoubtedly contribute to the popularity of those constructions of the mass culture that make the organization man of the underworld a figure of central importance. For critic and essayist Robert Warshow, however, the basis of the gangster's appeal to the imagination lies deeper. The gangster is what we want to be and are afraid we may become. He is thrown into the competitive crowd without any preparation or advantage, said Warshaw, and is forced to determine the pattern of his life and impose it on others by the strength of his personality. His career is a savage drive for success, and the typical gangster film presents a steady upward climb that is followed by an inevitable—and disastrous—fall. The gangster's life must end in failure, for every attempt to succeed is an act of aggression that at last leaves him isolated, guilty, and defenseless among enemies. The gangster film as fictional work, then, lays bare the modern sense of tragedy in a society that is hagridden by the idea of success. It is the *No* to the great American *Yes*, presented as entertainment and bound in a conventional form as rigid as Elizabethan tragedy or Restoration comedy.[102]

This interpretation of the meaning of the gangster, insightful though it may be, concentrates on the individual criminal. For a great many people, however, the most significant aspects of organized crime in America are the facts—or the alleged facts—that it is run by the Mafia and that it controls illicit gambling, the distribution of illegal drugs, and much of the prostitution in the United States. Pictured as a secret organization based on ties of kinship and ethnic solidarity, wedded to violence and operating outside the law, the Mafia reigns in popular thought as a dangerous conspiracy powerful enough to undermine the American social order. There is a sinister criminal organization known as the Mafia, the Senate Crime Investigating Committee, headed by Senator Estes Kefauver, said in 1951, and it operates throughout the United States and has ties in other countries. It has infiltrated legitimate business, protected its leaders from prosecution and punishment, corrupted the political process, and murdered untold numbers of people in gangland slayings.[103] Warnings about the power of organized crime were not new to the 1950s. "Before we can settle any other question, before any other question is

---

[101] *The Godfather* movies are said to be among the greatest money-making films of all time (see Conklin, *The Crime Establishment*, p. 1). They are, moreover, part of an enduring Hollywood tradition that stretches back to *Little Caesar* of the 1930s.

[102] "The Gangster as Tragic Hero," in *The Immediate Experience* (Garden City, N.Y.: Anchor Books, 1964).

[103] See Gus Tyler, ed., *Organized Crime in America* (Ann Arbor: University of Michigan Press, 1962), pp. 10–15.

worth settling," declared the *Saturday Evening Post* in the early 1930s, "we must get a decision on who is the Big Shot in the United States—the criminal or the government." [104]

Whether organized crime or the government has the upper hand in the United States is still unsettled, in the opinion of many, with the Mafia standing a good chance of coming out ahead. And there is a "lunatic fringe," according to Francis A. J. Ianni, which sees even greater plots than those identified by the Kefauver Committee. At various times, he notes, there have been reports that the Mafia was approached by the Ghanaian government to get rid of the embarrassing exiled Nkrumah; that the Cosa Nostra (the term, as we shall see, is sometimes used interchangeably with Mafia) "was issuing guns to black nationalists in Chicago as middleman for a southern white extremist seeking to stir racial wars in the North; that the New Orleans *Mafia* engineered the assassination of John F. Kennedy for Lyndon Johnson and his associates; that the *Mafia* was using Italian supplied guns and ships in Haiti to protect the regime of the late President Duvalier and their gambling interests against rebels backed by the CIA; and most recently, that the *Cosa Nostra* organized attacks on pacifist students by 'hard-hat' construction workers in New York." [105]

Disclosures that the CIA and individuals from the ranks of organized crime have been involved in plots to assassinate Castro have made the "lunatic fringe" appear more prescient than lunatic. There is much debate, nevertheless, about the nature of organized crime, its precise structure, and the extent of its power. In particular, questions have centered on the Mafia.

The Mafia: Reality or Myth? Despite the frequent discussions of the Mafia in the press, the dramatic testimony before government committees, and the analysis of Mafia structure by a number of American criminologists, more than a few social scientists have expressed considerable doubt about the existence of the Mafia as a nationally organized criminal syndicate staffed by Italian-Americans and bound by the rules of *Omerta*, the code of secrecy. [106]

Donald R. Cressey is one of the most eminent criminologists who have supported the claim that the Mafia is more than the invention of an overheated imagination. Because he was one of the sociological consultants to the President's Commission on Law Enforcement and Adminis-

[104] Ibid., p. 5.

[105] *A Family Business* (New York: Russell Sage Foundation, 1972), p. 7.

[106] Ianni has called these contrasting views of the Mafia "one of the most extraordinary sociological puzzles of the times" (*A Family Business*, p. 8). For a discussion of the issue in the literature of criminology, see John F. Galliher and James A. Cain, "Citation Support for the Mafia Myth in Criminology Textbooks," The American Sociologist 9 (May 1974), pp. 68–74.

tration of Justice, his views are worth considering at some length. "Upon being invited to work for the Commission," he has written, "I was not at all sure that a nationwide organization of criminals exists. Discussions with my friends and colleagues indicated, and continue to indicate, that this skepticism is widely shared. I changed my mind. I am certain that no rational man could read the evidence that I have read and still come to the conclusion that an organization variously called 'The Mafia,' 'Cosa Nostra,' and 'The Syndicate' does not exist. Henry S. Ruth, Jr., Deputy Director of the President's Commission, invited law enforcement and investigative agencies to submit reports on organized crime to the Commission. A summer spent reading these materials, exploring other confidential materials, and interviewing knowledgeable policemen and investigators convinced me."[107]

A nationwide alliance of at least twenty-four tightly knit "families" exists in the United States, Cressey concluded, placing the term *families* in quotation marks to indicate that not all members are actually related by blood or marriage. The members of these families are all Italians and Sicilians, or of Italian and Sicilian descent; those on the Eastern seaboard refer to the national organization as Cosa Nostra ("Our Thing") rather than Mafia. The identity of those holding key positions in the families—boss; underboss; lieutenants, or captains; counselor; and soldiers, or button men—is known to law enforcement officials, as are the names of those who occupy other positions, such as buffer, money mover, enforcer, and executioner. The families are linked to one another, and to non–Cosa Nostra syndicates, by agreements or treaties, and by common deference to a commission made up of the leaders of the more powerful families. The members of this system control most of the illegal gambling in the United States and act as the principal loan sharks. They are the major dealers in narcotics and have infiltrated a number of labor unions, through which they extort money from employers and cheat the union rank-and-file. They have a virtual monopoly on several legitimate businesses, such as the sale and distribution of juke boxes and vending machines, and they own numerous enterprises, including restaurants, bars, hotels, trucking companies, and factories. They also "own" a number of government officials, including judges, at the local, state, and federal levels.[108]

This portrayal of organized crime in the United States makes the Mafia appear to be a powerful national criminal group, ethnically restricted and operating with impunity outside the law. If, in fact, the Mafia now functions as a nation within a nation, and if, as many writers have claimed, stricter enforcement of the existing criminal law would have little im-

[107] *Theft of the Nation* (New York: Harper & Row, 1969), p. x.
[108] Ibid., p. x–xi.

Ripping Out the Label That Says "Made in Sicily"

Most Americans take for granted that the heart of organized crime is a secret criminal conspiracy of Sicilian origins that is variously called the Mafia or Cosa Nostra. Belief in the Mafia, once derided, has grown steadily over the last few decades until today it is a journalist's cliché, and the cornerstone of public policy against organized crime. We repudiate that approach.

We do not believe that criminal groups, whether consisting of Italians or others, are nearly so organized as theories about the Mafia imply. The appropriate way to understand criminal organization is not in terms of formal lines of authority and responsibility—as in the analogies to a corporation or military unit that pervade the literature on the Mafia—but as a series of endlessly shifting alliances among men who are endangered on all sides, by the police and by each other.

We reject the chronology that sees a single chain of continuous development linking present-day American organized crime to a Sicilian past.

We know that much in that reputed chronology—from the origins of the Mafia in a Sicilian

revolt against the French in 1282 to the 1931 gangland murders of scores of old-time "greasers" by ambitious organizers of a modern Mafia—is demonstrably false. We strongly suspect that other commonly accepted "facts" are false as well.

We reject the premise that organized crime is dominated by a single ethnic group. True, criminal groups are often composed of individuals with the same ethnic origins, since shared ethnicity is one basis for the trust that cooperation requires. But the ethnic origins important in criminal groups differ by place and, even more so, by type of criminal activity. The notoriety of Italian-American gangsters simply reflects an obsession with the Mafia that leads law-enforcement agencies so to concentrate their energies on Italians that much is known about them and little about others.

Debate over organized crime has inevitably swirled around the question of whether there is a Mafia—the wrong question, unfortunately. Given the prominence of Italian-American gangsters over the last half century, simply to answer, "No, there is not a Mafia," appears to many to stand reality on its head; but acceptance of the "Mafia" notion brings with it a false emphasis on the cultural origins of organized crime that obscures its actual roots in American society.

According to theories about the Mafia, organized crime is alien to American life, arising from the values of a specific ethnic group—values antithetical to mainstream America. Although Mafiologists have often Americanized the Mafia by likening it to General Motors, underneath the analogy the belief remains intact that organized crime is the fault of some outsiders.

The "Mafia" view has led Americans to see organized crime as an ethnic conspiracy motivated by a tradition of criminality and a sense of particularistic loyalty alien to a democratic, industrialized society.

What this view ignores is the link between the activities of criminal groups and a wider range of activities that are inherently American and fundamentally linked to a market economy. The activities labeled "organized crime" are not simply vice crimes; more important is their entrepreneurial character. When viewed apart from traditional assumptions about lower-class crime and immigrant groups, they become part of a much wider problem that includes white-collar crime.

Illegal practices in the nursing-home industry; electrical-industry price-fixing of the early 1960's; the collapse of the Equity Funding Corporation of America—all are part of the same spectrum. Together with traditional organized criminal activity, they represent the extension of entrepreneurial behavior into areas normally proscribed, for the pursuit of profit and often in response to illicit demand. By this description, the loan shark is a banker; the drug and cigarette smuggler is a wholesaler; and the bribe-taker is a power-broker. Organized crime cannot be dealt with effectively until the current preoccupation with criminal conspiracy is traded for such a wider view of illicit enterprise.

The popular notion of "Mafia" has led to an insatiable fascination with the trappings and ritual of a secret criminal conspiracy, stimulated by romantic concoctions like "The Godfather." The consequences would be serious enough if they ended with a simplistic equation between Italians and organized crime. But official attempts to understand and control organized crime have fallen victim to the same fascination, which the Justice Department's promises to eschew the word "Mafia" do little to end.

Despite the millions spent to fight it, organized crime flourishes. It should be obvious that current strategies for its control are bankrupt. This is because the concept on which they are founded is bankrupt. It is time for a new view that focuses on the dynamics of American life rather than romantic imaginings about Italians.

pact—even if the police were authorized to use electronic surveillance to a greater extent than is now the case—then the following recommendation by Cressey for a policy of appeasement might seem reasonable. He has argued that "our State Department and Department of Defense rightfully engage in negotiations with cold-war and hot-war enemies. Once Cosa Nostra has been precisely defined as a unit, in somewhat the same way the Soviet Union and Cuba are identified as units, then there can be 'tacit or explicit understandings analogous to what in the military field would be called limitations of war, the control of armament, and the development of spheres of influence.' " [109]

A number of other writers, however—including Albini, Bell, Hawkins, Horton and Leslie, Ianni, Turkus and Feder, and Tyler—contend that the present existence of a nationwide bureaucraticized criminal syndicate staffed exclusively by Italian-Americans is simply not supported by the evidence. [110] Gordon Hawkins is perhaps the most caustic of these critics. He claims that the question of whether the Mafia is a reality is similar in many respects to theological disputes about the existence of God. The Mafia is described, he says, as invisible, nonmaterial, eternal, omnipresent, and omnipotent; and, like a belief in God, a belief in the Mafia requires an act of faith—for proof of its existence appears woefully inadequate. The Kefauver committee claimed again and again that the Mafia threatened the nation; but evidence consisted largely of repeated assertions; and later investigations, such as by the McClellan committee (1963) and the President's Commission on Law Enforcement and Administration of Justice, provided little additional documentation. Facts to support allegations of initiation rites, organizational structure and discipline, patterns of mutual aid, and precepts binding on all Mafia members have failed to materialize. The meeting at Apalachin, New York, at the home of Joseph Barbara, on November 14, 1957, at which some fifty-eight men—the number varies from one report to another—were picked up by the police is often cited as proving the existence of a national criminal syndicate. In actuality, argues Hawkins, the purpose and nature of the meeting have never been established, and the conviction on a criminal charge of all the men arrested was reversed on appeal. [111]

[109] See ibid., p. 323.

[110] See Joseph L. Albini, *The American Mafia: Genesis of a Legend* (New York: Appleton-Century-Crofts, 1971); Daniel Bell, "Crime as an American Way of Life," *Antioch Review* 13 (June 1953), pp. 131–54; Gordon Hawkins, "God and the Mafia," in John E. Conklin, *The Crime Establishment*, pp. 43–72; Paul B. Horton and Gerald R. Leslie, *The Sociology of Social Problems* (New York: Appleton-Century-Crofts, 1960); Francis A. J. Ianni, *A Family Business*; Burton B. Turkus and Sid Feder, *Murder, Inc.: The Story of the Syndicate* (New York: Permabooks, 1952); and Gus Tyler, *Organized Crime in America.*

[111] Hawkins, "God and the Mafia," pp. 67–70.

Is the Mafia, then, simply the stuff of legend? Or are the skeptics failing to see a real but elusive, nationally organized criminal conspiracy? The truth of the matter probably falls somewhere between the two positions. Before the Second World War the Mafia might have existed as a well-demarcated social group composed of Italians and Sicilians with entrenched criminal customs—particularly in Chicago and New York. But it has probably been replaced by a more ordinary species of organized crime that goes by various names, recruits from many sources, and enforces silence not by blood oaths and other rituals but by the mundane threat of retaliation. While there may well be cooperation among local gangs on occasion (such as the mutual use of wire services for gambling, money lending, and information sharing), the existence of a national governing board appears doubtful. The internal organizational structure of local gangs around the country remains largely unknown, despite the impressive organizational chart presented by the President's Commission on Law Enforcement and Administration of Justice.[112] As Cressey himself has pointed out, "Our knowledge of the structure which makes either Cosa Nostra or 'organized crime' organized is only a little better . . . than the knowledge of Standard Oil which could be gleaned from interviews with gasoline-station attendants."[113] Social relationships within a gang are more likely to be patterned on the ties of kinship than on the formal roles of a business bureaucracy, although some division of labor and elements of hierarchy are surely present.[114] Organized crime, then, is undoubtedly a feature of the American scene, but it is probably neither quite the Mafia of legend nor a casual grouping of crooks.[115]

The Role of Organized Crime in Society

If our knowledge of organized crime in the United States is still far from precise and marked by a good deal of heated debate, some aspects of racketeering seem clear. A number of ethnic groups, including Irish, German, Jewish, and Italian immigrants, supplied a variety of illicit goods and services in the years before Prohibition.[116] It was the Eighteenth Amendment, however, that presented a major opportunity for large-scale profits, although few people at the time seemed aware of the problems of enforcement. "We shall see," said the first Prohibition com-

[112] Task Force Report: Organized Crime (Washington, D.C.: Government Printing Office, 1967).

[113] Theft of the Nation, p. 110.

[114] See Ianni, A Family Business.

[115] For reports about the organization of the Mafia and recent struggles among a number of rivals to merge as the Boss of All Bosses, see "After the Don: A Donnybrook," Time (November 1, 1976) and Nicholas Gage, "A Gambino Who's Who, Who Isn't," The New York Times (October 24, 1976). But see also Joseph L. Albini, "The Italians and the Mafia: Reflections on the Passing of a Myth." Paper presented at the 1976 Annual Meeting of the American Sociological Association.

[116] See Tyler, Organized Crime in America, Part III.

missioner, "that liquor is not manufactured, nor sold, nor given away, nor hauled in anything on the surface of the earth, or under the earth, or in the air."[117] Gangsters, however, quickly discovered that such rhetoric offered few obstacles to the illegitimate entrepreneur, and liquor was manufactured, sold, given away, and hauled in large quantities.[118]

With the repeal of the Eighteenth Amendment in 1933, organized crime—now staffed largely by Italian-Americans, in cities such as Chicago and New York—was forced to look for other sources of revenue. Gambling and, later, drugs proved to be highly profitable enterprises; and groups of criminals carved out their spheres of influence in a series of gang wars that added "Tommy gun," "going for a ride," and "hit man" to the American lexicon. After World War II, organized crime extended its interest in labor racketeering, invested in legitimate business, and maintained its extortionate monopoly on gambling and drugs. Today the provision of illicit goods and services is probably largely a local affair conducted by individuals drawn from a variety of ethnic groups.[119] The activities of organized crime continue to be periodically exposed by governmental investigations; gangland slayings continue to be reported sporadically in the newspapers, although the number of such murders appears to be a good deal smaller than it was during the 1920s reign of gangland chief Al Capone; and the public's fascination with organized crime persists. But the handful of convictions secured by law enforcement agencies, often heralded as great victories against the mobsters, seems to have little effect on the flow of illicit goods and services.

The persistence of organized crime on a large scale in the United States for more than fifty years must be explained in terms that go beyond the personalities of particular gang leaders or a secret "brotherhood of evil" supposedly transported to America from Sicily.[120] Organized crime can probably best be interpreted as an illegal, social institution that performs important functions valued by many people, aside from the obvious activity of supplying illicit goods and services in wide demand. These functions link organized crime to a wider social world of respectability

[117] See Andrew Sinclair, *Prohibition: The Era of Excess* (Boston: Little, Brown, 1962).

[118] For an engaging history of this boozy period, see Mark Sullivan, *Our Times*, vol. VI (New York: Charles Scribner's Sons, 1933).

[119] See, for example, John A. Gardiner, *The Politics of Corruption* (New York: Russell Sage Foundation, 1970).

[120] As Ianni has pointed out, it is important to distinguish between *Mafia* as an organization and *mafia* as an attitude or state of mind. The latter, to a Sicilian, is a sense of pride, a sense of family and honor that required every man to seek protection for himself and his loved ones when the state is too weak to perform this function (see *A Family Business*, pp. 24–25). It is quite possible that *mafia* was brought to the United States by Italian immigrants and continues to shape much of organized crime and portions of the Italian-American community. The concept is similar in many respects to that of *machismo* in the Hispanic community.

and help explain why racketeering continues to flourish despite repeated exposés and the promises made in reform campaigns. As Robert Merton has pointed out, in his analysis of the political machine in American cities, corrupt political organizations have provided the legitimate community with services that are otherwise unavailable, such as personalized assistance to the poor and guidance through the bureaucratic maze of governmental agencies for the business entrepreneur. Until such benefits can be found elsewhere, any attempt to get rid of the political machine is likely to be futile.[121] Organized crime, Merton and a number of other writers have concluded, functions in a similar way. Urban rackets persist, says Daniel Bell, because they have provided many people with a means of social mobility. The early Italian immigrants found the more obvious big-city paths from poverty to prosperity preempted; and many of them, coming from unskilled, rural backgrounds, were forced into such dead-end jobs as railroad section hands, dock workers, and barbers. The second and third generations, however, became wise in the ways of the urban slum. If Italians were excluded from positions of power and influence in the Catholic church—largely dominated by the Irish— and from the desirable jobs on the city payroll, the illicit routes to wealth were wide open. The money flowing to organized crime brought individual success, but even more important, it provided funds for local political contributions that greatly enhanced the position of the Italian community as a whole. Bootlegging, gambling, and drugs helped ease the way for an ethnic group struggling to find its place in the sun; and if much of society has branded organized crime an unmitigated evil, there are many for whom it has had a far more benign meaning.[122]

The existence of the Mafia, or Cosa Nostra, then would seem to be a far less important question than precisely how organized crime is bound by functional ties to a society that continues to clamor for the extinction of the mobster. We must keep in mind Merton's assertion that periodic efforts at "political reform," "turning the rascals out," and "cleaning house" are little more than ritualistic gestures that are bound to be ineffective as long as these functional ties are ignored.[123] Since the structural features supporting organized crime—the possibility of large profits, ease of police corruption, and ethnic groups denied legitimate access to achievement—remain largely untouched, the problem will continue for some time.

[121] See Merton, *Social Theory and Social Structure* (New York: The Free Press, 1968), pp. 126–32.

[122] See Bell, "Crime as an American Way of Life," pp. 131–54. For an earlier analysis along the same lines, see William F. Whyte, "Social Organizations in the Slums," *American Sociological Review* 8 (February 1943), pp. 34–39. See also Francis A. J. Ianni, *Black Mafia: Ethnic Succession in Organized Crime* (New York: Simon & Schuster, 1974).

[123] *Social Theory and Social Structure,* p. 135.

Conclusions

The idea that "you can't legislate morality" is common in American popular thinking. Thus, for example, it has often been said that Prohibition was bound to be a failure; the law should not have interfered in such a matter; it should have left the issue to be regulated by individual conscience. Similar arguments are frequently encountered today with regard to gambling, sexual behavior, the use of illegal drugs, and other offenses found in the heterogeneous category of crimes against morals, health, and public safety.

However, whether the criminal law *should* be used to control such behavior and whether it *can* be so used are complex questions of both value and fact, not to be answered by clichés. How undesirable is the activity thought to be and should it be declared illegal by society? What standards are used to reach such judgments and whose standards are they? If the behavior should be controlled, is the criminal law the proper instrument? How effective can the criminal law be? What are the social and economic costs of using the criminal law and are they warranted by the outcome? These questions must be confronted if discussions about "legislating morality" are to take on substance.

Many of the offenses in the category of crimes against morals, health, and public safety are said to be crimes without victims. But this does not mean that the crimes do not involve a harm or that the harm is of no importance, since many people see these crimes as violations of moral values and believe that such violations should be punished or deterred no less than violations of property and physical safety. (Even those critics who feel that the criminal law has overreached itself with regard to victimless crimes may be willing to agree that some acts with no immediately discernible physical injury or loss of property—such as perjury, malfeasance in office, false arrest, or the invasion of privacy—should continue to be defined as crimes.)

In recent years the claim that clear-cut harms are caused by victimless crimes, either to the self or to others, has been much eroded. Perhaps of greater importance, the argument that these crimes are immoral has also lost much of its force for a large segment of the population; or at least a great many more people are now willing to publicly declare they no longer find the behavior morally wrong. The result is a strong pressure to decriminalize such activities as the use of marijuana, gambling, and homosexual relationships between consenting adults.

The arguments for decriminalization have received additional support from a large body of evidence that indicates our society pays a high price for its attempts at control in these areas. The prohibition of the so-called vices has opened the door to organized crime; the penalization of public drunkenness has absorbed a large portion of police resources; and the marijuana laws have alienated large numbers of young people from the system of legal authority. The benefits of these attempts at control appear to be small. There is little to suggest that gambling, the illicit use of drugs, or alcoholism is markedly reduced by police activities—although it might be argued that the law's prohibitions have at least held such behavior within reasonable bounds.

This does not mean that the majority of Americans have come to accept the concept of decriminalization. It does suggest that a significant portion of the criminal law in the United States today is subject to much dispute. Some people feel that the government has no reason at all to be in this area and that the state is simply imposing the viewpoint of a few "moral entrepreneurs" on an ill-served majority.[124] Others are convinced that the offenses involved are trivial, lacking in serious immorality, and excessively penalized. Still others are ambivalent, uncertain of their judgments, and not at all sure that the costs of law enforcement are worthwhile. And still others are certain that if victimless crimes are not suppressed, regardless of any proven harm to the self or to others, American society will become another Sodom or Gomorrah.

In short, there is enough difference of opinion to warrant a good deal of caution in treating the criminal law in the area of victimless crimes as reflecting a normative consensus. The conflicts concerning the allowable forms of sexual relations, the use of drugs, and gambling would appear to be part of a larger theme—the persistent debate over the right to differ and be different. In every society it is only a small segment of the great arc of potential patterns of social behavior that is permitted to find legitimate expression; the rest is consigned to the category of deviance. A major problem for American society today is to understand and deal with deviance that is prohibited by the criminal law and punished by the state but which might better be controlled by other means or left alone altogether.

Recommended Readings

Gilbert Geis, *Not the Law's Business* (Washington, D.C.: Government Printing Office, 1972) offers an eminently clear and illuminating account of how the criminal law tries to regulate moral behavior. The reader should also see Edwin M. Schur, *Crimes Without Victims* (Englewood Cliffs, N.J.: Prentice-Hall, 1965). An interesting and worthwhile debate concerning the concept of victimless crime is found in Edwin M. Schur and Hugo Adam Bedau, *Victimless Crimes: Two Sides of*

[124] See Howard S. Becker, *Outsiders: Studies in the Sociology of Deviance* (New York: The Free Press, 1963).

a Controversy (Englewood Cliffs, N.J.: Prentice-Hall, 1974). The legal issues and policy questions that are encountered in trying to regulate the use of marijuana—commonly viewed as a crime without a victim—are clearly analyzed in John Kaplan, *Marijuana—The New Prohibition* (New York: World, 1970) and Erich Goode, *Drugs in American Society* (New York: Alfred A. Knopf, 1972).

Organized crime, often seen as a response to society's criminalization of gambling, prostitution, and the use of drugs, is discussed in Donald R. Cressey, *Theft of the Nation* (New York: Harper & Row, 1969); Francis A. J. Ianni and Elizabeth Reuss-Ianni, eds., *The Crime Society* (New York: New American Library, 1976); and John E. Conklin, ed., *The Crime Establishment* (Englewood Cliffs, N.J.: Prentice-Hall, 1973). John A. Gardiner, *The Politics of Corruption* (New York: Russell Sage Foundation, 1970) is particularly valuable, offering a detailed look at organized crime from a sociological perspective.

Chapter 6
Political Crime

Crimes such as theft, robbery, murder, assaults, gambling, and prostitution, along with juvenile delinquency, have traditionally absorbed much of the attention of criminology. The social changes of the last decade or so, however, marked by a profound questioning of the existing social order, have stirred a growing interest in another type of criminal behavior that has long been neglected—namely, political crime. Both attacks on the political order that society is unwilling to tolerate (such as sedition and violent protest) and the illegal use of political power by those holding public office (such as the burglaries committed by the FBI in the name of national security) are included in the concept of political crime and promise to play a much larger role in criminological thought than has been true in the past.

Some criminologists, however, argue that almost all crimes are political in character and that our thinking about the political nature of criminal behavior should be greatly extended. The decision to call certain behavior criminal, it is said, is made by those who rule society and control the political process. Crimes are those acts that are seen as threatening the people who hold the reins of power and who fear for the system of privilege they have created.[1] The stigma of criminality, it is said, obscures the political nature of the behavior in question.[2]

This argument was touched on earlier, in the discussion of the conflict theory of the criminal law, and we will examine it further in Chapter 7 when we consider sociological theories of crime causation. The important point for the moment, however, is the claim that the category of political crime should include more than illegal acts of political protest and

[1] See, for example, William J. Chambliss, "The State and the Criminal Law," in William J. Chambliss and Milton Mankoff, eds., *Whose Law? What Order?* (New York: John Wiley & Sons, 1976), pp. 101–02; and Richard Quinney, "A Critical Theory of Criminal Law," in Richard Quinney, ed., *Criminal Justice in America* (Boston: Little, Brown, 1974), pp. 1–25.

[2] See Barry Krisberg, *Crime and Privilege: Toward a New Criminology* (Englewood Cliffs, N.J.: Prentice-Hall, 1975).

the malfeasance of public officials. Until we understand how the threats to the power of an elite are defined as crimes, assert a number of criminologists, we will be unable to understand the political meaning of crime and why society reacts to crime the way it does. The assertions in this area are frequently part of a larger political argument concerning the inadequacies of a capitalistic social order and are often colored by political preferences. It is clear, however, that the concept of political crime in the criminology literature is not a neat, fixed category, but a subject of important controversy.

In this chapter we will first examine the concept of crimes against ideology. We will then turn to the question of political dissent, including the long-standing tension between the First Amendment of the Constitution and the attempt to control sedition, the various interpretations of the political rebel, and the difference between aberrant and nonconforming behavior. Our third concern will be political crime in the form of governmental lawlessness. Finally, we will look briefly at the view that crime in general has a political character which must be taken into account.

The Criminal Law and Crimes Against Ideology

Much of the prohibited behavior discussed under the heading of crimes against morals, health, and public safety is commonly called victimless crime because specific individual victims and tangible harm are said to be lacking. Many people, however, would not agree that no harm has been done; in their view these crimes represent an attack on important values that deserve protection no less than property or the person. It may be unjust for the law to intervene in these areas, and the law may be grossly ineffective in trying to control the behavior in question. The first is a value judgment and the second is a question of fact. But whether just or unjust, effective or ineffective, the Anglo-American legal tradition has a long history of involvement with behavior viewed as an affront to what are claimed to be basic normative judgments; efforts to show harm to somebody or something are often added in what appears to be a rationalization or an afterthought.

The attempt to use the criminal law to protect values is nowhere more evident than in the case of political crimes. As we shall see in this chapter, the concept of political crime is difficult to pin down precisely, but one major component is that the object of attack is not a person or property but an idea of what the social order should be. In place of a victimized person we have a victimized ideology—a set of articulated values, rather than a single value, setting forth the proper distribution and exercise of political power within society. Attacks on this ideology can call forth the harshest punitive reactions and are viewed as more serious, more threatening, than a host of physical assaults or larcenies. They are also considered more threatening than other victimless crimes, for it is held that they endanger not simply the ethos of work, for example, or sexual morality, but the fundamental framework of the social order.

Although political crimes should thus be of considerable interest in the study of criminal law and its violation, the topic has, until fairly recently, remained much neglected by criminologists. "Although political crime is the oldest and perhaps most recurring criminal phenomenon of history," notes Stephen Schafer, "and because of its impact by all means the most important, it has been largely ignored in criminological studies and has been the subject of little research or analysis. It is almost as if it were considered a kind of criminological satellite, some strange body of law violation revolving around the body of ordinary crimes."[3] The political upheavals of the 1960s and '70s, however, captured the attention of numerous criminologists who now see the problems of political crime as a central concern of the field.

Political Dissent

Treason and Sedition

Treason, regarded by early legal commentators as the most serious of all breaches of the law, is the only crime defined by the Constitution of the United States. As a charter for a nation founded in revolution against a monarchy, the Constitution understandably abandoned the traditional concept of treason as disloyalty to the king and placed in its stead the idea of disloyalty to the newly emerged society. According to Article III, "treason against the United States shall consist only in levying war against them, or in adhering to their enemies, giving them aid and comfort." Killing the king, counterfeiting the great seal, compassing or imagining the death of our Lord the King—all these English definitions of treason had vanished. By express provision of the Constitution, in Article IV, it was added that "no person shall be convicted of treason unless on the testimony of two witnesses to the same overt act, or on confession in open court." The Founding Fathers, well read in English history, were keenly aware of the unproven charges and the trifling dissent that had sent many to their death in the past.

Many states have constitutional or statutory provisions for the punish-

[3] *The Political Criminal: The Problem of Morality and Crime* (New York: The Free Press, 1974), p. 7.

ment of treason, so that an act against a particular state may constitute treason as well as an act against the federal government. Treason is probably far less significant for modern society, however, than the crime of sedition, for it is in this offense that the issue of disloyalty to the government frequently arises in troublesome form to challenge the existing political order.

The concept of sedition can be traced back in English law to the statute *De Scandalum Magnatum*, enacted in 1275, which provided for imprisonment of anyone who disseminated false news or "tales" that could result in discord between the king and his people.[4] With the invention of printing and the rise of the modern state, the offense became transformed into seditious libel, and written as well as spoken criticism of the rulers of the state was declared a crime. "The ground of the criminal proceedings," said Sir William Russell in the early part of the nineteenth century, "is the *public mischief*, which libels are calculated to create in alienating the minds of the people from religion and good morals, rendering them hostile to the government and the magistry of the country; and, where particular individuals are attacked, in causing such irritation in their minds as may induce them to commit a breach of the public peace."[5] By the time of the American Revolution, some measure of freedom of expression had been won. Discussions in legislative assemblies were protected from charges of seditious libel, and the press, according to the doctrine of "no previous restraint," was free to make public criticisms of government officials without prior censorship. However, the vulnerability to a charge of seditious libel after publication remained.[6]

With the adoption of the Bill of Rights amending the Constitution, American society made a sharp break with the English legal tradition, for the First Amendment declared that "Congress shall make no law respecting the establishment of religion or prohibiting the free exercise thereof; or abridging the freedom of speech, or of the press, or the right of the people peaceably to assemble, and to petition the government for a redress of grievances." In this matter, the legal system of the United States, so often cherishing the common law of England, moved off in a new direction. Criticism of the government and public discussion of competing ideologies were to be free of the taint of criminality.

As Mark Twain has said, however, "It is by the goodness of God that

Freedom of Speech Versus Public Order

---

[4] Edward G. Hudson, *Freedom of Speech and Press in America* (Washington, D.C.: Public Affairs Press, 1963), pp. 8–9.

[5] Quoted in ibid., p. 8.

[6] See Zechariah Chafee, Jr., "Freedom of Speech in the Constitution," in Howard Mumford Jones, ed., *Primer of Intellectual Freedom* (Cambridge, Mass.: Harvard University Press, 1949), p. 47.

in our country we have those three unspeakably precious things: freedom of speech, freedom of conscience, and the prudence never to practice either of them."[7] In 1798, less than ten years after the adoption of the
First Amendment, Congress enacted the Alien and Sedition Acts, which
made it a criminal offense to write, print, utter, or publish any false,
scandalous, or malicious criticisms of the United States, the Congress, or
the President. Although the truth of the criticisms could be entered as a
legal defense, the aim of the legislation was primarily to silence those
who opposed the patriotic clamor for a war with France; and when
Thomas Jefferson became President, he pardoned or released all those
convicted or awaiting trial.

The Alien and Sedition Acts proved to be merely the first in a long
series of attempts by the federal and state governments to use the criminal law to limit the expression of political dissent. Despite the apparent
protection afforded free speech by the First Amendment, legislative enactments and judicial decisions have again and again declared that there
is a point at which criticism of the government and its policies poses too
great a danger to society to be tolerated. The dissenter must be punished
in the name of public safety. By the middle of the twentieth century,
there were more than three hundred state statutes (some of them dating
back to colonial times) directed against subversive acts and utterances, in
addition to such federal legislation as the Espionage Act (1917), the Sedition Act (1918), the Smith Act (1940), the National Security Act (1947), the
Immigration and Nationality Act (1952), and the Communist Control Act
(1954).[8] Most of these laws—generally aimed at ideologies from the far
left that lawmakers have regarded as most threatening to American institutions—have been spawned since 1900 and reflect the tensions of economic depressions and international conflicts, both hot and cold.[9] And
public sentiment, as revealed by opinion surveys, has frequently shown
a good deal of support for the idea that free speech can be dangerous.
Samuel Stouffer, for example, in a national study of attitudes toward
communism and civil liberties made in 1954, the year the Senate condemned Senator Joseph McCarthy, found that of the approximately 5000
respondents in the sample, 68 percent believed that an admitted Communist should not be allowed to make a speech in the community. Some
89 percent believed that if such a person were teaching in a college, he or
she should be fired. (Approximately 60 percent said that atheists should

[7] Quoted in Richard Harris, "Annals of Law," *The New Yorker* (June 14, 1974), p. 38.

[8] See William B. Prendergast, "Do State Antisubversive Efforts Threaten Civil Rights?"
The Annals of the American Academy of Political and Social Science 275 (1951), pp. 124–31; see
also Marshall B. Clinard and Richard Quinney, *Criminal Behavior Systems* (New York: Holt,
Rinehart and Winston, 1973), Chapter Six.

[9] Prendergast, "Do State Antisubversive Efforts Threaten Civil Rights?" p. 124.

also be prohibited from public speaking.) [10] As public sentiments like these have been converted into legislative prohibitions, it has been the task of the Supreme Court to determine the constitutionality of the legislation and to draw a clear line between licit and illicit speech.

The central problem the Supreme Court has faced has been to find the point at which the expression of political dissent can be said to create a real or substantial danger to public safety and order and to weigh that danger aganst competing social values. The Court has always argued that free speech is not an absolute right and that the government may legitimately impose limitations. "The most stringent protection of free speech would not protect a man in falsely shouting fire in a theater and causing a panic," said Justice Oliver Wendell Holmes. At the same time, the First Amendment is designed to protect free speech as an individual interest—that is, the need of men and women "to express their opinions on matters vital to them if life is to be worth living." [11]

In trying to solve the dilemma, the Supreme Court has reached a series of decisions that are frequently confusing. "The justices have never agreed in the past, nor do they agree today," noted David Fellman several decades ago, "on any single theory or doctrine, or even upon any collection of words and phrases with which to dispose of cases presenting free speech issues." [12] His comment is still valid. At different times the Court has held (1) that to be prohibited by the criminal law the words used must be "of such a nature as to create a clear and present danger that they will bring about the substantive evils that Congress has a right to prevent"; (2) that a clear and present danger was not necessary and that "a single revolutionary spark may kindle a fire that, smoldering for a time, may burst into a sweeping and destructive conflagration"; (3) that First Amendment rights have a preferred position in our constitutional law and that statutes which invade such rights are presumptively invalid; (4) and that the individual's right to free speech must give way to the state's right to suppress the utterance of offensive, derisive, or annoying words to any person in a public place, since utterances of this type "are of such slight social value as a step to truth that any benefit that may be derived from this is clearly outweighed by the social interests in order and morality." [13] Proclaiming these rather ambiguous—and contradictory—principles, the Court has swung back and forth between the

---

[10] *Communism, Conformity, and Civil Liberties* (New York: John Wiley, 1966), Chapter Two. These sentiments were often translated into action. See Paul Lazarsfeld and Wagner Thielens, Jr., *The Academic Mind* (Glencoe, Ill.: The Free Press, 1958).

[11] See Chafee, "Freedom of Speech in the Constitution," p. 63.

[12] "The Supreme Court as Protector of Civil Rights: Freedom of Expression," *The Annals of the American Academy of Political and Social Science* 275 (May 1951), p. 61.

[13] See Henry J. Abraham, *Freedom and the Court* (New York: Oxford University Press, 1967), Chapter Five.

poles of freedom and repression, attuned, it would seem, to the public mood as well as to the logic of the law. The judges follow the election returns, said Mr. Dooley—a pseudonym for Finley Peter Dunne, the shrewd humorist and journalist writing at the turn of the century—and few would quarrel with him.

Defining Political Crime Although freedom of speech has long been a complex issue in the question of how and why our society marks certain types of political dissent as a crime, in recent years the problem of political dissent has grown still more complicated. Both opposition to the existing political structure and society's reaction to such opposition have a tendency to escape their obvious boundaries: first, "ordinary" crimes can be invested with political meaning and used as symbolic means of expressing dissent; and, second, those expressing political dissent, both legally and illegally, can be treated as "ordinary" criminals, with the enforcement of the criminal law used as a means of striking back at opponents of the government and its policies. Thus, for example, behavior ranging from vandalism to random acts of physical violence may be defined by individuals as an expression of a political ideology in conflict with the ideology embedded in law; and political dissenters may be prosecuted for loitering, driving without a taillight, trespassing, violating fire ordinances, and other minor offenses. In both cases what can be called "ordinary" crime has become "politicized." Affluent, politically conscious youths, among whom radical ideas have found their most vigorous adherents, form a special stratum of the nation's population, argues Robert Kelly. "A phenomenon that is increasingly widespread among them is stealing and shoplifting, carried off under the rubric of 'ripping off' the system, or revolutionary reappropriation of goods and services. . . . Many of those who steal and pilfer genuinely feel themselves to be part of a revolutionary vanguard whose role is to subvert an allegedly debased and hopelessly philistine world."[14] Similarly, the police may feel that they are acting in defense of the beleaguered ideology of the status quo when they arrest dissenters for minor violations of the law—as, for example, when the police arrested civil rights workers James Earl Chaney, Andrew Goodman, and Michael H. Schwerner for infractions of the traffic laws, before the three were murdered in Neshoba County, Mississippi, in 1964.[15]

The ideological quality of "politicized" acts, in which the underlying meaning may not be immediately or readily discernible, is also to be

[14] Robert J. Kelly, "New Political Crimes and the Emergence of Revolutionary Nationalist Ideologies," in R. Serge Denisoff and Charles H. McCaghy, eds., *Deviance, Conflict and Criminality* (Chicago: Rand McNally, 1973), p. 236.

[15] See Jethro K. Leberman, *How the Government Breaks the Law* (Baltimore: Penguin Books, 1973), p. 129.

found in some forms of civil disobedience, in which the law being violated has little to do with the governmental policy being opposed. The illegal blocking of a road, for example, may be a means of protesting military bombings or racism in public policies. Any attempt to understand the behavior outside its political context is obviously fruitless.[16]

In analyzing political crime, then, as in analyzing all forms of social behavior, we cannot ignore the meanings that individuals attach to their behavior; much political crime is important because of its latent rather than manifest content, and the behavior itself covers a bewildering spectrum of activities. Nevertheless, as a working definition, most political crimes probably fall into the following categories: (1) acts prohibited by the criminal law that are undertaken in an attempt to change the existing structure of political power; (2) illegal efforts to seize or maintain political power, as in a coup d'état or the wrongful imprisonment of political opponents; (3) refusals to obey the law on the basis of political or ideological beliefs; and (4) either failure to enforce the law or discriminatory enforcement of the law for political ends, as in cases of political favoritism and political harassment. The crucial feature of political crimes, then, is the political character of the lawbreaker's objectives.[17] Depending on purpose as an element in defining political crime does, of course, present certain hazards, since purposes are often difficult to establish and invite subjective interpretation. Nonetheless, many writers concerned with the problem of political crime follow such usage either implicitly or explicitly, and it would appear to open up the most fruitful lines of inquiry.

With purpose as the crucial element in the definition of political crime, a number of attempts have been made to describe political criminals. Typically, they are seen as different from run-of-the-mill offenders; and their behavior, it is argued, must be interpreted in a different light. Marshall Clinard and Richard Quinney, for example, have asserted that, in general, political criminals do not view themselves as criminals. For most political offenders, violations of the law are committed to make a political point or to bring about political change. The goals of the political offenders, they claim, "are not personal, but are deemed desirable for the larger society. The actions are usually public rather than private. The po-

The Nature of the Political Criminal

---

[16] See Robert T. Hall, *The Morality of Civil Disobedience* (New York: Harper & Row, 1971); Ernest van den Haag, *Political Violence and Civil Disobedience* (New York: Harper & Row, 1972); Robert A. Goldwin, ed., *On Civil Disobedience* (Chicago: Rand McNally, 1968).

[17] The restricted concept of "political crime" discussed in legal circles is not very useful for sociological purposes. As Schafer has indicated, the term is "a somewhat artificial and arbitrary product of international law which facilitates the process of extradition and the possibility of offering asylum for certain fugitive criminals" (*The Political Criminal*, p. 28).

litical offender regards his behavior as important for a larger purpose. Political offenders carry on their activities in pursuit of an idea."[18]

Clinard and Quinney make a distinction between persons who use illegal means in attempting to change the system of power, and persons in positions of governmental power who misuse their office for political purposes. Both are referred to as political criminals, although much of the analysis clearly applies only to the former. Thus, for clarity of presentation here, the former will be referred to as *political rebels*, the latter as *governmental lawbreakers*.

Mabel Elliott, writing at a time when the memory of conscientious objectors during World War II was still fresh in people's minds, has drawn a similar picture of the political rebel: "Although some political offenders are persons without integrity who have yielded to the extensive bribe paid either by foreign powers or by local groups, the vast majority are conscientious adherents to a political philosophy which threatens the existence of the government they are opposing. Political offenders thus represent a paradox for they are criminals who carry on their illegal activities in search of their ideals. They are not imbued with sordid schemes for extracting vast sums of money from unsuspecting victims, nor are they motivated by basic desires to destroy or kill although these crimes may be necessary in the pursuit of their ideals. They are generally idealists," she concluded, "devoted to a cause (however mistaken it may be) which they place higher than patriotism or personal safety."[19]

Other criminologists have come to much the same conclusion, although they may sometimes describe political rebels in less appealing terms, attributing to them arrogance, self-righteousness, romanticism, and intolerance of those who disagree.[20] In any event, political rebels have often been viewed as motivated by an idealistic, unselfish hope for a better world and deliberately choosing political rebellion as an appropriate means. In general, their actions are portrayed as fitting the model of *nonconforming*, rather than *aberrant*, behavior (these are the two major modes of deviance described by Robert Merton). According to Merton, nonconformists publicly announce their deviance, challenge the legitimacy of the accepted norms, desire to change the norms they violate, act for disinterested purposes, and claim to be conforming to the deepest values of the society. Aberrants, in contrast, are secretive, acknowledge the legitimacy of the rules they violate, are concerned with escaping sanctions for deviations from the norms rather than with changing the

---

[18] *Criminal Behavior Systems*, pp. 159–60.

[19] *Crime in Modern Society* (New York: Harper & Row, 1951), p. 180.

[20] See, for example, William A. Stanmeyer, "The New Left and the Old Law," in Cherif Bassiouni, ed., *The Law of Dissent and Riots* (Springfield, Ill.: Charles C. Thomas, 1971), pp. 47–56.

norms themselves, act in their own interests, and make no claim to conforming to society's ultimate values.[21]

It is possible that a greater variety of motivational patterns underlies political rebellion than this portrayal suggests. Much of the recent writing about political crime has sprung from an effort to interpret the protests against the Vietnam War and racial discrimination in the United States, and sympathy with these causes may sometimes lead to an overly flattering account of the protesters. An analysis of persons on the right subverting the political process or violating the constitutional guarantees of individuals and groups—persons such as members of the Ku Klux Klan—might lead to a more complicated picture of the nature of political rebellion. Furthermore, a concern with creating a model of *the* political rebel probably renders ideological orientations far more rationally articulated than they often are. Behavior can be tinged with ideology rather than completely formed by it; a vague sense of social injustice as well as a finely wrought political philosophy can inform violent dissent.

Given these limitations, however, the description of political rebellion offered by writers such as Clinard and Quinney is of prime importance in extending our comprehension of the dynamics of criminal behavior. It is clear, they argue, "that an understanding of the political offender requires a conception of man that is quite different from the one usually employed by criminologists. The view that the criminal is produced by a variety of impersonal forces beyond his control is inadequate for the study of the political offender. Man alone is capable of considering alternative actions, of breaking from the established order. A purposive, voluntaristic conception of man and his behavior is thus essential to the study of human behavior in general and political crime in particular.

"For the most part," they add, "criminologists have concentrated their attention on the conventional (supposedly pathological) offender who challenges the existing system. That a criminal could have a moral conscience has not been seriously entertained by students of crime. No longer, however, is such a narrow view of crime possible. Indeed, the underlying character of much criminal behavior is political in nature, rather than being merely deviant or pathological."[22] The idea of *principled deviance* has emerged as an important theme in modern criminology and promises to lead to significant changes in the understanding of crime causation.

---

[21] See Robert K. Merton and Robert Nisbet, *Contemporary Social Problems*, 2nd ed. (New York: Harcourt Brace Jovanovich, 1976), pp. 29–32.

[22] *Criminal Behavior Systems*, pp. 163–64.

The social changes of the last decade or so, marked by a profound questioning of the existing social order, have stirred a growing interest in a type of criminal behavior that has long been neglected—political crime. Both the illegal use of political power by those in office and the attacks on the political order that society is unwilling to tolerate must be included in the concept.

Governmental Lawlessness

Most of the foregoing discussion of political crime has concentrated on illicit political dissent, or political rebellion—that is, attempts to change society's political institutions by illegal means. But, as indicated in the definition of political crime, another category consists of the illegal use of legitimate authority for political purposes. The problem here is not one of treason or sedition, but of the abuse of power; those in government rather than those trying to alter or overthrow it are the criminals.

As Franklin H. Giddings pointed out as long ago as 1898, one of the most important meanings that can be attached to the term *political crime* "is that of the crime perpetrated by governments for alleged reasons of state and by politicians for alleged reasons of expediency or for political advantages." The comment appears in an introduction to Louis Proal's *Political Crime* and is quoted by Schafer as an example of the long tradition of thought that sees the powerful as maintaining their privileged position by acts of illicit aggression, intimidation, and economic swindling.[23] Nonetheless, until the rise of what has been termed critical criminology (see pp. 14–22), this viewpoint achieved little prominence in the analysis of political crime. A vague, diffuse awareness of wrongdoing by those in official positions had long shaped the attitudes of many Americans toward governmental power, it is true; but not until the 1960s and 1970s did it flower into a vigorous assertion by a number of criminologists that political authority in the United States is fundamentally dishonest, bloody-minded, and ready to use a variety of technological devices for the suppression of political liberty.[24]

But the idea that those in government can be violators of the criminal law is difficult for many people to accept, according to Jethro Leberman. Although not all governments abide by the proposition that the state is subservient to the law, he argues, "the orthodox view is that it doesn't happen here. This is not merely the official line; it is the unblushing opinion of sincere citizens throughout the nation that our government is a doer of good and that our good will should be accorded it."[25] Furthermore, even if the evidence of criminal behavior on the part of public officials becomes inescapable, many people tend to interpret such behavior far differently from that of the robber, the rapist, or the murderer. Wrongdoing by the government is apt to be excused, claims Leberman, because there is a widespread attitude that "a government cannot be expected to obey laws that are inconvenient or unsuited to the needs of the

[23] *The Political Criminal,* Chapter 4.

[24] See, for example, Stanley Aronowitz, "Law, the Breakdown of Order, and Revolution," and Bertram Gross, "Friendly Fascism, A Model for America," in Richard Quinney, ed., *Criminal Justice in America* (Boston: Little, Brown, 1974), pp. 394–414 and 414–29.

[25] *How the Government Breaks the Law,* pp. 19–20.

times, for what good is governmental power if it cannot be used? If social illness from government crimes is the price we must pay for law and order, we ought to be willing to bear it. . . . The government must have a healthy contempt for the law if it is to govern at all." [26] Thus, he says, the President of the United States, the military services, the Attorney General and other executive officials, prosecutors, judges, members of Congress, and the police may break the law—yet find their lawbreaking accepted by society.

Those social commentators who are most critical of the public's willingness to accept governmental lawlessness in the name of law and order are frequently the same writers who are willing to excuse civil disobedience in the name of a humane and just vision of law and order—an irony of which Leberman is aware. [27] We might question the extent to which the wrongdoing of public officials is actually viewed as excusable by Americans in the aftermath of the Watergate disclosures; and there are, in many instances, serious problems of converting allegations of crime into legal proof, of disentangling criminal acts from other types of illegal behavior, of distinguishing personal and political ends—and maintaining some degree of objectivity in an area filled with political passion. Nonetheless, there is a substantial record of proven crimes committed by public officials in their governmental capacities that must be encompassed by any theory attempting to deal with political crime and must be taken into account by any program designed to deal with the "crime problem" in America. [28]

The list of crimes committed by public officials is a long one and includes the dismissal of persons from their jobs for revealing governmental corruption; discriminatory prosecution on the basis of political opinions; the manufacturing of evidence, including the use of perjured testimony; unlawful sentencing; the premeditated and unlawful repression of legal dissent; entrapment; illegal wiretapping; illegal search and seizure; unlawful arrests; illegal treatment of prisoners; illegal denial of the right to vote; illegal awards of state and federal contracts; bribery to influence the political process; unlawful use of force by the police; and military war crimes. [29] Politicians have long used their official position to

[26] Ibid., pp. 22–23.

[27] The government, unlike the individual engaged in civil disobedience, *must* submit to the rule of law, argues Leberman, because of its great power and because evasion of the law by the government in the case of some social good stimulates far-reaching lawlessness (ibid., Chapter One).

[28] See Frank Mankiewicz, *U.S. v. Richard M. Nixon* (New York: Ballantine Books, 1975), Appendix.

[29] Ibid. See also Theodore L. Becker and Vernon C. Murray, eds., *Government Lawlessness in America* (New York: Oxford University Press, 1971); for a brief bibliography, see Clinard and Quinney, *Criminal Behavior Systems.*

Questionnaire on Official Corruption

The following questions are offered to assist citizens in determining whether official corruption or an atmosphere that is conducive to official corruption might exist in their State or city government.

Each question is so worded that an affirmative answer tends to indicate the presence of corruption or an atmosphere that is conducive to corruption. It should be emphasized and clearly understood that one or even a few affirmative answers do not constitute a conclusive showing of corruption, however. Further inquiry into laws and regulations would be necessary for that. And only official investigation and prosecution could establish the existence of criminal activity.

But this list of questions gives the citizen a good start in determining the possible integrity of local government.

Questions

1. Are municipal contracts let to a narrow group of firms?   Yes____ No____
2. Is competitive bidding required?   Yes____ No____
   On contracts of what dollar amount?   Amount____
3. Does the mayor or Governor have inadequate statutory authority and control over the various departments of the executive branch?   Yes____ No____
4. Are kickbacks and reciprocity regarded by the business community as just another cost of doing business?   Yes____ No____
5. Is double parking permitted in front of some restaurants or taverns but not in front of others?   Yes____ No____
6. Is illegal gambling conducted without much interference from authorities?   Yes____ No____
7. Are government procedures so complicated that a middleman is often required to unravel the mystery and get through to the right people?   Yes____ No____

These questions have been excerpted from a questionnaire prepared by the National Advisory Commission on Criminal Justice Standards and Goals for its *Report on Community Crime Prevention*.

8. Are zoning variances granted that are generally considered detrimental to the community? Yes____ No____
9. Are officeseekers spending more of their personal funds campaigning for political positions than the cumulative salary they would receive as incumbents during their term of office? Yes____ No____
10. Do city or State officials have significant interests in firms doing business with the government? Yes____ No____
11. Would officials benefit financially from projects planned or under way? Yes____ No____
12. Is moonlighting by government personnel not regulated? Yes____ No____
13. Is it common knowledge that jury duty can be avoided or a ticket fixed? Yes____ No____
14. Do the police discourage citizens from making complaints or pressing charges? Yes____ No____
15. Are court fines regarded as a source of revenue for the municipality? Yes____ No____
16. Are records of official government agencies closed to public inspection? Yes____ No____
17. Are records of disciplinary action against government employees closed to inspection? Yes____ No____
18. Are citizens barred from public meetings and from access to what should be public records? Yes____ No____
19. Do State workers have to contribute a percentage of their wages to the party's campaign chest? Yes____ No____
20. Can public employees who wish to retire receive their pensions despite pending charges of misconduct? Yes____ No____

advance their personal interests, of course, and corruption of the political process for individual economic gain is a recurring theme in American life. The criminal depredations of local governments at the turn of the century in the granting of contracts and franchises, the Teapot Dome scandal, the payment of bribes to secure military contracts, the influence peddling by members of Congress and their administrative aides—these are familiar examples of the illegality that has so often tainted the practice of politics. In recent years the misuse of political office for personal profit has led to the conviction of Representatives John Dowdy and Frank Brasco; Martin Sweig, an aide to Speaker of the House John McCormack; Robert Baker, top aide to senate majority leader Lyndon Johnson; and Robert T. Carson, administrative assistant to Senator Hiram L. Fong.[30] In 1974, Vice President Spiro T. Agnew was sentenced to three years' probation and fined $10,000 for tax evasion on bribes paid to him by Maryland contractors.

While such crimes as these have been largely ignored by American criminology and deserve far more attention, they have usually involved the illegal use of political office for private ends and probably should be viewed as a species of property offense rather than as political crimes committed with a political objective transcending individual aggrandizement. The distinction, however, is admittedly blurred on a number of occasions. Thus, there are some political analysts who interpret the criminal behavior of the White House staff in the Watergate burglary and the subsequent obstruction of justice as largely a matter of individual careerism. These were the acts, says George Higgins, "of rather limited men, who had espied in the paranoia of the Administration what certainly seemed to be windfall opportunities to redeem lost hopes of self-aggrandizement by doing dirty deeds."[31] Other writers, however, are more inclined to view the criminal acts of the Nixon Administration as rooted in political ideology. "The men of the Nixon Administration," says Jonathan Schell in a perceptive analysis of the presidential scandals, "were intolerant of the shaping, restraining influence of American law. Instead of responding to the imperatives of the Constitutional system, they responded to the imperatives of another system, whose requirements and form were determined, in large measure, by national security. And since the Nixon Administration had become persuaded that the struggle on the home front against rebellious Americans was more important to the national defense than the war effort in Vietnam, the methods it used at home, even in legal encounters, were, increasingly, the methods of war."[32] It was concern for national security—distorted,

[30] See Congressional Quarterly, *The Washington Lobby* (Washington, D.C.: Congressional Quarterly, Inc., 1974), p. 46.
[31] *The Friends of Richard Nixon* (New York: Ballantine Books, 1975), p. xvii.
[32] *The Time of Illusion* (New York: Alfred Knopf, 1976), p. 156.

carelessly overriding all other considerations, meshed with a hatred of political dissent—rather than a quest for personal gain, that formed the basis for the crimes of Watergate, argues Schell.

Criminology has not yet analyzed political crime in a systematic fashion and separated such offenses clearly from other types of wrongdoing, but the need to confront the problem of political crime in the form of governmental lawlessness must rank high on the list of future areas of research. This would seem to be particularly true with regard to the lawless operations of governmental bureaucracies such as the CIA and the FBI, since it has been argued that the institutionalized criminal activity of these agencies has exerted a greater influence on American social structure than have the aberrations of a Watergate.[33]

The nature and extent of the operations of the CIA are still far from clear. What has been revealed, however, indicates that the CIA has been involved in some 900 foreign interventions over the past two decades; has clandestinely manipulated the governments of other countries; has engaged in assassinations; and has supported an extensive program of domestic surveillance. "In contrast to Watergate," says Taylor Branch, "the C.I.A. investigations proved that abuses of power have not been limited to one particular Administration or one political party. They also established facts that few people were prepared to believe—such as that distinguished gentlemen from the C.I.A. hatched assassination plots with Mafia gangsters."[34]

The CIA

The evidence shows that many thousands have died as a result of secret CIA paramilitary operations, it has been argued, although the congressional investigating committee did not, at the request of the intelligence agency, publish casualty figures.[35] The exact legal status of the activities of the CIA, however, has not been established. The CIA appears to defend its foreign operations on the same grounds as Barabas in Christopher Marlowe's play *The Jew of Malta*, written in the sixteenth century: Barabas claimed that he was innocent of fornication because the offense had been committed in another country (an argument, as John Brooks has indicated, that is likely to be used by American corporations to justify the bribery of foreign officials.[36]) The programs of domestic surveillance would appear to be illegal and possibly criminal, although a claim of immunity against criminal prosecution may be raised on the grounds that the activity was ordered by high authority. The United

[33] See Noam Chomsky, "Introduction," in Cathy Perkus, ed., *Cointelpro: The FBI's Secret War on Political Freedom* (New York: Monad Press, 1975), pp. 9–38.

[34] "The Trial of the CIA," *The New York Times Magazine* (September 12, 1976).

[35] Ibid.

[36] See Brooks, "Annals of Business: Funds Gray and Black," *The New Yorker* (August 9, 1976). See also Robert L. Borosage and John Marks, eds., *The CIA File* (New York: Grossman, 1976).

States Court of Appeals for the District of Columbia overturned the conviction of Watergate defendants Bernard Barker and Eugenio Martinez for the burglary of the office of Daniel Ellsberg's psychiatrist, arguing that the lower court was in error in not permitting the defendants to show that they had acted in good faith on a command from legitimate authority.[37] The same ruling may shield CIA agents accused of illegal acts.[38]

But whether or not they are judged to be criminal by the courts, such activities warrant the close attention of criminology as it attempts to understand the definitions of crime constructed by society. The CIA may or may not be one of the "janissaries of property" (the phrase is I. F. Stone's) protecting American capitalism at home and abroad.[39] It clearly offers an important case study in the problem of the abuse of governmental power, for which a solution has yet to be found.

The FBI   An exploration of the FBI's role in suppressing political dissent in the United States is perhaps even more crucial to an understanding of political crime. The illegality of the behavior of those in positions of power appears to be less ambiguous—and the misuse of power for frankly political purposes is brought sharply into focus.[40] The FBI has publicly acknowledged that it committed 238 burglaries since 1942 for "national security" reasons and that "numerous entries" have been made against unnamed "domestic subversive targets."[41] Phones have been tapped without authorization, informants have been employed and then encouraged to take an active role in illegal behavior, threatening letters have been sent, and property has been vandalized.[42] The targets of these oppressive tactics have frequently *not* been threats to national security or persons intent on the criminal subversion of democratic society. Rather, the FBI has deliberately followed a policy of harassment against those individuals and groups whose political opinions fall outside the narrow bounds of the established political consensus.[43] Documents and depositions made public during the last several years, says Chomsky, "lay bare a systematic and extensive program of terror, disruption, intimidation, and instigation of violence, initiated under the most liberal Democratic

---

[37] Ellsberg, a former Pentagon official, had given a secret Defense Department study of the Vietnam War to the press in 1971; and the Nixon Administration, which had ordered the burglary, was apparently seeking information to discredit Ellsberg.

[38] See Anthony Marro, "FBI Bag Jobs," *The New Republic* (July 17, 1976).

[39] Stone, "The Threat of the Republic," *The New York Review* (May 26, 1976).

[40] See John Crewdson," Criminal Charges Believed Supported in Inquiry on FBI," *The New York Times* (November 9, 1976).

[41] "When the FBI Could Break In, It Kept Doing So," *The New York Times* (April 4, 1976).

[42] See Milton Viorst, "FBI Mayhem," *The New York Review* (March 18, 1976).

[43] See Chomsky, "Introduction," p. 9.

Above the Law

Congress has now investigated the FBI and has uncovered an agency afraid of the subversive but even more distressed about open society and democratic government. For forty years, the FBI has operated on a theory of subversion that assumes that people cannot be trusted to choose among political ideas. The FBI has assumed the duty to protect the public by placing it under surveillance. For these long years, the FBI has watched over America's internal security threat and in the end that threat has turned out to be the democratic political process itself.

The executive and the Congress apparently share the bureau's concerns, because they have not terminated FBI intelligence operations. Today the FBI still conducts surveillance of

The Lawless State: The Crimes of the U.S. Intelligence Agencies by Morton H. Halperin, Jerry J. Berman, Robert L. Borosage, and Christine M. Marwick (New York: Penguin Books, 1976). Copyright © Center for National Security Studies, 1976. Reprinted by permission of Penguin Books and International Creative Management.

Americans engaged in lawful political activity. Its informer network is still in place and in operation. Its field offices may still be committing burglaries and illegal wiretaps, as the Socialist Workers party suit has shown. COINTELPRO [The F.B.I.'s counterintelligence program] has been formally ended, but other disruption programs continue. The exact scope of the bureau's activities is unknown, but its focus has not been altered. The bureau is still concerned with the opinions of men and women rather than solely with their illegal acts. The Justice Department has issued *strict* guidelines to prevent a recurrence of past "mistakes," but agents believe those guidelines authorize the bureau to continue investigating "subversive activities." The guidelines leave the matter open by permitting limited inquiries into lawful conduct. Even if that were not the case, the guidelines are only tentative rules that can be changed tomorrow by a worried executive concerned about the next political turmoil.

administrations and carried further under Nixon."[44] Among the groups subjected to such attacks were the Puerto Rican independence movement, the civil rights movement, black nationalist movements, segments of the peace movement, the radical Students for a Democratic Society, and the New Left in general, as well as the Communist party and the Ku Klux Klan.[45]

For some analysts, the harassment of political unorthodoxy by the FBI can be largely attributed to the reactionary attitudes and political opinions of J. Edgar Hoover, director of the FBI from 1924 until his death in 1972.[46] Others, more concerned with the functional significance of a national police force in contemporary America, are inclined to view the misuse of power by the FBI as rooted in the continuous struggle between democracy and property. The FBI, it is claimed, is a secret police force (because much of its activity has been kept hidden from the public) which has consistently allied itself with propertied interests to suppress political dissent, whether illegal or not.[47] This contention is open to question, as is the belief that there exists a monolithic commitment on the part of the American ruling elite to the repression of political dissent by the FBI. What is unquestionable, however, is that in recent years the FBI, subject to little outside supervision or control, has waged a systematic campaign against a variety of dissident groups, and that in many instances the threat of criminal behavior posed by these groups appears to have been insignificant.

Several reasons have been suggested for criminology's neglect of the various forms of governmental lawlessness. (The one possible exception is the illegal activities of local police.[48]) One is that the field has too narrow a scientific conception, rendering the topic unsuitable for investigation. Another is that the discipline is imbued with a zeal to control deviant behavior or with a fear of offending the ruling elite. It also appears likely, however, that until fairly recently many—perhaps most —criminologists looked upon governmental crime as the aberration of a handful of individuals that was far outweighed by the lawabiding actions of most public officials. An open, democratic society tended to be self-correcting, it was thought, and standards of behavior among public officials were probably on the rise.

[44] Ibid., p. 10.

[45] Ibid., pp. 17–18.

[46] See David Wise, "The Campaign to Destroy Martin Luther King," *The New York Review* (November 11, 1976).

[47] Stone, "The Threat of the Republic."

[48] For an outstanding analysis of how and why the police violate the law in reaction to political dissent, see Rodney Stark, *Police Riots: Collective Violence and Law Enforcement* (Belmont, Calif.: Wadsworth, 1973).

The events of recent history, including the Watergate break-in and cover-up and disclosures concerning the CIA and the FBI, have undermined such optimistic assumptions.[49] Even among those social scientists wary of tirades against the "soulless capitalism of modern America," or the "rise of neo-fascism in the United States," the threat of governmental lawlessness is no longer seen as a relatively minor aspect of political crime. "If repression is not yet as blatant or as flamboyant as it was during the McCarthy years," argues Henry Steele Commager, "it is in many ways more pervasive and more formidable. For it comes to us now with official sanction and is imposed upon us by officials sworn to uphold the law: the Attorney General, the FBI, state and local officials, the police, and even judges."[50] The area of governmental lawlessness is recognized as an important one, then, but the task of sociological analysis has only just begun.

Critical Criminology and the Politics of Crime

As indicated at the beginning of this chapter, some writers claim that all or almost all crime is political in character; they argue that the criminal law is simply an instrument designed by the ruling class to protect itself, its possessions, and its privileges from attack from below. Crimes, from this viewpoint, are acts of political revolt, prohibited and punished by the criminal law allegedly for the general public good but actually in the selfish interest of those in power.

Central to this interpretation is the portrayal of the capitalist social order as an exploitative system in which the suppression of the have-nots by the haves is an iron necessity. "The stratification of society into social classes," says William Chambliss, "where there are substantial (and at times vast) differences in wealth, power, and prestige inevitably leads to conflict between the extant classes. It is in the course of working through and living with these inherent conflicts that the law takes its particular content and form. It is out of the conflicts generated by social class divisions that the definition of some acts as criminal or delinquent emerges."[51] Barry Krisberg, arguing in a similar vein, asserts that "the concept of private ownership is based upon a form of wealth that depends upon the theft of labor power. Criminal laws and systems of law enforcement exist to promote and protect a system based upon this conception of property, and these laws and systems of organized violence or

---

[49] See Perkus, *Cointelpro*.

[50] "Is Freedom Dying in America?" *Look* (July 14, 1970), quoted in Gross, "Friendly Fascism, A Model for America," p. 415.

[51] "The State and the Criminal Law," p. 101.

coercion are thus linked intimately with those persons who possess the most private property."[52]

As suggested in Chapter 2, arguments like these often mingle political preference, theory, and factual claims in an indifferent fashion; and the central idea—that the criminal law is a deliberately created device to insure the dominance of a ruling class in capitalist society—is apt to be established by repeated assertion rather than empirical proof.

For some criminologists, however, the major flaw in such arguments lies not in their lack of clarity or absence of evidence but in the fact that they do not go far enough. The study of crime in capitalist society, it is claimed, must not be restricted to those acts declared criminal and punished by the state. Instead, we must examine violations of politically defined human rights, which include "truly egalitarian rights to decent food and shelter, to human dignity and self-determination rather than the so-called right to compete for an unequal share of wealth and power. A socialist, human-rights definition of crime frees us to examine imperialism, racism, capitalism, sexism, and other systems of exploitation which contribute to human misery and deprive people of their human potentiality."[53] Because criminology has largely restricted itself to a study of violations of the existing criminal law, argues Tony Platt, it has reflected and reinforced the values of the state and the status quo.[54] What is needed is a criminology committed to the abolition of inequalities in wealth and power.[55] Only by freeing criminology from a narrow legalism can the worth of criminology be revealed. "Actions that clearly ought to be labeled 'criminal' because they bring the greatest harm to the greatest number," declares the American Friends Service Committee, "are in fact accomplished officially by agencies of the government. The overwhelming number of murders in this century has been committed by governments in wartime. . . . The largest forceful acquisitions of property in the United States have been the theft of lands guaranteed by treaty to Indian tribes, thefts sponsored by government. The largest number of dislocations, tantamount to kidnapping—the evacuation and internment of Japanese-Americans during World War II—was carried out by the government with the approval of the courts.[56] Our concept of crime, then, it is asserted, must be enlarged to include the acts of violence and exploitation endemic to capitalism—particularly American capitalism—that have not been designated as crimes by the legal system.

[52] *Crime and Privilege,* p. 13.

[53] Tony Platt, "Prospects for a Radical Criminology in the USA," in Ian Taylor et al., eds., *Critical Criminology* (London: Routledge & Kegan Paul, 1975), p. 103.

[54] Ibid., p. 96.

[55] See Taylor et al., "Critical Criminology in Britain: Review and Prospects," in Taylor et al., *Critical Criminology,* p. 44.

[56] See *Struggle for Justice.* A Report on Crime and Punishment in America Prepared for the American Friends Service Committee (New York: Hill & Wang, 1971), pp. 10–11.

The demand for criminology to move beyond "legalism" is not new. In the late 1930s, for example, Thorsten Sellin argued that the study of crime should not be confined to the arbitrary definitions of penal codes and the rules of the common law, but should be based on scientific definitions established by scientists.[57] Sellin's objective, however, was apolitical. The effort to extend the definition of white-collar crime to include those corporate activities that are legal but are regarded as immoral by critics on the political left has long been a controversial issue. Academic criminology has resisted such attempts to broaden its scope, however, insisting that the legal doctrine *Nullum crimen sine lege, nulla poene sine lege* ("No crime without law, no punishment without law") not only provided a definition of crime but also staked out the limits of the discipline.

The claim that the concept of crime should be restricted to acts prohibited and punished by the legal system was an important element in the struggle between the entrepreneurial class and an entrenched aristocracy in the eighteenth century, notes Chambliss.[58] As an element in modern industrial society, however, it may well impede the examination of injustice, cruelty, and the callous disregard for others that do *not* fall within the scope of the criminal law. "For example," says Chambliss, "neither legislature nor appellate court in the United States would consider the question of whether it is criminal for a motion picture magnate to spend $20,000 on a birthday party for his daughter while people are starving a few blocks from the night club he rented for the occasion. . . . It is simply assumed as part of the prevailing definition of reality that such an issue is 'beyond the pale' of lawmaking institutions."[59] Since the behavior is not a crime, it is beyond the pale of criminology as well.

It is true that there are many acts—such as acts of racism and sexism—that many people find morally reprehensible and that are ignored by the criminal law. It is also true that criminology has largely confined itself to the content of the criminal law. The claim that criminology must convert itself into a political movement and concern itself with the major faults of American society is, however, an assertion of preference. Many criminologists—probably most—believe that academic study and political action are not the same and should be kept distinct, no matter how much society stands in need of reform. And an adherence to a legalistic concept of crime, as Richard Quinney has pointed out, does not necessarily place one on the side of oppression. What behavior is declared criminal by the state remains an important object of study, even for those concerned with other ills of society.[60] Nonetheless, few writers in the

---

[57] See *Culture Conflict and Crime* (New York: Social Science Research Council, 1938).

[58] See Chambliss, "The State and the Criminal Law," p. 83.

[59] Ibid., p. 80.

[60] See "A Critical Theory of Criminal Law,"

field of criminology today would deny the need for the discipline to become more attuned to the extent to which the criminal law is used to buttress the existing political, economic, and social structure. A large share of the credit for this significant change in outlook must be accorded to those writers who identify themselves with a critical or radical criminology.

Conclusions

We do not yet have a systematic, empirically based explanation for the political protest that increased in the United States during the last decade or so and that, on occasion, turned to violence and confrontation in the streets. The beginnings of such an explanation, though, do exist.[61] The following factors have surely played a part: the growing disenchantment with the conventional forms of political action, particularly among such segments of the population as blacks and the young, who felt that their voices were not being heard; the development of large-scale governmental bureaucracies which often seemed far beyond the control of the ordinary citizen; a war that was seen by an ever-increasing number of people as a useless tragedy but which the government, using a series of deceptions and falsehoods, refused to end; law enforcement officials who often viewed political dissent as little short of treason and who provoked rather than curbed violence in many instances; and the ready response of the mass media to dramatic gestures of political dissent that would win a large audience.

Attempts to explain governmental lawlessness are also in their infancy, and the task is complicated by the fact that such political crimes range from the illegal acts of local police and judges to perjury committed to hide a military massacre. A significant part of government lawlessness, however, is directed to the suppression of political dissent, both legal and illegal, and contains a common theme—an excessive fear that the expression of dissident political doctrines will somehow destroy American institutions or the "American Way of Life." Such fear is perhaps understandable, in part, as a kind of national neurosis that has long afflicted a society of diverse religious and cultural traditions; extremes of socioeconomic status; and successive waves of immigration that have introduced new customs and different styles of thought. America has been viewed by a number of social analysts as a country that has needed to be flattered or cajoled into coherence—and, in the viewpoint of some,

[61] See, for example, Jerome H. Skolnick, *The Politics of Protest* (New York: Ballantine Books, 1969); see also Irving Howe, "The New 'Confrontation Politics' Is a Dangerous Game," *The New York Times* (October 20, 1968).

coerced if necessary. Radical dissent has long been feared—a fear existing side by side with a varying commitment to freedom of expression—and the events of the 1960s brought the contradiction sharply into view. The Vietnam War, which is clearly emerging as one of the great turning points in the American experience, was a crucial factor, for it both engendered widespread hostility toward the government and served as a justification for the illegal actions on the part of government officials who were convinced that dissent in wartime was dangerously subversive.

Americans have been through a miserable decade as far as their government is concerned, notes TRB's column in *The New Republic*, through the events of the Vietnam War, Watergate, and beyond; and the issue of political crime has been a significant part of that trauma.[62] The difficult question for criminology is the extent to which those events are to be viewed as an aberration or as an inevitable expression of modern America's political and economic structure. Because the answer is by no means simple, criminology's interpretation of political crime, based on the American experience, remains uncertain. What is certain is that the "crime problem" is taking on new dimensions, and the question of political crime is in the process of moving from the periphery of the field to the center.

Recommended Readings

An excellent introduction to the subject of political crime can be found in Stephen Schafer, *The Political Criminal: The Problem of Morality and Crime* (New York: The Free Press, 1974). Also very useful is the chapter on political criminal behavior in Marshall B. Clinard and Richard Quinney, *Criminal Behavior Systems* (New York: Holt, Rinehart and Winston, 1973). *The Politics of Protest* by Jerome H. Skolnick (New York: Ballantine Books, 1969), which we recommended for the study of collective violence, is valuable here for the light it throws on political dissent.

In the area of crimes committed by public officials for political purposes, Jethro K. Leberman, *How the Government Breaks the Law* (Baltimore: Penguin Books, 1973) and Theodore L. Becker and Vernon C. Murray, eds., *Government Lawlessness in America* (New York: Oxford University Press, 1971) are especially worthwhile. In recent years, detailed accounts of illegal behavior on the part of the FBI and the CIA have raised many disturbing questions about the misuse of political power. The reader should consult Morton H. Halperin, Jerry J. Berman, Robert L. Borosage, and Christine M. Marwick, *The Lawless State: The Crimes of the U.S. Intelligence Agencies* (New York: Penguin Books, 1976) and David Wise, *The American Police State* (New York: Random House, 1976).

---

[62] See TRB, *The New Republic* (November 20, 1976).

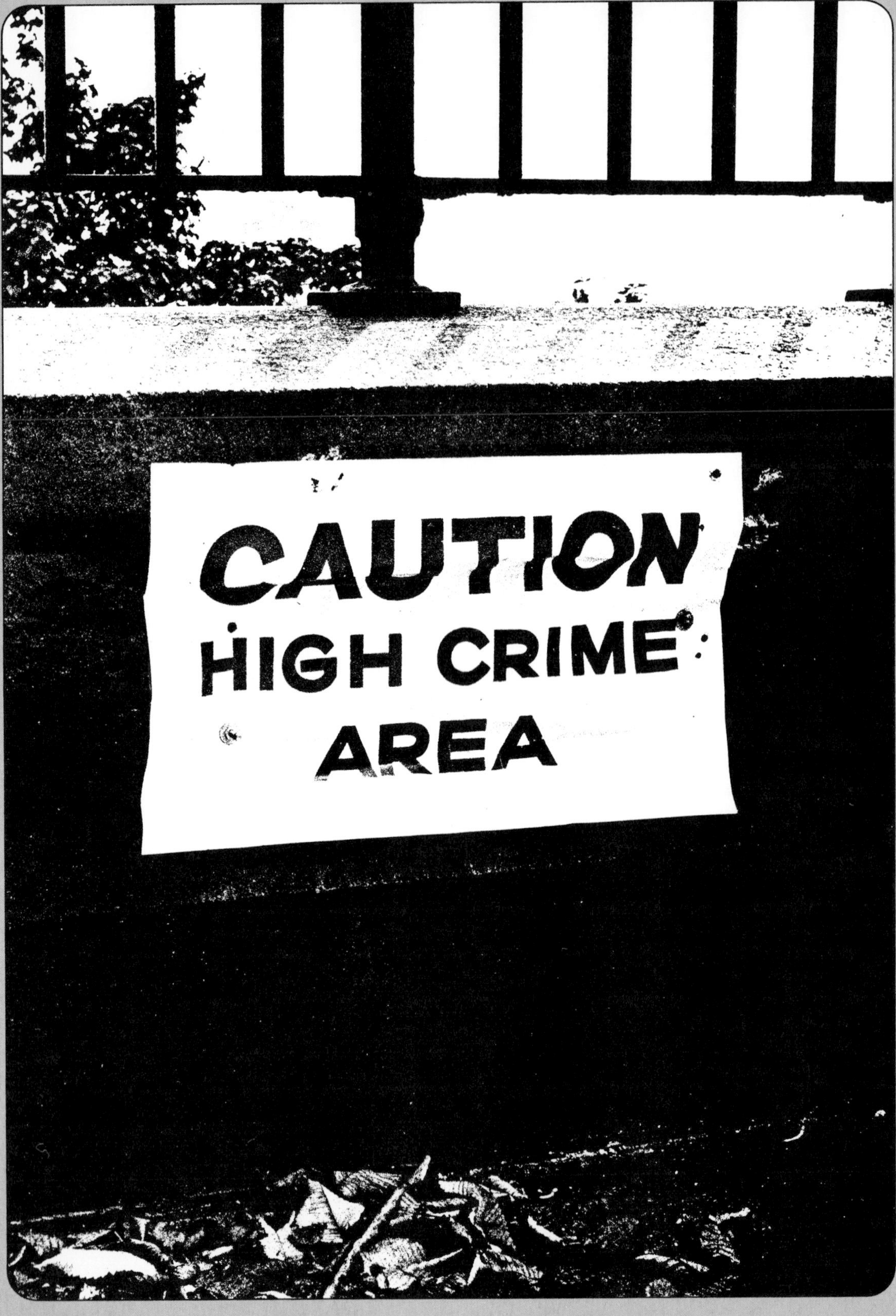
CAUTION
HIGH CRIME
AREA

Part 3

The Causes
of Crime

Cause was originally a legal concept in Greek thought and referred to human actions that resulted in damages for which compensation could be sought. The concept was too useful to be kept confined to the legal sphere, however, and was appropriated by philosophers concerned with the workings of the world.

Despite efforts to "depersonalize" the concept of cause, it has continued to convey a suggestion of a person choosing and acting, of personal responsibility. This connotation has proven troublesome for modern science in its attempt to find an order in the universe that is free of anthropomorphic notions. "Many influential scientists and philosophers have argued that the notion of cause plays a diminishing role in modern science," notes Ernest Nagel, "especially in the more advanced branches of it, such as mathematical physics, and that the notion is a relic of a primitive, anthropomorphic interpretation of the various changes occurring in the world."[1] But if it is difficult to say exactly what is meant by cause, Nagel points out, and to eliminate the connotations of intent (and some philosophers of science prefer not to use the term *cause* at all), the concept itself continues to have wide cur-

rency. It continually crops up in everyday usage and in the investigations of social scientists and natural scientists, and it appears to be an indispensable element in trying to understand the world about us.[2] There is rough agreement that if event A is "contiguous" in space and time to event B, precedes B, and can be shown theoretically to result in B by some understandable process, then event A can be said to be the cause of event B if event B occurs when the event A is present and fails to occur when the event A is absent. To this it can be added that the relationship between cause and effect is generally seen as involving multiple causal elements, as being probabilistic rather than certain, and contingent upon other events that usually remain unknown.[3]

In recent years a number of criminologists have also asserted that studies of causation are passé. Previous efforts to find the causes of crime have been in error, it is argued, because criminals have been seen as different in character, personality,

[1]"Types of Causal Explanation in Science," in Daniel Lerner, ed., *Cause and Effect* (New York: The Free Press, 1965), pp. 11–12.

[2]Ibid., p. 12.

[3]Excellent discussions of causation are presented in Morris R. Cohen and Ernest Nagel, *An Introduction to Logic* (London: Methuen, 1948), Chapter XVII; and L. S. Stebbing, *A Modern Introduction to Logic* (London: Methuen, 1948), Chapter XVII. For a more recent discussion, with particular attention to the social sciences, see Walter L. Wallace, *The Logic of Science in Sociology* (Chicago: Aldine-Atherton, 1971).

or past social experiences from those who abide by the law. In reality, it is said, criminals and noncriminals are much alike in their characteristics, differing only in their present situation or in their involvement in complex, symbolic processes that cannot be captured by the crude concepts of a mechanical causality. If criminals do differ from noncriminals in their social characteristics, this is not the cause of their illegal behavior; rather, these social characteristics are the reasons why society labels some persons criminal and ignores others. Studies of crime causation are dismissed by some, in short, not so much because the concept of cause is useless but because its application to criminal behavior is misleading or fruitless.

It is true, as we shall see in Chapters 7 and 8, that attempts to find the causes of criminal behavior have produced only limited results. We do not yet know enough about antecedent factors to predict with much accuracy which individuals will commit crimes in general or specific types of crime; and predictions for the crime rates of social groups or aggregates are little more than extrapolations. Nevertheless, studies of crime causation have served several useful purposes. They have managed to debunk a number of theories, such as those centering on the causal role of bio-logical characteristics; and they have shown the limited influence of other factors, such as broken homes, that have long been viewed as dominant by the public at large. Furthermore, if precise predictions are not yet possible—no more in criminology than in other areas of the social sciences—our understanding of the causal processes probably at work in crime has been much enlarged. The role of the social environment (such as the influence of delinquent gang membership), the pressures toward criminal behavior that are built into the social system (such as society's emphasis on economic success), the processes by which the meaning of crime is symbolized and transmitted (such as the acquisition of a criminal self-concept by means of argot) have all been illuminated. The causes of crime are now seen as a complex meshing of personal characteristics, social structure, culture, and patterns of social interaction imbued with symbolic meanings that emerge over time. If the causal analysis of crime has not yet yielded the precise predictions that science holds forth as an ideal, the goal is not necessarily hopeless—although we may do well to temper our hopes for the future with a keen awareness of the many problems of definition, data collection, and theory construction still to be solved.

Chapter 7
Social Structure, Culture, and Crime

Criminological theories are often not so much proven wrong as simply pushed to one side in favor of newer interpretations. The hope of the social sciences, of course, is to achieve an elegant simplicity, and perhaps in time the explanation of crime will form a coherent whole. Criminology, however, has grown by a slow process of accretion—in the manner, let us say, of a coral reef rather than a building designed from scratch—and today there are many theories, sometimes conflicting, sometimes complementary, having a number of variables seen as exerting a partial influence under certain circumstances. The amount of influence and the details of the circumstances often remain unspecified.[1]

In the nineteenth century, as people increasingly turned to science for a better understanding of human nature, criminal behavior proved to be an area of great interest for the emerging intellectual disciplines of anthropology, psychology, and sociology. Crime was both a pressing social problem in a time of growing industrialization and urbanization, and an intriguing, long-standing puzzle in human conduct that challenged the imagination of a scientific era.

In the eyes of the law, the causes of crime may have seemed simple enough. The legal system was built around the idea that the likelihood of crime was a product of the interplay between humankind's innate wicked passions—malice, lust, and greed—and the force of state-inflicted punishments. If penalties were quick and certain, and sufficiently outweighed the possible gratification of the criminal act, the individual would remain in the ranks of the law-abiding. If such penalties were lacking, people's wicked passions would be sure to find overt form. Given the threat of penalties, it was assumed that free will and the exercise of reason would determine the outcome and that most people would choose the path of greater pleasure and less pain. As faith in free will

[1] See Don C. Gibbons, "Observations on the Study of Crime Causation," *American Journal of Sociology* 77 (September 1971), pp. 262–78.

declined, however, along with the eighteenth century's trust in rationality, and the sanctions of the state appeared to be far from effective, the view of crime causation embedded in the legal tradition appeared less and less convincing. Other explanations found a growing audience.

Much of the initial scientific or quasi-scientific interest in crime involved a search for some aspect of the physical world that caused people to violate the law—first in the physical environment, in the form of geography and climate and, after Darwin, in man himself. Supposedly atavistic traits of a primitive form of man, excessive development of portions of the brain, and bodily anomalies—as we saw in Chapter 1—were announced as causes of crime and enthusiastically accepted by the public. To believe that lawbreakers must be marked by defects that set them apart from those who conformed to the law was comforting. Evil actions had an evil source, a biological inferiority certified by science, and thus the moral world fell into an understandable pattern. And efforts to find such characteristics have, in fact, continued into the present century. The studies of identical and fraternal twins undertaken by Johannes Lange to determine the effects of genetic similarities and differences; the examination of families exhibiting criminality generation after generation; and the work of E. A. Hooton, William H. Sheldon, and others with regard to a presumed link between body type and crime have been founded on the idea that crime is somehow due to an inadequate biological inheritance.[2] In recent years, the possibility that an anomalous combination of sex chromosomes is associated with crimes of violence has aroused much attention and is now a subject of considerable controversy.[3] In general, however, biological explanations of crime have repeatedly failed to withstand critical examination; and most criminologists today believe that in light of the available evidence, such explanations are of little use in understanding criminal behavior.[4]

By the beginning of the 1900s, much of the search for the causes of crime was shifting from the body to the psyche. As pointed out in Chapter 1, in the first several decades of this century interest focused on defective intelligence and then moved to a concern with unconscious

[2] See Johannes Lange, *Crime as Destiny* (New York: Boni, 1930); A. H. Estabrook, *The Jukes in 1915* (Washington, D.C.: Carnegie Institution, 1916); E. A. Hooten, *The American Criminal* (Cambridge, Mass.: Harvard University Press, 1939); William H. Sheldon, *Varieties of Delinquent Youth: An Introduction of Constitutional Psychiatry* (New York: Harpers, 1949).

[3] See Ernest B. Hook, "Behavioral Implications of the Human XYY Genotype," *Science* 179 (January 1973), pp. 139–50; and Saleem A. Shah, *Report on the XYY Chromosomal Abnormality* (Washington, D.C.: National Institute of Mental Health, 1973).

[4] "Laid to rest over and over, biological determinism keeps coming back to life," note Bernard Rosenberg and Harry Silverstein. "We can only marvel at the power of this phoenix which is regularly resurrected on the ashes of all criminological data so far adduced, inferred, collected, or imagined," (Rosenberg and Silverstein, *The Varieties of Delinquent Experience* [Waltham, Mass.: Blaisdell, 1969], p. 2).

conflicts. Crime, it was said, was a bursting forth of id impulses, and the criminal was acting out what most civilized men and women had learned to restrain. The criminal was still regarded as abnormal, but now the abnormality was in the mind.

There are many types of mental abnormality, of course, but five major ones have been distinguished as relevant to a theory of crime causation. First, inferior intelligence may be linked to crime because the feebleminded individual is easily led into illegal acts or is unaware of the risks that attach to his actions. Second, a variety of internal conflicts may erupt into criminal behavior that the individual recognizes as reprehensible but cannot control. Third, the individual may be characterized by a moral apathy, or indifference; the criminal act is known by the individual to be counter to the normative dictates of society, but, because of a so-called psychopathic personality, the commission of the act evokes little or no emotion on his part. Fourth, the individual may be of normal intelligence, appear to control his behavior, and hold the moral values of the society, but he or she has become divorced from reality. Acting under the sway of delusions, the individual strikes back at persecutors in a paranoid fantasy or plays the part of an avenger of imaginary wrongs. And fifth, the individual may suffer from an altered state of consciousness and be unaware of his actions, as in amnesia.[5]

These types of mental abnormality undoubtedly appear in some criminals and can reasonably be considered a cause of their illegal behavior. The crucial question, however, is whether it can be shown that criminals in general differ significantly from noncriminals in the incidence of mental abnormality causally related to crime.

The accumulated evidence of social science research after World War I indicated that the criminal population probably did *not* differ markedly from the conforming members of society, either in terms of mental disorders or personality deviations.[6] Representative samples of criminals were almost impossible to obtain, it was true; measures of crime and mental abnormality were admittedly imprecise; and the question was obscured by the chauvinism of academic disciplines. But the available data did not support the contention that mental defects or abnormal personality structure could serve as a general explanation of criminal behavior; and competing explanations of crime, drawn from sociology, became widely accepted.

[5] See Gregory Zilboorg, *The Psychology of the Criminal Act and Punishment* (New York: Harcourt, Brace & World, 1954); F. A. Wittock, *Criminal Responsibility and Mental Illness* (London: Butterworth, 1963); Edward Glover, *The Roots of Crime* (New York: International University Press, 1960).

[6] See K. F. Schuessler and D. R. Cressey, "Personality Characteristics of Criminals," *American Journal of Sociology* 55 (March 1950), pp. 476–84.

A sociological perspective on the problem of crime had been evolving gradually since the early part of the nineteenth century; indeed, the recognition of the influence of the social environment on human behavior had long been a part of society's lore about the causes of crime. Poverty, slums, and the bad example of others as circumstances that increased the likelihood of crime were certainly not the original discoveries of academic theorists.[7] As sociology developed as an intellectual discipline, however, it attempted to set such ideas on a scientific footing and to build an explanation of crime that fitted into a growing body of knowledge about the social origins of human behavior. Well before the middle of the present century, the explanations of crime offered by sociology were concerned almost exclusively with the question of why, because of past or present social experience, presumably normal people might come to commit criminal acts.

With varying degrees of emphasis and explicitness, much of the current sociological theorizing about crime causation is based on a frame of reference that involves three major elements: social values, social structures, and social norms.

Social value systems and individual goals The value system of society expresses in broad outline the things or social situations considered desirable or worthwhile. Values serve as the criteria by which the individual chooses his or her goals—ends that will not come into existence unless an effort is made to achieve them. The idea of choice or volition, then, is very much a part of sociological thinking about crime, even if the concept of free will is no longer employed. "Free will," notes David Matza, "as the phrase itself implies, takes will out of context, converting it inexorably into an abstraction of as little use as any other." But, he adds, the concept of will is indispensable in understanding social behavior, including crime, although we must remember that "will is the conscious foreshadowing of specific intention capable of being acted on or not. It is a sense of option that must be rendered in context."[8]

It is commonly argued, in other words, that criminal behavior, like other forms of behavior, can best be understood as a consciously chosen means to reach certain goals. Whether the goals of criminal behavior are the same as those of noncriminal behavior is, however, debatable. A number of criminologists discuss the goals of criminal behavior at a highly abstract level; and it is often assumed that, in broad terms, these goals correspond to those of law-abiding behavior—economic gain, for

---

[7] See David Rothman, *The Discovery of the Asylum* (Boston: Little, Brown, 1971).
[8] David Matza, *Becoming Deviant* (Englewood Cliffs, N.J.: Prentice-Hall, 1969), p. 116.

example, or prestige, or the release of emotional tension. Other criminologists see important differences in the goals of criminal and noncriminal behavior or in the value systems underlying the choice of goals; thus, for example, it is claimed that a significant variation in the values of middle- and lower-class cultures accounts for differences in crime rates.[9] Empirical research concerning the issue is, unfortunately, relatively limited.[10] In any event, sociological theories of crime usually interpret illegal behavior as a means to an end; and the possibility that crime can usefully be viewed as an end in itself or as a form of "expressive action" (an activity, that is, undertaken for its own sake, such as engaging in religious ritual or the enjoyment of music or art) has tended to be slighted.[11] The idea of individuals engaging in crime for the sheer pleasure of wrongdoing, in the manner of Shakespeare's Iago, is generally rejected as a significant possibility.[12]

Social structure and the availability of means The system of interrelated social positions—or social structure—provides the individual with a set of statuses that are acted out in a variety of role performances. In much (but not all) of the sociological theorizing about crime, it is assumed (1) that social position plays a major part in determining whether the means of achieving goals are available to the individual and (2) that a large portion of criminal behavior involves people's inability to reach their goals by legal means. Theories differ as to how the social structure restricts the availability of means for certain individuals or social groups and why some people are less able than others to tolerate the frustration of restricted means. But from this perspective crime is conceptualized as an alternative that is seized because legitimate channels of achievement have been blocked or simply do not exist. As some writers have pointed out, however, just as *legal* means may be unavailable, it is no less true that access to *illegal* means may be restricted.[13] Not everyone can enter organized crime, embezzle, or become a professional thief—and thus,

[9] See Walter B. Miller, "Lower Class Culture as a Generating Milieu of Gang Delinquency," *Journal of Social Issues* 14 (1958), pp. 5–19.

[10] See, however, John P. Clark and Eugene P. Wenniger, "Goal Orientations and Illegal Behavior among Juveniles," *Social Forces* 42 (October 1963), pp. 49–59. The question of the goals of criminal behavior is accorded much greater prominence in psychology or psychiatry—where the issue is treated in terms of motive—than in sociology. Even so, these disciplines have devoted little systematic attention to the problem.

[11] For a discussion of the important distinction between instrumental and expressive action, see Talcott Parsons, *The Social System* (Glencoe, Ill.: The Free Press, 1951).

[12] In the late nineteenth century, one textbook on criminology devoted a chapter to "pure meanness" as a cause of crime, but the idea has disappeared. See Arthur MacDonald, *Criminology* (New York: Funk & Wagnalls, 1893).

[13] See Richard A. Cloward and Lloyd E. Ohlin, *Delinquency and Opportunity* (New York: The Free Press, 1960).

when we ask why individuals engage in crime, we must consider the accessibility of both legitimate and illegitimate paths of achievement.

Social norms and internal and external pressures The individual experiences the normative system of society as social pressure arising in interaction with others who reward and punish different forms of behavior, presumably pushing his or her actions in morally approved directions. Where earlier thinkers had made much of state-inflicted sanctions as a device for channeling behavior, modern sociological explanations of crime have tended to exclude the punitive measures of the law from systematic analysis or at least to discount them.[14] Instead, the main theoretical emphasis in the area of external social pressures is placed on normative influences brought to bear on the individual by the social groups of which he or she is a member, and on more diffuse pressures of normative expectations or cultural demands flowing from society at large through the mass media, the example of public figures, and other public sources of information and attitudes.

The neglect of state-inflicted sanctions in sociological explanations of crime can be attributed in part to the rejection of the concepts of free will and human rationality mentioned earlier, as well as the apparent ineffectiveness of punishments imposed by the legal system. In the view of most criminologists, the idea that people look to the future, estimate the chances of punishment, calculate the advantages and disadvantages of alternative courses of action with mathematical precision, and then decide whether to engage in crime has little resemblance to reality. And then, of course, there is the question of why some individuals engage in crime while others do not, when they are all presumably subject to the sanctions of the state. In any event, in its study of the role of social pressures in crime causation, sociology has centered most of its attention on the variable influence of family, friends, neighbors, fellow workers, and others with whom the individual interacts on a face-to-face basis; and on the influence of the larger world—the normative structure or culture of society—to which the individual is linked by a complex web of symbolic communication.

Insofar as these social pressures are frequently seen as being on the

[14] There is, however, a growing interest in this area. See, for example, Austin T. Turk, *Legal Sanctioning and Social Control* (Washington, D.C.: National Institute of Mental Health, 1972); Charles R. Tittle, "Crime Rates and Legal Sanctions," *Social Problems* 16 (Spring 1969), pp. 409–23; Jack P. Gibbs, *Crime, Punishment and Deterrence* (New York: Elsevier, 1975); Theodore G. Chiricos and Gordon P. Waldo, "Punishment and Crime," *Social Problems* 18 (Fall 1970), pp. 200–17; Franklin E. Zimring and Gordon J. Hawkins, *Deterrence* (Chicago: University of Chicago Press, 1973); and Isaac Ehrlich, "The Deterrent Effect of Capital Punishment: A Question of Life and Death," *The American Economic Review* 65 (June 1975), pp. 397–417.

side of conformity to the law, the theoretical interests of many criminologists center on why these pressures are weak or nonexistent for particular individuals or social groups, thus increasing the likelihood of crime. It is also clear, however, that social pressures may be on the side of nonconformity to the law. A pattern of behavior labeled criminal by the legal system may be held forth implicitly or explicitly as an approved or admired form of behavior by the social group or subculture of which the individual is a member, as in the case of some forms of gang delinquency. The question then is why such countervailing standards of conduct exist. In such cases, the person views the criminal behavior as right, not wrong, although the extent to which a complete reversal of norms can take place remains a debatable point.

In addition to the external normative system, there are forces at work within the individual, commonly referred to as *internalized* norms (in lay terms these would probably be called the *voice of conscience*). Such forces may or may not be in accord with external demands, and it is important to avoid the error of regarding the individual as no more than a reflection of the social milieu.[15] Furthermore, these internalized norms are not used to evaluate conduct in a simple, consistent fashion. Such judgments are usually dependent on the specific details of the social context in which the conduct takes place. But human behavior is channeled to a large extent by the normative judgments arising within the self, and it is assumed that these norms play a vital role in determining whether individuals engage in crime.

In short, the frame of reference often used in sociological explanation of criminal behavior involves a set of elements that includes social values, social structure, and social norms, experienced by the individual as goals, the availability of means, and external and internal pressures toward conformity and deviance—a system of vectors, as it were, in which crime is seen as the result of forces operating both within the individual and in the social environment.

These forces, conceived of as being largely social in origin, are imbued with an ethical or normative character that distinguishes the wellsprings of human behavior from the causes analyzed in the natural sciences, but the language employed is often mechanistic in tone—much too mechanistic and deterministic for some critics. The image of people struggling with moral dilemmas, however, acting selfishly and unselfishly, making choices, and trying to balance their desires against what is expected of them can often be seen just beneath the surface of the most depersonalized and abstract theorizing. If the frame of reference appears

[15] See Dennis Wrong, "The Oversocialized Conception of Man," *American Sociological Review* 26 (1961), pp. 184–93.

overly simple, with its limited set of variables, it is well to remember that attempts to formulate sicentific explanations represent an effort not to capture the infinite details of empirical reality but to discover the basic principles that give reality an understandable form.

Some sociologists feel uncomfortable with these theories of crime causation on other grounds. One group claims that talk of causation in the area of crime is largely irrelevant or misleading, since the important reality is *not* some alleged difference between individuals that causes their behavior to flow into criminal or noncriminal channels. Instead, it is argued, the crucial issue is the process by which society attaches the label of criminal to some people rather than others, and the way society makes this decision may have little to do with objectively determined differences in either behavior or individual characteristics. (We will examine this viewpoint in the next chapter.) Other writers argue that the search for the causes of something as general as crime is a fool's errand. Research on the "causes of crime," declare Norval Morris and Gordon Hawkins in an admittedly high-handed decree, should be prohibited. The concept of crime is too diverse, they say, the knowledge likely to be gained too meager, the results too abstract to make the effort worthwhile.[16]

It is true, of course, that criminology needs to develop specific explanations for specific types of crimes; and a single, all-embracing theory that would lay bare the causes of *all* crimes, or crime in general, might be little more than a tautology. At the same time, it does not follow that crimes are unrelated forms of behavior, and general causal factors probably link a variety of broad categories of criminal acts. Furthermore, in addition to the need for limited theories, there is a need for a more comprehensive explanatory scheme that can help fit these theories together and show their relatedness. In any event, the causal explanation of crime at a fairly general and abstract level has long been one of the central themes in criminology and will undoubtedly continue to be so in the future, and it is to an examination of such explanations that we now turn.

Crime causation theories fall into three main categories that have long dominated sociological thought. One group of explanations concentrates on the breakdown of social controls under conditions of social disorganization. A second category focuses on the strains and tensions that are inherent in the normal functioning of society and that produce, under certain circumstances, a state of anomie, or normlessness. A third group of theories looks for the causes of crime in subcultures existing within society in which the normative structure has been turned upside down

[16] See *The Honest Politician's Guide to Crime Control* (Chicago: University of Chicago Press, 1970), Chapter Two.

and crime is an approved or accepted form of behavior. These different theoretical orientations are partly a matter of emphasis and are often in agreement, but there are important points of conflict among them as well. All three orientations are in use today, and each has its particular contribution to make to a comprehensive view of crime causation.

Crime and Social Disorganization

The contrast between a small, stable, cohesive society and a large, rapidly changing social order filled with inconsistencies and disagreements is a fundamental theme in sociological thought. Different terms were used in the writings of Tönnies, Emile Durkheim, Simmel, Maine, and others—*Gemeinschaft* and *Gesellschaft*, mechanical and organic solidarity, status and contract—but the underlying idea of two sharply different forms of society was the same. The first is a social order in which the extended kinship group, neighborhood, guild, and parish loom as major institutions, serving to bind people together in intimate relationships. One's place in society is largely assigned or fixed at birth rather than achieved by individual effort, and the norms that govern proper conduct find their authority in the weight of tradition. What has been done in the past is what should be done now, simply because it has always been so. The other social order is under the sway of large, impersonal social organizations, and the sense of an intimate community has for the most part vanished. A respected place in society is a prize to be won, and social mobility keeps personal relationships in a constant state of flux. The social rules no longer find their justification in unquestioned custom, but depend on considerations of utility for their legitimacy. The world has become rationalized, and the forces of social control are to be found in the bureaucratic agencies of the state rather than in the personal contact of small groups.

It is the historical shift of Western societies along the line drawn between these two theoretical poles that has provided much of the empirical data with which sociological theory has been concerned. Many writers have seen the great change in the form of human relationships, in which urbanization and industrialization have played a major role, as a crucial element in the causation of criminal behavior.[17]

In the formative years of American sociology, at the beginning of this century, evidence of the impact of urbanization and industrialization on the social landscape was everywhere at hand; and sociologists set about describing how this transformation produced a host of social problems,

[17] See Karl Polanyi, *The Great Transformation: The Political and Economic Origins of Our Times* (Boston: Beacon Press, 1960), for a particularly illuminating account.

including crime. As people are drawn from rural areas into the city or are caught up in the vast waves of immigration, they leave behind them small, homogeneous communities in which parents, other relatives, and elders can keep a firm grip on the process of socializing the young and in which adults are enmeshed in a network of close, continuous, and consistent relationships. These so-called primary-group relationships provide the channels for the flow of social pressures to conform. Moving to the metropolis (or finding their village, town, or small city overwhelmed by urbanization) and employed by the large organizations of modern industrial society, great masses of people find that they have been cut off from primary-group relationships. The nuclear family is split away from the larger kinship group, and the neighborhood no longer forms a stable, close-knit unit. The close bonds of friendship are apt to be replaced by the fleeting contacts of city life, and religious organizations and other voluntary associations lose their strength.

For some people, particularly those at the bottom of the social scale who fail to clamber upward in the new economy, traditional social relationships are more than weakened—they are seriously disrupted. Their neighborhood is now a slum. The family is severed by separation or divorce or finds its unity destroyed by prolonged unemployment of the father or the necessity for the mother to work. The social groups offering close personal relationships—those that are the major agencies of socialization and social control—have either vanished or become seriously undermined. Social isolation becomes extreme, and at some point the social environment becomes totally disorganized and the structure of people's lives collapses.[18] The result is a high rate of deviant behavior, including alcoholism, illegitimacy, suicide, crime, and delinquency.

In this theoretical orientation, it is assumed that the intact family, the sound neighborhood, the small work group, the circle of like-minded friends, and voluntary associations are all on the side of conformity to the norms of society, especially the legal norms. The absence of such groups has two effects: it releases the individual's impulses to engage in criminal behavior and it exposes the individual to patterns of criminal behavior or opportunities for crime existing in the community. The sources of the individual's impulses to crime are usually traced to emotional disturbances arising in families damaged by poverty, the frustrations of those who have failed in the struggle for success, and the inevitable tensions flowing from the vicissitudes of daily life. The temptation to crime existing in the community springs from the example set

[18] The term *social disorganization* has been used in a variety of ways in sociology, and no single definition is universally accepted. The term is used here in a relatively restricted sense, to refer to the destruction or loss of significance of those social groups providing close personal relationships.

by admired lawbreakers, the lure of gambling dens, houses of prostitution, bars, and the like, in deteriorating sections of the city; and the opportunity for illicit gain presented by warehouses, stores, and offices in commercial areas.

This viewpoint came to dominate much of the sociological theorizing about the causes of crime in the early 1900s; and textbooks in criminology, drawing on the American experience of rapid city growth, national and international migration, and the shift from agriculture to industry, discussed the plight of the demoralized urban poor in detail.[19] The idea that the criminal was frequently marked by a defect of body, mind, or character had by no means vanished, but the emphasis was on the "abnormal" or "pathological" social conditions that existed in portions of the city and impaired the process of socialization and the mechanisms of social control. The supposed link between social disorganization and personal demoralization was clearly expressed in the influential writings of Charles Cooley:

> We are dependent for moral health upon intimate association with a group of some sort, usually consisting of our family, neighbors and other friends. It is the interchange of ideas and feelings with this group and a constant sense of its opinions that makes the standards of right and wrong seem real to us. We may not wholly adopt its judgments, or that of any member of it, but the social interplay is necessary to keep the higher processes of the mind in action at all. Now it is the general effect of social displacement to tear us away more or less completely from such groups. When we move to town or go to another country, or get into a different social class, or adopt ideas that alienate us from our former associates, it is not at all certain that we shall form new relations equally intimate and cogent with the old. A common result, therefore, is a partial moral isolation and atrophy of the moral sense. If the causes of change are at all general we may have a great population made up largely of such displaced units, a kind of "anarchy of spirits" among whom there is no ethical or settled system of moral life at all, only a confused outbreak of impulses, better or worse.[20]

The criminogenic quality of city life, particularly for those in the poorer sections, was central in the thinking of Clifford Shaw, Henry McKay, and others who explored the concepts of human ecology, or the study of human beings in relation to their physical environment. The use

---

[19] See, for example, John Lewis Gillin, *Criminology and Penology* (New York: The Century Company, 1926); Fred E. Haynes, Criminology (New York: McGraw-Hill, 1930); Stuart Queen and Delbert Mann, *Social Pathology* (New York: Thomas Y. Crowell, 1925).

[20] Charles H. Cooley, *The Social Process* (New York: Charles Scribner's Sons, 1918), pp. 180–81.

of land in the metropolis, it was argued, was to be viewed as a product of patterns of economic and social change, with various sections of the city taking on their own special characteristics, including rates of crime and delinquency.[21] Following in the footsteps of the cartographic school of criminology established in the nineteenth century by Quetelet, Guerry, Mayhew, and other writers who had focused on territorial variation in crime, Shaw and his associates at the Institute for Juvenile Research in Chicago mapped the areas of the city in which delinquents lived and calculated rates based on the number of reported delinquents and population size.[22] The homes of delinquents were found to be concentrated in those areas marked by proximity to industry and commerce, physical deterioration, decreasing population, absence of home ownership, the presence of blacks and recent migrants, and the absence of "constructive agencies intended to promote well-being and prevent maladjustment."[23] According to Shaw and McKay,

> children who grow up in these deteriorated and disorganized neighborhoods of the city are not subject to the same constructive and restraining influences that surround those in the more homogeneous communities further removed from the industrial and commercial centers. These disorganized neighborhoods fail to provide a consistent set of cultural standards and a wholesome social life for the development of a stable and socially acceptable form of behavior in the child. Very often the child's access to the traditions and standards of our conventional culture are restricted to his formal contacts with the police, the courts and the schools and various agencies. On the other hand his most vital and intimate social contacts are often limited to the spontaneous and undirected neighborhood play groups and gangs whose activities and standards may vary widely from those of his parents and the larger social order. These intimate and personal relationships rather than the more formal and external contacts with the school, social agencies and the authorities become the chief sources from which he acquires his social values and conceptions of right and wrong.[24]

[21] Clifford R. Shaw and Henry D. McKay, "Social Factors in Juvenile Delinquency," in National Commission on Law Observance and Enforcement, *Report on the Causes of Crime* (Washington, D.C.: Government Printing Office, 1931), vol. I, Chapter 5. For a comprehensive critique of the ecological approach in the study of crime, see Terence Morris, *The Criminal Area* (London: Routledge & Kegan Paul, 1957).

[22] The need to distinguish clearly between places where delinquents lived and places where delinquencies were committed would be noted by later commentators, but in light of Shaw and McKay's theoretical orientation the choice of delinquents' residence was appropriate.

[23] Shaw and McKay, "Social Factors in Juvenile Delinquency," vol. II, Chapter 5.

[24] Ibid.

A host of such studies in the United States and in other countries, covering adult crime as well as juvenile delinquency, produced similar findings which were similarly interpreted. There was an inverse relationship between the status of an area, as measured by a variety of socioeconomic characteristics, and violations of the criminal law; and the relationship was to be attributed to the erosion of conventional personal ties, occurring most frequently among the urban poor, and the consequent lack of restraints on the individual and exposure to pressures toward deviant behavior.[25] (An emphasis on these pressures, flowing from nonconventional, intimate contact and supporting criminal and delinquent behavior, would later appear in the work of those concerned with a deviant subculture.)

It might seem that the idea of the urban poor being pushed in the direction of crime and delinquency by economic needs would have been given greater weight than the removal of social controls by these ecological theorists and other writers concerned with social disorganization. That economic necessity was a direct cause of crime had been discredited, however, by a large number of investigations extending over a period of many years. These studies indicated there was no consistent relationship between crime and income when variations in income were examined (1) historically, in terms of business cycles; and (2) cross-culturally, in terms of national differences in average income levels. In times of economic depression, financial need would presumably go up and the crime rate should increase; in fact, empirical data failed to reveal such a pattern.[26] The comparison of crime rates in different countries with different levels of economic well-being had received relatively little system-

[25] See Gwynn Nettler, *Explaining Crime* (New York: McGraw-Hill, 1974), Chapter 5. The author discusses much of the recent work on this topic, including Karl Schuessler, "Components of Variations in City Crime Rates," *Social Problems* 9 (Spring 1962), pp. 314–23; R. J. Chilton, "Delinquency Area Research in Baltimore, Detroit, and Indianapolis," *American Sociological Review* 29 (February 1964), pp. 71–83; B. L. Bloom, "A Census Tract Analysis of Socially Deviant Behaviors," *Multivariate Behavior Research* 1 (July 1966), pp. 307–20; D. C. Cartwright and K. I. Howard, "Multivariate Analysis of Gang Delinquency," *Multivariate Behavior Research* 1 (July 1966), pp. 321–72; S. L. Boggs, "Urban Crime Patterns," *American Sociological Review* 30 (December 1965), pp. 899–908; S. Turner, "The Ecology of Delinquency," in T. Sellin and M. E. Wolfgang, eds., *Delinquency: Selected Studies* (New York: John Wiley & Sons, 1969); C. F. Schmid and S. E. Schmid, *Crime in the State of Washington* (Olympia: Washington State Planning and Community Affairs Agency, 1972); O. R. Galle et al., "Population Density and Pathology," *Science* (April 7, 1972), pp. 23–30. For a general review of this field, with an emphasis on English materials, see Morris, *The Criminal Area*.

[26] In 1937, Sellin summarized the work that had been done in this area over a period of more than one hundred years, but could not find evidence of any definite, consistent relationship. See Thorsten Sellin, *Research Memorandum on Crime in the Depression* (New York: Social Science Research Council, 1937). See also George B. Vold, *Theoretical Criminology* (New York: Oxford University Press, 1958), Chapter 9. For a more recent review, see Leon Radzinowicz, "Economic Pressures," in Leon Radzinowicz and Marvin E. Wolfgang, eds., *The Criminal in Society* (New York: Basic Books, 1971), pp. 420–42. For arguments support-

atic attention, as was noted in Chapter 3. Such data as were available, however, did not seem to indicate that the wealthier nations of the world were blessed with lower crime rates; indeed, if any conclusion could be drawn, it might well be the reverse.[27]

There existed, then, the paradoxical finding that although the crime rate and the socioeconomic status of geographical areas in the city frequently varied together in an inverse relationship, no such co-variation was discernible when the socioeconomic status of individuals changed with fluctuations in the business cycle or varied among countries with different levels of economic development. The resolution, from the viewpoint of those sociological theories that stressed social disorganization as a cause of crime, was to be found in the premise that the crucial factor in crime causation was not poverty or economic need but the social situation that accompanied poverty under certain conditions—namely, the breakdown of agencies of social control and the disappearance of intimate, conventional social ties.

This interpretation was buttressed, it was argued, by the fact that crime was infrequent among poor people who had maintained the primary-group relationships necessary for the control of crime. Thus, for example, the degree of social integration—and low crime rates—of Japanese-American and Jewish enclaves in the poorest sections of the city were often cited as impressive arguments for the idea that poverty and crime did not necessarily go together.[28] Similarly, it was pointed out that poverty in rural areas frequently did not erode primary-group ties to the same extent as in an urban setting, and thus the rural poor could be expected to have lower crime rates than the urban poor—an expectation confirmed by the available data.

This perspective on crime causation, rising into prominence after the turn of the century and serving as the theoretical underpinning for a great deal of research, continues to influence much of the writing on the sources of criminal behavior. The Moynihan Report on the problems of the black family in America, with its description of the "tangle of pathology," is only one of many recent sociological analyses that locate the root of deviant behavior in general and crime in particular in the disorganized life of the urban poor, with an emphasis on the breakdown of the family and the neighborhood.[29] And it is probably true that the disorga-

---

ing the idea of a relationship between crime and unemployment, see Daniel Glaser and Kent Rice, "Crime, Age, and Employment," *American Sociological Review* 24 (October 1959), pp. 679–86; and Marcia Guttentag, "The Relationship of Unemployment to Crime and Delinquency," *Journal of Social Issues* 24 (January 1968), pp. 105–14.

[27] See *Report on the Causes of Crime*.

[28] Norman S. Hayner, "Delinquency Areas in the Puget Sound Area," *American Journal of Sociology* 39 (November 1933), pp. 314–28.

[29] See Lee Rainwater and William L. Young, *The Moynihan Report and the Politics of Controversy* (Cambridge, Mass.: The M.I.T. Press, 1967).

nized life of the urban poor in the United States today is a potent source of criminal behavior, a social force that continues to contribute to the likelihood of crime long after the impact of urbanization and industrialization on impoverished classes first caught the eye of American sociologists. At the same time, this approach to the causes of crime is only one part of the story—and may, indeed, be misleading, if it is taken as providing a comprehensive picture.

Social Disorganization and Its Critics

In the eyes of such critics as C. Wright Mills, much of the writing in American sociology about social disorganization in the period between world wars I and II did little more than reflect a distaste for the modern world of industry and large cities on the part of the textbook authors who looked back with nostalgia to their own rural and small-town antecedents. "Social disorganization" was simply the loss of the world they had known in their youth, and they accepted too readily the norms of the respectable middle class as the standard by which all deviant behavior should be measured. By placing such a heavy emphasis on the family and the neighborhood, said Mills, these writers managed to miss the significance of the larger society in which these groups were lodged.[30]

Some of Mills' criticisms of the concept of social disorganization—which were part of a larger ideological attack on the conservatism of American sociology—were valid enough, in the sense that many sociologists did appear to elevate the conventional, middle-class, small-town family and style of life to the status of an ideal. There remained, however, the empirical question of whether the breakdown of primary-group controls was in fact associated with crime and delinquency. And despite the faith in "good" neighborhoods and "good" families as great protectors against deviant behavior, a growing body of evidence indicated that such groups were much less important than was commonly supposed.

The intact family, with the parents in harmony, the father employed, and the mother at home, had been a crucial element in the theory about the importance of primary-group relationships in preventing crime and delinquency.[31] And the data did show that, in general, such families produced fewer delinquents and criminals than did broken families or families marked by unemployment of the father or the employment of the mother outside the home. The data, however, were not always con-

---

[30] C. Wright Mills, "The Professional Ideology of Social Pathologists," *The American Journal of Sociology* 49 (September 1943), pp. 165–80.

[31] See, for example, T. Earl Sullenger, "Juvenile Delinquency a Product of the Home," *The Journal of Criminal Law and Criminology* 24 (March–April 1934), pp. 1088–92; and Nathanial Cantor, "The Causes of Crime," *The Journal of Criminal Law and Criminology* 23 (March–April 1933), pp. 1029–34.

sistent and the differences that did appear were frequently small.[32] The definition of an impaired family or a broken family varied among different studies; the question of whether a break in the family preceded or followed criminal behavior was not always clearly answered; the rating of the quality of family life was often highly subjective; and many of the studies were marred by methodological flaws that made their findings dubious.[33] As it became clear that broken homes were not the overriding factor that many had thought, theories about the causal role of the family shifted to the quality of discipline in the home, the nature of the emotional relationships among family members, and other home conditions and child-rearing practices. As the crude categories of broken and unbroken family structures were replaced by more subtle characterizations of family life, however, the results proved to be no more conclusive than before. Under certain conditions and to a varying degree, a unified, loving, conforming family did appear to have a part to play in keeping individuals out of trouble—but this rather vague conclusion was far removed from the confident assertions of earlier writers who had no doubt that weak or absent primary groups were the basic cause of criminal behavior.

In 1965 Herman Mannheim could assert that the term "broken home" had been more overworked, misused, and discredited than any other term in the history of criminology. For many years, he noted, the broken home had been universally proclaimed as the most obvious explanation of both juvenile delinquency and adult crime. Now, however, it was "often regarded as the 'black sheep' in the otherwise respectable family of criminological theories, and most writers shamefacedly turn their backs to it."[34] The statement may have been somewhat exaggerated, and

[32] The important studies of Clifford R. Shaw and Henry D. McKay, for example, indicated that the ratio of broken homes among delinquent boys and boys from a control group was approximately 1.18 to 1. See Shaw and McKay, "Social Factors in Juvenile Delinquency," pp. 261–84; and Jackson Toby, "The Differential Impact of Family Disorganization," *American Sociological Review* 22 (October 1957), pp. 505–12.

[33] Thus, for example, the often-cited investigation of juvenile delinquency undertaken by Sheldon and Eleanor Glueck was based on a sample of delinquents from correctional schools and nondelinquents from public schools in Boston in 1939. See Sheldon and Eleanor Glueck, *Unraveling Juvenile Delinquency* (New York: Commonwealth Fund, 1950). The structure of the family, however, is frequently a major factor in the decision of whether to send a juvenile to a correctional school, with the boy from a broken home most likely to end up by being institutionalized. As a consequence, it is to be expected that the proportion of boys from broken homes would be higher in correctional institutions than in the public schools for reasons that have nothing to do with broken homes as a cause of delinquency. See Richard S. Sterne, *Delinquent Conduct and Broken Homes* (New Haven: College and University Press, 1964), p. 45.

[34] Herman Mannheim, *Comparative Criminology* (Boston: Houghton Mifflin, 1965), p. 618. For an analysis of the major studies in this area, see Lawrence Rosen, "The Broken Home and Male Delinquency," in Marvin E. Wolfgang et al., eds., *The Sociology of Crime and Delinquency* (New York: John Wiley & Sons, 1970), pp. 489–95.

Karen Wilkinson has suggested that the fluctuating fortunes of broken homes as an explanatory variable may be due to sociologists' changing attitudes toward divorce.[35] But it was true that a number of empirical studies served to throw a good deal of doubt on those sociological theories that made the erosion of conventional primary groups—particularly the family—the major element in the causation of crime and delinquency.

Even more important was an attack from another quarter. Theories about the criminogenic qualities of disorganized social life in the urban slum had been largely addressed to the fact that crime and delinquency were concentrated in the ranks of those in the lower portion of the socio-economic scale. But the crime and delinquency that the theories were trying to explain was the criminal behavior that reached official recognition by the police and the courts. In the decades after the shock of the 1929 stock market crash—and the publication of the Wickersham Commission's Report on Crime in 1931—the literature of criminology began to pay greater attention to the fact that a large amount of criminal behavior did not reach official recognition and that much illegal behavior was widely diffused throughout the social system. The examination of white-collar crime was one part of this changing emphasis, but the idea that crime was by no means simply a lower-class phenomenon also found expression in an increasing interest in "conventional" illegal behavior occurring outside the lower class (such as middle-class delinquency) and in crimes that showed few clear links with poverty, such as professional theft, confidence games, the widespread use of drugs, and check forgery.

The diverse nature of crime and delinquency had long been noted, and writers in the field of criminology had certainly not been so naive as to believe that people from the middle and upper classes did not commit crimes. Before the 1930s, however, the bulk of the illegal behavior analyzed in sociological theories of crime causation was apt to take the form of conventional crimes, such as larceny, robbery, rape, assaults, and the gang delinquency coming to the attention of the police in the poorer sections of the city. Because such offenses were in fact most likely to be committed by the poor, there was an understandable tendency to rely on social characteristics associated with economic deprivation as explanatory factors—and to elevate such explanations to the level of a general theory of crime and delinquency.

With the growing interest in a wide range of criminal behavior found throughout the society, however, new explanations were required. Sociological theories of crime causation began to pay more attention to possible sources of criminal behavior that could be found operating

[35] See Karen Wilkinson, "The Broken Family and Juvenile Delinquency: Scientific Explanation or Ideology?" *Social Problems* 21 (June 1974), pp. 726–39.

throughout the structure of American society, and less attention to the disorganized lives of those who had failed in the process of urbanization and industrialization. With this shift came a greater stress on the amount of crime exhibited by social groups or social aggregates, rather than on the criminal careers of individuals. An interest in crime rates rather than the incidence of crime, notable in the ecological approach to illegal behavior, now became prominent throughout much of American criminology.

The change was evident in general sociological theory as well. Thus, for example, Talcott Parsons, helping to bring the writings of Emile Durkheim into the mainstream of American sociological thought in *The Structure of Social Action*, first published in 1937, emphasized Durkheim's interest in explaining group rates of suicide rather than particular cases. Parsons illustrated the argument with the problem of unemployment. Personal inefficiency, he pointed out, "may well explain why one person rather than another is unemployed at a given time. But it is extremely unlikely that a sudden change in the efficiency of the working population of the United States occurred which could account for the enormous increase in unemployment between 1929 and 1932. The latter is a problem of rate, not of incidence."[36] After the experience of the Great Depression, explanations of social problems based on social malfunctioning rather than on individual failure were sure to capture a large audience.

Crime and Social Structure

In 1895 the noted French sociologist Emile Durkheim had argued that crime is found in all societies and is, indeed, inevitable. The important question is why some societies have more crime than others and why crime rates vary over time.[37] As societies move in the direction of greater complexity—and as the mechanical, unthinking solidarity of a traditional social order based on common interests and generally shared values gives way to division of labor, impersonality, and a multitude of social

Early Theories

---

[36] See Talcott Parsons, *The Structure of Social Action* (Glencoe, Ill.: The Free Press, 1949), p. 324.

[37] See Emile Durkheim, *The Rules of Sociological Method*, trans. Sarah Solovay and John Mueller and ed. George Gatlin (Glencoe, Ill.: The Free Press, 1950), Chapter III. For crime *not* to exist, said Durkheim, all the members of society would need to agree on what was right and what was wrong, and be willing and able to adhere to what was right. But such uniformity is clearly out of the question, given the fact that the immediate social milieu, hereditary antecedents, and social experiences vary from one individual to the next. The result is "diversified consciousness," and with it comes deviation from the norms, including the legal rules.

differences—the social norms and their underlying moral sentiments begin to lose their customary force. "In traditional society," says Anthony Giddens, summarizing Durkheim's thesis, "men are subject to the tyranny of the group, and the individual is subordinated to the pressure of collective sentiments. With the growth of a division of labor and a weakening of group solidarity, men escape the tyranny of traditional controls but now find themselves subject to the tyranny of their own inexhaustible desires."[38] A situation of normlessness, or *anomie,* comes into existence, in which individuals strive to reach their goals by the most effective means that come to hand, regardless of the moral prohibitions of society; or the ideal of altruistic action in behalf of group welfare is replaced by an institutionalized *egotism* in which society places a positive value on the unrestricted pursuit of individual interests.[39] The result is a high rate of deviant behavior, the price paid for the emergence of modern society.[40]

But Durkheim did not present an extensive, explicit theory of crime causation. His writings have served as a source for a number of important explanations of criminal behavior, as we shall see shortly when we examine Merton's theory of anomie, but this has come about more by reading between the lines than building on a well-developed argument.[41] In any event, sociological theories of crime that have looked to the nature of the social order as a cause have usually taken the concept of "modern society" and divided it into more specific types.[42]

[38] Anthony Giddens, "Durkheim's Political Sociology," *Sociological Review* 19 (November 1971), p. 494.

[39] See Ian Taylor, Paul Walton, and Jock Young, *The New Criminology* (New York: Harper & Row, 1973), Chapter 3, for an important effort to place Durkheim's views on crime within the larger body of sociological theory.

[40] Durkheim argued that crime is not only inevitable but can be beneficial as well. "Crime implies not only that the way remains open to necessary changes but that in certain cases it directly prepares these changes. Where crime exists, collective sentiments are sufficiently flexible to take on a new form, and crime sometimes helps to determine the form they will take. How many times, indeed, it is only an anticipation of future morality—a step toward what will be!" The illustration he gives is Socrates paving the way for independence of thought. See Durkheim, *The Rules of the Sociological Method,* p. 71.

[41] The result, as Albert Cohen has pointed out, is that some of Durkheim's ideas about crime have had a confused history in the sociological literature. See Cohen, *Deviance and Control* (Englewood Cliffs, N.J.: Prentice-Hall, 1966), Chapter 7.

[42] "Modernity" as a cause of crime, however, is still to be found in statements such as the following: "The evidence is substantial that social, industrial, and commercial progress is accompanied by an increase in criminal activity. For as you expand the bounds of human freedom and economic and social potential, you equally expand the bounds of potentiality for crime. As legitimate opportunities increase, so also do illegitimate opportunities. . . . Industrialization seems to carry with it urbanization, which in turn carries with it the anonymity, isolation, frustration, discontent, and the enormous criminogenic potential of the city. . . . In this sense, juvenile delinquency and crime are functional and not dysfunctional; they are, at the present level of our knowledge, costs that must be paid for other socially valuable developmental processes in the community" (Morris and Hawkins, *The Honest Politician's Guide to Crime Control,* pp. 49–50).

The criminogenic potential of two forms of society—capitalism and socialism—has long interested a number of criminologists. Willem Bonger (1876–1940), writing from the perspective of Marxist socialism, put forth the argument that crime is caused by capitalism, and socialism is its cure.[43] Every society, Bonger said, is divided into the rulers and the ruled, and the former dictate the shape of the criminal law; even though most crimes probably entail acts that are harmful to both groups, an act will not be punished unless it threatens the interests of those who rule. In a capitalist society, the motivation for violating the criminal law is bred by the system of unrestrained competition held in place by force rather than consensus. The capitalist state, Bonger argued, is before all a system of police. Social relations are based on exploitative exchange and the threat of state-inflicted violence rather than cooperation and trust; and since in a capitalist social order money is the primary means of fulfilling the innate human desire for pleasure, the social environment drives people to obtain money without regard for morality or altruistic considerations.

Those who live in poverty are impelled to commit crimes not only because of their desperate economic need but because the intensely competitive spirit of capitalism destroys the social sentiments in humans, making each an enemy of the other. And if the crime rate among the bourgeoisie is less than that among the proletariat, at least as measured by official statistics, it is because the legal system discriminates in favor of the haves against the have-nots. The selfish, exploitative actions of the bourgeoisie are made legal, whereas the same kind of behavior on the part of the proletariat is penalized.

The solution to the problem of crime, then, is to attack it at its source, which is the system of competition based on economic production for private profit. Only socialism, in which the means of production are held in common and property is distributed according to the maxim "to each according to his need," can establish the social solidarity that will make the motivation of criminal behavior disappear. A residue of crime will persist, it is true, even in a socialist society, but it will be the limited activity of pathological individuals and will fall within the sphere of the physician rather than the judge.[44]

As Turk has suggested, Bonger's theory supplies many insights and hypotheses for research, but the argument is flawed at several points. Few serious scholars would disagree with Bonger's description of the

[43] Until relatively recently, Bonger has been somewhat neglected by American criminologists. His work has often been accorded a nod and then ignored. His writings are now readily available in an abridged form and with an excellent introduction by Austin Turk. See Willem Bonger, *Criminality and Economic Conditions* (Bloomington: Indiana University Press, 1969).

[44] Ibid., pp. 3–12.

social conditions found in the era of rugged capitalism, says Turk, but Bonger fails to recognize the extent to which criminal behavior is found in all societies, capitalist, socialist, or otherwise. The concepts of egoism and altruism in Bonger's theory are too vaguely defined to be useful, and allow one to impute egoism to those whose behavior is considered reprehensible—criminals, for example, or capitalists—and altruism to those whose behavior is viewed as commendable. And the idea that socialism provides a cure for crime assumes far too easily that an equitable distribution of property will eradicate the motivation to break the law, particularly for nonproperty offenses. Bonger would have us believe, Turk argues, that in a socialist society the great mass of the people will be altruistic, always willing to do what they can to benefit the collectivity. Each person will understand how to act for the common good; and coercion, direction, and coordination will be unnecessary. This utopian vision, however, does not match what is known about human behavior, and the problem of deviance and control is almost certainly an aspect of all societies, both future and present.[45]

Even if Bonger's Marxist-socialist approach failed to receive the explicit recognition of many American criminologists, traces of Bonger's thought can be found running through much of the writing in American criminology, not in the form of an analysis of capitalism in general as a cause of crime but in the form of a suspicion that economic enterprise in the United States is a significant part of a distinctive American culture that is highly conducive to criminal behavior. The competitive spirit of American society, the social mobility—both horizontal and vertical—engendered by social and economic change, the diversity of values and norms produced by immigrants seeking new opportunities, the constant stimulation of material aspirations by the mass media, the stress on individualism, the heterogeneity and complexity of industrial America, the inevitable failure for some individuals in the general scramble for success—all have been viewed as components of a unique social configuration. The "pecuniary nexus"—that bundle of values, attitudes, and activities focused on making money rather than making things—which Veblen had seen as peculiar to capitalism might be at the center of all

[45] Ibid., pp. 12–18. Data on crime in the Soviet Union are skimpy at best, and the nature of the criminal law in that country makes any comparisons with the United States extremely difficult. See Herbert A. Bloch and Gilbert Geis, *Man, Crime, and Society* (New York: Random House, 1970), pp. 69–71. See also Walter D. Connor, *Deviance in Soviet Society: Crime, Delinquency, and Alcoholism* (New York: Columbia University Press, 1972); furthermore, it can be argued that the Soviet regime bears little correspondence with the socialism that Bonger had in mind. The available data, however, suggest that the Soviet Union is by no means a crime-free society, despite the contention of Soviet writers that in the U.S.S.R. the fundamental social causes of crime have already disappeared. See A. A. Gertsenzen, "The Community's Role in the Prevention of Crime," *Soviet Review* 2 (January 1961), pp. 14–27, quoted in Bloch and Geis, *Man, Crime, and Society*, p. 69.

The Social Sources of Crime

One of the authors of this book was at one time director of the United Nations Asia and Far East Institute for the Prevention of Crime and Treatment of Offenders in Tokyo. In that position he was occasionally questioned by trainees from rather backward Asian countries with low delinquency rates, who, seeing signs of increasing delinquency rates in their countries, wished his advice on how this trend might be inhibited. He found the answer not difficult. He urged them to ensure that their people remained ignorant, bigoted, and ill-educated; that on no account should they develop substantial industries; that communications systems should be primitive; and that their transportation systems should be such as to ensure that most of the citizens lived within their own small, isolated vil-

From Norval Morris and Gordon Hawkins, *The Honest Politician's Guide to Crime Control* (Chicago: University of Chicago Press, 1970), p. 49. Reprinted by permission of Norval Morris and the University of Chicago Press.

lages for their entire lives. He stressed the importance of making sure their educational systems did not promise a potential level of achievement for a child beyond that which his father had already achieved. If it was once suggested that a child should be able to grow to the limit of his capacity rather than to the ceiling of his father's achievement, he pointed out, the seeds of the gravest disorder would be laid. He stressed the universal human experience that village societies are entirely capable of maintaining any discordance or human nonconformity within their own social frameworks and never need to call on centralized authority to solve their problems. He would take time to sketch, with a wealth of detail, the horrors of increased delinquency and crime that would flow from any serious attempt to industrialize, urbanize, or educate their communities. He would conclude with a peroration against the establishment of an international airline.

this, but for a number of criminologists it has been the pecuniary nexus bearing the stamp "Made in the United States" that serves as a major source of crime.[46]

"Every society has its characteristic laws and crimes which express something deeper in its nature," said Donald Taft, in an influential statement that traced the causes of crime to the nature of American society.[47] People have been apt to think of crime as something done *to* society rather than as an aspect of social relations, he argued, but the fact is that crime in the United States is a reflection of some of our society's fundamental characteristics. Assume there is a culture that is dynamic, complex, materialistic, with slums reserved for those who fail in the competitive process; assume there is a culture split along racial, ethnic, and socioeconomic lines, lacking primary groups controls, permitting gigantic swindles and white-collar crime to go unpunished, influenced by a frontier tradition of violence and a puritanical tradition of repressing basic human drives; assume there is a culture that is marked by a confusion of moral standards and that gives great prestige to the most exploitative and antisocial behavior (such as the activities of powerful corporations)—assume, that is, said Taft, the existence of a social order such as the one existing in the United States, add a variety of "nonsocial practices" such as gambling and the questioning of religious and familial authority, and the result must be high levels of criminality.[48] "In this sense," Taft concluded, "we get the criminals we deserve."[49]

Other criminologists—Sutherland, for example—have provided a similar indictment of American society. The competitive, fluid, diversified, individualistic social order that has been created in the United States is a breeding ground for crime, Sutherland argued; and once again we are presented with a picture of a simple, harmonious, agricultural society that is beset by problems, including a rising crime rate, as it is transformed into an urban, industrial social order.[50] But the loss of control due to the breakdown of conventional primary groups, so heavily emphasized by criminologists writing from the perspective of social disorganization, receives much less attention than the new norms and values permeating contemporary American society and bidding for the individual's allegiance. A child encounters a mix of old and new standards even within his own home, said Sutherland, for no parent can act consistently

[46] See Thorstein Veblen, *Theory of the Leisure Class* (New York: Macmillan, 1912).
[47] Donald Taft, *Criminology* (New York: Macmillan, 1956), p. 28. (The first edition appeared in 1942.)
[48] Ibid., p. 341.
[49] Ibid., p. 342.
[50] See Edwin H. Sutherland, *Principles of Criminology* (New York: J. B. Lippincott, 1939), Chapter Five. The same argument continues to be found in more recent editions (with Donald R. Cressey) of this influential work.

in modern life.[51] And these new standards of behavior, part of the normal culture, no longer emphasize the traditional virtues of thrift, hard work, honesty, and a concern for the community. Instead, big-time spending, something for nothing, the fast buck, and the spirit of every person for himself—or herself—have come to pervade the American scene, paving the way for widespread violations of the law.[52]

The analysis of the criminogenic quality of American society presented by Taft and Sutherland has strong overtones of an offended morality, even though the argument is cast in the neutral terms of the social sciences.[53] There is also a tautological element in relying on culture as an explanation of cultural behavior patterns. Culture, by explaining everything, can end up explaining nothing. Moreover, although American culture may indeed have developed in such a way that it encourages violations of the legal rules, the empirical data linking culture and crime rates is minimal, and the assertion remains more a hypothesis than a tested theory. Comparisons between the United States and other countries are few and inconclusive, as we have seen, and would pose complex methodological and conceptual difficulties if they were to be seriously attempted. Such comparisons would seem to be essential, however, to any theory that points to the culture of a society as a cause of crime.[54] And if the culture of the United States is taken as a causal variable, the question of why the crime rate varies among different social groups remains unanswered, since all social groups can be presumed to be exposed to that culture, without additional theoretical specification to the contrary.

Despite these strictures, however, the attempt to trace the causes of criminal behavior to the normal functioning of American society marked a significant advance in the understanding of crime. First, it opened the door to the examination of a wide range of social factors, rather than the relatively narrow concentration on primary-group relationships that had previously characterized the theories of social disorganization. Normative conflict, political corruption, racial discrimination, the example set by white-collar crime, traditions of violence, social mobility—all became relevant, and the virtues of conventional life styles were no longer so easily assumed. Thus such writers as Taft and Sutherland encouraged a

[51] Sutherland, *Principles of Criminology*, p. 70.

[52] Ibid., pp. 71–75.

[53] At times these writers come surprisingly close to a sort of homespun radicalism that is not particularly ideological in character but that does bear a resemblance to a Marxian critique of the pathologies of American capitalism. See Walter D. Connor, "Deviant Behavior in Capitalist Society—The Soviet Image," *The Journal of Criminal Law, Criminology, and Police Science* 61 (December pp. 554–64).

[54] See Marshall B. Clinard and Daniel J. Abbott, *Crime in Developing Countries: A Comparative Perspective* (New York: John Wiley & Sons, 1973).

fuller development of *sociological* theories of crime causation as opposed to alternative modes of explanation.[55]

Second, the theorists that looked to American society and its culture for the causes of crime did not accept the implicit dictum that "bad" effects must have "bad" causes. Alleged "social pathologies," such as the family suffering from divorce or the wicked temptations of city life, were much deemphasized; and the bland, often unarticulated, provincial value judgments that frequently dominated sociological theorizing about deviant behavior tended to be replaced by a more sophisticated view of cultural diversity.

Third, and perhaps most important, the interest in crime as a form of normal behavior—normal in that it is shaped by the values and norms of society at large—helped to open up the analysis of criminal behavior as a matter of conscious choice. To speak of values and norms involved a consideration of goals and decisions to respond or not respond to social demands for conformity. The criminal was no longer to be viewed simply as an organism blindly reacting to biological urges, or as a person driven by unconscious wishes, or as an undifferentiated unit in an ecological aggregate with a specified probability of becoming a criminal. Instead, crime was now more apt to be seen as a meaningful act, as a selected path of goal achievement; and the criminal, by extension, was more apt to be seen as a human being.

These orientations—still somewhat inchoate in the 1930s and 1940s—helped prepare the ground for two major developments in the study of crime causation: theories centering on the concepts of anomie and subculture. "New" perspectives on a topic are more often than not a matter of gathering up diverse, existing strands of thought and weaving them into a cogent, coherent whole; and the theories built on anomie and subculture are no exception. They embody ideas—about the criminogenic quality of unlimited ambitions, the lack of opportunities for legitimate success, alternative norms and values, and the distinct life styles in different segments of the population—that had been part of the thinking

[55] Psychology, social psychology, and sociology are all undoubtedly necessary for a full understanding of criminal behavior, along with such other fields of intellectual specialization as anthropology, history, political science, and law. It can be argued, however, that it is the task of sociology to explore the possible contributions of its own special perspective rather than to seize on the findings of its sister disciplines. In any event, when he was preparing the first edition of his textbook in criminology, Sutherland pointed out that his principal interest "was opposition to the view . . . that sociology is a synthetic science, organizing and interpreting the findings of other sciences. In contrast, I insisted that sociology is a specialized science with special problems." See Albert Cohen, Alfred Lindesmith, and Karl Schuessler, eds., *The Sutherland Papers* (Bloomington: Indiana University Press, 1956), p. 14. Sutherland's *Principles of Criminology* probably had a greater impact on the development of criminology in the United States in the first half of this century than any other single work.

about crime for many years. But now these ideas were systematically formed into two explicit theoretical perspectives that were widely used after World War II as explanations of crime—and, in fact, continue to hold a prominent place in much of the current work in the field.

An influential essay on anomie by Robert Merton, published in 1938 and revised a number of times since then, has been included in numerous anthologies and is often used as a starting point by those criminologists who attempt to link crime and social structure.[56] "Without any doubt," it has been asserted, "this body of ideas, which has come to be known as 'anomic' theory, has been the most influential single formulation in the sociology of deviance in the last 25 years, and Merton's paper, in its original and revised versions, is possibly the most frequently quoted single paper in modern sociology."[57]

Crime and Anomie

The problem that Merton set for himself was to explain the origins of deviant behavior, including crime and delinquency, not in terms of biological drives or personality traits but in terms of normal social organization. His interest, like that of other sociologists who centered their attention on the nature of society as a social system, was focused not on the behavior of particular individuals but on the *rate* at which certain types of behavior occurred for the system as a whole or in portions of the system such as the different social classes; and, as in the writings of so many social scientists influenced directly or indirectly by Freudian thought, his underlying imagery frequently took the form of a hydraulic system in which pressure built up at various points (for social reasons, however, rather than the workings of id, ego, and superego) and behavior burst forth in an unregulated fashion, or was vented slowly by means of safety valves, or found new channels of expression.

Society, said Merton, is to be seen as made up of culture and social structure. Culture consists of the system of values and norms establishing the goals that individuals pursue and in laying out the boundaries of the behavior patterns that are socially acceptable as means of achieving them. Social structure refers to the organized set of social rela-

[56] See Robert K. Merton, "Social Structure and Anomie," in *Social Theory and Social Structure* (New York: The Free Press, 1967, 1968), Chapter VI. The original essay was reprinted in the 1949 edition of this work. See also Robert K. Merton, "Social Structure and Anomie: Revisions and Extensions," in Ruth Nanda Anshen, *The Family* (New York: Harper & Row, 1949); and Robert K. Merton, "Social Conformity, Deviation, and Opportunity-Structures: A Comment on the Contributions of Dubin and Cloward," *American Sociological Review* 24 (April 1959), pp. 177–89. For a listing of the applications of the concept of anomie, see Marshall B. Clinard, ed., *Anomie and Deviant Behavior* (New York: The Free Press, 1964), Chapter 1, and the annotated bibliography by Stephen Cole and Harriet Zuckerman in the same volume.

[57] Albert K. Cohen, "The Sociology of the Deviant Act: Anomie Theory and Beyond," *American Sociological Review* 30 (February 1965), pp. 5–14.

tionships in which the members of society play their various roles. And it is a peculiar feature of American society, Merton argued, that the theme of material success pervades the culture, placing a high premium on economic affluence and social ascent for all, while at the same time the possibility of achieving material success is sharply curtailed for many, by reason of their location in the social structure. There is a "built-in," chronic disjunction between the prizes all are urged to win and the means available for winning them. The result is that for a large number of people failure is inevitable and systemic.

To lose out in the competitive struggle carries a double sting. The unsuccessful person not only fails to secure those goods, services, and symbols of prestige that he and society value; he is also held responsible for his failure, which more often than not is attributed to a lack of moral stamina or personal worth. The corollary of the concept of the self-made man is the self-unmade man, Merton argues, and American society teaches its members that those who fail have only themselves to blame.[58] In such a situation, the strong temptation is to win at any cost—by fair means if possible, by foul means if necessary. The result is a greatly increased likelihood that the society will move toward a state of anomie in which the rules guiding behavior into rightful or legal channels lack their accustomed force. In a society where material success is a socially defined expectation for all yet attainable by only a few, the probability of deviant behavior is bound to be high, particularly in those social groups where the discrepancy between the goals and the realities of achievement is greatest.

Deviance can take a number of different forms, according to Merton, depending on the individual's position in the social structure, and include innovation, ritualism, retreatism, and rebellion (see Table 1). *Innovation* refers to an acceptance of the goals held forth by the culture but a rejection of the institutional means permitted by the norms. *Ritualism* involves the rejection of culturally defined aspirations accompanied by a compulsive attachment to the social rules, even though their purpose has disappeared. *Retreatism* describes the abandonment of both the goals and the means of achievement expected or permitted by society. Unable to win material success by legitimate means, and unable or unwilling to resort to means prohibited by the norms, the person renounces the competitive struggle altogether and falls into apathy or indifference. Finally, *rebellion* refers to the creation of a new set of goals and new norms governing appropriate means. The ambitions advocated by the culture and the accepted patterns of achievement are both rejected; instead of retreating into a mood of defeatism or withdrawal, however, individuals construct a new world filled with alternative goals and means.

[58] See Merton, *Social Theory and Social Structure*, Chapter VII.

Table 1. A Typology of Modes of Individual Adaptation

Modes of Adaptation	Culture Goals	Institutionalized Means
I. Conformity	accepted	accepted
II. Innovation	accepted	rejected
III. Ritualism	rejected	accepted
IV. Retreatism	rejected	rejected
V. Rebellion	rejected and replaced	rejected and replaced

SOURCE: Reprinted with permission of Macmillan Publishing Co., Inc. from *Social Theory and Social Structure* by Robert K. Merton, p. 194. Copyright © 1967, 1968 by Robert K. Merton.

Innovation and rebellion are most immediately relevant to theories of crime causation. Innovation would presumably include robbery, larceny, organized crime, embezzlement, white-collar crime, professional theft, and other offenses committed for material gain. Such forms of behavior constitute an effective if illegal way of obtaining the monetary rewards so highly valued in American society. The greatest pull toward deviant behavior of this sort is to be found in the lower classes, says Merton, where lack of education and job skills often make conventional success impossible, but a discrepancy between ends and means can also be found at many points along the socioeconomic scale. Businessmen at the edge of financial disaster, corporation executives under pressure to secure high profits, and monopolists intent on absorbing their competitors can also succumb to the temptation to use illegal methods to achieve their goals.

Rebellion may be restricted to a few, notes Merton, such as alienated adolescents teaming up in gangs to form a distinctive subculture, in which the behavior prohibited by society is seen as normatively justified or correct. But rebellion can also take the form of a revolutionary movement involving large segments of the population, as well as political crimes in which individuals use force or violent protest to change the political system or express their opposition to it. In these cases, deviance becomes a deliberate, self-conscious effort to effect social change and takes on the appearance of nonconforming rather than aberrant behavior.[59]

Merton's discussion of anomie leaves a number of questions unanswered and contains some assumptions that are arguable. Why is one mode of adaptation to goal frustration chosen over another? How do

[59] Ibid., p. 245.

norms become eroded when goals are not achieved?[60] What is the precise distinction between ends and means?[61] What influence do social groups and interaction between social groups have? Does material success rank as high—among as many people—as Merton suggests? How must the theory of anomie be modified to take into account the evidence of the widespread incidence of property crime among the middle class?[62]

These are important questions and indicate some of the limitations of the concept of anomie in explaining criminal behavior. But if the concept of anomie cannot support a detailed theory of crime causation (and, indeed, it was never intended for such a role), it is clear that the structurally induced frustration of material aspirations is a potent source of economic crime in American society. The virtue of Merton's formulation is that it indicates how the causes of such crime may be found in the lack of articulation between the culture and the social structure. Where Taft, Sutherland, and other American criminologists had pointed vaguely to a loose array of criminogenic aspects of American society, Merton systematically explored the theme of success as a cause of crime and reopened the question—introduced by Durkheim—of how normlessness arises.

Crime as Conformity

Differential Association The social theorists that we have examined so far have tended to see crime as a violation of the norms of society and the self. The possibility that crime may represent a normatively approved form of behavior is based on a very different theoretical perspective. From this viewpoint, crime is not a form of deviance, but the reverse: it is behavior that conforms to the social norms and values that are held by the person's immediate social groups and which the person has internalized. Crime is seen as simply a particular pattern of behavior that—like any other—may be demanded or expected by the social milieu.

Crime as conformity has long been recognized in discussions of the causes of criminal behavior; and Mayhew's description of the London

[60] The process, however, has begun to receive more attention in recent years. See Robert K. Merton, "Anomie, Anomia, and Social Interaction: Contexts of Deviant Behavior," in Marshall B. Clinard, ed., *Anomie and Deviant Behavior*, pp. 213–42.

[61] The pursuit of money without respect to approved means can be described as an excessive emphasis on goals. It is equally logical, however, to say that money is a means for the attainment of happiness and that the pursuit of money is an excessive emphasis on means at the expense of ends. See Ralph Turner, "Value-Conflict in Social Disorganization," *Sociology and Social Research* 38 (May–June 1954), p. 304. Is material success, then, a means or an end? It is very probably both—but if that is the case, the theoretical distinction between ends and means has a diminished usefulness.

[62] See Clinard, "*Anomie and Deviant Behavior*, Chapter 1.

underworld, as well as Charles Dickens' account of the socialization of Oliver Twist at the hands of Fagin, helped to create a familiar picture of crime being learned as easily as more conventional patterns of behavior. And between 1900 and World War II American social theorists concerned with crime causation gave ever greater attention to this view of illegal behavior—crime, for an increasing number of criminologists, came to be perceived as a normal response to an "abnormal" culture to which the individual happened to be exposed.

The development of this idea can be traced, in part, to the work of Thorsten Sellin and other writers interested in the problems of acculturation confronting immigrant groups in America.[63] In part, also, the theme of a normative support for criminal or deviant behavior is to be found in the work of Clifford Shaw, Harvey Zorbaugh, Nels Anderson, and other members of the Chicago school of sociological thought who, as David Matza has indicated, were keenly aware of a cultural diversity with a variety of normative standards underlying both conventional and unconventional behavior.[64] The writings of Edwin Sutherland, however, proved to be most influential in this area, particularly his explication of the theory of differential association that first appeared in 1939.[65]

Criminal behavior, said Sutherland, is neither biologically inherited nor invented afresh by each individual; it is learned. The learning occurs mainly within intimate social groups; impersonal agencies of communication, such as the mass media, are relatively unimportant. The criminal behavior that is learned includes the techniques of committing crimes, which are sometimes complicated and sometimes simple; and the motives, drives, rationalizations, and attitudes that are conducive to such behavior. What distinguishes these motives and drives is that they involve a cultural rejection of legal norms. A person becomes a criminal

[63] The cultural basis of deviant behavior is well expressed in the following example presented by Sellin:

> A few years ago a Sicilian father in New Jersey killed the sixteen-year-old seducer of his daughter, expressing surprise at his arrest since he had merely defended his family honor in a traditional way. In this case a mental conflict in the sociological sense did not exist. The conflict was external and occurred between cultural codes or norms. We may assume that where such conflicts occur, violations of the norms will arise merely because persons who have absorbed the norms of one cultural group or area migrate to another and that such conflict will continue so long as the acculturation process has not been completed (Thorsten Sellin, *Culture Conflict and Crime* [New York: Social Science Research Council, 1938], p. 69).

[64] See Clifford R. Shaw, *The Jack-Roller* (Chicago: University of Chicago Press, 1930); Harvey Zorbaugh, *The Gold Coast and the Slum* (Chicago: University of Chicago Press, 1929); Nels Anderson, *The Hobo* (Chicago: University of Chicago Press, 1923). Matza's book offers an outstanding analysis of the Chicago school and its perspective on deviant behavior. See David Matza, *Becoming Deviant* (Englewood Cliffs, N.J.: Prentice-Hall, 1969).

[65] See Sutherland, *Principles of Criminology.*

or delinquent, Sutherland argued, because he or she encounters an excess of definitions favorable to violation of the law over definitions favorable to law-abiding behavior. This excess of definitions favorable to the violation of law is due, in turn, to a preponderance of associations with criminal behavior patterns over noncriminal behavior patterns, with the former outweighing the latter in terms of frequency, duration, priority, and intensity. The learning process is the same as any other, and the needs and values of which criminal behavior is an expression are the same as those underlying noncriminal behavior.[66] Criminal behavior, in short, is not based on idiosyncratic motives or blind passions. Instead, crime is part of a cultural tradition that is transmitted through social interaction and in which crime is normatively approved and admired. Circus grifting, in the form of crooked gambling, and the work of the professional thief, such as pickpocketing and the con game, were cited by Sutherland as excellent examples of behavior declared illegal and immoral by society but admired and respected by subgroups; and an understanding of such behavior needs to take into account the group traditions, the esprit de corps, and the deference paid to competence, even though the activity involved is contrary to the law.[67]

Sutherland's theory of differential association has had a marked impact on American criminology.[68] The theory, as George Vold has pointed out, "is not especially unique or new, in and of itself, but it attempts a logical, systematic formulation of the chain of interrelations that makes crime reasonable and understandable as normal, learned behavior without having to resort to assumptions of biological or psychological deviance. It is a peculiarly 'sociological' theory in that it centers attention on social relations—the frequency, intensity, and meaningfulness of associations—rather than on the individual's qualities or traits, or on the characteristics of the external world of concrete and visible events."[69] Despite the widespread appeal of Sutherland's formulation, however, various writers have found the theory of differential association less than illuminating.

The theory, it can be argued, is flawed in three important respects. First, it ignores such crucial issues as why cultural definitions favorable to the violation of law exist in the first place. People may indeed learn to be criminals, just as they learn other forms of social behavior; but until we can explain why the pattern of criminal behavior is there to be

[66] See Cohen, Lindesmith, and Schuessler, *The Sutherland Papers*, pp. 8–10.

[67] See Edwin H. Sutherland, *The Professional Thief* (Chicago: University of Chicago Press, 1937).

[68] See Donald R. Cressey, *Delinquency, Crime, and Differential Association* (The Hague: Martinus Nijhoff, 1964).

[69] George B. Vold, *Theoretical Criminology* (New York: Oxford University Press, 1958), p. 192.

learned, our understanding of crime is woefully inadequate. Furthermore, Sutherland's discussion provides no clues to why some persons are more exposed than others to patterns of criminal behavior (or less exposed to patterns of conforming behavior). The theory, that is to say, ignores, social structure, in spite of Vold's assertion about its "peculiarly sociological" character. We are left with an extremely mechanical formula that does little more than tell us that crime breeds crime.

Second, Sutherland's theory of differential association is often ambiguously worded, making it difficult to develop and assess the theory and subject it to empirical verification. A number of the concepts appear to do little more than express a hope for the precision of quantification, rather than refer to clear-cut variables rooted in either sociology or psychology. Thus, for example, several critics have pointed out that "an excess of definitions favorable to the violation of law over definitions unfavorable to the violation of law"—an idea that lies at the heart of the theory—cannot be determined with any precision in specific cases. The necessary scales of measurement do not exist, even if there were agreement on the meaning of the terms.[70] Similarly, Sutherland's reference to the frequency, duration, priority, and intensity of associations seems to be based on a rather simple analogy with mechanical engineering: the longer and harder the application of force, the more likely it is that an object will give way. The social meaning of the terms, unfortunately, remains unanalyzed.

Third, and perhaps most important, Sutherland's theory of differential association comes dangerously close to being a tautology. If criminal behavior is motivated and not simply a compulsive or uncontrollable act, it is difficult to imagine a crime as *not* being based on "definitions favorable to the violation of law." A crime, after all, is a violation of law. To say that such behavior is caused by motives, drives, and attitudes favorable to such behavior is not very helpful.[71] Nontheless, Sutherland's theory of differential association played a vital part in directing the attention of criminology to the subcultural support of criminal behavior, and the idea of normatively approved deviance has come to dominate much of the theory and research in the field.

The concept of *subculture* has not been the exclusive possession of criminology, and a number of social scientists have used it in analyzing a

Delinquent Subcultures

[70] Cressey, *Delinquency, Crime, and Differential Association,* Chapter V. This work provides both an excellent summary of the criticisms of Sutherland's theory and an extended effort at refutation.

[71] For an excellent discussion of the pitfalls of tautological explanations in sociology, see Ralph Turner, "The Quest for Universals in Sociological Research," *American Sociological Review* 18 (December 1958), pp. 604–11.

wide variety of sociological phenomena.[72] Its most intensive employment, however, has probably been in the areas of adult crime and juvenile delinquency. In 1955 Albert Cohen did much to develop a comprehensive and systematic view of subculture as a causal factor in deviant social behavior.[73]

A number of psychogenic theories have been offered as an explanation for juvenile delinquency, Cohen noted, such as the idea that delinquency is an expression of innate antisocial impulses or a symptom of emotional disturbance engendered by frustration, deprivation, insecurities, anxieties, guilt feelings, and conflicts.[74] A growing number of students of juvenile delinquency, however, believe that the only important difference between the delinquent and the nondelinquent lies in the degree of exposure to a delinquent subculture, he argued; and this subculture formed the focus of his theoretical concern. The most interesting and important question, said Cohen, was not *why* a child would adopt the cultural pattern to which he or she was exposed. Rather, the difficult issue too long ignored by criminologists was why a delinquent subculture existed in the first place. Why does it persist in certain neighborhoods of American cities? A subculture is never a random growth, said Cohen. It has its characteristic niche in society, its own particular flavor, quality, style— the origin of which was the crucial datum demanding an explanation.

When we examine the delinquent subculture as it is presented in the literature of juvenile delinquency, Cohen continued, we must be struck by the fact that it is typically nonutilitarian, malicious, and negativistic. It is nonutilitarian in the sense that much of the stealing that absorbs the interest of many gangs is not a rational means to a necessary end. Rather, stealing is frequently engaged in simply "for the hell of it," for the satisfaction it provides in its own right. "There is no accounting in rational and utilitarian terms for the effort expended and the danger run in stealing things which are often discarded, destroyed or casually given away," Cohen points out. "A group of boys enters a store where each one takes a hat, a ball or a light bulb. They then move on to another store where these things are covertly exchanged for like articles. Then they move on to other stores to continue the game indefinitely. They steal a basket of peaches, desultorily munch on a few of them and leave the rest to spoil. They steal clothes they cannot wear and toys they will not use. Unquestionably, most delinquents are from the more 'needy' and 'unprivileged' classes, unquestionably many things are stolen because they are intrinsically valued. However, a humane and compassionate regard for their

[72] See David O. Arnold, ed., *The Sociology of Subcultures* (Berkeley, Calif.: The Glendessary Press, 1970).

[73] *Delinquent Boys* (New York: The Free Press, 1955).

[74] Ibid., Chapter 1.

economic disabilities should not blind us to the fact that stealing is not merely an alternative means to the acquisition of objects otherwise difficult of attainment."[75]

Contrary, then, to many of the interpretations of criminal and delinquent behavior in the field of criminology that stressed the consciously instrumental quality of many illegal acts, Cohen's view of juvenile theft emphasized its *expressive* content. And the expressive content of much juvenile delinquency, he argued, including both property and nonproperty offenses, was *malicious* in character. There was an apparent enjoyment in the discomfiture of others, a delight in the defiance of social taboos.[76] The satisfaction involved elements of spite, contempt, ridicule, and challenge illustrated by McKay's account of an incident in which a child defecated on the teacher's desk.[77] Finally, said Cohen, the delinquent subculture was *negativistic* in that delinquent behavior was not simply permitted or accepted with a bland indifference. Instead, the norms that characterized many of the boys' gangs flourishing in large American cities were notable for their "negative polarity" to the norms of respectable, middle-class society. The delinquent subculture, in effect, took the larger culture in which it was embedded and turned that culture upside down. Disdain for property rather than respect; aggressiveness and a readiness for violence rather than self-restraint; a demand for immediate gratification rather than a willingness to save and wait—these became the normatively approved values of the delinquent world and gave moral support to the behavior that led the juvenile into conflict with the law.

Cohen was unwilling to make the sweeping claim that exposure to a delinquent subculture is the exclusive cause of juvenile crime, but a belief in the central role of the delinquent subculture is clearly evident in his book. If an individual is exposed to a delinquent subculture, the result is likely to be delinquent behavior. One can scarcely help acquiring the ways of thinking and doing that are peculiar to a subculture, he notes, if one is a full-fledged participant.[78] We come back, then, to the more difficult question of how such behavior comes to receive normative support—and Cohen provided a possible answer.

Whatever the inadequacies of delinquency statistics, Cohen argued, we must conclude that juvenile delinquency and the delinquent subculture have been overwhelmingly concentrated in the male, blue-collar sector of the population. And the reason for this concentration is that among the working class we find the highest degree of social frustration.

[75] Ibid., p. 26.
[76] Ibid., p. 27.
[77] Ibid., p. 28.
[78] Ibid., p. 12.

Urged by middle-class society to value success, long-range goals, respectability, and the ability to make friends and influence people, the youthful working-class male finds himself seriously handicapped. The patterns of socialization in the working-class family, the lack of influence, the discrimination by primary and secondary school teachers who have little sympathy for working-class life styles—all serve to reduce the working-class child's chances for getting ahead. "It may confidently be said," claims Cohen, "that the working-class boy, particularly if his training and values be those we have here defined as working-class, is more likely than his middle-class peers to find himself at the bottom of the status hierarchy. . . . To the degree to which he values middle-class status, either because he values the good opinion of middle-class persons or because he has to some degree internalized middle-class standards himself, he faces a problem of adjustment and is in the market for a 'solution.' "[79]

The "solution" is the delinquent subculture—a set of norms and values holding forth standards of achievement within the reach of the working-class boy. Unable or unwilling to attain middle-class goals, the working-class boy turns to the patterns of aggression, vandalism, and theft where success *is* possible, and thus escapes the intolerable frustrations and anxieties that attend the unmet expectations of a predominantly middle-class society. Thus the delinquent subculture is created and maintained by working-class boys facing similar problems of adjustment. For these boys the subculture reopens the door to masculine self-respect.

Albert Cohen's thesis is open to criticism on a number of grounds. Lewis Yablonsky, for example, has claimed that delinquent gangs rarely exhibit the cohesiveness and normative consensus suggested by Cohen.[80] Solomon Kobrin has pointed out that the poor sections of large American cities are likely to vary and that a delinquent subculture is not apt to flourish when, as is often the case, the area is dominated by adult criminals engaged in illicit enterprises.[81] Walter Miller has argued that the most important influence on the behavior of adolescent gangs in lower-class communities is the cultural system of the community itself, rather than a separate system devised by the delinquent subculture and oriented to the deliberate violation of middle-class norms.[82] The "focal concerns," or values of toughness, smartness, and daring, run through

[79] Ibid., p. 119.
[80] See Lewis Yablonsky, "The Delinquent Gang as a Near Group," *Social Problems* 7 (Fall 1959), pp. 108–17.
[81] See Solomon Kobrin, "The Conflict of Values in Delinquency Areas," *American Sociological Review* 16 (October 1951), pp. 653–61.
[82] See Walter B. Miller, "Lower-Class Culture as a Generating Milieu of Gang Delinquency," *Journal of Social Issues* 14 (1958), pp. 5–19.

A Lot of Heart

A Cobra swung on one of the fellows, and he come down with his knife out. That means he's not scared to go to jail and pay whatever the consequences is.

If a group of boys say, going to break into a store or truck, and I tell this boy to do it and he does it, the people say he got a whole lot of heart—he not afraid of anything. He'll just go on and do everything the other person tell him to do.

A person who got heart, he not scared to do anything. Like we break in a liquor lounge or something, he not worried about being busted. He's game for it. Or like we in a fight, and we outnumbered say four to two. This man will stand up there and fight with you no matter what. If you all go down, he there with you. You all both go down together.

If you don't show heart people call you a punk, and they don't want to hang with you. A punk is a person who like get into a fight with somebody and he don't fight back. Or like if say me and you and somebody else, we going to rob somebody, and one of us be scared and won't do it. Then they say he punked out.

The delinquent subculture takes the larger culture in which it is embedded and turns that culture upside down. A disdain for property, a readiness to violence, and a demand for immediate gratification become the values of the delinquent world.

lower-class society, Miller argues, and are not to be interpreted as the peculiar traits of a delinquent subculture.

James Short and Fred Strodtbeck have claimed that problems of status within the adolescent gang are probably more important than those connected with the individual's position in society at large.[83] Albert Reiss and Albert Rhodes—along with numerous other writers—have raised serious doubts about the negative correlation between delinquency and social class that lies at the heart of Cohen's argument.[84] And John Kitsuse and David C. Dietrick, in what is probably the most thorough review of Cohen's thesis, have questioned his methods and logic as well as the accuracy of his characterization of delinquent behavior.[85]

Many of these criticism are well founded, and it is clear that the concept of the delinquent subculture as a nonutilitarian, malicious, and negativistic attack on middle-class values is by no means a complete theory of delinquency, let alone of adult criminality. Cohen's ideas concerning the sources and functions of a delinquent subculture may require a good deal of qualification, and some details are obviously subject to further modification and empirical testing. Nonetheless, his work has done much to take causal explanations in criminology beyond the simple learning-theory approach advanced by Sutherland. Whether or not all or much delinquent behavior is explicitly opposed to normative conformity, and whether or not the primary function of the subculture is to reduce status anxiety, the concepts involved are essential to an understanding of juvenile delinquency. Cohen's analysis, in short, has made an invaluable contribution to sociological theories that focus on normative support for criminal behavior.

The Subculture of Violence

The normative support for criminal behavior is nowhere more striking, perhaps, than in the social approval of violence that is encountered in a number of subcultures in other countries. In Colombia, Mexico, Italy, and India, as Marvin Wolfgang and Franco Ferracuti have indicated, there are towns, communities, regions, and tribes in which violence has become an accepted part of life, a respected—in fact, demanded—means of settling disputes and answering insults to one's honor.[86] Over an eighteen-year period, for example, the *Violencia Colombiana* is said to have taken more than 200,000 lives as armed groups struggled in bitter

[83] See James F. Short and Fred L. Strodtbeck, "Why Gangs Fight," *Transaction* 1 (September–October, 1964), pp. 25–29.

[84] See Albert J. Reiss and Albert Lewis Rhodes, "Delinquency and Social Class Structure," *American Sociological Review* 26 (October 1961), pp. 720–32.

[85] See John J. Kitsuse and David C. Dietrick, "Delinquent Boys: A Critique," *American Sociological Review* 24 (April 1959), pp. 208–15.

[86] See Marvin Wolfgang and Franco Ferracuti, *The Subculture of Violence* (London: Tavistock Publications, 1967), pp. 271–84.

feuds in which criminal violence was no longer a breach of normative expectation but its very opposite.[87] In the village of Acan in the Tarascan area of Mexico, countless homicides, woundings, and gunfire exchanges have taken place over a thirty-five-year period. "Political controversies include violence as a normal means of struggle," say Wolfgang and Ferracuti. "Homicide is not sadistic and is carried out by the quickest possible means. . . . Men must demonstrate their 'valor' or face loss of prestige and estrangement from political and social life. Homicide is justified and even prescribed. Violence erupted at the beginning of the century during the agrarian revolution and has never been abandoned as an accepted means of achieving political success."[88]

In such situations, argue Wolfgang and Ferracuti, criminal behavior is a cultural product, in that it has become a matter of training and indoctrination—and its absence, rather than its presence, is likely to be met with ostracism and punishment. And it is in this sense that the two sociologists speak of a subculture of violence, a social group in which violent behavior is not a breaking through of deviant impulses rooted in biological defects, psychopathology, or status frustration, but rather an expression of a subgroup's norms and values. After reviewing much of the literature concerned with the explanation of violence in a variety of disciplines, they conclude that the origins of a subculture of violence within the larger society are not yet precisely known. In their view, however, it is reasonable to believe that in the United States a subculture of violence is prevalent predominantly among young, lower-class males, particularly nonwhites. It is in this segment of society that the concept of *machismo* is most likely to flourish and physical violence, in the form of homicide and assault, to become a familiar companion.[89] As Wolfgang, in an earlier study of homicide in Philadelphia, has pointed out:

> . . . The significance of a jostle, a slightly derogatory remark, or the appearance of a weapon in the hands of an adversary are stimuli differentially perceived and interpreted by Negroes and whites, males and females. Social expectations of response in particular types of social interaction result in differential "definitions of the situation." A male is usually expected to defend the name and honor of his mother, the virtue of womanhood . . . and to accept no derogation about his race (even from a member of his own race), his age, or his masculinity.
>
> Quick resort to physical combat as a measure of daring, courage, or defense of status appears to be a cultural expression, especially for

---

[87] See Germán Guzmán, Orlando Fals Borda, and Eduardo Umaña Luna, *La Violencia en Colombia* (Bogotá: Universidad Nacional, 1962).

[88] Wolfgang and Ferracuti, *The Subculture of Violence*, p. 282.

[89] Ibid., pp. 151–55.

lower socio-economic class males of both races. When such a culture norm response is elicited from an individual engaged in social interplay with others who harbor the same response mechanism, physical assaults, altercations, and violent domestic quarrels that result in homicide are likely to be common. The upper-middle and upper social class value system defines subcultural mores, and considers many of the social and personal stimuli that evoke a combative reaction in the lower classes as "trivial." Thus, there exists a cultural antipathy between many folk rationalizations of the lower class, and of males of both races, on the one hand, and the middle-class legal norms under which they live, on the other.[90]

The subcultural approach to the explanation of violent crime, then, envisions a segment of society in which a portion of the mores stands at variance with those of the larger social order. Individuals socialized into the subculture do not view their behavior as deviant, although the larger society does and declares it illegal. Unlike Cohen, who sees the source of a delinquent subculture in status frustration, Wolfgang and Ferracuti are unwilling to posit any such problem-solving function for the subculture of violence. It is possible, however, that a subculture of violence can be analyzed in functional terms—as the response of a segment of society that has become isolated or alienated from the institutions of legitimate authority of the larger society. Unable or unwilling to rely on the dispute-settling capabilities of the formal legal system, members of the subgroup must depend on their personal prowess to defend their persons and their possessions in a dangerous world. The ability to do so becomes elevated into a prime virtue, and a test of that virtue is to be found in the readiness to respond to attacks on one's honor—that is, one's claim to be treated with respect. Such an interpretation would appear to be worth investigating, for much of what is referred to as *machismo* appears to be similar to the concept of *mafia* (see Chapter 5) and to arise under the same circumstances.

Subcultural interpretations offer one of the most promising lines of investigation in the effort to find the causes of criminal behavior. Undoubtedly many criminal acts involve a violation of the norms from the viewpoint of both society and the individual who breaks the rules. But it is also apparent that a great deal of criminal behavior is of a different character. Society may indeed declare the behavior criminal and threaten to punish it accordingly. For the individual socialized according to a contrary viewpoint, however, the behavior may appear in a very different light—and when we try to explain such behavior, we are in effect trying

[90] Marvin Wolfgang, *Patterns in Criminal Homicide* (Philadelphia: University of Pennsylvania Press, 1958), pp. 188–89.

to explain conformity instead of deviance. The problem, from the viewpoint of sociological theory, is to understand more clearly how subcultures come into existence and maintain themselves, in what way and to what extent subcultural norms are acquired, and how the contradictions between the subculture and the larger society are resolved in the minds of subgroup members.[91]

A major difficulty is that in many cases subcultural norms do not stand in explicit opposition to the norms of the larger society. Instead, they are apt to appear as a variation of the norms of the larger culture, with patterns of qualifications, evasions, excuses, and special emphasis that may permit—or even encourage—illegal behavior but do not demand it. Thus, as we have seen, numerous writers have pointed out that the culture of the urban lower classes differs from that of the larger society at a number of significant points, including the norms governing the use of violence, but that does not mean the use of force is defined as a positive good. Instead, the circumstances under which violence is seen as acceptable or necessary are broadened in ways not recognized by the larger society, and violence emerges obliquely, as it were—a product of a subculture but not something that can be traced to an explicit normative injunction.

Conclusions

Sociological theories concerning the causes of crime have changed over time, reflecting changes in the field of general sociology of which criminology is a part. A growing sophistication in the explanation of social behavior is evident in the explanation of crime and delinquency, and the simplistic approach of earlier years has been replaced by a sharp awareness of the difficulties in predicting and understanding violations of the criminal law.

All types of social behavior pose serious problems when it comes to theories of causation, of course, and an optimistic faith that sociology would soon achieve the interpretive power and clarity of the natural sciences is now seen as an error. Despite the argument heard in recent years, however, that criminology is mistaken in attempting to uncover the causes of crime, there is little reason to believe that such attempts

---

[91] The concept of subgroup is seriously in need of clarification in sociology. Milton Gordon's analysis of *subsocieties* (social units smaller than the national society and containing a large network of groups and institutions extending through the life cycle of the individual) and *subgroups* (gangs, play groups, the factory, the hospital, the office, etc.) provides an important distinction, but much remains to be done. See Gordon, *Assimilation in American Life* (New York: Oxford University Press, 1964).

will cease. While it may be true that such subjects as the substance of the criminal law and the process of labeling deserve more attention than they have received in the past, studies in these areas are not likely to eliminate the long-standing concern with the roots of criminal behavior—nor, indeed, should they do so.[92] It must be admitted that criminology is still a long way from a comprehensive understanding of the causation of criminal behavior. But this is simply to say that criminology is no further advanced than sociology in general. That so much remains unknown is no proof that it is unknowable, and we should be skeptical of those who urge abandoning the search for the principles of social life merely on the grounds that such principles have not yet been found.

Human variability, the moral curbs on experimentation, and society's reluctance to provide the large amount of resources needed for research have limited the accomplishments of the social sciences. In addition, in the field of criminology, research has been hampered because criminal behavior frequently involves strong feelings of guilt, the opprobrium of others, and the threat of punishment by the state. Understandably, the great bulk of illegal behavior remains hidden—and the criminologist is in the position of a person who tries to draw a picture of a rare animal that has often been described but seldom seen. When crime does swim into the public ken, in the form of official statistics, the data are apt to be so distorted by the process of their collection and reporting that their scientific usefulness is sharply restricted. To this must be added a remarkable lack of consensus among social scientists concerning the concepts they have employed in their analysis of criminal behavior. The definition of crime and delinquency has often varied from one study to the next, making it difficult to build a body of coherent knowledge.

No less important, sociological theorizing about the causes of crime has frequently been addressed not to the great variety of crime but to some limited portion—crimes against property, or crimes of violence, or juvenile delinquency. This specialized approach may indeed be necessary, but we are left with a number of partial interpretations that often appear inconsistent and whose relationships to a comprehensive view of crime causation are never made clear. Furthermore, many significant types of crime, such as the political crime of public officials or property offenses committed by upper-middle-class persons which are *not* white-collar crimes in Sutherland's sense, have been overlooked by much of the sociological theorizing about the causes of crime. Our maps of reality contain large blank areas that have been left unexplored—due, in no small measure, to the ability of the rich and powerful to protect themselves from sociological scrutiny.

[92] See Gibbons, "Observations on the Study of Crime Causation." See also the comments of Charles Logan, in Simon Rottenberg, ed., *The Economics of Crime and Punishment* (Washington, D.C.: American Enterprise Institute for Public Policy Research, 1973), pp. 55–58.

Despite these pitfalls, sociological theories of crime causation have managed to illuminate the relationship between criminal behavior and the social order in which it exists. In particular, they have increased our awareness of the extent to which criminal behavior frequently "makes sense" to the actor in specific social situations. In most instances, criminal behavior is not simply a wild outburst of anger, a compulsive act beyond control, an unthinking response to a deprivation, or the delayed expression of childhood traumas. Instead, as we are now much better able to see, crime is often the pursuit of goals widely understood and accepted; and, as such, it is frequently permitted or condoned—if not actually demanded—by the norms of certain social groups. Crime, that is to say, may often not be the act of a person whom society has failed to socialize, but may be instead the behavior of a person who has absorbed society's norms all too well. It is this illumination of the age-old puzzle of criminal behavior that the sociological perspective has helped to provide.

Recommended Readings

The reader will find Gwynn Nettler's *Explaining Crime* (New York: McGraw-Hill, 1974) a clear, well-organized survey of all the major theories of crime causation. Particular sociological approaches to crime causation, such as those involving the concepts of subculture, ecology, and anomie, can be found in Albert Cohen, *Delinquent Boys* (New York: The Free Press, 1955); Terence Morris, *The Criminal Area* (London: Routledge & Kegan Paul, 1957); Robert K. Merton, "Social Structure and Anomie," in *Social Theory and Social Structure* (New York: The Free Press, 1967, 1968); and Richard A. Cloward and Lloyd E. Ohlin, *Delinquency and Opportunity* (New York: The Free Press, 1960). For a clear, concise review of Sutherland's influential theory of differential association, see Donald R. Cressey, *Delinquency, Crime, and Differential Association* (The Hague: Martinus Nijhoff, 1964). *The Journal of Criminal Law, Criminology, and Police Science* contains many articles on various aspects and theories of crime causation; other journals the reader will find useful include *The American Sociological Review, American Journal of Sociology, Social Problems, Sociological Quarterly, Journal of Research in Crime and Delinquency, Law and Society Review,* and *Crime and Delinquency.*

For a skeptical view of the effort to find the causes of crime, the reader should see George B. Vold, *Theoretical Criminology* (New York: Oxford University Press, 1958), Chapter 11; and Norval Morris and Gordon Hawkins, *The Honest Politician's Guide to Crime Control* (Chicago: University of Chicago Press, 1970), Chapter Two. The reader should also consult Travis Hirschi, *Causes of Delinquency* (Berkeley: University of California Press, 1969).

Chapter 8
Symbolic Interaction and Crime

The various disciplines of the social sciences can be thought of as different ways of looking at a single social reality. Economics, history, anthropology, political science, psychology, sociology—each, using its own concepts, vocabulary, theoretical perspectives, and methods, examines a particular facet of human behavior, prepared at times to borrow from a sister discipline if it proves useful (or fashionable), but usually pursuing its special vision. Occasionally, in a burst of imperialistic zeal, one of the social sciences will declare that its viewpoint is the most inclusive, and graciously offer to integrate what is known about social behavior. Such offers are consistently declined. More frequently, each discipline simply makes a series of assumptions about those aspects of human behavior falling outside its purview, taking as established what other fields regard as problematical and concentrating its inquiries on a restricted segment of social life.

Yet if the social sciences have usually been characterized by tunnel vision, there has also been a persistent tradition of cross-disciplinary perspectives. One notable example is the field of study called social psychology, which attempts to join an interest in the individual and an interest in the social structure, treating the actor and the social setting as interrelated subjects of investigation.[1]

Social psychology has taken a variety of forms, depending on whether psychology, anthropology, or sociology has played the most influential part. When sociology has dominated the mixture, however, much of the theory and research has carried the label "symbolic interactionism" in reference to the crucial influence of language and other means of symbolic communication on human relationships.[2] The interpretation of

---

[1] See Harold B. Gerard, "Social Psychology," *International Encyclopedia of Social Sciences* (New York: Macmillan and Free Press, 1968), vol. 14, pp. 459–73.

[2] See Alfred R. Lindesmith and Anselm L. Strauss, *Social Psychology* (New York: Holt, Rinehart and Winston, 1968), Chapter 1. "The term 'symbolic interactionism' is a somewhat barbaric neologism that I coined in an offhand way," says Herbert Blumer, "in an article

criminal behavior from this perspective will occupy our attention in this chapter—although it must be admitted that the theories under examination do not always fit neatly under the label that is supposed to cover them.

As Lindesmith and Strauss have indicated, the study of social behavior from the viewpoint of symbolic interactionism has frequently been marked by a distinctive intellectual style—a quality that may help explain why it is attractive to some social scientists and not to others. Nonetheless, the social interactionist position occupies a large and significant part of social psychology and shapes many of the explanations of crime causation. According to Lindesmith and Strauss, five theoretical orientations underlie this perspective. They are as follows: (1) *A dominant concern with the meaning the individual attaches to his or her behavior.* We cannot understand human conduct through observation alone, it is argued, or by simply categorizing it according to some conceptual framework created by the social scientist.[3] We must know how the individual himself views his actions. (2) *An emphasis on the individual's behavior as a cause, rather than as an effect of environment or personality.* Human action, that is to say, is frequently examined as an independent variable, whereas the usual approach in sociology or psychology would be to relegate the individual's behavior to the status of a dependent variable, viewing the actor as more acted upon than acting. (3) *A concern with the complexities and ramifications of the individual's actions.* Rather than focusing on a narrowly defined aspect of behavior, the symbolic interactionist is apt to be interested in the multiple meanings of the individual's acts, the unforeseen contingencies and new patterns of behavior coming into existence, until at times the behavior under examination becomes nothing less than the individual's life history. (4) *An emphasis on the contingent quality of social interaction.* Patterns of human behavior, it is said, follow a changeable course with each phase growing out of the one that precedes it. Human action, deviant or otherwise, argues Albert Cohen, is

---

written in *Man and Society* [Emerson P. Schmidt, ed. (New York: Prentice-Hall, 1937)]. The term somehow caught on and is now in general use" (Herbert Blumer, *Symbolic Interactionism: Perspective and Method*[Englewood Cliffs, N.J.: Prentice-Hall, 1969], p. 1).

[3] The following statement by John Dewey and James Tufts is cited with strong approval by an influential advocate of a symbolic interactionist perspective on deviance: "Of one thing we may be sure. If inquiries are to have any substantial basis, if they are not to be wholly up in the air, the theorist must take his departure from the problems which men actually meet in their own conduct. He may define and redefine these; he may divide and systematize; he may abstract the problems from their concrete contexts in individual lives; he may classify them when he has detached them; but if he gets away from them he is talking about something which his own brain has invented, not about moral realities" (quoted in Jack D. Douglas, ed., *Deviance and Respectability: The Social Construction of Moral Meanings* [New York: Basic Books, 1970], p. 3).

something that typically develops and grows in a tentative, groping, advancing, backtracking, sounding-out process. And as an advocate of an interdisciplinary viewpoint, Cohen warns us that we should not think in terms of variables that describe initial states on the one hand and outcomes on the other, but should instead think in terms of *processes* whereby acts are built, elaborated, and transformed.[4] (5) *A commitment to the concept of freedom of action.* Unlike those social scientists who adhere to a belief in a strict determinism in human affairs, symbolic interactionists are likely to stress the alternative lines of conduct open to the individual. While freedom of action is not unbounded, the individual can control his actions—indeed, he can even learn to control such reflex actions as contraction of the eye pupil. Human behavior, it is argued, is *not* a mechanical response to external events and situations but is, at least in part, a voluntary matter.

These theoretical orientations differ in many ways from most of the approaches discussed in Chapter 7. In addition, symbolic interactionist theorists emphasize different research methods. They tend to prefer participant or informal interviews to surveys and questionnaires, qualitative to quantitative analysis; and they are relatively indifferent to problems of sampling and replication.

This theoretical and methodological school of thought has produced a body of literature that is extensive, lively, and rich in factual detail, conveying the smell, taste, and feel of deviant lives. It is also filled with perceptive insights about how individuals interacting with their peers and members of officialdom come to exhibit criminal behavior. Juvenile delinquents, confidence men, drug addicts, embezzlers, skid-row alcoholics, and armed robbers are among those who have been described and analyzed from this point of view. Such analyses are apt to concentrate on the discrepancy between what society says it is doing and what it does, and to show a strong concern for the underdog or the outcast who is caught up in the machinery of the law.

Against these virtues we must place the shortcomings found in some of these writings: the too easy cynicism, the lack of precision in handling concepts, the doubtful generality of certain findings, and the tendency of a concern for the underdog to turn into a bias that distorts the facts. Despite the current criticsm of symbolic interactionism, however, it has opened up a stimulating line of theoretical development in criminology, and its creative energies are far from spent.[5]

---

[4] See Albert K. Cohen, "The Sociology of the Deviant Act: Anomie Theory and Beyond," *American Sociological Review* 30 (February 1965), pp. 5–14.

[5] See Edwin M. Lemert, "Beyond Mead: The Societal Reaction to Deviance," *Social Problems* 21 (April 1974), pp. 457–68.

The Influence of Freudian Theory

As we saw in Chapter 1, the idea that crime is rooted in some form of mental illness or psychic aberration dominated much of the thinking about the crime problem in the United States in the early part of this century. The psychoanalytic theories of Freud, in particular, seemed to offer a profoundly enlightening explanation of criminal behavior, especially with regard to the bizarre acts of violence and the sexual offenses that stirred strong public reactions. Freudian theory was also widely accepted as a basis for constructing a rational method of treating the criminal.

Psychiatry had been dealing with "mentally disturbed" persons long before Freud, and the distinction between *organic disorders*, resulting from injury or disease, and *functional disorders*, for which there was no apparent physical basis, was well known. Freudian theory, however, provided a systematic analysis of functional disorders, pointing to causal processes where previous case histories had been filled with elaborate descriptions.[6]

According to the Freudian viewpoint, the individual comes into the world filled with primitive, untamed instincts. The perfectly normal infant, says a noted British psychiatrist, "is almost completely egocentric, greedy, dirty, violent in temper, destructive in habit, profoundly sexual in purpose, aggrandizing in attitude, devoid of all but the most primitive reality sense, without conscience or moral feeling, whose attitude to society (as represented by the family) is opportunist, inconsiderate, domineering and sadistic. . . . In fact, judged by adult social standards, the normal baby is for all practical purposes a born criminal."[7] Gradually, however, the psychological drives contained in the portion of the mind's structure labeled the *id* are brought under control by the *ego* (the perceptions, memory, and other mental processes that link the individual to social and physical reality) and the *superego* (the values and norms that the individual has absorbed from other persons, particularly the father and mother). Below the level of consciousness a continual struggle goes on between the superego and the forces of the id that have been repressed but not destroyed. As the id impulses attempt to break into consciousness and overt action, they arouse feelings of guilt and anxiety stemming from the disapproval of the superego. For the individual who has successfully completed the process of psychosexual development, who has met and solved the traumas of childhood and passed through the oral, anal, and phallic stages of sexual growth, unacceptable impulses of the id can be transformed and sublimated into socially approved

[6] George B. Vold, *Theoretical Criminology* (New York: Oxford University Press, 1958).

[7] Edward Glover, *The Roots of Crime* (New York: International Universities Press, 1960), p. ix.

forms. For the person who has not been able to complete this process successfully, the primitive drives of the id are uncontrollable and are expressed in criminal acts.[8] "The only difference between the criminal and the normal individual," claimed Franz Alexander and Hugh Staub in an influential statement of the psychoanalytic position, "is that the normal man partially controls his criminal drives and finds outlets for them in socially harmless activities. This power of controlling, and the domestication of the primitive, unsocial tendencies is acquired by the process of education. In other words, criminality, generally speaking, is not a congenital defect but a defect in the bringing up. . . . Our contention will become clearer if we could imagine that all the children of the world between the ages of two to six should suddenly become physically superior to the adult and were thus able to dominate the adult to the same degree as the adult dominates the child. These children, let us imagine further, would then set themselves to act out all their phantasies. These Gulliverian giant children dominating a world of dwarf-like adults would present a hundred-per-cent criminality in action."[9]

Thus, for example, an "educational mistake in the process of weaning" may leave the child unable to control the basic drive to grasp and dominate—and, as an adult, the individual may then show a tendency to violent action, an inability to tolerate frustration. A failure to resolve the Oedipus complex, which Freud saw as an inevitable aspect of parent-child relationships, may mean that a boy fails to identify with his father and as a consequence fails to internalize the normative demands of adult authority. If the individual experiences injustice, the supergo may lose its inhibitory power. The superego serves as a representative of society; and if society is unfair and not to be trusted, so too is the superego. Hence the ego need no longer seek the superego's approval by renouncing instinctual pleasure, and antisocial impulses are freed to find expression in action. This is a typical psychoanalytic interpretation of the roots of criminal behavior; and for those who found it persuasive, the prevention of and cure for crime were obviously not punishment (which could reinforce criminal behavior by satisfying an unconscious desire for retribution) but psychotherapy.[10]

There is the question, of course, of whether the psychoanalytic view of

[8] For an excellent, brief account of psychoanalytic theory discussed within the context of social psychology theories in general, see Morton Deutsch and Robert M. Krauss, *Theories in Social Psychology* (New York: Basic Books, 1965), Chapter 5.

[9] *The Criminal, the Judge, and the Public* (New York: Macmillan, 1931), pp. 35–36.

[10] Influential psychoanalytic interpretations of criminal and delinquent behavior are to be found in August Aichhorn, *Wayward Youth* (New York: Viking Press, 1935); Franz Alexander and William Healy, *Roots of Crime* (New York: Knopf, 1935); Robert M. Lindner, *Rebel Without A Cause* (New York: Grune & Stratton, 1944). In general, however, crime has been of marginal interest for psychoanalytic theory.

the causes of crime is true, false, or simply unprovable. Sociology, as Alex Inkeles has suggested, has long shown hostility toward psychoanalysis and has been quick to discount its claims. This attitude may stem in part from the fact that psychoanalysis was gaining prominence at the very time when sociology was trying to establish itself as a scientific discipline and warring against various forms of psychological reductionism.[11] In any event, in the decade after World War II many sociologists became convinced that despite the imaginative sweep of Freudian theory, a psychoanalytic approach to social behavior in general and crime in particular had not been able to develop a body of substantiating evidence according to accepted scientific method.[12] It was certainly true, as a number of writers pointed out, that the work of Freud and his followers had revolutionized the way we *talk* about ourselves and others.[13] Many Freudian concepts—such as sibling rivalry, projection, dream symbolism, and unconscious aggression—had become part of the culture, albeit in watered-down form. The idea that human behavior was the result of a process in which the individual interacted with others in the social environment linked Freudian thought to other emerging viewpoints in social pathology, even if the social environment of psychoanalysis often appeared to be confined largely to the bedroom and the bathroom. Perhaps most important, psychoanalytic thought encouraged an interest in the symbolic quality of social behavior and led to the explanation or interpretation of the individual's actions as a matter of choice or decision (even though they might be unconscious ones), rather than viewing the individual as a lump of matter shoved around by "social forces" or "personality traits." But the influence of orthodox psychoanalytic theory gradually diminished after a period of intense interest shown by many social science specialties, including criminology. Other theoretical orientations attempting to describe how the individual and the milieu were joined came into prominence.

Deviance and the Interactive Process

The tradition of social psychology in American thought had been established by writers such as Charles Cooley, Edward Ross, John Dewey, W. I. Thomas, Florian Znaniecki, and George Mead.[14] Mead left

[11] See Alex Inkeles, "Psychoanalysis and Sociology," in Sidney Hook, ed., *Psychoanalysis, Scientific Method, and Philosophy* (New York: New York University Press, 1959), Chapter 6.
[12] See Barbara Wooton, *Social Science and Social Pathology* (New York: Macmillan, 1959), pp. 236–37.
[13] See Charles Rycroft, "Actions Speak Louder Than Words," review of Roy Schafer, *A New Language for Psychoanalysis,* in *The New York Review of Books* (May 27, 1976), p. 12.
[14] Fay Berger Karp, *American Social Psychology* (New York: McGraw-Hill, 1932).

the deepest mark, perhaps, although not so much through his writings as through an influence on students who later shaped the field. The work of Herbert Blumer, in particular, carried forward Mead's theories, giving them a clearer, more persuasive form.

Human behavior, says Blumer, is an interactive process, and to understand it our theories must be built on three fundamental premises. First, individuals act toward things on the basis of the meanings that the things have for them. "Things," Blumer declares, include physical objects like trees or chairs, other human beings, institutions such as government, and ideals. (The "meaning" of things is not explicitly defined by Blumer but would appear to include such matters as factual knowledge of the physical world, an awareness of the emotional states of one's self and of others, evaluations of good and bad, and judgments of what is desirable and what is undesirable.) Few scholars would see anything wrong with this first premise, says Blumer. "Yet," he argues, "oddly enough, this simple view is ignored or played down in practically all of the thought and work in contemporary social science and psychological science. Meaning is either taken for granted and thus pushed aside as unimportant or it is regarded as a mere neutral link between the factors responsible for human behavior and this behavior as the product of such factors." [15] It is an error, however, to concentrate on the initiating factors and the resulting behavior to the exclusion of the intervening variable of meaning that occupies a vital—and problematical—part of the causal chain.

Second, meaning is not to be found as an intrinsic quality of the thing itself, as an invariable feature of objective reality, nor is the source of meaning to be located in the person's mind or psychological organization. Instead, meaning arises out of interaction between people. "The meaning of a thing for a person grows out of the way in which other persons act toward the person with regard to the thing. . . . Thus, symbolic interactionism sees meaning as social products, as creatures that are formed in and through the defining activities of people as they interact." [16]

Third, it is a mistake to think that meaning is used by a person in a mechanical fashion. Instead, it should be recognized that the use of meaning involves a process of interpretation. "The actor selects, checks, suspends, regroups, and transforms the meaning in the light of the situation in which he is placed and the direction of his action," explains Blumer. "Accordingly, interpretation should not be regarded as a mere

[15] Blumer, *Symbolic Interactionism*, pp. 2–3.
[16] Ibid., pp. 4–5.

automatic application of established meanings but as a formative process in which meanings are used and revised as instruments for the guidance and formation of action." And in this formative process the actor interacts not only with others but also with himself, communicating with himself in a silent dialogue to produce interpretations that influence his actions.[17]

Studies Based on Social Interactionist Theory

Blumer's perspective on social interaction lies behind the work of a large number of sociologists who in the 1950s and 1960s began to examine deviant behavior (including criminal behavior) by means of procedures such as participant observation and informal interviewing, often in small exploratory studies, aimed at understanding human actions from the actors' point of view.[18] A slum environment, patterns of childhood socialization, socioeconomic position, membership in a subculture, social disorganization—all these became far less important than a process of interaction in which the individual's perception of himself and the way he is perceived by others, growing out of an exchange of meanings that could not be fixed in advance, were the source of deviance.

Thus, for example, in Becker's often cited analysis of the use of marijuana, it is pointed out that the novice does not usually get high the first time he smokes marijuana. Several attempts are usually necessary, since the individual must learn to inhale the correct quantity of air to produce intoxication. The technique is picked up by participating in social groups where the drug is used. Furthermore, says Becker, even after the technique is acquired, the person must learn to recognize the symptoms of being high, to identify the physical and psychological effects of smoking and to separate what is pleasurable from what is not. This knowledge is also obtained by talking to others. Finally, one more step is needed if the individual who has learned to get high is to continue using the drug.

[17] Ibid., p. 5.

[18] The following writers exemplify the developing interactionist viewpoint in the area of deviance: Howard S. Becker, "Becoming a Marijuana User," *American Journal of Sociology* 59 (November 1953), pp. 235–42; David Matza, *Becoming Deviant* (Englewood Cliffs, N.J.: Prentice-Hall, 1969); Edwin M. Lemert, *Social Pathology* (New York: McGraw-Hill, 1951); John I. Kitsuse, "Societal Reactions to Deviant Behavior," *Social Problems* 9 (Winter 1962), pp. 247–56; David Sudnow, "Normal Crimes: Sociological Features of the Penal Code," *Social Problems* 12(Winter 1965), pp. 255–75; Kai T. Erikson, "Notes on the Sociology of Deviance," *Social Problems* 9 (Spring 1962), pp. 307–14; Richard D. Schwartz and Jerome H. Skolnick, "Two Studies of Legal Stigma," in Howard S. Becker, ed., *The Other Side: Perspectives on Deviance* (New York: The Free Press, 1964), pp. 103–17; Albert J. Reiss, Jr., "The Social Integration of Queers and Peers," in Becker, *The Other Side,* pp. 181–210; Irving Piliavin and Scott Briar, "Police Encounters with Juveniles," *American Journal of Sociology* 70 (September 1964), pp. 206–14; J. L. Simmons, *Deviants* (Berkeley, Calif.: The Glendessary Press, 1969); Aaron V. Cicourel, *The Social Organization of Juvenile Justice* (New York: John Wiley & Sons, 1968); Erving Goffman, *Asylums* (New York: Anchor, 1961); Harold Finestone, "Cats, Kicks, and Color," *Social Problems* 5 (July 1957), pp. 3–13.

"He must learn to enjoy the effects he has just learned to experience," Becker argues. "Marihuana-produced sensations are not automatically or necessarily pleasurable. . . . The user feels dizzy, thirsty, his scalp tingles; he misjudges time and distances. Are these things pleasurable? He isn't sure. If he is to continue marihuana use, he must decide that they are. Otherwise, getting high, while a real enough experience, will be an unpleasant one he would rather avoid." [19]

Many other forms of deviant behavior, it is claimed, involve a similar sequential learning of definitions, or meanings, in a process of interacting with one's self and others. The reasons for deviant behavior are to be sought not in the defective childhood socialization of the individual; or in such configurations of the individual's characteristics as age, sex, and social class; or in the contradictions of modern industrial society. Instead, the explanation is assumed to be found in the development and transformation of the symbols that form the stuff of human communication. In short, it is in words we find our destiny. The phrases and sentences we have learned from others and which we modify and repeat to ourselves lie at the heart of our actions.

In James Bryan's study of prostitution, the learning that takes place involves two interrelated dimensions, one philosophical and the other personal. [20] The former, according to Bryan, involves the imparting of a value structure in which prostitutes serve an apprenticeship, learn that people in general and men in particular are corrupt or easily corruptible, that all social relationships are part of a con game, and that prostitution is simply a more honest or at least no more dishonest act than the everyday behavior of "squares." [21] The personal dimension concerns the informal norms of behavior governing the relationships of prostitutes with one another, with customers, and with pimps. During her training period, the prostitute gradually comes to perceive the customer as a legitimate target of exploitation and other prostitutes as intelligent, self-interested, and trustworthy. She learns how to make "pitches" on the telephone, how and when to obtain her fee, and how to deal with the sexual habits of specific customers. These new perceptions and techniques, acquired over a period of several months, provide an explanation of prostitution. [22]

[19] Howard S. Becker, "Becoming a Marihuana User," p. 239.

[20] James H. Bryan, "Apprenticeships in Prostitution," *Social Problems* 12 (Winter 1965), pp. 287–97.

[21] Ibid.

[22] See also Norman R. Jackson, Richard O'Toole, and Gilbert Geis, "The Self-Image of the Prostitute," *The Sociological Quarterly* 4 (Spring 1963), pp. 150–60. An explanation of prostitution from a structural-functional viewpoint, which stresses the sources of the demands for the services of a prostitute, stands in sharp contrast. See Kingsley Davis, "Sexual Behavior," in Robert K. Merton and Robert Nisbet, *Contemporary Social Problems,* 2nd ed. (New York: Harcourt Brace Jovanovich, 1976), pp. 246–50.

Albert Cohen, in his study of delinquent behavior, places a similar stress on the interactive process. As indicated in Chapter 7, Cohen argues that the working-class young male faces continual failure in meeting the dominant, middle-class standards of achievement. Unable to succeed along lines permitted by society, he seeks alternative avenues of achievement that will be acceptable to his peers. The difficulty is that all members of society, including working-class young males, have been exposed to powerful pressures demanding conformity and have internalized the conventional norms. How can a set of alternative norms come into existence?

The answer, says Cohen, is to be found in interaction among individuals with similar problems of adjustment. A person makes a gesture toward cultural innovation—such as according respect to vandalism or physical aggression—in the hope that it will strike a responsive and sympathetic chord in others and not elicit hostility, ridicule, or punishment. It is a small, tentative, and ambiguous gesture that allows the individual to retreat and not to become identified with an unpopular position if his reception proves unfavorable. If the probing gesture provides a solution for tensions common to the youngster's peers, it is likely to initiate a process of mutual exploration and joint elaboration of a subculture of delinquency. Thus, by a series of *exploratory gestures,* the young, working-class male proceeds into delinquency—a form of behavior in which he can succeed. "By a causal, semi-serious, noncommittal or tangential remark I may stick my neck out just a little way, but I will quickly withdraw it unless you, by some sign of affirmation, stick *yours* out," notes Cohen. "I will permit myself to become progressively committed but only as others, by some visible sign, become likewise committed. The final product, to which we are jointly committed, is likely to be a compromise formation of all the participants to what we may call a cultural process, a formation perhaps unanticipated by any of them. Each actor may contribute something directly to the growing product, but he may also contribute indirectly by encouraging others to advance, inducing them to retreat, and suggesting new avenues to be explored. The product cannot be ascribed to any one of the participants; it is a real 'emergent' on a group level."[23]

Cohen thus provides an analysis of delinquent behavior from the delinquent's viewpoint, to be joined to his functional analysis of the delinquent subculture—a dual attack on the problem of delinquency that is infrequently encountered in criminological literature.[24]

[23] Albert K. Cohen, *Delinquent Boys* (New York: The Free Press, 1955), pp. 60–61. A similar tentative, groping movement toward deviance is embodied in Matza's concept of "the invitational edge" of deviance. Here too the stress is on the idea that the individual *may* break the law, but that is an outcome dependent on a long string of contingencies. See Matza, *Becoming Deviant.*

[24] Cohen, "The Sociology of the Deviant Act: Anomie Theory and Beyond."

The emphasis on the course of action as seen by the actor is perhaps most apparent in Donald Cressey's study of embezzlement, which was mentioned in Chapter 3. According to Cressey, when a person in a position of fiscal responsibility has financial problems that he is embarrassed to share with others—losses at the race track, the expenses of maintaining an extramarital relationship, a failing business—he is likely to think of the opportunities his job offers for obtaining the money he needs without anyone knowing. Once he sees his position in this light, the meaning of his situation is transformed, and the likelihood of crime increases. But these two conditions—a financial problem that cannot be shared, a recognition that legitimate duties can be turned to illegitimate use—must be followed by a third, Cressey argues, before the person will violate the trust placed in him. He must come to see his illegal action as noncriminal, or justified, or as an act of irresponsibility for which he cannot be held accountable.[25] In effect, the individual finds a way of rationalizing his action, but before the action has occurred rather than after. "We began using the 'rationalization' terminology," says Cressey, "when it was discovered that the application of certain key verbalizations to his conduct enables the individual to 'adjust' his conceptions of himself as a trusted person with his conceptions of himself as a user of trusted funds for solving a non-sharable problem."[26] The rationalization thus serves as motivation and it makes the individual's behavior intelligible both to other people and to himself.[27]

Cressey's study of embezzlement first appeared in 1953; and, as the author indicates in his preface to the current edition, it appears to fit better with the study of social behavior from the individual's viewpoint than with the quantitative, simplified cause-and-effect orientation that dominated so much sociological thinking shortly after World War II. In any event, Cressey's concern with rationalizations has added a significant dimension to symbolic interactionism as a mode of explanation for criminal behavior; and, as we shall see later in this chapter, his study of embezzlement has influenced a number of criminologists who see the manipulation of moral meanings as a crucial part of the interactive process leading to violations of the criminal law.

Analysis of criminal behavior from a symbolic interactionist point of view manages to convey much of the individual's experience as he or she engages in illegal activity. Conscious purposes, attitudes toward the law,

[25] Donald R. Cressey, *Other People's Money: A Study in the Social Psychology of Embezzlement* (Belmont, Calif.: Wadsworth, 1971), p. 85.

[26] Ibid., p. 94.

[27] See C. Wright Mills, "Situated Actions and Vocabularies of Motive," *American Sociological Review* 5 (December 1940), pp. 904–13. Cressey traces the use of the concept through the work of T. W. Richards, *Modern Clinical Psychology* (New York: McGraw-Hill, 1946); K. Young, *Personality and Problems of Adjustment* (New York: F. S. Crofts, 1946); and R. T. LaPiere and P. R. Farnsworth, *Social Psychology* (New York: McGraw-Hill, 1946).

one's perception of one's self, of one's social situation, and of one's peers emerge as important elements in an involved process in which an internal psychic dialogue shapes outward actions. Crime can be seen as more than a mechanical response to an external stimulus, so that the criminal can be understood as something different from an experimental animal struggling in its cage. Criminal behavior becomes meaningful, rather than the compulsion of a sick mind or the probable consequence of a particular social environment. At the same time, the interactionist perspective has left a number of theoretical issues unresolved.

First, much of the literature based on this perspective is descriptive rather than causally explanatory. Despite frequent assertions that behavior must be seen as an outcome of a process, the precise sequence of required steps is seldom specified. Statements claiming that events *may* be related in a complex series cannot be taken as the equivalent of a rigorously demonstrated causal chain. It can be argued, of course, that the process of symbolic interaction resulting in crime is too complex to be reduced to a precise series of correlations that indicate not simply correlation but causation as well. This may be true, but it is important to distinguish between events that are viewed as inherently incapable of being analyzed in specific, cause-and-effect terms and those that cannot be so analyzed at the present time because of our ignorance. Adherents of the interactionist perspective are not, in general, inclined to draw a line between the two.

Second, the analysis of criminal behavior from a symbolic interactionist viewpoint has frequently—and often deliberately—failed to raise the question of which people are most likely to become involved in the sequence of events that lead to crime. Such an issue, it is said, is misleading, because the sources of crime do not lie within the individual but are to be found instead in the interactive process among individuals. "The conventional style of studying deviance has focussed on the deviant himself and has asked its questions mainly about him," says Becker. "Who is he? Where did he come from? How did he get that way? Is he likely to keep on being that way? The new approach sees it as always a process of interaction between at least two kinds of people: those who commit (or are said to have committed) a deviant act and the rest of society."[28] This "new approach" developed into labeling theory, in which how and why society reacts to real or alleged deviance is of greater interest than deviance itself. We will examine this theory in a moment, but the important point here is that the interactionist perspective is primarily concerned with the process of becoming deviant, rather than with identifying the distinguishing characteristics of the criminal.

[28] Becker, *The Other Side,* p. 2.

The difficulties with this position are that, first, it represents a premature closure of the possibility that there are in fact important individual differences associated with violations of the law; and second, it may lead to an indifference to the cultural or structural sources of deviant behavior. If it is assumed that anybody can become deviant or criminal, that it is simply a matter of engaging in a particular process of social interaction and that variation in the larger social context is of no importance, both the individual *and* the social structure are likely to be slighted—and this is precisely what a social-psychological approach is supposed to avoid.

Labeling Theory

In the accounts of criminal behavior discussed above, the lack of attention paid to the societal element in social interaction is perhaps most significant with regard to the role of the state and its battery of official sanctions. "That anyone—sociologists especially—could write as if the authoritative fact of ban was of minor importance in the process of becoming deviant is hardly believable," says Matza. "To ignore the impact of ban is tantamount to suggesting that Leviathan can be irrelevant in the lives of ordinary men who fall within its oppressive ambit."[29] But this is precisely what happened, he points out, in the first half of this century. "The role of the sovereign, and by extension, instituted authority, was hardly considered in the study of deviant behavior. That lofty subject, unrelated to so seamy a matter as deviation, was to be studied in *political* science. There, as in the curriculum in government or political sociology, Leviathan had little bearing on ordinary criminals. And in criminology, the process of becoming an ordinary criminal was unrelated to the workings of the state."[30] In the last three decades or so, a growing body of literature that can be entitled labeling theory has sought to rectify the error.

Secondary Deviance

In 1951, with the publication of *Social Pathology*, Edwin Lemert helped to set the study of deviant behavior—including crime—on a new course.[31] In the early history of sociology, he pointed out, sociologists concerned with the ills of society simply drew on their intuitive sense of morality or followed the lead of the social reformers of the time to place the tags of *good* or *bad* on various social conditions. Like General Custer, said Lemert, their tactics were simple; they rode to the sound of the guns.

[29] *Becoming Deviant*, p. 143.
[30] Ibid., p. 144.
[31] *Social Pathology* (New York: McGraw-Hill, 1951).

Gradually, however, the study of social problems became more sophisticated. It was soon recognized that reform movements often create more problems than they solve, with the reform movement itself sometimes becoming the social ill in need of remedy, as in the case of Prohibition. And no less important, it became even more plain that the values cherished by society play a significant part in producing behavior that reform groups disapproved of and sought to eliminate. As a consequence, sociologists grew more sensitive to the issue of who defines a particular situation as a social problem and why such definitions are brought into play. The time had come, Lemert argued, to make a sharp break with the outlook of an older generation of social pathologists, to abandon the archaic idea, based on the practice of medicine, that human beings can be divided into the normal and the pathological—or, if some such division must be made, to divest the term "pathological" of its moralistic overtones.[32]

Lemert paid far more explicit and systematic attention to the social reactions to deviant behavior than other sociologists before him. Admiration, awe, envy, sympathy, fear, repulsion, disgust, hate, and anger were the elemental stuff from which society formed a response to those who broke the rules, he argued, and must be taken into account by any theory that attempted to explain the behavior in question. A great variety of subjective motives and objective external events may underlie an initial deviant act, or *primary deviance;* but once society responds to the act, a new factor comes into play. Individuals begin to "react symbolically to their own behavior aberrations and fix them in their social-psychological patterns."[33] Society is most likely to respond if the deviant act is repeated by the person and has high visibility (for example, drug use, prostitution, juvenile delinquency, homosexuality); and the response of society is most likely to become a causal element if the individual incorporates society's response into his own concept of self and reorganizes his social roles on that basis. When this occurs, the behavior is called *secondary deviation.* The important point is that society's reactions to violations of the rules are not merely an effect of deviant behavior but a causal element as well.

One deviant act will seldom provoke a sufficiently strong societal reaction to bring about secondary deviance, said Lemert. "Most frequently there is a progressive reciprocal relationship between the deviation of the individual and the societal reaction, with a compounding of the societal reaction out of the minute accretions in deviant behavior, until a point is reached where ingrouping and outgrouping between society and the deviant is manifest. At this point a stigmatizing of the deviant occurs

[32] Ibid., p. 21.
[33] Ibid., p. 75.

in the form of name calling, labeling, or stereotyping."[34] The sequence of interaction leading to secondary deviation, then, is roughly as follows: (1) primary deviance; (2) societal penalties; (3) further deviation; (4) stronger penalties; (5) further deviation with hostility and resentment possibly beginning to be directed toward those doing the penalizing; (6) a crisis point where the community takes formal action and stigmatizes the deviant; (7) a strengthening of the deviant conduct as a reaction to the severe actions of society; and (8) finally, an acceptance of deviant social status and an attempt to adjust to the corresponding role.[35] By attempting to treat a social problem—crime, let us say, or alcoholism, or a physiological abnormality like blindness or stuttering, rather than a moral deviation—society was very apt to worsen the ill rather than improve it. In the act of singling out and labeling the aberration, society ensured its perpetuation. Some twenty years after the first publication of his argument, Lemert was ready to reverse the causal sequence that sociologists had traditionally accepted. Rather than accepting the position that deviance leads to social control, Lemert asserted that "I have come to believe that the reverse idea (*i.e.*, social control leads to deviance) is equally tenable and the potentially richer premise for studying deviance in modern society."[36]

In the late 1950s and the 1960s the concept of labeling was enthusiastically adopted by a number of younger sociologists who began to give the idea an added twist. As Lemert pointed out, the concept of labeling always had the potential for serving as "a convenient vehicle for civil libertarians or young men of sociology to voice angry critiques of social institutions."[37] If established society was deeply implicated in the causation of disapproved behavior, then established society must shoulder the blame for norm violation no less than those who violated the norms. If one identified with the poor and the oppressed who were blamed by society for the conduct that society itself produced, then a scientific analysis of those who did the blaming was far more attractive than a dissection of those who were blamed.[38] In approaching the explanation of crime and other forms of deviant behavior from this vantage point, the adherents of labeling theory soon began to place a heavy stress on the problematical nature of the link between deviant behavior and the sanctions of society.

The relationship between deviance and the opprobrium of society can take four forms (see Table 1). Type IV, involving those who conform to

[34] Ibid., pp. 76–77.

[35] Ibid., p. 77.

[36] Edwin M. Lemert, *Human Deviance, Social Problems and Social Control* (Englewood Cliffs, N.J.: Prentice-Hall, 1976), p. ix.

[37] Ibid., p. 91.

[38] See William Ryan, *Blaming the Victim* (New York: Vintage Books, 1971).

The lawbreaker draws on the social and cultural setting to construct a system of meanings and interpretations that motivates his crime and makes it explicable to others. A Charles Manson creating an apocalyptic vision of a war between the races, a Bonnie Parker glorifying the life of the outlaw in the 1930s, a man from the ghetto creating a life style of flashy elegance by means of pimping—these are examples of "constructed causes" of crime.

Table 1. Deviant Behavior and Societal Reactions[a]

	Occurrence of Deviant Behavior	Labeling and Sanctioning by Society
Type I	Yes	Yes
Type II	Yes	No
Type III	No	Yes
Type IV	No	No

[a]Some writers might question this table on the grounds that the occurrence of deviance is always problematical rather than a matter of "yes" or "no"—an issue we will touch on in the following pages.

SOURCE: Reprinted with permission of Macmillan Publishing Co., Inc. from *Outsiders* by Howard S. Becker. Copyright © 1963 by The Free Press, a Division of the Macmillan Company.

the rules and do not suffer the sanctions of society, does not concern us here; the other three types, however, involve cases that have provided much of the substance for the concerns of labeling theory. Why are some of those who engage in deviant behavior singled out for labeling and sanctioning by society (type I)? Why do some of those who violate the rules escape official recognition (type II)? Why are some individuals who have not violated the norms stigmatized and treated as deviant (type III)? More colloquially, these experiences are contained in the accusatory questions often directed against the legal system: Why do some people get stuck for what everybody is doing? Why do some people get away with it? Why are some people hassled when they haven't done anything?

The Personal Bias Factor From the viewpoint of labeling theory, a large part of the answer to these questions is to be found in the prejudices and class biases of those who enforce the law. As we saw in Chapter 3, white-collar crime often escapes prosecution because of the middle-class or upper-class status of the offender; and in our examination of the police and the courts in Chapters 10 and 11 we shall see how persons in the upper reaches of society often manage to get preferential treatment. Singling out certain individuals for punishment is a frequent occurrence, however, as well as ignoring criminal activity, and involves juvenile delinquents as well as adult criminals.

In a study conducted by Irving Piliavin and Scott Briar, for example, it was found that police reactions to suspected adolescent offenders were strongly influenced by the race, class, and demeanor of the suspect and were not merely a reflection of the evidence pointing to a violation of the law. The disposition of juveniles could range from outright release to official reprimand to arrest and confinement—and the course followed, Piliavin and Briar point out, can have profound consequences. Arrest may lead not only to restrictions of educational and occupational opportunities but may, in a process of stigmatization, reinforce deviant behavior and serve as a catalytic agent initiating a delinquent career.[39] Serious crimes, such as robbery, homicide, assault, rape, or theft, usually resulted in an arrest of the youth involved. The bulk of the offenses coming to the attention of the police, however, involved minor violations of the law, and in these cases an assessment of the character of the juveniles played a major part in the decision of the police. But because the police officers had only limited information about the juveniles, "both the decision made in the field—whether or not to bring the boy in—and the decision made at the station—which disposition to invoke—were based largely on cues which emerged from the interaction between the officer and the youth, cues from which the officer inferred the youth's character. These cues involved the youth's group affiliation, age, race, grooming, dress, and demeanor. Older juveniles, members of known delinquent gangs, Negroes, youths with well-oiled hair, black jackets, and soiled denims or jeans (the presumed uniform of 'tough' boys), and boys who in their interaction with officers did not manifest what were considered to be appropriate signs of respect tended to receive the more severe dispositions."[40]

Similar findings have been described by Aaron Cicourel, although in his account of the interaction between juveniles and probation officers the stress on demeanor is even greater. "When we merely abstract information from official records," says Cicourel, "so that structural comparisons are possible (e.g., broken home, low income, ethnicity, negative social character), the contingencies of unfolding interaction, the typifications (theories of 'good' and 'bad' juveniles, families, etc.), are excluded from our understanding of how legal or other rules were invoked to justify a particular interpretation and course of action. . . . Knowledge of how reports are assembled is needed to transform the formal report descriptions into processual statements about the public and private ideologies of law-enforcement agencies."[41] At the heart of this process, he argues, is the interpretation by officials of such things as the physical appearance of juveniles, their facial expressions, and so on. The classification as delinquent, with all its profound consequences for the individual's future, is not so much a matter of the factual details concerning the individual's deviation from or conformity to the law as of the

---

[39] Piliavin and Briar, "Police Encounters with Juveniles."
[40] Piliavin and Briar, "Police Encounters with Juveniles," p. 210.
[41] Cicourel, *The Social Organization of Juvenile Justice*, pp. 121–22.

probation officer's reaction to the presentation of self made by the suspected offender. In analyzing the interaction between probation officers and alleged delinquent teenagers with records of theft, burglary, and sexual nonconformity, Cicourel points out that "if the girl was described as a 'punk' or a 'bitch' in conjunction with her stealing activities, the likely disposition is to send the juvenile to the Youth Authority. But a juvenile who is 'appealing and attractive,' and who 'wants very much to be liked and relates in a friendly manner to all around her,' is a prime candidate for clinical interpretations as opposed to criminal implications. Finding 'problems' in the home is not difficult, but there is no way for the observer to decide such matters independently if he relies solely upon documents. The transformation of the juvenile into a sick object permits all concerned to suspend the criminal imputations of her acts, even though the penal code sections are quoted each time the police report theft or burglary."[42] It is demeanor, then, rather than the realities of norm violations, that is likely to determine whether the criminal sanctions of the states are called into play. Labeling criminals and delinquents cannot be viewed as an exact reflection of criminal and delinquent behavior—and the act of labeling, arising in the interaction between the alleged offender and law enforcement officials, becomes a crucial factor in shaping the individual's subsequent conduct.

The Negotiated Outcome

It is not to be assumed, however, that all labeling is based on the personal biases of officials with regard to race, class, or conceptions of proper appearance. Organizational expectations or demands also play an important part in law enforcement decisions. Robert Emerson has provided an illuminating analysis of how the juvenile court, guided by pressures from community agencies like the police and the schools, considerations of available treatment facilities, and its own ideology concerning delinquency and its cure, reacts to the children who appear before it. The study, says Emerson, was undertaken from the theoretical viewpoint that sees deviance as the product of the way agents of social control respond to perceived norm violations; and his attention centered on the juvenile court's distinctive role in the labeling process.[43]

A major factor in the decisions made by juvenile court officials was the perceived moral character of the juvenile offender. In general, three main types were distinguished. First, there were those juveniles characterized as "normal" children. They were assumed to be acting on the basis of conventional motives, and their entanglement with the law was attributable largely to "accident." Second, there were delinquents who were seen as "hard-core" or "criminal-like" and who were believed to be

[42] Ibid., pp. 131–32.
[43] Robert M. Emerson, *Judging Delinquents* (Chicago: Aldine, 1969), p. vii.

maliciously motivated, consciously pursuing illegal ends, and marked by a deep hostility to society and its surrogates. And, third, there were "disturbed" children, who were seen as being driven into senseless and irrational violations of the law by obscure motives and inner compulsions.[44]

The juveniles appearing before the court are placed in these categories not on the basis of objectively established evidence, Emerson argues, but as the result of interaction and communication involving the delinquent, his family, complainants, law enforcement officials, and the court itself. The version of moral character finally accepted is *negotiated*, Emerson stresses, rather than *proven*, and reflects a variety of organizational considerations, the success or failure of "presentation strategies," and reactions to justifications, excuses and other defensive measures.[45] The decisions of the court are subjected to other compromises and modifications, stemming from the policies of the psychiatric clinic, the reform school, and other community agencies that have a stake in the handling of the juvenile offender. The social reaction to the juvenile delinquent, then, which plays such a large part in shaping both how the individual sees himself and how others see him, is strongly influenced by bureaucratic operations that transcend the personal views of officials.[46]

The studies that have been cited to illustrate the use of labeling theory in the interpretation of illegal behavior have been concentrated in the area of juvenile delinquency—and it is probably no accident that when labeling theory has been applied to deviant behavior in the form of law violations, juvenile delinquency and offenses involving drugs and sexual nonconformity have most often been selected for analysis. These crimes—variously and vaguely defined and subject to much public disagreement—appear most suited to "negotiated" outcomes. "Some specific forms of deviation may . . . lend themselves less readily to labeling analysis than do others," Edwin Schur has suggested.[47] Deviant acts that are not repeated by the individual or fail to undergo elaboration are difficult to explain from the labeling viewpoint, he argues, and thus a discrete act of homicide seems to incorporate fewer labeling processes than does long-term addiction to drugs.[48]

[44] Ibid., Chapter 4.

[45] Ibid., Chapters 5 and 6.

[46] For an excellent examination of the far-reaching consequences of legal labeling, see Richard D. Schwartz and Jerome H. Skolnick, "Two Studies in Legal Stigma," *Social Problems* 10 (Fall 1962), pp. 133–38.

[47] Edwin M. Schur, *Labeling Deviant Behavior: Its Sociological Implications* (New York: Harper & Row, 1971), p. 21.

[48] It has been argued, however, that even the legal rules defining homicide are far from clear, thus opening the door to a "negotiated" outcome. See Charles L. Black, Jr., *Capital Punishment* (New York: W. W. Norton, 1975).

Other limitations of labeling theory are evident, such as the frequent tendency to slide into a kind of solipsism in which it is suggested that deviance is no more than a subjective reaction. Social groups create deviance, Becker has claimed, "by making the rules whose infraction constitutes deviance, and by applying these rules to particular people and labeling them as outsiders. From this point of view, deviance is not a quality of the act the person commits, but rather a consequence of the application by others of rules and sanctions to an 'offender.' The deviant is one to whom that label has successfully been applied; deviant behavior is behavior that people so label."[49] Similarly, Kai Erikson has asserted that "deviance is not a property *inherent* in certain forms of behavior; it is a property *conferred upon* these forms by the audiences which directly or indirectly witness them. Sociologically, then, the critical variable is the social audience rather than the individual actor, since it is the audience which eventually determines whether or not any episode of behavior or any class of episodes is labeled deviant."[50] Many sociologists, of course, have long recognized that all categorizations of social behavior, scientific or otherwise, involve a social process and that classifications—including typologies of criminal or deviant behavior—are indeed human-produced and not something "inherent" in nature.

It is understandable that in trying to emphasize the uncertain relationship between society's application of the label *deviant* and the actual occurrence of deviant behavior, a number of writers overemphasize the novelty of their position by asserting that the reacting social audience is the critical variable. But it is unfortunate that the assertion has sometimes been taken to mean that "the reality of the individual's behavior is irrelevant" or that "deviance exists only in the eye of the beholder." Establishing the *existence* of an individual's behavior, as overt actions that did or did not occur, is one issue; presumably the question can be answered in such a fashion that observers can agree. The *characterization* of that behavior, in terms of the imputation of motive, for example, or the classification as deviant, is another issue, whether one employs commonly accepted social definitions or a scientific framework (itself a matter of accepted meanings in a scientific community).[51] The adherents of labeling theory have sometimes confused the two or stated their position in such a way that confusion has easily followed. As a consequence, the analysis of deviant behavior, including crime, often makes it appear that the reactions of agencies of social control are inevitably arbitrary and entail the unjust oppression of those whom society has decided to ca-

---

[49] Howard S. Becker, *The Outsiders* (New York: The Free Press, 1963), p. 9.

[50] "Notes on the Sociology of Deviance," Becker, *The Other Side*, pp. 10–11.

[51] See Melvin Pollner, "Sociological and Common-sense Models of the Labeling Process," in Roy Turner, ed., *Ethnomethodology* (Baltimore: Penguin Books, 1974), pp. 27–40.

tegorize as violators of the norms.[52] Far more precise knowledge is needed about when and why there is a discrepancy between the occurrence of criminal behavior and the labeling of the individual as criminal, and when and why there is variation in the social reaction to those who have allegedly violated the criminal law. When this knowledge is coupled with a better understanding of how these forms of labeling are related to the individual's subsequent deviant behavior, labeling theory will begin to fulfill the claims advanced in its name by its enthusiastic followers.

The Manipulation of Moral Meanings

In his study of embezzlement, Cressey identified a number of factors that he claimed were necessary and sufficient causal elements. Among these was the ability to rationalize the theft of money placed in one's trust, so that the illegal act was no longer regarded as morally reprehensible. It was this idea that Sykes and Matza singled out and advanced as a general causal factor underlying a good deal of juvenile delinquency and, by implication, much adult crime as well.

Only infrequently, they argued, do juvenile delinquents see their illegal behavior as fully legitimate, despite the claims of some criminologists that in deviant subcultures it was possible to find the norms of conventional society turned upside down. The world of the delinquent is embedded in the larger world of those who conform, and most juveniles cannot fail to internalize a large share of society's standards of behavior. Somehow these demands for conformity must be faced and answered—or neutralized—before the juvenile is likely to engage in delinquency.[53]

The evidence supporting the claim that delinquents cling to conven-

[52] Peter Manning has argued that the labeling perspective has been exhausted for such reasons as these, and that a "conceptual ennui is spreading like a grey fog, bringing with it a concomitant waning in interest, commitment, and attachment to deviance studies" (Manning, survey essay "On Deviance" in *Contemporary Sociology* 2 [March 1973], pp. 123–28). His criticisms are both accurate and important, but his pessimism concerning labeling theory seems premature. For other critical comments on the labeling perspective, see Walter R. Gove, "Societal Reaction as an Explanation of Mental Illness: An Evaluation," *American Sociological Review* 35 (October 1970), pp. 873–84; John Hagan, "Labelling and Deviance: A Case Study in the Sociology of the Interesting," *Social Problems* 20 (Spring 1973), pp. 447–58; Joseph W. Rogers and M. D. Buffalo, "Fighting Back: Nine Modes of Adaptation to a Deviant Label," Social Problems 22 (October 1974), pp. 101–18; Charles Wellford, "Labeling Theory and Criminology: An Assessment," *Social Problems* 22 (February 1975), pp. 332–45; Walter R. Gove, ed., *The Labelling of Deviance* (New York: John Wiley & Sons, 1975); and Alvin Gouldner, "The Sociologist as Partisan: Sociology and the Welfare State," *The American Sociologist* 3 (May 1968), pp. 103–16.

[53] Gresham M. Sykes and David Matza, "Techniques of Neutralization: A Theory of Delinquency," *American Sociological Review* 22 (December 1957), pp. 664–70.

tional norms—even though their behavior is outside the law—takes a number of forms. First, many delinquents exhibit feelings of shame and guilt when they are apprehended, and not merely as a manipulative gesture to appease those in authority. If delinquents were completely socialized into a deviant subculture, they might be expected to show indignation or a sense of martyrdom. But this is only occasionally the case—and then the sense of martyrdom often seems to be based on the fact that others "get away with it," and the indignation appears to be directed against the ineptitude or bad luck that led to their arrest. Second, juvenile delinquents frequently accord admiration and respect to law-abiding persons, often with the declaration that such persons are "really honest." A great deal of resentment may be expressed if illegal behavior is imputed to significant figures in the delinquent's immediate social environment or to heroes in the world of sport and entertainment. Third, many studies have shown that juvenile delinquents often draw a sharp line between those who, in their view, can be victimized and those who cannot. In general, the potentiality for victimization appears to be a function of social distance between the delinquent and others, and maxims such as "Don't commit vandalism against a church of your own faith" or "Don't steal from your friends" are often encountered. The "wrongfulness" of delinquent behavior is apparently often recognized. In short, no matter how deeply enmeshed in patterns of illegal behavior the delinquent may be, the delinquent has been exposed to demands for conformity that are frequently incorporated into his or her value system. It is the paradoxical fact of delinquency arising in such a situation that requires explanation.

Neutralization Techniques

The answer to the question of how the delinquent can violate norms without abandoning them, it is argued, is to to be found in "techniques of neutralization," whereby disapproval flowing from internalized norms and from those who conform is neutralized, turned back, or deflected in advance. Justifications or rationalizations, which are seen as valid by the delinquent but seldom by society at large, precede the deviant behavior and make it possible by protecting the individual from the restraining voice of conscience and the possible condemnation of others. In this way the delinquent has his cake and eats it too, for he remains committed to the norms of society and yet so qualifies their imperatives that violations become "acceptable" if not "right." [54]

Sykes and Matza distinguish five major techniques of neutralization.

[54] See M. D. Buffalo and Joseph W. Rogers, "Behavioral Norms, Moral Norms, and Attachment," *Social Problems* 19 (Summer 1971), pp. 101–07. See also Joseph W. Rogers, *Why Are You Not a Criminal?* (Englewood Cliffs, N.J.: Prentice-Hall, 1977).

The first is the denial of responsibility ("I couldn't help it"). The delinquent defines himself as not being responsible for his illegal behavior, and he does so for reasons that often extend beyond mere accident or some similar negation of personal accountability. The delinquent may claim that his acts are the result of external forces beyond his control, such as unloving parents, bad companions, or a slum neighborhood. Or the delinquent may argue that he has been thrown into a rage by no fault of his own and can no longer restrain himself. By learning to view himself as more acted upon than acting, the delinquent prepares the way for illegal behavior that violates the norms but does not necessitate a frontal assault on them.

The second technique is the denial of injury ("I didn't really hurt anybody"). The criminal law has long made a distinction between crimes that are *mala in se* and *mala prohibita*—that is, between acts that are wrong in themselves and acts that are illegal but not immoral—and the delinquent can and does make the same kind of distinction in evaluating the wrongfulness of his behavior. In the eyes of the delinquent, however, wrongfulness may turn largely on the question of whether anyone will clearly be hurt by the illegal act, and this is a matter open to a variety of interpretations. Vandalism, for example, may be thought of as mere mischief, since it is claimed that the persons whose property has been destroyed can well afford it. Similarly, auto theft may be viewed as "borrowing" and gang fighting as a private quarrel, an agreed-upon duel between two willing parties.

The third technique of neutralization is the denial of the victim ("They had it coming to them"). Even when the delinquent accepts responsibility for his illegal behavior and is willing to admit that his actions involve an injury or hurt, the moral disapproval of self and others may be neutralized by an insistence that the injury is not wrong in light of the circumstances. The injury, it may be claimed, is a rightful form of retaliation or punishment. Assaults on homosexuals or alleged homosexuals, attacks on members of minority groups who are said to have "gotten out of place," vandalism as revenge on an unfair teacher or school officials, thefts from a "crooked" store owner—all may be, in the eyes of the delinquent, justified hurts inflicted on a transgressor.

Fourth, there is the condemnation of the condemners ("Everybody's picking on me") or, as Lloyd McCorkle and Richard Korn have phrased it, a rejection of the rejectors.[55] The delinquent shifts the focus of attention from his own illegal behavior to the motives and behavior of those

[55] Lloyd W. McCorkle and Richard Korn, "Resocialization Within Walls," *The Annals of the American Academy of Political and Social Science* 293 (May 1954), pp. 88–98.

who disapprove of his violations of the law. His condemners, he may claim, are hypocrites, deviants in disguise, or impelled by personal spite. This definition of the conforming world may be particularly important when it turns into cynicism directed against those assigned the task of enforcing the law or expressing the norms of conventional society. Police, it may be said, are corrupt, stupid, and brutal. Teachers always show favoritism, and parents always "take it out" on their children. The delinquent, in effect, has changed the subject of the conversation in the dialogue between his own deviant acts and the reactions of others; and by attacking others, the wrongfulness of his own behavior is more easily repressed or lost from view.

The fifth technique of neutralization is the appeal to higher loyalties ("I didn't do it for myself"). Internal and external social controls may be neutralized by sacrificing the demands of social norms to the demands of immediate social relationships, such as the gang, the friendship clique, or the ethnic group. The conflict between the claims of friendship and the claims of law is an old-age human problem. If the delinquent frequently resolves his dilemma by insisting that he must always "help a buddy" or "never squeal on a friend," even when it throws him into serious difficulties with the law, his reasoning remains familiar to the law-abiding. The delinquent is unusual, perhaps, in the extent to which he uses such justifications for violations of society's norms, but it is a matter of degree rather than kind. In short, the delinquent does not necessarily repudiate the imperatives of society, despite his failure to follow them. Rather, the delinquent may see himself as caught up in a dilemma that must be resolved, unfortunately, at the cost of violating the law.[56]

The five slogans that give expression to each of the neutralization strategies, it is claimed, prepare the juvenile for delinquency. These definitions of the situation represent glancing blows at the dominant normative system rather than the creation of an opposing set of norms; and they are extensions of patterns of thought prevalent in society rather than something newly created. The crucial point, however, is that by lessening the effectiveness of social controls, neutralization increases the likelihood of delinquent behavior and can be expected to have the same effect on adult criminality.

Sykes and Matza point out that techniques of neutralization are not simply idiosyncratic constructs or personal rationalizations developed on

---

[56] For an empirical study of the conflict between the claims of friendship and general social obligation (or, in the jargon of sociology, between particularistic and universalistic demands) see Samuel A. Stouffer and Jackson Toby, "Role Conflict and Personality," in Talcott Parsons and Edward A. Shils, eds., *Toward a General Theory of Action* (Cambridge, Mass.: Harvard University Press, 1951), pp. 481–96.

an ad hoc basis. As Daniel Glaser indicates, however, they fail to pay systematic attention to the way in which delinquent subcultures serve to create, reinforce, and transmit the perceptions of social reality that allow individuals to violate the law.[57] In a study undertaken by Albert Reiss, for example, it was found that for young males engaging in homosexual prostitution the rationales developed and sustained in peer groups were a major factor in allowing young males to avoid guilt feelings and to continue in a lucrative activity.[58] Lower-class status and membership in a minority group would appear to be particularly important as a possible social source of techniques of neutralization for some types of crime—such as offenses against property or violence directed against members of the white middle class; but a governmental role, suffused with an ideology of service or national security, can also provide rationales for breaking the law in the name of some higher purpose. These possible links between social structure and techniques of neutralization still remain largely unexplored.[59]

The reduction of guilt feelings arising from the anticipated response of self and others to deviant behavior is only one way in which social norms can be rendered inoperative. Walter Reckless and his associates have suggested that the individual's self-concept may also play a vital part in determining whether the person will be delinquent. If the juvenile defines himself as a "good boy," they argue, he will be "insulated" from pressures to engage in delinquent behavior. "It is proposed that a socially appropriate or inappropriate concept of self and others is the basic component that steers the youthful person away from or toward delinquency, and that those appropriate or inappropriate concepts repre-

The Role of the Self-Concept

[57] See Daniel Glaser, "Role Models and Differential Association," in Earl Rubington and Martin S. Weinburg, *Deviance: The Interactionist Perspective* (New York: Macmillan, 1973), pp. 369–72.

[58] Albert J. Reiss, Jr., "The Social Integration of Queers and Peers," *Social Problems* 9 (Fall 1961), pp. 102–20.

[59] For an empirical examination of the theory of techniques of neutralization, see Richard A. Ball, "An Empirical Exploration of Neutralization Theory," in Mark Lefton, James K. Skipper, Jr., and Charles H. McCaghy, eds., *Approaches to Deviance* (New York: Appleton-Century-Crofts, 1968), pp. 255–65; Joseph W. Rogers and M. D. Buffalo, "Neutralization Techniques: Toward a Simplified Measurement Scale," *Pacific Sociological Review* 17 (July 1974), pp. 313–31; Thomas Brian Prat and John H. McGrath, III, "Techniques of Neutralization: Young Adult Marijuana Smokers," *Criminology* 8 (August 1970), pp. 185–93; Charles H. McCaghy, "Drinking and Deviance Disavowal: The Case of Child Molesters," *Social Problems* 16 (Summer 1968), pp. 43–49; Michael J. Hindelang, "The Commitment of Delinquents to Their Misdeeds: Do Delinquents Drift?" *Social Problems* 17 (Spring 1970), pp. 502–09; and Herman Schwendinger and Julia Schwendinger, "Delinquent Stereotypes of Probable Victims," in Malcolm Klein, ed., *Juvenile Gangs in Context* (Englewood Cliffs, N.J.: Prentice-Hall, 1967), pp. 81–105.

sent the differential responses to various environments and confrontations of delinquency patterns. With self and other concepts operating in appropriate and inappropriate directions, the normal good boy in the high delinquency area, the normal bad boy in the high delinquency area, the normal good boy in the good environment and the normal bad boy in the good environment can be understood."[60] The problem of handling sanctions from the self and others in anticipation of illegal behavior is not the central issue, from this point of view. Instead, the important fact is that delinquent behavior is or is not allowed to occur because of a particular self-image. A "good boy" presumably does not even have to consider delinquent behavior as a possibility.

It is possible, of course, that a good self-concept does not lead to good behavior, but that good behavior results in a good self-concept—if a causal chain does in fact exist. Reckless has indicated that a set of questions assumed to measure self-concept has done "a pretty fair job of spotting the boys in the slums of the inner city who were headed for trouble and those in the same areas who were not headed for difficulty with the law."[61] The questions, however, appear to be a rather discordant mix, some dealing with perceptions of adults ("Are grown-ups usually against you?"), for example, and some with the individual's past history of stealing.[62] In addition, the concept of "insulation" is not examined in any detail; and, as in the case of techniques of neutralization, the basis of the social-psychological variables in the social structure remains no more than a suggestion, rather than being systematically analyzed.

Despite these defects, theories that have looked to the individual's efforts to deal with the moral implications of his or her actions have raised an important issue. The internalization of norms and the impact of normative pressures both from within the self and from external figures are not an either/or affair, not simply present or absent, operative or inoperative. Instead, the role of norms in social life, the way in which they affect the psychological functioning of the individual as he interacts with

[60] Walter C. Reckless, Simon Dinitz, and Barbara Kay, "The Self Component in Potential Delinquency and Potential Non-Delinquency," *American Sociological Review* 22 (October 1957), p. 570. See also Walter C. Reckless, Simon Dinitz, and Ellen Murray, "Self-Concept as an Insulator Against Delinquency," *American Sociological Review* 21 (December 1956), pp. 744–46.

[61] Walter C. Reckless, *The Crime Problem* (New York: Appleton-Century-Crofts, 1973), p. 87.

[62] For an attempt to measure self-concept using the semantic differential technique developed by Osgood and his associates, and to examine the relationship between self-concept and delinquency in a midwestern city, see Michael Schwartz and Sheldon Stryker, *Deviance, Self and Others* (Washington, D.C.: American Sociological Association, 1970).

himself and with others, appears to be filled with ambiguity, ambivalence, inconsistency, vacillation, distortion of reality, and rationalization. By recognizing and trying to take into account these "messy" details of the individual's relationships with society, the interpretation of deviant and criminal behavior becomes "naturalistic"—that is, committed to the philosophical view that strives to remain true to the nature of the phenomenon under study.[63]

A full explanation of criminal behavior cannot avoid the individual's perception of the normative or moral order in which certain acts are declared illegal; nor can it avoid the individual's reaction to the ethical dilemmas in which he finds himself. It is the concern of criminology for this aspect of criminal behavior that has, indeed, helped to make the study of crime a subject of continuing interest for sociological theory in general. "Since sociology, like any scientific discipline, has from its beginnings been inspired by the problems of human society which its practitioners have felt to be crucial for our own existence," says Jack Douglas, "it is easy to see why sociologists have always considered the problem of social order to be their one fundamental problem. And, given the crucial importance of moral rules in constructing social order in our Western societies, it is also easy to see why Western sociologists have taken social morality and its violations, which they have called 'deviance' for the last decade or so, to be a second crucial problem of social order. As a result, the sociology of deviance has formed much of the core, the foundation of sociology."[64] Crime and deviant behavior are not identical, of course, but there is a large area of overlap. In so far as crime is seen as a moral problem for both the actor and the audience, the study of crime is firmly linked to the larger discipline of the study of society.

Firsthand Accounts

Life stories of professional criminals have long been popular with the law-abiding public. Titillating glimpses of the underworld, frank confessions of a blithe disregard for the law, a narrative laced with exotic criminal argot and generally serving to win the author a good deal of sympathy and admiration despite his wrongdoing—the genre is familiar.

In the 1930s such accounts were elevated to a prominent place in the literature of criminology with the publication of Clifford Shaw's *The Jack-*

---

[63] For an excellent discussion of naturalism as an essential viewpoint in the study of social behavior, see Matza, *Becoming Deviant*, Chapter 1.

[64] Douglas, *Deviance and Respectability*, p. viii.

Roller and Edwin Sutherland's *The Professional Thief.*[65] Chic Conwell, the professional thief who provided the reminiscences on which Sutherland's book was based, was a keen and articulate observer, and Sutherland constructed a number of generalizations concerning the nature of professional crime which were quickly incorporated into criminological theory. Other firsthand accounts by criminals subsequently found their way into academic criminology, but in the 1960s their number began to increase sharply and the range of criminal behavior reported on was much enlarged.

These reports pose a number of difficulties. Firsthand accounts of crime are apt to be self-serving, as we have seen, and it is difficult to separate fact from fancy. Offenders who are able and willing to see their recollections committed to paper may be far from representative of the groups for which they speak. The selection of accounts for an academic audience may, on occasion, reflect a romanticized view of the criminal as a scapegoat or as an antihero—as an amusing and admirable rogue who has set his hand against established society with all its blandness and hypocrisies. If these limitations are kept in mind, however, the abbreviated life stories provide data that can be valuable both for the development of new theories and the assessment of existing interpretations of criminal behavior.[66]

The wealth of illuminating detail that makes firsthand accounts so valuable is illustrated by Carl Klockars' presentation of the life story of a professional fence. Vincent Swaggi (a pseudonym) has run a successful business in buying and selling stolen property for over twenty-five years, and his story offers numerous insights into the sources of criminal behavior. Thus, for example, in analyzing the subcultural norms that guide the social interaction of the fence and the thief, the following incident offers a glimpse of the process at work:

> This morning a guy came in with a camera. He's a booster, high-class though, jacket and tie, real respectable-looking colored guy. He's got a newspaper in his hand an' in the newspaper he's got this camera. Now he musta just got it 'cause it still had the store tags on it. I think

[65] Clifford Shaw, *The Jack-Roller* (Chicago: University of Chicago Press, 1930); Edwin H. Sutherland, *The Professional Thief* (Chicago: University of Chicago Press, 1937).

[66] See Duane Denfeld, ed., *Streetwise Criminology* (Cambridge, Mass.: Schenkman Publishing Company, 1974); Harry King, *Box Man*, ed. Bill Chambliss (New York: Harper & Row, 1972); Bruce Jackson, *Outside the Law* (New Brunswick, N.J.: Transaction Books, 1972); Charles H. McCaghy, James K. Skipper, Jr., and Mark Lefton, eds., *In Their Own Behalf: Voices from the Margin* (New York: Appleton-Century-Crofts, 1968); Pedro R. David, ed., *The World of the Burglar* (Albuquerque: University of New Mexico Press, 1974); Jack D. Douglas, *Observations of Deviance* (New York: Random House, 1970); Robert W. Winslow and Virginia Winslow, *Deviant Reality: Alternative World Views* (Boston: Allyn and Bacon, 1974); and Carl B. Klockars, *The Professional Fence* (New York: The Free Press, 1974).

A Career in Crime

Steve: I've been a career criminal since I was eight years old. I don't know whether I'm like the people that have talked to you already; I just want to tell you what I know about criminal justice. I've experienced the total criminal justice system; been through everything past and present that they have to offer. I started as I said at eight years old. My criminal career was, I think, an accident. I came from a good home and went to a Catholic school and had pretty nice experiences as a child. At some point in time, however, things happened. I trace my beginning in this to riding my bicycle on the sidewalk and in so doing this I ran into an elderly old lady and knocked her down. At this point it became hit-and-run bicycle. This got me to the attention of the police. I think at the time I was somewhat scared. It wasn't too bad an experience because they didn't do too much. They told me I couldn't ride my bike for thirty

days. I lost the shock of this thing after a few days and soon was back on the street riding with another fellow on a Sunday morning and it was raining so we went into an old garage and started a small fire which soon spread and burned the building down. Now I'm an arsonist. This time they sent me to juvenile hall and locked me up. The first thing they do in any jail, and a thing that I can't help but equate with the criminal justice system, is that they take all your clothes off. A great deal of my life I've spent running around naked. The Home wasn't a bad place but it was a scary place for an eight-year-old boy. I met kids there that were much more sophisticated than I. I didn't like it so I ran home. Out of this I learned how to steal cars. We used to steal the night watchman's car at the old Brewery. We did it every night and finally got caught. My timing is terrible, because I seem to get arrested at a point in time when the authorities want to try new things. So at ten years old they sent me to reform school.

From Robert Winslow and Virginia Winslow, *Deviant Reality: Alternative World Views* (Boston: Allyn and Bacon, 1974). Reprinted by permission of Allyn and Bacon, Inc.

they said five sixty-five, five eighty, somethin' like that. Anyway, he said he wanted two hundred for it.

"Two hundred?" I says to him. "Sure it's worth two hundred if you had the whole thing, but you only got part of it there."

"What do you mean?" he said. "This is the way they had it right on the counter."

"Look," I tell him. "See these holes?" I show him all the holes and places where you put the lights and all that kind of stuff. "This thing don't work unless you got all the parts an' everything goes with it. You want two hundred from me, buddy, you gotta go back and get the rest of that stuff." Now I know he ain't goin' back to that store.

"Aw, come on, Vince," he says. "You gotta give me something for it. How about seventy-five dollars?"

Now I know I got 'em. Once they mention a price they gotta come down. They can't go up. "I'll tell you," I said, "I know you, you're a hard-working fella and you can use the dough, so I'm gonna give you forty for it."[67]

The thief accepts. But the interesting point, notes Klockars, is not that the fence has managed to trick the thief into accepting $40; rather, it is why the thief demanded $200 at the start. There is, says Klockars, a norm that has governed the asking price of thieves for centuries: "When you take something to a fence you should try to get a third of the value of the goods."[68] And the reason this norm exists, he argues, is that goods can usually be purchased wholesale on the legitimate market for half their retail price. To make the illegitimate transaction attractive—that is, profitable—to the fence, the price must be dropped to approximately one third. "For centuries thieves have been asking for a third of the ticket price because they couldn't get half of it," argues Klockars. "I suggest that this is the only tenable argument in support of a norm that has existed for centuries in the trade between fences and thieves. What else would he ask for—two-fifths, three-sevenths, four-ninths? For many small thieves these fractions do not exist! Even if they knew about them they would be unable to calculate the proportion of the price they represented. The assumption that there are fractions between one-half and one-third can be made only for sellers more sophisticated than the class of petty thieves who have operated without them for at least two hundred years."[69]

[67] Klockars, *The Professional Fence* pp. 88–89. Reprinted with permission of Macmillan Publishing Company, Inc. Copyright © 1974 by The Free Press, a division of the Macmillan Publishing Company, Inc.

[68] Ibid., p. 87.

[69] Ibid., p. 88.

Many of the accounts written in recent years have centered on the use of drugs. The offenders have frequently been articulate and willing and anxious to talk, seeing themselves as part of a counterculture or an anti-establishment movement. Thus, for example, in the account of James Carey, a twenty-four-year-old drug user, the members of the "straight" world are viewed as hypocritical, rigid, unable to be spontaneous:

> They're afraid of our place. They're afraid of our divergence from their solid norm, because they're so afraid to step out of theirs. You know they couldn't. They couldn't anymore go and turn around and grow a beard and wear dirty clothes and not wash for several days than—most of the hip people that I know are, have more, stand more on principle, than those people. It seems to me that those people aren't really taking their principles seriously, they're not taking too much at all seriously . . . so that they really get an insane sick thing out of putting everything down, you know. Like an angry drunk, clean slob, frat rat. He's angry at everything you know. He's angry at his next door neighbor. But it's a game there—They call each other bad names all the time and they call some people on the street bad names all the time. Because that's their game—call everybody down you can.[70]

The immorality, the lack of seriousness, the sickness of society become part of the explanation of deviant behavior in the mind of the deviant. Where earlier writers in criminology would have often been inclined to dismiss such self-revelations as no more than a smoke screen hiding the "underlying" motives for breaking the rules, many sociologists today, analyzing social behavior within the framework of symbolic interactionism, are apt to take such statements as indicative of values and beliefs that play a significant part in the causation of the individual's behavior.

One of the greatest values of these accounts, perhaps, is that they allow the criminologist to see how the lawbreaker draws on the social and cultural setting to construct a system of meanings and interpretations that both motivate the individual and make the individual's action explicable to himself and to others. The individual, in a sense, quarries the social milieu to arrive at his own determinants, which carry a distinctive stamp and yet are clearly rooted in the social environment. A Charles Manson creating an apocalyptic vision of a war between the races, using bits and pieces of the mass culture, including the songs of

[70] James Carey, "Involvement in the Drug Scene," in Douglas, *Observations of Deviance*, p. 290.

the Beatles; a thief pointing to the inequalities of American life and the unfairness of a system that lets the wealthy offender go free; a man from the ghetto, creating a life style of flashy elegance by means of pimping —these are possible examples of "constructed causes" of crime that are not direct expressions of the culture, the individual's place in the social structure, or the individual personality but which emerge in a process of social interaction in a particular social and cultural setting in a particular time and place.[71] The firsthand accounts of criminals help to lay bare this process in a way that no other source of data can match.

Conclusions

The sociological theories of crime causation discussed in Chapter 7 some-times appear rather crude, whether they center on the idea of subcultures or the structure of society as a whole. They are often illuminating and are undoubtedly an advance over those explanations of crime that looked to devils in the mind or stigma of the body. They are still inadequate, how-ever, in that they cannot predict with any accuracy who will engage in crime and who will not, or (at a less individualistic level) the relative crime rates of different social groups—beyond a repetition of last year's official figures. No matter how fashionable it may have become in recent years to discount an interest in such predictions or how difficult it is to achieve this kind of predictive knowledge, it is doubtful if the various social sciences, including criminology, can avoid being evaluated in terms of their ability to perform such a task.

The social-psychological theories presented in this chapter face much the same problem, despite the attention devoted to the complexities of the interactive process and the subjective view of the actors. The "natu-ralistic" flavor of symbolic interactionism—that is, the concern with de-tails of social behavior as *experienced* by the individual rather than as *perceived* by the observer—lends the social-psychological accounts of criminal behavior a certain verisimilitude; it does not necessarily create a science. If it is argued that labeling theory has taught us to avoid the error of confusing the social categorization of behavior with what people actually do (and thus to avoid the mistake of trying to construct predic-tive statements about behavior that may or may not exist), this does not mean that the problem of causal explanation has been done away with.

---

[71] The investigation of the Manson murders offers a good illustration of how an ap-parently inexplicable crime becomes understandable as the world of meanings and values created by the offenders is uncovered. See Vincent Bugliosi (with Curt Gentry), *Helter Skelter* (New York: W. W. Norton, 1974).

There is still the question of why the social agencies that label behavior act in one fashion rather than another.

It cannot be said, though, that criminology has had no success in building an important body of empirical generalizations and theoretical interpretations. On the contrary, criminology has managed to eliminate many of the pseudo-explanations that so often obscure the sources of social behavior, and it has uncovered—if not precisely delimited—many of the variables that cause violations of the law. Still, the vital question is not the extent to which criminology has succeeded in the past in explaining criminal behavior, but rather in what direction criminology is likely to move in future research. On this issue a number of points seem clear.

Theories explaining criminal behavior have long stressed the importance of barriers to the legitimate paths of achievement. Frustration—and particularly economic frustration—has often been seen as the major factor leading to illegal acts. If success and pleasure, riches and recognition, and the relief of anger were all readily accessible through lawful behavior, who would take the dangerous, guilt-ridden criminal path? "Very few" has traditionally served as the obvious answer. Criminal behavior, then, has been seen as a second choice, as a means forced on the individual when the preferred course is not available. Gradually, however, it has come to be recognized that the blockage of legitimate paths of satisfaction forms the *context* in which the erosion of norms governing the use of illegal means, inadequate socialization, the emergence of delinquent subcultures, and the like are crucial variables. The inability to achieve the ends valued by society may indeed be a necessary condition for the outgrowth of criminal behavior in the great majority of cases. But something more is required before the individual will seek to achieve his or her ends by breaking the law, and it is this "something more" (particularly in terms of the symbolic meanings individuals attach to their actions) that has increasingly served as the focus of research. It seems likely that this avenue of investigation will continue to provide important theoretical developments for some time.

The growing emphasis on the idea that the "garden variety" of crime, such as robbery, burglary, and assault, forms but a small portion of all crime also promises to produce significant theoretical changes. Just as the concept of white-collar crime required a new look at the assumptions linking crime and socioeconomic status, so too the concept of political crime appears likely to spawn a number of important works that will reexamine accepted ideas, including those about the aims of criminal behavior and the nature of the cultural environment that supports illegal activity.

Finally, it seems probable that future research in criminology will place increasing emphasis on both the psychological variables operating within the individual *and* on the configuration of the social structure in which the individual functions. The definition of criminal behavior and the designation of particular individuals as criminal are so enmeshed in the structure of society that any attempt to understand crime as an abstract entity floating free of both time and space is bound to be inadequate—and criminology has grown sophisticated enough to avoid such an error. It is no less clear that individual interpretations of the norms, perceptions of social reality, and alternative values are vital elements in shaping behavior, and these must be studied further rather than determined by assumption or post hoc reasoning. If the mystery of crime causation is to be solved, a social-psychological approach will surely play a part. An analysis of the criminal act as a consciously selected solution to a problem, an examination of the economic and political setting in which such problems and solutions arise, a study of the social reactions to criminal behavior, and a sharp sense of the historical context—all are necessary for an adequate explanation of violations of the criminal law.[72] It can be expected that in the decades ahead our knowledge of these issues will be substantially increased.

Recommended Readings

The sophistication and insight provided by the symbolic interactionist perspective on deviant and criminal behavior is well illustrated by David Matza, *Becoming Deviant* (Englewood Cliffs, N.J.: Prentice-Hall, 1969). A thoughtful critique of this perspective is provided by Edwin M. Lemert in his book *Human Deviance, Social Problems and Social Control* (Englewood Cliffs, N.J.: Prentice-Hall, 1976). An authoritative review of labeling theory is provided by Edwin M. Schur, *Labeling Deviant Behavior: Its Sociological Implication* (New York: Harper & Row, 1971). The reader will find an especially lucid, interesting application of labeling theory in Robert M. Emerson, *Judging Delinquents* (Chicago: Aldine, 1969).

The first-hand accounts of criminals are, as we have indicated in the text, both intriguing illustrations of theory and a source of ideas for further research and theory construction. The following are particularly recommended: Clifford Shaw, *The Jack-Roller* (Chicago: University of Chicago Press, 1937); Edwin H. Sutherland, *The Professional Thief* (Chicago: University of Chicago Press, 1937); Harry King, *Box Man*, ed. Bill Chambliss (New York: Harper & Row, 1972); Bruce Jackson, *Outside the Law* (New Brunswick, N.J.: Transaction Books, 1972); Carl B. Klockars, *The Professional Fence* (New York: The Free Press, 1974); Malcolm Brady, *False Starts* (New York: Penguin Books, 1976). Jean Evans, *Three Men* (New York: Alfred A.

[72] See Ian Taylor, Paul Walton, and Jock Young, *The New Criminology* (New York: Harper & Row, 1974), Chapter 9.

Knopf, 1956) is not, strictly speaking, a first-hand account—it is subtitled, in fact, *An Experiment in the Biography of Emotion.* Nonetheless, it provides an excellent presentation of the actor's behavior from the actor's viewpoint in the actor's own words.

Part 4

The State
Versus
the Accused

When society sets about catching those who have broken the law, there is always the danger that the innocent will be swept up along with the guilty. Since Anglo-American legal tradition regards the punishment of a person who is innocent as an intolerable wrong, and since the individual is considered innocent until proven guilty, society has surrounded the *suspected* offender with a great variety of rights limiting the efficacy of the police and the courts. "There can be no possible doubt," it has been said, "that without the restraints which the law insists upon, the police would catch and prosecutors could convict far more law breakers than they do now. But deterring criminals is not the only objective of our penal system. There are other equally important objectives, such as maintaining a decent respect for man's dignity and preserving an atmosphere of freedom."[1]

[1]See David Fellman, *The Defendant's Rights* (New York: Rinehart, 1958), p. 8.

Restraints on the authority of the police to arrest, protection against unreasonable searches and seizures (including protection against the invasion of privacy by illegal wiretaps), the right to bail, to have a lawyer, to have a speedy, fair trial in the public view, to be free of coerced confessions—all of these and more are deliberate limitations on the power of the state in the enforcement of the criminal law. We are guided, it is said, by the principle that it is better to let ten guilty persons go free rather than punish one who is innocent. The result is a loss of effectiveness, if we think of effectiveness as being measured by the ratio between crimes committed and criminals detected, apprehended, convicted, and punished. Yet the loss has been held acceptable, for this in part is what Emile Durkheim meant when he said that crime is one of the costs of a free society. If we institute the measures necessary to eliminate crime or reduce it drastically, society no longer will be free. The machinery of law enforcement is therefore constrained by a large body of rules—known as the laws of criminal procedure—that represent a compromise between two conflicting goals: the punishment of the criminal and the freedom of the law-abiding.

The public is not always happy about this compromise, and not all segments of society view the rights of criminal defendants with the same equanimity.[2] In the United States in the 1950s and 1960s, for example, many people claimed that under the direction of Chief Justice Earl Warren, the Supreme Court was hamstringing the police, showing less interest in the welfare of the public than in the welfare of the criminal, and wrecking the system for the administration of criminal justice because of a doctrinaire attachment to the rights of suspected offenders. And the police have frequently found themselves caught in a crossfire between the law's demands for the protection of defendants' rights and the public's interest in effective law enforcement.

The conflict between effectiveness and individual liberties may in theory be resolved by a knowing sacrifice of the former in the laws of criminal procedure, and our society may in fact often offer the suspected criminal numerous legal protections. A great deal of dispute concerning the issue remains, however; perhaps most important, practice frequently departs from legal ideals. The following chapters will be concerned with both the theory and the realities of criminal procedure, from the time crime comes to the attention of the police to the point at which the accused offender is judged guilty and penalized or judged innocent and set free.

[2]See Raymond Mack, "Do We Really Believe in the Bill of Rights?" *Social Problems* 3 (1956), pp. 264–69.

Chapter 9
The Machinery of Justice: From Arrest to Trial

The legal rules that are supposed to guide the process by which suspected offenders are detected, apprehended, and brought to trial are referred to as the law of criminal procedure. The application of these rules to reality brings the substantive criminal law to life, changing a set of abstract prohibitions into specific judgments of innocence and guilt.

The process is subject to error, and the socioeconomic status of the defendant has a significant impact on the outcome, despite the Anglo-American legal tradition's ideal of equality before the law. But what is possibly most striking in the United States today is the extent to which a variety of legal devices designed to control the power of the state in its uneven conflict with the suspected criminal do not function as intended.

Many of these legal devices—such as trial by jury, bail, the confrontation of accusers, and arrest warrants—have their roots in the distant past. Over the years, a number of the legal protections provided the defendant—such as freedom from self-incrimination—have been enlarged by judicial decisions and legislative enactments; and new devices—such as the provision of counsel for indigent defendants—have been added. The changes in the United States in the 1960s, it has been argued, are particularly important. "Few, if any, areas of the law have undergone as significant changes during the last decade as criminal procedure," it has been asserted. "Indeed, the change in criminal procedure has been so rapid and far reaching that some commentators have characterized it as a legal 'revolution'. . . . Almost every Supreme Court term since 1960 has been marked by several major decisions in the constitutional-criminal procedure area."[1]

It has become increasingly evident, however, that many of the protections now embedded in the law of criminal procedure are frequently undermined by the realities of law enforcement in American society. Arrest warrants, designed to provide judicial restraint on police actions, often fail to do so. The use of bail, designed to protect defendants from unnecessary confinement as long as their presence at trial can be assured, frequently is employed as a means of preventive detention. The grand

[1] See Jerold H. Israel and Wayne R. LaFave, *Criminal Procedure in a Nutshell: Constitutional Limitations* (St. Paul, Minn.: West, 1971), pp. 1–2.

jury, intended to serve as a screening device to set free those who have been charged with crime on the basis of inadequate evidence, seldom performs this function. And trial by jury, supposed to provide an impartial judgment of peers, has become—in case after case—a time-consuming and expensive process which the defendant and the prosecutor agree to avoid in exchange for leniency.

One reason for the subversion of the law of criminal procedure in practice is that the greater the extent to which the rights of criminal suspects are accorded full recognition, the heavier becomes the burden of the administration of justice for society. It is a burden that American society is often unwilling to bear. The bureaucratization of the legal profession is also a factor, in that the defense attorneys are often more concerned with their professional position or with their relationship to the court than with the interests of their clients. The pressure on the police to "win the war against crime" is a third contributory cause, with the public ready to wink and look the other way when the rights of suspected offenders are sacrificed to the demand for swift action.

In examining criminal procedures, then, we must remember that the legal rights of suspected criminals, constructed with such care over the years and often seen as one of the great accomplishments of the Anglo-American legal system, are a statement of what should be rather than of what is. The nature and source of the discrepancy are rapidly gaining a more prominent place in criminological studies.

In this chapter we will first examine the way in which suspected offenders are arrested by the police and held in jail pending trial, and the use—and misuse—of bail. After looking at the criminal statutes with regard to evidence and the protections against self-incrimination, we will turn to screening devices, such as the preliminary examination and the grand jury. Finally, we will consider the ways in which the defendant can respond to the formal accusation of crime and the process of plea-bargaining, whereby the suspected criminal can win a reduction of the charge or the penalty as a reward for cooperating with the court.

Catching the Criminal

A criminal act usually becomes known to the police in one of three ways: the crime may be committed in the presence of the police, as when law enforcement officers encounter a robbery in progress; the crime may be uncovered by police investigation of suspicious circumstances, as when the police find a door or window that has apparently been forced open; or the crime may be reported to the police by private citizens. The last is

Discovering Crime

by far the most common method, at least in metropolitan areas.[2] Police patrols undoubtedly uncover some crime, and police investigations of "suspicious circumstances" form a vital component of police work.[3] But the bulk of offenses enter the system of criminal justice on the basis of complaints made by private citizens (usually by telephone), and this public pressure plays a large role in shaping the nature of police activity in American society.[4]

The police, of course, do not respond to all the complaints with equal alacrity. Some complaints are ignored because they are thought to be frivolous or the muddled accusations of a drunk. Others will go unattended because in the judgment of the police they involve a civil rather than a criminal wrong. Still others may receive little or no attention because the police believe a cooperative witness cannot be found, thus making conviction unlikely, or because the matter does not seem serious enough to warrant the time and effort of police intervention. The following account of police reaction to a complaint from a slum dweller concerning an apparent robbery attempt provides a good illustration:

> At precinct headquarters an individual had come in to report a suspicious circumstance. He informed the lieutenant that the driver of a vehicle had pulled alongside him and had forced him to the side of the road. The man said that he thought the driver of the other car planned to rob him. He had recorded the license number of the car and passed this on to the police indicating that he thought this should be investigated. This officer had sat at the desk in a precinct in which there had been four holdups during the course of the evening and a great deal of other activity. He apparently did not think much of the information which this man had provided. He somewhat dutifully recorded it, and informed the man that they would attempt to give it some attention. When the man left the station, the officer ripped up the information with the comment that they had enough to do without following up leads such as this.[5]

It is also clear that crimes brought to the attention of the police and officially recorded form only a small portion of all crimes and are far from a

---

[2] See Donald McIntyre, Jr., *Law Enforcement in the Metropolis* (Chicago: American Bar Foundation, 1967), Chapter 1.

[3] It has been argued that one of the most important effects of police patrols is that they serve the functional equivalent of "showing the flag," a symbolic affirmation of armed authority, and deter crime rather than discover it. See Donald Cressey, "Introduction," Part III, in Gresham M. Sykes and Thomas E. Drabek, eds., *Law and the Lawless* (New York: Random House, 1969), pp. 271–82.

[4] See Albert J. Reiss, Jr., *The Police and the Public* (New Haven: Yale University Press, 1972).

[5] McIntyre, *Law Enforcement in the Metropolis*, p. 6.

representative sample. Many detected crimes are not reported to the police. Many crimes are never detected, either by police or private citizens. The "detection of crime," then, in the sense of bringing offenses into the public record and eliciting an official reaction, is a complex social process in which the interests of private citizens and the police intermingle to shape the outcome.

Complaints or information concerning crime come to the police mainly from victims, annoyed neighbors, jealous relatives, business competitors, persons motivated by a sense of civic responsibility, and informants.[6] The factors influencing the way the police will react to this flow of information have been analyzed by Jonathan Rubinstein in a perceptive account of police work in Philadelphia. Whether complaints are considered "believable" emerges as a crucial issue, notes Rubenstein, and such judgments cut across racial and class lines. "In every part of the city," he points out, "patrolmen are making judgments daily, based on their notions of local legitimacy. These are unavoidable because each man must make quick decisions without help from his sergeant. Often the requests require immediate action to prevent the escape of persons accused of serious crimes. Any officer begins his career by accepting as truth whatever he is told, but his experiences quickly encourage caution. Even after he has developed cues and techniques for assessing the validity of claims made upon him, he will be conned into exertions and dangers. Each time this happens, his suspicion of things he is told deepens and the circle of people he is likely to believe shrinks."[7]

The extent to which crimes are detected by police investigations undertaken outside the scope of routine patrol activities remains unknown. It is in this area of crime detection, however, that a variety of special surveillance techniques—such as wiretapping, the use of film or tape, and other forms of electronic eavesdropping, and undercover operations—are to be found; and it is the use of these techniques that has done much to bolster the image of an oppressive police state looming on the horizon as a threat to a free society. As David Fellman notes,

In spite of the fact that most states have statutes forbidding wire-tapping, and the enactment by Congress of Section 605 of the Federal Communications Act, and in spite of court decisions on the subject, wire-tapping today flourishes as a wide-open operation at the federal,

[6] The last category is particularly important in the case of offenses involving narcotics. It has been estimated, for example, that 50 percent of all persons arrested by the Federal Bureau of Narcotics are converted into "special employees"—that is, informants—in return for reduced charges or a minimum sentence. The policy, it is said, is to convert every arrested male who is willing into a special employee, in order to apprehend major interstate shippers (McIntyre, *Law Enforcement in the Metropolis*, pp. 10–13).

[7] Jonathan Rubinstein, *City Police* (New York: Farrar, Straus and Giroux, 1973), p. 199.

state, municipal, and private levels. Private parties as well as governmental agencies resort to wire-tapping for a tremendously wide range of purposes. Some government attorneys have maintained that there is a basic distinction between "intercepting" and "divulging" telephone communications and that Section 605 forbids only the latter. Since the Department of Justice taps telephone wires regularly, it has steadfastly refused to prosecute other federal and state officials and private persons who do so.[8]

Much of the concern expressed in the laws of criminal procedure for the rights of the suspected offender has resulted in safeguards around the accused *after* arrest. Techniques of surveillance, however, threaten the rights of the individual—most notably the right of privacy—*before* he is caught up in the processes of the criminal law, and protection against the intrusive power of the state in this area remains relatively undeveloped.[9]

The Power to Arrest In early English history, when the laws governing arrest first began to be developed, placing a suspected offender in custody carried a great potential for harm. There were no professional police forces, and arrests by private persons, by means of hue and cry, could easily spring from spite. The individual might be detained for years awaiting trial, and the jails and dungeons of the time were pestholes in which starvation and typhoid fever were commonplace. Arrest was likely to be a calamity, no matter what the outcome of the trial; and as a consequence a strict body of law came into being that severely circumscribed the powers of those who sought to make arrests. Our present laws bear the mark of this past concern.[10]

Although the laws of criminal procedure in America differ among the various states, as does the substantive criminal law, it is possible to make some broad generalizations concerning the power to take a suspected offender into custody. First, an arrest may be made by a private person, but only under certain limiting conditions subject to statutory variation. According to the common law, a private person may make an arrest when a felony has been committed in his presence and he has reasonable grounds to believe that the person to be arrested committed the crime. This power appears in a number of state penal codes. If the person arrested turns out to be innocent, however, the private citizen mak-

---

[8] *The Defendant's Rights* (New York: Rinehart, 1958), p. 144.

[9] A rapidly growing body of literature deals with the right of privacy and its invasion by law enforcement agencies. See Arthur R. Miller, *The Assault on Privacy* (Ann Arbor: University of Michigan Press, 1971). See also Columbia Human Rights Law Review, *Surveillance, Dataveillance, and Personal Freedoms* (Fairlawn, N.J.: R. E. Burdick, 1973).

[10] See Fellman, *The Defendant's Rights*, p. 12.

ing the arrest can be sued for false arrest, which may help explain why such arrests are so rare.

Second, a police officer is authorized to arrest persons committing either a misdemeanor or a felony in his presence; and in such situations—termed an *on-view arrest*—a warrant to arrest is not required. In addition, a police officer is authorized to make an arrest when he has reasonable grounds to believe that a felony has been committed and the person arrested is the offender, if it appears that the offender may escape or evidence be destroyed, even though the crime has not been committed in the police officer's presence. Once again, a warrant is not required, and in many states the police officer is protected from a civil suit for false imprisonment if his suspicions turn out to be unfounded.[11] When a misdemeanor is committed, but not in the presence of a police officer, a warrant is required if an arrest is to be made.

Most arrests are on-view arrests. "The exigencies of most crime situations," notes McIntyre, "call for an immediate decision by the police officers as to whether a suspect should be taken into custody. As an authority to arrest, the arrest warrant does not accommodate the need to act on the spur of the moment."[12] In reality, then, the control of police power that may be provided, at least in theory, by the need to obtain a warrant for an arrest from an independent judicial agency is much reduced. Indeed, many of the warrants to arrest are secured *after* the suspect is already in custody, and represent not a judicial review of the decision to arrest but a desire by the police to be protected from possible civil suits, an effort to demonstrate the legality of the arrest in a future trial, or an indication that the prosecuting attorney wishes to proceed with the case and not discharge the suspect.[13]

On occasion, the police power to arrest is subject to serious abuse, as when the police overstep the legal restrictions in an effort to curb the activities of individuals believed to be engaged in criminal behavior but for whom clear evidence of wrongdoing is lacking. In the "tip-over," for example, police may raid places where petty gambling, prostitution, and the after-hours sale of liquor are thought to be occurring, and arrest the individuals involved with no intention of taking the cases into court. The police power to arrest can also be said to be abused, however, on the

[11] Peace officers with the power of arrest may include, in addition to the police, court officers, prison guards, harbor masters, an agent for such organizations as the Society for the Prevention of Cruelty to Animals, and sheriffs. See Hazel B. Kerper, *Introduction to the Criminal Justice System* (St. Paul, Minn.: West, 1972), pp. 236–39. For a comparison of American and English legal rules and practice in the matter of arrest, see Delmar Karlen, *Anglo-American Criminal Justice* (New York: Oxford University Press, 1968).

[12] McIntyre, *Law Enforcement in the Metropolis*, p. 50.

[13] See Wayne R. LaFave, *Arrest: The Decision to Take a Suspect into Custody* (Boston: Little, Brown, 1965).

many occasions when the police decide *not* to arrest suspected offenders even though the criminal conduct can easily be proved. The offense may be thought to be trivial, the conduct may be viewed as reflecting the standards of a community subgroup and best ignored, or the status of the offender may win him immunity.[14] As Frank J. Remington has said:

> It is obvious that arrests are not made for every offense which comes to the attention of the police. So great has been the proliferation of criminal statutes that arrest of all violators would cause a breakdown of the criminal justice system. There must therefore be a limitation upon the number of persons subjected to the criminal process. As a practical matter, this limitation must take place, in large part, at the arrest stage since this is ordinarily the first official decision relating to the offender's conduct. The power and responsibility which this discretion gives the police is immense. Too often the existence of discretion is denied and its exercise is, therefore, left without guidance and control from the legal system.[15]

At the arrest stage, then, there is an emphasis on some offenses and a disregard of others. Just as the police recognition of the existence of crime is shaped by a variety of social forces, producing a body of "crimes known to the police" that is far different from crimes actually committed, so too is police reaction to known crimes in terms of arrest influenced by numerous pressures, resulting in a socially selected group of offenses— and offenders—to be handled by the legal system. In some instances the process is clearly unjust, as when a tough, swearing boy from the slums is placed in jail and a well-mannered juvenile from the suburbs is left untouched, though the two have committed the same offense. In other instances, the nonenforcement of the law is widely accepted as the preferable course—as in the case of adultery, where the cost of enforcement, involving as it does the invasion of privacy, is unacceptable even for those who believe that adultery rightfully falls within the province of the criminal law.

The crucial point is that, for better or worse, discretion in the use of the power of arrest by the police is inevitable. The law enforcement agencies can handle only so many arrests. A choice must be made, and it is a choice that probably must remain in the hands of those engaged in the day-to-day enforcement of the law. The question of the criteria to be used in making that choice must still be resolved, however; and the legislature, the courts, and the police have failed to develop an explicit

[14] Ibid., Part II.
[15] Frank J. Remington, "The Law Relating to 'On the Street' Detention, Questioning, and Frisking of Suspected Persons and Police Arrest Privileges in General," in Claude R. Soule, ed., *Police Power and Individual Freedom* (Chicago: Aldine, 1962), p. 20.

policy subject to public review. Between the laws of arrest and the realities of apprehending suspected criminals are the informal norms of police practice and the judgments of individual police officers. Until these informal elements are brought under community control, the rights that are provided criminal suspects in legal theory are likely to be violated in practice. [16]

A large number of those arrested by the police in the United States each year are never brought to trial. Charges are dropped because witnesses fail to appear or are unwilling to testify; the police believe that the fact of arrest is itself sufficient to forestall future criminality; the arrest turns out to be illegal and thus prevents the evidence against the accused from being presented in court; or the evidence against the accused is not sufficient for a conviction, and the prosecutor wishes to avoid a battle he cannot win. But for those suspected offenders who are to be prosecuted and brought to trial, the legal system must ensure appearance in court on the appointed day. One traditional device has been incarceration in a local jail.

Jailing Suspected Offenders

Places of detention for suspected offenders awaiting trial have a long and sordid history, and the conditions in such institutions in the United States today remain appalling. Overcrowded, filthy, swarming with vermin, lacking a minimum of facilities for men and women held in debilitating idleness—this accurately describes all too many local jails, which differ but little from the brutal debtor's prisons and lockups of an earlier age. [17] The following description of an Atlanta jail is typical:

> The jail was far worse than the state prisons I had just seen. Inside a relatively modern interior in a modest, busy part of town was a cramped, dark, dank interior. Large, four-sided cages each held sixteen men, with disheveled beds and an open toilet. Inmates were kept inside these cages twenty-four hours a day throughout their often prolonged stays at the Atlanta jail. There is no privacy and no activity at all, artificial air and light, and nothing to do day and night. A dismal atmosphere, a constant din and a wretched stench pervaded the place. [18]

The number of persons placed in jail far exceeds the number of persons sentenced to prison in any given year, and a large proportion of the

[16] Civilian review boards, once envisioned as a potentially effective means of controlling police behavior, appear to have faded from public attention. See Andrew H. Malcolm, "Civilian Boards on Wane as Watchdogs of Police," *The New York Times* (February 10, 1975).

[17] See Richard McGee, "Our Sick Jails," *Federal Probation* 35 (March 1971), pp. 3–8.

[18] See Ronald Goldfarb, *Jails: The Ultimate Ghetto of the Criminal Justice System* (Garden City, N.Y.: Anchor Books, 1975), pp. 5–6.

former have not been convicted of a crime. Indeed, many of them will never be convicted.[19]

If the appearance of the suspected offender at the time of his trial could be assured, pretrial detention in the local jail would be unnecessary—and this, in theory at least, is the primary function of bail. The right to bail is deeply rooted in the Anglo-American legal tradition and appears in a number of state constitutions. Whether the federal Constitution makes bail a right, however, is subject to controversy. The Eighth Amendment declares that "excessive bail shall not be required, nor excessive fines imposed, nor cruel and unusual punishments inflicted." Some legal scholars argue that this says nothing about a right to bail but merely declares that bail shall not be excessive if it is imposed. Others maintain that there would be little point in prohibiting excessive bail if bail could be denied altogether at the whims of the prosecution.[20] In practice, however, most offenses are regarded as bailable, except perhaps in cases of first-degree murder in which the evidence is thought to be clear and convincing or in which the defendant is shown to have intimidated witnesses or attempted to bribe jurors.[21]

The arguments about bail have tended to center largely on the amount of money involved and the form that it takes. The money for bail can be furnished in cash or by bond. In the latter case, a document is signed by the accused and other persons acting on his behalf ("sureties"), guaranteeing the appearance of the accused at the time of trial. If the accused does not appear in accordance with the directives of the court, the cash is supposed to be forfeited or the face amount of the bond is to be paid to the state by the sureties. Since suspected offenders are often unable to furnish the cash for bail and often lack friends or relatives who are able or willing to act as sureties, they must rely on professional bail bondsmen, who charge a fee that usually ranges from 10 to 20 percent of the face value of the bond. In theory, then, the legal system has set up economic incentives that will serve to assure the appearance of the defendant at the time of his trial, making incarceration unnecessary.

The great majority of suspected offenders released on bail appear in court as scheduled. A study of eighty cities in the United States has indi-

---

[19] One study, for example, has indicated that of 31,187 persons detained in Wisconsin county jails overnight or longer in 1956, only 6,811 were sentenced prisoners. See Sanger B. Powers, "Day-Parole of Misdemeanants," *Federal Probation* 22 (December 1958), pp. 42–46. The *Uniform Crime Reports* indicate that in 1972 approximately 60 percent of the persons held for prosecution were found guilty of the offense for which they were charged. See *Uniform Crime Reports—1975* (Washington, D.C.: Government Printing Office, 1976), p. 217. See also *Sourcebook of Criminal Justice Statistics—1974* (Washington, D.C.: Government Printing Office, 1975), pp. 426–27.

[20] See Kerper, *Introduction to the Criminal Justice System*, pp. 276–77.

[21] Ibid., p. 276.

cated that the forfeiture rate is less than 10 percent in eight out of ten cit-ies.[22] But the forfeiture rate, as Paul Wice points out, must be interpreted with a good deal of caution, since it may be only a crude measure of how frequently accused offenders actually jump bail. Courts have a good deal of discretion in deciding when a forfeiture has occurred. "In cities wish-ing to reform their bail system," he notes, "and [to] permit increasing numbers of defendants to obtain their pretrial release, [courts] will liter-ally interpret when a forfeiture has taken place. They may stipulate that a forfeiture has occurred only after the defendant has had a day or two in which to come to court and has been reminded of his tardy appearance. This approach will usually result in a city having a low or at least respect-able forfeiture rate."[23] On the other hand, the forfeiture rate may be increased sharply if a defendant is categorized as failing to appear when he is a few minutes late or if the initial failure to appear and all sub-sequent failures to make scheduled appearances are counted as separate events—as may be the case when a city wishes to discredit a liberaliza-tion of bail procedures.

The bail bondsman has frequently been portrayed as an unsavory character, living on the margin of the underworld and able to charge ex-orbitant fees because of the helplessness of the suspected criminal. This stereotype no longer fits reality, it has been claimed, and the occupation is on the way to becoming respectable.[24] In any event, it is clear that if the bondsman is to stay in business, he must be a shrewd judge of which defendants are likely to stay and which are likely to disappear; and interviews with bail bondsmen indicate that they use a number of criteria for the selection of "reliable" defendants.[25] The nature of the crime the individual is accused of committing, including the severity of the potential sentence, is an important factor in the opinion of bonds-men. The best risks are said to be professional criminals and individuals linked to organized crime. Bad risks include first offenders who have never been in prison (and who may panic as the time of their trial ap-proaches), prostitutes, drug addicts, and armed robbers. The reasons for avoiding the last type are summarized by one Washington bondsman:

A guy that takes a gun and goes into a store or bank must have it in the back of his mind that he'll use it if he has to. Now if I bail him and can't produce him in court, I've got to go get him. He didn't hesitate to pull a gun when he held you up and I make a good target, big as I am. Besides that the bonds in these cases run high, making potential losses

[22] Paul Wice, *Freedom for Sale: A National Study of Pretrial Release* (Lexington, Mass.: D. C. Heath, 1974), Chapter 4.
[23] Ibid., p. 66.
[24] Ibid., pp. 50–54.
[25] Ibid., pp. 55–58.

greater. Taking someone who has gone to the gun just isn't worth the risk. Besides a guy charged with that kind of offense knows he may be going away for a long time and that increases the chances he'll skip.[26]

In addition, though, bail bondsmen place a good deal of stress on the defendant's community ties. Close links with friends, relatives, family, neighborhood, job—these are often viewed as the social cement that holds the suspected offender in place and assures his appearance in court. For those intent on reforming the system of bail in the United States, this last point is thought to be of prime importance, since it offers the basis for a far more just and effective system than now exists in most cities.

The existing bail system has been criticized on a number of grounds. The chance to be free on bail while awaiting trial is closely tied to the suspected offender's economic standing. The suspect drawn from the ranks of the poor, unable to post bond for himself, unable to find friends or relatives who can do so, and unable to convince a professional bondsman to take on the risk of acting as his surety, is far more likely than the middle-class offender to remain imprisoned.[27] The lower-class suspect is thus often kept in jail while awaiting trial, despite the traditional right to freedom before conviction in the Anglo-American legal system. This occurs, in part, because the police often charge a suspected offender with a more serious crime than is warranted. As Wice points out:

> The police realize that because of constitutional guarantees they can only delay and interrogate the defendant for a brief period of time. They also realize and are angered by the fact that the defendant often posts bail so rapidly he is out on the street before the patrolman has completed the arrest report. A final irritant to the police, which encourages them to engage in this overcharging tactic, is their belief that because of current plea-bargaining practices the defendant is frequently able to have his original charge significantly reduced in exchange for a guilty plea. . . . Due to these various irritations and fears that the defendant is "beating the system" and thereby humiliating the police, the police therefore seek to punish the defendant by charging him with a serious crime. These serious charges usually result in the judge setting a very high bond and so the defendant is often unable to raise the required amount.[28]

Judges also may set high bail in a deliberate effort to keep suspected offenders confined, in an informal preventive detention program. Con-

[26] Quoted in Wice, *Freedom for Sale*, p. 57.
[27] See Charles E. Ares, Anne Rankin, and Herbert Sturz, "The Manhattan Bail Project," *New York University Law Review* 38 (January 1963), pp. 67–92.
[28] Wice, *Freedom for Sale*, p. 6.

trary to both the letter and the spirit of the law, which holds that only *convicted* offenders may be imprisoned for their crimes, many judges use their discretion in setting the amount of bail to keep an individual locked up because he is *potentially* dangerous—in the opinion of the judge. If the individual is viewed as a "bad risk," likely to commit more crimes while awaiting trial, the judge may simply set bail at an amount that the defendant cannot possibly obtain and thus ensure his continued confinement. Such abuses of bail are a national phenomenon of long standing; some fifty years ago Arthur Beeley concluded his classic study of the Chicago bail system by pointing out that "the present system [of bail], in too many instances, neither guarantees security to society nor safeguards the rights of the accused. The system is lax with those with whom it should be stringent and stringent with those with whom it could safely be less severe." [29]

Various attempts to reform the system have been made over the years, and Paul Wice's book—on which this discussion has drawn heavily—provides an excellent, up-to-date summary. Some of these efforts, such as those in Illinois, Washington, D.C., and Pennsylvania, have taken the form of allowing the defendant to gain release by paying a percentage (8 to 10 percent) of the total bond to the court. If a defendant has his bail set at $1000, for example, he pays $100 to the court. If he fails to appear, he owes the court the entire $1000; if he does appear at the appointed time, 90 percent of his payment of $100 will be refunded and the remaining 10 percent will be used to cover the costs of administering the program. The objective is to reduce the cost of bail and eliminate the bondsman—although where bondsmen are prohibited by statute, many of them have become small-loan agents charging defendants inflated interest rates on the money needed by the defendants to pay 10 percent of the original bond. [30] Other efforts at reform have followed the lead of the Manhattan Bail Project, conducted by the Vera Foundation and the New York University School of Law and based on "pretrial parole" or release on personal recognizance—that is, a formal agreement to appear in court as ordered. In this approach suspects are carefully screened and selected according to such criteria as length of residence, employment record, and ties with relatives. [31] Despite these encouraging experiments, however (which provide good reason to believe that the pretrial release of suspected offenders can be accomplished at less cost and with more fairness, without sacrificing the need to assure the defendant's appearance at the time of trial), the system of bail in most cities continues as a blatant example of economic discrimination. And insofar as the system is used for the purpose of preventive detention, our society persists in imprisoning

---

[29] *The Bail System in Chicago* (Chicago: University of Chicago Press, 1966), p. 160.
[30] See Wice, *Freedom for Sale*, pp. 9–10.
[31] See Ares, Rankin, and Sturz, "The Manhattan Bail Project."

suspected offenders without trial in gross violation of our legal system's most fundamental traditions.

Obtaining Evidence The evidence necessary to secure the conviction of the suspected criminal is gathered by law enforcement agencies to a large extent from the same sources as those supplying the information that a crime has been committed. The activities of the police, the reports of victims and witnesses, and the accounts of paid informants provide the "facts" indicating that a particular person is to be held accountable for a specific crime.

There is the danger, however, that the police will become overzealous in their task of collecting evidence. The fear of an abuse of the power of the state in the enforcement of the criminal law is a recurring theme in Anglo-American political and legal thinking—a fear founded on the suppression of religious and political dissent by a tyrannical monarchy in former times and no less oppressive acts of government bureaucracies in the present era.[32] In response to this fear, the legal system has slowly surrounded the suspected criminal with a set of defenses against the state's power to gather evidences of wrongdoing, particularly with regard to searches and self-incrimination.

Even when an arrest is made without a warrant, the police may search the suspect's person and his surroundings. "When an arrest is made," said the Supreme Court in the case of *Chimel v. California*, "it is reasonable for the arresting officer to search the person arrested in order to remove any weapons that the latter might seek to use in order to resist arrest or effect his escape. . . . And the area into which an arrestee might reach in order to grab a weapon or evidentiary items must, of course, be governed by a like rule."[33] An aimless searching of a larger area is prohibited, as is the search for weapons or evidence when no arrest has actually occurred.[34] Forms of searching that "would shock the conscience of an ordinary citizen" because of the method or the amount of force used are similarly prohibited—and thus it is unlawful to use a stomach pump or forced vomiting to obtain material that the suspect has swallowed and might be used as evidence.

If a warrant is obtained from the court to authorize the search of a premise, the law requires that the place to be searched and the things to

---

[32] For a current expression of this distrust of law enforcement agencies with strong political overtones, see Anthony Platt and Lynn Cooper, eds., *Policing America* (Englewood Cliffs, N.J.: Prentice-Hall, 1974).

[33] *Chimel v. California*, 395 U.S. 752 (1969).

[34] It has long been the custom of police to stop suspicious persons for questioning and to search them for weapons without arresting them. These "stop-and-frisk" situations pose a number of legal problems, but recent decisions of the Supreme Court have declared that the practice is permissible. See Jerold H. Israel and Wayne R. LaFave, *Criminal Procedures in a Nutshell* (St. Paul, Minn.: West, 1971), Chapter 2.

be seized must be described in detail; there must be reasonable grounds to believe that contraband or evidence of a specific crime can be uncovered; and the warrant must be based on a formal affidavit or sworn complaint. The law's concern for these safeguards can be seen emerging in seventeenth- and eighteenth-century England, when a general warrant authorizing a search was no more than a license to go on a "fishing expedition" to seize whatever incriminating evidence might be found that would imperil a person who had displeased those in authority. In the United States, the desire to restrain the power of the state flowered in the Fourth Amendment to the Constitution, in which it was declared that "the right of the people to be secure in their persons, houses, papers, and effects, against unreasonable searches and seizures, shall not be violated, and no Warrants shall issue, but upon probable cause, supported by Oath or affirmation, and particularly describing the place to be searched and the persons or things to be seized."

The safeguards provided by the Bill of Rights were originally confined to the operations of the federal government; the individual states were under no obligation to be equally concerned in their laws of criminal procedure about the rights of criminal suspects. (The states had their own bills of rights, but in most cases these provided suspected offenders with less protection than the first eight amendments to the Constitution.)[35] After the passage of the Fourteenth Amendment, in 1868, however, which provided that no state shall deprive any citizen of life, liberty, or property without due process of law, a series of decisions by the Supreme Court began to make many of the provisions of the Bill of Rights binding on the states. The problem was to make sure that the safeguards provided by the Bill of Rights were realized in fact as well as in theory—and this was a particularly difficult matter with regard to police practices in obtaining evidence. As Justice Robert Jackson had noted, "An illegal search and seizure usually is a single incident, perpetrated by surprise, conducted in haste, kept purposely beyond the court's supervision and limited only by the judgment and moderation of officers whose own interests and records are often at stake. . . . There is no opportunity for injunction or appeal to disinterested intervention. The citizen's choice is quietly to submit to whatever the officers undertake or to resist at risk of arrest or immediate violence."[36] In 1914 the Supreme Court ruled that evidence gathered illegally could not be used in a criminal prosecution at the federal level, and in 1961 the so-called exclusionary rule was extended to cover prosecutions by the states as well.[37] Finding

[35] See Irving Brant, *The Bill of Rights: Its Origin and Meaning* (New York: New American Library, 1965).
[36] *Brinegar v. United States*, 338 U.S. 160, 182 (1949) (dissenting opinion).
[37] See *Mapp v. Ohio*, 367 U.S. 643 (1961).

Search and Seizure

Mr. Justice Clark delivered the opinion of the court.

Appellant stands convicted of knowingly having had in her possession and under her control certain lewd and lascivious books, pictures, and photographs in violation of § 2905.34 of Ohio's Revised Code. As officially stated in the syllabus to its opinion, the Supreme Court of Ohio found that her conviction was valid though "based primarily upon the introduction in evidence of lewd and lascivious books and pictures unlawfully seized during an unlawful search of defendant's home. . . ."

On May 23, 1957, three Cleveland police officers arrived at appellant's residence in that city pursuant to information that "a person [was] hiding out in the home, who was wanted for questioning in connection with a recent bombing, and that there was a large amount of policy paraphernalia being hidden in the home." Miss Mapp and her daughter by a former marriage lived on the top floor of the

From *Mapp v. Ohio*, 367 U.S. 643, 81 S.Ct. 1684 (1961).

two-family dwelling. Upon their arrival at that house, the officers knocked on the door and demanded entrance but appellant, after telephoning her attorney, refused to admit them without a search warrant. They advised their headquarters of the situation and undertook a surveillance of the house.

The officers again sought entrance some three hours later when four or more additional officers arrived on the scene. When Miss Mapp did not come to the door immediately, at least one of the several doors to the house was forcibly opened and the policemen gained admittance. Meanwhile Miss Mapp's attorney arrived, but the officers, having secured their own entry, and continuing in their defiance of the law, would permit him neither to see Miss Mapp nor to enter the house. It appears that Miss Mapp was halfway down the stairs from the upper floor to the front door when the officers, in this highhanded manner, broke into the hall. She demanded to see the search warrant. A paper, claimed to be a warrant, was held up by one of the officers. She grabbed the "warrant" and placed it in her bosom. A struggle ensued in which the officers recovered the piece of paper and as a result of which they handcuffed appellant because she had been "belligerent" in resisting their official rescue of the "warrant" from her person. Running roughshod over appellant, a policeman "grabbed" her, "twisted [her] hand," and she "yelled [and] pleaded with him" because "it was hurting." Appellant, in handcuffs, was then forcibly taken upstairs to her bedroom where the officers searched a dresser, a chest of drawers, a closet and some suitcases. They also looked into a photo album and through personal papers belonging to the appellant. The search spread to the rest of the second floor including the child's bedroom, the living room, the kitchen and a dinette. The basement of the building and a trunk found therein were also searched. The obscene materials for possession of which she was ultimately convicted were discovered in the course of that widespread search.

At the trial no search warrant was produced by the prosecution, nor was the failure to produce one explained or accounted for. At best,

"There is, in the record, considerable doubt as to whether there ever was any warrant for the search of defendant's home." The Ohio Supreme Court believed a "reasonable argument" could be made that the conviction should be reversed "because the 'methods' employed to obtain the [evidence] were such as to 'offend "a sense of justice," ' '" but the court found determinative the fact that the evidence had not been taken "from defendant's person by the use of brutal or offensive physical force against defendant . . ."

The State says that even if the search were made without authority, or otherwise unreasonably, it is not prevented from using the unconstitutionally seized evidence at trial, citing Wolf v. People of State of Colorado, 1949, 338 U.S. 25, 69 S.Ct. 1359, in which this Court did indeed hold "that in a prosecution in a State court for a State crime the Fourteenth Amendment does not forbid the admission of evidence obtained by an unreasonable search and seizure." On this appeal, of which we have noted probable jurisdiction, it is urged once again that we review that holding.

it impossible to secure a conviction based on evidence that had been obtained by violating the safeguards surrounding the suspected criminal, the police would refrain from such behavior—or so the Court hoped.

It seems probable that the police have modified their behavior in light of the exclusionary rule, but it is also probably true that both the spirit and the letter of the law are frequently violated by the police. In many cases the police trick suspected offenders into giving their permission for a search, thus doing away with the need for a warrant. A suspect may be charged with a felony in situations where a charge of a misdemeanor would be more fitting, in order to justify an on-view arrest with its attendant powers for securing evidence. In some cases the police may claim that they saw the suspected offender make a movement—such as dropping drugs to the sidewalk—giving them probable cause to believe that a felony had been committed; an arrest—and a search for incriminating evidence—becomes legitimate, even though the suspect's behavior is no more than a story contrived by the police to justify their actions. As Morton Hunt notes:

> A policeman who searches a person or a person's car without probable cause will, if he finds anything incriminating, invent a probable cause. In California, for instance, highway patrolmen have recently been swearing, in case after case, that they searched the suspect or his car because, when pulled over to the side of the road by the patrolman, the suspect made a "furtive gesture," as if to hide contraband. As Justice Stanley Mosk of the California Supreme Court recently wrote, "The furtive gesture has on occasion been little more than a subterfuge in order to conduct a search on the basis of mere suspicion or intuition."[38]

Despite the decisions of the courts, then, law enforcement agencies have all too often pushed beyond boundaries set by the legal rules. The emphasis of the Court on the protection of the right against unreasonable search and seizure has created a great deal of bitterness, both among those who carry the responsibility of enforcing the criminal law and those members of the public who believe that "law and order" have been endangered. The police have claimed that the Supreme Court has frequently shown little awareness or appreciation of the difficulties of law enforcement and has been inclined to place the rights of suspected criminals over the right of the public to be protected. On the other hand, those who supported the legal safeguards of suspected criminals have claimed that the police show little understanding of the need to control the power of the state and that the protection of the public need not suf-

---

[38] Morton Hunt, *The Mugging* (New York: Atheneum, 1972), p. 232.

fer if the police are more adroit and persistent within the limits set by the law.[39]

As might be expected, this dispute has often pitted liberals against conservatives, and the bitterness of the argument became extreme in the 1960s. The need to protect political dissent had long been the very foundation of the claim that the power of the state must be curbed in the prosecution of those who were said to have violated the law—even though those suspected of murder, robbery, rape, and other such crimes, rather than those engaging in political dissent, made up most of the court's business. In the 1960s, the need to surround those who disagreed with the government with every protection seemed obvious to those on the left side of the political spectrum—and the disputes about the legal rights of ordinary criminals reached a singular intensity.

The arguments about search and seizure have been matched by those concerning self-incrimination. According to the Anglo-American legal tradition, the burden of proof in a criminal prosecution rests on the state; the defendant is under no obligation to help the state, nor should he or she be forced into doing so by torture or threats of other punishment. The image of men and women broken on the wheel to make them confess to treason or heresy has been replaced by the picture of a suspect subjected to more subtle forms of coercion; but the fear of brutal interrogation by the state remains, and in American society the Supreme Court has grappled with the problem in a series of important decisions.

Self-
Incrimination

The decisions stand as landmarks in the development of the rights of the suspected offender—and once again, as in the decision concerning search and seizure, the purpose of the Supreme Court has been to control police activity by threatening to exclude evidence obtained by illegal means. Direct legal action against particular police officers has proved largely ineffective, since law enforcement agencies are reluctant to prosecute, evidence is not readily available, and juries are unwilling to convict; and the Court has tried another path in implementing constitutional rights.[40]

The Fifth Amendment of the Constitution asserts that no person shall be compelled in any criminal case to be a witness against himself. As we have seen, however, the protections provided by the first eight amendments have only gradually been extended from the federal to the state level. Although the Supreme Court had reached, over the years, a number of decisions concerning the admissibility of confessions in cases involving federal law, it was not until 1936, in *Brown v. Mississippi*, that

---

[39] Herbert L. Packer, "Two Models of the Criminal Process," *University of Pennsylvania Law Review* 113 (November 1964), pp. 1–68.

[40] See, however, Robert H. Sulnick, *Civil Litigation and the Police: A Method of Communication* (Springfield, Ill.: Charles C. Thomas, 1976).

The law of criminal procedure protects the legal rights of the suspected offender by placing numerous restraints on the power of the police. Many people feel that the law has gone too far in this direction, but perhaps the central problem is that the safeguards are too often a myth rather than a reality.

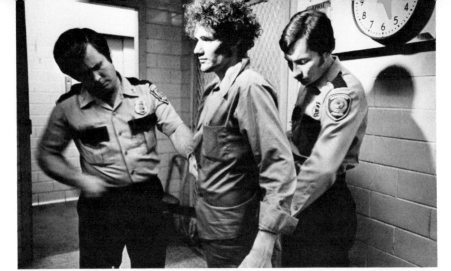

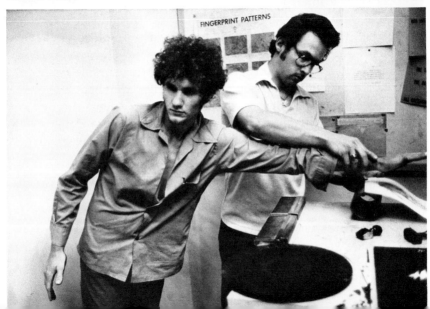

the Court ruled on the legality of a confession used in a case in a state court.[41] And in this case the Court relied not on the Fifth Amendment but on the Fourteenth, arguing that the confessions involved (they had been obtained by brutally beating the suspects) should be excluded on the grounds that the confessions were unreliable and thus violated the concept of due process of law. Later decisions excluded confessions on other grounds, such as that they were obtained by offensive police practices, that the defendant's ability to exercise free choice was significantly impaired, that the questioning was too prolonged, and that the suspect was held incommunicado. In 1964, in *Malloy v. Hogan*, the Supreme Court finally declared that the right to remain silent embodied in the Fifth Amendment was binding on the states; and in the same year, in *Escobedo v. Illinois*, the Court held that the Sixth Amendment right to counsel was essential—the accused must be advised by his lawyer of his privilege against self-incrimination. In 1966, in *Miranda v. Arizona*, it was announced that the privilege against self-incrimination is fully applicable when the accused is interrogated by the police before the trial, at both the state and federal levels.

Among these decisions the two that have caused the most dispute are the *Miranda* and *Escobedo* rulings. The use of force in obtaining confessions was undoubtedly a frequent occurrence in the past, although precise figures are lacking.[42] Rubber hoses, clubs, electric shocks—all have been part of the "third degree" and probably continue to be used, although on a more limited scale.[43] But if the use of physical force to extract confessions has decreased, the use of psychological coercion has not; and the latter came under the fire of the Supreme Court in the *Miranda* decision. "Again we stress that the modern practice of in-custody interrogation is psychologically rather than physically oriented. . . . Interrogation still takes place in privacy. Privacy results in secrecy and this in turn results in a gap in our knowledge as to what in fact goes on in the interrogation rooms. A valuable source of information about present police practices, however, may be found in various police manuals and texts which document procedures employed with success in the past, and which recommend various other effective tactics. These texts are used by law enforcement agencies themselves as guides. It should be noted that these texts professedly present the most enlightened and effective means presently used to obtain statements through custodial interrogation. By considering these texts and other data, it is possible to describe procedures observed and noted around the country."[44]

[41] Israel and LaFave, *Criminal Procedures in a Nutshell*, p. 215.
[42] See National Commission on Law Observance and Enforcement, *Report on Lawlessness in Law Enforcement, Report No. II* (Washington, D.C.: Government Printing Office, 1932).
[43] See Hunt, *The Mugging,* pp. 103–07.
[44] *Miranda v. Arizona,* 384 U.S. 436 (1966).

The book that particularly caught the attention of the Court was *Criminal Interrogation and Confessions,* by Fred Inbau and John Reid.[45] "To protect ourselves from being misunderstood," said the authors, "we want to make it unmistakably clear that we are not advocates of the so-called 'third-degree' . . . but we approve of such psychological tactics and techniques as trickery and deceit that are not only helpful but frequently necessary in order to secure incriminating information about the guilty."[46] But it was precisely these psychological tactics and techniques of trickery and deceit that the United States Supreme Court held unjustifiable and sought to eliminate.

The authors of *Criminal Interrogation and Confessions* provided a discussion of twenty-six techniques for obtaining an admission of guilt from suspected offenders. The techniques were simple, easily applied, and showed a psychological shrewdness common among those who manipulate social relationships professionally. The guilt and anxiety felt by the suspect were to be lessened by a sympathetic demeanor on the part of the police to a point where a confession of wrongdoing would become psychologically bearable. If two or more companions were being questioned about their involvement in a crime, one could be played off against the other by the creation of distrust and suspicion between them.

Inbau and Reid urged the interrogator to display an air of confidence in the "subject's" guilt, to undermine the suspect's self-assurance. "When the interrogator enters he should greet the subject in somewhat the same manner as a doctor greets a patient," they recommended, "cordially, but not in an overly friendly manner, and there should be no offer of a handshake. . . . At the beginning of the interrogation the interrogator's chair may be two or three feet from the subject's chair, but after the interrogation is under way the interrogator should move his chair in closer, so that, ultimately, one of the subject's knees is just about in between the interrogator's two knees."[47]

The suspect, said Inbau and Reid, should be watched for any sign in his demeanor that might betray him and place him in a more vulnerable position.[48] Pulsation of the carotid artery, staring at the floor or ceiling rather than looking the interrogator "straight in the eye," swallowing and wetting the lips because of a dry mouth—all could be taken as indications of guilt feelings and used to convince the suspect that a confession was the best remedy. "A criminal offender," they argued, "and particularly one of the emotional type, derives considerable mental relief

[45] Fred E. Inbau and John F. Reid, *Criminal Interrogation and Confessions* (Baltimore: Williams and Wilkins, 1962).
[46] Ibid., pp. 203–04.
[47] Ibid., p. 22.
[48] Ibid., p. 29.

and comfort from an interrogator's assurance that anyone else under similar conditions or circumstances might have done the same thing. He is thereby enabled to at least partially justify or excuse in his own mind his offensive act or behavior."[49] Sympathizing with the suspect, telling him that anyone else might have done the same thing in his place, minimizing the moral seriousness of the offense, suggesting a "less revolting and more morally acceptable" motivation or reason for the offense than that which is known or presumed, condemning the victim—all are techniques to reduce feelings of guilt and thus make easier the confession of wrongdoing.[50]

If these techniques proved ineffective or inappropriate, there remained other ways of manipulating the situation so that the suspected offender would become willing to confess. One method that elicited specific mention by the Supreme Court was the "Mutt and Jeff," act in which a show of friendliness is deliberately alternated with a display of anger. The technique, according to Inbau and Reid, may be applied somewhat as follows:

> Interrogator *A*, after having employed a sympathetic, understanding approach throughout his interrogation, expresses his regret over the subject's continued lying. *A* then leaves the room. Interrogator *B* enters and he proceeds to berate the subject, by referring to him as a rather despicable character, or perhaps as one who probably has been in a penitentiary or at least in prior police difficulties. (Or, *B* may enter while *A* is still in the room, and *B* can start his efforts by admonishing *A* for wasting his time on such an undesirable person; whereupon *A* will leave the room with pretended hurt feelings over the subject's refusal to tell him the truth. . . .
>
> The psychological reason for the effectiveness of the friendly-unfriendly act is the fact that the contrast between the methods used by each interrogator serves to accentuate the friendly, sympathetic attitude of the first one and thereby renders his approach more effective.[51]

From these representative samples of interrogation techniques, said the Court, it was clear that the object was to deprive the suspected offender of outside support, to undermine his will to resist, to persuade, trick, or cajole him out of exercising his constitutional right to remain silent.[52] And the remedy, in the eyes of the Court, was a cautionary an-

[49] Ibid., p. 34.

[50] Ibid., pp. 34–55. The discussion of techniques of neutralization in Chapter 8 appears to be particularly germane.

[51] Ibid., pp. 58–59.

[52] As Jerome Skolnick pointed out in a review of Inbau and Reid's work, the book might more properly be entitled *The Cop as Con Man: or How to Succeed in Trickery and Falsehood*

nouncement. The suspected offender was to be fully informed of his constitutional rights by the police at the time of his arrest in the so-called Miranda warning.[53] The police officer must tell the suspect: (1) you have the right to remain silent; (2) if you do not remain silent, what you say may be used against you; (3) you have a right to be represented by counsel during questioning and therafter; and (4) if you cannot afford to hire your own counsel, a lawyer will be provided for you at state expense. The indigent had been entitled to the right to counsel at all "critical stages" in criminal proceedings since *Gideon v. Wainwright,* decided in 1963.[54] Now he was to be told in plain words that this was so. (The police officer, in fact, frequently carries a small card on which the Miranda warning is printed and from which he may read to make sure that he does not overlook any of the points—and he may also hand the card to the accused to read.) Without the required warning, no admissions or confessions of the suspected offender can be introduced as evidence at trial, and the police are under strong pressure to make sure that the warning is in fact delivered.

The fury aroused by the *Miranda* and *Escobedo* decisions could hardly be explained on the ground that the Supreme Court had introduced a radically new view of the rights of criminal suspects. The Miranda decision, after all, simply represented an effort to ensure that the poor and the ignorant would have the same legal rights as the well-to-do and the educated had long enjoyed.[55] And although the critics of the Court predicted that the police would be severely handicapped in their battle against crime if they were forced to caution suspected offenders about their right to remain silent, the available evidence suggests that the Miranda warning has had little impact on either suspects' willingness to confess or the rate of conviction. This may be so because the warning is often presented in a perfunctory manner or may not be understood by the suspect, but several studies have indicated that the readiness to confess frequently persists even when suspects are aware of their legal

Without Ever Breaking the Law. See Skolnick, *American Sociological Review* 28 (April 1963), pp. 327–28.

[53] The details were enunciated by the Supreme Court in *Escobedo v. Illinois* and *Miranda v. Arizona,* in which it was made clear that the warning must be given not simply at the time of arrest but whenever an inquiry into a crime ceases to be a general inquiry and suspicion begins to focus on an individual. Furthermore, the warning is to be given when the individual is under such restraint that he is not free to walk away from the scene, even though no formal arrest has been made. See Kerper, *Introduction to the Criminal Justice System,* p. 250. In a 1969 decision (*Frazier v. Cupp*), the Supreme Court indicated that under some circumstances a confession could be admissible even though the police lied to the suspect, as Inbau and Reid pointed out in a later edition of their book.

[54] See Anthony Lewis, *Gideon's Trumpet* (New York: Random House, 1966).

[55] Hunt, *The Mugging,* p. 119. For a critical analysis of the *Miranda* decision, see Jan Gorecki, "Miranda and Beyond—The Fifth Amendment Reconsidered," *University of Illinois Law Forum,* No. 3 (1975), pp. 295–312.

rights.[56] Plea bargaining, which we will consider in a moment, is certainly an important factor and is usually based on an admission of guilt, and the psychological pressures attacked by the *Miranda* and *Escobedo* decisions can still be brought to bear, of course, after the Miranda warning has been given.

The right not to testify against one's self is, then, a vital part of our legal tradition, cherished by legal thinkers and held forth as the very hallmark of justice—but it is a right that is not exercised by the majority of criminal suspects. The Supreme Court has strengthened and extended the right to remain silent, placing the burden of proving guilt firmly on the government; yet it is estimated that 95 percent of all those convicted of a crime in the United States each year—both felonies and misdemeanors—have entered a plea of guilty.[57] Perhaps at no other point in the administration of the criminal law is the discrepancy so great between the assumptions of our legal system and the day-to-day realities of the law in operation.

Screening Devices

The criminal justice system is akin to a machine that sweeps up *suspected* offenders and that must then separate the guilty from the innocent. Ideally, of course, the innocent will be few, but it is inevitable that a number of persons will be arrested by mistake or run afoul of the law when there is insufficient evidence to warrant further prosecution. It is important to set such individuals free as quickly as possible, preferably before the time-consuming, costly, and stigmatizing experience of a formal trial. The Anglo-American legal system has developed two mechanisms designed to undertake this task—the preliminary examination and the lodging of a formal accusation. Both are supposed to screen out wrongfully suspected offenders at an early stage in criminal proceedings, although the preliminary examination has proved the more successful.

Preliminary Examination When a person is arrested and charged with a misdeameanor, a *preliminary examination* (also called a *preliminary hearing* or an *examining trial*) is usually not employed.[58] When the charge is a felony, however, in most

[56] See "Interrogation in New Haven: The Impact of Miranda," *The Yale Law Journal* 76 (July 1967), pp. 1519–1648; and Richard H. Seeburger and R. Stanton Wettick, Jr., "Miranda in Pittsburgh—A Statistical Study," *University of Pittsburgh Law Review* 29 (October 1967), pp. 1–26.

[57] See Donald J. Newman, *Conviction: The Determination of Guilt or Innocence Without Trial* (Boston: Little, Brown, 1966), p. 3.

[58] "The adjudication process in its simplest form is the handling of minor offenders (persons charged with a misdemeanor punishable by not more than 90 days confinement or a

states the accused must be brought before a magistrate without delay, and the court must determine whether there is sufficient evidence to proceed with the prosecution. (While the federal Constitution does not mention the right to such an examination, state constitutions or statutes usually provide for the procedure.) The magistrate does not determine the guilt or innocence of the suspected offender at this point, and the proceedings are generally informal; the suspect is normally not interrogated, and strict rules of evidence are seldom called into play. The magistrate must decide whether the state has established probable cause—that is, whether in the light of the evidence presented by the prosecution the accused *may* be guilty of the crime charged. If so, the suspect will be held for further action; if not, the suspect will be dismissed.[59] "Everyone threatened with the charge of the commission of a crime has two rights," a federal judge has said. "One is, of course, the right to a fair and impartial trial upon which the question of his guilt is determined; the other is the no less valuable right, and practically the more valuable right, that he shall not be even called upon to answer to a criminal charge until some duly constituted tribunal has passed upon the preliminary question of whether he ought to be brought to trial."[60]

The practical value of the preliminary hearing becomes apparent when a large number of cases are thereby eliminated—because witnesses fail to appear, for example, or the evidence of the police proves to be inadequate. Some fifty years ago, *The Illinois Crime Survey* noted that more than one half of defendants may be discharged because a probable cause for their detention has not been established.[61] More recent data, however, suggest that in some jurisdictions a large proportion of defendants now waive their right to a preliminary hearing.[62] The reasons why suspected offenders are willing to bypass the preliminary examination are not completely clear, but two possibilities can be noted. First, sophisticated lawbreakers are well aware that the testimony of witnesses elicited in the preliminary examination is available to the prosecutor at the trial—and this testimony, taken under oath with the details of the

---

$100 fine). Usually, the morning after he is arrested the defendant is brought before a court of limited jurisdiction such as a magistrate or police court and asked to plead guilty or not guilty. If he pleads guilty, he may be sentenced immediately. If he pleads not guilty, he may be tried, often immediately if the arresting officer or other witnesses are present. The defendant may have a jury trial, although one is not usually requested" (McIntyre, *Law Enforcement in the Metropolis*, p. 117).

[59] See Fellman, *The Defendant's Rights*, pp. 19–22.

[60] *United States v. Fitzgerald*, 29‡. 2nd 573, 574 (E.D. Pa. 1928).

[61] Arthur V. Lashly, Director, and John W. Wigmore, Editor, *The Illinois Crime Survey* (Chicago: Illinois Association of Criminal Justice, 1929).

[62] A study in Detroit indicated that in 1956, for example, approximately 72 percent of those charged with serious offenses failed to take advantage of their legal right to a preliminary examination. See McIntyre, *The Defendant's Rights*, p. 119.

crime still fresh, may prove damaging at a later date.[63] Second, those defendants who are convinced that pleading guilty in return for a reduced charge and a lesser sentence is their best course of action may see the preliminary hearing as merely adding an unnecessary delay, increasing the time spent in jail. In such cases, an immediate move to sentencing is preferable.[64]

That the right to a preliminary hearing is frequently waived must be kept in mind, along with the fact that the right is available and often results in the dismissal of charges that cannot be supported by the evidence. Flexible, informal (sometimes unduly so), public, and relatively straightforward, the preliminary examination provides a more or less effective device that helps to keep the legal system from becoming clogged with its own errors.[65]

Formal Accusation	After the suspected criminal has appeared before a magistrate in the preliminary hearing and the court has decided that there is good reason to believe that the state has established a *prima facie* case against the suspect (a case that supports a conclusion of guilty unless contradicted and overcome by other evidence), it becomes the responsibility of the prosecuting attorney to prepare a formal accusation. In some states, the prosecuting attorney has the authority to lodge a formal accusation subject to judicial review (in which case it is referred to as an *information*); in other states, the accusation is presented by the prosecuting attorney to a grand jury for approval (in which case it is referred to as an *indictment*).[66] "Both accusation by an official—sheriff, constable, or the like—and accusation by a body of the freemen of the vicinage were about equally ancient in

[63] See Lewis Mayers, *The American Legal System* (New York: Harper & Brothers, 1955), p. 122.

[64] See Newman, *Conviction*, p. 202. See also Frank W. Miller and Robert O. Dawson, "Non-Use of the Preliminary Examination: A Study of Current Practices," *Wisconsin Law Review* 252 (March 1964); and Note, "Preliminary Hearing—An Interest Analysis," *Iowa Law Review* 164, 167 (Fall 1965).

[65] For a critical view of the realities of the preliminary hearing, see Ernest W. Puttkammer, *Administration of Criminal Law* (Chicago: University of Chicago Press, 1953). For a discussion of how the preliminary hearing has been used as an opportunity to fix cases by professional criminals, see Edwin H. Sutherland, *The Professional Thief* (Chicago: University of Chicago Press, 1937), Chapter 8. "In the United States," it has been pointed out, "the quality of the preliminary hearing varies greatly with the quality of the magistracy. In some areas . . . it is conducted with relative decorum. But the situation is sometimes very bad in rural areas where justices of the peace are inexperienced or incompetent and it is at its worst in some large cities where magistrate courts are of poor quality. In such courts it is not unusual to find a noisy, crowded courtroom with policemen, defendants, bondsmen, and lawyers milling together in great disorder" (Karlen, *Anglo-American Criminal Justice*, p. 148). But the decorum of the court may not be reflected in the quality of the legal proceedings. See Eisenstein and Jacob, *Felony Justice*.

[66] In general, it is the states east of the Mississippi that use the indictment; the others tend to use the information.

England, their origins being traceable to the twelfth century, the period in which began the centralization of royal justice."[67] Both methods are subject to a good deal of debate concerning their virtues and vices.

The *grand jury*—so named to distinguish it from the *petit*, or *trial*, jury, consisting usually of twelve jurors—varies in size in different jurisdictions but may contain as many as twenty-three members. They are sworn "to make inquiries about crime, to keep the proceedings secret, and to present no charges for malice nor to leave any unpresented for fear, favor, or affection." Generally speaking, the prosecuting attorney (who may also be called the state attorney or district attorney) presents a written accusation—termed a *bill*—with the supporting evidence to the grand jury. If the majority of jurors agree that the accusation is supported by the evidence and warrants a trial, the bill is endorsed a *true bill*, signed by the foreman of the grand jury, and submitted to the court, where it is now labeled an *indictment*.

The *information* is simpler in operation and is said to have the advantage of placing the responsibility for the prosecution of a crime directly and clearly in the hands of the prosecuting attorney, rather than diffusing that responsibility in a body of laymen meeting irregularly. In reality, however, the grand jury has seldom been more than a rubber stamp for the wishes of the prosecuting attorney, and the substitution of the information for the indictment represents a change of procedure rather than of substance.[68] The relative unimportance of the decision-making power of the grand jury is attested to by the fact that in the overwhelming majority of instances the cases presented for prosecution are accepted by the grand jury—and thus in practice its usefulness as a screening device is negligible.[69]

The presentation of a formal accusation—whether by information or indictment—is, in any event, a vital step in the stages between arrest and trial. First, it places a great deal of power in the hands of the prosecuting attorney, who controls the decision of which cases will come to the attention of the court. Within rather wide limits, the prosecuting attorney can choose the violations of the criminal law that will make up a community's proven criminality. Second, the formal accusation brings into play

---

[67] Mayers, *The American Legal System*, p. 146. The American attachment to the grand jury is to be found in the Fifth Amendment to the Constitution, in which it is declared that "no person shall be held to answer for a capital, or otherwise infamous crime, unless on a presentment or indictment of a Grand Jury. . . ." It is a requirement that has not been extended to the states under the due process clause, and the use or nonuse of a grand jury is determined by state law.

[68] Ibid., p. 148.

[69] England abolished grand juries in 1933, mainly on the grounds that they were cumbersome, expensive, and time-consuming. See Karlen, *Anglo-American Criminal Justice*, p. 153.

a right that is regarded as essential in the just treatment of suspected offenders—the right of the defendant to be informed of the crime with which he or she is charged. It was not until the end of the seventeenth century, in English law, that the defendant gained the right to be so informed prior to trial. In the United States, the fear that such a right might be lost required an explicit provision in the form of the Sixth Amendment to the Constitution.[70] But the idea of adequate notice is now firmly entrenched as a fundamental requirement of criminal proceedings; and vaguely worded charges, general accusations lacking specificity, and accusations of wrongdoing not clearly contained in the criminal law are all considered invalid.

It is also true, however, that notice is largely confined to the nature of the accusation, and the defendant is generally not informed of the evidence that will be used against him. This is in contrast to civil proceedings, in which litigants are either encouraged or compelled to disclose the evidence prior to trial. But criminal procedure, notes Mayers, "is still on the whole dominated by the concept of 'surprise'—the belief that the truth will more surely be disclosed at the trial if the prosecution conceals its prospective evidence from the defense, thus precluding the manufacture of rebuttal evidence."[71]

One other problem concerning the grand jury should be noted. In a number of states, the grand jury has the authority to investigate a variety of areas for possible wrongdoing, such as public corruption, misconduct in office by government officials, prison brutality, and organized crime. With this authority goes the power to subpoena witnesses, to grant immunity, and to compel testimony under threat of a jail term for contempt if witnesses refuse to cooperate. On many occasions grand juries have undoubtedly performed their investigative task satisfactorily, functioning in a manner analogous to England's Royal Commissions and Tribunals of Inquiry. It has been argued, though, that in the United States the power of the grand jury has often been misused for political purposes, particularly in the 1950s, during a time of anticommunist hysteria, and in the 1970s, when remnants of the radical left had gone underground. In the 1950s, notes Charles Goodell, "a stream of suspected communists were brought before grand juries where federal prosecutors pressed inquiries into witnesses' political beliefs and affiliations, and those of their acquaintances. It was rarely made clear what crime, if any, was being in-

---

[70] Mayers, *The American Legal System*, p. 151.
[71] Ibid., p. 152. For a discussion of variation by state and possible future changes with regard to pretrial disclosure or discovery of evidence, see Israel and LaFave, *Criminal Procedure in a Nutshell*, pp. 51–55.

vestigated, and indictments were not forthcoming to justify the probes.
. . . The Nixon Administration's fondness for the people's panel (i.e.,
the grand jury) is rooted in this aberration of the fifties, not in the colonial grand juries and the tradition underlying the Fifth Amendment. In
the 1970s, the grand jury has almost completely replaced the moribund
and powerless antisubversive committees of the earlier era."[72]

Special prosecutors from the Justice Department have called witnesses
before grand juries in cities scattered around the country and questioned
them in the most general terms about their associations, political activities, conversations, and sources of information and opinion; and then,
when the witnesses refused to testify and were given immunity and
again refused to testify, the witnesses have been imprisoned. "It is such
'investigatory' grand juries that the Justice Department lawyers assembled in Los Angeles and Boston to look into the distribution of the
Pentagon Papers," notes Nathan Lewin. "Using the subpoena power of
the grand jury, federal prosecutors compelled newsmen, academics, and
even senatorial aides to appear and be asked questions about the Pentagon Papers." One teacher was taken to jail for refusing to disclose the
names of other scholars with whom he had discussed the Pentagon
Papers and for declining to state whether he had discussed the Pentagon
Papers with Daniel Ellsberg during the six months before their publication.[73]

The function of the grand jury to hear evidence presented by the prosecuting attorney and decide whether an indictment is justified is wedded, then, to the authority to make far-reaching investigations that are
easily converted into political inquiries. The first function has been
largely subverted, it has been argued, by the fact (in the words of attorney F. Lee Bailey) that the modern grand jury is "a flock of sheep led by
the prosecutor across the meadows to the finding he wants." The second
function, according to some legal writers, means that the grand jury has
been a sort of time bomb ticking away in the Anglo-American legal system for over eight hundred years, posing the danger of political suppression. Taken together, the two conclusions have led a number of
commentators to urge that the grand jury be abolished in the United
States, with its screening function absorbed by the preliminary hearing,
or that its power and procedures be subjected to serious reexamination.

[72] Charles E. Goodell, "Where Did the Grand Jury Go?" *Harper's* (May 1973), p. 16.
[73] Nathan Lewin, "The Misuse of Grand Juries," *The New Republic* (December 23–30,
1972), pp. 18–20. In January 1974 the Supreme Court declared that the exclusionary rule did
not apply to material gained from illegal wiretaps for the questioning and indictment of individuals appearing before the grand jury. See "Court Says Grand Juries May Use Illegal
Evidence," *The New York Times* (January 9, 1974).

The Negotiated Plea

The last stage of criminal proceedings before the trial itself is commonly called the *arraignment*.[74] At this time the defendant must offer a plea or make a formal answer to the charge against him. The defendant is brought to court and the judge reads the indictment or information, asking if the document states the correct name. The judge then inquires, "How do you plead?"[75] The defendant—or his lawyer—may make a legal objection to the charge (such as questioning the jurisdiction of the court in the matter); enter a plea of guilty; declare his innocence; or, in the states where it is permitted, enter a plea of *nolo contendere*. The last means "no contest" and is equivalent to a plea of guilty, but it cannot be used in a civil suit as evidence that the defendant has admitted guilt.

A plea of guilty obviously saves the judicial system a good deal of time and expense—and, in fact, as was pointed out earlier, the great majority of defendants do plead guilty. Indeed, if this were not true, the legal system would be overwhelmed. Already handicapped by too few judges, limited courtroom space, and inadequate staffs, the legal system is severely overburdened.[76] If only a small percentage—say 10 percent—of the defendants now pleading guilty decided instead to enter a plea of innocent and to demand a trial, the number of trials would increase by 100 percent, the backlog of cases awaiting trial would soar, and the jails would be overflowing. It is a spectacle that our society has no wish to contemplate, and the collapse of the legal system is avoided by making sure that the great majority of defendants continue to plead guilty and do not demand a full, formal trial.[77]

Pleas of guilty are encouraged by offering defendants an exchange: if the defendant promises to plead guilty, the state will reduce the penalties it will inflict or indirectly reach the same result by changing the crime of which the individual is accused from a more serious to a less serious category. The fundamental characteristic of crime—the punishment of prohibited behavior by the state—is thus compromised in the interest of administrative efficiency.

This is not the only reason that defendants may be urged to enter a guilty plea to a reduced charge or that a relatively light sentence may be

---

[74] In some states the term *arraignment* is used to refer to the defendant's first appearance before a magistrate, rather than to the presentation of the charge prior to trial.

[75] See Kerper, *Introduction to the Criminal Justice System*, pp. 288–90.

[76] See *Lagging Justice, The Annals of the American Academy of Political and Social Science* 328 (March 1960), for a symposium of articles dealing with the problem. See also Arthur Rosett and Donald R. Cressey, *Justice by Consent: Plea Bargaining in the American Courthouse* (Philadelphia: J. B. Lippincott, 1976).

[77] For a fictional portrayal of the disastrous consequences that would follow an increase in pleas of innocence, see James Mills, *One Just Man* (New York: Simon & Schuster, 1974).

given by the judge for such a plea. Prosecuting attorneys may believe that the harsh penalty attending conviction of a more serious charge will do more harm than good in a particular case or that conviction of the more serious crime is unlikely. Newman has indicated the complex factors that may underlie the reduction of charges:

> The experienced prosecutor, in anticipation that acquittal at trial is likely, will frequently reduce a charge in spite of evidence objectively sufficient to sustain it. In general, prosecutors hesitate to try cases where (a) a long mandatory sentence will follow conviction; the defendant is young, respectable, or inexperienced; and the offense is of a minor nature; (b) the conduct involved in the offense, while technically criminal, is not generally considered morally reprehensible; (c) the activities of the police in obtaining the evidence are likely to be viewed by the court or the jury as improper and perhaps more blameworthy than the conduct of the defendant; or (d) the characteristics of the defendant, such as youth or respectability, or the particular circumstances surrounding the offense are such that the criminal conduct will probably appear justified or mitigated to a jury.[78]

It can also be argued that when judges give relatively light sentences to those pleading guilty, something more than the desire to speed the flow of cases through the court may be involved. A plea of guilty may be viewed by some judges as a sign of remorse, the first step on the road toward rehabilitation, and leniency in sentencing is therefore appropriate. This viewpoint may be extended to include the converse situation; that is, if a defendant pleads innocence and is then convicted, he has compounded his crime by committing perjury in denying it at trial, and severity rather than leniency in sentencing is warranted.[79] The key element in the exchange of leniency for a plea of guilty, however, seems to be the need to make manageable the workload of the court.

Many observers of the legal system find plea bargaining objectionable.[80] The promise of leniency, whether implicit or explicit, is nothing more than a form of coercion, it is said, and is just as improper as threatening the defendant with greater punishment if he insists on pleading innocent. In either event, the defendant is placed in a situation in which he will be penalized for exercising his constitutional right to a

---

[78] Newman, *Conviction*, p. 72.

[79] Ibid., p. 62. See also *Note, Yale Law Journal,* 66, 204 (1956), pp. 212–17.

[80] "Plea bargaining is one of the controversial and often criticized features of the criminal justice system," notes Lesley Oelsner, in an article in *The New York Times* discussing the public outcry that followed the Watergate prosecution disposing of cases by inducing guilty pleas in return for reduced charges. A similar outburst attended the prosecution and conviction of Vice President Spiro Agnew. See Lesley Oelsner, "Watergate Plea Bargaining," *New York Times* (June 23, 1974).

trial, and to claim that a threat of a more severe sentence in return for a plea of innocence is somehow wrong whereas a promise of a less severe sentence in return for a plea of guilty is somehow right is little more than fancy logical footwork. The legal system's unwillingness to face this fact finds expression in the hypocritical dialogue that takes place between the defendant and the judge when the defendant enters a plea. In situations where plea bargaining has occurred and both the judge and the defendant know it, the judge asks the defendant if he has been offered any promises or received any threats to make his plea of guilty. The defendant says no, and the judge accepts his answer, but everyone in the courtroom is aware of the deception involved.

Moreover, it is argued, plea bargaining creates the danger that persons who are in fact innocent may be induced to plead guilty because the circumstantial evidence against them appears strong or because their poor reputations or past records make acquittal unlikely.[81] And those defendants who are too naive or too unfamiliar with the workings of the criminal court to engage in plea bargaining may be given sentences that are wildly different from those given defendants who do so. "Differential opportunity for plea negotiation typically results in disparate sentences, a major problem for correctional authorities," Newman indicates. "In prison, particularly, offenders quickly learn of this 'cop out' process and quite obviously compare their own sentences with those of other inmates guilty of similar crimes. It is a difficult correctional task to convince an inmate to accept a sentence perhaps three times as long as that of another who has successfully bargained."[82]

For those who argue in favor of plea bargaining, such claims are held to be unconvincing. In practice, it is said, guilty pleas by innocent persons are rare, and sentence disparity is not markedly affected by leniency shown those pleading guilty. Few judges base their sentencing solely on whether the defendant pleads guilty or innocent. And, in any event, whatever defects such a procedure may have, they are far outweighed by the administrative advantages.[83] Unless the great majority of defendants in criminal cases are willing to forego the determination of their guilt or innocence by means of a trial, the legal system shaped with such care over the centuries will no longer be able to function. A penalty less than that called for by the crime with which they are charged is the only feasible means to avoid such a collapse.

Some social scientists have claimed that the flood of cases in the criminal courts is much less important as a cause of plea bargaining than is commonly supposed. In a study of two Connecticut circuit courts, for ex-

[81] Newman, *Conviction*, p. 66.
[82] Ibid., p. 43.
[83] Ibid., p. 66.

ample, Malcolm Feeley comes to the conclusions that plea bargaining has long been a feature of the American legal system and does not represent a breakdown of once well-established adversarial procedures; that at the present time courts with a large volume of cases in relationship to staff are not more inclined to produce guilty pleas than are courts whose workload is more manageable; and that it has not been demonstrated that all cases should go to trial or that guilty pleas are necessarily undesirable.[84]

The evidence, however, is far from conclusive. It is true, as Feeley indicates, that settling cases with a plea of guilty is an old practice, but on the whole it seems more likely that the practice has increased rather than remained constant. And the reason for the lack of relationship between the size of the workload and the number of guilty pleas may be that after the backlog of cases reaches a certain point, variation in workload makes little difference: a court with x number of cases is under as much pressure as a court with twice that number.

The author of this study is right, nonetheless, in warning us to be suspicious of the idea of a golden age of justice somewhere in the past. The full exercise of the defendant's rights (including a trial in court with the burden of proof on the prosecution) has probably been an ideal rather than a reality for most suspects, as indicated earlier, for reasons that go beyond the size of the court's workload. Until more evidence to the contrary is at hand, however, it appears reasonable to contend that the pressure of cases in the criminal court has increased in recent years and has been an important factor in making the prosecutor willing to arrange a diminished penalty for the defendant in exchange for a plea of guilty.

From a practical viewpoint, the argument for the necessity of plea bargaining in the United States today is probably correct, if one assumes that the number of suspected offenders passing through the criminal justice system will not decrease and that the United States will be unlikely to appropriate significant sums of money to enlarge the capacity of the courts. It may well be true that the majority of suspected offenders who plead guilty are in fact guilty of some crime even though it may not be either the one with which they were originally charged or the one that finally appears in the accusation that leads to a guilty plea. It may even be true that plea bargaining provides a measure of mercy, easing harsh penalties embedded in the criminal law. But having said this, it is important to point out that plea bargaining as it now exists represents a fundamental contradiction in the Anglo-American tradition. It is a basic

---

[84] See Malcolm M. Feeley, "The Effects of Heavy Caseloads." Paper delivered at the annual meeting of the American Political Science Association, 1975. See also James Eisenstein and Herbert Jacob, *Felony Justice: An Organizational Analysis of Criminal Courts* (Boston: Little, Brown, 1977).

assumption in our legal system that the individual is assumed to be innocent until proven guilty—and *proven* is generally taken to mean proven in a court of law following the rules of evidence and with the defendant aided by counsel. In plea bargaining, however, the proof of guilt remains largely an informal matter, based on the defendant's confession and discussions with police, defense attorney, prosecuting attorney, and judge, with scant opportunity for the standards of legal evidence to be applied.[85] Unlike a public trial, plea negotiation is carried on in private, where prejudice and personal opinion can flourish and the uninformed defendant stands at a serious disadvantage.

Conclusions

In this chapter we have examined the steps by which a crime comes to the attention of the police, suspected offenders are identified and arrested, apprehended suspects are screened to eliminate the more obviously mistaken cases, and the remaining defendants are required to enter a plea to the charge that has been brought against them.

The phases of criminal procedure are carefully hedged with numerous safeguards to protect the suspected offender from the oppressive power of the state. "It is not without significance," Justice William O. Douglas has said, "that most of the provisions of the Bill of Rights are procedural. It is procedure that spells much of the difference between rule by law and rule by whim or caprice. Steadfast adherence to strict procedural safeguards is our main assurance that there will be equal justice under law."[86]

Many people, however, are quite convinced that the American legal system has gone much too far in protecting suspected offenders and has been all too willing to sacrifice the safety and welfare of the law-abiding members of society in the quest for equal justice. We have turned the legal process into a game, it is said, in which the need to protect society from the depredations of criminals has been lost from view. The state has set up so many rules designed to help the defendants that the police are left in the position of trying to win a race in which they must carry one hundred pounds of extra weight and wear clodhoppers, while the suspected criminal is allowed to wear only a jogging suit and run in

[85] A confession, it should be noted, is not the same thing as a guilty plea. "A confession relates a set of facts (*i.e.*, 'I shot him'), whereas a plea is an admission of all elements of a formal criminal charge (*i.e.*, 'guilty of murder in the second degree'). The confession requires knowledge of a factual situation; the plea, however, implies a sophisticated knowledge of law in relation to the facts" Newman, *Conviction*, p. 23.

[86] *Joint Anti-Fascist Committee v. McGrath*, 341 U.S. 123, 179 (1951) (concurring opinion).

sneakers. And at the sidelines of this game are the judge, who continually rules in favor of the defendant, and the public, betting and cheering, encouraging first one side and then the other.

These criticisms of the laws of criminal procedure suffer from a major defect—their neglect of the fact that the safeguards surrounding the defendant are so often no more than paper safeguards. In the matter of arrest, laws concerning the need for warrants or reasonable grounds for believing a felony has been committed are often ignored. The protections afforded by the *Miranda* and *Escobedo* decisions may indeed be extended, but seem to have little effect on the ability of the police to extract confessions by psychological coercion. The right to a preliminary hearing—a right that could play a crucial role in separating the innocent from the guilty, if the English experience is any guide—is frequently waived. Other screening devices, such as the grand jury, have become little more than a vestigial organ or have become transformed into a means for snuffing out political dissent. The right to counsel, long regarded as one of the bulwarks against unfair or illegal practices, has indeed been extended, but there is sufficient evidence available to raise serious doubts about the amount of protection actually offered by many defense attorneys. The central problem, then, may not be one of providing suspected offenders with too many safeguards; instead, the important issue may be that the safeguards are still too often a myth rather than a reality. Supreme Court decisions have frequently promised much only to have their promises undone by practice.

A number of people seem to believe that the Bill of Rights is a fine idea, but that it is wasted on criminals. As Joseph O'Meara of the Notre Dame Law School has pointed out, however, "The simple truth is that you have to be for the Bill of Rights or not; you can't be for the Bill of Rights for yourself and your friends; it's all or nothing. A break in the dike imperils the whole countryside, not just the area adjacent to the break. There is only one protection against the flood and that is to contain it entirely."[87] The problem of achieving that ideal of justice is one of the most serious issues confronting the administration of the criminal law in the United States today.

Recommended Readings

For readers interested in a further examination of criminal procedure, it is useful to first explore the legal aspects of the issue in a legal textbook like Jerold H.

[87]See Joseph O'Meara, "Freedom of Inquiry Versus Authority: Some Legal Aspects," *Notre Dame Lawyer* 31 (December, 1955), p. 11.

Israel and Wayne R. LaFave, *Criminal Procedure in a Nutshell: Constitutional Limitations* (St. Paul, Minn.: West, 1971). A discussion of the law well balanced by an account of the actual administration of the laws of criminal procedure is to be found in Donald McIntyre, Jr., *Law Enforcement in the Metropolis* (Chicago: American Bar Foundation, 1967) and Lloyd L. Weinreb, *Denial of Justice: Criminal Process in the United States* (New York: The Free Press, 1977).

Specific aspects of criminal procedure are presented in Wayne R. LaFave, *Arrest: The Decision to Take Into Custody* (Boston: Little, Brown, 1965); Arthur Rosett and Donald R. Cressey, *Justice by Consent: Plea Bargaining in the American Courthouse* (Philadelphia: J. B. Lippincott, 1976). Morton Hunt, *The Mugging* (New York: Atheneum, 1972), recommended earlier for the light it throws on such crimes as robbery, provides a readable account of the criminal law in operation.

Chapter 10
The Police

In the United States today there are approximately 15,000 law enforcement agencies at the federal, state, and local levels of government. The overwhelming majority of them are local agencies, found in counties, cities, and towns.[1] They range in size from one- or two-man police forces in rural areas to mammoth police departments in major metropolitan centers, such as New York City, which has some 29,000 employees, or Chicago, with 15,000.[2] Although the nature of police work obviously varies a good deal, as do the problems of police–community relationships, the bulk of the literature on police structure and functioning is based on studies of large, urban law enforcement agencies; and this fact must be kept in mind in examining the assertions about the role of the police in American society.

Even while the necessity of the police in maintaining law and order has been recognized, the police have been viewed with much suspicion since the emergence of modern police organizations in the nineteenth century. And, indeed, for a democratic social order, the existence of a quasi-military force in the midst of civilian society has posed an enduring dilemma that has yet to be resolved. Suspicion of the police has its roots in two major issues that have been mentioned in previous chapters. First, there is the long-standing fear that the police will be used by those in positions of political power to suppress dissent. Second, there is the awareness that in their zeal to enforce the law, the police may frequently overstep the limits erected by society and sweep up the innocent along with the guilty. These uneasy attitudes toward the police have fluctuated in American history—along with the widespread feeling that the police are courageous men and women doing a difficult job and must be supported at any cost.[3]

[1] See *Sourcebook of Criminal Statistics—1974* (Washington, D.C.: Government Printing Office, 1975), p. 32.

[2] See *Uniform Crime Reports—1976* (Washington, D.C.: Government Printing Office, 1977), pp. 228–36.

[3] It should be kept in mind that even during the tumultuous years of the 1960s, the majority of Americans believed that the police were doing a good or excellent job in enforcing the

The debate over the police has probably been most intense in congested urban areas, where law enforcement is all too likely to take on the appearance of a species of class warfare. Those arrested are usually drawn from among the poor, the uneducated, and the politically powerless; and those enforcing the law are apt to be identified as the minions of a small group of people variously described as the ruling elite, the rich and the powerful, or the Establishment. But in the 1960s, as racial antagonisms flared and Vietnam War protests spilled into the streets, contention surrounding the police became bitter and emotional to an unprecedented extent.

It is in the context of turmoil that we must examine recent criminological writing about the police—but it is probably fair to say that the analysis of the structure and functioning of the police has *never* been free of political and ideological considerations. The police have traditionally represented authority and the preservation of the status quo; the critics of the police have most often viewed themselves as aligned with the downtrodden and those who favored social change. If discussions concerning the police have often been marked by emotion-laden statements, we should hardly be surprised. The place of the police in society symbolizes profound issues in social thought.

History of the Police

"Most people obey most laws willingly," says Michael Banton in his article in the *Encyclopaedia Britannica*, "whether or not there is a policeman looking on. They comply with the laws because they believe them right and perceive that in the long run it is in everybody's interest to observe them."[4] But this sort of voluntary compliance, he adds, is more common in some communities than in others. Small, homogeneous communities, in which each person's behavior is subject to constant scrutiny and such informal controls as ridicule, gossip, and the allocation of esteem, most nearly approach the theoretical model of the self-regulating social group. This form of social life—or the approximation of it—began to break down with the advent of the industrial and urban revolution, as was noted in Chapter 7. As the small, intimate community, with its simple system of social control, began to be displaced by large, impersonal

---

law, that the police were very good or reasonably good in respecting the rights of citizens, and that almost all policemen were honest. In general, blacks were more critical than whites, and the lower the individual's income the less favorable his views of the police were likely to be. See Philip H. Ennis, *Criminal Victimization in the United States* (Washington, D.C.: Government Printing Office, 1967), pp. 52–60.

[4] See "Police," *Encyclopaedia Britannica*, Macropaedia, vol. 14 (1975), p. 662.

groupings, the need for new forms of regulation seemed more and more necessary; and in response to this need the modern, bureaucratic police force emerged.[5]

The control of crime in earlier times was not exclusively a matter of unstructured, spontaneous reactions. In England, before the Norman Conquest, local associations of private citizens were pledged to the maintenance of law and order. "Every man was responsible not only for his own actions but also for those of his neighbors. It was each citizen's duty to raise the 'hue and cry' when a crime was committed, to collect his neighbors and to pursue a criminal who had fled from the district. If such a group failed to apprehend a law-breaker, all were fined by the crown."[6] These groups first consisted of ten families and were called *tithings;* later, ten tithings were grouped together to form *hundreds.* A hundred was placed in the charge of a constable, a local nobleman who had command over the group's weapons and equipment. At a still later date, as the society grew in size and complexity, hundreds were joined to form a *shire,* a geographical area equivalent to a county. An official—a *reeve*—was appointed by the Crown to supervise each shire. The *shire-reeve* was the ancestor of tens of thousands of sheriffs to come.[7]

In the following centuries, law enforcement in England underwent many changes, including the separation of judicial and police functions, the decline of the local pledge system, and the creation of fragmented civic associations like the Bow Street Horse and Foot Patrol in London. But the sudden rush of social growth and social change attending industrialization and urbanization in the 1700s and 1800s overwhelmed what was basically a small, part-time, uncoordinated effort to deal with crime. The Industrial Revolution, says one writer, "created the proletariat, an unfixed, propertyless peasantry of the mills. And with the appearance of this class came the modern police problem. . . . This is the still unsettled question of how to achieve a stabilized political order for communities which contain so large an element of population inherently unstable as to *means of livelihood* and *place of residence*—the two points upon which all the older systems were based."[8] Roving gangs of thugs, sporadic outbreaks of violence, and the growing threat of the desperate poor living in urban squalor all gave strength to the argument that a full-time, well-trained police force was a necessity.[9] The Gordon Riots in London in

[5] See Roger Lane, *Policing the City: Boston 1822–1885* (Cambridge, Mass.: Harvard University Press, 1967).

[6] See President's Commission on Law Enforcement and Administration of Justice, *Task Force Report: The Police* (Washington, D.C.: Government Printing Office, 1967), pp. 3–12.

[7] Ibid. See also William Alfred Morris, *The Medieval English Sheriff to 1300* (Manchester, England: University of Manchester, 1927).

[8] Asher Brynes, *Government Against the People* (New York: Dodd, Mead, 1946), p. 164. Italics in the original.

[9] See Patrick Pringle, *Hue and Cry* (London: W. Morrow, n.d.).

1780, during which anti-Catholicism flared into violence that lasted for four days and completely overwhelmed the civil authorities, had been particularly disturbing. And the French Revolution seemed to raise the specter of widespread rebellion, as did the subsequent Napoleonic wars—at least in the mind of a ruling class that feared the spread of foreign and subversive ideas. In 1829 Sir Robert Peel, in his capacity as England's Home Secretary, convinced Parliament that the time had come to organize a professional law enforcement body, and the London police—quickly nicknamed "bobbies"—came into existence.

The United States, in the early part of the nineteenth century, was experiencing a similar period of social upheaval. As cities became large manufacturing centers, the urban poor, lacking the strength and cohesiveness that trade unions would later provide, competed with one another for jobs; and the plight of propertyless masses produced something close to a proletarian civil war. Riots erupted in 1835, and in 1837 in Boston the native-born workers fought the immigrant Irish laborers in clashes resembling the Gordon Riots. In 1838 the antagonism between the whites and the blacks of Philadelphia broke into open warfare; and in 1844 antiforeign riots burst out in Baltimore, Philadelphia, and New York. Added to these disturbances were election riots and fighting between street gangs. In 1845 New York City followed London's example and created a municipal police force, with Chicago, New Orleans, Cincinnati, Philadelphia, and Boston soon following suit.[10] The shift of police power from the hands of private citizens to government bureaucracies was virtually complete.

Both in England and in the United States, the early police forces were greeted with a good deal of hostility and suspicion, and numerous social commentators were ready to argue that uniformed agents of law enforcement had no place in a democratic society. "When Sir Robert Peel finally won acceptance of his police plan," says one writer, "he was denounced as a potential dictator. Even the respectable London *Times* urged revolt and a national secret body was organized to combat the police."[11] In American cities the police were criticized for the violent fighting that frequently broke out between the day shift and the night shift, who saw themselves as rival organizations rather than as members of a unified system; personnel standards were often compromised in the attempt to staff rapidly growing departments; and the inability to attract competent candidates, because of low salaries, helped to diminish the prestige of the police in the mind of the public.[12]

[10] See Brynes, *Government Against the People*, Chapter Four. See also A. F. Costello, *Our Police Protectors: History of the New York Police* (New York: Charles F. Roper, 1884); and Charles P. McDowell, *Police in the Community* (Cincinnati: W. H. Anderson, 1975), pp. 1–37.

[11] George Berkley, *The Democratic Policeman* (Boston: Beacon Press, 1969), p. 5.

[12] See *Task Force Report: The Police*.

The most significant problem, however, was the extent to which the police were subject to political control. "Rotation in office enjoyed so much popular favor," declares one writer, "that police posts of both high and low degree were constantly changing hands with political fixers determining the price and conditions of each change. . . . The whole police question simply churned about in the public mind and eventually became identified with the corruption and degradation of the city politics and local government of the period."[13]

For many people, the solution to the problem of the lowly position of the police was clear: the police must become professionals.[14] Beginning slowly in the early 1900s and accelerating after the end of World War I, serious efforts were made to reform the police, and steps were taken to institute programs of training, raise educational requirements, develop scientific methods of crime detection, increase salaries, win freedom from political interference, and rationalize the administrative structure that had grown up on a piecemeal basis.

This push toward professionalization, so often encountered in the study of occupational groups, has continued to the present day. It has proved to be a mixed blessing, as Abraham Blumberg and Arthur Niederhoffer have indicated. While the various elements undoubtedly result in more efficient police operations, professionalization carries a number of problems in its train. When professionalism is concerned primarily with technical expertise and proficiency, and is filled with the jargon of the academic world but has not absorbed the humanistic values of the traditional professions, claim Blumberg and Niederhoffer, it is dangerous for the police and the society they are supposed to protect. "To date," they argue, "the police would appear to be more interested in power than in the conventional norms and values of a profession. They applaud and vigorously seek the autonomy of the professional but are rather superficial and perfunctory in developing the kind of systematic knowledge base, academic involvement and research orientation, colleagueship, service ideal, critical self-analysis, and nonbureaucratic controls that are usually the hallmark of professionalism."[15]

The appearance of professionalism rather than the substance, they

[13] Bruce Smith, Sr., *Police Systems in the United States* (New York: Harper, 1960), pp. 105–06.

[14] Professionalism is typically regarded as including a high degree of autonomy, training, control through collegial bodies, systematic extension of knowledge, the acceptance of a code of ethics, a sense of public duty, and the existence of professional societies rather than union-like bargaining agents. See James Q. Wilson, *Varieties of Police Behavior* (New York: Atheneum, 1971), pp. 29–30.

[15] Abraham S. Blumberg and Arthur Niederhoffer, "The Police in Social and Historical Perspective," in Arthur Niederhoffer and Abraham S. Blumberg, eds., *The Ambivalent Force: Perspectives on the Police* (Waltham, Mass.: Ginn, 1970), pp. 13–14.

point out, can create a struggle for power between an entrenched administrative oligarchy—the Old Guard—and an innovative younger group using the jargon, style, and ideological slogans of professionalism, which may be simply a disguise for a personally centered careerism. The demand for increased educational requirements can lead to cynicism and frustration among old timers who fear the competition of the college-educated; and those police officers who try to upgrade their skills by obtaining college training may find themselves caught in an acute conflict between the local bureaucratic loyalties of the police force and the cosmopolitan, questioning traditions of academic life. Professionalism can be maintained only as long as the police have high prestige in the public eye—and this can lead to a powerful push to cover up mistakes and to falsify official reports to give an appearance of ever-greater success in combating crime. Professionalism also increases the demand within the police department for a rigorous, impersonal enforcement of the law—but this may sharpen the conflict between the police and the community, for the latter is likely to find full enforcement of the law an irritant. Perhaps most important, a frequent concomitant of police professionalism is the growing militarization of urban police departments seeking greater efficiency through centralization and rigid internal controls.

The problem of fitting the concept of the police to a democratic society, then, is much more complex than easy slogans about the need for professionalization suggest. Over time, the tasks assigned to the police have changed considerably from the days when chase and capture followed hue and cry. Frequently finding themselves at the cutting edge of social change in large American cities, embroiled in social problems that extend far beyond their control or mandate, the police struggle with issues that are not merely a matter of professional *expertise* that can be brought to their task but also include the question of what precisely that task should be.

Function and Structure of the Police

A great deal of the work that engages the police has very little to do with the detection and apprehension of people who have violated the criminal law. Directing traffic, granting permits for taxicabs and parades, locating missing persons, escorting cars of political dignitaries, rescuing cats and dogs, controlling crowds at public events (including fires and the opening of new supermarkets), licensing amusement parks and theaters, providing emergency services for the ill and injured, inspecting public places for conformity with safety regulations—all these and more absorb much of the time and resources of local police forces and are marginally related at best to the popular view of the police as crime fighters. When James Wilson made a study of police behavior in eight communities in the mid-1960s, he found that a large share of citizen complaints radioed to patrol cars did *not* involve violations of the criminal law but matters that could best be described as requests for service.[16] Similar patterns have been observed in other studies, such as the one conducted by Elaine Cumming, Ian Cumming, and Laura Edell, who analyzed the incoming telephone calls at the complaint desk of a metropolitan police department over a period of several days. The police, they suggest, are inundated by requests for aid in numerous personal problems that only occasionally involve crime. The stereotype of the police as agents of the legal system in the administration of justice needs serious revision.[17] Poor, uneducated people, they argue, are apt to use the police in the way that middle-class people use family doctors and clergymen—and the police, ill-trained to fill this helping role, are pressed into service on a twenty-four-hour basis, very often against their wishes.

Another large segment of police work deals with behavior that might be classified as touching on violations of the law but does not involve murder, theft, robbery, rape, or aggravated assault. Instead, the police are confronted with cases of domestic quarrels, complaints about noisy neighbors and trespassing, bothersome drunks, and kids hanging around on street corners. "Only about one tenth of the calls afforded, even potentially, an opportunity to perform a narrow law enforcement function by stopping a burglary in progress, catching a prowler, making an arrest of a suspect being held by another party, or investigating a suspicious car or an open window," says Wilson in discussing his data concerning police operations in the Syracuse Police Department. "In fact, very few of *these* will result in arrests—there will be no prowler except in a woman's imagination, the open window will signify an owner's oversight rather than a thief's entry, the 'suspicious' car will be occupied by a respectable citizen, and the burglar, if any, will be gone. Almost a third of all calls—and the vast majority of all nonservice calls—concern allegations of disorder arising out of disputes, public and private, serious and trivial."[18]

It is necessary, says Wilson, to distinguish between the functions of *maintaining order* and *law enforcement*, as a number of other writers who have studied the police at first hand have argued for some time.[19] The

---

[16] *Varieties of Police Behavior*, pp. 17–19.

[17] See Elaine Cumming, Ian Cumming, and Laura Edell, "Policeman as Philosopher, Guide and Friend," *Social Problems* 12 (Winter 1965), pp. 276–86.

[18] *Varieties of Police Behavior*, p. 19.

[19] Ibid., Chapter One. See also Michael Banton, *The Policeman in the Community* (London: Tavistock, 1964) and Egon Bittner, "The Police on Skid-Row: A Study of Peace-Keeping," *American Sociological Review* 32 (October 1967), pp. 699–715.

use of the dichotomy maintaining order and law enforcement is perhaps unfortunate, since it suggests that maintaining order does not involve the legal rules. In fact, these studies make it clear that the police are involved in three different types of activities: (1) *formal* application of the criminal law, involving the use of arrest, detention, judicial determination of guilt or innocence, and judicial sanctioning for serious offenses, such as robbery; (2) *informal* application of the criminal law, involving the use of the individual policeman's discretion, judgment of responsibility, and application (or nonapplication) of sanctions to minor offenses such as public drunkenness; and (3) the provision of services that have nothing to do with the criminal law—such as rescuing cats from trees. It is to point up the contrast between the policeman acting on his own to provide services and enforce the criminal law (often his own version of it) and the use of the full panoply of the legal system that the terms maintaining order and law enforcement are commonly used, but law enforcement is involved in both. While the terms are sometimes confusing, the important issue is the reality that is being examined.

On the one hand, the policeman on the street struggles with the varied disputes and problems arising in the life of the community—and generally in the poorer sections of the community; his purpose is to keep things calm, to avert large disorders, to achieve a rough sort of justice, and to avoid the time-consuming and possibly disruptive operations of the formal system of adjudication and sanctioning. On the other hand, the policeman attempts to prevent crime and to apprehend wrongdoers, to catch a burglar or a car thief or some other criminal whose offense is considered to be a clear-cut breach of the legal rules and whose behavior warrants the imposition of formal punishment by the state. The first is a matter of preventing *disorder*—that is, behavior defined as "not right" or "unseemly," such as a teenager shouting in the street or racing a car at night, a radio being played too loudly in the middle of the night in the next-door apartment, an aggressive panhandler, or people "looking like hippies" and loitering in public places.[20] The second is a matter of controlling moral wrongdoing or a situation perceived as a serious threat to community safety, where the public expects and demands not simply informal conflict resolution but also symbolic affirmation of the law's constraints. As Wilson indicates, the drunk, the teenager, the person next door, the panhandler, and the hippie are likely to feel that their behavior is *not* disorderly, that people should mind their own business, that the policeman has no right to intervene. In the case of a theft or a burglary, a fight in a tavern, or an assault on an unfaithful lover, however, there may be widespread agreement that the police have a right to take action. In both situations the policeman encounters a series of problems, as we

[20] Wilson, *Varieties of Police Behavior,* p. 16.

The work of the police is a blend of different activities, and much of it bears little resemblance to public stereotypes constructed from television dramas of high-speed chases and violent shootouts.

shall see shortly, that have much to do with the emergence of what can be called the policeman's "working personality"—that is, a typical style or pattern of response to the demands generated by the policeman's role.

The work of the police, then, is a blend of different activities, and much of it bears little resemblance to public stereotypes constructed from television dramas of high-speed chases and violent shootouts. Jerome Skolnick, undertaking a study of law enforcement, quickly discovered that detective work was far closer to his intended subject matter than the activities of the police officer on patrol. "I soon learned," he says, "that patrol work is minimally connected with legal processing. To be sure, some street behavior is relevant to the policeman's role as a legal actor. On the street, the policeman has the greatest potential for discretionary judgment not to invoke the criminal law. . . . Nevertheless, I thought that the typical activities of a patrolman were not those of a *law* officer, but rather those of a *peace* officer."[21]

In fulfilling the functions both of law enforcement and the maintenance of order, the individual policeman clearly exercises a good deal of discretion, both in terms of the situation in which he decides to intervene and the action he decides to take. The exercise of discretion is inevitable, as indicated in Chapter 9, but the problem of how to supervise, review, and thus control the policeman's use of discretion remains; and it is a problem that is greatly complicated by the organizational structure of the police.

Like many organizations operating on a twenty-four-hour basis, the police are divided into three eight-hour shifts. Each shift has its own lore and each is viewed in a special light by policemen, as the following remarks by policemen suggest:

> Four (in the afternoon) to twelve is great for working, lots of action, but it's hell on your life. You feel like you're always working or getting ready to go to work. No time for yourself.

> Daywork is all bullshit but you get to meet some nice people and make a lot of contacts.

> I won't kid you fellas, last out (12 midnight to 8:00 A.M.) is rough. I tried everything but I could never go to sleep in the morning when I got home. And then maybe you got to go to court. Man, when the sun comes up, it's murder. You just have to drink a lot of coffee and keep shaking your head. But it's part of the job.[22]

[21] *Justice Without Trial* (New York: John Wiley & Sons, 1966), p. 33.

[22] Jonathan Rubinstein, *City Police* (New York: Farrar, Straus & Giroux, 1973), pp. 63–64. In a number of cities, each district is policed each day by three squads, while a fourth squad is off. Each squad works for six days and then takes two days off; each week each squad works a different shift, and over a four-week period the patrolmen have worked on all three shifts.

The important fact for the moment, however, is not that policemen learn that different shifts have different characteristics and come to prefer a particular one; rather, the reason multiple shifts are significant is that they result in discontinuities in command and control that make it difficult to establish and maintain uniform standards for the individual policeman's discretionary use of power. Other organizations operating around the clock, such as certain types of manufacturing plants or transportation services, are faced with a similar problem.[23] But whereas a factory is concerned with adherence to a well-defined schedule, the police are faced with the need to supervise something more elusive—namely, the discretionary use of power. The temporal fracturing of police organizations obstructs the establishment of consistent policies in a sphere of activity that is ambiguous at best.

Further complicating the task of administration, a police force, unlike an office or a factory, scatters its personnel over large geographical areas. Maintaining supervisory contact is a constant difficulty, and one- or two-man patrols are left to do their job largely on their own. The geographic dispersal of police work has, in fact, long been a problem in the establishment of an effective chain of command.

In the early part of the nineteenth century, Colonel Charles Rowan, the first commissioner of London's police force, attempted to meet the issue by demanding that policemen walk a prescribed route at a prescribed pace, so that supervisors could know where their men were at all times.[24] Unfortunately, criminals were no less able to keep track of patrolmen, and the plan was soon abandoned. Technological advances led to the installation of call boxes, to be replaced in this century by the two-way radio in squad cars and walkie-talkie radios worn on the belt, but the basic problem remains. The police supervisor's need to keep track of the people under his command accounts in large measure for the vast quantity of paperwork that is the bane of the police officer's existence—and it is a poor substitute for the ease of control that comes with continual face-to-face contact.

Police organizations are marked by one other feature that has profound consequences for the functioning of the police in the community. In most cities in the United States, the recruitment base of the police is greatly restricted by formal policies and informal custom. A survey conducted by the International Association of Chiefs of Police indicated that almost 75 percent of the responding departments required preservice residence in the community for periods of time ranging from six months to five years.[25] This parochialism, in part a result of the Great Depression, when

---

[23] See Wilbert E. Moore, *Man, Time, and Society* (New York: John Wiley & Sons, 1963).
[24] Rubenstein, *City Police,* Chapter One.
[25] *Task Force Report: The Police,* p. 130.

the scarcity of jobs led many communities to give preference to local residents, also finds expression in the opposition of the police to the concept of *lateral entry*, or the filling of higher positions by persons from outside the particular police force. "Under existing police structures," it has been pointed out, "nearly all local enforcement agencies restrict advanced appointments to personnel within the department. . . . A consequence is that America's police personnel are virtually frozen into the departments in which they started."[26]

In addition, there are the restrictions imposed by ethnic selection. "The Irish cop" may be a cliché, but it is worth remembering that at the turn of the century Irish immigrants found the police department an important avenue of social mobility; and the Irish still dominate the police force in a number of large cities, long after the days when positions in city government were a crucial source of jobs for ethnic groups tied to the big-city political machine.[27] Today, the use of ethnic criteria in police recruitment is probably most evident in the lack of representation of blacks and the Spanish-surnamed on the police force in many cities. Even where they have managed to fill a fair share of available positions, their entry into the police force has often been grudgingly accepted.[28]

The most striking restriction on the recruitment base of the police may be that of social class. The low educational requirements, the low pay, and the public image of the job as one involving much physical danger and social conflict have all conspired to make police work relatively unattractive to the college-educated middle class.[29] People going into police work have generally come from the lower rungs of the socioeconomic ladder—and since the upper rungs of the police hierarchy have largely been staffed by those rising through the ranks, police departments have tended to be predominantly lower or lower-middle class in origin.[30]

These restrictions in the recruitment of the police, whether introduced by the police themselves as a matter of policy or caused by public attitudes toward the police, give rise to several problems. First, they can impede the process of finding competent personnel. Promotions from within, for example, greatly reduce the pool of potential talent. "An

[26] Ibid., p. 142.

[27] See James Q. Wilson, "Generational and Ethnic Differences Among Career Officers," *American Journal of Sociology* 69 (March 1964), pp. 522–28.

[28] John Darnton, "Color Line a Key Police Problem," *The New York Times* (September 28, 1969). See also Nicholas Alex, *Blacks in Blue: A Study of the Negro Policeman* (New York: Appleton-Century-Crofts, 1969).

[29] See Wilson, *Varieties of Police Behavior*, Chapter Nine.

[30] Studies of the police that include data on such indicators of socioeconomic status as education have found that few policemen have completed college, and many have not completed high school. See, for example, *Task Force Report: The Police*, p. 126. In recent years, however, the socioeconomic level of police recruits has probably been rising.

officer whose special skills are in oversupply in his own department cannot move to a department where those skills are in demand," it has been noted. "An officer who seeks to improve his situation by moving from a small department where opportunities for advancement are few to a large department where they are numerous cannot do it, nor can a city officer who would like to work in a small community follow his inclinations. A department that cannot fill important jobs adequately from its own ranks is precluded from seeking experienced officers elsewhere."[31] Second, the failure to hire members of minority groups has the consequence, it has been argued, of both alienating large numbers of people with whom the police must deal and depriving the police of personnel who would be invaluable because of their background. Third, because the police are so largely recruited from the lower and lower-middle classes, it has been said, they are all too apt to be marked by the authoritarianism, intolerance, and racial prejudice allegedly found in those segments of the population.[32]

We will examine some of these arguments later in the chapter. At the moment, it is sufficient to point out that by limiting the potential pool of candidates from which the police are drawn, in terms of residence, ethnic group, and social class (as well as sex), police departments are likely to show a high degree of social homogeneity. This in turn would appear to be an important precondition for the social solidarity that has been remarked so often in studies of the police in American communities. "All occupational groups share a measure of inclusiveness and identification," says Jerome Skolnick. "People are brought together simply by doing the same work and having similar career and salary problems. . . . However, police show an unusually high degree of occupational solidarity."[33] Isolation from the larger community, odd working hours, public hostility, the threat of danger—all these conditions may act to drive the police together. But the lack of social differentiation within police departments intensifies the effect of these pressures, creating a monolithic organizational structure that resists outside scrutiny or interference.[34] "Never squeal on a fellow cop" becomes an overriding maxim, and the private citizen is held at bay.[35]

[31] Task Force Report:The Police, p. 142.

[32] See Bernard Locke and Alexander B. Smith, "Police Who Go To College," in Niederhoffer and Blumberg, The Ambivalent Force, pp. 144–47. See also David H. Bayley and Harold Mendelsohn, Minorities and the Police (New York: The Free Press, 1969).

[33] Justice Without Trial, p. 52.

[34] See David J. Bordua and Albert J. Reiss, Jr., "Command, Control, and Charisma: Reflections on Police Bureaucracy," American Journal of Sociology 72 (July 1966), pp. 68–76.

[35] See William A. Westley, "Secrecy and the Police," Social Forces 34 (March 1956), pp. 254–56.

The Occupational Personality of the Police

On his first day as a policeman a rookie may capture an armed felon, be cracked on the head with a rock, be offered sexual favors, free food, or money; he may be confronted by a naked woman, screaming hysterically, or a belligerent drunk who outweighs him by fifty pounds; or if he begins on last out, he may spend the entire tour trying to fight off the desire to sleep. He has no control over what he will learn first, and when he will learn it, because he has no control over what he must do. Regardless of what occurs, he is obliged to be immediately what he has chosen to become, although his colleagues know he has only the vaguest appreciation of what that is. The department has told him that he is expected to "prevent crime, protect life and property, arrest law violators, assist the public, preserve the public peace, regulate public conduct and control and expedite the flow of vehicular traffic." He does not know whether he can do any of these things, and the only way he can find out is by being what he is officially—a policeman. He acquires bits and pieces of knowledge, information, and experience which he alone can put together to make himself independent, effective, and valuable to his colleagues. While he is learning to do his work, he is also defining for himself the nature of his place on the street, discovering the contradictions inherent in his position as a guardian of the "public" peace, and the ambiguities of being a regulator of people's conduct.[36]

This perceptive account of a tyro policeman's day well describes the problems confronting the patrolman. It has been argued that the patrolman responds to these problems in a standardized fashion, not because policemen come from similar class backgrounds or because those drawn to police work are born with similar personality structures, but because the job itself is a great socializer, inculcating attitudes, habits, and modes of perception. The study of the policeman's personality thus illuminates one of sociology's major areas of interest—the influence of experience on social behavior.

Suspicion The patrolman soon finds that the most innocent-appearing element may in fact be a warning that a crime has taken place or is about to do so. A line of empty pop bottles along the length of a building may be the ammunition supply for a juvenile gang fight. A man sitting by himself in a car near a playground may be a child molester. A pounding noise, unidentifiable, may be someone trying to break into a building. An expensive car in a poor neighborhood or an old, battered car in a wealthy neighborhood may both be signs of trouble. Someone moving too

[36] Rubinstein, *City Police*, pp. 127–28.

quickly or too slowly, someone staring at a police officer or avoiding his gaze, someone carrying a suitcase on a residential street—all become "suspicious characters," possibly up to no good and to be kept under surveillance.[37]

Training for law enforcement, it has been pointed out, "can produce a revision of unconscious expectations of violence and crime. This does not mean that the law enforcer necessarily comes to exaggerate the prevalence of violence. It means that the law enforcer may come to accept crime as a familiar personal experience, one which he himself is not surprised to encounter. The acceptance of crime as a familiar personal experience in turn increases the ability or readiness to perceive violence where clues to it are potentially available."[38] The policeman's dominant characteristic, claims one writer speaking of the British police, "is neither those daring nor vicious qualities that are sometimes attributed to him by friend or enemy, but an ingrained conservatism, an almost desperate love of the conventional. It is untidiness, disorder, the unusual, that a copper disapproves of most of all; far more, even, than of crime, which is merely a professional matter. Hence his profound dislike of people loitering in the street, dressing extravagantly, speaking with exotic accents, being strange, weak, eccentric, or simply any rare minority of their doing, in fact, anything that cannot be safely predicted."[39]

The American policeman is no less inclined to be sensitive to anything out of the ordinary, to identify certain kinds of people as "symbolic assailants," to use Skolnick's term, who because of their gestures, language, or dress are thought to be prone to violence. The policeman's perception of dangerous situations is illustrated, Skolnick suggests, by the warning signs listed in an article instructing police in the problem of selecting persons for field interrogation. The list included the following items:

Persons who do not "belong" where they are observed

Automobiles which do not "look right"

Businesses opened at odd hours or not according to routine or custom

Exaggerated unconcern over contact with the officer

Unescorted women or young girls in public places, particularly at night in such places as cafes, bars, bus and train depots, or street corners

"Lovers" in an industrial area (make good lookouts)

[37] Ibid., Chapter Six.
[38] H. Toch and R. Schute, "Readiness to Perceive Violence as a Result of Police Training," *British Journal of Psychology* 52 (November 1961), p. 392.
[39] Colin McInnes, *Mr. Love and Justice* (London: New English Library, 1962), p. 74 (quoted in Skolnick, *Justice Without Trial*, p. 48).

Catching Crooks

For five months PFF, Inc., was one of Washington, D.C.'s, most successful enterprises. Its friendly staff specialized in typewriters, television sets and other appliances, and on good days fifteen cars would be lined up outside its warehouse to do business. Last week, however, the company suddenly closed shop, to the acute embarrassment of its 200 regular customers. PFF, Inc., it turned out, stood for Police–FBI Fencing, Incognito—a fencing ring owned and operated by the cops. At a going-out-of-business party they dubbed "The Sting," PFF agents blew their cover by arresting scores of thieves, implicating an assistant U.S. attorney, and recovering $2.4 million in stolen property. "It was the smoothest mass arrest I've seen in 24 years in the bureau," gloated FBI official Nick Stames.

PFF, Inc., was modeled on a similar caper by the New York City police last year. Six Washington policemen and federal agents moved into an abandoned warehouse in the fall. They distributed PFF business cards, hung several Playboy centerfolds at the warehouse entrance to hide a camera that would photograph every wide-eyed customer, and sat back to await business.

They didn't wait long. As word spread through the streets, Washington thieves walked through the door lugging typewriters, stereo systems, firearms and electric stoves. One man brought a heart–lung resuscitator stolen from a suburban hospital. There was a bearskin rug, a silver candelabrum, and some not-very-well-counterfeited $50 bills. All told, PFF agents purchased 3,500 items, including 1,500 credit cards, eighteen cars and trucks and $1.2 million worth of government checks stolen from a vault at the Department of Housing and Urban Development. They paid bargain prices: $400 electric typewriters went for $25 apiece, and the $1.2 million in HUD checks for a mere $750.

As the ruse wore on with almost tedious success, the cops began to work into their roles. They noticed that the customers assumed they must be mafiosi, and so they took to calling themselves "Rico Rigatone" and "Angelo Lasagna." They cooked up spicy meatballs on a hot plate, peppered their small talk with words like "ciao," and talked darkly of the "don" in

New York for whom they were working. Their visitors were impressed. Several described the tricks of their trade in fascinating detail, all recorded on video tape. One man demonstrated how he sprang open rows of apartment mailboxes with karate chops. Another asked whether PFF needed a hit man. Fill out an application he was told, and he did—including among his references a hitherto unsolved murder in Maryland.

Finally, short of "buy money" and burdened with paperwork, PFF decided to liquidate its assets. It announced a formal party for prize customers to celebrate the firm's success and to meet the don "who is so proud of what you did for us." The clients arrived in dinner jackets and dutifully checked any guns at the door. One hood showed up in handcuffs—he had just escaped from a street arrest by the city police—and asked his hosts to cut them off. "We said, 'Here's another set for you'," recalled Lt. Robert Arscott, one of the company's phony fences. All told, 108 men were arrested that night.

At the same time FBI agents arrested assistant U.S. attorney Donald E. Robinson at his Maryland home. Robinson was charged with accepting $700 in bribes to help "protect" PFF, and he was immediately fired. By early last week police had rounded up 25 more people and had begun investigating 10,000 crimes ranging from use of stolen credit cards to murder.

Enforcement: The arrests shed some interesting light on Washington law enforcement. Most of the thieves had prior records and many had been freed on parole. The man who snatched the HUD checks was on parole after serving five years of a 24-year sentence for armed robbery. He had been arrested more than six times since—yet his parole had never been revoked. Several had told their probation officers they were working for PFF, and the officers evidently did nothing to find out what sort of business it did.

Although some people believed that the Stingers might have been guilty of entrapment, legal authorities thought not. The police never encouraged their customers to commit a crime—in fact they turned down offers from 100 people who volunteered to steal to order. Police–FBI Fencing, Incognito, sounded like just what the Law Enforcement Assistance Administration had in mind when it suggested recently that police departments needed to find more creative ways of catching crooks.

Solicitors or peddlers in a residential neighborhood

Loiterers around public rest rooms

Hitchhikers

Lone male sitting in car near shopping center who pays unusual amount of attention to women, sometimes continuously manipulating rear-view mirror to avoid direct eye contact

Person wearing coat on hot days

Cars with mismatched hub caps, or dirty car with clean license plate (or vice versa)

Uniformed "deliveryman" with no merchandise or truck[40]

To the private citizen, this list may seem to indicate a degree of suspiciousness bordering on paranoia; but to the police, the items appear perfectly reasonable. While well aware that many of these situations are innocent, the police also realize that some are not. There is no way to tell one from the other without investigation; and the police, made mistrustful by experience, are led to treat them all with caution.

Cynicism The world of the police is often a world of decaying flophouses and poverty-stricken streets, of pimps, whores, thieves, petty hustlers, drunks, quarreling spouses, and drug addicts. It may be somewhat melodramatic to describe it as a jungle, but it is undeniably a seamy environment, in which one commonly encounters deceit, selfishness, cruelty, and greed. It is hardly surprising that the policeman comes to view his fellow man with a skeptical eye, looking for base motives and frequently finding them. The behavior of his colleagues may also give him reason to doubt the virtue of human nature. Bribery, brutality, and false testimony are encountered among his fellow officers and provide a discouraging picture of the official world. Added to this, the work of the police frequently appears to be an illusionary method of combating crime. The arrested thief who is immediately back on the street boasting of his invulnerability, the felon returned to the neighborhood from prison who quickly resumes a criminal career, and the juvenile lounging on the corner who obviously has nothing but contempt for the patrolman and the law make police effectiveness a joke.[41]

Another important source of policemen's cynicism is the fact that as agents of society they hold a grant of power that others are anxious to manipulate or control for their own purposes. The police become well aware that they may be used, and they are quick to look for selfish mo-

[40] Thomas F. Adams, "Field Interrogation," *Police* (March–April 1963), p. 28.

[41] See Arthur Niederhoffer, "Police Cynicism," in Niederhoffer and Blumberg, *The Ambivalent Force*, pp. 179–83.

tives. "When the police arrive to look for a prowler, examine a loss, or stop a fight, the victim and suspect are agitated, fearful, even impassioned," says one writer. "But the police have seen it all before and they have come to distrust victim accounts (to say nothing of suspect explanations) of what happened. Instead of offering sympathy and immediately taking the victim's side, the police may seem cool, suspicious, or disinterested because they have learned that 'victims' often turn out not to have been victimized at all—the 'stolen' TV set never existed or was lost, loaned to a boyfriend, or hidden because the payments were overdue; the 'assault' was in fact a fight which the 'victim' started but was unable to finish."[42] Aware that crimes may be reported when none have occurred, just as crimes that have occurred may not be reported, the police become wary; both the supposed suspect and the supposed victim are viewed with cynicism—that special form of suspicion in which virtue is always taken as a mask for vice.

A frequent complaint about the behavior of the police concerns their harsh, swift reaction to any act they define as an affront to their authority. They are "touchy" to an extreme degree, if they believe a private citizen is ridiculing them or challenging their power; and the person who does not move along quickly enough when ordered to do so, who records a policeman's badge number during a fracas in the street, or who questions a police officer's actions may be accused of flouting authority, and roughly handled as a consequence.

Touchiness

Such situations arise not only in mass disturbances; they frequently occur when the police are engaged in "maintaining order." They often involve minor offenses and vague infractions of the law, such as "disorderly conduct"—the very areas in which the authority of the police is likely to be most problematical. As Albert Reiss has indicated, arrests for minor violations are apt to provoke citizens' claims that authority is being exercised arbitrarily and unjustly, and bystanders are likely to interfere on similar grounds. Furthermore, police officers often intervene in such situations on their own initiative rather than in response to a complaint. When this happens, Reiss argues, the police "cannot begin with the usual queries to parties about 'What's the trouble here?' or 'Who called the police?' Rather, they try to assert authority by such means as commands: 'Break-it-up,' 'move on,' or even more commonly 'get your ass out of here.' "[43]

Unfortunately for the police, these commands often prove to be ineffective; as Banton has pointed out, in a heterogeneous society that pro-

[42] Wilson, *Varieties of Police Behavior*, pp. 24–25.
[43] Albert J. Reiss, Jr., *The Police and the Public* (New Haven: Yale University Press, 1972), p. 58.

vides some latitude in its definition of proper conduct, the official position of the policeman, with its symbols of uniform and badge, is frequently inadequate to secure compliance.[44] When the police speak of their authority, Wilson has indicated, they mean the right to ask questions, get information, and have their orders obeyed. When the police officer is unable to exercise authority by the mere fact of his presence, he may be called on to prove himself, to "show who is boss." For some, says Wilson, size alone may be sufficient; others may find an assured tone of voice is enough; still others, though, will resort to shouting, pushing, and cursing.[45]

The policeman, then, cannot take the authority attached to his role for granted. He is obligated to intervene in circumstances where the proper course of action is ambiguous and where, in his view, his presence may be resented. Trying to control the situation on the basis of his authority, he finds that the trappings of his office are not sufficient. He must become personally involved, and he is constantly uncertain whether his personal exercise of authority will be successful. As a consequence, the policeman is understandably sensitive to any doubt that may be cast on his power, and he tends to react strongly to any slight, real or imagined.

Prejudice It is often claimed that the police are highly prejudiced against members of minority groups, particularly blacks and the Spanish-surnamed, and treat them with a brutal disregard for either legal rights or human dignity. In recent years, the politically alienated young and members of the counterculture have asserted that they too have become special targets of police hostility; and the outbreak of police violence at the Democratic National Convention in Chicago in 1968 is pointed to as a dramatic example of the long-standing tendency of policemen to hate and fear the outsider.

Now the evidence indicates that policemen frequently *are* prejudiced against members of minority groups, that they deeply distrust expressions of political discontent, and that they resent those they characterize as hippies. But these are attitudes, it should be noted, that the police share with many private citizens; and policemen, in large measure, reflect the biases of the society from which they are drawn. Thus, for example, in the study conducted by Bayley and Mendelsohn, white police officers and a sample of the general public were asked if they would be upset if a member of their immediate family married a black. Some 85 percent of the policemen answered yes—and 84 percent of the public

[44] Banton, *The Policeman in the Community*, p. 168. See also James R. Hudson, "Police-Citizen Encounters That Lead to Citizen Complaints," *Social Problems* 18 (Fall 1970), pp. 179–93.

[45] Wilson, *Varieties of Police Behavior*, pp. 32–33.

gave the same answer. About 33 percent of the officers and 44 percent of the public said they would be upset if the marriage involved a Puerto Rican or Chicano; 14 percent of the officers and 25 percent of the public would be upset if the marriage were with a Jew.[46]

The crucial question, however, is whether the police, in their official capacity, express their prejudices overtly against members of minority groups, the poor, and youths with long hair. Again the answer is yes. The police do *not* treat all members of the public alike, and there is good reason to believe that large segments of the population think, quite correctly, that they are singled out for special attention. Our task, at the moment, is to understand why the police discriminate against some members of society.

Prejudice obviously has something to do with the matter. Policemen use their position to harass those they dislike, sometimes engaging in petty acts simply to embarrass or inconvenience the poor, the young, or the members of minority groups.[47] At other times, the prejudice can burst into violence, in the form of a beating or worse.[48] But the most persistent discriminatory behavior of the police is their tendency to devote extra surveillance to certain groups and to arrest people from such groups on the slightest suspicion. Prejudice alone does not explain this behavior.

According to the police, blacks, hippies, and the poor are singled out for special attention not because the police are intent on harassing these groups but because the groups are especially prone to commit crimes. They must be watched more carefully and arrested more frequently under suspicious circumstances because such arrests so frequently turn out to be justified. When the police stop and question a poorly dressed black in a wealthy white residential neighborhood at three o'clock in the morning, it has been suggested, the police believe they are acting in a reasonable fashion—and, even more important, they believe they are acting justly.[49] "No one would accuse the police of acting unjustly if they stopped and questioned a man wearing a mask and carrying a sack of burglar tools near a bank at three o'clock in the morning," says Wilson. "Even though he might be entirely innocent—say, a reveler on his way home from a costume party—our instinct, formed by experience, suggests a high probability of felonious intent."[50] When the police direct their suspicions against a member of a minority group, a poor person, or

[46] *Minorities and the Police,* pp. 144–47.

[47] See Skolnick, *Justice Without Trial,* p. 80.

[48] See, for example, Paul Chevigny, *Police Power: Police Abuses in New York City* (New York: Pantheon Books, 1969).

[49] Wilson, *Varieties of Police Behavior,* pp. 38–39.

[50] Ibid., p. 38.

an adolescent in what they consider unusual circumstances, they claim that they act in a no less sensible manner. "The great majority of suspicion stops occur in poor neighborhoods, because that is where street crime is the greatest, where the most drugs are sold in the streets, and where people are the least safe," Rubinstein argues. "In some of these neighborhoods policemen stop people for reasons many people might consider reprehensible. . . . He [the policeman] knows that many people would think him prejudiced or cynical . . . , but he also knows that these people have not seen what he has seen. The patrolman stops a black man in a white neighborhood because he feels the person does not belong there. This may be an unwholesome perception, but the policeman's experience tells him it is by and large valid. The policeman making the stop is not questioning the personal right to walk there but the infrequency of its occurrence."[51]

From a strictly factual point of view, the police are probably correct when they argue that blacks, the poor, and the young have higher crime rates than the rest of the population, if we are talking about such "conventional" crime as theft, robbery, rape, and assault. It is unlikely that these groups have higher rates simply because the police watch them more closely and arrest their members more frequently than others.[52] Furthermore, the police are probably correct when they claim that it is not mere prejudice that leads them to single out particular groups for special attention. Unquestionably the police frequently use their estimation of the relatively higher rate of crime as an excuse, and a variety of social biases are disguised behind a scrim of statistics. Nonetheless, numerous reports by keen observers make it appear likely that the police often honestly believe that their discriminatory behavior results in greater effectiveness in fighting crime.

But even if discriminatory tactics do allow the police to detect more crimes and apprehend more criminals, such practices cannot therefore be declared acceptable. Portions of the community are often far from satisfied with the situation. Moreover, the question of the legality of discriminatory treatment remains.[53] Clearly, in many instances the police have overstepped the law as they have interfered in people's lives without probable cause, no matter how accurate their predictions of certain groups' crime rates. The exercise of police power in a specific situation must, in theory, be based on specific present knowledge and not statis-

[51] *City Police*, p. 263.

[52] "Scholars who believe otherwise," notes Wilson with some acerbity, "are, in my view, either still suffering from a romantic or Marxist illusion that the proletariat was untouched by original sin or else they were raised in a glass jar" (*Varieties of Police Behavior*, pp. 40–41).

[53] See Charles A. Reich, "Police Questioning of Law-Abiding Citizens," *Yale Law Journal* 75 (June 1966), pp. 1161–72.

tical generalizations, even though such generalizations are a valid summary of similar events. It is a restriction the police frequently feel they must ignore.

Policemen, then, do exhibit typical traits as they go about their work. They are inclined to be highly suspicious of anything out of the ordinary, cynical about the truthfulness of what people tell them, sensitive to any signs of disrespect for their authority, and quick to discriminate against certain people on the basis of stereotypes. It may be thought that these are aspects of a personality structure for which police work holds a specific allure; it has been claimed, for example, that psychological testing indicates policemen are more suspicious, more ready to take risks, and more aggressive than the general run of the population.[54] The writers whose work has been discussed here, however, have taken a contrary and perhaps more illuminating approach. While there may be some degree of meshing between personality traits and occupational role, it is argued, the characteristics of suspicion, cynicism, touchiness, and prejudice, often seen as underlying much police behavior, are best analyzed as products of the job itself. It is the voice of duty—as perceived by the policeman—that summons his style rather than something buried in the psyche.[55] A clear resolution of these conflicting claims must, however, wait on future research.

The Police and the Community

Public attitudes toward the police, as we have seen, have been tinged with suspicion and hostility since the first modern police force was established. Community antagonism toward the police creates numerous problems, such as difficulties in recruitment, impaired police morale, lack of public funds, and an unwillingness on the part of the public to cooperate with the police.[56] It is to be expected, then, that the police have long felt the need for more harmonious police–community relationships. The issue has taken on a special prominence in the last several decades. "The need for strengthening police relationships with the com-

Antagonism and Support

[54] Clifton Rhead et al., "The Psychological Assessment of Police Candidates," *American Journal of Psychiatry* 124 (May 1968), pp. 1573–80. See also Martin Symonds, "Emotional Hazards of Police Work," in Niederhoffer and Blumberg, *The Ambivalent Force*, pp. 58–64.

[55] For an excellent review of the relevant literature, see Joel Lefkowitz, "Psychological Attributes of Policemen: A Review of Research and Opinion," *Journal of Social Issues* 13 (Winter 1975), pp. 3–26.

[56] *Task Force Report: The Police*, pp. 144–45. For an excellent comparative study of the police, see David H. Bayley, *Forces of Order: Police Behavior in Japan and the United States* (Berkeley: University of California Press, 1976).

munities they serve is critical in the Nation's large cities and in many small cities and towns as well," notes the President's Commission on Law Enforcement and Administration of Justice. "The Negro, Puerto Rican, Mexican-American, and other minority groups are taking action to acquire rights and services which have been historically denied them. As the most visible representative of the society from which these groups are demanding fair treatment and equal opportunity, law enforcement agencies are faced with unprecedented situations on the street which require that they develop policies and practices governing their actions when dealing with minority groups and other citizens."[57] With much of their work concentrated in the poverty-stricken areas of large cities, the police have found themselves at the center of the social discontent that has flared into the open in American society; and again and again the police have discovered that there are those who consider them not a source of protection and support but the enemy.

The feeling of the police that they are a beleaguered force is evident in a number of surveys. In one study, 70 percent of the policemen interviewed thought the prestige of police work was fair or poor while only 29 percent said good and 2 percent said excellent. "Relations with the public" was selected as the number-one problem by the police.[58] A survey of police officers undertaken by the Commission on Law Enforcement in eight precincts in three large cities found that the "prestige and respect one gets from a job" was ranked next to last among factors that police officers said they liked about police work. When asked what they had liked least about police work when they entered the force, 22 percent cited lack of public respect; only the hours worked rated lower.[59]

Other evidence, however, strongly suggests that the police have a distorted view of public attitudes. As was pointed out earlier, most community members are likely to approve of the police and respect their work and may indeed tend to glorify the police as daring fighters of crime. "Contrary to the belief of many policemen," notes the Commission on Law Enforcement, "the overwhelming majority of the public has a high opinion of the work of the police."[60] Public opinion polls and special surveys undertaken for the commission indicate that most members of the public believe that the police are doing an excellent job, that they provide sufficient protection to people in the neighborhood, and that they act properly toward private citizens.[61]

At the same time, sizable segments of the public do *not* share these

[57] *Task Force Report: The Police,* p. 144.
[58] Skolnick, *Justice Without Trial,* p. 50.
[59] *Task Force Report: The Police.*
[60] Ibid., p. 145.
[61] Ibid., pp. 145–46.

sentiments. The poor, members of minority groups, and the young, in particular, are apt to be a good deal more suspicious of the police than is the rest of the community. According to numerous surveys, a relatively high percentage of people in these groups believe that the police are ineffective, discourteous and disrespectful to the disadvantaged, and prone to use brutality.[62] In addition, a large, articulate portion of the public that is generally well off and has rarely encountered the abuse of police power feels a deep suspicion of the police on political or moral grounds. The denigration of the police as "pigs" during the 1960s can be viewed as an extreme, momentary expression of a persistent doubt about the police as an instrument of a too-powerful state.

In its attitudes toward the police, then, the community is not a homogeneous entity but is composed of at least four distinct elements. First, there are those who have little in the way of social, economic, or political power and are extremely hostile toward the police. Second, there are the poor and members of minority groups living in urban ghettos who approve of the police and see them as an important source of support in a disorganized world. Third, there are those who, while firmly entrenched in the social order, are attuned to the abuse of police power on ideological grounds and can readily gain a public platform for their views. And, finally, there are members of the dominant white majority who strongly support the police and believe that any hint of criticism is the opening wedge for criminal anarchy. The fact that the community is actually a multiplicity of communities tends to make the analysis of police–community relationships less easy and to complicate the task of resolving the problems that have been identified.

Attitudes toward the police are, moreover, not simply a reflection of firsthand experience, nor are they formed in a social vacuum. Reactions to these uniformed symbols of power are apt to spring from deep levels of unarticulated emotion.[63] Feelings about drug use, the virtues of work, the sacredness of the American flag, sexual permissiveness—all these and more are likely to color judgments about the police; specific facts about police performance may be less important than a general ideological stance or a dim memory of parental authority. It is not surprising, then, that improving police–community relationships has turned out to be no easy task.

Despite the awareness of the need for widespread community support, the police have been slow to develop programs specifically directed to that end. A survey conducted in 1964 by the International Association of

Police–Community-Relations Units

[62] Ibid., pp. 146–49.

[63] See, for example, Pete Hamill, "The Revolt of the White Lower Middle Class," *New York* Magazine (April 14, 1969).

Chiefs of Police and the United States Conference of Mayors found that only a small fraction of large cities or cities with a sizable population of blacks had extensive community-relations programs and many of these programs did not have community-relations units within the police department itself.[64] The situation does not appear to have improved much since that time. One reason for the slowness of the police in developing more effective programs may be the belief that "every policeman is a community-relations officer." But probably even more important is the view held by many police officers that community-relations work is in fundamental conflict with the task assigned them. Few top administrators really believe in programs designed to improve police–community relations, and such activities are likely to be defined as "dabbling in social work" or "negotiating with persons hostile to the police"—thus granting those persons a legitimacy they do not deserve.[65]

A perceptive analysis of the tensions created by community-relations programs is provided in an account of the experience of the San Francisco Police Department.[66] In 1962, Police Chief Thomas Cahill established a community-relations bureau on the urging of the National Association for the Advancement of Colored People and the National Conference of Christians and Jews. Implicit in the creation of this unit, according to Skolnick, was the belief that a new concept of police work was required to meet the needs of a changing society. Police work could no longer consist simply of the detection and apprehension of criminals but must include efforts to prevent crime by developing an understanding of the problems of people living in the ghetto. By helping to alleviate the frustrations of urban-slum life, the police would reduce crime.

This new concept touched off a struggle within both the San Francisco Police Department and the community. On one side of the battle were those who believed in traditional forms of police work; on the other were those convinced that the police must act as a social service agency to help the poor. The points of conflict were numerous. First, the establishment of a special police–community-relations unit appeared to be an open admission that the police department had failed in this area in the past—an admission that many were unwilling to make. Second, the police officers assigned to the unit wore civilian clothes even though they had not attained the rank of detective. Many policemen in the department considered this a sign of disrespect for fellow officers or part of a sinister plot to disparage the uniform. Third, the work of the police–community-rela-

[64] *Police–Community Relations Policies and Practices,* (Washington, D.C., 1965), p. 9.
[65] See *Task Force Report: The Police,* p. 152.
[66] See Jerome H. Skolnick, *Research Contributions of the American Bar Foundation* (Chicago: American Bar Foundation, 1968), pp. 3–28 (reprinted in Niederhoffer and Blumberg, pp. 223–38).

tions unit was considered "social work" by some other policemen and became part of a formula that is not uncommon in American society: social worker = socialism = communism. (One police captain referred to the unit as the "Commie Relations Unit," notes Skolnick, and the tendency for the police to see subversion in attempts at police reform is familiar to other observers.) Fourth, as the police–community-relations unit began to win the confidence of the poor, blacks, homosexuals, hippies, and prostitutes, many policemen felt that the image they had of themselves as strong, aggressive, masculine fighters of crime was being destroyed. The loss of a traditional identity was apparently painful to many. Finally, a serious source of conflict was the informal complaint procedure developed by the unit as part of its effort to be responsive to the needs of people living in the ghetto. In effect, the unit became an "ombudsman" for the city of San Francisco and in the process incurred the antagonism and distrust of a variety of city agencies, such as the welfare department, the fire department, and the schools, that came to feel their authority was being undermined. Police outside the unit came to view it as an internal security force, aloof, mysterious, and possibly revolutionary.

Lieutenant Dante Andretti, the dedicated and highly effective commanding officer of the police–community-relations unit, came to the conclusion that 90 percent of the San Francisco Police Department was opposed to the program. By 1966, the opponents of the unit were triumphant; Andretti was eased out and the unit ceased to exist as an effective part of the police department. "The head of a police-community relations unit steps immediately into a polarized world," Skolnick argues. "If he is to remain on congenial terms with his colleagues, he cannot represent the interests of the minorities. On the other side, if he is to gain the confidence of minority groups, he is required to break down the castelike lines that separate the police and the policed in our urban ghettoes."[67] There are three possible forms that programs to improve police–community relations can take, he concludes. The first is a determined effort to build relationships of confidence with people living in the ghetto; the second is an attempt to improve the image of the police, concentrating on the press and contacts with responsible citizens; and the third is an effort to scatter police–community affairs among local stations under the direction of district captains, thus deemphasizing the role of a special police–community-relations unit. The first is likely to alienate powerful elements in the community and the police department, thus leading to the destruction of the program; and the second and third are likely to be ineffective in accomplishing their assigned task. The outlook for substantial improvement in such programs would therefore appear rather bleak.

[67] Skolnick, *Research Contributions to the American Bar Foundation*, p. 233.

**Community
Control**   A number of other devices have been employed in the hope of achieving
more harmonious relations between the police and members of minority
groups. Citizen advisory committees have been established to open
channels of communication between the police and the community; but
because these committees are generally composed of well-established
members of the business world and the clergy, and other leaders, communication with the poor and minority groups is likely to be limited.
Membership in such committees, it has been pointed out, is apt to include only those people who agree with the police and who do not cause
trouble. Such an approach is essentially self-defeating.[68]

Other efforts have included so-called sensitivity training, in which the
police are supposed to learn how to shed their prejudices; the psychological screening of police recruits to eliminate individuals who are blatantly hostile to minorities; recruit training and in-service training in
police–community relations; civilian review boards for handling complaints about police brutality and harassment; ombudsman programs;
and special efforts to increase minority-group representation on the police force.[69] None of these, however, can be said to have been markedly
successful in reducing the bitterness that has so often marred the interaction between those who police and those who are policed. The reason, it
has been argued, is essentially a simple one. In many American cities
today a large segment of the population views the police as little more
than an occupation army. "The only way to police a ghetto is to be
oppressive," says novelist James Baldwin, giving a voice to this attitude.
"None of the police commissioner's men, even with the best will in the
world, have any way of understanding the lives led by the people: they
swagger about in twos and threes patrolling. Their very presence is an
insult, and it would be even if they spent their entire day feeding gum-
drops to children. They represent the forces of the white world, and that
world's criminal profit and ease, to keep the black man corralled up here,
in his place."[70]

From this point of view, the problem of police–community relations is
not a matter of "poor communications," "lack of sensitivity," or an insufficient number of blacks on a predominantly white police force.
Rather, the reason for the difficulty is that the poor—and particularly
poor blacks—are apt to be politically helpless and subject to the capricious control of a white majority that forces them to obey laws not of
their making. The solution, it is argued, lies in an "indigenous" police
force that is created, staffed, and controlled by ghetto residents.[71]

[68] *Task Force Report: The Police,* pp. 156–57.
[69] Ibid., Chapter 6.
[70] James Baldwin, *Nobody Knows My Name* (New York: Dell, 1962), p. 65.
[71] See Robert Mast, "The Police–Ghetto Relations: Some Findings and a Proposal for
Structural Change," *Race* 3 (April 1970), pp. 447–62; see also Terry Ann Knopf, *Youth Pa-*

This concept rose to prominence in the latter part of the 1960s, when the relations between the police and ghetto residents in many cities appeared to be at the point of rupture. It was greeted with a singular lack of enthusiasm by city officials. Whatever might be the need to ease tensions among different segments of the community, the idea of dividing the power of the state was simply unacceptable. Beyond this, the creation of an "indigenous police force" presented a host of practical problems. Allocating tax resources, defining the geographical limits of ethnic communities in heterogeneous neighborhoods, deciding which laws could be subject to variable enforcement, dealing with people traveling from one subcommunity to another, providing police for a variety of ethnic groups within the same subcommunity—all appeared to be beyond satisfactory solution.[72]

If the creation of dissimilar and independent police forces for different parts of the city does not appear feasible, the idea inherent in the concept of "indigenous police" is an important one. In a democratic social order, the police are expected to be fair in their enforcement of the law and accountable to those who are policed. They are not to be an alien force imposed on a community, an autonomous body ruling by coercion, or the agents of a tyrannical state, but the servants of society maintaining a commonly accepted body of law in an evenhanded fashion. The realization of this ideal is a continuing problem—and particularly in those sections of large cities where the poor and members of minority groups are concentrated. If the people who find the police a friend rather than an enemy fail to see that many do not share their good fortune and that it is necessary to make sure the police are fair and accountable to all, the tensions inherent in the policing function will continue as an embittering and divisive element in American communities.

Police and Corruption

If the enforcers of the law are breakers of the law, who is to be trusted?

Criminal activity on the part of the police is deeply disturbing to the American public, arousing great indignation and concern; yet such activity sometimes also elicits a yawn, as if the corruption of police officers is to be expected, an inevitable accompaniment of law enforcement.

Whether inevitable or not, crimes committed by the police in the course of their official duties have marred police work in the United

trols: An Experiment in Community Participation (Boston: Brandeis University, Lemberg Center for the Study of Violence, 1969); and George Nash, The Community Patrol Corps (New York: Bureau of Applied Social Research, Columbia University, May 1968).
[72] See Mary C. Sengstock, "Community Control of the Police: Assessing the Problem." Paper presented at the American Sociological Association, 1973.

States since the inception of modern police forces in the nineteenth century.[73] When full-time police supported by public funds were introduced into American cities, government corruption at the local level was an open scandal. The police were immediately drawn into patterns of political patronage, influence peddling, and other forms of malfeasance that characterized the city political machine.[74] By the turn of the century, police officers in many urban communities were deeply implicated in prostitution, gambling, and the provision of other illegal services, thus enforcing what was in effect an illicit system of licensing operated for the profit and with the approval of city officials and local business interests.[75] Prohibition greatly increased both the profits of such enterprises and the money paid in bribes to the police, with narcotics later taking the place of liquor. And to this record of corruption must be added theft, burglary, rolling drunks, and shaking down merchants—all of which have been a problem in police behavior in a number of cities on different occasions.[76]

Why does such behavior occur? One explanation, particularly common among law enforcement officers, can be called the "bad apple" theory. In every occupation, there are bound to be some who are willing to cut corners, to commit dishonest or criminal acts in pursuit of gain. The fault lies in personal charcter—and thus it would seem to make sense to argue, as does the President's Commission on Law Enforcement and Administration of Justice, that "the most fundamental method of maintaining integrity in law enforcement is through careful selection of personnel. All of the selection techniques available today must be used, including comprehensive background investigations and reliable tests to determine attitude and emotional stability. . . ."[77] By implication, most of the apples in the barrel are sound, and police corruption is a matter of a few carelessly selected officers with poor moral fiber giving many honest officers a bad name.

Comforting though this viewpoint may be, it provides little understanding of how or why policemen become involved in corrupt behavior. It ignores the pervasiveness of corruption in many police departments and the condoning of criminal behavior by those policemen who do not

[73] No precise figures are available, but many observers agree that a number of European countries exhibit a lower degree of police corruption than does the United States. A common explanation involves the American passion for suppressing immoral behavior by means of the criminal law, a matter that will be discussed later. See George Berkley, *The Democratic Policeman*, pp. 124–25. See also Lawrence W. Sherman, ed., *Police Corruption: A Sociological Perspective* (Garden City, N.Y.: Anchor Books, 1974).

[74] See *Task Force Report: The Police*, Chapter 7.

[75] Lincoln Steffens, *The Shame of the Cities* (New York: McClure & Phillips, 1904).

[76] *Task Force Report: The Police*, pp. 208–09.

[77] Ibid., p. 214.

engage in such behavior themselves. It overlooks the extent to which police corruption is not simply the failure of a few but an integral part of police work in American society.

That police connivance in the provision of illegal services has been almost impossible to eradicate must be attributed, in large part, to the huge sums of money that America spends on its vices and the ambiguity of the status of those vices in the public mind. Graft and extortion put too many dollars in the pockets of public officials to be counteracted by reformers armed with little more than a call for improved public morality.

The behavior to be suppressed by the police often appears innocuous, and the figures from the underworld who offer the bribes can find convincing reasons for police compliance. Here is the way one West Coast police official described how a bookie attempted to influence him:

> These people really work on you. They make it seem so logical—like you are the one that is out of step. This bookie gave me this kind of line: "It's legal at the tracks, isn't it? So why isn't it legal here? It's because of those crooks at the capitol. They're gettin' plenty—all driving Cads. Look at my customers, some of the biggest guys in town—they don't want you to close me down. If you do they'll just transfer you. Like that last jerk. And even the Judge, what did he do? Fined me a hundred and suspended fifty. Hell, he knows Joe Citizen wants me here, so get smart, be one of the boys, be part of the system. It's a way of life in this town and you're not gonna change it. Tell you what I'll do. I won't give you a nickel; just call in a free bet in the first race every day and you can win or lose, how about it? [78]

Such cajolery apparently often proves persuasive, and few large-city police departments in the United States, it is said, have managed to eliminate the systematic, steady payoff.[79] So-called vice work, involving high arrest quotas for prostitution, narcotics, and gambling, is carried out in a context of bribery that allows vice to flourish. Few persons are punished even when arrests are made. In New York City in 1970, for example, out of more than 9000 arrests for gambling, only seventy people went to jail. In Philadelphia, in the same year, 4720 persons were charged with gambling and five went to jail. The pattern of large numbers of arrests and few convictions is widespread and of long duration—and many policemen become aware that, despite impassioned newspaper editorials and the public rhetoric of police administrators, the eradication of vice is not the purpose of the police.[80]

[78] Ibid., p. 209.
[79] Rubinstein, *City Police*, p. 376.
[80] Ibid., pp. 376–80.

The large-scale bribery of the police by the suppliers of illicit services is built on top of a pattern of widespread petty corruption. From the day he starts as a raw recruit, the policeman finds himself being offered favors. The shopowner persuading the policeman to ignore the parking violations of his customers; the motorist trying to get a speeding ticket "fixed"; the merchant offering merchandise in exchange for increased surveillance of his store; the towing companies, ambulance drivers, garage owners, and lawyers who will pay a fee if the policeman will steer the victims of automobile accidents their way; the free meals and special prices—all involve the offer of money or goods and the expectation of a favor in return.

Some observers have claimed that such patterns of reciprocity, so common in police work, pave the way for the acceptance of large bribes from organized crime.[81] (In New York City, policemen refer to those who accept small favors as "grass eaters"; those who accept large sums of money are labeled "meat eaters.") Other writers are inclined to doubt that the course of corruption is an inevitable downward slide from a free cup of coffee to domination by mobsters, but they do see police work being impaired by businessmen who secure preferential treatment by means of petty bribery.[82] Even if petty payoffs to the police do not necessarily lead to serious wrongdoing in every case, it does seem likely that the task of maintaining strict standards of professional conduct is made more difficult by the ubiquitous practice of payoffs. The distinction between petty and serious is a subjective matter, and it is all too easy to alter one's attitudes to fit one's needs or desires. As a result, the concept of official honesty is apt to become blurred.

It has been suggested that the amount of police corruption differs according to the administrative style of different police departments.[83] Furthermore, it has been pointed out, many individual policemen are not involved in payoffs from organized crime and have a minimal involvement in trading off small favors, although only a few seasoned police officers can completely avoid the latter form of entanglement.[84] City size and cycles of city government reform are also factors that influence the levels of police corruption. But despite this variation, any analysis of the structure and functioning of the police must take into account the fact

[81] See Former Denver Police Officer, as Told to Mort Stern, "What Makes a Policeman Go Wrong?" *Journal of Criminal Law, Criminology, and Police Science* 53 (March 1962), pp. 97–101.

[82] See Rubinstein, *City Police*, p. 418.

[83] See Wilson, *Varieties of Police Behavior*.

[84] For a vigorous statement in support of those policemen who have the courage to combat the corruption found in police work, see David Durk, "Viva la Policía," in Abraham S. Blumberg, ed., *Law and Order: The Scales of Justice* (New Brunswick, N.J.: Transaction Books, 1973), pp. 285–92.

that in general corruption is a chronic problem. The enforcement of the law is compromised at numerous points by people in legitimate businesses as well as by criminals, and the sources of these compromises are to be found not simply in the moral character of the police officer but also—and probably to a greater extent—in the web of relationships that make up the social structure of the community.

The Police as Oppressors

New Left radicals and black nationalists openly advocated the use of confrontation tactics in dealing with the police, noted Seymour Martin Lipset at the end of the 1960s. The killing of the police in ghetto areas was defined by some as a form of self-defense rather than murder. "The current tensions between the police and New Left student and black nationalist radicals probably involve the most extreme example of deliberate provocation which the police have ever faced," Lipset asserted. "The tactics of the campus-based opposition rouse the most deep-seated feelings of class resentment. Most policemen are conservative, conventional, upwardly mobile working-class supporters of the American Way, who aspire for a better life for their families. Many of them seek to send their children to college. To find the scions of the upper-middle class in the best universities denouncing them as 'pigs,' hurling insults which involve use of the most aggressive sexual language, such as 'Up against the wall, Mother F——,' throwing bricks and bags of feces at them, is much more difficult to accept than any other situation which they have faced."[85]

Many of these tensions lessened, went underground, or were transformed with the end of the Vietnam War and the political and economic changes of the early 1970s, although many of the underlying conflicts had not been resolved. But the idea of cop as pig—of the policeman, that is, as a brutal agent of an oppressive society—continues in one form or another in the thinking of a number of writers.

An analysis of the police function as an expression of political and economic domination is presented by Richard Quinney, who approaches the problem from the standpoint of "critical Marxian philosophy."[86] As capitalism is threatened by its own contradictions, he argues, the legal system is increasingly used to maintain domestic order; in the name of "criminal justice," the national government—an instrument of the ruling

---

[85] "Why Cops Hate Liberals—and Vice Versa," *The Atlantic* (March 1969), p. 82.
[86] Richard Quinney, *Critique of Legal Order: Crime Control in Capitalist Society* (Boston: Little, Brown, 1974).

classes—is now building a comprehensive, coordinated system of repression.[87] "The contradiction within advanced capitalist society is that a system which violates human sensibilities in turn calls for resistance and rebellion by the population," asserts Quinney. "And the more such resistance occurs, whether in outright political acts or in behavior that otherwise violates the rules of such a society, the more the state must bring its repressive forces to bear on the people. The state's failure to respond would allow changes that would undoubtedly spell the end of the kind of political economy upon which that society rests. Thus today in America we are witnessing the repression of a society that refuses to use its resources to solve its own problems. To protect the system from its own victims, a war on crime is being waged."[88] And the war on crime within the United States, Quinney argues, is inseparable from wars waged abroad in the name of American imperialism. "The war waged against the people of Indochina is part of the same war waged against the oppressed at home," he asserts, since both are part of an effort to avoid changing the national corporate economy.[89] The technology developed by the armed forces—such as the new forms of weapons and means of surveillance—is applied to domestic turmoil, and military operations abroad and crime control at home become identical in objective and technique.[90]

We have encountered a portion of this argument before in examining the nature of the criminal law and political crime. Here the emphasis is on the class-bound interest of law enforcement bureaucracies and advisory groups rather than the control of the substance of the criminal law by a ruling elite. The President's Commission on Law Enforcement and Administration of Justice, the presidential commissions on violence and riots, the Law Enforcement Assistance Administration, the Senate Subcommittee on Criminal Laws and Procedures, the Committee for Economic Development, the Federal Bureau of Investigation, the Justice Department—all are attacked as being those agencies of the power structure that devise the overall strategies for combating crime and maintaining the status quo of capitalism. These groups, it is charged, are under the management of the ruling elite and have no intention of introducing fundamental changes into the social order to solve the problem of crime.

[87] Ibid., p. 109.
[88] Ibid., p. 132.
[89] Ibid., pp. 93–94.
[90] Ibid., pp. 122–23. For a collection of readings that share this approach to crime and crime control, see Richard H. Quinney, ed., *Criminal Justice in America* (Boston: Little, Brown, 1974). See also Anthony Platt and Lynn Cooper, *Policing America* (Englewood Cliffs, N.J.: Prentice-Hall, 1974) and Evelyn Parks, "From Constabulary to Police Society: Some Implications for Social Control," in Milton Mankoff, ed., *The Poverty of Progress* (New York: Holt, Rinehart and Winston, 1972).

There is merely talk of "reform," which, for Quinney, is no more than a method of emasculating resistance to the oppressive character of existing social and economic arrangements.[91]

It is true that these groups, headed by persons who cannot be counted as members of the lower class, are clearly not interested in radical social change; they do show a readiness to seize on new technologies and to employ military methods. And in the 1960s and 1970s, particularly after the revelations of the crimes of Watergate and subsequent disclosures, it became apparent that government bureaucracies involved in law enforcement have misused their power in many ways.

Quinney's argument, however, is designed to say more than this. Capitalism is the basic cause of these oppressive governmental agencies, he contends, and only in a socialist society can such oppression be avoided—a viewpoint that echoes the thought of Bonger (see Chapter 7). It is not the socialism of the Soviet Union and some East European countries that he has in mind, but a vision of what socialism might be as described by Michael Harrington: democratic, decentralized, and with participatory control by the individual.[92]

Quinney, then, is writing within the long tradition of social criticism that has looked to capitalist social structure as the source of most social ills and has envisioned an egalitarian society as the cure. The argument is specifically directed against the large-scale governmental bureaucracies in the United States engaged in creating a centralized program of national law enforcement.

It is difficult to assess the validity of such theoretical viewpoints, for they are often presented as self-evident truths without empirical support. The fact that socialist societies like those of the Soviet bloc are marked by police systems far more brutal and oppressive than the police in a capitalist nation like the United States cannot be pushed to one side by appealing to a hypothetical socialism. The economic link between the effort to control crime in the United States and wars waged abroad in the name of American imperialism is tenuous. Most important, however, the existence of a national policy of repressive law enforcement as a necessary or probable consequence of the social and economic structure of American society is not demonstrated. Rather than being the unique expression of American capitalism—a conclusion not to be reached by fiat—the growth of law enforcement bureaucracies indifferent to the rights of individuals may be fostered by an imperial presidency obsessed with problems of

---

[91] See also Anthony Platt, *The Politics of Riot Commissions* (New York: Macmillan, 1971) and Jeff Gerth, "The Americanization of 1984," *Sundance Magazine* 1 (April–May 1972), pp. 58–65 (reprinted in Quinney, *Criminal Justice in America*).

[92] See Michael Harrington, *Socialism* (New York: Saturday Review Press, 1972), pp. 36–54.

national security,[93] or may be associated with the development of an urban, industrial social order.

Although the argument of Quinney and other writers approaching the problem of law enforcement in a similar vein is open to question, their examination of federal agencies and advisory groups involved in the policing of crime should not be ignored. National groups establish long-range objectives, standards of performance, technologies and technological resources, training courses, and research programs. It is crucial to come to an understanding of such groups, both as an important influence on the operation of local police and as expressions of the use and abuse of governmental power. The radical critique of these structures has helped to bring them into the light after long neglect by criminology.

Conclusions

One of the most striking things about the role of the police in the United States today is the ambivalence with which policemen are so often viewed by the public. This is not simply a matter of conservative, "hard-hat" support versus the skepticism of liberals or the hostility of ghetto residents. Rather, it is an uncertainty in which trust and doubt, respect and dislike, are mingled in bewildering contradiction.

This ambivalence, it can be argued, springs from the tension inherent in trying to fit public agents of social control into a context of democratic structure. Almost everyone recognizes the need to be protected from violence and from attacks on one's property; and in a large-scale, urban society, marked by mobility and anonymity, implementing that need seems to call for a professionally trained, publicly supported police force. As the police attempt to accomplish their task, however, they are subjected to strong public pressures to go beyond the limits of their legal power, despite the discriminatory treatment of private citizens that is so often involved. These pressures stem in no small measure from the view that the ratio between crimes committed and criminals apprehended is unsatisfactory, bringing police effectiveness continually into question.[94] The problem in the United States has been greatly complicated by (1) the attempt to suppress the so-called vices by means of the criminal law in face of the large public demand for illegal services; and (2) the long-

[93] See Morton H. Halperin, Jerry L. Berman, Robert Borosage, and Christine M. Marwick, *The Lawless State: The Crimes of the U.S. Intelligence Agencies* (New York: Penguin Books, 1976), pp. 1–12. See also David Wise, *The American Police State* (New York: Random House, 1976).

[94] See Peter K. Manning, "The Police: Mandate, Strategies, and Appearances," in Jack Douglas, ed., *Crime and Justice in American Society* (Indianapolis: Bobbs-Merrill, 1971), pp. 149–93.

standing alliance between the police and the political machine. Both have served to lower the standing of the police in the eyes of a public that already suspects them of infringing on democratic liberties. The low standing of the police, coupled with relatively minimal job requirements, has tended to restrict the recruitment base of the police to the lower end of the socioeconomic scale, thus adding strong class differences to the conflicts between the police and the rest of society and increasing the possibility of polarization by furthering police solidarity in the face of a hostile public. When the police are in fact used as an instrument for the suppression of political dissent—which has occurred often enough in a disorganized fashion at the local level in the past and which became particularly threatening at the national level in the 1960s and 1970s—the tensions between the concepts of the police and the democratic state near the breaking point in the eyes of many. Even those who are most politically conservative are apt to find themselves caught up in the mood of ambivalence.

These problems transcend the alleged authoritarian personality structure of policemen or excessive racial prejudice. And they also appear to be problems that cannot be attributed to capitalism per se or explained by any well-tested theory of the inevitable emergence of the police state. Instead, they seem to be rooted in a complex interlocking of aspects of modern democratic social structure, the Anglo-American legal system, specific patterns of historical events in the United States—and the stubborn difficulties in the detection and apprehension of those who violate the law.

Recommended Readings

An excellent collection of readings dealing with current issues in police work is found in Arthur Niederhoffer and Abraham S. Blumberg, eds., *The Ambivalent Force: Perspectives on the Police* (Waltham, Mass.: Ginn, 1970). Other useful anthologies containing recent articles on the police are Jim Munro, ed., *Classes, Conflict, and Control: Studies in Criminal Justice Management* (Cincinnati: Anderson, 1976) and Daniel B. Kennedy, ed., *The Dysfunctional Alliance* (Cincinnati: Anderson, 1977). For the issue of police corruption, the reader should see Lawrence W. Sherman, ed., *Police Corruption: A Sociological Perspective* (Garden City, N.Y.: Anchor Books, 1974).

Michael Banton, *The Policeman in the Community* (London: Tavistock, 1964) provides valuable comparative material; Jerome H. Skolnick, *Justice Without Trial* (New York: John Wiley & Sons, 1966) is particularly illuminating on the role of the detective. For a view of the political implications of the police, the reader should see Anthony Platt and Lynn Cooper, eds., *Policing America* (Englewood Cliffs, N.J.: Prentice-Hall, 1974).

Private police have become a major element in crime control in the United States. The reader will find both of the following valuable: James S. Kakalik and Sorrel Wildhorn, *U.S. Department of Justice Study of Private Police*, Vol. I–IV, (Santa Monica, California: The Rand Corporation, 1971) and National Advisory Committee on Criminal Justice Standards and Goals, *Report of the Task Force on Private Security* (Washington, D.C.: Government Printing Office, 1976).

Chapter 11
The Criminal Court: Procedures and Personnel

In many primitive societies the task of determining the innocence or guilt of those suspected of committing a crime has been assigned to supernatural forces. Omens, ordeals, religious oaths, trials by battle, and similar devices have been employed, in the belief that the gods will point to those who have broken the law. In some cultures, poison is administered to the accused, on the theory that the guilty will die and the innocent will be spared.[1] In others, the suspected offender is made to hold a piece of heated iron in his or her hand; and a festering wound is supposed to mark the wrongdoer.[2] In early English history, guilt or innocence was established in a battle between two armed antagonists, on the principle that divine intervention would give might and thus victory to the right—a form of trial apparently used infrequently but not formally abolished until 1819.

In modern societies a pervasive secular view of the world has tended to make the proof of criminal wrongdoing a matter of empirical evidence. But there is an important split concerning the best method to be used. Some societies (including the United States) whose laws are based on the Anglo-Saxon legal tradition, place their faith in a system of adversaries—a sort of trial by combat, but one that depends on logic and proof, the weapons of science, rather than the sword. This is referred to as the *adversarial*, or *accusatory*, system, and it assigns the task of discovering the truth to two opposing lawyers who elicit the facts in the case favorable to their side and present them to an impartial judge or jury playing a relatively passive role in the fact-finding process.[3] Other societies,

[1] See George Harley, "The Mano of Liberia," in Carleton S. Coon, ed., *A Reader in General Anthropology* (New York: Holt, Rinehart and Winston, 1948), pp. 344–74.

[2] See, for example, Andre J. K. Kobben, "Law at the Village Level: The Cottica Djuka of Surinam," in Laura Nader, ed., *Law, Culture, and Society* (Chicago: Aldine, 1969), pp. 117–40. See also William J. Tewksbury, "The Ordeal as a Vehicle for Divine Intervention in Medieval Europe," in Paul Bohannon, ed., *Law and Warfare* (Garden City, N.Y.: Natural History Press, 1967), pp. 267–70.

[3] Too insistent questioning of a witness by a judge may be viewed by an appellate court as being inconsistent with the judge's role of neutral referee. As far as the jury is con-

deriving their legal systems from Roman law, rely on the *inquisitorial* system. The judge takes a far more active part and does most of the questioning to discover the facts. The role of the lawyers at the time of the trial is much reduced, since most of the evidence has already been assembled by a judicial officer of the court. Thus it has been argued that under the Soviet legal system, based on the inquisitorial model, the criminal trial can be viewed as "an appeal from a pretrial investigation," and the so-called trial is simply a recapitulation of the data collected by the pretrial investigator.[4]

The inquisitorial system has a number of advantages, according to some judicial scholars: reliance on professionally trained and responsible judges for the supervision of criminal investigations and the expert preparation of cases for trial rather than a fumbling, improvised solicitation of testimony.[5] But the idea of the inquisitorial system seems to run counter to the idea of a fair trial embedded in law in the United States. "The rules of due process," notes Abraham Blumberg, "as expanded and strengthened by the Supreme Court are predicated on the existence of an adversary system of criminal justice. The rules envision a 'combative' procedural system wherein prosecution and defense (who are admittedly possessed of unequal resources) will clash. After the dust has settled, the data which determine guilt or innocence will have emerged."[6] Blumberg goes on to assert that this ideal of an adversary system does not, unfortunately, have a counterpart in reality in the United States today.

Numerous other writers in the fields of law and criminology have come to the same conclusion in recent years. "The assumption that anyone accused of a crime in the United States has a right to a full adversary trial of his guilt or innocence—with well-prepared advocates for each side, carefully overseen by an able, even-handed judge, searching diligently for the truth and satisfying all legal rules and safeguards—is fundamental to the American system of justice and to the populace's confidence in it," argues Leonard Downie. "Yet with few exceptions, this concept has become little more than a still celebrated myth both in the folklore of the law and in formal jurisprudence."[7] The discrepancy

---

cerned, it has been pointed out that "it is perhaps one of the most curious features of our jury trial procedure, though seldom the subject of remark, that the persons charged with evaluating the testimony of the witness [that is, the members of the jury] are in effect inhibited from asking him any question" (Lewis Mayers, *The American Legal System* [New York: Harper & Brothers, 1955], p. 156).

[4] George Feifer, *Justice in Moscow* (New York: Simon and Schuster, 1965), p. 86.

[5] See Raymond Moley, *Our Criminal Courts* (New York: Minton, Balch, 1930), pp. 36–40.

[6] Abraham S. Blumberg, *Criminal Justice* (Chicago, Quadrangle Books, 1967), p. 26.

[7] Leonard Downie, Jr., *Justice Denied: The Case for the Reform of the Courts* (Baltimore: Penguin Books, 1971), p. 26. See also Jerome H. Skolnick, "Social Control in the Adversary System," *Conflict Resolution* 11 (March 1967), pp. 52–70.

between the way the courts are supposed to function and the way they function in fact is a fault that imperils the structure of American justice, declares Harry W. Jones.[8] And the President's Commission on Law Enforcement and Administration of Justice is no less critical. "No findings of this Commission," it is declared, "are more disquieting than those relating to the conditions of the lower criminal courts. . . . No program of crime prevention will be effective without a massive overhaul of the lower criminal courts. The many persons who encounter these courts each year can hardly fail to interpret that experience as an expression of indifference to their situations and to the ideals of fairness, equality, and rehabilitation professed in theory, yet frequently denied in practice."[9]

The message conveyed by these and other observers of criminal-trial proceedings in the United States today is plain: the adversary system is not functioning the way it is supposed to—and, in fact, has virtually ceased to exist. Individuals are often convicted of crimes other than the ones they have committed, and even more frequently they are not convicted of crimes they did commit. The rights erected by the law for the protection of the suspected offender during trial proceedings are not being observed, compromising the ideal of justice at many points. And the explanations offered for these failures of the criminal-trial process are much the same from one account to another. The machinery for the adjudication of criminal cases has been overwhelmed by the press of numbers. The American public has been unwilling to absorb the costs of enlarging the capacity of the judiciary or to confront the political problems that would be created by increasing the number of judicial posts, which are viewed as political plums by competing political parties. As a consequence, the increasing number of cases coming to the court due to a growing population and a rising crime rate has far outstripped the judiciary's ability to deal with each case according to established standards of justice. The court has two alternatives: either the standards can be applied, creating an ever-growing backlog of cases and interminable delays; or the standards can be abandoned, getting rid of the cases relatively quickly but sacrificing the search for "the truth, the whole truth, and nothing but the truth" that is undertaken by opposing lawyers.

Since the court is a bureaucratic structure, it is argued, and part of the state machinery for the administration of the criminal law, it is not surprising that the pressures for "efficiency"—the rapid disposition of cases—prevail. Justice is cut and trimmed to fit the needs of governmental administration. Our society, says Blumberg, has produced a

[8] See Harry W. Jones, ed., *The Courts, the Public, and the Law Explosion* (Englewood Cliffs, N.J.: Prentice-Hall, 1965).
[9] *Task Force Report: The Courts* (Washington, D.C.: Government Printing Office, 1967), p. 29.

bargain-counter, assembly-line system of criminal justice.[10] "Judge, prosecutor, defense attorney, policeman, and clerk are working partners struggling to keep their heads above water as the flood of cases rises. Is it not natural that, for them, expediency should take precedence over justice, eventually becoming one and the same in the minds of bureaucrats?" asks Downie. And he quotes an exasperated chief judge of the General Sessions Court of Washington, D.C., who complains that criminal courts have become "factories where defendants are processed like so many sausages."[11]

These critical views of the criminal court ignore a good deal of variation that exists. Some courts in the United States bear little resemblance to such portrayals. More studies are needed of the extent to which the problems of the courts are matters of long standing rather than a recent development, an issue that we encountered in Chapter 10.[12] Although a vast number of errors are unquestionably being made in the present system, in that pleas and convictions frequently bear little relationship to the behavior in question, there are no verifiable measurements of the problem.[13] And a passionate devotion to the adversarial system should not obscure the fact that partisan lawyers contending in court can obscure the truth as well as uncover it. Given these qualifications, however, the general picture of an institution with a great discrepancy between ideals and reality does appear valid. In this chapter it will be our task to examine the present plight of the criminal court and the trial process in detail.

The Social Organization of the Criminal Court

There are fifty-one different court systems in the United States: one for the federal government and one for each state. Each of these systems contains many courts of different kinds, specialized both in geographical jurisdiction and area of substantive law. Within each system, in general, the courts are arranged in a hierarchical fashion. On the bottom are *trial courts*, or *courts of original jurisdiction*, which provide the first hearing of a case; above these are *appellate courts*, which review the decisions of the

---

[10] Blumberg, *Criminal Justice*, p. 5.

[11] Downie, *Justice Denied*, p. 33.

[12] See Lawrence M. Friedman, *A History of American Law* (New York: Simon and Schuster, 1973).

[13] Defendants have been interviewed after plea bargaining and sentencing to ascertain their attitudes toward their guilt, but the interpretation of their answers presents a formidable task. See Abraham S. Blumberg, "Lawyers with Convictions," in Abraham S. Blumberg, ed., *Law and Order: The Scales of Justice*, 2nd ed. (New Brunswick, N.J.: Transaction Books, 1973), pp. 67–83.

courts of original jurisdiction; and at the top is a *supreme court*, to which cases may be appealed for a final ruling. When a case involves a violation of both state and federal law—when, for example, there is a question concerning search and seizure prohibited by the United States Constitution—it may move from one of the state systems to the federal system and be carried up to the United States Supreme Court, which stands as the final arbiter.

There is considerable variation in the names given to the different types of courts in each state system. The highest state court is variously referred to as the *court of appeals,* the *supreme court of errors,* the *supreme judicial court,* or simply the *supreme court.* The intermediate courts of appeal are generally called *appellate courts.* The courts of original jurisdiction for criminal cases are typically divided into two categories. One is composed of courts that deal with minor offenses or misdemeanors, and they go by such names as the *municipal court,* the *justice of the peace court,* the *police court,* and the *lower court.* The second category handles felonies; the names for these courts include *district court,* the *circuit court,* the *superior court,* and the *court of common pleas.*[14] The courts dealing with the vast flood of misdemeanors have received the sharpest criticism. It is there that the dignity and decorum supposed to accompany the judicial process is most likely to be lacking. "An observer in the lower criminal courts ordinarily sees a trial bearing little resemblance to those carried out under traditional notions of due process," it has been pointed out. "There is usually no court reporter unless the defendant can afford to pay one. One result is an informality in the proceedings which would not be tolerated in a felony trial. Rules of evidence are largely ignored. Speed is the watchword. Trials in misdemeanor cases may be over in a matter of 5, 10, or 15 minutes; they rarely last an hour even in relatively complicated cases. Traditional safeguards honored in felony cases lose their meaning in such proceedings; yet there is still the possibility of lengthy imprisonment or heavy fine."[15]

The Role of the Judge

After the Revolution, Americans reacted against the highly centralized judicial system dominated by English royal governors and set about creating a decentralized judiciary in which judges were to be relatively autonomous. "Each court was in organization a legal principality in itself," says Lewis Mayers, speaking of the decades following Independence. "Thus was developed that pattern of extreme decentralization of

---

[14] For an excellent brief description of state and federal court systems, see Hazel B. Kerper, *Introduction to the Criminal Justice System* (St. Paul, Minn.: West, 1972), Chapter VI. See also Mayers, *The American Legal System.*

[15] *Task Force Report: The Courts,* p. 31; see also Jones, *The Courts, the Public, and the Law Explosion.*

the judicial machinery which almost everywhere characterizes our court organization to this day, and which presents so marked a contrast to the judicial organization of the continental countries and Great Britain."[16] One result has been that judges in American society are subject to relatively little supervision and control, particularly in the day-to-day operations of the court. (In Colorado, for example, the judges of the Supreme Court have ruled that no bar association or court can institute disciplinary proceedings against any judge for any reason.[17]) The sentencing power of the judges is indicative of their freedom from control: in most jurisdictions today, the trial judge's sentence cannot be changed by an appellate court if the sentence is within statutory limits, no matter how harsh or arbitrary it may be.[18]

The movement for political reform that swept over Europe in the early part of the nineteenth century, and found expression in the United States as Jacksonian democracy, had as one of its aims the popular control of the judiciary; and from that time to the present day American society has struggled with various aspects of the issue—such as how to select judges and how to remove those who are incompetent or corrupt—trying to balance judicial independence and judicial accountability. The result has been a somewhat mixed affair, in which decentralization and judicial autonomy have been coupled with the selection of judges on a political basis. In more than half the states, judges are selected by popular vote, and over 80 percent of the judicial positions in America are filled on an elective basis.[19] Judges are thus likely to be attentive to popular pressures for "efficiency" flowing from a public that has consistently been unwilling to provide the necessary funds. The slipshod procedures of many criminal courts, the hasty trials, and the excesses of plea bargaining undertaken in the hope of keeping the workload within manageable proportions are frequently among the consequences.[20]

The burden of large caseloads is often increased by the inefficient use

[16] *The American Legal System,* p. 57. The striking extent of decentralization in America was noted by Alexis de Tocqueville in *Democracy in America* (New York: New American Library, 1964), pp. 62–72.

[17] See Gresham M. Sykes, "Cases, Courts, and Congestion," in Nader, *Law, Culture, and Society,* pp. 327–36.

[18] *Task Force Report: The Courts,* p. 65. The judge's legal decisionmaking is influenced by the possibility that his decisions will be reversed by the appellate court, thus tarnishing his professional reputation. Nonetheless, the influence of the appellate court on the trial court remains limited, particularly with regard to administrative matters.

[19] *Task Force Report: The Courts,* p. 66. Except for parts of Switzerland, the United States is the only democratic society in which judges are still selected by popular vote.

[20] The autonomy of the judge, coupled with a sensitivity to community opinion, can also lead to a humane, fair, and flexible application of the law. Most of the literature on the problems of the American judiciary appears to take the view that such an outcome is unlikely.

of judicial manpower.[21] The structure of the judicial role is a significant causal factor. Many courts are composed not of a single judge sitting in isolated magisterial splendor but of a number of judges, each responsible for a category of the court's many responsibilities, such as criminal charges, civil cases, and divorces—and these judges are not easily transferred from one task to another. In creating a trial calendar that uses the judges' time to the best advantage, cases should be scheduled so that there is always one case before one judge in an orderly sequence. No judge should be left inadvertently idle for lack of a case to be heard, and no case should go untried for lack of an available judge. In fact, however, this goal of full utilization of judicial personnel is seldom achieved.

The court's failure to use the judges' time with maximum effectiveness is due in part to the inevitable mishaps, such as illness and emergencies, that attend the scheduling of human events. In addition, the trial calendar frequently exhibits "holes," or unused time, owing to two factors that are linked to the administration of the court. First, the length of time required for a trial is often overestimated by the court, and thus short trials leave many judges unoccupied. Second, many cases scheduled for trial suddenly reach a settlement before their trial date falls due. If no other cases can be substituted—and frequently they cannot, because the announcement of a settlement comes so close to the scheduled trial date—the court again is left with vacant time.[22]

The creation of a court calendar is a gamble, and a balance must be struck between being two ambitious and too cautious. The temptation in many courts is to err on the side of caution, to overestimate trial time, and to schedule too little work rather than too much. A judge in his chambers with nothing to do is not in the public view and is far less likely to arouse criticism and indignation than lawyers in the halls of the courthouse clamoring for their cases to be heard when no judge is available. Given the administrative independence of the judiciary, little can be done about the judges and the court clerks who are guided by the safe and comfortable administrative course.[23]

[21] See Hans Zeisel, Harry Kalven, Jr., and Bernard Buchholz, *Delay in Court* (Boston: Little, Brown, 1959).

[22] The problem of early settlement is usually to be found in civil rather than criminal cases, but nonetheless it affects the total use of judicial personnel. If a case has been scheduled for trial, settlement may become more likely because lawyers may prefer settlement to the uncertainties of trial. It is also possible that lawyers may delay working on a case in detail until it is certain that the case will go to trial. As this process comes into play, a mutually acceptable settlement is more likely to emerge and a trial becomes unnecessary. Robert Merton has analyzed the phenomenon of the self-fulfilling prophecy in which the prediction of an event makes its occurrence more likely. See Robert Merton, *Social Theory and Social Structure* (New York: The Free Press, 1967, 1968), Chapter IX. Here we seem to be dealing with the phenomenon of the self-defeating prophecy.

[23] For a general discussion of court congestion, see Maurice Rosenberg, "Court Congestion: Status, Causes, and Proposed Remedies," in Jones, *The Courts, the Public, and the Law Explosion*, pp. 29–59.

The court provides, in theory, an "impartial" referee institution, transcending factional disputes—the mundane embodiment of the Roman goddess of justice with her sword and her scales and a blindfold over her eyes to demonstrate her neutrality. To ensure that neutrality, American society has decentralized the judiciary and given each court a large grant of unfettered power, hoping to shield the administration of justice from political pressures—and then, wary of such independence, has made most judicial positions subject to popular election. The results of this mixture may be hard to pin down—the system is, after all, unique—but whatever its virtues in a democratic society, the arrangement contributes to administrative laxness in many courts. It also helps to breed a frequent indifference to the laws governing procedure and a willingness to push criminal cases through the system with an undue haste.

The prosecutor is, perhaps, an even more important figure than the judge in the great majority of criminal cases. The prosecutor makes the decision to bring a case to trial or to drop it because the evidence is inadequate or because the time and effort necessary for a conviction do not appear to be justified. The prosecutor represents the state in plea-bargaining negotiations and frequently hammers out the final terms of the agreement, with the judge merely serving as a rubber stamp.[24]

The Role of the Prosecutor

The great discretionary power of the prosecutor to decide who will be prosecuted, and under what conditions, is euphemistically called "selective enforcement," notes Morton Hunt, and is justified "on the grounds that the prosecutor's and the court's limited time must be used to society's greatest advantage against the worst and socially most destructive criminals: in practice it often means that prosecutors go after the sure wins and drop the chancy cases, in order to look as good as possible."[25]

One reason prosecutors desire an impressive string of court victories is that, like many judges, they are elected to office. There is a public prosecutor or attorney general for each state, but he or she usually has limited responsibilities for the prosecution of crime. The bulk of the work is done by county officers (variously known as the county, district, or state attorney or prosecutor) who are elected locally and who are not subordinate to the attorney general of the state.[26] A lawyer who loses cases—and

[24] Downie, *Justice Denied*, pp. 185–86. The overriding power of the prosecutor rather than the judge is a central theme in the defendant's view of the criminal court. See Jonathan D. Casper, *American Criminal Justice: The Defendant's Perspective* (Englewood Cliffs, N.J.: Prentice-Hall, 1972).

[25] *The Mugging* (New York: Atheneum, 1972), pp. 178–79. For a discussion of the historical roots of the prosecutor's discretionary power in English and French law, see Brian A. Grosman, *The Prosecutor: An Inquiry into the Exercise of Discretion* (Toronto: University of Toronto Press, 1969).

[26] Mayers, *The American Legal System*, p. 104. In the federal system, local prosecutors, known as United States attorneys and found in each of the eighty-nine federal judicial dis-

he need not lose many—when he is acting as the people's representative in the fight against crime will soon find his competence called into question. He may well lose his job in the next election.

The job of prosecuting attorney pays less than most forms of private practice, one reason being that the position frequently involves less than full-time work. The official duty of the prosecutor is to prosecute all criminal cases and, in most jurisdictions, to represent the local government in civil disputes; but the prosecutor is often free to practice law privately when not so engaged. This pattern of an outside practice is common in rural counties and smaller cities, but it is also encountered in large urban areas—and conflicts of interest between the prosecutor's public duties and private interests are almost inevitable.[27] Even more important, however, the poorly paid job of prosecuting attorney is attractive in many instances mainly because it is a stepping stone in a political career. A misstep can be serious, and the risk of losing cases in court looms as a dangerous threat indeed. It is in light of the highly political orientation of the prosecutor's office that we begin to understand more fully the prosecutor's willingness to enter into plea bargaining, since a plea of guilty obviously does not pose the danger of a disastrous upset in the glare of a public trial. When the pressures of caseload are also taken into account, it is hardly surprising that such a small percentage of criminal cases reaches the trial stage, there to be exposed to the full array of devices, so cherished by the Anglo-American legal tradition, for establishing innocence or guilt.

There are men and women who undertake the responsibilities of the prosecutor's office for idealistic reasons, as Morton Hunt has argued. The idealists, however, are apt to be in the minority, and experience is likely to turn their hopes of doing important and constructive work for society into cynicism, indifference, or a sense of futility. Hunt quotes one young lawyer leaving a district attorney's office after four years as an assistant—a spokesman, argues Hunt, for many young lawyers:

> Often I felt I did significant public service—I sometimes got cases dropped that didn't warrant prosecution at all, I got others dismissed where there had been incorrect police conduct (and maybe educated the police a little by so doing), and, most important of all, I protected the public by getting some of those who were likely to harm them out of the way for a while. But sometimes when I'd look at the volume of cases we couldn't handle or had to drop, or had to bargain down to almost nothing, I would wonder what good my long, hard hours of work were doing. It was like putting a Band-Aid on a mortal wound.[28]

tricts, are under the authority of the Attorney General, who is in charge of all prosecutions by the United States government.

[27] *Task Force Report: The Courts,* p. 73.

[28] *The Mugging,* pp. 181–82.

The prosecution of criminal offenders by the state, then, has been decentralized in much the same fashion as the judicial function; and yet, like the judge, the prosecutor has also been made a creature of politics, subject to the vagaries of public elections. The prestige of the judge—and the pay—are a good deal higher than that of the prosecuting attorney. The dignity of his office no doubt protects the judge from many of the gross political pressures often facing the district attorney. The criticisms directed against the prosecutor's office—such as the quick turnover of personnel, the lack of professional training, the political ambition of incumbents, and the absence of uniformity under a highly fragmented system—are directed less frequently against the judiciary. Nonetheless, both the prosecutor and the judge are under public pressure to "make the system work"; and that means, in general, that the millions of criminal cases swept up each year by the police are to be handled with dispatch and a minimum of cost without blatantly offending standards of justice. Some writers argue a considerable degree of fairness characterizes the prosecution of crime in the United States, because prosecutors learn their ambitions are best served by dropping most of the cases where the evidence is of doubtful legality.[29] Other writers offer no such solace, arguing that the work of the prosecuting attorney amounts to nothing less than legal oppression of the innocent or another illustration of the willingness of the ruling few to punish those who challenge them.[30] The reality of the matter would appear to lie somewhere between these positions. Prosecuting attorneys are neither inadvertent heros nor villains. Instead, the work of the prosecutor must be viewed as a mixed affair in which attempts to provide justice are often undone or at least compromised by a variety of factors. Idealism, corruption, a high level of skill, mediocrity, and incompetence are all to be encountered.

The Lawyer for the Defense

The search for the truth in trial proceedings in the United States is assumed to be best undertaken by means of an adversarial system, as we have seen. Partisan lawyers for the prosecution and the defense, each arguing their particular version of a case, are thought to reveal the facts in a way that would be impossible for a single person, no matter how neutral he or she might try to be. This view is contrary to that of continental legal systems and to the principles underlying the scientific ethos (discussed in Chapter 1), which hold that finding the truth requires an impartial search for the facts. The Anglo-American devotion to the adversarial system is commonly justified by the idea that those involved in the administration of criminal justice tend to follow the folk belief "Where there's smoke, there's fire," even though the suspected offender

[29] Ibid., p. 184.
[30] See, for example, Robert Lefcourt, ed., *Law Against the People* (New York: Random House, 1971), pp. 21–37.

is supposed to be innocent until proven guilty. If the search for truth starts from a position less than completely neutral, it may be necessary to provide competing positions that will cancel bias.

The lawyer's partisan commitment to his or her client can—and often does—pose complex ethical issues. The following fictional account is illustrative:

> A lawyer is called on the telephone by a former client who is unfortunately at the time a fugitive from justice. The police want him and he wants advice. The lawyer goes to where his client is, hears the whole story, and advises him to surrender. Finally, he succeeds in persuading him that this is the best thing to do and they make an appointment to go to police headquarters. Meanwhile the client is to have two days to wind up his affairs and make his farewells. When the lawyer gets back to his office, a police inspector is waiting for him, and asks whether his client is in town and where he is. Here are questions which the police have every right to ask of anybody, and even a little hesitation in this unfortunate lawyer's denials will reveal enough to betray his client.[31]

"Of course," says the author of this account, "he lies. And why not?"

Partisan lawyers in conflict are held out as the ideal in the Anglo-American legal system. The law claims that a lawyer for the defense is necessary, and further assumes that the lawyer for the prosecution and the lawyer for the defense are of roughly the same competence, for otherwise the forensic duel will be unfair.

"The right to be heard would be, in many cases, of little avail if it did not comprehend the right to be heard by counsel," said the United States Supreme Court nearly five decades ago. "Even the intelligent and educated layman has small and sometimes no skill in the science of law. . . . Left without the aid of counsel he may be put on trial without a proper charge, and convicted upon incompetent evidence, or evidence irrelevant to the issue or otherwise inadmissible. He lacks both the skill and knowledge adequately to prepare his defense even though he has a perfect one. He requires the guiding hand of counsel at every step in the proceedings against him. Without it, though he is not guilty, he faces the danger of conviction because he does not know how to establish his innocence."[32]

In 1963 the Supreme Court held that the Constitution requires the appointment of a defense lawyer for felony defendants who are too poor to

---

[31] Charles P. Curtis, "The Ethics of Advocacy," in John J. Bonsignore et al., eds., *Before the Law* (Boston: Houghton Mifflin, 1947), p. 181.
[32] *Powell v. Alabama*, 287 U.S. 45, 68–69 (1932).

hire one.[33] In addition, in a few states poor defendants are entitled to the appointment of a lawyer when they are charged with certain misdemeanors—a right granted by judicial decision, rule of court, or statute. Approximately 60 percent of all felony defendants—and 25 to 50 percent of all misdemeanor defendants—are unable to contribute any money to the cost of their defense.[34] Defense lawyers for the poor are provided in a number of ways. In the assigned counsel system, used in the majority of jurisdictions, lawyers in private practice are appointed by the court on a case-to-case basis. In some communities, the appointed lawyers are largely the younger members of the bar; in others, seasoned veterans are apt to be selected.[35] In either event, the fees—paid from state or county funds—are low.[36] In the defender system, used in most of the other jurisdictions, salaried lawyers devote all or part of their time to the defense of the poor. Some defender offices are supported by charitable foundations and other private agencies; some are supported by state or local government appropriations; again, salaries tend to be low.

Many observers of the criminal courts agree that despite the assigned counsel system and the defender system the indigent are not likely to find adequate legal representation; furthermore, the defendant who can afford to hire his own lawyer frequently does not do much better. Competent and experienced defense attorneys devoted wholly to the client are the exception rather than the rule. In plea bargaining, for example, the aid provided by counsel may not serve his client's best interests. The defense lawyer has many close ties with the court—the judge, his staff, the prosecuting attorney; despite his supposed adversary role, he is actually part of a legal structure in which he is under great pressure to make things go smoothly. In the case of a private attorney, argues Blumberg, a large fee depends on an impressive performance, but an impressive performance depends in large measure on the cooperation of the court. "Court personnel," he notes, "are keenly aware of the extent to which a lawyer's stock in trade involves precarious staging of a role. . . . For this reason alone, the lawyer is bound to the court system. Therefore, court personnel will aid in the creation and maintenance of that impression. There is a tacit commitment to the lawyer by the court organization, apart from formal etiquette, to aid him. This augmentation of the lawyer's stage-managed image is the partial basis for the quid pro quo which

[33] *Gideon v. Wainwright,* 372 U.S. 335 (1963). For a full discussion see Anthony Lewis, *Gideon's Trumpet* (New York: Vintage Books, 1966).

[34] Lee Silverstein, *Defense of the Poor in Criminal Cases in American State Courts* (Chicago: American Bar Foundation, 1965), pp. 8–9.

[35] *Task Force Report: The Courts,* p. 59.

[36] In one county, notes Hazel Kerper, pointing to the low sums involved, attorneys are expected to turn their fees over to the local bar association for the support of the county law library. See Kerper, *Introduction to the Criminal Justice System,* p. 440.

exists between the lawyer and the court organization. It tends to serve as the continuing basis for the higher loyalty of the lawyer to the court organization while his relationship with his client, in contrast, is transient, ephemeral, and often superficial."[37] The service the defense lawyer can perform in return for the court's cooperation is to persuade his client to plead guilty. Blumberg studied 724 male defendants pleading guilty in a large metropolitan court handling only felonies, and his data indicate that in 56 percent of the cases it was the defense lawyer who first suggested that the defendant enter a guilty plea. The defense lawyer, according to Blumberg, is thus pushing the client toward the convenient leniency of a negotiated plea rather than possible freedom to be won by a trial. The lawyer–client relationship is turned into a confidence game, with the client playing the role of the mark.[38]

Blumberg may be more cynical about the behavior of defense lawyers in criminal cases than the facts warrant. Furthermore, it may well be that a determination to take every case to trial would be detrimental to many defendants, as well as being an administrative burden. Blumberg is probably correct, however, when he argues that in many instances the defense lawyer is not working simply for the defendant but is also serving the court's need to induce guilty pleas to speed the flow of cases. Such tactics may be particularly frequent among defense lawyers who are paid with state funds. A public defender, argues Sudnow, "will not cause any serious trouble for the routine motion of the court conviction process. Laws will not be challenged, cases will not be tried to test the constitutionality of procedures and statutes, judges will not be personally degraded, police will be free from scrutiny to decide the legitimacy of their operations. . . ."[39] In return, the prosecuting attorney does not insist that the judge or the jury "throw the book" at the defendant, and both the public defender and the prosecuting attorney work together to dispatch the business of the court as quickly and easily as possible, with little regard for the defendant's best interests.

The need for adequate counsel extends far beyond the plea-bargaining process and trial proceedings. Police questioning; preliminary examination; arraignment; obtaining bail; dealing with an employer, landlord, or creditor; pretrial investigation; seeking an appellate review; sentencing; probation and parole revocation hearings—all may require the aid of a skilled lawyer dedicated to one's cause. Many lawyers involved in criminal defense work, however, are neither skilled nor unswerving in their commitment to their client. Defense lawyers are often inadequate be-

[37] Blumberg, *Law and Order,* p. 73.
[38] Ibid., p. 69.
[39] David Sudnow, "Normal Crimes: Sociological Features of the Penal Code in a Public Defender Office," *Social Problems* 12 (Winter 1965), p. 273.

cause law schools traditionally have offered few courses in criminal law or criminal procedure; and for many young defense lawyers at a criminal trial, the process is essentially one of trial and error, with their first clients bearing the consequences.[40] The low pay, the stigma that so often attaches to the criminal lawyer, the lack of decorum encountered in the criminal court, and the tendency of defense lawyers to lose more cases than they win (not because they are incompetent but because most defendants whose cases reach trial are convicted) mean that the most able members of the legal profession are not likely to enter the practice of criminal law.[41] The defendants in criminal cases able to pay for a lawyer—but not able to afford, say, a famous attorney such as F. Lee Bailey or Edward Bennett Williams—find their choice limited. "In many of our larger cities," it has been pointed out, "there is a district criminal bar of low legal and dubious ethical quality. These lawyers haunt the vicinity of the criminal courts seeking out clients who can pay a modest fee. Some have referral arrangements with bondsmen, policemen, or minor court officials. They negotiate guilty pleas and try cases without investigation, preparation, or concern for the particular needs of their clients. Because the prosecution is frequently willing to recommend a light sentence in exchange for a guilty plea in a routine case, the dispositions which these lawyers arrange often appear satisfactory to the defendants and other laymen who are ignorant of the fact that the result owes little to the capability of the lawyer. Fed by this ignorance, the reputation of the courthouse lawyer grows, and he attracts a substantial portion of the paying criminal business. The insufficiency of his performance thereby comes to taint in large measure the image of all defense counsel."[42]

Unfortunately, then, the inadequacies of the American legal system appear to be a dominant theme in the evaluation of the role of the defense attorney in the United States. In spite of a long-standing faith in a fair meeting between more or less equal adversaries as the cornerstone of a just legal order, American society has not yet managed to turn that faith into a working reality. There are two main reasons. First, most of the defendants in criminal cases are poor, and second, society has been unwilling to provide the funds needed to achieve its ideals of justice. Able to pay only a modest fee or no fee at all, defendants are frequently represented by lawyers who stand at the beginning of their career or at the margin of their profession. When lawyers of presumably average or

[40] Downie, *Justice Denied*, p. 165.

[41] *Task Force Report: The Courts*, pp. 57–59. In recent years, the practice of criminal law has gained in prestige, particularly in the eyes of younger lawyers beginning their careers. In general, however, it remains something of a pariah among the specialties of the law.

[42] *Task Force Report: The Courts*, pp. 57–58.

better ability are provided by a public-funding system, they may give their first allegiance to the government that pays them and to the judicial apparatus—and the need for speed in the hard-pressed court, with an inadequate capability due to inadequate funding, is all too apparent. The client gets short shrift.

The Trial

Although only a small proportion of criminal cases reach the trial stage— and this is often a summary, informal affair without a court recorder or even a court clerk—the elaborate criminal trial with a jury and long lists of witnesses to be examined and cross-examined must still be viewed as a significant element in the administration of justice. The anticipated results of a trial are an important factor in plea bargaining, in much the same way that jury awards in civil litigation are influential in shaping out-of-court settlements. And, perhaps more important, the full-blown criminal trial, with all the formal legal procedures brought into play, provides a picture of how the law conceives of justice, thus giving us a standard against which we can measure what happens in reality—and which, at times, influences the actions of the police and others who need to bring their evidence to court.

Criminal trials exert a potent fascination on many people, and for good reason. When the accused fights for his life and liberty against the state, a conflict that is the very stuff of drama is created and then resolved in the public view, with the persons in the play—real people and not actors—ignorant of the outcome along with the audience. In the United States, in the nineteenth century, criminal trials were a source of entertainment in rural areas; and when judges traveled an extensive circuit, "court day" was a major happening to be attended with picnic lunches. Today, on the national level, an important criminal trial is still a significant event at which normative values are expressed in dramatic form. As we have seen, Thurman Arnold called such proceedings the passion play of a secular society, seeing in them a united people reaffirming its norms. In contrast, in the divisive climate of the 1960s, the trial of the Chicago Seven was described by Dwight MacDonald as a *Kulturkampf*, a battle between divergent cultures.[43]

In addition to the drama of the conflict between the state and the ac-

[43] See Mark L. Levine, George C. McNamee, and Daniel Greenberg, eds., *The Tales of Hoffman* (New York: Bantam Books, 1970). This is an edited official transcript of the trial that followed the Chicago riots during the Democratic National Convention in 1968. Dwight MacDonald's introduction makes it clear that a new form of "juro-drama" has come into existence.

cused, there is the drama of another struggle occurring in the court-room—the struggle to discover the truth, regardless of whether it aids or hinders either the prosecution or the defense. The lawyers for each side must now be joined in a combat that will result in the disclosure of the facts of the case. To this end, the law has designed an intricate set of procedures to lay bare the guilt or innocence of the accused.

The first step, in trials using a petit (trial) jury, is termed the *voir dire*— **Jury Selection** that is, the questioning of prospective jurors by the lawyers for the prosecution and the defense to see if they will "speak the truth."[44] (The ancient French phrase points to the Norman Conquest and the introduction of French legal concepts into English law.) The jury, the triers of fact, that "hunk of laity," in the words of Rebecca West, was originally composed of neighbors of the accused who, as so-called compurgators, would swear to the guilt or innocence of the defendant. Over time, however, as the close, communal, and stable world of an agricultural society was replaced by an impersonal, urban social order, the jury became a group of ordinary men and women who were expected to listen to the testimony of others concerning the case and to come to a fair and accurate judgment.[45] It was a peculiar notion, in a way; amateurs, deliberately chosen as such, were to be the arbiters of truth, and the collective good sense of the common people would arrive at the facts that would determine the guilt or innocence of the citizen accused by the state. For a long time, it is true, the judge could overturn the judgment of a jury that was thought to be mistaken; but with the Bushell case, in 1670, the jury finally won the right to arrive at a decision without fear of what the trial judge might do if he disagreed.[46]

Today, the prospective members of the petit jury questioned at the *voir dire* are drawn by lot from a list of community residents. Generally, a list of registered voters is used. Persons may be excluded from the list by law because they are over sixty-five years of age; defective in sight or hear-

[44] In general, the right to trial by jury does not extend to offenses categorized as "petty"—that is, offenses that do not entail heavy penalties or social opprobrium. The right to trial by jury, when it does exist, may be waived by the defendant. It has been estimated that out of six to seven million prosecutions per year, nearly a million of which are for serious crimes, only about 125,000 result in jury trials. "Nonetheless," it has been said, "they are of immense importance: they are the test cases, the examples, the models which guide the rest of criminal justice behavior" (Hunt, *The Mugging*, p. 20).

[45] See Morris J. Bloomstein, *Verdict: The Jury System* (New York: Dodd, Mead, 1972).

[46] Before this time, juries might be punished if their decisions conflicted with that of the judge hearing the case. Bushell, the foreman of a jury that arrived at the acquittal of two defendants charged with "tumultuous assembly," much to the displeasure of the court, was fined and imprisoned and then freed. This was apparently the last attempt to question the legal right of a jury to reach whatever verdict it decided was right. See Moley, *Our Criminal Courts*, pp. 115–16.

Anatomy of a Murder

Only a small proportion of criminal cases reaches the trial stage. Nonetheless, the criminal trial must be viewed as a significant element in the administration of justice, and its inherent drama has long fascinated the public.

Adam's Rib

Compulsion

Twelve Angry Men

ing; fill the occupational role of lawyer, doctor, minister, fireman, or policeman; or have been convicted of a felony. No person may be excluded from jury duty because of characteristics viewed as irrelevant by the law, such as race, class, or sex.

The list of those who can serve on the jury is clearly not an exact reflection of all citizens living in the community; and since the selection of prospective jurors from the list for the *voir dire* is supposed to be based on chance, those appearing at the *voir dire* are frequently not a cross-section of the community's population. The lawyer for the defense or the prosecution (usually the former) may object to the composition of the panel of prospective jurors, on the grounds that illegal criteria of selection such as race, class, or sex have been used, but such attacks are seldom successful. There are undoubtedly discriminatory forces at work in many court systems, as evidenced by the fact, for example, that blacks are vastly underrepresented in selection for jury service. The task for the lawyer, however, is not to mount a persuasive argument that discriminatory forces are at work in general but that discrimination has been exercised in the selection of the panel of prospective jurors now before the judge. The underrepresentation of blacks at other times, made plain by the accumulated statistical data, is no proof that discrimination has been practiced in the present case. A "jury of one's peers," then, in the eyes of the law, generally refers to a group of fellow citizens selected without the use of such criteria as race, class, or sex, regarded as irrelevant to the fact-finding function, rather than to a group of people representing a particular mix of demographic characteristics.

Nonetheless, at the time of *voir dire*, the lawyers for each side are entitled to challenge prospective jurors with respect to their fitness for jury service, regardless of how they have been selected. First, one lawyer or the other may declare a candidate for the jury unacceptable without any reason being given—the so-called peremptory challenge. (The allowable number of such challenges varies from one state to another and according to the type of offense, but generally ranges from six for a minor felony such as larceny to twenty for a case of murder.) Second, prospective jurors may be challenged for cause, without any limitation of number, where it is shown that bias, previous knowledge of the case, attitudes toward capital punishment that might attend conviction, and similar factors are likely to interfere with a fair evaluation of the testimony. The lawyers for the defense and prosecution, then, to a limited extent, can mold the jury to their liking—if they can predict accurately whether particular types of people will favor their client.

Lawyers commonly assert that experience has given them some rough knowledge about selecting jurors likely to be favorable to one side of a case or the other. It is sometimes claimed that the prosecution will find business executives, the well-educated, and persons with administrative responsibilities inclined to view defendants with an unsympathetic eye. Poor people, those on the left side of the political fence, and members of minority groups are likely to believe in defendants' innocence. If a sexual offense is involved, the prosecution will find women jurors an advantage.[47]

Whether or not these claims are valid, lawyers do try to use their challenges to pack the jury in their favor. In recent years defense lawyers have shown an increasing willingness to call the social sciences to their aid. In the trial of Angela Davis, a militant black teacher who was accused of murder, kidnapping, and conspiracy, for example, a group of five psychologists advised the defense lawyers concerning the racial attitudes of prospective jurors and their probable reactions to the defendant's particular style and characteristics. "All the influence of factual evidence and legal shenanigans notwithstanding," says Wayne Sage," innocence is, to a large extent, in the eye of the beholder."[48] The aim of the defense lawyers, then, was to pick those jurors who would be sure to see innocence, and in this they were aided by the five psychologists.[49] After a *voir dire* that lasted for three and a half weeks, a jury was selected and the trial that followed resulted in an acquittal.

There are serious problems in using the social sciences in this way, since it can be turned into manipulation of the jury's task to arrive at the truth. Enough defendants, says Amitai Etzioni, have been freed with the help of social scientists in jury stacking to disturb observers on all sides. In a number of well-publicized trials—the Harrisburg conspiracy trial, the Camden 28 trial, the Gainesville Eight trial, the trial of the Attica defendants, the Mitchell–Stans trial, and the trial of Indian militants at Wounded Knee—social scientists were called on to aid the defense.[50] The procedures used in the Harrisburg conspiracy trial, involving protests

[47] The noted defense lawyer Clarence Darrow claimed that Prohibitionists, Presbyterians, Baptists, Scandinavians, and the wealthy were likely to convict; Jews, agnostics, the Irish, and those who liked to laugh were good for the defense. See James Kann, "Picking Peers," *The Wall Street Journal* (August 12, 1974). These stereotypes are often wrong, of course, and it has been pointed out that a peremptory challenge based on the characteristics of the prospective juror may be no more than an expression of the lawyer's prejudice. See Bloomstein, *Verdict*, p. 73.

[48] Wayne Sage, "Psychology and the Angela Davis Jury," *Human Behavior* 2 (January 1973), pp. 56–61.

[49] The ability of social scientists to pick favorable jurors may be somewhat exaggerated. As the defense attorney asked about a juror's opinion of Afro hairstyles, says Sage, the psychologists watched for the slightest involuntary eye movements away from either the attorney or Angela Davis, on the assumption that such a glance indicated an uneasiness the juror did not want to admit. The significance of such involuntary eye movements, of course, may be largely fictional.

[50] Amitai Etzioni, "Science: Threatening the Jury Trial," *The Washington Post* (May 26, 1974).

against the Vietnam War, illustrate the techniques that can be employed. The social scientists advising the defense took a survey of a random sample of people in the area from which the jurors would ultimately be selected; established the relationship between the backgrounds of those in the sample and a seven-item scale measuring tolerance for protest activities; and constructed a picture of the "ideal juror"—that is, one most likely to favor the defendants. Then, working with the defense lawyers, the social scientists rated each prospective juror. After weeks of questioning and using both challenges for cause and peremptory challenges, a jury was selected—and the trial that followed resulted in a deadlocked jury on the conspiracy charges, with ten for acquittal and two for conviction.[51]

"It would be foolish and dangerous to maintain that we fully determined the composition of the jury," say the social scientists who worked on the case, "or that we knew exactly what we were doing at the time. . . . In selecting the Harrisburg jurors, the defense used a complex combination of subjective impressions, hearsay, objective information, and data from our survey."[52] In general, however, the attempt to apply the techniques of the social sciences to the selection of jurors appeared to be fairly successful. Although the social scientists involved felt some moral qualms about what they were doing, they concluded that criminal trials provide great opportunities for "direct, practical" research—but they worried that some day the prosecution might also find such tactics attractive.

The moral dilemmas involved in the application of these techniques are not as easily dismissed as those writers suggest, however. The use of challenges for cause and peremptory challenges is designed to eliminate bias, not create it. That jury stacking is a common practice among trial lawyers does not justify further abuse of the system with the techniques of the social sciences. The liberal causes that have motivated social scientists to engage in this work have tended to obscure the fact that they are attempting to create biased rather than impartial juries—which is tampering with the jury, despite the talk of opportunities for direct, practical research.

Presentation of Evidence After the jury is selected, the trial is ready to begin. The prosecution usually opens the case, explaining briefly to the jury the nature of the charge against the accused and what facts the government intends to establish. The prosecution then introduces its witnesses. After the prosecuting attorney has questioned each witness, the defense attorney has the right to question—or cross-examine—him. The process of cross-ex-

[51] Jay S. Schulman et al., "Recipe for a Jury," *Psychology Today* 6 (May 1973), pp. 37–84.
[52] Ibid., p. 83.

amination has been characterized by John Henry Wigmore, an authority in the field of evidence, as the greatest legal engine ever invented for the discovery of the truth.[53] With the completion of the prosecution's case, the defense makes its opening statement in a similar manner and introduces its witnesses, who are then cross-examined by the opposing side.

The examination and reexamination of witnesses, which form the substance of the criminal trial, are governed by so-called rules of evidence that have grown up largely as part of the common law. Certain types of testimony are prohibited from being brought before the jury, primarily on the grounds that such evidence is almost certain to take the jurors away from the truth rather than bring them closer to it.

Hearsay evidence is generally treated as inadmissible in a criminal trial. It is argued that when a witness testifies not to what he has seen or heard but to what somebody else has told him, there is no opportunity for confrontation and cross-examination in the courtroom. "A woman may say, 'I know the defendant was there that night because my brother told me he was there,' " explains Kerper. "If the defendant cross-examines only the woman, he can get no information as to when and under what conditions the brother saw the defendant, nor whether the brother had good eyesight, disliked the defendant, or any other fact that might discredit his testimony. The law therefore says that the woman's testimony is hearsay and not admissible. If the state wants the brother's testimony, it will have to call the brother to the witness stand, where he can be examined and cross-examined about the occasion when he saw the defendant."[54]

So-called privileged communications may also be excluded, such as those between husband and wife, lawyer and client, doctor and patient, and priest and penitent. Although one reason is that the law finds testimony arising from such intimate relationships difficult to verify—thus presenting some of the problems of hearsay evidence—another is the desire to protect the privacy of such relationships. The information may be true, but it is not to be used in the interest of other objectives of society.

Perhaps one of the most important restrictions on the evidence that may be introduced in court involves the defendant's past criminal record. The defendant is protected by the Fifth Amendment from self-incrimination; and this means that he can choose not to testify. Moreover, the judge is not allowed to comment on the defendant's refusal to testify as being possibly indicative of guilt. If the defendant does not testify, the prosecution cannot introduce testimony concerning any crimes

[53] See Francis L. Wellman, *The Art of Cross-Examination* (New York: Collier Books, 1962).
[54] Kerper, *Introduction to the Criminal Justice Systems*, p. 312.

that he may have committed in the past. Prior crimes, it is argued, have nothing to do with proving the defendant guilty of the crime with which he is now charged; and putting such evidence before the jurors will only prejudice them against the accused. If the defendant does decide to testify in his own behalf, however, the prosecution can question him about his criminal record at length, on the grounds that such evidence is relevant to his credibility as a witness.

The rules of evidence are many and complex, and their rationale is not always clear. In general, their purpose is to speed the logical and orderly presentation of the case, to protect a social interest (such as maintaining the privacy of lawyer–client relationships) that transcends the resolution of the conflict immediately before the court, and to prevent evidence from being presented to the jury that would create prejudice or that could be easily misinterpreted. The last is, perhaps, the most important purpose, and in it we can see a compromise typical of the Anglo-American legal system. The task of finding the truth by a group of lay people is viewed as a democratic right. "Just as popular election helps to legitimize legislatures to members of a society," it has been argued, "lay participation on juries provides legitimation for the judicial process. Legitimacy, according to democratic theory, is enhanced when people feel they have participated in the promulgation of the laws by which they are governed. Legitimacy is similarly enhanced when people believe it within their power to participate, via the jury, in the application of the law."[55] Having assigned the task to lay people, however, the law exhibits its misgivings and carefully hedges in the fact-finding function of the jury. Many of the rules of evidence, says Jerome Frank, have been perpetuated primarily because the competence of the jury is doubted; as a consequence of this distrust, jurors frequently cannot learn of matters that would lead a person of average intelligence to a correct knowledge of the facts.[56]

The arguments concerning the effectiveness of the American jury system are heated and difficult to resolve. There are those who claim that a fair or objective jury is impossible to obtain, that juries lack the intellectual skills to deal with the issues that confront them, and that juries ignore the facts and usurp the judge's role of deciding questions of law.[57]

[55] "The Case for Black Juries," *The Yale Law Journal* 79 (January 1970), pp. 531–49. This interpretation is relatively new. The origin of the jury had no connection with the concept of democracy, and in the American colonial period a property qualification for jurors was still universal. See Barnaby C. Keenen, *Judgment by Peers* (Cambridge, Mass.: Harvard University Press, 1949).

[56] Jerome Frank, *Courts on Trial: Myth and Reality in American Justice* (Princeton: Princeton University Press, 1949), pp. 108–25.

[57] For an analysis of this argument, see Harry Kalven, Jr., and Hans Zeisel, *The American Jury* (Boston: Little, Brown, 1966), Chapter 11.

Other analysts disagree. They see the jury system as one of the truly great achievements of English and American jurisprudence, as the palladium of our liberties.[58] One extensive study of the jury system in the United States suggests that juries are quite capable of following the evidence and understanding the cases before them and that judges and juries are likely to come to the same conclusion when considering the same set of facts.[59] The pros and cons of the jury system are not likely to be settled by this sort of empirical research, however. Disagreement between the judge and the jury may be either a virtue or a vice of the jury system, depending on one's viewpoint. For those who are skeptical of the jury system, a jury coming to a decision that "flies in the face of the evidence" is obvious proof of its incompetence or irresponsibility. For those who admire the jury system, such a decision may be taken as indicative of the community's ability to determine innocence or guilt no matter what the law may say. An ideal of logical, competent fact-finding stands opposed to an ideal of democratic participation and community influence.[60]

The exact sequence of events at the close of the trial varies from state to state and is fixed by statute. In general, the prosecution sums up the major part of its argument, the defense presents the whole of its position, and the prosecution then has the final word. The closing statements of the opposing attorneys can, on occasion, be masterful displays of forensic skill, filled with fiery rhetoric that makes it seem as if all the forces of good and evil are struggling with one another in the courtroom; at the very least, the prosecution and the defense will usually go beyond the immediate facts at hand and appeal to the jurors' emotion.[61]

The Summing Up and Instructions to the Jury

Following the closing statements of the prosecution and the defense, the judge instructs the jury in the relevant law, so that once the jury has reached a decision concerning the factual evidence, it can decide if a verdict of guilty or innocent is warranted according to the legal rules. The opposing attorneys often present the instructions they would like to see given to the jury. The judge may use these, select from them, or prepare

[58] See, for example, Lloyd E. Moore, *The Jury: Tool of Kings, Palladium of Liberty* (Cincinnati: W. H. Anderson Company, 1973) and Walter R. Hart, *Long Live the American Jury* (Case Press, 1964).

[59] Harry Kalven, Jr., and Hans Zeisel, *The American Jury.*

[60] See Justice Murphy, dissenting, in *Moore v. New York,* 333 U.S. 565, 569 (1948). In the dissenting opinion, it was argued that attempting to improve the quality of the jury by systematically excluding all but the "best" or most learned of jurors is invalid. Such "blue ribbon" panels, it was said, "are completely at war with the democratic theory of our jury system, a theory formulated out of the experience of generations."

[61] For an excellent account of a criminal trial from start to finish, including appellate proceedings, see Philip B. Heymann and William H. Kenety, *The Murder Trial of Wilbur Jackson: A Homicide in the Family* (St. Paul, Minn.: West, 1975).

his own instructions.[62] And it is at this stage that the judge must instruct the jury concerning the doctrine of "beyond a reasonable doubt."

According to the law, the state must provide enough evidence to prove the guilt of the accused beyond a reasonable doubt. "Beyond a reasonable doubt does not mean beyond any doubt at all or absolute certainty," says Kerper, using language often found in legal texts. "Rather, a reasonable doubt is a doubt that a reasonable man might have after hearing all the evidence. If a single juror entertains such a doubt when the opposing attorneys finish their arguments, the verdict must be not guilty."[63]

What does this mean? One legal scholar points out that the words "beyond a reasonable doubt" have never been precisely defined by the law but that they somehow convey to the jury that its task is a solemn one to be performed with great care, since life or liberty is at stake.[64] This is still rather indefinite, and many judges and lawyers are convinced that few jurors really understand what they are told with regard to level of proof. There are few scientific data on hand, however. "The fact is that we do not know and perhaps do not want to know the impact of instructions on the mysterious dynamics of deliberation," says one observer. "Too much or too precise knowledge may not be healthy for a system which lives largely by myth and assumption."[65]

The jurors are supposed to start with the assumption that the defendant is innocent, and it appears that the criminal law is in fact asking the jury to perform a logical operation similar to that involved in testing a null hypothesis in statistics. Assuming that the defendant is innocent, what is the probability that the prosecutor's array of evidence demonstrating the defendant's guilt could arise by chance alone? If the probability is very low, the assumption that the defendant is innocent must be rejected and its contrary accepted—namely, that the accused is guilty. If, on the other hand, the probability is very high that such an array of evidence pointing to guilt could arise even though the defendant were innocent, the assumption of innocence must be maintained. The jurors, however, are not dealing with matters that are easily quantifiable, and the statistician's concepts of the null hypothesis, tests of significance, and so on cannot help them. They must proceed on a more or less intuitive basis, keeping in mind the Supreme Court's admonition "to avoid being misled by suspicion, conjecture, or mere appearance."[66]

[62] The judge must be careful at this point, for his instructions to the jury can be used as the basis of an appeal for a new trial on the grounds that he misled the jurors. See H. Richard Uviller, *The Process of Criminal Justice: Adjudication* (St. Paul, Minn.: West, 1975), pp. 750–53.

[63] See Kerper, *Introduction to the Criminal Justice System*, p. 188.

[64] See Delmar Karlen, *The Citizen in Court* (New York: Holt, Rinehart and Winston, 1964), Chapter 3.

[65] See Uviller, *The Process of Criminal Justice*, p. 750.

[66] Ibid., p. 760. In Scottish law, the jury can straddle the question of guilt versus innocence and return a verdict of "not proven."

Having undergone the questioning of the *voir dire* and having heard the testimony of witnesses, the cross-examination of opposing lawyers, the summations of the case by each side, and the judge's instructions, the jury must now retire to discuss the case in private and reach a verdict.

In states where a jury of fewer than twelve persons is permitted or where a unanimous verdict is not required, the task of reaching a decision is sometimes eased. Nonetheless, jury deliberations are difficult and time-consuming and may become deadlocked. If a jury fails to agree within a reasonable time and reports that there is little likelihood that agreement can be reached, a mistrial may be declared and the case may be dismissed or begun again with another jury.

In the early history of the jury system, the members of the jury were kept together without food, drink, fire, or light until they were able to arrive at a verdict.[67] In part, this spartan confinement was designed to speed the jurors' deliberations, but there was also the intention of protecting the jury from outside pressure or influence. Today, the jurors are generally not secluded during a trial that may go on for days; once the jury retires, however, every effort is made to keep them isolated.

The judge usually informs the members of the jury that they have a duty to consult with one another and that a juror should not hesitate to reexamine his or her position if convinced that it is erroneous. Nevertheless, each juror must decide for himself what the decision should be, and no juror should surrender honest convictions about the case solely because other jurors disagree or because it is thought necessary to reach a verdict.

Great care is taken to keep the jurors from considering any evidence other than that introduced by the lawyers during the trial. Jurors are not allowed to take notes during the trial and use them in their deliberations, on the grounds that taking notes is distracting and may represent a distorted version of what was said. (They may, however, request that portions of the trial transcript be read to them.) Jurors are not allowed to discuss the trial with anyone outside the courtroom, to watch television reports or to read newspaper accounts concerning the case, or to bring tomes on law or books on other subjects into the jury room.[68] A violation of any of these rules may result in a mistrial—as may bribery of a juror,

[67] Delmar Karlen and Charles W. Joiner, *Trial Cases and Appeals* (St. Paul, Minn.: West, 1971), p. 341.

[68] Unlike England, where the coverage by the mass media of trials in progress is sharply restricted, in the United States newspaper and television reports are apt to be full of sensational material that will never be allowed into evidence. For a discussion of the issues involved in criminal trials and freedom of the press, see *The Rights of a Fair Trial and Free Press* (Chicago: American Bar Association, 1969); see also Paul P. Ashley, *Say It Safely: Legal Limits in Publishing, Radio, and Television* (Seattle: University of Washington Press, 1966), Chapter 16, and Leonard Davies, "An Unfettered Judiciary Lurks Behind 'Gag' Orders," *Rocky Mountain News* (December 28, 1975).

deciding the issue by the toss of a coin, or proof that a juror concealed bias during the *voir dire*. The jurors, in short, are to be kept shielded from any contaminating influence, the privacy of their discussions to be protected to forestall retaliation, and they are bound to a standard of impartiality.

What really happens in the jury room, however, remains something of a mystery. According to one writer, "the working of a juryman's mind is the unknown quantity, the missing link in the trial of legal cases."[69] Jerome Frank, a judge whose work was cited earlier, has claimed that logical decisions grounded in facts are rare and that juries habitually reach a verdict by the occurrence of some chance event. A number of other judges have been similarly skeptical about the jury's truth-finding function. But direct observation of juries on a systematic basis is lacking, and the validity of such judgments remains unknown. In 1955 a research team from the University of Chicago attempted to remedy this situation by hiding microphones in the heating system of a jury room in Wichita, Kansas, with the permission of the judge, the prosecution, and the defense. Only the jurors and the witnesses were unaware the jury had been bugged. When the project, which had been granted $400,000 by the Ford Foundation, became known to the public, there was a great outcry; and federal legislation was passed to prohibit any such ventures in the future.[70]

The research team then turned to another procedure: mock jury deliberations in which the jurors were persons drawn by lot from regular jury pools. The persons playing the roles of jurors listened to a recorded trial, deliberated, and reached a decision. Their deliberations were recorded and scored in terms of a set of categories indicating the nature and the extent of social interaction.[71] These experiments suggested that in picking a foreman of the jury, persons with the occupational position of proprietor would be selected more frequently than would be accounted for by chance and women would be selected less frequently; that persons selected as foremen would be more likely to engage themselves in the deliberations than other jurors; that occupational status would be linked to

[69] Robert Stewart Sutliffe, *Impressions of an Average Juryman* (New York: D. Appleton, 1925), p. 5.

[70] "Reaction to the news that deliberations of juries in Wichita, Kansas, had been microphoned and recorded was virtually all one way," noted one report. "The metropolitan press and representatives of all shades of the political spectrum vied with one another in expressing a sense of outrage" ("Eavesdropping on Jurors," *The Commonweal* [November 4, 1955]). See also " 'Ear' in the Jury Room," *Newsweek* (October 17, 1955).

[71] See Fred L. Strodtbeck, Rita M. James, and Charles Hawkins, "Social Status in Jury Deliberations," *American Sociological Review* 22 (December 1957), pp. 713–19. See also Harry Kalven, Jr., "Report on the Jury Project of the University of Chicago Law School." Conference on Aims and Methods of Legal Research, University of Michigan Law School, Ann Arbor (November 5, 1955).

participation even among those not selected as foreman; and that jurors who participated the most in deliberations would be likely to have the greatest influence on the final decision. Other studies have been based on interviews with jurors after actual trials or inferences drawn from a general knowledge of group dynamics. Despite these analyses, however, jury deliberations remain an enigma.[72] Just as the doctrine of privileged communication has taken precedence over the fact-finding function of the jury and denied certain information to the jurors, so too has society's regard for the privacy of the jury transcended the interest of the social scientist in jury deliberations and virtually eliminated the jury room as a possible area of research.

After the jury has reached a decision, the jury returns to the courtroom to announce its verdict to the judge, the lawyers for the prosecution and the defense, and the defendant, who must be present. The judge asks if the jury has reached a decision, the foreman presents the written verdict to the judge, and the verdict is read aloud by the judge or the bailiff.[73] (The attorney for the losing side has the privilege of asking that the members of the jury be polled to report their individual votes.) If the verdict is "not guilty," the defendant is released. If the verdict is "guilty," the defendant is kept in custody, with the time of sentencing dependent on whether a pre-sentence investigation is to be made and on the condition of the court docket.

Verdict and Appeal

With an acquittal, the case is at an end. According to the Fifth Amendment of the Constitution, no person shall be "subject for the same offence to be twice put in jeopardy of life or limb." Almost all the states offer a similar protection, ensuring that a person cannot be prosecuted for the same cime once he or she has been declared "not guilty" by the court.[74] If the verdict is guilty, the case may be far from closed. The lawyer for the defense may ask the judge to declare a mistrial, or, that failing, he may file an appeal asking that the case be reviewed by a higher court. If the judge has said something highly prejudicial during the trial or made a serious error, he may be willing to grant a motion for a mistrial on almost any grounds to avoid the embarrassment of having his decision overthrown when the case is reviewed by an appellate court. In general, though, the declaration of a mistrial by the trial judge is rare,

[72] See James Marshall *Law and Psychology in Conflict* (Indianapolis: Bobbs-Merrill, 1966), p. 96.

[73] See Kerper, *Introduction to the Criminal Law System*, p. 323.

[74] A conviction in a state court, however, does not bar prosecution in a federal court for an act that is declared a crime by both state and federal law. The Supreme Court has ruled that this would not be double jeopardy, since a United States citizen owes allegiance to two sovereignties and may be liable for punishment for infractions of the laws of both. See David Fellman, *The Defendant's Rights* (New York: Rinehart, 1958), p. 190.

and appellate review is the more common course if further action is to be taken.

The right of appeal in criminal cases was not clearly established until the nineteenth century and is still limited in a variety of ways. (The Supreme Court, for example, is not required to review cases submitted to it.) But the right is now strongly rooted in custom if not in law, and the indigent defendant is entitled to the assistance of a lawyer provided by the state and a free transcript of the trial record. For the approximately 90 percent of criminal defendants who plead guilty and forego trial, no appeal is possible; for those who go through a jury trial and are convicted, an appeal is not at all uncommon. "It is almost a matter of course for an American defendant," says one criminal justice scholar, "either operating on his own independent means, or, if indigent, through the assistance of court-appointed counsel, to exhaust all possibilities of appellate review, carrying his case as far as the appellate system allows. . . ."[75]

When a case appears before the judges of the appellate court, it is not retried with the opposing lawyers and the witnesses and a jury repeating the earlier performance. Instead, the appellate court usually confines itself to the printed record of the trial and is primarily concerned with the legality of the lower-court proceedings. When a verdict is overturned or a case sent back for a new trial, a new view of the guilt or innocence of the defendant is generally not the cause, but the fact that the defendant has been convicted by unfair methods. "This is why appeals are so numerous and yet so rarely result in the freedom of the appellant," says Morton Hunt. "Our higher courts, and in particular our Supreme Court, have granted prisoners easy access to the appellate machinery, but for larger ends than those of the defendants themselves. The odds in favor of any defendant's winning his freedom through the appellate process is minuscule: many appeals are not heard at all, less than a fifth of those that are heard result in reversals, and the great majority of these result in reconviction after retrial."[76] The primary purpose of appellate review, then, is to make sure that the procedures of the lower courts are in good working order. A conviction may be set aside because of errors in the indictment, the selection of the jury, the admission or exclusion of evidence, the conduct of police investigators, or the instructions to the jury; and the case is sent back to the lower court to be tried again. Much more rarely, a conviction may be reversed and the defendant freed because the appellate court finds the evidence insufficient to establish proof of guilt.

Many observers, particularly those whose politics tend to be conservative, claim that the process of appellate review is much abused. Since the

[75] Delmar Karlen, *Anglo-American Criminal Justice* (New York: Oxford University Press, 1967), p. 215.
[76] *The Mugging,* p. 380.

execution of sentence is usually deferred while an appeal is pending, there is a great incentive to appeal a case on grounds that have no merit, merely to delay punishment. Appellate review undoubtedly postpones a final judgment and the imposition of sanctions. The delay involved, however, can hardly justify allowing a wrongful conviction to stand.[77] A possible solution would be some system of preliminary screening that would get rid of frivolous cases without restricting the right to appeal. Such a system could also help reduce the growing workload that is clogging the appellate courts no less than original trials are clogging the lower courts.

Political Trials

In trying to assess criminal trials in the United States, the legal rules and procedures specifying how such trials should be conducted must be separated from the question of how those procedural norms are implemented. While many people argue that the procedural norms, imperfect and in need of improvement though they may be, are better than any alternative system so far devised, many others are quick to point out that criminal trial proceedings are in fact frequently far from just.

The failure to achieve an ideal of justice must often be marked down as the inadvertent result of trying to fit grossly inadequate resources to overwhelming needs. But some criminal trials violate the ideal of justice without any such excuse. They are *deliberately* unjust, a combination of false charges and blatant judicial impropriety with the clear aim of reaching a conviction no matter what the evidence may be. More often than not, such trials are politically motivated; their target is those who threaten or appear to threaten the status quo.

All trials are political, in a sense, says Theodore Becker. "Since courts are government agencies and judges are part of 'the system,' all judicial decisions can be considered political. . . ."[78] Still, he adds, to call a case involving a traffic accident a political trial would rob that phrase of much of its meaning. We need more precise conceptual distinctions.

The trials of Jesus, Captain Dreyfus, Socrates, Joan of Arc, and Sir Thomas More were all political trials, he suggests; in each case men in power believed that the defendant posed some threat to the status quo. "This is not to say that Jesus or Sir Thomas More broke no laws," Becker argues. "Rather, that perception of a direct threat to established political

---

[77] An extreme example of postponing the execution of sentence can be found in the case of Caryl Chessman, who was convicted in California in 1948 of robbery, kidnapping, and attempted rape. Sentenced to death, he was not executed until May 2, 1960, because of a long series of appeals.

[78] Theodore L. Becker, ed., *Political Trials* (Indianapolis: Bobbs-Merrill, 1971), p. xi.

power is a major difference between political trials and other trials."[79] But if the concept is to be useful, he points out, we must recognize four different types of political trials. In the first type, the crime involves an overt, explicit attack on the political order, or a breach of national security, and the judicial proceedings are fair and impartial. In the second, the defendant is made a target of criminal proceedings for political reasons, but is charged with a nonpolitical offense. The political nature of the trial is covert, but the judicial proceedings are still a model of legal propriety. In the third type of political trial, the crime in question is political in character, but the proceedings are a caricature of due process. And in the fourth, the person is accused of a nonpolitical crime for political reasons; the legal proceedings are again a sham. (Becker lists the following as examples of these four types: the Spiegel trial in West Germany; the trial of Reies Lopez Tijerina in New Mexico; the trial of the Soviet writers Andrei Sinyavsky and Yuri Daniel, as well as the trial of the Chicago Eight; and last, the trial of Nigeria's Chief Enahoro.)[80] The first type of political trial is inevitable in modern societies, including democracies, claims Becker, and should be regarded as legitimate; the last three types are a cause for concern, either because they are a "shabby façade" behind which the government gets rid of dissenters or because they involve intolerable acts of injustice.

For other observers, the distinctions between types of political trials are less important than the new political note that has been introduced into American judicial proceedings by the trials of radical dissenters in the 1960s and 1970s. Until recently, says David Sternberg, the prevailing and largely uncontested model of criminal trials assigned a passive and unimportant role to the *audience*. Defendants in criminal trials, including the trials of political radicals, were also inclined to take a passive attitude, generally accepting the traditional structure and procedures of the court without challenging its fundamental legitimacy.[81]

Suddenly, however, in a number of trials involving radical defendants, the accepted decorum of the court has been shattered by the traditionally passive audience assuming an active role, and by the lawyers for the defense sharing the alienated style of their clients. The trial becomes a moment in the Living Theatre, in the words of Dwight MacDonald, a species of avant-garde dramatic presentation; and the boisterous behavior of both the audience and the defendant challenges the authority of the legal system. The defendants, says Sternberg, "see themselves as political prisoners trapped by a power structure of laws created by societal

---

[79] Ibid., p. xi.

[80] Ibid., pp. xiii–xiv.

[81] "The New Radical-Criminal Trials: A Step Toward a Class-for-Itself in the American Proletariat?" in Richard Quinney, ed., *Criminal Justice in America* (Boston: Little, Brown, 1974), pp. 274–94.

groups hostile to their interests. The court is both an agent for these groups and institutions—most significantly, monopoly capitalism, racism, colonialism, the military-industrial complex, and incipient fascism—and also an oppressive power group in its own right."[82]

The tactics used to challenge the authority of the legal system are varied. Defendants may abuse the judge or prosecutor, ignore the proceedings, refuse to stand when the judge enters or leaves the courtroom, or otherwise show hostility to or disrespect for the court. (In Chicago, Abbie Hoffman and Jerry Rubin appeared in court in black judicial robes.) The audience may cheer or boo or chant encouraging slogans. These forms of guerrilla theater, Sternberg suggests, are already becoming a thing of the past, as the legal system learns how to cope with such behavior.[83] But their importance, he says, lies in the influence they may have exerted on the political consciousness of all criminal defendants at other stages in the administration of justice. Working-class poor people, black and white, may suddenly refuse "to cooperate any longer with the prosecutor in the 'betrayal' system of plea-copping which has so successfully divided indicted persons and suffocated class consciousness."[84] Having learned that the authority of the legal system need no longer be accepted, says Sternberg, criminal defendants will develop solidarity as a quasi-class and bring the system to a halt by refusing to accept the bribe of a lesser sentence for a plea of guilty.

A small increase in the proportion of those demanding a trial could indeed seriously disrupt the administration of justice. That criminal defendants will soon develop such a sense of unity that they will forego self-interested plea-bargaining on an ideological basis seems unlikely, however. Furthermore, it seems unlikely that middle-class white radicals can serve as models of defiance for the great majority of criminal defendants, no matter how skillful such radicals have been in staging "juro-drama." Nonetheless, Sternberg's analysis of the difficulties posed by the disruptive tactics of defendants and spectators in recent political trials and the self-defeating attempts at coercion by the court focuses attention on some of the assumptions underlying trial proceedings. If the legal system is not accepted as legitimate, and if people refuse to limit their part in the drama to the roles assigned them or refuse to play any part at all, no amount of force can turn the outward form of court proceedings into the inward reality of a fair trial. If, in a criminal trial, the judge *or* the prosecution *or* the defense *or* the witnesses do not act on a voluntary basis, the fact-finding function of the court is jeopardized and the results are not to be trusted.

[82] Ibid., p. 281.

[83] At the 1972 trial of Soledad Brothers John Clutchette and Fleeta Drugo, Sternberg points out, a bullet-proof structure separated the defendants from the spectators, thus interfering with the interaction on which courtroom disruption must depend.

[84] Sternberg, "The New Radical-Criminal Trials," p. 292.

Sentencing

With the completion of the trial and the announcement of the verdict, the court must now impose sentence upon those declared guilty. In some states, this task is assigned to the jury; in others, the convicted offender may choose between being sentenced by a jury or a judge; and in some states, such as California, an administrative body determines the offender's period of imprisonment. In general, however, sentencing is regarded as the responsibility of the judge, and perhaps nowhere else in legal proceedings is the power of the judge more evident. The sentence that he assigns is not subject to review by any other government official or office. "In all Western countries, except the United States," it has been said, "grossly excessive sentences are subject to routine review and correction by appellate tribunals. The great majority of jurisdictions in the United States, however, vest sentencing power solely within the discretion of the trial judge, with appellate review available only to correct sentences which do not conform to the statutory limits."[85]

Statutory provisions attempt to reduce the judge's discretion or compel a certain type of sentence in four major ways. First, the law may state flatly that a person convicted of a particular crime must be imprisoned for a specific number of years. Second, the law may specify that a particular offense calls for a minimum period of time the offender must spend in prison before he can be considered for parole or a maximum period of time beyond which he cannot be kept confined. Third, the law may require that a person who has been convicted repeatedly of crimes must be punished more severely for the present crime.[86] And fourth, the law may insist that a person convicted of several offenses at one trial must serve consecutive rather than concurrent sentences. Many of these statutory provisions are flouted in practice, however, by judges who refuse to displace their own judgment with what they consider to be pointless rigidity. They may view mandatory sentences as unduly harsh and—no less important—as interfering with plea bargaining. There is persuasive evidence of nonenforcement of mandatory sentencing provisions, notes the President's Commission on Law Enforcement and Administration of Justice. Convictions for offenses carrying severe mandatory sentences are rare, and "where prosecutors have sought the imposition of long mandatory sentences, the courts often have refused to enforce the statutes or have narrowed their application. In Detroit, for example, the judges' opposition to the mandatory 20-year minimum sentence for sale of nar-

---

[85] *Task Force Report: The Courts*, p. 25.

[86] In some states, driving while intoxicated is a misdemeanor for the first conviction. On the second conviction, the offense is treated as a felony. Statutes may double the penalty for the second conviction of a crime and triple it for the third. Many states require life imprisonment for offenders convicted of two or more felonies.

Unequal Justice

Disparity is wide even among judges sitting in the same court. A study early this year of misdemeanor cases in Detroit's Recorder's Court found that black defendants, even when represented by a lawyer, drew jail terms twice as often as whites. It also found that defendants—white or black—who appeared in court in work clothes stood a much greater chance of going to jail than did defendants wearing sports clothes or coats and ties. The charges of discrimination were hotly denied by one of the Recorder's Court judges, who said the study was "superficial" because it was based on only 787 cases.

However, an earlier, more extensive survey of the same court found that one judge imposed prison terms on 75% to 90% of the defendants while another judge, more liberal in imposing fines and probation, sentenced only 35% of his

From Glynn Mapes, "Unequal Justice: A Growing Disparity in Criminal Sentences Troubles Legal Experts," *The Wall Street Journal* (September 9, 1970). Reprinted with permission of *The Wall Street Journal*, © Dow Jones & Company, Inc., 1970. All rights reserved.

cases to jail terms. The toughest judge in the court consistently imposed prison sentences twice as long as those of the most lenient judge.

White collar crime is rife with sentence disparity. Indeed, when the affluent are convicted of crimes, the punishment is often lenient compared with sentences imposed on poor people for everyday offenses.

Last year in Federal court in Manhattan, for example, a partner in a stock brokerage firm pleaded guilty to an indictment charging him with $20 million in illegal trading with Swiss banks. He hired himself a prestigious lawyer, who described the offense in court as comparable to breaking a traffic law. Judge Irving Cooper gave the stockbroker a tongue lashing, a $30,000 fine and a suspended sentence.

A few days later the same judge heard the case of an unemployed Negro shipping clerk who pleaded guilty to stealing a television set worth $100 from an interstate shipment in a bus terminal. Judge Cooper sentenced him to one year in jail.

cotics is so great that they have almost refused to accept guilty pleas to that offense and have instructed defense counsels and prosecutors to negotiate for a reduction of the charge to possession or use."[87]

Judges frequently manage to retain a good deal of discretion, then, despite the efforts of legislators to make the punishment fit the crime according to their view of the matter; and the charge is frequently made that judges' use of discretion in sentencing is often wildly capricious. Personal bias about particular types of offenses and types of offenders, private philosophies of punishment, and various conceptions of the public safety can all influence the penalty assigned by the judge, along with (so it is said) the state of the judge's digestion.

Numerous studies do indicate that the sentences handed out by different judges are strikingly inconsistent.[88] One investigation, for example, found that among ten judges sitting in the same court over a twenty-month period, one judge imposed prison terms in about 35 percent of the cases, while another judge used prison sentences at more than twice that rate. One judge consistently imposed prison sentences twice as long as those of the most lenient judge, and judges who imposed the most severe sentences for some crimes imposed the lightest sentences for others.[89] Similarly, when judges at workshop sessions of the Federal Institute on Disparity of Sentences were given sets of facts about a number of crimes and asked to select an appropriate penalty, the results varied markedly. "One case," it is reported, "involved a 51-year-old man with no criminal record who pleaded guilty of evading $4,945 in taxes. At the time of his conviction he had a net worth in excess of $200,000 and had paid the full principal and interest on the taxes owed to the government. Of the 54 judges who responded, 3 voted for a fine only; 23 judges voted for probation (some with a fine); 28 judges voted for prison terms ranging from less than 1 year to 5 years (some with a fine). In a bank robbery case the sentences ranged from probation to prison terms of from 5 to 20 years."[90]

Disparities in the sentencing record of different judges do not necessarily mean that the judges are guided by such irrelevant considerations as personal prejudice. The cases coming before different judges can and do vary a great deal, both in terms of officially recorded characteristics

[87] *Task Force Report: The Courts*, p. 16. The attempt of New York State to combat the narcotics problem with mandatory life sentences for drug pushers has encountered similar difficulties. See "Rockefeller's Drug Law: How Well Has It Worked?" *The New York Times* (July 20, 1975). See also Nathan Lewin, "Platitudes About Crime," *The New Republic* (July 5 and 12), 1975, pp. 19–21.

[88] See Peter W. Low, "Inconsistencies Within the Sentencing Structure," in Leon Radzinowicz and Marvin E. Wolfgang, eds., *The Criminal in the Arms of the Law* (New York: Basic Books, 1971), pp. 525–29.

[89] *Task Force Report: The Courts*, p. 23.

[90] Ibid., p. 23.

(such as type of crime, age of the offender, and previous criminal record) and less tangible factors that may be relevant in sentencing. The judge, indeed, is given discretion precisely because no two cases are exactly alike and sentencing cannot be reduced to a neat formula that obviates the need for individualized evaluations. Unless careful statistical controls have been employed, we must be skeptical of the claim that disparities in sentencing necessarily reflect the judge's temperament and social attitudes, rather than the gravity of the various cases.[91] At the same time, consistency among judges does not necessarily mean that the judges have arrived at a rational solution. Judges may agree about a foolish sentence just as they may disagree about a sensible one.

The variation among states in the laws concerning sentencing certainly makes little sense, and the differences in sentencing among judges for the same crime committed by criminals with the same background can hardly be justified. But it cannot be assumed by those who would reform sentencing procedures that the achievement of uniformity can be taken as an indication that sentencing has become rational. Sentencing councils (in which judges discuss appropriate penalties for different kinds of crimes and criminals), training institutes, statutory changes—all may help to produce a neat schedule of crimes and the attendant penalties that judges will follow without fail. Yet consistently placing x type of criminal in prison for five years and y type for ten may be no more rational than determining the length of sentence by throwing dice, unless it can be clearly shown that years in prison are in fact related to the purposes that punishment is supposed to serve. And that has yet to be done, as we shall see in later chapters.

In the lower criminal courts dealing with petty misdemeanants and minor offenders, fines rather than prison terms are routinely imposed. Since many offenders cannot pay the fines and since those who cannot pay are commonly jailed, a large share of minor offenders end up behind bars. Although imprisonment for private debts has largely been abolished in the United States, debts to the state as part of a criminal sentence are another matter. Many jurisdictions retain comparatively harsh sanctions for nonpayment of fines. (Only in 1966 did the New York Court of Appeals declare unconstitutional a statute permitting the court to im-

---

[91] Edward Green, *Judicial Attitudes in Sentencing* (London: Macmillan, 1961). See also Theodore G. Chiricos and Gordon P. Waldo, "Socioeconomic Status and Criminal Sentencing: An Empirical Assessment of a Conflict Proposition," *American Sociological Review* 40 (December 1975), pp. 753–72; David F. Greenberg, "Socioeconomic Status and Criminal Sentences: Is There an Association?" *American Sociological Review* 42 (February 1977), pp. 174–76; Andrew Hopkins, "Is There a Class Bias in Criminal Sentencing?" *American Sociological Review* 42 (February 1977), pp. 176–77; Charles E. Reasons, "On Methodology, Theory, and Ideology," *American Sociological Review* 42 (February 1977), pp. 177–81; and Theodore G. Chiricos and Gordon P. Waldo, "Reply to Greenberg, Hopkins, and Reasons," *American Sociological Review* 42 (February 1977), pp. 181–85.

prison a defendant for one day for each dollar of his fine not paid.[92])
Moreover, the ability to pay a fine depends on the defendant's wealth,
and the use of fines as a penalty for criminal offenses is inherently discriminatory. As Morris Cohen has indicated, money damages mean imprisonment for the poor and release for the rich, violating the concept of
equal justice.[93] It has been suggested for years that the number of offenders imprisoned for nonpayment of fines might be reduced if offenders could pay their debt to the state on the installment plan.[94] The
idea has never been widely accepted, perhaps in part because the paperwork involved seemed burdensome.

Indeterminate Sentences The discretion of the judge in determining the offender's sentence is
overshadowed in a number of jurisdictions by the discretion lodged in
the hands of administrative boards to determine the length of imprisonment under the provisions of statutes calling for the use of indeterminate
sentences. According to such laws, convicted offenders are to be kept
imprisoned for a period of time not to exceed a specified maximum, with
the actual length of sentence set by a sentencing authority. A system of
parole, in which imprisoned criminals are released prior to the expiration of the sentence imposed by the court, is a functional equivalent.
Since the sentence of so many offenders is determined by one or the
other of these methods, notes one report, "it is extremely rare for a convicted criminal . . . to know, at the time 'judgment' is formally imposed
by the court, precisely how long he actually will be retained in confinement."[95]

The concept of the indeterminate sentence is closely linked to the concept of rehabilitation, as we shall see in Chapter 12. The important point
at the moment, however, is that the use of discretion by such administrative bodies as a sentencing authority or a parole board has been criticized no less strongly than the use of discretion by the judge of the
criminal court. Characterized as arbitrary, unfair, harsh, and secretive,
these administrative bodies have come under increasing attack in recent
years. Recent Supreme Court decisions appear to signal a growing con-

[92] *Task Force Report: The Courts*, p. 18.
[93] See "Moral Aspects of the Criminal Law," *The Yale Law Journal* 49 (April 1940),
pp. 1009–26.
[94] Ronald L. Goldfarb and Linda R. Singer, *After Conviction* (New York: Simon and Schuster, 1973), pp. 126–31. See also *Task Force Report: The Courts*, p. 18.
[95] See *Fair and Certain Punishment*. Report of the Twentieth Century Fund Task Force on
Criminal Sentencing (New York: McGraw-Hill, 1976), p. 97; see also Caleb Foote, "The Sentencing Function," in *Annual Chief Justice Earl Warren Conference* (Cambridge, Mass.: The
Roscoe Pound American Trial Lawyers Foundation, 1972), pp. 17–32.

cern for legal constraints.[96] The striking fact is that the Anglo-American legal system has treated the rights of the suspected offender with great care before conviction but has long neglected the rights of the convicted offender with regard to the severity of the sentence. The report of the pre-sentence investigation, used to some degree or another by most courts and sentencing boards in felony cases, is not available to the convicted offender or his counsel by right; yet this report (often containing hearsay information and unsupported opinion) may have a vital impact on the offender's punishment. The sentence itself is the judge's or administrative agency's estimate of the appropriate penalty, for which no justification need be offered and which is not subject to review by higher authority. Penalties range from probation to life imprisonment, yet no one is empowered to challenge the sanctions that are applied.

Many of those involved in sentencing offenders have grown disillusioned in dealing with the long parade of criminals appearing in the courts and the prisons; their sentencing decisions have become routine. Others remain deeply involved in the problems of administrating justice and continue to look for the penalty appropriate to each case.[97] Even when an effort is made to place sentencing on a rational basis, however, resources are often lacking. Thus, for example, it may be believed that a delinquent with a steadily worsening record needs to be sent to a reformatory, but the reformatories may be so overcrowded that there is no alternative to placing the delinquent on probation. Conversely, it may be believed that an adult offender is best placed on probation if he can find a job, but the lack of employment opportunities may make this course appear unwise. (The high correlation between the unemployment rate and the prison commitment rate is much in need of investigation.[98]) Seldom able to predict with much accuracy who is likely to stay out of trouble, lacking any sure sense about the extent to which punishment will serve as a deterrent for particular offenders, and doubtful about imprisonment as a means of rehabilitation, those responsible for sentencing must struggle with the problem as best they can in a society in which the issue of identifying the guilty often receives far more attention than ascertaining what should be done with those found guilty. Almost all criminologists and legal scholars are agreed that the indeterminate sentence as it is now used is a part of the problem rather than a solution.

---

[96] *Fair and Certain Punishment*, pp. 107–15.

[97] See, for example, Donald Dale Jackson, *Judges* (New York: Atheneum, 1974).

[98] See Paper No. 5. *Estimating the Social Costs of National Economic Policy: Implications for Mental and Physical Health, and Criminal Aggression*. A Study Prepared for the Joint Committee, Congress of the United States (Washington, D.C.: Government Printing Office, 1976).

The Juvenile Court

Approximately 25 percent of all persons arrested in the United States in 1976 were under eighteen years of age.[99] A large majority fall within the provisions of the laws governing juvenile delinquency and are handled with the special procedures of the juvenile court. Here, no less than in the criminal court for adult offenders, American society is confronted with the difficult problem of assigning fairly, accurately, and expeditiously responsibility for violations of the law. The youthfulness of the suspected offenders, however, has opened the door for alternative ideas about the nature of the wrongdoer, the purposes of sentencing, and the proper balance between the rights of the individual and the power of the state—and these ideas have changed markedly in recent years.

"Until fairly recently," it has been said, "a book describing the law for children in juvenile courts could have been written in a very few pages. Indeed, it could have been concisely summarized by declaring that virtually all of the formal rules of law governing proceedings in other courts may be ignored in the juvenile court. The focus of the proceedings was on helping the child who had been brought to the court; and, for this, only the diagnostic kindness of the judges was called for. . . . Yet, in the process, severe punishments were sometimes meted out: but that was rarely admitted, and even when acknowledged, seemed to require no greater degree of legal formality."[100] In the past several decades, however, the juvenile court has come under increasingly sharp attack, and there has been a strong movement to redefine juvenile justice in legal terms rather than those of child welfare.

The origins of the juvenile court are commonly traced to the courts of chancery, established in England in the fifteenth century, that were founded on the principle of *parens patriae:* the king, as "father of his country," had the right to act in lieu of parents who were unable or unwilling to perform their proper parental function.[101] The courts of chancery, however, dealt with neglected and dependent children rather than with children accused of crimes, and it has been argued that juvenile courts should be viewed as a product of contemporary administrative and quasi-judicial tribunals. The *parens patriae* theory is simply an ex post facto justification for practices that originated with the modern

---

[99] See Department of Justice, *Uniform Crime Reports—1976* (Washington, D.C.: Government Printing Office, 1977), p. 170.

[100] Stanford J. Fox, *The Law of Juvenile Courts in a Nutshell* (St. Paul, Minn.: West, 1971), p. vii.

[101] See H. Warren Dunham, "The Juvenile Court: Contradictory Orientations in Processing Offenders," *Law and Contemporary Problems* 23 (Summer 1958), pp. 508–27. See also Robert G. Caldwell, "The Juvenile Court: Its Development and Some Major Problems," *Journal of Criminal Law, Criminology, and Police Science* 51 (January–February 1961), pp. 493–511.

treatment of juvenile offenders.[102] In any event, it is agreed that the first juvenile court as we know it today came to life at the end of the nineteenth century in Chicago, after nearly a century of developments in the handling of the youthful offender. The founding of the House of Refuge for juveniles in New York in 1825; the establishment of reform and industrial schools in Massachusetts in 1847; the use of a special commissioner in Chicago in 1861 to hear and decide minor charges against boys between six and seventeen years of age; the separate hearing of children's cases in Boston in 1870; the provision of separate sessions, dockets, and court records for juvenile cases in New York in 1892—all were part of a trend toward different legal procedures for children and adults that culminated in the Juvenile Court Act of the Illinois legislature in April 1899.[103]

Why did the juvenile court come into existence? Anthony Platt has argued that the creation of the juvenile court was part of a "child saving" movement in the United States in the latter part of the nineteenth century that was heavily influenced by middle-class and upper-class feminist reformers intent, as they found their traditional domestic role undermined by social change, on finding a career in a "moral enterprise." Types of adolescent behavior that had been ignored or handled informally in an earlier era were seized upon by these reformers, who in a sense "invented" juvenile delinquency to provide themselves with a special area of social concern, defining delinquency as an individual pathology and suggesting such remedies as recreation and the restriction of illicit pleasures.[104]

While it is true that state intervention in juvenile violations of the law increased in the nineteenth century and that feminist reformers found careers in working on the problem of juvenile delinquency, this is not quite the same thing as proof that "child savers" defined delinquency into existence, as Platt has seemed to suggest.[105] In a later version of his argument, however, Platt has claimed that changing patterns of handling juvenile delinquents are to be traced at least in part to the corporations interested in maintaining a disciplined labor force, and here the historical evidence appears to be stronger.[106] In any event, Platt is correct in his thesis that a new philosophy concerning juvenile delinquents emerged

[102] See *Task Force Report: The Courts*, p. 2.

[103] Ibid., p. 3. See also Robert M. Mennel, *Thorns and Thistles: Juvenile Delinquents in the United States. 1825–1940* (Hanover, N. H.: Published for the University of New Hampshire by the University Press of New England, 1973).

[104] See Anthony M. Platt, *The Child Savers: The Invention of Delinquency* (Chicago: University of Chicago Press, 1969).

[105] The phrase "child savers" is evidently less than a compliment in Platt's writing and appears to echo the indignation of *The Child Buyer*, the title that John Hersey gave to one of his novels.

[106] Anthony M. Platt, "The Triumph of Benevolence: The Origins of the Juvenile Justice System in the United States," in Quinney, *Criminal Justice in America*, pp. 356–89.

with the development of a modern, industrial, urban America that could no longer handle juveniles defined as delinquents with traditional methods. It was a philosophy in which a belief in treatment or therapy helped to limit the youthful offender's legal rights in the juvenile court. In 1905 an attempt was made to challenge the constitutionality of the legislation creating the juvenile court on the grounds that the juvenile's rights were ignored, but to no avail. The juvenile was not to appear in the juvenile court for a trial, it was declared, because it was a hearing to aid the child, and the right to a trial by jury and other legal safeguards were not required.[107] The idea of the juvenile court spread with great rapidity; by 1920 juvenile courts were to be found in all but three states, and in 1945 the list was completed with the appearance of the juvenile court in Wyoming.[108]

If questions about the defendant's rights were largely ignored in the enthusiastic rush to cure rather than punish the youthful offender, there were a number of social scientists who continued to express their doubts about the procedures of the juvenile court. Notice of the charges, right to counsel, right to confrontation and cross-examination, privilege against self-incrimination, right to a jury trial, right to a transcript of the proceedings, right to appellate review—all were lacking for the youthful offender who was dealt with by the juvenile court. The aim of the proceedings was laudable, said Paul Tappan in 1946. "The desire," he noted, "is to avoid the stigma which grows out of court contact and adjudication and, particularly where the offense involved is of no great seriousness, to prevent the sentencing to an offender's status and to formal correction. The aim, too, is to break with the legal approach of adjudging defendants on the proof of a given criminal act, holding it more scientifically appropriate to determine through social and biological information whether a case needs treatment and, if so, what sort is required."[109] Unfortunately, he pointed out, informal procedures designed to evaluate the child's character and the causes of his misbehavior (rather than to determine whether he committed an illegal act for which he should be held accountable) resulted in proceedings akin to those of the infamous Court of the Star Chamber.[110] The juvenile court, argued

[107] *Commonwealth v. Fisher*, 213 Pa. 48, 53, 62 Atl. 198, 200 (1905). As with other forms of social change, a new structure was attended by a new vocabulary: *petition* was used instead of *complaint*, *summons* instead of *warrant*, *initial hearing* instead of *arraignment*, *finding of involvement* instead of *conviction*, *disposition* instead of *sentence*. See *Task Force Report: The Courts*, p. 3.

[108] Caldwell, "The Juvenile Court: Its Development and Some Major Problems."

[109] Paul W. Tappan, "Treatment Without Trial," *Social Forces* 24 (March 1946), pp. 306–11.

[110] The Court of the Star Chamber, created by an act of Parliament in 1487, during the reign of Henry VII, was designed to achieve swift, sure, secular trials like those of the ecclesiastical courts, by ignoring nearly all the safeguards provided by the common law. The result, it has been said, was to make "*injustice* swift, sure, and terrible" (Irving Brant, *The Bill of Rights* [New York: New American Library, 1965], p. 95).

H. Warren Dunham, has inevitably broadened its jurisdiction because of the reform spirit in which it was founded. The supposedly benevolent court, acting in lieu of the parents, has a tendency to deal with all cases involving children. As a result, the difference between criminal and noncriminal behavior is apt to be obscured, and children are subjected to the control by the state, including imprisonment, for reasons that have little to do with violation of the law.[111] And it is true, of course, that the definition of delinquency has become much extended including not only cases of children who have committed an act that would be a crime if committed by an adult, but also cases of children who have violated regulations concerning curfew, school attendance, the use of alcohol and tobacco, and children who are designated as beyond control, ungovernable, incorrigible, runaway, or in need of supervision. The last two groups account for more than 25 percent of all children appearing in the juvenile court.[112]

The chorus of criticism grew stronger in the 1950s and the early 1960s, a part of an escalating sensitivity to civil liberties.[113] By the middle of the 1960s it became apparent that the juvenile court movement, begun with such enthusiasm at the turn of the century, had failed to fulfill its promise of fair and enlightened rehabilitation of the youthful offender. Roscoe Pound had called the juvenile court one of the great social inventions of the nineteenth century; slightly more than half a century later, many people were ready to call it a social disgrace. The programs of "treatment" to which the court assigned those labeled delinquent showed few signs of effectiveness; the label delinquent was all too often a class-bound moral judgment based on vague standards; and the juvenile was frequently denied the most elementary features of due process in the procedures of the juvenile court. In 1967 the disenchantment with the juvenile court found concrete expression in a decision of the Supreme Court concerning a fifteen-year-old boy by the name of Gerald Gault.

In June 1964 Gerald Gault and a friend, Ronald Lewis, were taken into custody by the sheriff of Gila County, Arizona. Gerald was on probation at the time as a result of having been in the company of another boy who had stolen a wallet from a woman's purse. Gerald was now taken into custody because a neighbor, Mrs. Cook, claimed that he had made an obscene telephone call to her.

When Gerald was taken into custody, both his mother and father were at work; no notice that he had been picked up by the police was left at the home. The next day a probation officer by the name of Flagg filed a

[111] Dunham, "The Juvenile Court: Contradictory Orientations in Processing Offenders."
[112] Task Force Report: The Courts, p. 4.
[113] For an excellent extended bibliography, see Jeffrey F. Glen and J. Robert Weber, The Juvenile Court: A Status Report (Rockville, Md.: National Institute of Mental Health, Center for Studies of Crime and Delinquency, 1971).

formal petition with the juvenile court that made no reference to any specific charges—it simply claimed that "said minor is under the age of 18 years and in need of the protection of this Honorable Court [and that] said minor is a delinquent minor." At the hearing before the judge, Mrs. Cook, the complainant, did not appear. No testimony was taken under oath. No transcript or recording of the hearing was made. Gerald Gault was questioned by the judge, and Officer Flagg testified that he recalled the boy had "admitted making one of these [lewd] statements." A few days later, the judge committed Gerald as a juvenile delinquent to the State Industrial School for the period of his minority—that is, until he was twenty-one. The case reached the U.S. Supreme Court not on appeal, which is not permitted for juvenile delinquents in Arizona, but on a writ of *habeas corpus*. [114] The Arizona Supreme Court had been in error in affirming Gerald Gault's detention, it was declared, and he was to be given an entirely new hearing.

The Arizona Supreme Court had held that (1) advance notice of the charges against a delinquent was unnecessary because "the policy of the juvenile law is to hide youthful errors from the full gaze of the public"; (2) representation of counsel for a minor is discretionary with the judge of the juvenile court; (3) juveniles did not have to be advised that they need not incriminate themselves because "necessary flexibility for individualized treatment will be enhanced by a rule which does not require the judge to advise the infant of a privilege against self-incrimination"; and (4) cross-examination of witnesses was not essential. On all of these points, said the U.S. Supreme Court, the Arizona Supreme Court was mistaken. Since so-called treatment could not be shown to be successful in achieving rehabilitation and was, in fact, usually little more than punishment under another name, the juvenile accused of breaking the law must be provided with such constitutional protections as notice of the charges and representation by counsel provided other defendants threatened with punishment by the state.

The Gault decision left many issues unresolved, as Alan Neigher has indicated, for while it may be true that the Fourteenth Amendment and the Bill of Rights are now not for adults only, the Fourteenth Amendment and the Bill of Rights are not yet for children completely. Questions concerning juveniles' rights with respect to searches and seizures, grand jury indictments, public trials, and so on are still not answered. [115] None-

---

[114] *In Re Gault*, 387 U.S. 1 (1967). A writ of *habeas corpus* (literally, "you have the body") commands a person having custody of another to bring him or her into court to show whether the detention is legal.

[115] See Alan Neigher, "The Gault Decision: Due Process and the Juvenile Court," *Federal Probation* 31 (December 1967), pp. 8–18. For an excellent review of changes in the law concerning juvenile delinquents since the Gault decision, see Monrad G. Paulsen and Charles H. Whitebread, *Juvenile Law and Procedure* (Reno, Nev.: National Council of Juvenile Court Judges, 1974).

theless, the Gault decision was viewed as a legal landmark that provided defendants in the juvenile court with at least a minimum of procedural safeguards.

The decision, however, has had less of an impact than its admirers would have supposed. First, many juveniles have waived their crucial right to counsel, due in no small measure to the pressure applied by juvenile judges reluctant to have defense lawyers in their courtroom no matter what the law may say.[116] Second, even when juveniles have in fact been represented by counsel, the defense attorney often finds it difficult to play the traditional role of an aggressive advocate of his client's cause. In many instances, the lawyer is subjected to the same pressures that are encountered, as we have seen, by the defense attorney for adult criminals. In addition, the lawyer who represents an alleged juvenile offender may be more or less convinced that the juvenile court really does offer a hope of rehabilitation. As a consequence, he may be unwilling to fight to the end to get his client freed, using every legal technicality that comes to hand, when he believes that the juvenile is seriously in need of help.[117]

As a result of the Supreme Court decision in the Gault case, juveniles in many jurisdictions have undoubtedly won a measure of justice that did not exist before. But the juvenile court continues to pose many problems in the administration of the criminal law despite a number of decisions, the Gault case included, that have extended the rights of juveniles. The ways in which judges and lawyers play their roles in the courtroom proceedings are no less important for achieving a fair trial than are the rules of criminal procedure.

Conclusions

As indicated in Chapter 2, a *crime* is defined as an act that has been prohibited and made punishable by the state. The rationales for punishment are varied and subject to much dispute—a matter that will occupy much of our attention in the last chapters of this book. There are probably few people, however, who would quarrel with the idea that it should be the guilty who are punished and the innocent who are set free.

In the Anglo-American legal system, as in the legal systems of other modern industrial societies, disputes about guilt are resolved in a secular process taking the form of a *trial*—an attempt, as the word itself suggests,

---

[116] One study of juvenile court judges revealed that half had not received undergraduate degrees, a fifth had received no college education, and a fifth were not members of the bar. It is possible that a trained lawyer, well versed in current law, might appear threatening. See *Task Force Report: The Courts,* p. 7.

[117] See Charles E. Cayton, "Relationship of the Probation Officer and the Defense Attorney After Gault," *Federal Probation* 32 (March 1970), pp. 8–13.

to separate fact from fancy, the grain from the straw. And in the Anglo-American legal system, the facts are to be established and a decision reached in the trial by means of a peculiar division of labor. There are opposing lawyers each presenting the facts for one side of the case only. There is a group of so-called triers of fact, the jury, a collection of lay citizens selected at random to decide which evidence is false and which is true and what the verdict shall be. And there is a judge, a supposedly impartial referee to keep order and to instruct the jury in the law.

Does it work? The criminal court, most observers would seem to agree, probably convicts the innocent infrequently. One mistake is too many, of course, from the view of the wronged man or woman, and some terrible blunders have been made and continue to be made. When these are irrevocable—as when the death penalty has been carried out—the system must appear completely flawed.[118] In general, nonetheless, criminal court proceedings function to forestall a verdict of guilty where no guilt exists. If the system of opposing lawyers, trial by jury, and impartial judge commits many errors, it is more likely to be in the direction of reaching a verdict of not guilty when in fact the defendant is guilty; but this has long been viewed as an acceptable cost. Thus, for example, clear evidence of wrongdoing may be declared inadmissible on the grounds that the evidence was illegally obtained, with the court hoping that the police will be induced to be more law-abiding in the future.

Trial proceedings, however, form only a small part of the criminal court's work in separating the guilty from the innocent. In the bulk of the cases, the court's task is to ratify an agreement in which the defendant's admission of guilt is exchanged for a lesser penalty. And in this phase of the court's operations the assignment of guilt is often faulty. Persons are induced to plead guilty to crimes they did not commit, and persons guilty of a serious crime are convicted on a much less serious charge. Accuracy is sacrificed to expediency while justice looks the other way.

In both trial proceedings and plea bargaining, it is clear that money does make a difference. Hiring a private lawyer or a particularly skillful one, paying for investigative work, securing expert witnesses, obtaining a transcript, postponing a decision by being out on bail—these are but some of the activities that increase the likelihood of acquittal or a much reduced sentence and that are more easily available to the rich than to the poor. In this sense, the criminal court is discriminatory. Ordeal by battle was always vulnerable to the common-sense observation that victory was apt to go to those wealthy enough to hire the strongest and most skillful defender and that truth was likely to get lost in the scuffle. Despite society's attempts to provide a system of public defenders for a

---

[118] See Charles L. Black, Jr., *Capital Punishment: The Inevitability of Caprice and Mistake* (New York: W. W. Norton, 1974).

secular ordeal, there is still reason to be skeptical of the claim that all defendants are equally matched in their conflict with the state.

Finally, in the matter of sentencing, the criminal court is marked by both inconsistency and a lack of scientific knowledge about human behavior that could provide a rational schedule of penalties. Punishment is too often handed out on the basis of whim, tradition, or a crude estimate of how deterrence works; and a trial in which the guilt of the accused has been established after an expenditure of much time and effort devoted to finding the truth may be capped by a sentence determined by folk belief and bias.

The criminal court, then, appears to provide a mixed performance. Yet even those who are most critical of the administration of criminal law in the United States today have had little to suggest as an alternative way of doing things. There have been many proposals for improving the criminal court—by providing more resources, for example, or by strengthening the defendant's right—but the tone of the proposals is largely one of modest reform rather than radical innovation. This might be attributed to a considered judgment that the present procedures of the criminal court are about the best that can be hoped for in an imperfect world. It is also possible, however, that the lack of suggestions for fundamental changes in the system reflects the weight of legal tradition, which is a good deal heavier than might be expected, even in a rapidly changing society.

Recommended Readings

Abraham S. Blumberg, ed., *Law and Order: The Scales of Justice,* 2nd ed. (New Brunswick, N.J.: Transaction Books, 1973) provides an excellent introduction to some of the major issues now confronting the judicial system. An overview of the criminal court system in the United States, and its problems, can be found in the President's Commission on Law Enforcement and Administration of Justice, *Task Force Report: The Courts* (Washington, D.C.: Government Printing Office, 1967). For a collection of articles on possible changes in the court, the reader should see Herbert Jacob, ed., *The Potential for Reform of Criminal Justice* (Beverly Hills, Calif.: Sage Publications, 1974). Of particular importance is the problem of sentencing—a problem that has long been neglected. The report of the Twentieth Century Fund Task Force on Criminal Sentencing, *Fair and Certain Punishment* (New York: McGraw-Hill, 1976); John Hogarth, *Sentencing As a Human Process* (Toronto: University of Toronto Press, 1971); and Leon Radzinowicz and Marvin E. Wolfgang, eds., *The Criminal in the Arms of the Law* (New York: Basic Books, 1971) are worth examination.

The juvenile court poses special issues. Anthony M. Platt, *The Child Savers: The Invention of Delinquency* (Chicago: University of Chicago Press, 1969) and Jeffrey F. Glen and J. Robert Weber, *The Juvenile Court: A Status Report* (Rockville, Md.: National Institute of Mental Health, Center for Studies of Crime and Delinquency, 1971) give a good introduction to some of the major issues, and the latter contains a useful bibliography.

Part 5

Social
Reactions
to Criminal
Behavior

Punishment inflicted by the group for violation of group rules is surely one of the most ancient forms of human behavior. Nevertheless, a note often sounded in the following chapters is that we still know little about the effects of such punishment, either in terms of the individual wrongdoer or of society at large. We do know, however, that the punishment of crime has changed as the social structure has changed, and so, too has the end that punishment is supposed to serve.

In primitive societies, punishment for wrongdoing frequently took the form of retaliation inflicted in a blood feud, in which the kin group of the victim demanded vengeance from the kin group of the offender. With the rise of the nation-state and the centralization of political authority, the desire for retribution was supplemented by an explicit interest in deterring crime, using the threat of the death penalty and physical punishment. The eighteenth and nineteenth centuries witnessed the creation of the penitentiary, in which the desire for retribution and deterrence was mixed with a concern for the reformation of the offender—to be found, it was thought, in a small, carefully controlled community embedded in the body of the state. In the modern era, probation and parole have been advanced as the best path to the rehabilitation of the criminal, with therapy or "social reintegration," rather than "mere punishment," the proper objective of the penal process.

In recent years it has become increasingly evident that society has not yet found effective and humanitarian techniques capable of transforming criminals into law-abiding citizens. The system of criminal justice, despite much talk of corrections, rehabilitation, and reformation, can give little assurance that convicted criminals are not made worse rather than better; and some new methods of treatment—like operant conditioning and chemotherapy—raise complex moral, legal, and political issues, as well as scientific questions about their proven utility.

Today, in fact, penology is in disarray. Some criminologists urge a return to the goal of deterrence, claiming that if transforming the criminal's character eludes our grasp, we can at least secure conformity to the law by means of threats. Others argue that neither rehabilitation nor deterrence is a realistic goal and that the reduction of crime made possible by keeping offenders confirmed is the best that can be hoped for. Still others claim that the major problem is that the criminal law undertakes too much, trying to control such behavior as the use of drugs, public drunkenness, and gambling, and thus clogging the machinery of justice to the point where it can no longer function effectively.

Earlier generations of criminologists were inclined to believe that an enlightened pursuit of rehabilitation using the techniques of science was slowly but surely replacing an irrational desire for vengeance. Today, criminologists are probably more apt to argue that the goals of retribution, deterrence, and reform are all still to be found shaping the sanctions of the criminal law and that penal policy will continue to represent a shifting compromise among competing forces rather than a humane concern with rehabilitation alone. In any event, social reactions to crime present a field of study thronged with issues involving the nature of conformity and deviance that are no less intricate than the problems of the nature of criminal law, the causation of criminal behavior, and the separation of the innocent from the guilty.

Chapter 12
Crime and Punishment

Explanations of why a society adopts a particular system of criminal law and why the criminal law is violated occupy much of the attention of criminology. The explanation of why societies *react* to violations of the criminal law in a particular fashion is no less important, however, and the issue poses a number of major questions that are far from resolved.

When one examines the punishments inflicted on wrongdoers in different societies in different historical periods, one must be struck by the brutality and cruelty so commonly exhibited. Burning, branding, flogging, impaling, beheading, exiling, caging—these are but some of a long list of social sanctions, often imposed for crimes that today would be considered trivial. In the present era, when the death penalty and the official use of physical punishment have largely disappeared in a number of societies, convicted criminals continue to be locked away for long periods of time and made to suffer not merely the loss of liberty and material deprivation but the many psychological pains that attend imprisonment. Why does this occur? How is it justified?

There have been a variety of answers, as we shall see in this chapter; when the connection between crime and punishment is no longer taken for granted, the supposed inevitability of punishing criminals turns out to be a complex and troublesome problem. In general, the answers have fallen into three major groups. Criminals are punished, it is said, for the purpose of retribution, deterrence, or rehabilitation. Crime is a species of wrongdoing that calls for retaliation, either to bring the moral world back into balance or as a matter of plain vengeance. Crime is a violation of the law that must be prevented by threatening the potential wrongdoer. Crime is a form of lawlessness that can be stopped by reforming or rehabilitating the criminal, by changing the offender's personality or character, and this entails the imposition of penal sanctions.

After the beginning of the present century, the idea of rehabilitation or reform came to dominate much of the thinking in criminology. Retribution was generally regarded as a savage, irrational response left over from an age of barbarism and having no place in a civilized, humanitarian era. Punishment as a deterrent to crime was ineffective, it was said, founded on the discredited concept of free will and man as a rational calculator of future pains and benefits. History shows that severe punishments never reduce criminality to any marked degree, many criminologists contended, and the argument for deterrence was a rationalization, a disguise for a crude thirst for vengeance.[1]

This attitude was widespread in criminology by the end of World War II, and almost every criminology student was thoroughly indoctrinated with the idea that the punishment of criminals was a useless relic.[2] The proper aim of society, argued the new orthodoxy, was the rehabilitation of the offender; and if it required imprisonment so that one could maintain access to the patient, the punishing aspects of confinement should be reduced to the absolute minimum allowed by law. Indeed, said one writer, by 1950 it became evident that there had been a revolution in the way people regarded crime, the criminal, and methods of handling the convicted offender. The "rehabilitation ideal" ruled the field, in words at least, if not in deeds.[3] And it was not only criminologists, penologists, psychiatrists and enlightened judges who had embraced the idea of reforming the wrongdoer rather than making him suffer. Despite the frequent allegation that "the public," with its irrational demand for vengeance, was a major barrier to penal progress, a large segment of the population had also come to believe that punishment should serve a rehabilitative function. In the latter part of the 1960s, the Harris Poll asked a national sample of respondents about the purpose of the prison; a surprisingly high proportion seemed to believe that prisons should adhere to the ideal of rehabilitation (see Table 1).

There had always been those who were skeptical about the rehabilitative ideal, however, and in the last several decades the orthodox argument in criminology for the nonpunitive treatment of convicted offenders has increasingly been called into question. Moral philosophers have turned their attention to the establishment of a moral basis for retribution; social scientists have begun to examine more closely the deterrent effect of punishment; and all those concerned with individual rights have become more sensitive to the issue of so-called therapy or treatment for criminals, whether imposed or voluntarily accepted.

[1] For an influential statement of this position in a popular text, see Harry Elmer Barnes and Negley K. Teeters, *Horizons in Criminology* (New York: Prentice-Hall, 1951), pp. 337–38.

[2] See C. R. Jeffery, "Criminal Behavior and Learning Theory," *Journal of Criminal Law, Criminology, and Police Science* 56 (September 1965), pp. 294–300.

[3] Francis A. Allen, *The Borderland of Criminal Justice* (Chicago: University of Chicago Press, 1964), pp. 25–41. As the author points out, the language of therapy was often employed, wittingly or unwittingly, to disguise the true state of affairs existing in custodial institutions.

Table 1. Public Attitudes Toward the Purpose of Prison

Response	Emphasis Now Is	Emphasis Should Be
Punishing	13%	7%
Rehabilitation	48%	72%
Protecting Society	24%	12%
Not Sure	15%	9%

SOURCE: Louis Harris and Associates, "The Public Looks at Crime and Correction." Report of a survey conducted by Louis Harris and Associates for the Joint Commission on Correctional Manpower and Training in November 1967. February 1968, p. 7. Cited in Department of Justice, *Sourcebook of Criminal Justice Statistics—1974* (Washington, D.C.: General Printing Office, 1975), p. 218.

The rise of the rehabilitative ideal was seen, in the first part of this century, as a great step forward; many sociologists were attracted by its humanitarian viewpoint and its reliance on the scientific disciplines—particularly psychiatry. The present criticisms may seem like a cowardly retreat just at the moment of victory. In fact, the skepticism that now surrounds the ideal of reforming criminals represents a complex of several themes. There is a doubt about the claims of the behavior sciences, which have often promised more than they could achieve. "The bloom is off the scientific rose," it has been asserted, "and people realize that a sociologist or cultural anthropologist cannot solve all human problems."[4] There is an increasing fear that the state is threatening to become an agent of totalitarian control in the guise of a concern for the citizen's mental and physical well-being. And there is a reluctance on the part of the social scientist to be constrained by any orthodoxy, no matter how well-intentioned or humanitarian, that shuts off a possible line of inquiry, such as the deterrent effect of punishment.

That the rehabilitative ideal is now rather uneasily ensconced in criminological thought is not simply the result of a conservative return to a punitive orientation. The hope of controlling crime within a humane and just framework remains, but there is a far greater awareness of the moral, political, and scientific difficulties that lie in the way.

[4]Rudolph Gerber and Patrick D. McAnany, "Punishment: Current Survey of Philosophy and Law," *Saint Louis University Law Journal* 11 (Summer 1967), pp. 502–35 (reprinted in Leon Radzinowicz and Marvin E. Wolfgang, eds., *The Criminal in the Arms of the Law* [New York: Basic Books, 1971], pp. 113–44). This collection of readings offers a good sampling of the controversy now surrounding the question of punishment.

It is sometimes hypothesized that punishment inflicted by the state has its roots in the efforts of primitive societies to purge themselves of the defilement caused by a violation of religious or magical taboos. Punishment—a collective act undertaken by the community or selected representatives—is said to have been applied to individuals who had committed offenses defined as sacrilege, so that the community could avoid the disasters that would otherwise surely be inflicted on it by supernatural forces.[5]

While it may be true that punishment for some crimes represented an effort by some primitive societies to forestall collective retribution imposed by the gods, it is likely that the origins of most collective sanctions can be traced to a more mundane reality.[6] Social reactions to crime grew out of private acts of retaliation in which forms of wrongdoing, such as theft or illegitimate violence, were avenged either by a similar injury inflicted on the wrongdoer or by a money payment to the victim or his kin. This is the principle of *lex talionis,* an eye for an eye, a tooth for a tooth, underlying the penal codes of ancient Babylonian, Hebraic, Roman, and Islamic societies. The concept of crime as an injury to society had not yet clearly emerged—the offense harmed a private person, and the punishment was for his satisfaction or for the compensation of the members of his family. But by setting a schedule of appropriate penalties and seeing that the schedule was enforced, the community was beginning to involve itself in the matter.

Blood Feuds and Wergild

The principle of *lex talionis,* influenced by Germanic, Danish, and Christian sources, dominated the legal system of Anglo-Saxon society before the Norman Conquest. The vendetta, or blood feud, required that harm be avenged by a like injury inflicted on the malefactor or a member of his kindred. Vengeance, rather than being an impulsive act committed in a rage, was a carefully regulated duty imposed by the society.[7] But the blood feud was a disruptive element in a primitive society that could ill afford to see its members sacrificed to private demands for vengeance. Gradually a system of money conpensation, or *wergild* (literally, man-money) developed, in which a harm could be atoned for by a money

[5] For an analysis of punishment as a form of ritual cleansing, see A. R. Radcliffe-Brown, *Structure and Function in Primitive Society,* (New York: The Free Press, 1965), Chapter XII.

[6] See Max Radin, "Enemies of Society," *Journal of Criminal Law and Criminology* 27 (September–October, 1936), pp. 328–56.

[7] "Vengeance was no mere satisfaction of personal feeling," it has been pointed out, "but a duty that had to be carried out even when it ran counter to personal inclination, and a favourite theme in Germanic literature was provided by any situation when this duty clashed with other feelings, such as friendship or marital affection" (Dorothy Whitelock, *The Beginnings of English Society* [Harmondsworth, England: Penguin Books, 1952], p. 39).

payment to the injured party or his kin, with the amount dependent on the type of injury and the victim's social status. (If the harm was a deliberate act of malice, an additional fine—the *wite*— had to be paid to the king.) "The seventh century Kentish laws of King Ethelbert," says Christopher Hibbert, "among the earliest documents written in the English language, provided a list of fines for a variety of crimes from murder to fornication. The amount of compensation to be paid in each case was carefully stipulated and carefully graded. While a murderer might have to pay a hundred shillings, the compensation was limited to twenty shillings if the assailant only succeeded in smashing his enemy's chin bone. Every part of the body had its value, from fifty shillings for an eye or a foot to sixpence for a toe-nail. Injuries which interfered with a man's ability to work or fight were compensated for at a higher rate than those which disfigured him."[8]

The blood feud had been largely brought under control in England and replaced by the *wergild* system before the Norman Conquest, it has been claimed; the historical records, with their detailed schedules of payments, suggest that disputes were generally settled by fines or by the enslavement of those who could not pay.[9] In the turbulent centuries that followed the Norman Conquest, a series of social changes brought a new social structure, a new concept of lawbreaking, and new forms of punishment.

The Rise of Corporal Punishment Anglo-Saxon society, with thousands of village communities loosely governed by the king and his lords, and with land owned and cultivated by free men in common, had been changing gradually into a feudal social order. Peasants slowly sank in the social scale as they traded their freedom for the protection of a local lord. The Norman Conquest vastly accelerated this process, as the Norman kings struggled with the barons for dominance and all proved eager to exploit the prize that had been won. When the conquest had been completed, it has been noted, "England was in a most unsettled state. Large districts . . . had been ravaged; the forests were full of broken and landless men; the Norman knights who had come with William to make their fortunes were dispossessing Saxon thegns, seizing villages, and quarrelling with one another over the plunder."[10] A vital element in the struggle to achieve order and to assure the

[8] Christopher Hibbert, *The Roots of Evil: A Social History of Crime and Punishment* (Minerva Press, 1963), pp. 3–4.

[9] See Alan Harding, *A Social History of the English Law* (Baltimore: Penguin Books, 1966), pp. 13–15. However, it was always possible for the injured kindred to refuse a money settlement and carry on the blood feud if they preferred. See Whitelock, *The Beginnings of English Society*, p. 40. The exercise of such a choice appears to have continued into the twelfth century, but to a diminishing extent.

[10] C. E. Carrington and J. Hampden Jackson, *A History of England* (Cambridge, England: The University Press, 1937), p. 77.

king's hegemony involved gaining control of the judicial process and establishing a centralized legal authority. Slowly the king's courts became the recognized sources of law and justice, the definers of crimes, and the dispensers of punishment.

The concept of wrongdoing had long been transformed from an individual harm demanding a like injury as revenge to a harm involving the victim's kindred and calling for recompense to the kin group. Now, with the rise of strong, centralized governmental authority, the next step was taken: wrongdoing came to be defined as a crime, an injury to society that called for a social response. No longer was robbery or theft or murder to be atoned for by money payments to the kindred. Such wrongs disturbed the peace of the state, and were therefore to be controlled by the power of the state. And it is at this point that we begin to see the emergence of the idea of crime as a disturbance of the ethical balance of the universe, a violation of the right in the abstract, a sin.[11]

The shift from private wrong and private compensation to public wrong and state-inflicted penalties had three main causes, according to Georg Rusche and Otto Kirchheimer. First, as already noted, royalty wanted to extend its influence. (The king's coronation oath made him responsible for the maintenance of peace, giving him both the opportunity and the duty to enlarge his judicial powers.) Second, the feudal lords used the punishment of crimes as a means of increasing their domination over their subjects. (The barons' right to maintain their own courts for minor offenses was an important privilege and was not checked until the end of the thirteenth century.) And third, in many instances the administration of criminal justice was often financially rewarding, at least when it involved landowners and quarreling members of the nobility. Fines and forfeited estates proved to be an important source of royal revenue.[12] For persons convicted of crimes and unable to pay—who were drawn from what one social scientist has described as a largely anonymous and fugitive criminal population, many of them members of outlaw bands roaming the countryside—punishment was often quick, harsh, and arbitrary.[13] The use of the pillory and stocks, branding, mutilation, and various forms of capital punishment became commonplace.[14]

A fourth reason for the change in patterns of response to wrongdoing

[11] See Frederick Howard Wines, *Punishment and Reformation* (New York: Thomas Y. Crowell, 1895), Chapter Three. See also Nicholas N. Kittrie, *The Right to Be Different* (Baltimore: Penguin Books, 1971), Chapter 1. One of the major tasks of governance is to establish the legitimacy of state power. This frequently involves the declaration that the use of state power is directed to the interest of society as a whole.

[12] See Georg Rusche and Otto Kirchheimer, *Punishment and Social Structure* (New York: Columbia University Press, 1939), Chapter II.

[13] Harding, *A Social History of the English Law*, Chapter 3.

[14] See Brian Ashley, *Law and Order* (London: B. T. Batsford, 1967).

was that the extended kinship group was fast disappearing as a major element of the social structure. Without the backing of the kindred, fewer individuals were able to make the payments that had supported the system of *wergild*. Furthermore, the weakening of the extended kinship group entailed the loss of a potent form of informal social control. The self-regulating community, as a small group of persons linked to a specific place, bound by blood ties, and in face-to-face contact, was coming to an end. New measures for the inhibition of illegal behavior were needed, and the solution was sought in brutal corporal punishments inflicted by the state. It was a pattern that would last well over five hundred years.

Branding and mutilation marked the wrongdoer in a simple fashion that all could recognize: the loss of ears for seditious words, the amputation of a hand for theft, and so on. Treason, an attack on the king and thus the state itself, called for particularly horrendous penalties. In the sentence pronounced against the Earl of Carlisle in the reign of Edward II, in the fourteenth century, it was declared that "the award of the court is that you be drawn, hanged, and beheaded; that your heart, and bowels, and entrails, whence came your traitorous thoughts, be torn out, and burnt to ashes, and that the ashes be scattered to the winds; that your body be cut into four quarters, and that one of them be hanged upon the tower of Carlisle, another upon the tower of Newcastle, a third upon the Bridge of York, and the fourth at Shrewsbury; and that your head be set upon London Bridge, for an example to others that they may never presume to be guilty of such treason as yours against their liege lord." [15]

For both the traitorous member of the nobility and the "anonymous and fugitive" thief or robber, the idea behind their punishment was much the same: the penalties inflicted by the state should be so terrifying that none would dare to break the law. "The sanguinary punishments and tortures of old are no evidence of blood-thirstiness or sadism on the part of those who used them," Thorsten Sellin has argued. "They rather testify to the fact that those who designed them could conceive of no better, that is more efficient, way of securing protection of the social values which they treasured." [16] Possibly this is true, for there is little doubt that as the Anglo-Saxon social order gave way to a centralized state, the idea of crime control by means of deterrence dominated the thinking of those in power. In a society that possessed no effective means of communications, no police, and only a rudimentary record-keeping system, many criminals found it fairly easy to escape capture and conviction. By raising the stakes—by making punishment even more

15 Wines, *Punishment and Reformation*, pp. 66–67.
16 See the "Foreword" in Rusche and Kirchheimer, *Punishment and Social Structure*, p. vi.

terrible for those wrongdoers who were caught and convicted—the state hoped to create a more potent antidote to crime. Thus, for example, it came to be believed that the death sentence was not enough; the criminal must not only be executed but his body must be preserved with tar and hung in iron hoops for years in the public view, so that all might contemplate with horror the consequences of breaking the law.[17] Nonetheless, there is more than a touch of sadism in the many methods of inflicting pain—the rack, the wheel, the boot, and those other machines for torture that bloody the pages of history. Public executions were festive occasions; in France, the introduction of the guillotine, in 1792, was greeted with numberless songs and jokes. "Models of it were made in wood, in ivory, in silver, and in gold, and sold as parlor ornaments and toys for children," notes one writer. "A somewhat fashionable closing ceremony with which to wind up a dinner in an aristocratic house was for the noble hostess to produce a *figurante* supposed to represent Danton, Robespierre, or Marat, and with a toy guillotine cut off his head, when, instead of blood, a tiny stream of crimson perfume flowed from the neck, in which the ladies at the table hastened to dip their dainty lace handkerchiefs."[18]

No matter how harsh the punishments, however, or how frequently imposed, the problem of crime would not go away. By the latter part of the eighteenth century, the deterrent effect of brutal penalties was beginning to be viewed with some doubt, and a growing segment of the population regarded them with revulsion. The number of crimes carrying the death penalty continued to increase, it is true; by 1780, it had risen to 350 offenses.[19] But it became more and more difficult to secure convictions for offenses that many believed were far too trivial to warrant the strong penalties demanded by the law. "The English revolt against capital punishment began in the second quarter of the eighteenth century," says Frank Hartung. "Juries either acquitted the accused or found them guilty of stealing 39 shillings (the theft of 40 shillings was capital) regardless of the sum they confessed to stealing or were proved to have stolen. Banks appealed . . . to the government to abolish the death sentence for forgery, as the law against it became practically inoperative. Victims refused to prosecute, witnesses to testify, and juries to convict."[20] The number of crimes for which the death sentence could be inflicted began to fall and was reduced to four by 1861. And the decline

[17] See Leon Radzinowicz, *A History of English Criminal Law and Its Administration from 1750* (New York: Macmillan, 1948), Vol. I, Part III.

[18] Wines, *Punishment and Reformation*, pp. 58–59.

[19] See Frank E. Hartung, "Trends in the Use of Capital Punishment," *The Annals of the American Academy of Political and Social Science* 284 (November 1952), pp. 8–19; see also Jerome Hall, *Theft, Law and Society* (Boston: Little, Brown, 1935).

[20] Hartung, "Trends in the Use of Capital Punishment," p. 11.

of capital punishment was accompanied by a decline in the mutilations, brandings, and prolonged floggings that had provided society's standard answer to crime for so many centuries.

Convict Labor A growth of humanitarianism and doubts about corporal punishment's deterrent effect were only a part of the reason why punishment for crime began to assume new forms. The state also began to see that convicted criminals represented an important source of labor that might be put to productive use.

For several centuries, England had had a superabundance of labor, as the enclosure of land (first for raising sheep and the production of wool, and later for more efficient, large-scale agriculture) forced men and women off the farms and into the towns or into roving bands of beggars. Convicts had long provided a crucial source of galley slaves, it is true, since the harsh, hazardous nature of the work made it difficult to recruit free men. But this was an exception and ended with the advent of technical improvements in the art of sailing in the eighteenth century.[21] In general, there was little to be done by those convicted of breaking the law that could not be done more effectively by law-abiding workers who were in abundant supply. This situation was changed by the discovery of new lands to be colonized.

The systematic transportation of criminals to the American colonies began in 1717 with an act of Parliament that allowed the courts to place convicted offenders in the custody of private contractors who could then sell the services of their charges in the New World.[22] The death rate among those thus exiled was high, both on board ship and in the plantations, where the working conditions were appalling. Those that survived were often absorbed into the general population, although precise data as to the number of criminals transported and their eventual fate are lacking. In any event, the American Revolution closed the New World as a dumping ground for criminals convicted in England, and a new means of handling the convicted offender had to be found.

For some ten years many criminals were confined in the "hulks" floating in the rivers and ports of England—the ships that had been used for transporting criminals to America and now converted to nautical prisons.[23] Then, in 1786, the first shiploads of convicts were transported to Australia, recently discovered by Captain Cook.[24] It was a disastrous

[21] See Rusche and Kirchheimer, *Punishment and Social Structure*, Chapter IV.

[22] See Hibbert, *The Roots of Evil*, pp. 139–50; and A. G. L. Shaw, *Convicts and the Colonies* (London: Faber and Faber, 1966).

[23] In the late 1920s, a "hulk" still survived and was brought to New York harbor and exhibited to crowds of the curious.

[24] L. L. Robson, *The Convict Settlers of Australia* (Carlton, Australia: Melbourne University Press, 1970).

venture, initially, with the involuntary settlers beset by famine and disease. As the colonization of Australia advanced with the arrival of free citizens and as the discovery of gold and the expansion of sheep husbandry opened new opportunities for economic gain, Australian society split into two hostile factions—the "emancipists," who wished to give transported criminals a voice in the government, and the "exclusionists," who were steadfastly opposed to convict colonists.[25] The latter position prevailed. A high crime rate, the terrorization of rural areas by escaped convicts, the ill treatment of convict laborers by employers, the organization of convicts into gangs that plundered city neighborhoods—all argued in favor of bringing the transportation of convicted criminals from England to an end.[26] In 1837, following an investigation, the government decided that dealing with the crime problem by shipping criminals to distant colonies should cease.

England continued to experiment with the transportation of criminals on a small scale for a number of years. The penal colony at Australia's Norfolk Island supervised by Alexander Maconochie was to have a significant impact on correctional philosophy in later years—particularly its adherence to the concept of the mark system, in which a prisoner earned his way to freedom by the demonstration of good behavior. And penal colonies continue as a component of the treatment of criminals in a number of countries, including France, the Soviet Union, Mexico, and Greece.[27] But by the middle of the nineteenth century, the handling of the criminal in England—still a major influence on American penal practices despite the rupture of the war for independence—had moved in a new direction. The criminal was not to be sent into exile; rather, he was to be encapsulated in the body of the state, there to be usefully employed and reformed, as well as serving as a deterrent for others.

The imprisonment of the convicted offender had previously been regarded as a preliminary step in the legal process, a period in limbo in which the suspected offender awaited trial or the convicted criminal looked forward to the hangman's noose or the lash. Slowly the idea developed that the imprisonment of the criminal was itself an appropriate penalty for criminal behavior, since it provided society with an opportunity to lead the wrongdoer into the ranks of conformists.

Imprisonment

This new view concerning the handling of the criminal was grafted on a much older idea about what to do with those persons who could not or would not work. "In the sixteenth century," it has been pointed out,

[25] See Wines, *Punishment and Reformation*, Chapter IX.
[26] Hibbert, *The Roots of Evil*, p. 144.
[27] See, for example, Donald P. Jewell, "Mexico's Tres Marias Penal Colony," *Journal of Criminal Law, Criminology and Police Science* 48 (November/December 1957), pp. 410–13.

"there began to be erected here and there houses of correction or work-houses, not punitive nor reformatory but rather repressive in their character and purpose, designed for the detention not of criminals so much as vagabonds."[28] A house known as Bridewell, given to the city of London by the king, was used as a lodging place for those wandering without work, and it served as a model for many others. Called houses of correction, they were designed to bring vagrants and others back to respectability by means of disciplined labor, and the distinctions among the unemployed, petty criminals, lazy apprentices, and so on were never precisely drawn. All were seen as standing in need of control through honest toil.[29]

The idea of imprisoning criminals in something like a house of correction continued to grow. It seemed a promising method for handling not simply minor offenders but more serious offenders as well, a humane and efficient alternative to the corporal punishments that were coming under increasing criticism. Interest in the idea increased when criminals could no longer be shipped to the American colonies, then dropped off as they were sent to Australia instead. At the beginning of the nineteenth century, the idea of imprisonment swept into ascendency. The criminal was to be reformed, not merely punished, by being forced to live in seclusion in an institution where he could be subjected to a regime inculcating the Christian virtues of honesty, sobriety, cleanliness, and industriousness—and where he could help to pay for his keep.[30] Thus the concept of the penitentiary came into being—that is, a place where the criminal could be brought to feel penitence and be made economically productive.

The American colonies, before the Revolution, differed but little from England in their methods of handling the convicted criminal. At the end of the eighteenth century, however, the United States began to show a decided flair for innovation in penal practices; the history of punishment would thereafter be largely an account of American events. As the penitentiary became the basic mechanism for dealing with criminals, says David Rothman, the fame of efforts in America spread so quickly "that almost no important visitor to the United States neglected to tour the

[28] Wines, *Punishment and Reformation*, p. 113.

[29] The appearance of houses of correction was also common on the Continent in the same period. Among the cities that developed a workhouse system were Amsterdam and Nuremberg (1588), Lübeck and Bremen (1613), Bern (1615), Hamburg (1620), Basel (1667), Vienna and Breslau (1670), Luneburg (1676), and Munich (1687). Nearly all of them, it has been pointed out, were in northern Europe and the Germanic states (Wines, *Punishment and Reformation*, p. 115). It was an area in which the Protestant ethic—with its belief in the virtues of disciplined labor—flourished.

[30] See James Heath, *Eighteenth Century Penal Theory* (London: Oxford University Press, 1963). John Howard (1726–1790), a noted British philanthropist, was particularly influential in introducing the concept of the penitentiary.

New York State penitentiary at Auburn, or the Philadelphia prison, and some, like Tocqueville and Beaumont, came to America expressly to investigate them."[31]

A primary source of the zeal for the penitentiary in the United States, Rothman argues, was the general acceptance of a new theory about the causes of criminal behavior. Crime was not due to inherited defects, to innate depravity, or some biological taint. Rather, it was said in this young and optimistic society, the cause of crime was to be found in the failure of the family and church to protect the individual from the corruptions pervading the community. This view, notes Rothman, led easily to the claim that a well-ordered institution could rehabilitate the offender. The steady and regular regime of the penitentiary "would inculcate the discipline that negligent parents, evil companions, taverns, houses of prostitution, theaters, and gambling halls had destroyed."[32]

The need to isolate the prison inmate from corrupting influences was widely accepted, but there was disagreement about how it should best be accomplished. The supporters of the so-called Pennsylvania system of imprisonment ranged themselves against those who preferred the Auburn system, and the debate reached a level of startling intensity. In the Pennsylvania system, embodied in the Eastern Penitentiary in Philadelphia, the inmate was to be kept in solitary confinement both day and night. He would work in his cell—weaving textiles on a hand loom, for example—and exercise in a small yard. His access to other persons would be limited to a handful of trustworthy guards and selected visitors. In the Auburn system, exemplified by the penitentiary at Auburn, New York, inmates would sleep in isolated cells at night, but during the day would be allowed to congregate in workshops and in mess halls. Absolute silence was required, however, and all communication was prohibited. Those inmates who were released from their cells to perform maintenance duties were to wear a mask or a hood at all times. Prisoners moving in a group were to march in lockstep, without speaking, each man's hand placed on the shoulder of the man in front of him.

Looking back from the vantage point of the present, the great debate between the partisans of the Pennsylvania and Auburn systems seems like an argument about the relative virtues of Tweedledum and Tweedledee. Both systems imposed a rigid discipline at a minimum level of subsistence, both sharply restricted the prisoners' interaction with others,

---

[31] David J. Rothman, *The Discovery of the Asylum* (Boston: Little, Brown, 1971), p. xiv. The report of de Tocqueville and Beaumont was important in shaping European practice. See Gustave de Beaumont and Alexis de Tocqueville, *On the Penitentiary System in the United States and Its Application in France* (Philadelphia: Carey, Lea, and Blanchard, 1833).

[32] Rothman, *The Discovery of the Asylum*, p. 82.

and both saw penitence and hard work as the means of reform. However, the economic inefficiency of the Pennsylvania system with its reliance on handicrafts—and the pernicious effects of continual solitary confinement—soon became apparent.[33]

Although the Auburn system came to dominate penal practice in the United States, neither system could claim success in rehabilitating the criminal, and it has been argued that the concept of the penitentiary as an institution where prisoners could be reformed through penitence and productive labor was already obsolete even as it emerged as the major device for handling the convicted offender. The Industrial Revolution, note Rusche and Kirchheimer, citing the studies of Sidney and Beatrice Webb, was making it more and more difficult to obtain any real profit from demoralized and indiscriminately assembled prisoners.[34] The hope of achieving reformation by making the prisoner reflect on his violations of God's laws was unrealistic in a world where it was the prison reformers rather than the prisoners who were apt to be religious. And the idea that the criminal could be made a law-abiding citizen after release from prison by seeing to it that he did not communicate with other criminals during his confinement was simply naive. Cut in stone over the threshold of the New Jersey penitentiary—erected in 1799—were the words "Labor, Silence, Penitence." Within less than fifty years, there were probably few people who still believed that the inscription offered a useful guide.

| The Reformatory Movement | Faith in the ability of society to find a way to rehabilitate the criminal is not easily eradicated. It is, one could suppose, deeply embedded in the religious traditions that view God as a shepherd who finds those who have strayed and returns them to the flock. In any event, at the end of the nineteenth century a new program for reforming criminals came into prominence. Called the reformatory movement, it flourished for some forty years. |

Prison reformers in Austria, Spain, and Ireland had been arguing for some time that if criminals were ever to be rehabilitated, they must be allowed to assume responsibility for their own improvement. They must

[33] In his annual report of 1839, the warden of the New Jersey State Prison indicated that solitary confinement was bad for the prisoners' health because it made normal methods of exercise impossible. Even worse, he said, was the effect on the mental health of the prisoners, leading to "solitary vices and mental degeneration" (Emil Frankel, "Crime Treatment in New Jersey, 1668–1934," *Journal of Criminal Law and Criminology* 28 [May–June 1937], pp. 98–99).

[34] See Rusche and Kirchheimer, *Punishment and Social Structure*, p. 110. In England, the commitment to penal servitude even when such labor served no economic purpose led to the use of the treadmill and a crank installed in the prisoner's cell to be turned for no other reason than to keep the prisoner busy. See Barnes and Teeters, *New Horizons in Criminology*, pp. 719–20.

be allowed to *earn* their freedom, by acquiring habits of industrious, conforming behavior.[35] And since the reform of the criminal, not punishment, was to be the true purpose of his incarceration, the length of imprisonment could not be fixed in advance. The prison, said prison reformers at the time, should be used as a kind of moral hospital to which offenders would be sent until they were cured of their bad habits. It would be unfair to keep the criminal confined after he had been cured, and it would be foolish to release him before the cure had been accomplished. The only just and rational procedure, then, was to impose an indeterminate sentence, with the release of the criminal dependent solely on his demonstrated rehabilitation.

In 1870, at the first meeting of the American Prison Congress—a group of private citizens and public officials concerned with penology—the ideas behind the reformatory movement were made explicit in a statement of principles and enthusiastically adopted as a basis for prison reform. Most notably, it was declared that

Reformation, not suffering, should be the purpose of penal treatment of prisoners

Classification of prisoners should be patterned after the mark system then being used in Ireland

Rewards should be provided for good conduct

The prisoner should be made to realize that his destiny is in his hands

Indeterminate sentences should be substituted for fixed sentences

The aim of the prison should be to make industrious free men rather than orderly and obedient prisoners

Full provisions should be made for industrial training

Society at large should be made to realize its responsibility for conditions that lead to crime[36]

These ideas were mainly applied to young first offenders, particularly at the Elmira Reformatory in New York; and for a number of years the glowing reports of reformatory superintendents and observers filled the penal journals of the time.[37] Within a few decades, however, it began to

[35] As indicated earlier, the mark system installed by Maconochie was an important precursor. The work of Montesinos in Spain, Obermaier in Bavaria, and Crofton in Ireland were also significant influences on prison reformers in America. See Wines, *Punishment and Reformation*, Chapter X. See also Barnes and Teeters, *New Horizons in Criminology*, Chapter XXV.

[36] See Arthur Evans Wood and John Barker Waite, *Crime and Its Treatment* (New York: American Book Company, 1941), pp. 532–33.

[37] Barnes and Teeters, *New Horizons in Criminology*, p. 526.

be apparent that the reformatory movement was no more the answer to crime than the forms of punishment that had preceded it. The idea of the reformatory, greeted with prayers and song at the 1870 meeting of the American Prison Congress, was on the decline by 1910 in what seemed to be the inevitable cycle of penal innovation: an initial period of enthusiasm and high hopes for new methods, a brief time of attempted implementation, and then an aftermath of disillusionment and a sense of futility.

The reformatory movement failed, it has been claimed, not because its ideas were mistaken but because they were never really put into practice. Large inmate populations, an excessive concern with custody, a lack of well-designed vocational and educational programs with adequate resources, the difficulty of maintaining discipline and control within the insitutions—these conditions made it impossible to translate the ideals of the reformatory into reality. The statement of principles of the American Prison Congress was untested rather than proven wrong.[38] There is much truth in this argument, although it has been pointed out that when the idea of the reformatory has received something like a fair testing—as in the Borstal system in England—the results do not bear out the claims of the reformatory movement.[39] Nonetheless, reformatories continue to be built, and frequently there is an attempt to make them look more like a private school than a prison. But the sense of a correctional crusade that attended their introduction has long since vanished.

From Elmira to Attica A prison can be called a penitentiary or a reformatory—or, as it is commonly referred to today, a correctional facility[40]—but it remains a place of punishment, a place where people are kept confined under conditions of acute deprivation for long periods of time.[41] Whatever might have been the hopes for reforming criminals in such institutions, it was recognized at an early date that prisons could also breed crime by building resentment that would later find expression in further lawlessness or by schooling the inmate in criminal attitudes and techniques. With the declining faith in the rehabilitative function of the prison, the problem of avoiding the crime-generating aspects of prison life took precedence. If the prisoner could not be made better, at least he should not be made worse. Many of the changes introduced into prisons from World War I to the present time, despite the rhetoric of rehabilitation, can be seen as attempts to mitigate the corrosive abnormalities of custodial institutions.

[38] Ibid., pp. 529–39.

[39] See Alan Little, "Penal Theory, Penal Reform, and Borstal Practice," *British Journal of Criminology* 3 (January 1963), pp. 257–72.

[40] See President's Commission on Law Enforcement and Administration of Justice, *Task Force Report: Corrections* (Washington, D.C.: Government Printing Office, 1967), Chapter 9.

[41] An analysis of custodial institutions will be presented in Chapter 13.

Between the 1930s and the 1960s, state prison systems were divided into institutions providing varying degrees of custodial security for different types of inmates. Diagnostic centers for classifying inmates made their appearance. Educational and vocational programs were offered in many custodial institutions, although they were generally of poor quality and lacking in resources. Medical services were improved, and, for a brief time, great interest was shown in the possibility of permitting some degree of inmate self-government. The brutality that had so long characterized the treatment of prisoners, even in the reformatories, began to decline. Visiting privileges and recreational facilities were extended, and hobby work was frequently encouraged. These changes were viewed as an attempt to reduce the punishing features of prison life by making the prison bear a closer resemblance to the free community outside the walls. If their impact on the prisoner's criminal proclivities was doubtful, they at least made life within the prison tolerable.

Not all thought of reformation was abandoned. In small experimental institutions for juvenile delinquents, staff members sometimes felt that they had found an effective way of dealing with the offender, even if their methods did involve a high ratio of staff to inmates.[42] Various forms of psychotherapy were introduced into a number of institutions by psychologists and psychiatrists who were convinced that emotional problems lay at the heart of criminal behavior.[43] In general, though, the ideal of reforming criminal offenders within the custodial setting became a goal discussed in the annual reports of state correctional systems, in the studies of presidential commissions, or in public speeches, rather than the working philosophy of prison administrators. If the zeal for using the prison as an instrument of reformation was rekindled, it was apt to be an individual enthusiasm and not a coherent program guiding the correctional system as a whole. The hope of reforming the criminal had, in fact, largely shifted to another area.

The idea of *parole*, or releasing prisoners when they were ready to return to the community instead of holding them for a fixed period of time, had received official recognition in the reformatory movement. The idea of *probation*, or suspending an offender's sentence contingent on his behavior in the community, was also of long standing.[44] It was not until

---

[42] See, for example, Lloyd W. McCorkle, Albert Elias, and F. Lovell Bixby, *The Highfields Story: An Experimental Treatment Project for Youthful Offenders* (New York: Henry Holt, 1958).

[43] By the middle of the 1960s, however, there were still only some seven hundred psychologists and psychiatrists treating the more than one million prisoners confined in custodial institutions in the United States. See *Task Force Report: Corrections,* Chapter Ten.

[44] The beginnings of probation are usually traced to Boston, where John Augustus, a shoemaker, bailed out minor offenders on a volunteer basis in the early part of the nineteenth century. See Charles Lionel Chute and Marjorie Bell, *Crime, Courts and Probation* (New York: Macmillan, 1956), Chapter 2.

the twentieth century, however, that these methods of handling the convicted criminal came into widespread use. More and more states gradually adopted both probation and parole as major elements in their correctional systems; and by the 1960s, two thirds of all convicted offenders in the United States were not kept in institutions but were, instead, supervised in the community. Social reactions to the criminal had been transformed, not with the sudden and dramatic introduction of a new method of punishment or treatment, but in a slow process of social change.[45]

"Treatment in the community" became an attractive alternative to imprisonment for a number of reasons. First, the cost of supervising an offender on probation or parole is far less than the cost of keeping him confined in an institution. Second, the nation's constantly growing population and rising crime rates threatened to overwhelm existing custodial institutions or else to require an extensive program of new construction. Third, the labor unions were becoming increasingly influential and opposed the use of prison labor, without which the prison was an even more costly enterprise. Finally, a growing portion of the public was disillusioned with the prisons' failure to reduce crime.

More and more people had come to believe that to lock up an individual for his crimes was as foolish as locking up a knife because it had cut its owner. The real task was to rebuild the individual's social relationships or to modify the community in which he was to live. The premise underlying treatment in the community, said the President's Commission on Law Enforcement and Administration of Justice in 1967, summing up the developing theory and practice of more than half a century, was that crime and delinquency are symptoms of failures and disorganization of the community as well as the criminal:

> In particular, these failures are seen as depriving offenders of contact with the institutions that are basically responsible for assuring development of law-abiding contact: sound family life, good schools, employment, recreational opportunities, and desirable companions, to name only some of the more direct influences. The substitution of deleterious habits, standards, and associates for these strengthening influences contributes to crime and delinquency.
>
> The task of corrections therefore includes building or rebuilding solid ties between offender and community, integrating or reintegrating the offender into community life—restoring family ties, obtaining employment and education, securing in the larger sense a place for the offender in the routine functioning of society. This requires not only efforts directed toward changing the individual offender, which has

[45] An analysis of parole and probation will be presented in Chapter 14.

The Crime of Imprisonment

Imprisonment as it exists today is a worse crime than any of those committed by its victims; for no single criminal can be as powerful for evil, or as unrestrained in its exercise, as an organized nation. Therefore, if any person is addressing himself to the perusal of this dreadful subject in the spirit of a philanthropist bent on reforming a necessary and beneficent public institution, I beg him to put it down and go about some other business. It is just such reformers who have in the past made the neglect, oppression, corruption, and physical torture of the old common gaol the pretext for transforming it into that diabolical den of torment, mischief, and damnation, the modern model prison.

From George Bernard Shaw, *The Crime of Imprisonment* (New York: Philosophical Library, 1946), p. 13. Reprinted with permission.

been the almost exclusive focus of rehabilitation, but also mobilization and change of the community and its institutions.[46]

Unfortunately, in a pattern not unlike the history of the reformatory movement, many critics argued that the idea of treatment in the community was seriously flawed even as it received the full stamp of official support. Very little was actually known about what should be done in the name of social reintegration, it was said, and much of the talk of rehabilitation, reformation, and the like on the part of social workers was nothing more than an "apostolic laying on of words," rather than part of a proven program of treatment.[47] The supporters of social reintegration hastened to point out—as had the supporters of the reformatory movement before them—that the idea of probation and parole had never received a fair trial. All too often treatment in the community meant little more than dumping convicted offenders into the streets, where—aside from a fifteen-minute conference with their supervisor once a month—they were left to sink or swim largely on their own. And it was true that despite the prolonged discussions in the professional journals about what probation and parole should be, the realities of the two methods often meant that caseworkers were overburdened and overwhelmed by their task.[48]

Nevertheless, the enthusiasm for treatment in the community began to show a marked decline in the latter part of the 1960s, in part because—once again—American society was extremely reluctant to supply the necessary funding. Research reports showing the minimal impact of treatment efforts began to appear, and the optimistic faith in imminent change in community institutions and underlying problems, such as poverty and racism, began to fade. Then, in 1971, the uprising at Attica Prison in New York State and its tragic aftermath served to bring the problems of penology directly into the public view and acted as a symbol for the end of an era in correctional philosophy. Inmates seized forty-three correctional employees as hostages and took command of a large section of the institution. Ten of the hostages and thirty-two of the inmates were shot to death by state troopers, guards, and local police officers when they stormed the prison and regained control.

The riot at Attica will surely be debated for years to come.[49] The Attica

[46] Task Force Report: Corrections, p. 7.

[47] See D. J. Hager, "Some Observations on the Relationships Between Social Science and Intergroup Education," The Journal of Educational Sociology 23 (January 1950), p. 279.

[48] Professional standards of casework are said to require a caseload of no more than fifty offenders. Less than 5 percent of all parolees are part of such a caseload, and the percentage is even smaller for those on probation. See Task Force Report: Corrections, p. 196. There is no conclusive evidence, it should be pointed out, that a caseload of fifty offenders is in fact the most effective.

[49] See, for example, Roger Starr, "Prisons, Politics, and the Attica Report," Commentary (March 1973); Tom Wicker, A Time to Die (New York: Quadrangle/The New York Times

Special Citizens' Commission, under the direction of Dean Robert McKay of the New York University Law School, made clear, however, that the idea that prisons could be turned into humane institutions or tolerable places to live in was simply not true, given the attitudes underlying penal administration in the United States today and the available resources.[50] As the accusations and counteraccusations of brutality and political maneuvering broke out into public debate in the wake of the Attica riot, disillusionment with correctional philosophy in the United States became commonplace. Penology, it was asserted, was intellectually bankrupt.[51]

Many people felt that such a condemnation of corrections was premature, that the erratic swings in public opinion were being fed by social commentators who had grown accustomed to disillusionment with American institutions and were quick to spot a crisis of confidence or intellectual bankruptcy in each day's headlines. Some years before, George Vold had sagely commented on the difficulty of judging the effectiveness of various methods of handling the convicted offender. We might emphasize the offenders who are salvaged and call the prison a success, he pointed out, since it is apt to be the most hardened criminals who are confined. If an individual does not commit a crime after being punished, has he reformed because of punishment or in spite of it? If an individual commits a crime after being treated, has treatment exercised a harmful influence or no influence at all? Is it possible that methods of handling the offender do reform, only to have that achievement undone by other forces, such as the nature of the community to which the criminal returns? Until we can answer these questions—a difficult task, at best, as we shall see when we examine punishment as rehabilitation—the evaluation of attempts at rehabilitation in the prison must remain uncertain.[52] Still, there seems little doubt that by the beginning of the 1970s the rehabilitative ideal that had so long dominated criminological thought was in serious trouble.

It is clear that America is in a time of profound questioning about what should be done with the convicted criminal. Elements of older

Book Company, 1975); and Norval Morris and Gordon M. Hawkins, "Attica Revisited: The Prospect for Prison Reform," *Arizona Law Review* 14 (1973), pp. 747–63.

[50] See *Attica: The Official Report of the New York State Special Commission on Attica* (New York: Bantam Books, 1972).

[51] See, for example, Big Change in Prisons: Punish—Not Reform," in *U.S. News & World Report* (August 25, 1975); Jessica Mitford, "Prisons: The Menace of Liberal Reform," *New York Review of Books* (March 9, 1972); Selwyn Raab, "City Prison Reform Plan Called Failure," *The New York Times* (August 10, 1975); *Struggle for Justice*. A Report on Crime and Punishment in America Prepared for the American Friends Service Committee (New York: Hill & Wang, 1971); Erik Olin Wright, *The Politics of Punishment* (New York: Harper & Row, 1973).

[52] See George B. Vold, "Does the Prison Reform?" *The Annals of the American Academy of Political and Social Science* 293 (May 1954), pp. 42–50.

When one examines the punishments inflicted on wrongdoers in different societies in different historical periods, one is struck by the brutality and cruelty so commonly exhibited.

The boot, a medieval instrument of torture.

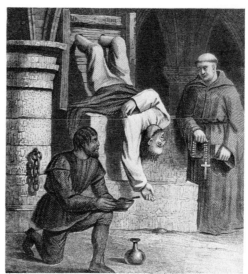

The stocks, fifteenth-century Europe.

The punishment for parricide in ancient China.

A tribunal of the Inquisition.

The Iron Maiden of Nuremberg.

The modern gas chamber.

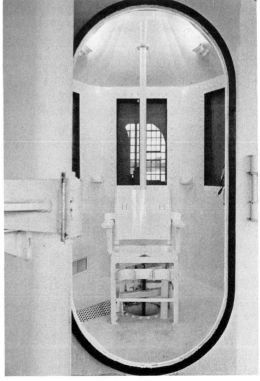

ideas persist and are haphazardly linked to newer orientations in a penal policy that satisfies few. Some offenders are exposed to group therapy sessions in fortress-like prisons, with unknown results. Other offenders are simply kept in custodial institutions with nothing to do— "warehoused," as the term has it—until the law requires that they be released. Some are in halfway houses that serve as a sort of decompression chamber between imprisonment and freedom. Still others are under the supervision of probation and parole officers guided by varying correctional philosophies and with disparate resources at their disposal. And, as we shall see in Chapter 14, some are now subjects in experimental programs that attempt to modify behavior by the use of the principles of operant conditioning, chemical "therapy," or enforced psychiatric counseling in institutions in which inmates are confined not under criminal law but under the authority of a civil commitment declaring them to be "defective delinquents."[53] If such variation were the result of a carefully wrought policy that maintained strict attention to the individual's needs and legal rights, present misgivings might be unwarranted. But it is not. The "correctional system" in the United States is a jerry-built structure hammered together out of the scraps of yesterday's enthusiasms, undergirded by premises of dubious scientific validity, and too often oblivious of the legal rights of the criminal, whose conviction is viewed as placing him beyond the protection of the law. The question that now confronts society is what to do next.

The Rationales of Punishment

In the decades after World War I, American criminology was apt to dismiss the punishment of criminals as a senseless relic of primitive societies. "The old argument was that punishment was necessary as a 'just retribution' or requital of wickedness," said Sheldon Glueck in 1928. "No thoughtful person today seriously holds this theory of sublimated social vengeance. . . . Official social institutions should not be predicated upon the destructive emotion of vengeance, which is not only the expression of an infantile way of solving a problem, but unjust and destructive of the purpose of protecting society."[54] In an analysis of eleven well-known criminology textbooks published between 1941 and 1960, Jackson Toby found that most writers took the position that punishment had no place in an enlightened penology; nonpunitive and individualized methods of treatment, such as probation, parole, and psychotherapy, would surely emerge as the humanitarian and rational

[53] See Phil Stanford, "A Model, Clockwork-Orange Prison," *The New York Times* (September 17, 1972).

[54] Sheldon Glueck, "Principles of a Rational Penal Code," *Harvard Law Review* 41 (February, 1928), pp. 453–82.

means of dealing with the offender.[55] After World War II, however, a small group of scholars began to reexamine the place of punishment in the administration of the criminal law.[56] As the belief in rehabilitation started to falter in the late 1960s and early 1970s, as the claims of curing criminals failed to materialize and people increasingly questioned psychiatric explanations of crime, the number of criminologists coming to believe that the matter of punishment might not be as simple as had previously been supposed began to grow.[57]

Of all the justifications for punishment, the idea that the commission of a crime throws the moral world out of a balance that is then restored by punishing the wrongdoer is perhaps one of the oldest.[58] Since the concept of a just and moral world, according to this argument, is one in which good behavior is rewarded and bad behavior penalized, we have a moral duty to punish the individual who violates the basic moral precepts embodied in the criminal law. The essence of punishment is the concept of the individual receiving his just deserts. "Against the doubt as to whether the state has any right to punish at all," said the legal philosopher Morris Cohen, "this theory maintains it to be a positive moral duty. It regards crime as a violation or disturbance of the divine or moral order. When Cain kills Abel, the very earth cries for vengeance. The moral order can then be restored, or the violation atoned for, only by inflicting evil (generally pain) upon the one guilty."[59]

Punishment as Retribution

[55] Jackson Toby, "Is Punishment Necessary?" *Journal of Criminal Law, Criminology, and Police Science* 55 (September 1964), pp. 332–37.

[56] See Norval Morris, "The Future of Imprisonment: Toward a Punitive Philosophy," *Michigan Law Review* 72 (May 1972), pp. 1161–80. Accusations of war crimes and the moral issues raised by the punishment of war criminals may well have been important causal factors.

[57] In 1974 Norval Morris—a highly respected writer in the field of criminology—was willing to argue in his analysis of needed prison reform that "penal purposes are properly retributive, deterrent, and incapacitative. Attempts to add reformative purposes to that mixture—as an objective of the sanction as distinguished from a collateral aspiration—yield neither clemency, justice, nor, as presently administered, social utility" ("The Future of Imprisonment," p. 1161). Ten or fifteen years earlier, many criminologists would undoubtedly have found this statement a reactionary cry for vengeance; today, many find it a reasonable position worthy of close attention. See also, Milton Goldinger, ed., *Punishment and Human Rights* (Cambridge, Mass: Schenkman, 1974); Ernest van den Haag, *Punishing Criminals: Concerning a Very Old and Painful Question* (New York: Basic Books, 1975).

[58] See, for example, Stanley E. Grupp, ed., *Theories of Punishment* (Bloomington: Indiana University Press, 1971); Ted Honderich, *Punishment: The Supposed Justifications* (London: Hutchinson, 1969); Edmund L. Pincoffs, *The Rationale of Legal Punishment* (New York: Humanities Press, 1966); Johannes Andenaes, *Punishment and Deterrence* (Ann Arbor: University of Michigan Press, 1974); H. L. A. Hart, *Punishment and Responsibility* (Oxford, England: Clarendon Press, 1968); Frank E. Zimring, *Perspectives on Deterrence* (Rockville, Md.: National Institute of Mental Health, Center for Studies of Crime and Delinquency, 1971); and Gertrude Ezorsky, ed., *Philosophical Perspectives on Punishment* (Albany: State University of New York Press, 1975).

[59] Morris R. Cohen, "Moral Aspects of the Criminal Law," *The Yale Law Journal* 49 (April 1940), pp. 1009–26.

From a sociological viewpoint, this theory of punishment is of great importance in two respects. First, the concept of retribution would appear to be a powerful influence in the public consciousness, helping to shape public reactions to the sanctions imposed by the legal system. Second, and no less important, the concept of "just deserts" has served as an important check on the power of the state to use unlimited punishments for the purpose of deterring the potential wrongdoer or to force therapy on those it pleases without regard to the illegality of their past behavior. Punishment, that is, must match the wrongdoing; it can only be inflicted on the individual who has broken the law, and the state is to be restrained from using any coercion it likes to insure conformity.

Without the concept of just retribution, C. S. Lewis has argued, society could punish the wife and children of the wrongdoer rather than the wrongdoer himself, since this might be even more effective as a deterrent. Moreover, the state could incarcerate those who are simply deemed dangerous, ignoring any actual violation of the law.[60] That American society is unwilling to engage in these practices must be attributed in part to the continuing influence of the *lex talionis* on society's concept of what is fair.

Punishment as Sublimated Vengeance

A second viewpoint holds that punishment inflicted by the state is a collective expression of the private desire for revenge. It is not a sense of moral duty or a sense of a moral world out of balance that drives people to inflict pain on the wrongdoer, it is said, but a wish for vengeance that has managed to garb itself in the robes of justice. The suffering of the criminal is a source of psychological satisfaction to those whom he has injured. The state is justified in acting as the agent of punishment because, it is argued, private individuals would otherwise seek vengeance on their own and society would be plunged into disorder.

In this argument, the individual's desire for vengeance when confronted with wrongdoing is often simply taken for granted, and variations in the readiness of society to inflict punishment are likely to be ignored. As Svend Ranulf has indicated in his classic monograph, however, the disposition to inflict punishment varies from one society to another depending on the social structure. He argues that the desire to see punishment imposed is especially strong in the social class that is usually known as the petite bourgeoisie, or lower middle class; and in societies where such a class is not a significant element, the disposition to inflict punishment will be practically nonexistent.[61] The bourgeois

---

[60] See C. S. Lewis, "The Humanitarian Theory of Punishment," *20th Century* 3 (Autumn 1948–1949), pp. 5–12.

[61] Svend Ranulf, *Moral Indignation and Middle Class Psychology* (Copenhagen: Levin & Munksgaard, 1938), p. 2.

psychology, he claims, is based on industriousness, orderliness, thrift, discipline, and sexual restraint—that is, a forced suppression of instinctive urges.[62] The criminal who breaks free of these controls is regarded with an envious resentment that finds expression in demands for the punishment of the wrongdoer, using the state as an instrument.

Jackson Toby, examining a similar strand of thought in the writings of Emile Durkheim, pointed out that "one who resists the temptation to do what the group prohibits, to drive his car at 80 miles per hour, to beat up an enemy, to take what he wants without paying for it, would like to feel that these self-imposed abnegations have some meaning. . . . The social significance of punishing offenders is that deviance is thereby defined as unsuccessful in the eyes of conformists, thus making the inhibition or repression of their own deviant impulses seem worthwhile."[63]

Testing this theory, however, poses great difficulties; and Ranulf's examination of a number of societies, including Nazi Germany and Puritan England, is inconclusive, because data linking the repression of impulses, resentment, and the inclination of the state to impose punishment are lacking. Nonetheless, social demands for punishment do vary, and these demands are frequently tinged with a certain envy of the criminal, who has managed to break through society's barriers. But if Ranulf's analysis helps to throw some light on where the desire for vengeance comes from, it still leaves unanswered the crucial question of whether punishment by the state is necessary to head off angry citizens bent on revenge.

If the state did not impose its penalties, some people probably would resort to private acts of revenge. But in many instances people might do nothing, particularly if a pattern of revenge were not institutionalized, the situation was one in which passions had cooled, and exacting revenge carried danger. Most important, however, there is no iron necessity for the state to choose between inflicting punishment and doing nothing. Other courses of action are possible, such as restitution by the state, or subjecting the offender to treatment. The state does not have to give the public what it wants—even in a democratic society—and is quite capable of suppressing disorders that may arise when the public finds its desires frustrated. The justification of punishment that rests its case on the necessity of state-inflicted sanctions in order to avoid public disorder appears to be weak, although a good deal of work remains to be done on the question of precisely what the public expects to be done to those who have broken the criminal law and what the public reactions are when these expectations do not materialize. (There is reason to believe, for example, that the public often wishes to see a sentence imposed

[62] Ibid., p. 43.
[63] "Is Punishment Necessary?" p. 334.

but quickly loses interest about whether the sentence is actually carried out.)

Punishment as Special Deterrence

The idea that punishing the individual who has broken the law in the past will deter that individual from breaking the law in the future is probably almost as old as the idea of punishment as retribution. In the first half of the present century, talk of deterrence became unfashionable among those who were convinced that probation, parole, psychotherapy, and the like were the only proper methods of dealing with the criminal. But the belief that the criminal who experiences punishment will be less likely to commit further crimes has continued to provide one of the major justifications for state-inflicted sanctions, both among those who administer the law and among a good part of the general public. Punishment, from this point of view, is a utilitarian matter aimed at reducing crime rather than demanding atonement, and is to be evaluated by how well it succeeds—although it is by no means free of the restrictions imposed by the concept of *just* punishment.

The disparagement of punishment's capacity to deter has been based in no small measure upon the decline of the concept of man as a rational creature carefully planning his future course of action, with self-interest as his goal. It is not true, however, argues Ernest van den Haag, that punishment can deter only if man consciously weighs future pains and benefits and deliberately chooses the happier path. "The mere risk of injury often restrains us from doing what is otherwise attractive," he says. "We refrain even when we have no direct experience, and usually without explicit computation of probabilities, let alone conscious weighing of expected pleasure against possible pain. One abstains from dangerous acts because of vague, inchoate, habitual, and above all, preconscious fears."[64] The threat of man-made injury in the form of punishment functions in much the same way as the threat of natural injury, he maintains, and the collapse of the rationalistic psychology of the eighteenth and nineteenth centuries should not lead us to suppose that state-inflicted penalties cannot play a significant role in the control of criminal behavior.

There is some question whether the threat of punishment by the state can be equated with the threat of "natural" injuries about which van den Haag speaks—just as the deterrent effect of punishment in training animals or in experimental psychology offers a hazardous basis for generalization concerning the deterrent effect of state-imposed sanctions.[65] In any event, many criminologists felt that no matter what the role of "pre-

[64] Ernest van den Haag, "On Deterrence and the Death Penalty," *Journal of Criminal Law, Criminology, and Police Science* 60 (June 1969), pp. 141–47.
[65] See Andenaes, *Punishment and Deterrence* Appendix 3.

conscious" fears might be, the fact that man is not a hedonistic calculator cast serious doubt on theories about the deterrent effect of punishment so carefully charted in classical criminology. And the empirical data, it was argued, gave little support to the idea that the threat of suffering made the individual pause and decide to stay within the law.

Pickpockets, busily at work amid the crowds attending the execution of a pickpocket at Tyburn, where open galleries for the public surrounded the gibbet, showed how small was the effect of punishment, said the critics of deterrence.[66] And if that illustration appeared somewhat fragmentary and out of date, more systematic and more recent data could be marshalled to show that the death penalty was far less of a deterrent than it was claimed to be. When states of roughly the same socioeconomic characteristics were compared, some of which had abolished the death penalty while others had retained it, their murder rates were found to differ hardly at all.[67] If the execution of criminals had no discernible impact on the murder rate, it was argued, the justification for such punishment on the grounds of deterrence was simply a smokescreen for sadism.

Similar arguments were commonly presented concerning the alleged failure of imprisonment. Police chiefs, judges, wardens, professors of criminology—all, noted Daniel Glaser, were frequently to be found claiming that 60 to 70 percent of those who have been imprisoned commit new crimes after their release.[68] Again, said the critics of deterrence, it was clear that state-inflicted penalties were of little use in controlling crime. Punishment, in reality, was no more than vengeance.

After World War II, as we have seen, a number of scholars began to express reservations about this blanket rejection of deterrence. "The prevalent academic attitude—it is hardly more—is that punishment is a useless relic of barbarism, a mere symbol of man's lust for vengeance, hence lacking in any rational support," said Jerome Hall. "The plain fact is that no such conclusion is established; the vehemence of the assertion is accompanied by fast and loose play with history and statistics."[69] The

[66] See Hibbert, *The Roots of Evil*, Chapter Three.

[67] See Karl F. Schuessler, "The Deterrent Influence of the Death Penalty," *The Annals of the American Academy of Political and Social Science* 284 (November 1952), pp. 54–62. The debate concerning the use of capital punishment has been one of the most heated in the field of criminology, and the literature is extensive. For excellent reviews of the topic, see Hugo Adam Bedau, ed., *The Death Penalty in America* (Garden City, N.Y.: Doubleday, 1968); Thorsten Sellin, *Capital Punishment* (New York: Harper & Row, 1967); and Arthur Koestler and C. H. Rolf, *Hanged by the Neck: An Exposure of Capital Punishment in England* (Baltimore: Penguin Books, 1961).

[68] Daniel Glaser, *The Effectiveness of a Prison and Parole System* (Indianapolis: Bobbs-Merrill, 1964), Chapter 2.

[69] Jerome Hall, "Criminology," in G. Gurvitch and W. E. Moore, eds., *Twentieth Century Sociology* (New York: Philosophical Library, 1945), p. 363.

claim that the absence or presence of the death penalty had little effect on the murder rate could well be true, but to generalize from that fact to the conclusion that all punishments were useless for controlling any type of crime was simply unwarranted.[70] The often-quoted figure of 60 or 70 percent of imprisoned criminals committing new crimes after release was probably a myth, said Glaser. It was based, he suspected, on the prior prison records of inmates confined in a small number of penitentiaries. Since offenders with prior imprisonment generally get longer sentences and are less likely to be paroled than criminals going to prison for the first time, recidivists are apt to accumulate in prison and become higher as a percentage of men *in* prison at any given time than as a percentage of offenders *received or released* by the prison in a given period.[71] Those studies that followed a cohort of offenders through prison and their subsequent careers are admittedly few in number and based on limited samples, Glaser argued, but they suggested that the proportion of ex-convicts that managed to stay free of crime might well be in the neighborhood of two thirds.[72]

In recent years, an increasing number of criminologists have come around to the position that the deterrent effect of punishment on the criminal is not nonexistent—rather, it is unknown. The assertion that state-inflicted penalties must be abandoned and the control of crimes must be sought in the reformation of the criminal's character because science has shown this to be the only effective course is now viewed as claiming more than has yet been established by the facts.

A large part of the difficulty in determining the deterrent effect of punishment is that society is understandably reluctant to experiment in this area. Finding out the exact effects of different kinds of penalties on different types of criminals for different types of crimes would require the rigorous controls of well-designed scientific research. Thus, for example, as Franklin Zimring has pointed out, it might be shown that criminals who are punished are more likely to commit crimes in the future than noncriminals or criminals who have somehow managed to avoid state-inflicted sanctions. This might be true because offenders who are punished have a marked proclivity for crime, or because being punished increases criminal tendencies, or because of some mixture of the

[70] See William J. Chambliss, "The Deterrent Influence of Punishment," *Crime and Delinquency* 12 (January 1966), pp. 70–75. "As important as these studies are in indicating that the death penalty is ineffective as a deterrent to murder," says the author, "their very broad interpretation has rendered a disservice to the more general issue of punishment as a deterrent to all kinds of criminal behavior. Such an expansive conclusion is obviously not justified since murder is, in many ways, a unique kind of offense often involving very strong emotions."

[71] Glaser, *The Effectiveness of a Prison and Parole System*, p. 14.

[72] Ibid., pp. 15–35.

two.[73] Before we can untangle these possibilities, however, we need to conduct either contrived or so-called natural experiments. The first are precluded by a value system (embodied in part in law) that prohibits treating human beings as guinea pigs; the latter are made difficult in the extreme by the fact that much criminal behavior is apt to be kept hidden. The result is that our knowledge of the deterrent effect of punishment remains fragmentary at best—and we continue to punish on the basis of hunch, common sense, and tradition.

Even when the illegal behavior is visible and reported rates of law-breaking can be taken as representative of actual crime rates, the interpretation of data is no easy matter. If, for example, a sudden rise in the rate of illegal behavior—such as speeding—leads to a program of rigorous enforcement of the laws and sharply increased penalties, which is then followed by a dramatic fall in the rate, it might be concluded that the new program of law enforcement has shown a clear-cut salutary effect. In fact, no such conclusion is warranted, because random variation over a period of time could be expected to show a large deviation of a rate from the mean to be followed by a rate closer to the average due to chance alone.[74]

The attempts to measure the deterrent effects of punishment, then, are beset by complex problems, and criminologists—if they are wise—must be cautious in their judgments. Classical criminology's view of man as a cool calculator may be in error; but so, too, quite possibly, is the view that sees the human actor plunging ahead on the course of his desire quite indifferent to the cost.

In much of the previous discussion, we have looked at the deterrent effect of punishment on the wrongdoer. But this is only half the story. What of the person who has never violated the law and who contemplates the dreadful prospect of state-inflicted sanctions? According to many criminologists and legal scholars, this is what deterrence is all about. We punish Peter, it is said, not because we believe that we can change the probable future course of Peter's conduct (he is by nature a knave), but because we think that by doing so we can keep Paul honest (he has always been so).[75]

This is the concept of general as opposed to special deterrence—the idea that punishment by the state is directed primarily not to the individual who has broken the law but to the great mass of law-abiding citi-

Punishment as General Deterrence

[73] Zimring, *Perspectives on Deterrence*, pp. 97–99.
[74] See H. Laurence Ross, "Determining the Social Effects of Legal Reform," *American Behavioral Scientist* (March/April 1970), pp. 493–509. See also Donald T. Campbell, "Reforms as Experiments," *American Psychologist* 24 (April 1969), pp. 409–24.
[75] Cohen, "Moral Aspects of the Criminal Law."

zens who totter on the edge. According to some writers, the general deterrent effect of punishment is by far the most important, and the impact of punishment on the convicted criminal—whether it increases his criminal tendencies or makes him more obedient to the law—is of minor significance. The social order is maintained by the regular punishment of the wrongdoer, reminding the law-abiding that the violation of the law carries its certain penalty.

Those who argue for the efficacy of punishment as a special deterrent must take two possibilities into account: first, that the experience of punishment may breed resentment, making future crime more likely; and second, that the threat of punishment may be far less potent to one who has already been publicly stigmatized. But aside from these considerations, the justifications of punishment as a means of deterring the convicted criminal or the law-abiding citizen are much the same: public order is maintained by appealing to the person's self-interest. If the penalty for crime outweighs its possible benefits, the individual contemplating a criminal act will hesitate and reconsider. Criminology, unfortunately, cannot yet demonstrate clearly how and when this process works. The present small boom in the study of deterrence nonetheless represents an important step forward, argues Franklin Zimring, and the role of deterrence in controlling crime will probably receive greater attention in the future.[76]

Punishment as Incapacitation Whatever the results of punishment may be in terms of exacting vengeance or deterring the criminal, one thing at least seems clear. While undergoing punishment in the form of imprisonment, the criminal is prevented from committing crimes against members of the free community. The incapacitating function provides a major justification for punishment, according to some criminologists; and talk of reformation, deterrence, and retribution is futile or misleading. By locking up persons who are known to be criminals and who are likely to commit crimes in the free community, we prevent crime.

There is a great difference, however, between punishing the individual for a crime he has committed in the past and punishing him for a crime he *may* commit in the future. In both cases, punishment or imprisonment may be restricted to those who are guilty of a crime. The reduction of criminal behavior may, in both cases, be the final aim of state-inflicted sanctions, and the criminal may indeed be unable to commit crimes against members of the outside community while in prison. But when incapacitation is taken as the proper way to curb crime, the length of the prison sentence is based on a guess about events that have

[76] Zimring, *Perspectives on Deterrence*, pp. vii–viii.

not yet occurred rather than on an act of behavior that has already taken place. Imprisoning people for crimes they have committed has long been accepted as part of the Anglo-American legal tradition; imprisoning people for crimes they might commit is a matter of vigorous dispute.

Nevertheless, at numerous points in the legal system of the United States today the terms of the individual's punishment are determined on the basis of what it is thought the individual will do in the future rather than on demonstrated wrongdoing in the past. At the plea-bargaining stage, the prosecutor's decision to reduce the charges frequently depends in part on his judgment of the defendant's future criminality. The granting of probation or parole is based partially on an estimate of what the convicted offender will do when he is at large in the community. Criminal statutes are often explicitly constructed around the idea that the recidivist is more likely to commit a new crime than the first offender and should therefore receive a longer sentence. The exercise of judicial discretion in sentencing is frequently based not simply on the enormity of the offense but on the judge's opinion of the offender's dangerousness. Thus, for example, when an individual has been convicted of several offenses simultaneously, the judge has the option of imposing sentences that run concurrently or consecutively. If he thinks the offender is likely to get into trouble, the judge is apt to choose the latter course. The Model Penal Code of the American Law Institute, presented to the states as a rational, coherent statement of the criminal law and its objectives, urges that dangerousness determine the sentencing of convicted criminals. The code's provisions for long prison terms for persistent, professional, psychologically disturbed, and dangerous or multiple offenders has profoundly influenced the criminal law in a number of states.[77]

If the concept of incapacitation, then, is frequently used in the punishment of criminals, the question arises whether future criminality can in fact be accurately predicted. "There is a seductive appeal to separating the dangerous and the nondangerous offenders and confining imprisonment principally to the former," notes Norval Morris. "It would be such a neat trick if it were possible; prophylactic punishment—the preemptive judicial strike, scientifically justified—designed to save potential victims of future crimes and at the same time minimize the use of imprisonment and reduce the time served by most prisoners."[78] Unfortunately, he concludes, future criminality cannot be predicted with any precision, even with the use of the most sophisticated clinical techniques.

As evidence, he cites the results of a ten-year study designed to measure the ability of a team of social scientists to identify dangerous of-

[77] See Morris, "The Future of Imprisonment," pp. 1165–66.
[78] Ibid., p. 1165.

fenders, based on clinical examinations, psychological tests, and a careful reconstruction of the individual's life history, using material drawn from the offender, his family, friends, neighbors, teachers, employers, and official records.[79] The team of social scientists was indeed able to pick two groups of prison inmates, one of which exhibited a higher rate of violent crime after release than did the other. As the directors of the project indicated, however, many of the prison inmates identified as dangerous did *not* engage in violent crime once they had gained their freedom, just as a number of those identified as "safe" turned out to be dangerous. And if all the inmates identified as dangerous had been kept confined, two men would have been kept wrongly in prison for every one correctly detained. This is one of the costs of keeping criminals confined on the basis of an estimate of what they might do, and many persons consider the cost too high. Other studies have shown that accurately predicting behavior after release is difficult and that offenders are likely to be kept imprisoned in the mistaken belief that they will surely break the law if they are freed.[80]

The idea, therefore, that dangerousness can be determined in advance—an idea that is fundamental to the justification of punishment as a method of incapacitation—is open to serious doubt. When the predictions are in error, it means that either a person is kept in prison who should be free or one is set free who should be confined. Both types of error are, of course, undesirable, but it is errors of the first type—so offensive to the law's concept of justice—that are more likely to occur. Officials charged with the task of setting the terms of punishment understandably take the cautious view that if there is a chance a convicted criminal will commit another crime, it is best that he or she be kept locked up as long as the law allows. As a consequence, many criminals become "false positives"—that is, individuals identified as dangerous who in fact will not commit another crime and are thus denied probation or parole or given a lengthy sentence without adequate reason.

There are some people who argue that such mistakes are warranted in light of the need to protect the public. Persons denied probation or parole or kept too long in prison have, after all, been convicted of a crime. They may be detained unnecessarily at times, but there is no way of knowing that in advance. If the free community is reluctant to confine a person wrongly, it is also under no obligation to risk the life and property of the law-abiding. Just as the criminal can be imprisoned to deter others, punishing the criminal not to deter or reform him but for the effect on the general public, so too can the convicted criminal be im-

---

[79] See Harry L. Kozol, Richard J. Boucher, and Ralph F. Garofalo, "The Diagnosis and Treatment of Dangerousness," *Crime and Delinquency* 18 (October 1972), pp. 371–92.

[80] See Ernst A. Wenk, James O. Robinson, and Gerald W. Smith, "Can Violence Be Predicted?" *Crime and Delinquency* 18 (October 1972), pp. 393–402.

prisoned who represents a minimum risk if set free. Both are justified on the grounds that the public safety takes precedence.

In support of this argument it has been pointed out that a relatively small number of criminals account for a large share of the crimes known to the police.[81]

A growing number of analysts are willing to conclude that the legal system in the United States today has little deterrent effect on these habitual offenders and that attempts to rehabilitate them are either nonexistent or—when present—notable for their lack of success. Indeed, argues James Wilson, citing a number of studies, we have in effect thrown up our hands. In the Pittsburgh Common Pleas Courts in 1966, well over half the white males convicted of burglary, grand larceny, indecent assault, or possession of narcotics, and who had a prior record, were placed on probation. In Wisconsin, 63 percent of the adult males convicted of a felony from 1954 to 1959 who had previously been convicted of felonies were placed on probation. In Los Angeles, according to a report published by the Rand Corporation in 1973, only 12 percent of those who had been convicted and imprisoned for burglary in the past and who were convicted of burglary once again were sent to prison. Between 1963 and 1969, the number of persons arrested in New York State on narcotics charges—mainly involving dealers—increased by more than 700 percent, but the proportion going to prison fell from 68 percent of those convicted to 23 percent.[82] This increasing use of methods other than imprisonment for handling offenders with a demonstrated criminal proclivity has not been the result of any great faith in probation, parole, and the like, argues James Wilson. Rather, it is because judges have come to believe in the rehabilitation of criminals; since prisons do not or cannot accomplish this task, convicted offenders might just as well be placed in the free community.[83]

What we should consider, says Wilson, is the possibility of abandoning entirely the rehabilitative theory of sentencing and corrections. We can continue to experiment with new corrective and therapeutic proce-

[81] See *Uniform Crime Report—1972* (Washington, D.C.: Government Printing Office, 1973), pp. 35–39. Data on "careers in crime" were published in 1971, 1972, and 1973, but not thereafter.

[82] See Martin A. Levin, "Urban Politics and Policy Outcomes: The Criminal Courts," in George E. Cole, ed., *Criminal Justice* (North Scituate, Mass.: Duxbury Press, 1972), p. 335; Dean V. Babst and John W. Mannering, "Probation Versus Imprisonment for Similar Types of Offenders," *Journal of Research in Crime and Delinquency* 2 (July 1965), pp. 61ff.; Peter W. Greenwood et al., *Prosecution of Adult Felony Defendants in Los Angeles County: A Policy Perspective* (Santa Monica, Calif.: Rand, 1973), p. 109; Harold D. Lasswell and Jeremiah B. McKenna, *The Impact of Organized Crime on an Inner City Community* (New York: Policy Sciences Center, 1972), p. 203. Cited in James Q. Wilson, *Thinking About Crime* (New York: Basic Books, 1975), pp. 165–66.

[83] Wilson, *Thinking About Crime*, p. 167.

dures, and we can continue efforts to make custodial institutions more humane. But the main function of the prison should be to isolate the criminal and to punish him. "It is a measure of our confusion that such a statement will strike many enlightened readers today as cruel, even barbaric. It is not. It is merely a recognition that society at a minimum must be able to protect itself from dangerous offenders and to impose costs (other than the stigma and inconvenience of an arrest and court appearance) on criminal acts; it is also a frank admission that society really does not know how to do much else."[84]

By incapacitating the offender in prison, we at least eliminate those crimes he would have committed had he been at large—and the reduction of crime achieved in this manner, Wilson suggests, can be substantial. Citing an unpublished study made by Shlomo and Reuel Shinnar of the school of engineering of the City College of New York, in which it was estimated that the crime rate in New York State could be reduced by approximately two thirds if every person convicted of a serious crime were imprisoned for three years, Wilson argues that the estimate may be too optimistic but that a sizable reduction of the crime rate is clearly possible.[85]

The costs of such a program may be more than we are able to afford, concedes Wilson. The propriety and the humaneness of three-year mandatory sentences are subject to debate. The willingness of defendants to plead guilty may be altered if a three-year sentence is the best that can be achieved, thus imposing tremendous burdens on the courts. But the central element, says Wilson, is that these are reasonable questions around which the facts can be gathered and intelligent arguments mustered; the justification for punishment on the basis of incapacitation should not be dismissed out of hand but deserves careful attention as a practical means of combating crime—which is, after all, a crucial objective in the handling of lawbreakers.

Since the policy proposed by Wilson is likely to at least double the institutional population in the United States, the cost would undoubtedly be declared exorbitant. Mandatory prison sentences—whether one, three, or five years—are not apt to be accepted by either the judiciary or the legislatures; and the problem of predicting future criminality—which must lie at the heart of any program of preventing crime by incarcerating those likely to commit a crime—remains unsolved. Nonetheless, the idea that incapacitation has a legitimate place in society's attempt to deal with crime will undoubtedly receive more attention in the future, even though

---

[84] Ibid., pp. 172–73.

[85] Ibid., pp. 200–01. For a skeptical view of the incapacitative function of imprisonment, see David F. Greenberg, "The Incapacitative Effect of Imprisonment: Some Estimates," *Law and Society Review* 9 (Summer 1975), pp. 541–79.

there are many people who view the concept as no more than an updated version of the philosophy that the best way to deal with criminals is to "lock 'em up and throw away the key."

"The most immediately appealing justification for punishment," says Herbert Packer, "is the claim that it may be used to prevent crime by so changing the personality of the offender that he will conform to the dictates of law; in a word, by reforming him. In that ideal many have seen the means for resolving the moral paradox of the utilitarian position: that punishment is an instrumental use of one man for the benefit of other men."[86]

Punishment as Rehabilitation

The process by which punishment might reform the criminal offender is still a matter of dispute. According to some scholars following the lead of Durkheim, punishment is a dramatic expression of social disapproval, plainly identifying certain behavior as wrong. The punishment of that behavior—or the threat of punishment contained in the punishment of others—serves a moral or educative function, and criminals and non-criminals alike learn in explicit, official terms where society draws the line between legitimate and illegitimate behavior. Thus, for example, it has been claimed that the fact that people are hanged for murder is one reason why murder is considered so dreadful a crime.[87] The argument, notes Johannes Andenaes, is sometimes asserted with great confidence but has little in the way of substantiating evidence, in terms either of research or practical experience.[88] Other social scientists have seen punishment as demonstrating to the wrongdoer the bankrupty of crime as a way of life, thus serving as a necessary precondition to any programs of rehabilitation.[89] Only by accepting responsibility for one's actions and recognizing that one's criminal acts are wrong is it possible for true rehabilitation to occur—and this acceptance and recognition (which in effect is the creation of a sense of guilt) is brought about by punishment.[90]

In general, however, the idea that reformation is to be won by pain or suffering (an echo, as it were, of the religious concepts of penitence and a state of grace) is rarely advanced by those involved in the administration of the criminal law at the present time, even though it may appeal to

[86] *The Limits of the Criminal Sanction* (Stanford, Calif.: Stanford University Press, 1968).

[87] Gordon Hawkins, "Punishment and Deterrence: The Educative, Moralizing, and Habituative Effects," *The Wisconsin Law Review* no. 2 (1969), pp. 550–65.

[88] Andenaes, *Punishment and Deterrence,* Chapter IV.

[89] Lloyd McCorkle and Richard R. Korn, "Resocialization Within Walls," *The Annals of the American Academy of Political and Social Science* 293 (May 1954), pp. 88–98; see also D. J. B. Hawkins, "Punishment and Moral Responsibility," *The Modern Law Review* 7 (November 1944), pp. 205–08.

[90] The deliberate inculcation of a sense of guilt appears to play an important role in some forms of milieu therapy. See Deborah and Kenneth Colburn, "Integrity House: The Addict as a Total Institution," *Society* 10 (May/June 1973), pp. 39–52.

some moral philosophers as a justification for punishment. For those who take the reformation of the criminal as their goal, punishment—particularly punishment in the form of imprisonment—is apt to be viewed simply as a necessary evil, a context of captivity in which reformation efforts like therapy, education, and vocational training are to be pursued. Insofar as imprisonment can be justified, it is seen as an opportunity for maintaining access to the patient or as the price that must be paid if correctional personnel are to carry out their rehabilitative programs.[91]

As humane as this argument may appear at first glance, it leaves many questions about the rightfulness or the utility of imprisonment unanswered. First, if the individual is involuntarily confined, his incarceration is a form of punishment no matter how humane or "treatment-oriented" the reason for his detention may be. Changing the name on the door of an institution from "prison" to "hospital" cannot change the fact of incarceration, and it is reasonable to suppose that any "treatment" of the criminal offender will be carried out under relatively spartan conditions, since the mentally ill—who do not carry the stigma of criminality—frequently experience severe deprivations. The problem of punishing the criminal cannot be avoided by labeling it therapy.

Second, an exclusive concern for the reformation of the criminal provides no firm limits on the length of time the individual is to undergo a program of treatment. If the offender is confined until he is declared cured, it may turn out that his period of detention far exceeds the period of imprisonment that would be accorded him under the guidance of a punitive philosophy. It is this possibility that Sheldon Glueck recognized and accepted some fifty years ago when he noted that if society reacts to the offender in terms of his criminal personality rather than his criminal acts, it is conceivable that a law-breaker defined as socially dangerous could be locked up for life for a minor offense.[92] Although this view has the virtue of logical consistency, few people would probably accept such a policy with equanimity, any more than they would accept the idea of permitting a murderer "cured" in a week to be set free immediately.[93]

Third, there is a question of how far the state should be allowed to go in altering the personality of the individual in the name of crime preven-

[91] There are some advocates of rehabilitation (particularly those psychiatrically inclined) who are unwilling to accept such a compromised position. There is no possible excuse for punishment, it is said, since crime is an illness. Consequently, it is both inhumane and futile to imprison the criminal. He must be treated, and prisons must be transformed or done away with completely. See, for example, Karl Menninger, *The Crime of Punishment* (New York: Viking Press, 1966), pp. 249–51.

[92] See Sheldon Glueck, "Principles of a Rational Penal Code," *Harvard Law Review* 41 (February 1928), pp. 453–82.

[93] See Gresham M. Sykes, "The Dilemmas of Penal Reform," *The Howard Journal* 10 (1960), pp. 194–200.

tion. While words like rehabilitation or reformation have a fine ring to them, brain-washing or conditioning convey a more sinister image; yet the psychological processes involved may be much the same. Extensive permanent personality change is not yet within the grasp of the social sciences, it is true, even though institutions such as Patuxent in Jessup, Maryland, have been called "clockwork-orange prisons" in reference to Anthony Burgess' novel about the reconstruction of the criminal of-fender's personality structure.[94] Nonetheless, society does have available physical means of altering the individual's personality, such as prefrontal lobotomy, and it appears likely that psychological techniques of person-ality transformation will soon be much more effective than they are at present. The state does have the power to alter profoundly the conditions of the individual's life, all in the name of rehabilitation, even though what the state does may have little demonstrated effectiveness in reach-ing its alleged goal.

These issues, as we shall see in more detail in Chapter 14, involve the most difficult questions about the nature of society's reaction to crime, and yet the adherents of rehabilitation have often either ignored them or simply assumed that the procedures of a humane concern for bringing the criminal back into the ranks of the law-abiding need no justification. In an era, however, when the benevolent state is suspect, when the claims of psychiatry are being much disputed, and when the moral supe-riority of those who make and administer the criminal law is no longer taken for granted, reforming the criminal offender is viewed by many as a questionable enterprise rather than an enlightened mode of curbing criminal behavior.

Conclusions

There is an aphorism that what is done to the criminal is an accurate index of the quality of a civilization. Presumably, as a society marches along the path of evolution, it gives up its more sanguinary forms of punishment, turns its attention to the improvement of the criminal's character, and tempers justice with mercy.

The "civilized" character of modern societies may be disputed but there is little question that societies embodying the Anglo-American legal tradition are less brutal in the punishment of the criminal than societies of the past. Attempts to rehabilitate the offender now play a far more influential role, and mercy has been partially institutionalized in the form of probation and parole. Nonetheless, there are many social

---

[94] See Phil Stanford, "A Model, Clockwork-Orange Prison."

commentators who doubt if this means penal policies are actually becoming as effective, just, or humane as some penologists have claimed. The extent to which deterrence is a necessary and legitimate part of the penal system has been much ignored, it is argued. Despite all the talk of rehabilitation, very little is known about how to accomplish it, and what is known about changing the attitudes or personality traits of criminals raises serious questions about whether such endeavors are acceptable in a just and humane society.

Efforts to explore the place of punishment in controlling crime cannot be dismissed simply as a reactionary attempt to reintroduce the brutal treatment of the criminal offender.[95] Similarly, a critical analysis of what is done in the name of rehabilitation cannot be brushed aside as an overly sensitive reaction to the threat of control of the individual's psyche by the state. The fact of the matter is that much of the conventional thinking in criminology about the proper treatment of the criminal is now in a state of disarray, and the future development of theory, research, and social policy is far from clear. What does seem plain is that the orthodoxies about the uselessness of punishment and the virtues of reformation are no longer easily accepted, and the issue of the proper relationship between crime and punishment promises to become a matter of debate and investigation rather than a repetition of platitudes.

Recommended Readings

Much of what is done to the criminal is rooted in the past. Frederick Howard Wines, *Punishment and Reformation* (New York: Thomas Y. Crowell, 1895) provides an excellent history of punishment that continues to be illuminating despite the early date of its publication. Another classic work in this area is Georg Rusche and Otto Kirchheimer, *Punishment and Social Structure* (New York: Columbia University Press, 1939). For an exploration of the rationales of punishment, the reader will find it worthwhile to consult Stanley E. Grupp, ed., *Theories of Punishment* (Bloomington: Indiana University Press, 1971); Ted Honderich, *Punishment: The Supposed Justifications* (London: Hutchinson, 1969); and Ernest van den Haag, *Punishing Criminals: Concerning a Very Old and Painful Question* (New York: Basic Books, 1975).

For the eighteenth- and nineteenth-century social experiments with punishment, and the rise of the penal institution in the United States, the reader should see David J. Rothman, *The Discovery of the Asylum* (Boston: Little, Brown, 1971). The disenchantment with imprisonment and the fall of the ideal of rehabilitation is discussed in Francis A. Allen, *The Borderland of Criminal Justice* (Chicago: Uni-

---

[95] It is true, of course, that the moral philosophers who are most vocal in arguing for the rightful place of punishment in society's reaction to crime seldom discuss the realities of punishment in detail; they might well recoil in distaste from the task of turning an academic argument into an actuality.

versity of Chicago Press, 1964). The idea of using punishment for deterrence has been looked at anew in recent years; Franklin E. Zimring, *Perspectives on Deterrence* (Rockville, Md.: National Institute of Mental Health, Center for Studies of Crime and Delinquency, 1971) provides a concise, logical discussion of the issues.

Chapter 13
The World of
the Prison

The social decision to confine criminals en masse, whether for the purpose of punishment, deterrence, or reform, had always carried one important implication in its train that was quite evident to the early proponents of imprisonment. If prisoners were allowed to interact freely with one another, custodial institutions might become, in effect, small-scale, criminal societies embedded in the body of the state.

The Pennsylvania and Auburn systems, with their emphasis on silence and isolation, were precisely designed to avoid such an outcome. As faith in the two systems declined, to be replaced by an enthusiasm for the less-constraining reformatory, it was hoped that the pernicious effects of increased social interaction among prisoners could be avoided by close surveillance and strict control imposed by the custodial staff. As things turned out, however, in one custodial institution after another, efforts to impose such a regime often proved futile. Inmates showed a remarkable tendency to develop an informal inmate social structure with values and norms at odds with the purposes of penal administrators.

In the beginning of this century, inmate social structure received scant scrutiny; the bulk of the criminological literature dealing with the prison concerned itself with two other issues. First, a great deal of discussion was devoted to how the prison could be made more effective as an agency of rehabilitation, with much attention paid to such matters as vocational training, education, and architectural design; and second, a good deal of humanitarian effort was directed to exposing conditions of prison life that were viewed as brutal, degrading, and reflective of an irrational desire for vengeance on the part of the public. Gradually, however, beginning with the work of Hans Reimer, Norman Hayner and Ellis Ash, Donald Clemmer, Kirson Weinberg, and Clarence Schrag, the informal social structure of the inmate population emerged as an issue of prime significance.[1]

[1] See Hans Reimer, "Socialization in the Prison Community," *Proceedings of the American Prison Association, 1937* (New York: American Prison Association, 1937), pp. 151–55; Norman S. Hayner and Ellis Ash, "The Prison Community as a Social Group," *American Socio-*

In the period immediately before World War II studies of the prison social structure were apt to be largely descriptive. With time, however, they became more analytical, more concerned with explaining social relationships in the prison; and in the 1950s and 1960s there developed what is sometimes referred to as a functional interpretation of the inmate social system.[2] Imprisoned criminals, it was argued, suffered from a number of frustrating circumstances imposed by their jailers to insure custody and the maintenance of internal order within a framework of material deprivation erected in the name of punishment. Inmates attempt to meet and counter these frustrations in a variety of ways, but in general their responses to the conditions of prison life are to be seen as ranged along a continuum that lies between two theoretical poles. On the one hand, prisoners can bind themselves together with ties of mutual aid, loyalty, and respect, presenting a united opposition to the officials; on the other hand, prisoners can try to exploit one another, betraying fellow inmates to the officials for their own gain and allowing the frictions of prison life to burst into open warfare.

The inmate code, or the norms of the inmate social system, is apt to stress inmate cohesion, for the more inmates stick together, the better able they are to alleviate the frustrating circumstances of prison life. The norms, however, are frequently violated; and despite the passionate avowals of solidarity expressed by prisoners, custodial institutions are likely to exhibit a good deal of force and fraud in inmate relationships.

---

logical Review 4 (June 1939), pp. 362–69; Donald Clemmer, The Prison Community (Boston: Christopher Publishing House, 1940); Kirson Weinberg, "Aspects of Prison's Social Structure," American Journal of Sociology 47 (March 1942), pp. 217–26; Clarence Schrag, "Social Types in a Prison Community," unpublished master's thesis, University of Washington, 1944. For a brief bibliography of early prison studies, see Gresham M. Sykes and Sheldon L. Messinger, "The Inmate Social System," in Richard Cloward et al., Theoretical Studies in Social Organization of the Prison (New York: Social Science Research Council 1960), pp. 5–19. An excellent brief review of changes in the study of the prison to 1969 is to be found in Sheldon L. Messinger, "Issues in the Study of the System of Prison Inmates," Issues in Criminology 4 (Fall 1969), pp. 133–44. A recent discussion of the prison literature is to be found in John Irwin, "Prison," in Contemporary Sociology 5 (July 1976), pp. 424–26.

[2] See Messinger "Issues in the Study of the System of Prison Inmates," p. 134; Lloyd W. McCorkle and Richard Korn, "Resocialization Within Walls," The Annals of the American Academy of Political and Social Science 293 (May 1954), pp. 88–98; Gresham M. Sykes, The Society of Captives (Princeton, N.J.: Princeton University Press, 1958); Richard Cloward, Donald R. Cressey, George H. Grosser, Richard McCleery, Lloyd E. Ohlin, Gresham M. Sykes, and Sheldon L. Messinger, Theoretical Studies in Social Organization of the Prison (New York: Social Science Research Council, 1960); Donald Cressey, ed., The Prison: Studies in Institutional Organization and Change (New York: Holt, Rinehart and Winston, 1961); Stanton Wheeler, "Socialization in Correctional Communities," American Sociological Review 26 (October 1961), pp. 697–712; David H. Ward and Gene S. Kassebaum, Women's Prison (Chicago: Aldine, 1965); Rose Giallombardo, Society of Women: A Study of a Women's Prison (New York: Wiley & Sons, 1966); and Esther Heffernan, Making It in Prison: The Square, The Cool and The Life (New York: John Wiley & Sons, 1972).

But it is in light of the need to solve the problems of confinement that we can begin to understand the ideal of inmate cohesion and the realities of inmate conflict that give rise to the mixture of social roles forming the social system of the prison population.[3]

It has been pointed out that this argument needs to take into account important differences among prisons.[4] The degree of deprivation imposed, the extent of the concern for rehabilitation, the degree of security—all may affect how inmates react to their confinement. It has also been pointed out that the predispositions of prisoners have received insufficient attention.[5] The degree of inmate cohesion may be influenced by the proportion of prisoners who identify themselves as full-time criminals or by the nature of the culture from which the inmate population is drawn. More important for the moment, however, is that in the late 1960s and early 1970s it became evident that in a large number of prisons in the United States a significant change was beginning to take place. Many inmates were finding a source of solidarity in ethnic militancy that had not existed before; and for prisoners, social scientists, and others attempting to analyze the prison experience, the confinement of convicted criminals began to be seen more and more in political terms.[6]

For a growing number of blacks, argued black prisoner George Jackson in a powerful indictment of American prisons, resistance had become the only hope. "The holds are beginning to slip away. Most of today's black convicts have come to understand that they are the most abused victims of an unrighteous order. . . . With the sure knowledge that we are slated for destruction, we have been transformed into an implacable army of liberation. The shift to the revolutionary anti-establishment position that Huey Newton, Eldridge Cleaver, and Bobby Seale projected as a solution to the problems of America's black colonies has taken firm hold of these brothers' minds."[7]

[3] See Sykes, *The Society of Captives*, pp. 82–83.

[4] See David Street, "Inmates in Custodial and Treatment Settings," *American Sociological Review* 30 (February 1965), pp. 40–55; and Charles R. Tittle, "Inmate Organization: Sex Differentiation and the Influence of Criminal Subcultures," *American Sociological Review* 34 (August 1969), pp. 492–505.

[5] See Irwin and Donald R. Cressey, "Thieves, Convicts, and the Inmate Culture," *Social Problems* 10 (Fall 1962), pp. 142–55; and Wheeler, "Socialization in Correctional Communities." See also Gordon Hawkins, *The Prison* (Chicago: University of Chicago Press, 1976).

[6] See, for example, Erik Olin Wright, *The Politics of Punishment* (New York: Harper & Row, 1973); *Struggle for Justice. A Report on Crime and Punishment in America* Prepared for the American Friends Service Committee (New York: Hill & Wang, 1971); Joan Smith and William Fried, *The Use of the American Prison: Political Theory and Penal Practice* (Lexington, Mass.: D. C. Heath, 1974); *Attica: The Official Report of the New York State Special Commission on Attica* (New York: Bantam Books, 1972); Roger Starr, "Prisons, Politics, & the Attica Report," *Commentary* (March 1973), pp. 31–37.

[7] *Soledad Brother: The Prison Letters of George Jackson* (New York: Bantam Books, 1970), p. 30.

For some prisoners, the new basis of solidarity involved something more than ethnic militancy; inmates, it was now said, must unite as *convicts*, as people held in bondage by an exploitative socioeconomic order. "We, the people of the convicted class," declared the Bill of Rights proposed by one of the many prisoner organizations beginning to emerge on the American scene, "locked in a cycle of poverty, failure, discrimination, and servitude, DO HEREBY DECLARE, before the World, our situation to be unjust and inhuman."[8] For prison officials, the rhetoric frequently appeared to be marked by a dangerous revolutionary flavor, and there were many complaints of "agitators," "militants," and "radicals." But if the world of officialdom often overreacted to any sign of resistance to their authority, it was clear that a new theme had been introduced into custodial institutions. Insofar as inmates had come to view themselves as political prisoners rather than imprisoned criminals, the nature of inmate cohesion had undergone a significant change—and the possibility of organized resistance to the regime of the custodians would appear to have been increased. The analysis of the informal social system of inmates had acquired a new dimension.

American Penal Institutions

On an average day in the United States there are approximately half a million adults and juveniles confined in jails, detention centers, or prisons. At least half of those detained are either awaiting trial or serving relatively short sentences for minor offenses.[9] Some twenty-four thousand persons are held in 35 federal institutions, ranging from short-term camps to adult penitentiaries, but a large number of federal offenders are also confined in state and local institutions.[10] In 1967 the President's Commission on Law Enforcement and Administration of Justice reported that the 358 state institutions are devoted to a variety of special population groups, with less than half used to house adult male felons. The same picture holds true today, and it is worth noting that 61 of these institutions were opened before 1900 and that 25 are now more than 100 years old. Security restrictions are classified as maximum in 15

[8] See Hearings Before Subcommittee No. 3 of the Committee on the Judiciary, House of Representatives, Ninety-second Congress. First Session on Corrections, October 25, 1971 (Washington, D.C.: Government Printing Office, 1971), p. 356.

[9] See David Peterson and Charles W. Thomas, *Corrections: Problems and Prospects* (Englewood Cliffs, N.J.: Prentice-Hall, 1975), p. 5.

[10] See Robert M. Carter, Daniel Glaser, and Leslie T. Wilkins, eds., *Correctional Institutions* (Philadelphia: J. B. Lippincott, 1972), pp. 99–100. See also *Prisoners in State and Federal Institutions* (Washington, D. C.: Government Printing Office, 1977).

percent of the state facilities, medium in 35 percent, minimum in 29 percent, and the remainder are described as mixed.[11]

A survey of the Department of Health, Education, and Welfare indicates that there are 220 state institutions for juvenile delinquents housing an average daily population of 62,000.[12] The average annual per capita operating cost of these institutions was approximately $3600, according to the 1967 *Report* of the Task Force on Corrections—the latest detailed study available at the national level—compared with $2000 for adult institutions. These averages conceal a good deal of variation; among juvenile institutions, for example, annual per capita costs can range from less than $1000 to almost $8000.[13]

A large share of the operating costs of custodial institutions for both adults and juveniles is devoted to feeding, clothing, and guarding prisoners. Although precise figures concerning institutional budgets on a national basis are not available, the proportion of custodial and service staff to rehabilitative staff is instructive. Approximately 95 percent of the employees in adult correctional institutions are assigned to custodial and service tasks; for juvenile institutions, the comparable figure is 83 percent.[14] As the *Task Force Report on Corrections* pointed out, programs of rehabilitation may appear admirable on paper but the reality is frequently disappointing.[15] The emphasis on custody and control, notes the American Correctional Association, is "universally prescribed by law, custom, and public opinion. Although at times such a concept may seem at variance with attempts to introduce rehabilitative services, it is doubtful that any . . . program which ignores this reality will long endure."[16] To talk of correction, then, is more often a statement of an ideal than a description of penal practice—and the verbal shift from "prison" to "treatment center," from "prisoners" to "residents," from "punishment" to "aversion therapy" is regarded by a number of critics as being nothing more than a sham manufactured to gull the public.[17]

Many custodial institutions are in rural areas, far from the towns and cities that supply most of the inmate population. In part this can be traced to an earlier interest in banishing offenders to remote locales, a faith in the curative powers of a country setting, and the desire on the

[11] President's Commission on Law Enforcement and Administration of Justice, *Task Force Report: Corrections* (Washington, D.C.: Government Printing Office, 1967), pp. 179–80.

[12] Ibid., pp. 143, 192.

[13] Ibid., pp. 144–45.

[14] Ibid., p. 51

[15] Ibid., p. 144. For a striking analysis of the discrepancy between paper programs and reality, see Rose Giallombardo, *The Social World of Imprisoned Girls* (New York: John Wiley & Sons, 1974).

[16] *Manual of Correctional Standards* (New York: American Correctional Association, 1966), p. 366.

[17] See Smith and Fried, *The Use of the American Prison*, p. 23.

part of rural legislators to create employment opportunities for their constituents.[18] Today, these rural locations pose serious problems in recruiting personnel, particularly at the professional level; and the rural background of the custodial staff often serves to increase the misunderstandings between the guards and the inmates. The recruitment of qualified people to fill the more than one hundred thousand positions in custodial institutions in the United States is generally a difficult task, and it has been argued that many of the problems of these institutions are the result of the unattractiveness of the work. The salaries, including those of teachers, social workers, and counselors, are relatively low.[19] The work is often dangerous, conditions are frequently oppressive, and little prestige is attached to being employed in a custodial institution. "As a result of these conditions," it has been pointed out, "administrators of correctional programs tend to have limited backgrounds. Too often they are promoted to their managerial posts from within the system, without adequate training experience, or fitness for their task. A number are also chosen largely on the basis of political considerations."[20]

The difficulties in securing adequate personnel are not, however, the prime cause of the problems custodial institutions face today. Instead, we must look to the nature of the tasks society assigns to such institutions—tasks that are frequently inconsistent, inherently difficult, and made still more difficult by limited means. Custodial institutions, particularly maximum- and medium-security institutions for adult offenders, must prevent escapes above all else. They must also maintain internal control over groups of individuals with long records of violent, aggressive behavior who would pose serious problems for the maintenance of orderly community life under the best of circumstances. They must somehow employ inmates at useful labor, for society has long decreed that imprisoned offenders must be as self-sustaining as possible. Finally, they are charged with the task of reforming, or rehabilitating, prisoners. Precisely what is meant by reformation is, however, far from clear, and it is doubtful that such a task could be accomplished in any case in the tense, frustrating circumstances of the custodial institution.

Custody The task of preventing escapes is performed with fair efficiency. As James V. Bennett, Director of the Federal Bureau of Prisons, pointed out,

[18] President's Commission on Law Enforcement and Administration of Justice, *Task Force Report: Corrections*, p. 4.

[19] According to the *Task Force Report: Corrections*, in 1967, the median starting salary for custodial employees in adult institutions was between $4000 and $5000 per year. It was even lower in juvenile institutions, and the rehabilitative staff did not fare much better (p. 6). There is little indication that the relative position of correctional workers in the labor force has improved since that time.

[20] *Task Force Report: Corrections*, p. 6.

"When one takes into consideration the antiquity of most prisons, the flimsiness of some prison structures, the Rube Goldberg character of the locking devices, the hit or miss standards used in selecting men for 'trusty' assignments, the extent of overcrowding, personnel shortages, and the increasingly more desperate character of the offender, there are few enough escapes."[21] Maintaining custody, however, involves much more than erecting a high chain-link fence or placing armed guards on a prison wall. If escapes are to be prevented, security measures must be taken throughout the institution. Constant checks of cells for materials that might be used in an escape attempt, a system of passes for moving about the institution, frequent counts of the inmate population—these are but a few of the steps that custodians believe necessary to keep their prisoners from fleeing. Aside from a small group of offenders with a long record of escape attempts, however, administrators find it difficult to identify which inmates pose a serious threat to custody.[22] Stringent security measures are often imposed on the entire population of prisoners with the full realization that for many it is unnecessary.[23]

Internal Control The task of maintaining control within the institution is usually regarded as only a step behind the maintenance of custody in importance. The offenders who end up in prisons, reformatories, and jails are likely to present numerous behavioral problems, both in terms of relationships among inmates and between guards and inmates. Exacerbating the existing criminal tendencies of many prisoners are the harsh frustrations of life in confinement and the prolonged intimacy of hundreds or thousands of people held together for months or years against their will. Despite the surveillance of the custodial staff, despite the locks and the bars and the constant counting of the inmates and the searching for weapons, violations of the rules such as drugs smuggled into the institution, homemade liquor, and "disturbances" are a commonplace. This is generally true no matter what kind of institution is involved or how efficient its administration is. Violence, theft, homosexuality, rackets of various sorts are all encountered, in spite of the public image of the custodial institution as the ultimate weapon against crime.

Work Utilizing the labor of inmates to move the custodial institution in the direction of self-sufficiency is also a perplexing problem. The demands of

[21] "Evaluating a Prison," *The Annals of the American Academy of Political and Social Science* 293 (May 1954), p. 11.
[22] See Norman Holt, *Escape From Custody* (Sacramento, Calif.: Research Division, California Department of Corrections, May 1974).
[23] See Gresham M. Sykes, *The Society of Captives* pp. 18–21. The dangers of attempting to escape, the great likelihood of being captured, and the anticipation of release in the not-too-distant future are sufficient to keep many inmates from trying to flee.

To talk of correction is more often a statement of an ideal than a description of penal practice—and the verbal shift from "prison" to "treatment center," from "prisoners" to "residents," from "punishment" to "therapy" is regarded by a number of critics as nothing more than a sham.

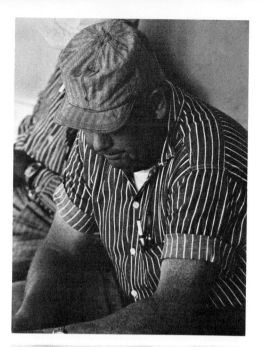

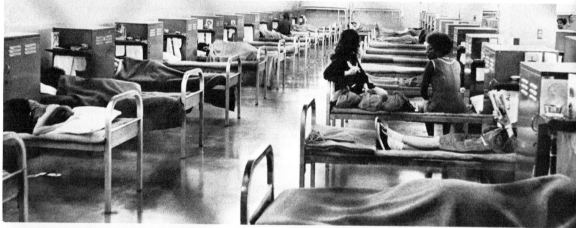

custody and the maintenance of order often mean that the efficient use of inmate labor must be sacrificed, along with programs such as vocational training and education. But other factors sharply limit the productivity of inmate labor as well. Whether the work of prisoners is viewed as a means of aiding the taxpayer, deterring criminal behavior, instilling "habits of industry," or preparing the prisoner for life in the free community, the attempts to fit imprisoned criminals into a rational economic enterprise are generally flawed.

The opposition of labor unions to prison labor has led to the widespread adoption of the state-use system, in which the products of penal labors are purchased exclusively by state agencies. This has greatly restricted the range and the level of occupations to be found in custodial institutions (items commonly manufactured in prisons include license plates, brooms, work clothes, and office furniture). Political pressure from the unions has also led to severe limitations on the capitalization of prison industries, with the result that the industrial machinery found in institutions is frequently outmoded, worn out, or inefficient. Inmates are often poorly trained and inexperienced; the rates of inmate turnover and absenteeism are high.[24] Perhaps even more important, however, is that in most states the inmates of custodial institutions are paid pennies a day for their work—if they are paid at all. (The District of Columbia, the Federal Bureau of Prisons, and some twenty states report paying wages to 90 percent or more of their imprisoned criminals. In five states, no more than 10 percent earn money, and six states prohibit inmate earnings altogether.) In thirty-three states, wages range from 4 cents to a high of $1.30 a day.[25] "Objections have been raised against inmate wages," notes Elmer Johnson. "Deprivation of earning capacity is viewed as part of punishment. Easing of the lot of the prisoner's family would reduce the deterrent effect of imprisonment. The cost of prison operations already is too great without the additional expense of paying wages."[26] As a consequence, prisoners are little motivated to perform their work with diligence or care.

The barriers to effective work programs have made it difficult for custodial institutions to keep their prisoners busy in a productive fashion. Many inmates (far more than are needed, in fact) devote their time to such housekeeping activities as stoking fires, cooking, barbering, washing clothes, and sweeping, while others are simply forced into idleness.

[24] It has been estimated that the productivity of prison inmates is about one fourth that of private industry. See *Crime in America: Causes and Cures* (Washington, D.C.: U.S. News & World Report, 1972), pp. 112–13.

[25] See Elmer Johnson, "Prison Industry," in George G. Killinger and Paul F. Cromwell, Jr., eds., *Penology: The Evolution of Corrections in America* (St. Paul, Minn.: West, 1973), pp. 291–301.

[26] Ibid., p. 301.

The precise impact of work experiences and vocational training in prison on the subsequent criminal careers of inmates is not known.[27] Nevertheless, it is widely agreed—particularly among penal administrators—that the failure to provide prisoners with meaningful work is a major problem and contributes greatly to the tensions of prison life.

The task of rehabilitation is seen by correctional personnel as including much more than vocational training. Education, psychological therapy, conjugal visits, inmate self-government, furloughs—all are likely to be viewed as somehow contributing to the prisoner's reformation.

Rehabilitation

As indicated in preceding chapters, the bulk of the criminal offenders arrested, indicted, convicted, and confined in the United States are drawn from the lower ranks of society. It is not surprising, then, that the educational level of prisoners is a good deal lower than that of the general population. About 61 percent of inmates in state prisons have not completed high school; the comparable figure for the general population is approximately 36 percent.[28] Since educational certification has come to be regarded as essential in an increasingly technological society, many correctional workers are convinced that remedying deficiencies in the schooling of inmates must be at the heart of any rehabilitation program. But because so many inmates have a history of failure in school—and have come to think of school as a place that is quick to get rid of "troublemakers"—educational programs face serious difficulties. "Training school and reformatory inmates are particularly likely not only to be far behind in school but to associate education with their failure and rejection," it has been pointed out. "Even if they come from higher income areas, inmates tend to be the most maladjusted people in their groups. Consequently, their academic attainments are often far below what their intelligence test scores indicate they are capable of attaining, and even the scores are often deflated by their hostility and insecurity in test taking, as is evident by sharp increases in score when their confidence is increased. The problem in instructing them is essentially to make learning a more relevant and rewarding experience for them, rather than a situation where they anticipate only failure and humiliation."[29]

It is a problem that has not been solved. Hampered by the lack of adequate teachers, appropriate instructional material, and classroom space,

[27] See Daniel Glaser, *The Effectiveness of a Prison and Parole System* (Indianapolis: Bobbs-Merrill, 1964), Chapter 11; Michael J. Miller, "Vocational Training in Prisons: Some Social Policy Implications," *Federal Probation* 36 (September 1972), pp. 19–21; Robert Martinson, "What Works?—Questions and Answers About Prison Reform," in Seymour I. Halleck et al., eds., *The Aldine Crime and Justice Annual 1974* (Chicago: Aldine, 1975), pp. 352–84.
[28] See *Survey of Inmates of State Correctional Facilities 1974* (Washington, D.C.: Department of Justice, 1976), p. 2.
[29] *Task Force Report: Corrections*, p. 53.

and restricted by the demands of security, education in custodial institutions lags far behind what its adherents have envisoned. Programmed learning, hailed with much enthusiasm in the 1960s as a promising approach to the problems of the alienated student, has failed to produce the hoped-for results. Other ideas, such as the inmate college, have come to be viewed with much distrust, particularly by prison officials who fear that revolution rather than rehabilitation is being brewed in the classroom. But perhaps of even greater importance is the growing recognition that the link between education and rehabilitation is far from demonstrated.

On the face of it, the idea that rehabilitation is fostered by education—whether in the form of classroom instruction, Dale Carnegie courses, Great Books seminars, or courses on hobbies and games—might seem eminently reasonable. "All of these activities hopefully augment the offender's social skills," says the *Report* of the Task Force on Corrections, "promote alternatives to illegitimate uses of leisure time in the institution and outside, and increase the offender's stake in conformity."[30] Just as in another, more religious era, sermons and Bible instruction were thought to offer the key to reform, so in this educational age schooling is often considered the means of assuring conformity to the law. Existing empirical studies are not, unfortunately, encouraging. "Nobody knows conclusively and precisely the effectiveness of correctional education," writes Daniel Glaser. "Statistics vary from one study to the next. When one defines 'success' for research purposes as the absence of post-release felony convictions or parole violations, some studies indicate that inmates who were in prison school succeed more than those who were not, while other studies have the opposite finding."[31]

Vocational training and schooling can be considered as part of a "social skills" view of rehabilitation: the offender's criminality is seen as stemming from an inability to adjust to the demands of society and to secure a worthwhile, rewarding place in the social order—most notably, in the form of a job. If the individual can be trained to overcome the handicap, the chances that the criminality will disappear are much increased. Many people engaged in corrections, however, take a different view. The causes of the individual's criminality, it is said, lie not in a lack of social skills but in a disordered personality. Psychotherapy is the path to rehabilitation; if the psyche can be changed in the custodial institution, conforming behavior after release is sure to follow.

Programs of psychotherapy in custodial institutions in the United States today are varied, but generally they are understaffed and limited

[30] Ibid., p. 54.
[31] "The Effectiveness of Correctional Education," *American Journal of Correction* 28 (March–April 1966), pp. 4–9.

in scope, both in the number and kind of inmates they treat and the type of treatment provided. Despite much talk of diagnosis, treatment, and the like, psychotherapy remains a goal on paper and a cliché of public speeches about penal reform rather than a well-established part of penal practice.

The programs of psychotherapy that do exist are most likely to take the form of group meetings. "Because of the shortage of clinically trained persons," notes the *Report* of the Task Force on Corrections, "as well as the presumed therapeutic advantages of group methods over one-to-one psychotherapy, the expansion of psychotherapeutic services in corrections in the past few decades has occurred primarily through group therapy."[32] The *Report* goes on to point out, somewhat ruefully, that most offenders have had more successful experience in crime and delinquency than in conventional modes of achievement. Changing their personalities in order to follow the path of conformity may not have much appeal. Furthermore, despite attempts to direct group discussion to an objective analysis of the causes of criminal behavior, meetings frequently degenerate into collective mythmaking and rationalization of misconduct. When group leaders prohibit discussion of the distant past or the distant future in order to encourage greater realism among the inmates, group therapy sessions may become little more than rambling conversation about how to cope with the problems of institutional life, which may be quite irrelevant to inmates' behavior after they are released.[33]

At the present time, Don Gibbons has concluded, so-called correctional work consists largely of unshared, intuitive procedures that are frequently vague and ambiguous, even to the correctional worker, and based on a crudely articulated behavioral theory that views most offenders as maladjusted. Treatment, he notes, is largely a matter of "someone doing something to someone else"—and that something may not be related to the problems of the offender.[34]

Robert Martinson, whose review of rehabilitative procedures was cited earlier, is no less pessimistic. He restricted himself to those reported studies conforming to the conventional standards of social science research—standards, he notes, that are rigorous but hardly esoteric. For evaluations of treatment methods to be considered acceptable, it is necessary that they include an independent measure of improvement (such as recidivism rates) and some control group. There should be sufficient data to judge the findings, with results beyond a preliminary assessment, and sample size should be large enough for purposes of compari-

[32] *Task Force Report: Corrections*, p. 52.
[33] Ibid., p. 52.
[34] "Some Notes on Treatment Theory in Corrections," *Social Service Review* 29 (1955), pp. 20–32.

son. A total of 231 studies were found meeting these criteria; and the results—in terms of revealing clear principles to be used in the rehabilitation of criminal offenders—were disappointing.[35]

Psychotherapy in particular, long viewed as a fundamental element in "enlightened" or "progressive" programs for the rehabilitation of criminal offenders, failed to show the results expected by those with a psychiatric bent. While a few studies suggested that counseling, or helping inmates with the psychological causes of their criminal behavior, was related to lower rates of recidivism, most of the studies indicated that psychotherapy had no effect or, indeed, might make matters worse.[36] In programs designed for young male inmates, such as those examined by Evelyn Guttman, Alvin Rudoff, and Stuart Adams, treatment effects appeared to be negligible.[37] Similar results, in general, were found in programs for youthful female offenders, although one study done by Adams showed an interesting if somewhat puzzling finding: if individual therapy was administered by a psychiatrist or a psychologist, the resulting parole suspension rate was almost two-and-a-half times higher than if treatment was administered by a social worker without specialized psychiatric training.[38] Group treatment did not seem to be any more or any less effective than individual therapy, and the results were equally inconclusive when programs for adults and youths were examined separately. So-called milieu therapy has sometimes been held out as the only effective form of treatment, on the grounds that any benefits derived from treatment are likely to be undone by the custody-oriented institutional context. In milieu therapy the entire institution is transformed into a therapeutic environment, with all its parts working consistently toward the reformation of offenders. But evaluations of such ventures have found little evidence that milieu therapy is effective in changing the

[35] Martinson's review of the literature was commissioned in 1966 by the New York State Special Committee on Criminal Offenders. When the project was completed, some four years later, state officials had changed their minds about the worth and proper use of the information that had been gathered; a law suit was necessary to free the material for publication. Like those messengers in ancient times who were killed when they delivered bad news, social scientists who show that data are lacking to support a desired public policy are apt to be unpopular. See Mirra Komarovsky, ed., *Sociology and Social Policy* (New York: Elsevier, 1975).

[36] Martinson, "What Works?—Questions and Answers About Prison Reform," pp. 359–62.

[37] See Evelyn S. Guttman, "Effects of Short-term Psychiatric Treatment on Boys in Two California Youth Authority Institutions," *Research Report No. 36* (California Youth Authority, 1963); Alvin Rudoff, "The Effect of Treatment on Incarcerated Young Adult Delinquents as Measured by Disciplinary History," unpublished master's thesis, University of Southern California, 1960; Stuart Adams, "Assessment of the Psychiatric Treatment Program: Second Interim Report," *Research Report No. 15* (California Youth Authority, December 13, 1959).

[38] Reported in Martinson, "What Work?—Questions and Answers About Prison Reform," p. 360. Martinson's article contains a lengthy bibliography of treatment studies that is particularly valuable.

criminal into a noncriminal. A study by James Robison and Marinette Kevotkian suggests that such treatment does reduce recidivism in the first year after release—but after two years, this effect disappears.[39] Others report no significant effects in a thirty-six-month period.[40] The Highfields Project in New Jersey is one of the best-known attempts to use milieu therapy and is often cited as a good example of what enlightened treatment can accomplish. A small number of delinquent boys are confined for a short period of time in a residential center at Highfields (a house and grounds once belonging to Charles and Anne Morrow Lindbergh) and exposed to "guided group interaction" five days a week. This process, it is asserted, plays a major part in the "Highfields experience" and is "directed toward piercing through . . . strong defenses against rehabilitation, toward undermining delinquent attitudes, and toward developing a self-conception favorable to reformation."[41] The results are said to be positive and clear—and evaluation studies indicate that the recidivism rate for delinquent boys sent to Highfields is lower than that for delinquent boys committed to more conventional confinement in a reformatory.[42] The difference between the two recidivism rates tends to disappear with the passage of time, however, and one reason for the supposed superiority of the Highfields program is that the boys sent to Highfields are more likely to come from and be released to communities with relatively low delinquency rates than are boys released from the reformatory. Furthermore, as Martinson has noted, more of the Highfields boys are discharged early from supervision, thus reducing the chances that recidivism will be detected; and different organizations—a probation agency for the Highfields boys and a parole agency for youngsters from the reformatory—are charged with determining whether the boys have kept out of trouble. This last point is particularly important, since there is strong evidence that reported treatment results are often due not to the treatment itself but to the biases and presuppositions of those charged with supervising the released offender.[43] Thus the advantages of milieu therapy have not yet been established unequivocably.

[39] James Robinson and Marinette Kevotkian, "Intensive Treatment Project: Phase II. Parole Outcome: Interim Report," *Research Report No. 27* (California Department of Corrections, Youth and Adult Corrections Agency, January 1967).

[40] Gene Kassebaum, David Ward, and Daniel Wilnet, *Prison Treatment and Parole Survival: An Empiral Assessment* (New York: John Wiley & Sons, 1971).

[41] Lloyd W. McCorkle, Albert Elias, and F. Lovell Bixby, *The Highfields Story: An Experimental Treatment Project for Youthful Offenders* (New York: Henry Holt, 1958), p. v. To a large extent, the program appears to be directed toward the task of creating an atmosphere of affection and respect in which the delinquent boy learns to take responsibility for his actions and their consequences.

[42] Ibid., Chapter X. See also Howard E. Freemand and H. Ashley Weeks, "Analysis of a Program of Treatment of Delinquent Boys, *American Journal of Sociology* 62 (July 1956), pp. 56–61.

[43] Martinson, "What Works?—Questions and Answers About Prison Reform," pp. 374–76.

Martinson's report has been attacked by some critics who believe that he is too negativistic and that he slights the fact that some rehabilitative efforts for some offenders under some conditions do appear to help.[44] Nonetheless, his major conclusion—that society has not yet found a sure way of reducing recidivism through rehabilitation—cannot be faulted. This is not to say the task is impossible; rather, it is a recognition of "the extraordinary gap between the claims of success made by proponents of various treatments and the reality revealed by good research."[45]

Programs of psychotherapy in custodial institutions are frequently described as highly successful in reducing recidivism, proclaimed as a significant contribution to the solution of the crime problem, and then, on close and rigorous examination, found to be of minor influence or none at all. The idea that a criminal personality can be restructured by group discussion, counseling, and the like is, of course, beguiling; but there is more than a touch of naiveté in the belief that the influence of the social conditions and the years of experience in the community that often play such a large part in crime can be undone with a limited number of brief therapeutic sessions conducted within a framework of involuntary participation. When efforts are made to transform the entire custodial institution into a therapeutic milieu and the inmate population is restricted to a small number of individuals considered amenable to treatment, the results are not easily utilized as the basis for a large-scale public policy for the handling of confined offenders.

Conjugal Visits Many custodial officials have little expectation of curing inmates of their criminality, either by schooling, vocational training, or psychotherapy. Believing there is not much they can do to improve prisoners, they hope at least to provide tolerable living conditions. A variety of programs and activities is included in the institutional regimen to ease the more abnormal aspects of life in confinement. The goal is not so much to cure as to make custody bearable—and to lessen the administrative problems faced by institution officials.

Various recreational programs, television, opportunities for the sale of hobby work, and religious services are all viewed as helping to reduce the tensions of imprisonment. Yet measures such as these barely begin to confront the problems of institutional life; and other devices, such as

---

[44] See Ted Palmer, "Martinson Revisited," in Robert Martinson, Ted Palmer, and Stuart Adams, *Rehabilitation, Recidivism, and Research* (Hackensack, N.J.: National Council on Crime and Delinquency, 1976), pp. 41–62. Martinson's analysis is now being subjected to extensive criticism. See, for example, Staff Report, Correctional Research and Evaluation Center, "Profile," *The Quarterly Journal of Corrections* 1 (1977), pp. 32–38.

[45] See Martinson, "California Research at the Crossroads," in Martinson, Palmer, and Adams, *Rehabilitation, Recidivism, and Research*, p. 63.

conjugal visits and inmate self-government, have been suggested as being far more important. In these matters, however, penal administrators are apt to become wary.

The sexual frustrations of prisoners, both male and female, provide a constant theme in the analysis of custodial institutions. Homosexual liaisons are common, and many penologists believe that much of the sexual perversion lending the custodial institution a hothouse atmosphere might be reduced if inmates were allowed visits from their spouses.[46] (As in the free community, however, a double standard exists: it is conjugal visits for male prisoners that provide the primary subject of debate; conjugal visits for women are not even considered.)

Social visits for inmates are allowed in most institutions (although often hedged about by many restrictions imposed in the name of security), and the concept of furloughs for inmates nearing release has gained wide acceptance. Congugal visits, on the other hand, are permitted in only a few institutions in the United States. Other countries, particularly in Latin America, have long provided for conjugal visits in prisons for male offenders, justifying the visits in part as a means of maintaining the family; the sexual needs of unmarried inmates have been met by allowing the visits of prostitutes. Norman Hayner's discussion of conjugal visiting in prisons in Latin America and Mexico represents one of the few attempts at comparative analysis.[47] In the United States, conjugal visits are permitted on a limited basis in Oregon, California, and Mississippi; in the case of Mississipi, the acceptance of the idea has been attributed to a rural emphasis on the stable family and the small, semi-isolated camp organization of the Mississippi State Penitentiary.[48] In general, however, American correctional officials have been reluctant to explore the possibility of conjugal visits, despite the apparent benefits. Poor facilities, a lack of custodial personnel, the difficulty of verifying marital status and of dealing with the demands of unmarried inmates—all have been cited as standing in the way of innovation; and behind these reasons is undoubtedly the fear of being seen as procurers dressed in official clothing. If prison administrators do try to solve the problem of inmates' sexual frustration, a greater use of home visits in some sort of a furlough program, rather than the widespread reliance on conjugal visits to the custodial institution, seems the most likely course.

---

[46] For an excellent discussion of homosexuality in custodial institutions, see John H. Gagnon and William Simon, "The Social Meaning of Prison Homosexuality," *Federal Probation* 32 (March 1968), pp. 23–29.

[47] "Attitudes Toward Conjugal Visits for Prisoners," *Federal Probation* 36 (March 1972), pp. 43–49.

[48] See Columbus R. Hopper, *Sex in Prison* (Baton Rouge: Louisiana State University Press, 1969).

Inmate Self-Government The reluctance of custodial officials to deal with the problem of prisoners' involuntary celibacy is matched by their lack of enthusiasm for inmate self-government. Some wardens have, on occasion, extolled the virtues of inmates' participation in the administration of the institutions, claiming that it aids communication between the inmates and the custodial staff and increases inmate morale, but most prison officials view the concept with suspicion. A survey of some fifty penitentiaries, with forty-four responses, found that only seven allowed prisoners to participate even in an advisory role, and this was restricted to such matters as recreation and entertainment programs.[49]

In the nineteenth century, in a few instances, confined offenders were permitted a small part in institutional administration, and a handful of officials praised the benefits of democracy for captive criminals. The most important experiment in inmate self-government, however, was performed by Thomas Mott Osborne shortly before World War I, first at Auburn and then at Sing Sing, with the establishment of the Mutual Welfare League. A body of delegates, elected by the inmate population, was given various responsibilities, such as maintaining discipline, running an employment bureau, and establishing a program of recreation and lectures. A brief period of success was followed by public accusations that criminals were being coddled, prison officials were being dominated by inmates, and the system was being manipulated by shrewd and unscrupulous prisoners for their own advantage. Although many of the charges were trumped up by Osborne's opponents, Osborne was forced to resign as warden.[50] Since that time, most prison officials have claimed that inmate self-government cannot succeed. If inmates were smart enough to govern themselves, it is argued, they would not be in prison in the first place. That inmates will inevitably exploit one another, subvert discipline into a kangaroo court, and use committee meetings to plan escape attempts are only a few of the objections put forward.[51]

With a few exceptions, then, custodial institutions in the United States today are totalitarian in their governance. All control is gathered into the hands of a ruling few—the custodians—and in theory the inmates form an undifferentiated mass, without organization and without leaders.[52]

---

[49] J. F. Baker, "Inmate Self-Government," *Journal of Criminal Law, Criminology, and Police Science* 55 (March 1964), pp. 39–47.

[50] See Frank Tannenbaum, *Osborne of Sing Sing* (Chapel Hill: University of North Carolina Press, 1933). See also Arthur Evans Wood and John Barker Waite, *Crime and Its Treatment* (New York: American Book Company, 1941), pp. 605–08. A similar effort to establish some degree of inmate self-government, undertaken by Howard B. Gill at the Norfolk Prison Colony in Massachusetts in the 1920s and 1930s, met the same fate.

[51] Baker, "Inmate Self-Government"; see also Glaser, *The Effectiveness of a Prison and Parole System,* Chapter Ten.

[52] See N. A. Polanski, "The Prison as an Autocracy," *Journal of Criminal Law and Criminology* 33 (May–June 1942), pp. 16–22; and Gerard De Gré, "Freedom and Social Structure," *American Sociological Review* 11 (October 1946), pp. 529–36.

When inmate leaders do emerge to express common grievances or to guide inmates in united action, custodial officials speak resentfully of conspiracies, revolutionary movements, and the like; such leaders do in fact challenge the fundamental pattern of power on which most custodial institutions are supposed to be constructed. It is just this challenge that dismays prison administrators in today's "politicization" of the prison, as we shall see later in this chapter.

The Social Structure of Custodial Institutions

Custodial institutions in the United States vary greatly in obvious ways, for there are institutions for men and for women, for adults and for youths, for felons and for misdemeanants. The degree of security ranges from the intricate locking devices and constant surveillance of the maximum-security prison to the casual confinement of a work camp for delinquent boys. The organizational goals may stress rehabilitation or the rigid control of behavior.

This variation is not to be ignored, and generalizations must be constructed with care. Nonetheless, custodial institutions can be viewed as forming a species of social organization marked by a number of distinguishing characteristics. First, no matter how much stress is placed on the reformation of the inmate or on allegedly enlightened concepts of therapy, custodial institutions generally *impose* a social order, a regimen, on those held captive. Second, although often differing in the conditions of confinement, custodial institutions usually inflict a number of deprivations on inmates, of which the loss of liberty is only one. The "pains of imprisonment" involve more than material discomfort or physical mistreatment—they pose serious psychological threats to the prisoner that cannot be ignored. And third, custodial institutions typically reveal an informal social system among inmates centering on reactions to the deprivations and frustrations of life in confinement, ranging from a highly individualistic to a collectivist response, but in general reflecting an attempt to circumvent the institutional rules and expressing hostility to the custodians. These characteristics may emerge more prominently in some types of institutions than in others, but the central fact is that all custodial institutions involve a punishing detention that prisoners must cope with as best they can. It is this configuration of circumstances that forms the framework for the social structure of the world of imprisonment.

The Custodial Staff

In most of society's institutions, officials play their roles in a bureaucratic hierarchy. As Max Weber pointed out, "For the needs of mass administration today, bureaucratic administration is completely indispensible.

The choice is between bureaucracy and dilettantism."[53] Even small institutions need the well-defined roles and impersonal standards of performance that are bureaucracy's hallmarks. In custodial institutions, however, the bureaucrat is a bureaucrat with a gun—quite literally so, in the case of guards in a maximum-security prison. Even in institutions where less emphasis is put on custody and control, the threat of force lies just beneath the surface.

But in the day-to-day activities of small-scale communities, the use of force is an uncertain and often ineffective means of channeling behavior. Force cannot be invoked on a routine basis to move hundreds of inmates through a mess hall or to fulfill the work assignments of the custodial institution. Official force may touch off inmate violence, and the officials are acutely aware that they are greatly outnumbered. The administrative staff, then, finds itself in need of other means to secure compliance but quickly discovers that such means are scant. Inmates are already being punished, more often than not, close to the limits allowed by law. There are few additional punishments that the custodians can inflict to secure obedience. Similarly, the law—and public attitudes—restrict any rewards that might be offered, and even the promise of "good time"—the reduction of a sentence in return for good behavior—is often seen as a distant benefit of small relevance to present conduct. In institutions where prisoners work, wages are abysmally low, as we have seen, and the hope of promotion cannot exist where inmates are deliberately forced into the equality of powerlessness.

As a consequence, the dominance of the administrative staff is frequently more apparent than actual.[54] Unwilling to rely routinely on force, limited in their stock of punishments and rewards, and unable to expect obedience from the prisoners on the basis of loyalty to the organization or a sense of mission, the officials are hard pressed to enforce regulations. Thus there is strong pressure on the officials to compromise—to overlook a number of infractions that are considered relatively trivial in exchange for compliance in areas considered significant. Inmates may be allowed to remain out of their cells without authorization, to cook food stolen from the institution's kitchen, to pass letters back and forth—and in return they are expected to refrain from violence, to perform their assigned tasks with at least a show of effort, and to maintain some degree of civility toward one another and the guards.

Custodians also fail to enforce the full array of institutional regulations

---

[53] *The Theory of Social and Economic Organization,* ed. Talcott Parsons (New York: Oxford University Press, 1947), p. 337.

[54] For a more extended discussion of the power position of custodial officials, see Sykes, *The Society of Captives,* Chapter Three; see also James B. Jacobs and Harold G. Retsky, "Prison Guard," *Urban Life* 4 (April 1975), pp. 5–29.

on the grounds of friendship. Custodians and inmates are thrown into proximity over a prolonged period of time, and it is inevitable that in many instances guards come to see those they guard as something other than enemies of society, to be suppressed at any cost. Bonds of friendship are established as the criminal in prison comes to be perceived as the man or woman in prison, and violations of the rules may be ignored as the guard no less than the prisoner tries to find a *modus vivendi* within the detailed rules of the custodial bureaucracy.

Finally, the authority of the custodial administrators is compromised by the tendency to shift the responsibility for many boring, monotonous chores into the hands of the prisoners. Making out lists, distributing mail, climbing stairs to unlock a cell—such tasks are often assigned to inmates due to laziness, indifference, or naiveté. Prisoners come to control much more of institutional life than is commonly acknowledged. In examining the social structure of the custodial institution, then, it is important to realize that officials do *not* reign as unquestioned dictators enforcing every rule. Instead, their power is splintered and compromised, with many "minor" infractions ignored. Thus the stage is set for more serious infractions—an escape attempt, a violent fight between inmates over an unpaid gambling debt, an assault on a guard with a homemade knife—that the custodians do not anticipate.

The degree of the corruption of authority varies from one institution to another, and even within an institution when changes occur in the administrative staff; and the picture is greatly complicated when, as is true in some institutions, the bribery of guards in the smuggling of drugs and other contraband items seriously undermines the administration of custodial authority.[55] In almost all custodial institutions, however, varied though they are, a basic sociological principle can usually be seen at work. If it is true that power corrupts and absolute power corrupts absolutely, it is also true that the maxim has another meaning: Power—even total power—is apt to be corrupted as it is exercised. No social organization corresponds exactly to the blueprint of the ruling few. The custodial institution is apt to be marked by an informal social system in the making of which the prisoners have a large hand.

The loss of liberty of movement is the defining element of a custodial institution, but that prisoners must live in a greatly shrunken world is only the beginning of their punishment. Many perceptive prisoners have

The Pains of Imprisonment

---

[55] See R. Theodore Davidson, *Chicago Prisoners: The Key to San Quentin* (New York: Holt, Rinehart and Winston, 1974), Chapter Six. According to the author, writing an anthropological account of the San Quentin Prison in the late 1960s, as many as thirty guards may have brought in illegal drugs, with each guard earning about $10,000 a year from his smuggling activities.

Prison Within the Prison

"Adjustment Center" is the name euphemistically attached by the Department of Corrections to that area of the prison where inmates are kept for punishment or "institutional convenience." Prisoners in the Adjustment Centers are defined as being in "isolation" or "segregation" status. Prisoners and correctional officers alike call the Adjustment Center "the hole"; reporters have labeled them "dangerous dungeons"[1] and "zoos."[2] There are Adjustment Centers located in the California prisons at San Quentin, Folsom, Soledad, Vacaville, Chino, Tehachapi, and, for youthful offenders, at the Deuel Vocational Institute at Tracy. They currently house about 720 inmates. 63% of Adjustment Center inmates are black or Chicano, although these groups comprise only 45% of the whole prison population.[3]

From Lynne S. Hollander, "The Adjustment Center: California's Prisons Within Prisons," *The Black Law Review* 1 (Summer 1971), pp. 153–54. Reprinted with permission of *The Black Law Journal*.

[1] "Prisons in Crisis" by Bob Williams, *Sacramento Bee*, Feb. 9, 1971.
[2] "Men Without Hope" by Tom Findley, *San Francisco Chronicle*, March 17, 1971.
[3] Note 1, Supra.

Conditions in the Adjustment Centers range from extreme to total sensory deprivation. Cells are approximately six feet by ten feet with a concrete floor and solid concrete walls on three sides (some have a very heavily screened window on one wall). The fourth wall has either a solid steel door with a small slot through which meals are served (the flap on the slot often being locked by guards at other times) or a barred door covered with heavy steel mesh. The cells are often filthy, foul-smelling, and infested with cockroaches and bedbugs. The inmate sleeps on a thin cotton pad placed either on the floor, on a cement pallet, or on rudimentary and often broken springs.

Each inmate eats all his meals alone in his cell. The diet is severely monotonous, and an inmate who "wastes" food or "fails in other ways to obey the rules" may be placed on an even more restricted "special isolation diet."[4] A Folsom Adjustment Center inmate describes the isolation diet this way: "The inmates in the hole call the stuff they feed us in here a dog biskit (sic). It's made by pressing left over foods

[4] Director's Rule 4509(6), California Department of Corrections.

into a block and then drying it out and cutting it into 3 by 5 inch squares, you get 2 per day—with one slice of bread. I don't eat the stuff, not solely because of pride, but because of the smell . . ."

For six months, a year, two, even five years the inmate lives in his Adjustment Center cell almost continuously. He is caged there at least twenty-three hours a day and often twenty-four. He is supposed to be let out for exercise at least one-half hour per day and to shower once every five days, but frequently he is not allowed out for several days at a time. Most of his personal property is taken away from the inmate. His canteen privileges are non-existent or severely limited. He is deprived of most reading material. He is given almost no recreational, educational, vocational or psychotherapeutic program. He has only limited access to the prison physician and rarely obtains adequate medical care. (One inmate recently sent out a message asking for medical attention and received a note back telling him to "call for help when the blood is ½ inch thick on the floor.")

The extreme severity of the physical conditions and restriction of experiences in themselves make the Adjustment Centers "emotion charged combustion chambers."[5] But the situation is compounded by the inmates' fears of cruelty, violence and brutal treatment. Inmates relate that their personal property is mutilated or stolen by the guards. They claim that guards throw hot coffee on them. They describe beatings by guards and unwarranted use of tear gas and mace. They assert that racial hostility is deliberately provoked and fostered by guards and staff, both as an expression of their own racial prejudice and as a means of control; as illustration they describe numerous "set-ups," wherein guards leave a prisoner's cell door open so that other inmates, known to be hostile to him, can attack him during their exercise period, and other techniques by which conflict is provoked between different racial groups.

These allegations are often so outrageous as to defy belief, but the consistent and repetitive nature of the reports seems to authenticate them. Whether or not every one is true, there is no doubt but that the inmates live in constant anxiety for their safety and well-being.

[5] "Prisons in Crisis" by Bob Williams, *Sacramento Bee,* Feb. 9, 1971.

written of the oppressive conditions of prison life that range from grinding monotony, boredom, and loneliness to brutal acts of violence inflicted by both guards and inmates.[56] The systematic neglect and gross sadism that so often marked prisons in the past have largely disappeared from American custodial institutions—although enough instances keep breaking into the public view to prick the conscience of a society that would like to believe it has left such barbarities behind. Nonetheless, imprisonment *is* punishing, and there are profound psychological threats confronting the inmates that are no less fearsome than the physical maltreatment they have replaced.[57]

First, whatever confinement may mean in terms of broken relationships with family and friends and a double loss of liberty (for the inmate is not only confined to the institution but within the institution as well), it also inflicts a deeper hurt, in that confinement represents a deliberate, moral rejection of the criminal by the free community. Indeed, as Walter Reckless had pointed out, the moral condemnation of offenders converts mere pain into punishment, and this condemnation confronts inmates by the fact of their involuntary seclusion.[58] It is sometimes claimed that criminals are so alienated from society that its moral condemnation does not touch them, and for a small number of offenders, such as the professional thief or the psychopathic personality described by William and Joan McCord, this may be true.[59] For the majority of imprisoned criminals, however, the evidence suggests that the threat to the prisoner's ego posed by society's rejection cannot be avoided. The prisoner is never allowed to forget that he can no longer claim to be a full-fledged, trusted member of society. Somehow this rejection by the free community must be warded off, turned aside, rendered harmless. Somehow the imprisoned criminal must find a device for rejecting his rejectors, if he is to endure psychologically.[60]

Second, by the conventional standards prisoners live in a condition of extreme material deprivation; they are often housed in cramped, barren cells and lacking the simple amenities most Americans take for granted. Medical services are provided, it is true, no matter how inadequate they

---

[56] For an excellent set of accounts of prison life today, in the inmates' own words, see Jamie Shalleck, ed., *Prison. Interviews by Leonard J. Berry* (New York: Grossman Publishers, 1972). The recollections of well-known writers and political figures who have been imprisoned—such as Dostoyevsky, Cervantes, Genet, Nehru—form an important part of the world's literary heritage, added to in recent years by Solzhenitsyn in Russia and some of the black activists who have been jailed in the United States. See, for example, George Jackson, *Soledad Brother*.

[57] For a more extended discussion of the following material, see Sykes, *The Society of Captives*, Chapter Four.

[58] See *The Crime Problem* (New York: Appleton-Century-Crofts, 1955), pp. 428–29.

[59] See *Psychopathy and Delinquency* (New York: Grune and Stratton, 1956).

[60] See McCorkle and Korn, "Resocialization Within Walls," pp. 99–111.

may be, and inmates are not forced to remain hungry, cold, or wet. There is usually an exercise yard, a shower once a week. But life in most institutions lacks those subtle symbolic overtones—such as a sense of mastery, competence, and worth—that modern Western culture finds in the world of possessions. When poverty cannot be excused as a blind stroke of fate or part of universal calamity, the impoverished individual is likely to feel under attack at the deepest layers of personality. Few prisoners are trained to accept asceticism as a means of spiritual salvation, and inmates cannot fail to see themselves as having lost control of those goods and services so commonly accepted as sure indicators of a person's value.[61]

Third, as we have seen, few custodial institutions allow conjugal visits. Prisoners must face the deprivation of heterosexual relationships for long periods of time; and if inmates are rejected and impoverished by the fact of imprisonment, they can also be said to be figuratively castrated by involuntary celibacy.

Some commentators have suggested that imprisoned males experience a reduction of the sexual drive and that the sexual frustrations of prisoners are less than they might appear to be.[62] Robert Linder has argued to the contrary, noting that prisoners' access to the mass media, pornography circulated among inmates, and constant discussions of sexual matters serve to keep sexual impulses alive.[63] In reality, the situation is undoubtedly mixed, depending on many factors, such as the age of inmates and the conditions of imprisonment. Furthermore, there are possibly important differences in the extent of homosexuality in institutions for men and for women, as we shall see later. Nonetheless, most analysts agree that (1) a great many inmates do suffer from a sense of heterosexual deprivation; (2) homosexual behavior is widespread in custodial institutions, with possibly one third of adult male inmates being involved at one time or another; and (3) much of the homosexual behavior, both for men and women, involves more than simple physical release. Symbolic meanings of domination, for example, and affection are of crucial importance.[64]

[61] Mirra Komarovsky's discussion of the psychological implications of unemployment would appear to be highly relevant to the inmates of custodial institutions, despite the difference in context. She notes, in *The Unemployed Man and His Family* (New York: Dryden Press, 1940), pp. 74–77, that economic failure provokes acute anxiety as humiliation cuts away at the individual's conception of his manhood. He feels useless, undeserving of respect, disorganized, adrift in a society where economic status is a major anchoring point.

[62] See Gagnon and Simon, "The Social Meaning of Prison Homosexuality."

[63] See "Sex in Prison," *Complex* 6 (Fall 1951), pp. 5–20.

[64] Gagnon and Simon note that two recent estimates of the number of women in female prisons engaging in homosexual behavior vary from 50 percent to 85 percent, with the variation probably due in part to differing definitions. "There are almost as many views of the extent, form, significance, and expression of homosexuality or pseudohomosexuality in

In addition to these more or less voluntary homosexual liaisons, homosexual rape is not uncommon. In an investigation of local correctional institutions in Philadelphia, officials from the district attorney's office and the police department concluded that sexual assaults are endemic in that city's prison system. They estimated that during the twenty-six-month period under investigation there were approximately 2000 sexual assaults, involving some 1500 individual victims and 3500 individual aggressors. The investigators found that "virtually every slightly built young man committed to jail by the courts is sexually approached within hours of his admission to prison. Many young men are overwhelmed and repeatedly 'raped' by gangs of inmate aggressors."[65] Similar accounts of homosexual rape are to be found in reports on state and federal institutions. Inmates' attempts to solve the problem of heterosexual deprivation by engaging in homosexual behavior frequently creates another problem that is no less devastating. In the tense atmosphere of the prison or the reformatory, latent homosexual tendencies may be activated in the individual without being translated into overt behavior and yet still arouse strong guilt feelings at either the conscious or unconscious level. The individual's sexual identity is likely to be called into question—a psychological onslaught that few can bear with equanimity.

A fourth pain of imprisonment involves the large body of rules and commands designed to control prisoners' behavior in minute detail. From the viewpoint of a great many inmates, this represents an intolerable domination, a deprivation of autonomy that is bitterly resented. It might be argued that for a number of imprisoned offenders, extensive control by the custodians provides a welcome escape from freedom and that institutional officials serve as an external superego reducing the anxieties created by an awareness of deviant impulses. This may sometimes be so, but the number of such cases appears to be small. It might also be argued that much of the regulation involves intrusion that is irritating or bothersome but no worse, and must be accepted because it is essential to the maintenance of custody and internal order. For many inmates, however, it is precisely the triviality of much of the officials' control that proves most galling. Many regulations governing inmates' lives serve no useful purpose, it is said, but are designed simply to humiliate prisoners, to force them back into the weak, dependent status of childhood.

------

prison as there are persons describing the phenomena," it has been pointed out (*Making It in Prison*, Heffernan, p. 89). It seems likely that for many prisoners, both male and female, who do engage in homosexual behavior, the behavior is often rare or sporadic rather than chronic; and much of the homosexuality that does occur in prison is not part of a life pattern existing before and after confinement, but is instead a response to the prison situation.

[65] See Alan J. Davis, "Sexual Assaults in the Philadelphia Prison System," in David M. Peterson and Charles W. Thomas, eds., *Corrections: Problems and Prospects* (Englewood Cliffs, N.J.: Prentice-Hall, 1975), pp. 64–75.

"Total institutionalization is synonymous with forced dependency," notes one writer. "The controls of prison which attempt to regulate lives, attitudes, and behavior are synonymous with those used during infancy."[66] Inmates are likely to react with rage.

The seeming pointlessness of many rules in custodial institutions may be due in part to what can be called the *principle of bureaucratic indifference*—that is, events that are important to those at the bottom of the heap are viewed with increasing lack of concern at each step up in the hierarchy. The rules, the commands, the decisions flowing down to the inmates are not accompanied by explanations, on the grounds that it is "impractical" or "too much trouble."[67] Some of the regulations imposed by the custodians may in fact be quite pointless, the result of an excess of caution that is simply not justified. And the lack of explanation may be a calculated policy, since to provide explanation implies that those who are ruled have a right to know and that if the explanations are not satisfactory the rules will be changed. The important fact for the moment, however, is that prisoners are frequently unable to understand why their lives are being controlled in such detail and deeply resent their loss of autonomy.

It is possible that the loss of autonomy is particularly painful in American society because of the insecurities produced by the delays, the conditionality, and the uneven progress so often experienced in gaining adult status. It is also possible that many criminals have had great difficulties in adjusting to figures of authority and so find the many restraints of prison life especially threatening as earlier psychological struggles are reactivated in more virulent form. In any event, inmates in a variety of custodial institutions commonly express their dislike of the petty humiliations, the enforced deference, the finality of authoritarian decisions—all features of childhood's helplessness. Of the many psychological threats confronting prisoners, few are better calculated to arouse acute anxieties than the attempt to reimpose the subservience of youth, and prisoners must somehow find a way of coping with the issue.

Fifth and last, the pains of imprisonment include forced association with other criminals for prolonged periods of time under conditions of severe deprivation. Rubbed raw by the irritants of custodial life, and frequently marked by long histories of aggressive behavior, inmates are likely to explode into violence or to take what they want from other inmates with the threat of force. The world of the prison can be anxiety-provoking even for the hardened recidivist, and inmates are apt to count

[66] See Kathryn Watterson Burkhart, *Women in Prison* (Garden City, N.Y.: Doubleday, 1973), p. 129.
[67] Sykes, *The Society of Captives,* pp. 73–75.

the deprivation of a sense of security as one of the most difficult problems with which they must deal.

Weaker inmates and those without friends or money to buy protection may find themselves in a particularly vulnerable position. But all inmates must face the possibility that they will be tested, that someone will push them to see how far they will go, to see if they will fight for the safety of their person or their possessions. If they fail, they will thereafter be an object of contempt, constantly in danger of being attacked by other inmates who will identify them as obvious victims.[68] Yet if they succeed, they may well become targets for new prisoners who wish to establish a reputation for toughness or daring. Thus both success and failure in defending one's self against the aggression of fellow prisoners may provoke fresh attacks, and no inmate stands assured of the future. The world of the maximum-security prison for adult males has been described as a gigantic playground—and the metaphor can be extended to a great variety of custodial institutions, for inmates are frequently caught up in an atmosphere of aggression and emotion where few are willing to call on external authority to settle disputes. It is a tense and troubling world, and no inmate can view it without some degree of apprehension.

The Inmate Social System   Individuals encountering a frustrating situation in the free community can react in a great many ways. But prisoners trying to solve the problems posed by confinement find their alternatives greatly reduced. They cannot walk away from their plight.

Most inmates are ill prepared to withdraw psychologically, although some prisoners do sink into a numb indifference to their surroundings. Most of them, at least until the recent past, have had little hope of bringing about major changes in the conditions of custody. The major mode of reaction has centered on the need to adjust to the rigors of imprisonment.

As sociologists have examined the patterns of adjustment in different kinds of custodial institutions over the past thirty years or so, two findings have emerged with special clarity. First, the reactions of inmates are not a grab bag of idiosyncratic responses but constitute a coherent whole that is remarkably similar from one institution to another. A set of related social roles labeled in terms drawn from prison argot forms an inmate social system that persists long after individual inmates have come and gone. And second, there exists in most custodial institutions an inmate code, or a set of maxims and normative injunctions that describes

---

[68] In the case of homosexual assaults, it has been pointed out, "after a young man has been raped, he is marked as a sexual victim for the duration of his confinement. This mark follows him from institution to institution" (Davis, "Sexual Assaults in the Philadelphia Prison System," p. 65).

how inmates *should* behave—and that is matched by inmate behavior in varying degrees, depending on a variety of circumstances.[69]

The code centers on the relationship of inmate to inmate and inmate to guard: *Never snitch on a fellow convict*, it is declared. *Play it cool, do your own time. Don't sell favors to other inmates, don't exploit other inmates. Never trust the guards.* The fundamental injunctions are two—inmates should stick together and inmates should oppose the custodians—and these norms find their embodiment in the role of the *right guy*, or *real man*, one who shares his limited stock of worldly goods with other inmates, never betrays his fellows, never starts a quarrel, and endures his captivity with dignity and courage. It is an ideal, of course, and few prisoners match their behavior completely to the code's image of the hero. Within the population of deviants, there is a great deal of deviant behavior, in that many inmates fail to conform to the norms of the inmate code; and the patterns of deviant behavior are also assigned argot labels that are similar from one institution to another.

The *rat*, or *snitch*, is widely recognized and berated, and the intensity with which inmates conveying information to the officials are condemned by their fellow inmates must be understood in light of the psychological threat the betraying inmate poses.[70] There is, of course, the danger that the escape attempt will be revealed or the smuggling operation exposed to the guards. In addition, however, the rat, or snitch, undermines the solidarity of all inmates, hurting not one inmate but many. The one social group in which the prisoner can find a sense of worth is endangered, and the person who poses that danger is treated with hatred and contempt.

Inmates who deal in the commodities stolen from institutional supply stores—such prisoners are called *merchants, racketeers*, and so on—are also likely to be accorded great opprobrium. They profit from the misery of their companions, and yet it is not merely economic gain at the expense of their fellows that is resented. By selling or trading, rather than freely sharing, they too violate the idea of inmate solidarity.[71] *Gorillas*,

[69] See Sheldon L. Messinger, book review, *American Sociological Review* 32 (1967), pp. 143–46. As Messinger indicates, the study of inmate social relations and culture has turned out to be one of those unusual areas in which there has been an extensive exchange of ideas among sociologists; studies have been built on what has been done before, and there has been a notable accumulation of findings.

[70] Not all inmates within an institution view ratting in exactly the same way. The meaning of betrayal can be fairly complex, and in some women's prisons a large number of inmates do not identify with the criminal world and may view ratting with ambivalence. For an excellent discussion of the social roles of those inmates identifying with the custodians, see Heffernan *Making It in Prison*, Chapter VII. Nonetheless, the polarization of inmates and guards appears to dominate many custodial institutions.

[71] See Vergil L. Williams and Mary Fish, *Convicts, Codes, and Contraband* (Cambridge, Mass.: Ballinger Publishing, 1974).

who use violence or the threat of violence to advance their own interests, are similarly viewed with dislike, although it is a dislike often tinged with the respect and deference that the weak accord the powerful. *Wolves*—aggressive homosexuals who coerce, seduce, or bribe other inmates into providing sexual services—violate the inmate ideal of stoic endurance (as well as the free community's ideas about sexual normality) and thus are apt to lose standing in the eyes of other prisoners.[72] Those prisoners who identify explicitly with the custodians, who echo official sentiments and take the side of the guards in the endless disputes that roil the surface of institutional life, are especially disliked. Called *centermen, junior guards,* or *inmate cops,* prisoners who present themselves as being at ease with officialdom are usually despised and distrusted by the rest of the inmate population, if, indeed, they are not beaten or sometimes killed.

Confinement and deprivation are probably not, in themselves, capable of accounting for the thievery, violence, and sexual exploitation encountered in custodial institutions; in certain wartime situations, for example, or in monasteries, the degree of social solidarity may be high.[73] But existence in a custodial institution is deliberately made miserable by a hostile staff, in the eyes of most prisoners; and the prisoners themselves bring to the institution long-standing behavior patterns involving violence and the exploitation of others. With no lofty purpose to justify their plight and frequently well versed in patterns of criminality, inmates might be expected to drift in the direction of a war of all-against-all.

That many custodial institutions do *not* exhibit continual conflict among large numbers of inmates can be attributed in large measure to the inmate code, with its demands for solidarity and mutual support. The inmate code is frequently violated by prisoners, it is true, and some inmates cynically proclaim in public their allegiance to their fellow prisoners while exploiting them in private. Nevertheless, the inmate code is usually sufficiently influential to produce some measure of solidarity within a population that is being pushed in the opposite direction by so many other forces; and most custodial institutions rest in a compromise between a war of all-against-all and inmate unity.[74]

[72] In institutions for males, so-called passive homosexuals are divided among those who engaged in homosexual behavior before coming to prison and those who become homosexuals because of fear or economic need. The former are often referred to as *fags* and the latter as *punks.* Both are viewed with much greater contempt than the aggressive *wolf.*

[73] See Erving Goffman, "On the Characteristics of Total Institutions: Staff–Inmate Relationships," in Donald R. Cressey, ed., *The Prison* (New York: Holt, Rinehart and Winston, 1961), pp. 68–106.

[74] In some institutions, such as jails and military prisons for short-term offenders, it appears likely that an inmate code demanding inmate solidarity plays a smaller part. Many prisoners do not wish to get involved and place a greater stress on "doing your own time," in anticipation of an early release. It has also been argued that inmates serving long sen-

The individual fulfilling the social role of the real man, or right guy, serves as the exemplar of the inmate code, and his behavior stands in admired contrast to the deviance of the snitch, the merchant, and the gorilla. Somewhat aloof, seldom complaining, enduring the rigors of imprisonment with dignity, ready to fight if necessary but not aggressive, loyal to other inmates and willing to share whatever he may have— the real man is a respected figure accorded the deference that flows to those who match a group's ideals. The concept of hard, silent stoicism has its roots in a vision of manhood and integrity that transcends the prison; self-restraint, reserve, toughness, emotional balance, and loyalty have long been considered virtues by many cultures, and they are virtues that thrive on adversity.[75] In fact, according to John Irwin and Donald Cressey, there is a thief subculture in the free community, and the norms embodied in the behavior of the real man are the norms of that subculture imported into the prison by "real" criminals, such as career burglars, robbers, and professional thieves.[76] The content of the thief subculture is not entirely clear, as Julian Roebuck has pointed out, nor is the concept of "real" criminal.[77] The important point for the moment, however, is not whether components of the inmate code (such as an injunction against siding with those in authority or a belief in sharing) exist to varying degrees in the free community; rather, it is that in the custodial institution the population of *prisoners* is held forth as the social group deserving the highest allegiance and the real man exhibits the behavior that all should try to match.

By stressing group solidarity, the inmates of custodial institutions can alleviate—although not eliminate—a number of the pains of imprisonment. A cohesive inmate society provides prisoners with a meaningful social group with which they can identify and which will support them in their battles against their condemners—and thus prisoners can at least in part escape the fearful isolation of the convicted offender. Inmate solidarity helps to solve the problem of personal security posed by the involuntary intimacy of men with long criminal records. Inmate solidarity, in the form of sharing or reciprocating gifts and favors, attacks a potent source of aggression among prisoners, the drive for material betterment

tences pass through a series of phases, with commitment to the inmate code relatively low at the beginning and the end of their prison terms. See Stanton Wheeler, "Socialization in Correctional Communities," *American Sociological Review* 26 (1961), pp. 699–712; see also Peter G. Garabedian, "Socialization in the Prison Community," *Social Problems* 11 (Fall 1963), pp. 139–52.

[75] See Robert Warshow, "The Gangster as Tragic Hero," *Partisan Review* (February 1948), pp. 240–44.

[76] "Thieves, Convicts, and the Inmate Culture," *Social Problems* 10 (Fall 1962), pp. 142–55.

[77] See "A Critique of 'Thieves, Convicts, and the Inmate Culture,'" *Social Problems* 11 (Fall 1963), pp. 193–200.

by means of force and fraud. A cohesive population of prisoners helps curb aggressive sexual attacks. And although autonomy cannot be regained, the respect paid to fortitude helps prisoners in their struggle to maintain personal integration in the face of punishments inflicted by the custodians.

According to this theoretical viewpoint, then, the inmate code has an important function for those held in custody, providing a solution of sorts to the problems created by the conditions of confinement. These problems, notes Messinger, involve symbolic dilemmas centering on the maintenance or reestablishment of the integrity of self; and the informal social system, created by the inmates as an answer to these difficulties, is founded on a pervasive opposition between inmates and custodial staff that seriously undermines the hope of rehabilitation.[78]

The inmate social system of the custodial institution varies more than is indicated by this sketch. In particular, it has been argued that (1) within institutions the inmate viewpoint is less monolithic than the foregoing suggests, with a significant number of prisoners who disagree with the inmate code; (2) custodial institutions vary in the extent to which they impose deprivations on inmates, with resulting differences in the reactions of prisoners; and (3) the characteristics of inmates need to be accorded a larger part in the explanation of inmate social systems.[79] Recent research on the nature of prison life has done much to enlarge our understanding of some of this variation, most notably in terms of the similarities and differences in prisons for men and women.

Prisons for Women

Because so few women are convicted of serious crimes that the facilities of neighboring states can be used when necessary, a few states have no prisons for women. One or two states imprison women in a separate section of a custodial institution for men. In general, however, women are confined in special prisons, relatively small in size; lacking the forbidding walls and other fortress-like aspects of men's institutions; and stressing the need for education, vocational training, and psychotherapy.[80]

[78] See "Issues in the Study of the System of Prison Inmates," p. 137.

[79] Ibid., pp. 137–40.

[80] See Edna Walker Chandler, *Women in Prison* (Indianapolis: Bobbs-Merrill, 1973). In 1974, women made up about 3.9 percent of the total prison population in state institutions. See *Survey of Inmates of State Correctional Facilities, 1974* (Washington, D.C.: Government Printing Office, 1976), p. 1. In 1977, the federal prison system announced the creation of a maximum-security prison for women—a move stimulated by the concern over the rising incidence of violent crimes, such as kidnapping and bank robbery, by women in recent years. See James F. Clarity, *The New York Times* (June 29, 1977).

The philosophy underlying prisons for women differs from that of custodial institutions for men, argues Rose Giallombardo; while male criminals are usually thought of as dangerous persons who must be suppressed, female offenders are likely to be viewed as disgraced, dishonored individuals who need protection. As a consequence, "treatment" in women's prisons is apt to concentrate on instilling standards of sexual morality, sobriety, and respect for the role of mother and homemaker—a task best accomplished, it is believed, under conditions approximating home life in the free community.[81] Women prisoners are usually housed in small groups in cottages or dormitories, and the matrons in charge are expected to be knowledgeable about housekeeping matters such as laundry, cooking, and good table manners.

As in prisons for men, however, the publicly announced programs bear only a faint resemblance to what happens in practice. The educational and vocational training are often inadequate, psychotherapy is frequently no more than an unfulfilled promise; and, despite the benign atmosphere of a cluster of cottages in a rural setting, custody is still likely to take precedence over all else.

Women in prison, no less than men, are confronted with a set of frustrating circumstances that threaten the confined criminal's identity and sense of personal worth. They are isolated from the law-abiding and made to feel contaminated and untrustworthy. Heterosexual contact is denied them, and the material standard of living is reduced to a minimum. Women too must live as children, without the autonomy commonly accorded adults. And although the degree of personal insecurity may be somewhat less in women's institutions than in men's, because the level of violence is apt to be lower, the anxieties over the safety of one's person and meager possessions still exist.

These problems are countered in part by the social relationships established among female inmates, as is true for male inmates. The informal social structure that is found repeatedly in women's prisons, however, differs markedly from that of male institutions. Of prime importance is that there is no equivalent to the argot role of the real man in custodial institutions for women. Self-containment and endurance are *not* regarded as ideal modes of adjustment to prison life, nor are loyalty and sharing viewed as especially admirable traits. A sense of inmate solidarity as a dominant value appears to be lacking.[82] A role

[81] Giallombardo, *Society of Women*, pp. 7–8.

[82] Inmates of either sex may see themselves as individually opposed to the custodial staff and the conforming world for which it stands, even if inmate unity is given a low value. See David Street, Robert D. Vinter, and Charles Persow, *Organization for Treatment* (New York: The Free Press, 1966), Chapter 9. This would appear to be frequently the case in women's prisons.

resembling "the structure of the 'right guy,' " says Giallombardo in her study of the Federal Reformatory for Women at Alderson, West Virginia, "who is such a dominant figure in the male prison, does not emerge in the female prison. . . . Concepts such as 'fair play,' 'courage,' and the like—which are consistent with the concepts of endurance, loyalty, and dignity associated with the 'right guy'—are not meaningful to the female."[83]

The lack of a flinty endurance can probably be attributed to cultural conditioning argues ex-prisoner Elizabeth Gurley Flynn. Women in prison, she says, "are far less restrained than men who are curbed by standards of manliness and who do not want to be considered cry-babies or sissies by their fellow prisoners. . . . To weep, have hysterics, shriek, scream, have 'spells,' are expected behavior patterns among women in prison. To be self-controlled, keep your chin up, be a good sport, be able to take it—it is expected of men, in daily life, in the army, and in prison. But women are deaf to such appeals."[84]

Similarly, Giallombardo attributes the lack of emphasis on inmate solidarity in women's prison to the difficulties women in America face in forming extended loyalties to other women on a relatively abstract basis. Women trained in competitive sexuality, she suggests, find it hard to put aside their habits of rivalry and to welcome the idea of sacrifice for the good of women as a group. The concept of sisterhood is difficult to establish after decades of enculturation to the contrary.

It was suggested earlier that stoical self-control and inmate unity are important factors in alleviating the pains of imprisonment. Since women appear to suffer the same pains of imprisonment as men do and since an inmate social system centered on inmate solidarity is unlikely to arise, is there any other response that can serve the same purpose?

The answer would appear to lie in homosexual relationships that are elaborated to create pseudo-family units. In account after account of custodial institutions for women, observers have noted the prominence of small groups in which members play the roles of husband, wife, father, mother, son, daughter, brother, and sister. In addition to the family units there are numerous inmate couples who may "go steady" for a time, perhaps going through a marriage ceremony or breaking up to form new alliances. The sociological literature on institutional adaptation, says Charles Tittle, suggests that female prisoners tend to establish relatively enduring primary relationships, whereas male prisoners tend

[83] Giallombardo, *Society of Women*, p. 130.

[84] *The Alderson Story: My life as a Political Prisoner* (New York: International Publishers, 1963), p. 86. Convicted of violating the Smith Act, which prohibits people from conspiring to advocate the violent overthrow of the government, Flynn was confined for several years in the same institution later studied by Giallombardo.

to organize themselves into what he terms "an overall symbiotic structure."[85]

The involvement of female inmates in family groups and homosexual couples is labeled with different argot terms in different institutions. In a comparative study of three institutions for delinquent girls, such involvement was variously referred to as the *racket*, the *sillies*, and *chick business*.[86] Those inmates who are said to be "gay on the outside," who acknowledge a serious commitment to homosexuality, consistently assume a male role, and intend to continue homosexual relationships when released may be called *stone butch, big hard daddy*, or *true butch*. The individual who plays the part of the woman in a lesbian relationship is the *true fem*. For inmates who assume a male role while imprisoned but who are not committed to homosexuality, the term *trust-to-be butch* may be employed; again, there is a complementary role in the *trust-to-be fem*. Inmates who are not sincere in their relationships, who "fool around" or "play the field," may be called *jive butches* or *jive fems*. They are viewed with some contempt, at least among those inmates who believe in forming a close bond with one individual for a prolonged period of time to see whether marriage would be desirable.[87]

The masculine pronoun is used to refer to anyone assuming the part of the male; and he communicates his masculinity by such symbolic devices as hair style, length of skirt, type of shoe, stance, walk, and mode of speech. A butch may marry a fem (and in some institutions the marriage may involve a "preacher," an exchange of vows, a certificate, and so on), and together they provide the nucleus around which a family unit may be formed. Son and daughter, brother and sister—each inmate in the family group performs his or her part according to the expectations of the outside world.

The elaboration and formalization of family structures may vary among custodial institutions, as Heffernan has suggested, but the consistent emergence of male and female roles is well established, and the function of these roles seems clear. They provide a basis for mutual aid, protection, and stable relationships offering affection and respect in a world where such matters have become acutely problematical. "In the impersonal atmosphere of the institution," says Giallombardo in describing a

---

[85] See Charles R. Tittle, "Inmate Organization: Sex Differentiation and the Influence of Criminal Subcultures," *American Sociological Review* 34 (August 1969), pp. 492–505. The tendency of women prisoners to form family units may be greatest in institutions for younger offenders, but the evidence is incomplete. See Heffernan, *Making It in Prison*, Chapter V. Inconsistencies in the accounts of custodial institutions may be the result of inaccurate observation. Temporal changes in inmate social structure, however, along with variation by type of institution, are probably more important.

[86] Giallombardo, *The Social World of Imprisoned Girls*.

[87] Ibid., pp. 146–47.

prison for young girls, "the adolescent inmates want above all to be accepted as human beings and to interact in primary relationships that are similar in nature to those which they had with some individuals in their civilian lives. To this end, the informal group is shaped in the image of the nuclear family. Only in this context can one begin to understand the seriousness with which the inmates declare their kinship ties and the special joy and satisfaction that the inmate reveals when she interrupts a conversation with another inmate as a member of her family approaches: 'Hey, this is my brother!' "[88]

The precise nature of homosexual relationships in custodial institutions for women is difficult to determine. The whole area of behavior, notes Heffernan, is usually discussed gingerly by both inmates and staff through the use of euphemisms like "people are doing those things," "everyone plays," and "tying in."[89] She suggests, however, following the work of Lowell Selling, that at least four different levels of affective relationships may occur.[90] First, inmates may form bonds of friendship similar to those recognized by the free community. Second, inmates may adopt nonconjugal family roles, taking on the rights and responsibilities typically assigned to mother, father, sister, brother, daughter, and son, with full awareness of the "play" element involved. (This form of "familying," notes Heffernan, appears to be common.) Third, inmates may "play" at marriage in the same way, interacting as husband and wife but not engaging in sexual intercourse. And finally, inmates may form a full homosexual liaison that involves both sexual relations and the public behavior expected of a married couple.

The four types of relationships are easily confused by the outsider. American culture, noted Giallombardo, "does not discourage a public display of affection between two women, such as using terms of endearment, embracing, holding hands, and kissing. Such behavior on the part of the male, however, would be immediately defined as homosexual."[91] The range of permissible gestures of affection accorded women undoubtedly accounts in part for the varying estimates of the incidence of homosexuality in women's prisons. The central issue in our analysis of inmate social structure, however, is not the amount of eroticism that exists, but the basis on which social groups are formed.

Female prisoners typically appear to model their social relationships on the patterns of marital and consanguine bonds found in the larger society. These patterns, like inmate solidarity among male prisoners, appear

[88] Ibid., p. 186.
[89] Heffernan, *Making It in Prison,* p. 89.
[90] See Lowell S. Selling, "The Pseudo-Family," *American Journal of Sociology* 37 (September 1931), pp. 247–53.
[91] *Society of Women,* p. 15.

to ease the pains of imprisonment. The different solutions worked out by men and women in custody can probably be attributed to enculturation. Men in prison may form a "buddy" system in which two close friends look out for each other, as they do in the army, but the formation of a closer bond or the formation of family units cannot be tolerated when the imputation of effeminacy is one of the most offensive of insults. (Homosexual liaisons among male inmates are usually based on domination and exploitation, and the aggressive wolf is careful to avoid any intimation of softness or affection that might detract from his image of masculine toughness.) The inmate population as a whole emerges as the crucial social unit demanding allegiance. Women prisoners apparently find the personal bonds of the family unit easier to adopt, either because an abstract unity of women is outside their experience or because the transformation of sexual roles is less anxiety-provoking than it is for males.[92] The possible impact of the women's liberation movement on the informal social system of female inmates has yet to be explored.

From Inmate to Convict

According to the sociological studies of custodial institutions prior to the latter part of the 1960s, the solidarity achieved by prisoners was clearly far from perfect. Inmates informed on one another frequently, despite the strictures of the inmate code; and although the social role of the right guy might be held out as a model, exploitation and violent fights often occurred. During the Second World War, imprisoned conscientious objectors sometimes achieved a high degree of unity and were able to confront their captors with a coordinated show of resistance. In a number of prison riots that broke out in the 1950s, prisoners were able on occasion to form disciplined groups that could act in concert, but the coalitions usually fell apart quickly as racial animosities, old feuds, and the realization of certain defeat took their toll.[93] In general, inmate soli-

[92] The tendency of women isolated from men to form family structures may transcend national boundaries. Giallombardo cites a study of Chinese women recruited for factory work during World War II who had to live apart from their families. A number of extended-family units were established, with both male and female roles. See Ju-K'ang T'ien, "Female Labor in a Cotton Mill," in Kuo-Heng Shih, *China Enters the Machine Age* (Cambridge, Mass.: Harvard University Press, 1944), pp. 185–87.

[93] See John Bartlow Martin, *Break Down the Walls* (New York: Ballantine Books, 1954). Between 1951 and 1953 Michigan, Louisiana, North Carolina, Idaho, Georgia, Kentucky, California, Massachusetts, Ohio, Illinois, Utah, New Mexico, Pennsylvania, Arizona, Washington, Oregon, and Minnesota all experienced major prison riots. For a discussion of the causes of prison riots, see Frank E. Hartung and Maurice Floch, "A Social-Psychological Analysis of Prison Riots: An Hypothesis," *The Journal of Criminal Law, Criminology, and Police Science* 47 (May–June 1956), pp. 51–57; Clarence Schrag, *The Sociology of Prison Riots*,

darity was apt to be a normative expectation that was often met but also often breached by behavior, with inmate social systems uneasily balanced between unity and internal disorder. In the 1960s, however, and in the early part of the 1970s, ethnic militancy emerged as the basis of cohesion for a significant number of prisoners, bringing with it a new view of the nature of the prison, the prisoner, and the possibilities of unified action.

A detailed analysis of race relations in American custodial institutions has not yet been written, and the following account must be viewed as tentative.[94] Nonetheless, it appears that Mexican-American, or Chicano, inmates in California prisons have formed ethnic alliances for some time, partly because of their cultural and linguistic isolation from other prisoners.[95] The alliances themselves often broke into warring factions, based on the gangs and *barrios,* or neighborhoods, from which the confined offenders were drawn. The unity that was achieved was also likely to be periodically shattered by an individualistic commitment to machismo, or masculine honor, that easily led to violence. According to R. Theodore Davidson, from about 1964 to 1972 there was a loose organization known as the *Baby Mafia* or *Family,* a group within a group composed of Chicano prisoners who dominated much of the large-scale smuggling and illegal trading within the California prison system. Members of the Baby Mafia were able to achieve a high degree of unity, but the group was eventually destroyed by a struggle for power attended by numerous killings.[96]

In both California and New York, where the formation of ethnic groups in prisons has been most prominent, the Black Muslims were able, in the 1950s and 1960s, to develop some solidarity. But the Black Muslims were relatively few in number, and much of their effort was directed to the recruitment of members for the Muslim organization out-

---

Proceedings of the American Correctional Association, 1960 (New York: American Correctional Association, 1961), pp. 136–46; Vernon Fox, "Why Prisoners Riot," *Federal Probation* 35 (March 1971), pp. 9–14; and Richard Wilsnack, "Explaining Collective Violence in Prison," in Albert K. Cohen, George F. Cole, and Robert G. Bailey, eds., *Prison Violence* (Lexington, Mass.: D. C. Heath, 1976), pp. 61–78.

[94] For an important pioneering effort, however, see Leo Carroll, *Hacks, Blacks, and Cons* (Lexington, Mass.: D. C. Heath, 1974).

[95] R. Theodore Davidson, *Chicano Prisoners: The Key to San Quentin* (New York: Holt, Rinehart and Winston, 1974), p. 54; see also John Irwin, *The Felon* (Englewood Cliffs, N.J.: Prentice-Hall, 1970), pp. 67–85.

[96] *Chicano Prisoners,* Chapter 5 and pp. 194–95. According to an account in *The New York Times* (May 14, 1973), "killings, knifings, terrorism and torture extending throughout the California penal system's 12 prisons and 16 work camps have become almost commonplace in a vicious struggle for power being waged by the two rival Mexican-American gangs. . . . Officials of the State Department of Corrections blame the internecine Chicano warfare for at least half of the 34 convict killings, and numerous knifings and beatings that have occurred in the last year among the 21,000 inmates of California's prisons."

side the prison or to securing rights of religious expression.[97] Prior to the early 1960s, then, the sense of ethnic identification in custodial institutions was largely apolitical—a basis for maintaining control of prison rackets, a means of expressing a common resentment of a shared discrimination, or the source of an appeal to a limited number of prisoners on the grounds of religion. Ethnic *militancy*—united action based on an explicit ideology and seeking changes in the structure of power—was relatively rare.

The political turmoil of the 1960s brought about a significant change in ethnic consciousness both within the custodial institution and in the larger society. The Black Muslims declined in influence in the mid-1960s, it has been argued, due to the split between the movement's spokesman, Malcolm X, and its leader, Elijah Muhammad; disillusionment with the theological analysis of the Nation of Islam; and the Black Muslims' refusal to define prison problems as a central issue.[98] A legacy of their work remained, however, according to John Pallas and Robert Barber, for "they helped destroy the barriers to political consciousness which have impeded prisoners in previous attempts to struggle against their oppression. The Muslims introduced disciplined organization among prisoners, the idea that collective action could be taken to achieve desired goals. They also introduced the notion of collective oppression to black prisoners, which counteracted the prison ideology of individual pathology. Although they located the source of that oppression in the 'white devil' and his institutions rather than in specific class-related institutions, their insistence upon the collective nature of that oppression marked an important step in the transformation of black consciousness."[99]

In the latter part of the 1960s, apparently, in a number of custodial institutions a radical political movement developed that attempted to transcend ethnic lines. "Nonwhite prisoners especially made quick connections between their struggles inside and the struggles of oppressed peoples around the world," contend Pallas and Barber. "These prisoners were joined by an influx of new prisoners, imprisoned for radical activities. Black, Puerto Rican, Chicano, and other nonwhite men and women active in radical movements, and an increasing number of whites arrested for offenses stemming from their opposition to the Indochina war, brought their politics and organizing talent to prisons. . . .

[97] See John Pallas and Robert Barber, "From Riot to Revolution," in Wright, *The Politics of Punishment,* pp. 243–45. Black Muslim activity was watched carefully by officials at Attica Prison as early as 1957 who were fearful of the "degree of intimacy and comradery beyond what prison officials felt to be a 'safe' level" (Smith and Fried, *The Uses of the American Prison* p. 57). See also *Attica: The Official Report of the New York State Special Commission on Attica* (New York: Bantam Books, 1972), pp. 122–23.

[98] Pallas and Barber, "From Riot to Revolution," pp. 246–47.

[99] Ibid., p. 246.

Since 1964, then, the prison struggle has consciously become a part of an international struggle."[100]

It is difficult to gauge the extent to which a unity based on an ideology of political oppression has actually been achieved among inmates—or whether such unity remains an ideal in the minds of a small number of politically sophisticated prisoners who hope to see confined offenders emerge as a new, powerful group on the American scene. The existence of a "revolutionary movement" is probably exaggerated, both by prison officials who are often convinced that they are confronted with a massive communist plot, and by radical inmates whose political ambitions outrun the realities of inmate social systems.[101] It appears most likely that prisons have come to present a mixed picture, with some inmates calling for unity on political grounds, others urging close-knit ethnic groupings for apolitical ends, and still others indifferent to the calls for such allegiances and determined to "pull their own time" or to exploit their fellows. There are numerous accounts of violent feuding among ethnic or social groups; inmates who identify with the Chicanos, blacks, Anglos, Nazis, and Hell's Angels often are caught up in bitter conflict.[102] There are also numerous accounts of inmates who have come to see all prisoners as sharing a common fate and who advocate the formation of a united front against the class and racial prejudice that they consider to be the cause of their confinement.[103] And there is a good deal of evidence that individualistic patterns of exploitation persist in the prison, along with ideas about inmates as a group in opposition to the guards. The relative frequencies of these different orientations are impossible to estimate with any precision, but the important point, perhaps, is not the nature of the mix but the fact that the inmate social structure is undoubtedly changing. The social role of the real man, or right guy, so central to

[100] Ibid., p. 249.

[101] "What is happening here," California's director of corrections is quoted as saying in an article in *The Reader's Digest*, "is a highly organized attempt to destroy our system of correctional justice. These agitators mean to bring anarchy to the prisons and, through them, to the streets of our cities. It is an explosive situation" (Nathan M. Adams, "Our Prisons are Powder Kegs," *The Reader's Digest* (October 1974), pp. 185–86.

[102] See, for example, Edward Bunker, "War Behind Walls," in Burton M. Atkins and Henry R. Glick, eds., *Prisons, Protest, and Politics* (Englewood Cliffs, N.J.: Prentice-Hall, 1972), pp. 60–76. According to some inmates, much of the feuding among different ethnic groups in the prison is deliberately cultivated by the guards, both to maintain control and to satisfy the guards' racial hostilities. See Hearings Before Subcommittee No. 3 of the Committee of the Judiciary, House of Representatives, Ninety-Second Congress, First Session on Corrections, October 25, 1971, *Serial No. 15* (Washington, D.C.: Government Printing Office, 1971).

[103] Herman Badillo and Milton Haynes, *A Bill of No Rights: Attica and the American Prison System* (New York: Outbridge & Lazard, 1972), pp. 7–12.

the inmate social system in the 1950s, has been supplemented—although perhaps not supplanted—by the social role of the political activist.[104]

The assertion of the prison activist—that confined criminals are political prisoners—frequently infuriates the administrators of custodial institutions, and for understandable reasons. The term *political prisoner* has often been, in the antitotalitarian traditions of American political thought, a badge of honor—one not to be appropriated by murderers, thieves, and rapists. But arguments about the rightfulness of the term *political prisoner* miss the point, as far as a sociological analysis of the prison is concerned, for they ignore the force of W. I. Thomas' famous principle that what men believe is no less important in understanding human behavior than what the independent observer calls reality. Inmates may come to see their crimes as political acts long after they were committed with apolitical motives; charges of class or racial bias may be greatly exaggerated in particular instances; and the idea that criminals are always the innocent victims of a repressive state may be mistaken. But the fact remains that many inmates have come to see themselves not as wrongdoers but as the casualties of an exploitative, racist social order. For many prisoners, the label *convict*, with its frank reminder of a political process, has become preferable to the label *inmate*, with its connotations of hospitalized patient—and thus of a "sickness" that needs to be cured. And as this shift in perception begins to take place, imprisonment for crime is likely to lose much of its moral authority.

When the custodial institution is seen as an instrument for the deliberate oppression of a class or a social group—and this has become the viewpoint not just of some confined criminals but of a significant portion of the free community—the idea of imprisonment inevitably escapes the bounds of criminology and becomes an issue for political debate.

---

[104] Something of the nature of the changed inmate consciousness can be found in the following statement of a prisoner from Auburn Prison: "I was a ghetto rat. I identified with all that the Establishment advocated as legitimate—capitalist luxury—never realizing that this was only to hook me on the opium of continuing to be a slave that sought only material gratification, and that did not strive to be a man and to be human, and most of all to be free. . . . The greatest thing that ever happened to me was to be incarcerated in the Tombs [the Men's House of Detention in New York City] with the beautiful brothers Richard Moore and William King. I finally came in contact with those people who thoroughly realized their condition. . . . One doesn't become a revolutionary by reading the book or shooting a few pigs; one has to submit one's self totally to serving the needs of the people. . . . I am a communist, a socialist, a Marxist-Leninist, a pupil of Mao, a follower of Che— the spear of the fist that from generation to generation has given his life, his will, his entire world to uplift the people's progress" (*From Behind the Walls of Auburn Concentration Camp, Prisoners Call Out: Freedom* [New York: Prisoners Solidarity Committee, 1971], pp. 23–24).

Conclusions

A number of years ago, a lawyer—obviously much concerned about the problems of penal policy—suggested in all seriousness that the solution was to be found in an orbital world prison. The space vehicle would revolve around the earth, self-sufficient in food and oxygen through the soil-less growth of plants and edible algae, a heavenly penal colony to help handle a world population of confined offenders estimated to number seven to ten million by the year 2000.[105] The sense of frustration giving rise to this zany proposal—the awareness that custodial institutions inflict much misery without returning much apparent benefit to society—is easy to understand.

In plain fact, the impact of imprisonment remains unknown. It is a cliché of modern criminology, Glaser has indicated, to argue that prisons are surely a failure, since two out of every three criminals confined commit crimes after being released and are eventually imprisoned once again. This is little more than a legend, according to Glaser, and the proportion of imprisoned criminals that revert to crime cannot be specified.[106] But even if the proportion were known, the impact of imprisonment would remain uncertain, since little or nothing is known about what would happen to comparable offenders who were not imprisoned. Would those who revert to crime do so whether they were imprisoned or not? Would those who no longer engage in crime follow such a path without regard to the penal treatment they receive? No systematic, scientific study of these questions, over a prolonged period of time, with rigorous controls for extraneous variables and precise measures of criminal behavior, has ever been made.[107]

In the mid-1970s a growing disenchantment with the concept of imprisonment became evident, for while a portion of the public continued to believe that prisons do the job they are supposed to do, a larger segment had become convinced that prisons do more harm than good. "If the choice were between prisons as they are now and no prisons at all, we would promptly choose the latter," asserted a report of the American Friends Service Committee. "We are convinced that it would be far better to tear down all jails now than to perpetuate the inhumanity and hor-

---

[105] See Luis Kutner, "A World Outer Space Prison: A Proposal," *Denver Law Review* 45 (Fall 1968), pp. 702–18. Establishing a colony in space may indeed be feasible in the near future. It is highly unlikely, though, that such an expensive venture will be devoted to the punishment of criminals. See Gerard K. O'Neill, *The High Frontier: Human Colonies in Space* (New York: William Morrow, 1977).

[106] Daniel Glaser, *The Effectiveness of a Prison and Parole System* (Indianapolis: Bobbs-Merrill, 1964), Chapter 2.

[107] See R. G. Hood, "Some Research Results and Problems," in Leon Radzinowicz and Marvin E. Wolfgang, eds., *The Criminal in Confinement* (New York: Basic Books, 1971), p. 159.

ror being carried on in society's name behind prison walls. Prisons, as they exist, are more of a burden and disgrace to our society than they are a protection or a solution to the problem of crime."[108] The demand for penal reform, stretching back to John Howard, Sir James Mackintosh, Elizabeth Fry, and Benjamin Rush in the eighteenth century, had once again found a voice.

The immediate events that pushed the prison into public consciousness in the early 1970s—the killing of three guards and three inmates at San Quentin on August 21, 1971, and the death of forty-three persons at Attica between September 9 and 13, 1971—were horrifying examples of a fundamental failure, it was argued. Jessica Mitford, in a review of *Struggle for Justice,* claimed that the philosophy of treatment presented as the underlying principle of modern custodial institutions was simply a convenient justification for secret procedures, unreviewable decisions, and unquestioned discretionary power over those in custody. "Treatment" was no more than a humiliating game, she argued, and she pointed with approval to the assertion of the American Friends Service Committee that the persistent branding of lawbreakers as sick or abnormal may be a mask to hide the hatred, fear, and revulsion that white, middle-class, Protestant reformers feel toward lower-class offenders who do not share their values. The resistance convicts offer to their systematic mistreatment, she concluded, must make us "confront the question, who is 'sick'? These courageous men or the society that condemns them to barbarities?"[109]

Such protests against the prison appeared to flow from a number of sources—the demonstrated harshness of prison life; sympathy with the war resisters and political dissidents jailed in the 1960s; the belief that blacks, Chicanos, and others were unfairly imprisoned and discriminated against even behind bars; the growing skepticism accorded psychiatry; the belief that much crime in areas such as drugs and gambling was not crime at all—and the inclination toward self-flagellation sometimes encountered among liberals. The advocates of treatment had *not* been able to prove their case, and the idea that penology was intellectually and morally bankrupt found an increasing number of adherents. And on this point, curiously enough, a number of proponents of punitive measures for convicted criminals and of believers in the futility of existing penal practice united.

Prisons, it was said, should cease pretending to "treat" criminals. Instead, prisons should return to the earlier concept of making the punish-

[108] *Struggle for Justice,* p. 23.
[109] Jessica Mitford, "Prisons: The Menace of Liberal Reform," *New York Review of Books* (March 9, 1972). Mitford's own book—*Kind and Usual Punishment: The Prison Business* (New York: Alfred A. Knopf, 1973)—helped to bring the prison problem to a wide audience.

ment fit the crime. Sentences should have a definite duration, they should be uniformly applied and talk of rehabilitation should be abolished. The whole person is *not* the concern of the law, it was claimed; rather the law should deal only with the individual's criminal acts.[110]

"My premise throughout is that penal purposes are properly retributive, deterrent, and incapacitative," argued Norval Morris, speaking not from a radical viewpoint but in the measured tones of a professor of law at the University of Chicago: "Attempts to add reformative purposes to that mixture—as an objective of the sanction as distinguished from a collateral aspiration—yield neither clemency, justice, nor, as presently administered, social utility. We may utilize our rehabilitative skills to assist the prisoner toward social readjustment, but we should never seek to justify an extension of power over him on the ground that we may thus more likely effect his reform."[111]

This argument may reflect the disillusionment with programs of social reform that flowered in the aftermath of the 1960s, a general loss of faith in social engineering that was evident in the areas of mental health, welfare, and education. Possibly, too, the economic hardships of the early 1970s have left their mark. It has become clear that the rehabilitation of criminals (if, indeed, it is possible) will probably require a very large expenditure of public funds, and public funds for all worthy purposes are in short supply. What does seem certain is that ideas about imprisonment and the proper role of the custodial institution are in a state of flux. The fortress-like walls of the American prison are still there for all to see and seem solid; the philosophical foundation appears to be crumbling.

Recommended Readings

Donald Clemmer, *The Prison Community* (Boston: Christopher Publishing House, 1940) offers the first full-length picture of the prison from a sociological perspective and contains much descriptive detail. For a so-called functional interpretation of the prison, the reader should see Gresham M. Sykes, *The Society of Captives* (Princeton, N.J.: Princeton University Press, 1958) and Richard Cloward et al., *Theoretical Studies in Social Organization of the Prison* (New York: Social Science Research Council, 1960). For an excellent analysis of prison life, with an alternative view, the reader should see John Irwin, *The Felon* (Englewood Cliffs, N.J.: Prentice-Hall, 1970). Rose Giallombardo, *Society of Women: A Study of a Women's Prison* (New York: Wiley & Sons, 1966) and Esther Heffernan, *Making It in Prison: The Square, The Cool and The Life* (New York: John Wiley & Sons, 1972)

[110] *Struggle for Justice,* Chapter 9.
[111] Norval Morris, "The Future Imprisonment: Toward a Punitive Philosophy," *Michigan Law Review* 72 (May 1974), p. 1161; see also Edwin M. Schur, *Radical Non-Intervention* (Englewood Cliffs, N.J.: Prentice-Hall, 1973).

provide excellent discussions of correctional institutions for women. For the "politicization" of the prison, the reader should see Erik Olin Wright, *The Politics of Punishment* (New York: Harper & Row, 1973) and Joan Smith and William Fried, *The Use of the American Prison: Political Theory and Penal Practice* (Lexington, Mass.: D. C. Heath, 1974).

Chapter 14
Probation, Parole, and the Therapeutic State

The brutality of prison life has convinced many people that if the criminal is to be rehabilitated, the task is best pursued outside the prison wall. Convicted offenders, it is argued, should be treated in the community, and treatment is basically a matter of integrating the individual into normal social life. If offenders must be confined for a period of time—for the purpose of punishment or because of the potential danger that they pose–they should be released on parole as quickly as possible when the punishment has been inflicted or the danger of repeated criminality is past. As far as correction is concerned, the goal is to be sought in the free world, not in the abnormal and frustrating society of the custodial institution.

Supervision in the community, for those whose sentences have been suspended or who have been released from prison before their sentences are completed, does appear to be associated with lower recidivism rates than does serving one's full sentence behind bars. Probation and parole would seem to be far more humane than imprisonment, and they are clearly cheaper. In the latter half of the 1960s, as indicated in Chapter 12, the President's Commission on Law Enforcement and Administration of Justice announced that correctional work in the United States was standing at the threshold of a new era and that the proper task of corrections included "building or rebuilding solid ties between offender and community, integrating or reintegrating the offender into community life-restoring family ties, obtaining employment and education, securing in the larger sense a place for the offender in the routine functioning of society." [1] These efforts must be undertaken without giving up the custodial and deterrent roles of corrections, the report added cautiously, particularly in the case of dangerous offenders, but the commitment to reform of the criminal rather than punishment was clear, along with the belief

[1] *Task Force Report: Corrections* (Washington, D.C.: Government Printing Office: 1967), pp. 6–7.

that it was in the community rather than in the prison that the effort must be made.

The enthusiasm of the President's Commission for probation and parole, reaffirming in an official voice the sentiments of several generations of reform-minded penologists and correctional workers, was not without its critics. Supervision in the community might indeed be associated with a lower likelihood of repeated crime than was imprisonment—but this was possibly due *not* to the effect of probation and parole, but to the attributes of those selected for such rehabilitative effort. Furthermore, as the President's Commission was forced to admit, very little was actually done to or for those on probation and parole. Low recidivism rates might be attributed to neglect as much as to "treatment."[2]

If social reintegration or corrections in the community is not the key to the reform of the convicted criminal, there are some persons working in the field of corrections who are convinced that curing criminality is by no means impossible. Some form of operant conditioning (based on the work of B. F. Skinner and other behavioral psychologists), it has been claimed, or the use of chemical therapies will provide society with a way of transforming the personality of those inclined to commit criminal acts—surely, precisely, permanently. Where crime was, conformity shall be, and treatment will have found a scientific footing.

Many people find such a vision of rehabilitation horrifying, for it appears to promise the certain ascendancy of what has been called the *therapeutic state*.[3] Acting in the name of the individual's welfare and the safety of society, the state imposes its view of proper thought and behavior on all, using the techniques of modern science rather than the clumsy punishments of the criminal law. The claims for a "chemical straitjacket" and programs of behavior modification far outrun what is presently possible, it is true, and a Clockwork Orange prison based on the novel by Anthony Burgess remains fiction rather than fact.[4] Nevertheless, both the use of various drugs in the name of therapy and the application of Skinnerian theory to captive criminals are sufficiently advanced to disturb

---

[2] The *Task Force Report: Corrections* contains almost no empirical evidence with regard to recidivism. In its discussions, "corrections" remains largely a hope of what might be done rather than a program of demonstrated effectiveness.

[3] See Nicholas N. Kittrie, *The Right to Be Different: Deviance and Enforced Therapy* (Baltimore: Penguin Books, 1973); see also Thomas S. Szasz, "Toward the Therapeutic State," in William J. Chambliss, ed., *Sociological Readings in the Conflict Perspective* (Reading, Mass.: Addison-Wesley, 1973), pp. 45–46.

[4] For public reactions to such means of dealing with the deviant, see "Chemical Straitjackets," *Time* (August 25, 1975); and Phil Stanford, "A Model, Clockwork-Orange Prison," *The New York Times* (September 17, 1972).

many critics, for they foresee the imminent development of powerful techniques for the control of people's minds as well as their actions. It is not merely criminals who will be manipulated by the state but political dissidents as well, and Big Brother will have come at last to reign over the personalities of a pacified population.

Performance does not yet match promise—or threat—and democratic societies still provide safeguards against the psychic destruction of non-conformists. New forms of dealing with the criminal are ominous enough, however, to warrant the most careful scrutiny by the social sciences, and we must be mindful once again of the constant tension that exists between the just and effective control of crime and the suppression of dissent in the administration of criminal justice.

In this chapter, we will first examine briefly the history of community corrections in the form of probation and parole and the question of whether they are supplanting or supplementing imprisonment. We will then turn to an analysis of the social role of the probation officer and the parole officer—the different ideas about what community-corrections workers should do and what in fact can be done. After discussing the extent to which probation and parole reduce recidivism, and the difficulties of evaluation research, the chapter will conclude by examining the rise of the therapeutic state, in which new modes of transforming criminals into noncriminals are beginning to appear, as society continues to try to "cure" criminality.

Origins and Development of Community Corrections

Probation, or supervision in the community in lieu of imprisonment, is sometimes said to have its roots in the early English common law in such practices as benefit of clergy, judicial reprieve, and recognizance. *Benefit of clergy* was a special plea by which certain types of offenders— members of the clergy, initially, and later all who could read—claimed the right to be tried in ecclesiastical courts, where penalties were often mild, sometimes amounting to no more than being "put to penance."[5] *Judicial reprieve* consisted of a temporary suspension of sentence so that the convicted offender could apply for a pardon or the case could be reviewed because the judge believed the evidence was suspect. *Recognizance* involved freedom given the offender in exchange for his promise, backed by a money bond or a personal assurance offered in public view, that he would offend no more.

The Rise of Probation

[5] David Dressler, *Practice and Theory of Probation and Parole* (New York: Columbia University Press, 1969), pp. 16–18.

It is extremely doubtful, however, that benefit of clergy had a direct influence on any immediate precursors of probation;[6] similarly, judicial reprieve and recognizance are better viewed as early, isolated attempts to deal with special situations than as true social ancestors of modern probation practices. The origins of probation can probably be attributed most accurately to the work of John Augustus, a Boston shoemaker, in 1841.

Working as a volunteer, Augustus attended to the immediate needs of released offenders for food, clothing, shelter, and work, in the belief that the fallen could be reformed. After first looking after drunkards, he progressed to a variety of criminals released by the courts. He finally found it necessary to turn over his shoemaking business to his son in order to devote all his time to his new vocation.[7] In 1878 Massachusetts followed his lead and enacted legislation formally establishing probation and providing for a paid staff; by 1900 six other states had followed suit. The use of probation continued to grow, despite a number of legal battles in which probation was decried as undue leniency; and at the present time probation is the most common form of correctional treatment, involving more than one million convicted offenders and probation officers.

The place of probation in the structure of government varies greatly among the states, sometimes appearing under the control of the executive branch and sometimes found within the sphere of the judiciary. There may be one probation agency for all offenders or separate agencies for felons and misdemeanants, and for adults and juveniles. Probation services may be organized on a statewide basis or divided among counties and cities.[8] "The question of where probation should be placed in the framework of government becomes more critical as its use expands and staff numbers increase," notes the National Advisory Commission on Criminal Justice Standards and Goals;[9] but perhaps even more important are questions about the substance of probation work and the limits of its effectiveness.

The Rise of Parole

Parole, or the prisoner's conditional release under supervision *after* a portion of the sentence has been served, also has a number of antecedents. The transportation of criminals to America and Australia, the English ticket-of-leave system, apprenticeship by indenture—all made their contribution to the idea that supervision and treatment in the free com-

---

[6] See United Nations, Department of Social Affairs, *Probation and Related Measures* (1951), quoted in George G. Killinger and Paul F. Cromwell, Jr., eds., *Corrections in the Community* (St. Paul, Minn.: West, 1974), p. 160.

[7] See Charles Lionel Chute and Marjorie Bell, *Crime, Courts, and Probation* (New York: Macmillan, 1956), Chapter 3.

[8] See National Advisory Commission on Criminal Justice Standards and Goals, *Report on Corrections,* 1973, in Killinger and Cromwell, *Corrections in the Community,* pp. 168–69.

[9] Ibid., p. 173.

munity was preferable to institutional confinement for those who had broken the law. *Transportation,* as indicated in Chapter 12, provided needed labor for England's colonial possessions, and thousands of convicted criminals escaped the gallows or branding on the condition that once they were shipped overseas they should never again return to England. For those who were confined in penal colonies, as in Australia, freedom became possible in a *ticket-of-leave system,* in which a declaration, signed by the colonial governor, excused convicts from further labor for the government and permitted them to live independently but within a circumscribed area.[10] In the American colonies, felons received from England became *indentured servants* and were bound for a specified period to be taught a trade while performing service for their master—a pattern continuing for juvenile offenders released from American correctional institutions until well into the nineteenth century.[11] Gradually, the idea of an indeterminate sentence took hold, with a maximum and a minimum period of imprisonment specified but with confinement for a period less than the maximum made possible on the basis of good behavior while in prison and a demonstrated readiness for life under supervision outside the walls. Starting first at Elmira and then spreading to the rest of the country, parole, for both adults and juveniles, is now found in every state, in a patchwork of statutory provisions. There is much variation among the states in the use of parole; in some states nearly all inmates from the state prison are released on parole, whereas in others only a small proportion enjoy the privilege. On the average, however, more than 60 percent of all persons released from state prisons in the 1960s were released on parole, and by the 1970s this figure had reached 70 percent.[12]

The increasing use of probation and parole can be viewed as the obverse side of a growing disenchantment with institutional solutions to the problems of the criminal, the mentally ill, the economically dependent, and the aged—a disenchantment, according to David Rothman, that became evident in the latter part of the nineteenth century. The Progressive era, he argues, marked a dividing point in public policy as new, noninstitutional programs began to rise into prominence. The first caretaker institutions to fall into disuse were orphan asylums, to be replaced by foster homes and liberalized adoption procedures.[13] The growth of public welfare programs led to the decline of the almshouse, and New Deal

Corrections in the Community

---

[10] Dressler, *Practice and Theory of Probation and Parole,* pp. 56–62.

[11]. Ibid., pp. 72–73.

[12] See Killinger and Cromwell, *Corrections in the Community,* p. 420. This figure does not include the more than one million persons released from jails, workhouses, and local institutions that seldom have parole services available.

[13] David J. Rothman, "Of Prisons, Asylums, and Other Decaying Institutions," *The Public Interest* (Winter 1972), pp. 3–17.

legislation helped to further these trends. Between 1920 and 1940 state mental hospitals became less important, as out-patient facilities for the mentally ill opened in metropolitan centers; and in the period after World War II, particularly after the passage of the Community Mental Health Act (1963), under which the federal government matched state funds, out-patient treatment programs grew increasingly popular.[14] "Over the course of the past several decades," Rothman declares, "without clear theoretical justification or even a high degree of self-consciousness, we have been completing a revolution in the treatment of the insane, the criminal, the orphaned, the delinquent, and the poor. Whereas once we relied almost exclusively upon incarceration to treat or punish these classes of people, we now frame and administer many programs that maintain them within the community or at least remove them as quickly as possible from institutions. Policy makers in each of these areas interpret their own measures as specific responses to internal developments—an advance in drug therapy or a dissatisfaction with prevailing penitentiary conditions—not as part of a general anti-institutional movement. But such a movement exists, and it must be seen in a comprehensive way if it is to be understood.[15]

Rothman's argument appears to outrun the facts. It is true, as he points out, that attitudes toward institutionalization changed at the end of the nineteenth century, and some institutions—such as the orphan asylum—have largely disappeared. It is also true that in the middle of the twentieth century the number of persons held in mental hospitals fell dramatically—from 613,628 in 1950 to 433,890 in 1970—and out-patient treatment in the community rose at a rapid rate.[16] It appears likely, however, that rather than a comprehensive movement toward deinstitutionalization, what has taken place is (1) the creation of *additional* programs of state supervision and control in the community, in the name of treatment; and (2) the substitution of one set of institutions for another. The population of mental hospitals has declined, for example, along with the number of patients in tuberculosis sanitoriums, but the use of reformatories for young offenders has expanded greatly, and the number of juvenile delinquents confined in training schools and detention homes almost doubled betwen 1950 and 1970.[17] Before 1950, the

[14] Ibid. See also Franklyn N. Arnhoff, "Social Consequences of Policy Toward Mental Illness," *Science* 188 (June 1975), pp. 1277–81. "Community treatment and the planned complete phasing out of the public mental hospital have become official policy of federal, state, and local government," argues Arnhoff, "with enthusiastic sanction from professionals and citizens' organizations" (p. 1277).

[15] "Of Prisons, Asylums, and Other Decaying Institutions," p. 3.

[16] See Morton Kramer, "Psychiatric Services and the Changing Institutional Scene." Paper presented at the President's Biomedical Research Panel, National Institutes of Health, Bethesda, Md., November 25, 1975 (mimeographed).

[17] Ibid.

Figure 1. Number of Probation and Parole Officers

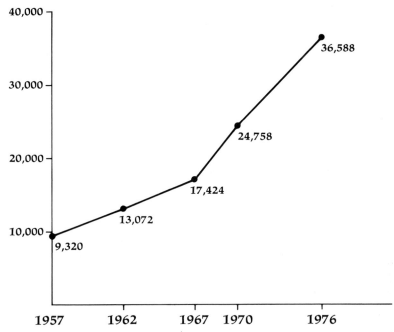

SOURCE: *Probation and Parole Directory* (Hackensack, N.J.: National Council on Crime and Delinquency, 1976), p. v. Reprinted by permission.

aged made up a significant portion of those confined in mental hospitals. Subsequently, nursing homes assumed a much larger role, and the number of the aged in such institutions grew from 217,536 in 1950 to 795,807 in 1970.[18] The net effect of such changes has been that the rate of persons confined in institutions of all types per 100,000 population in the United States increased slightly between 1950 and 1970 (from 1035.4 to 1046.6), along with what is probably a large increase in a variety of community-based treatment programs—although national data for the latter are lacking.[19]

As far as the treatment of convicted criminals is concerned, it appears that the use of probation and parole has increased greatly in the last forty years or so and that the majority of offenders under correctional supervision are now to be found in the community. Although the number of offenders under supervision in the community each year is unknown, the figures for the number of probation and parole officers provide a crude index (see Figure 1). It is also true that the rate of confinement in state and federal prisons per 100,000 civilian population in the United States fell from 130 in 1940 to about 100 immediately after World War II,

[18] Ibid.
[19] Ibid.

increased to 120 in the early 1960s, and dropped again—to 96.7 by 1970.[20] Then, however, in 1973, the number of inmates in prisons began to go up sharply and in 1976 reached its highest level in American history.[21] Treatment in the community has grown, in short, but the use of the correctional institution does not appear to have declined significantly in the last thirty years and may indeed be on the increase—if the trend in recent years proves to be more than a momentary aberration.

Much more data are needed to establish why these changes have occurred.[22] The spreading disillusionment with the effectiveness of imprisonment as a means of rehabilitation, discussed in Chapter 13, may have been offset by a growing attachment to the idea of incapacitation. Rising unemployment rates may also help explain the increasing number of inmates in the 1970s, since judges are reluctant to place convicted criminals in the free community when their chances of obtaining a job are much diminished. As to reasons for the growth of probation and parole, the rise of a well-organized group of semiprofessional workers with a stake in community-corrections careers is not to be discounted. And there is the possibility that the policy of isolating criminals and the mentally ill in custodial institutions is based on the public's perception of them as different in ethnicity and social class from the rest of society—and as this perception changes, the faith in custody changes as well.[23]

If these issues stand in need of research, it is nonetheless clear that community corrections have become the dominant method of handling convicted criminals and are widely regarded as the enlightened solution to the crime problem, both in the United States and in many other countries.[24] Probation and parole, in particular, are viewed by many as a rational alternative to the futility of imprisonment—even if what is actually

[20] See Bureau of the Census, *Persons in Institutions and Other Group Quarters* (Washington, D.C.: Government Printing Office, 1973), p. 350.

[21] See Steve Gettinger, "U.S. Prison Population Hits All-Time High," *Corrections Magazine* 11 (March 1976), pp. 9–20. See also *Prisoners in State and Federal Institutions* (Washington, D.C.: Government Printing Office, 1977).

[22] Changes in the annual number of felony convictions, for example, need to be taken into account in examining changes in the rate of different modes of treatment, along with such factors as changes in the average length of sentence. For an excellent discussion of some of the problems of research in this area, see Sheldon L. Messinger, "Review Symposium of Paul Lerman's *Community Treatment and Social Control: A Critical Analysis of Juvenile Correctional Policy*, *Journal of Research in Crime and Delinquency* 13 (January 1976), pp. 82–92. See also Irvin Waller and Janet Chan, "Prison Use: A Canadian and International Comparison," *Criminal Law Quarterly* 17 (December 1974), pp. 47–71.

[23] See Pauline B. Bart, "The Myth of a Value-Free Psychotherapy," in Wendell Bell and James A. Mau, eds., *The Sociology of the Future* (New York: Russell Sage Foundation, 1971), pp. 114–15. It is a striking fact that the rate of imprisonment per 100,000 population in 1970 was 206.9 for white males and 1102.2 for non-white males. See Kramer, "Psychiatric Services and the Changing Institutional Scene," p. 105.

[24] See *European Seminar on Probation: London, 20–30 October 1952* (New York: United Nations Publications, 1954).

done in the name of probation and parole and the eventual outcome are apt to receive relatively little attention.

The Social Role of the Probation and Parole Officer

Probation and parole differ in a number of respects; most notable, perhaps, is that probation is often a judicial function, under the control of the courts, whereas parole is generally an administrative function, under the control of a state agency. As a consequence, probation and parole may use different criteria in selecting offenders for community treatment and in determining revocation. But the treatment afforded the offender, the philosophy, and the practices of probation and parole work are apt to be much the same.

The precise nature of correctional work in the community is obscured by the jargon and inflated rhetoric that fill the journals in the field. Much of the writing about probation and parole by correctional administrators and practitioners is marred by excessive vagueness, unexamined assumptions about "normal" behavior, and the half-digested terminology taken from the social sciences.[25] The criminal, it is said, must be taught to live productively; the needs of the offender must be identified systematically and periodically, and measurable objectives based on those needs must be specified; probation services should be goal-oriented, directed toward removing or reducing individual and social barriers that result in recidivism; the community-corrections system must create a climate that will enable the probationer to move successfully from one status to another; treatment must consist of introducing the probationer to a better way of life, of providing motivation for constructive patterns of behavior, of giving support and guidance to those unable to solve their problems by themselves, and of providing an opportunity for the offender to work out ambivalent feelings . . . and so on and so on. Even more important, however, is that in the haste to lay claim to professional competence, serious inadequacies in the role of the probation and parole officer are too often accorded a minor position or ignored altogether.[26]

In general, what is done in the name of probation and parole takes three forms. First, the probation or parole officer may play the part of a *law enforcer*. His goal is to establish strict conformity to the orders of the court, on the part of his client, and a strong respect for authority, by

[25] For a critical view of the writing on probation and parole, see Carl B. Klockars, "A Theory of Probation Supervision," *The Journal of Criminal Law, Criminology, and Police Science* 63 (December 1972), pp. 550–56.

[26] For an outstanding exception, see Elliot Studt, *Surveillance and Service in Parole* (Institute of Government and Public Affairs, UCLA, 1972).

means of firm, consistent supervision. "What it simmers down to is police work," says a probation officer devoted to what has been described as the "junior G-man" model.[27]

Second, the probation or parole officer may view himself primarily as a *social worker*, whose main task is to steer the offender to social agencies in the community for help in solving such day-to-day problems as obtaining a job, finding a place to live, and securing medical care. "Probation and parole work is social work," asserts an influential writer in the field, trying to settle a long-standing problem of occupational definition, "with law enforcement and other adaptations."[28] Since the term *social worker* may lack prestige or carry connotations of leniency, the title *case manager* is preferred by some practitioners, but the underlying idea remains the same.[29]

Third, the probation or parole officer may see himself as a *therapeutic agent* or as a *psychiatric caseworker*, the latter term implying psychiatric skill that a social worker may not have. "Development of child guidance clinics in the 1920s and 1930s influenced particularly the juvenile courts and their probation staff," notes the National Advisory Commission on Criminal Justice Standards and Goals. "The terms 'diagnosis' and 'treatment' began to appear in social work literature and not long after in the correctional literature. Those terms come from the medical field and imply illness. A further implication is that a good probationer practitioner will understand the cause and be able to remedy it, just as the medical practitioner does."[30] The therapeutic agent must go beyond the everyday needs of the offender released into the community. "We take conscious pains in our every contact with the offender to demonstrate our concern about him and our respect for him as a human being," says Charles Shireman in an article in *Federal Probation*, trying to sum up the viewpoint. "We seize every opportunity to help the offender come to understand the nature of the shared, problem-solving, helping process by actually experiencing it. . . . We recognize, bring into the open, and deal directly with the offender's negative attitudes toward us as the representatives of social authority. . . . We 'partialize' the total life problem confronting the offender. . . . We help the individual perceive the degree to which his behavior has and will result in his own unhappiness."[31]

[27] Lewis Diana, "What Is Probation?" *The Journal of Criminal Law, Criminology, and Police Science* 51 (July–August 1960), pp. 189–208.

[28] Dressler, *Practice and Theory of Probation and Parole*, p. 103.

[29] See *Task Force Report: Corrections*, pp. 96–97.

[30] *A National Strategy to Reduce Crime: Report by the National Advisory Commission on Criminal Justice Standards and Goals* (New York: Avon Books, 1975), pp. 517–18. See also Roy Lubove, *The Professional Altruist* (New York: Atheneum, 1969), Chapter III.

[31] Charles Shireman, "Casework in Probation and Parole: Some Considerations in Diagnosis and Treatment," quoted in Klockars, "A Theory of Probation Supervision," pp. 55–52.

The relative virtues of these three viewpoints have dominated much of the discussion about what probation and parole should be and clearly involve deeply held sentiments. Unfortunately, when we examine the realities of community corrections, serious difficulties in converting any of the theoretical models into effective practice become apparent.[32] Furthermore, the impact of the different modes upon the criminality of the probationer or parolee remains largely unknown.

The major problem in playing the role of law enforcer is that the probation officer's knowledge of what the probationer is doing must depend to a large extent on what the probationer is willing to tell him. Information concerning the offender's adjustment on the job, in the neighborhood, or within the family must flow along a bond of trust established between the probation officer and the probationer, but this flow of information can be much restricted in an authoritarian relationship.[33]

The Law-Enforcer Model

The insistence on conformity to rules as the dominant theme in probation and parole work is further complicated by the detailed regimentation frequently imposed on the offender as the price of freedom from confinement. "The offender, often habitually unsuccessful in his attempts to adjust to the pressures and demands of society," argues one writer, "needs to have successful experiences—even if they are at first coerced. A definite 'shall and shall not' approach is often necessary until the client reaches the point where he can be comfortable with the restraints and constraints imposed on his conduct. . . ."[34] In the interest of securing these "successful experiences," the offender may be prohibited from changing jobs, moving, traveling, drinking, and socializing without the approval of the probation officer. In some states, the probationer or parolee may not marry, engage in business, sign contracts, or make purchases on credit without permission. A number of these restraints might be viewed as simply commonsense efforts to keep track of the offender—for example, to prevent him from renewing the gang membership that was instrumental in getting him into trouble in the first place. In many instances, however, the probationer is required to conform to standards of behavior far more strict and confining than those adhered to by most members of the community, and the conditions of

---

[32] See Lloyd F. Ohlin, Herman Piven, and Donald M. Pappenfort, "Major Dilemmas of the Social Worker in Probation and Parole," in Mayer N. Zald, ed., *Social Welfare Institutions* (New York: John Wiley & Sons, 1965), pp. 523–38.

[33] See Dale G. Hardman, "The Matter of Trust," in Killinger and Cromwell, *Corrections in the Community*, pp. 226–47; and Studt, *Surveillance and Service in Parole*, Chapter V.

[34] Claude T. Mangrum, "The Function of Coercive Casework in Corrections," *Federal Probation* 35 (March 1971), pp. 26–29. Efforts to resolve the tension between helping the offender to become autonomous and controlling him form a recurring issue in the literature of probation and parole. See Richard W. Tappan, ed., *Contemporary Corrections* (New York: McGraw-Hill, 1951), pp. 384–94.

probation and parole imposed by the legal system are sometimes little more than punitive measures dressed up as treatment. Dressler reports, for example, that one federal judge placed an overweight offender on probation with the stipulation that he lose fifty pounds. In another case, an unemployed man convicted of passing bad checks was required to wear in plain sight a card reading, "Do not cash my check—Because I have been convicted of felony check writing."[35] There is a serious question whether the regimentation so often demanded by those who believe in the law enforcement model is feasible and, if feasible, desirable.

The Social-Work Model The main difficulty with the social work view of probation is the frequently inflated notion of the ability of the community-corrections officer to shape the social reality in which the offender must live. The probation officer may indeed believe that the offender will be helped greatly if he can find a decent job, adequate housing, and supportive family and social ties. The literature is filled with references to "coordinating community agencies" and "fulfilling clients' needs." But in plain fact the probation officer often finds it extremely difficult, if not impossible, to marshall the resources thought to be essential to the offender's community adjustment. Jobs for ex-convicts may be virtually nonexistent; satisfactory living quarters hard to find; and medical care expensive, unavailable, or of little use.

In recent years, fired by the activist zeal of the 1960s, probation and parole workers have begun to speak of organizing community-welfare resources. Social work with the offender is no longer to be limited to a one-to-one relationship between probation officer and probationer; instead, the probation officer is to become an agent of social change, dealing with the community and mobilizing local leaders. Dressler has presented a fictional scenario to give this vision form: Many parolees in a hypothetical community are unable to get needed mental health services because the community lacks clinical facilities. Their parole officer discusses the matter with the director of the Community Health and Welfare Council. The director arranges meetings of social workers, ministers, doctors, educators, and public officials. An ad hoc committee enlists the aid of influential lay and professional people. "Stimulated and guided by the Council's director," Dressler hypothesizes, "and with the use of his professional staff as aids, the committee conducts a survey to determine how many units of mental health service are needed if all of those requiring it are to receive it promptly; how many units are currently available; and the difference between units required and units available. Armed with this information, the civic leaders, guided and assisted by the

---

[35] *Practice and Theory of Probation and Parole*, p. 238.

Council Director, mobilize community action, secure the funds and personnel needed to augment the mental health services in that area."[36]

There is a beguiling simplicity in this hypothetical chronicle, and the parole officer's dealings with community leaders surely sounds more attractive than the grubby work of unraveling the red tape of welfare agencies. Undoubtedly, a few community efforts are organized in this fashion. In general, however, the idea of probation and parole officers serving as agents of social change remains a hope that must be viewed with a skeptical eye. The social work approach to community corrections is largely a matter of making do with existing resources—and they are apt to be sadly limited.

The ambition to convert the work of the probation and parole officer into a form of psychotherapy is probably beset by the most serious difficulties. In the 1920s and 1930s, as we have seen, psychiatric social work, or social work with a strong Freudian flavor, rose into prominence; and the jargon of social workers became laced with terms like *ego defense, repression, trauma,* and *cathexis,* as social workers struggled to find a body of scientific knowledge in which they could ground their work and which would justify claims to professional status. This movement spilled over into probation and parole and helped to shape the view of the community-corrections officer as a therapeutic agent. "With developments in the fields of psychology and psychiatry, both of which have made their contributions to case work," argued Richard Chappell, "there has been a shift of emphasis in case work from the 'furnishing of services' to 'counseling.' . . . Most persons who have studied the methods and practices of successful probation services agree that the probation process is based primarily on case work skills, methods, and practices."[37] Probation, he claimed, must become treatment and "there must be respect for the individual, understanding of the motivation for his behavior, and a recognition that all forms of behavior which may be encountered are human responses to a given set of circumstances and have some meaning and relationship to the individual's total personality structure."[38] Crime, in short, was to be defined as a symptom, and the job of probation and parole was to supply a cure for the underlying psychic malady.

Three problems attend this viewpoint. First, the large caseloads that are usual in probation and parole work are apt to reduce counseling sessions to superficial interviews in which little is learned and still less accomplished in terms of changes in attitudes, values, or aspects of the

The Psychiatric-Casework Model

[36] Ibid., p. 163.
[37] "Probation: Case Work and Current Status," in Tappan, *Contemporary Correction,* pp. 384–85.
[38] Ibid., pp. 389–90.

The probation officer trying to use a social-work approach to community corrections finds that it is largely a matter of making do with existing resources—and the resources are apt to be severely limited.

personality structure. Few probation or parole officers are in fact trained in psychotherapeutic techniques, and what guidance is provided by the professional literature is apt to be excessively vague. A leading theorist of psychiatric casework, for example, explains that

> working from a process base the social worker conceives all phenomena as unique within classes or categories, as characterized by continuous change and direction toward an end, as embodying potential for such changes which itself shifts in the course of time. He uses a process, a professional social work process, to affect processes, that is, the life process of an individual, group, or community, in order that the processes may have the best possible chance for self-realization in relation to a purpose which has brought worker and cientele together.[39]

The sociologist, it must be admitted, is hardly in a position to criticize others for their obscurities, but this sort of description of therapy is not likely to be very useful to the probation officer.

Second, no matter how much the aim of therapy is stressed, the social role of the probation and parole officer involves the legal obligation to supervise the behavior of the offender according to the terms set by the court and to report rule violations that can lead to the revocation of the offender's probationary status. The probation officer and the probationer are thus unavoidably bound in an authoritarian relationship; and if the power of the community-corrections officer over the life of the offender is sometimes cloaked by friendship and trust, the fact of power remains, and neither of them can ignore it.

Some writers in the field of community corrections claim that the authoritarian relationship poses no serious threat to the goal of treatment and may indeed be an aid. "The assertion is sometimes made that the methods of casework cannot be applied in the authoritative setting of probation," says Ben Meeker. "Experience has shown otherwise. Authority per se does not preclude casework. . . . The authority of the child welfare worker may differ from that of a probation officer in degree but hardly in kind. The clients of both are seldom so from choice. Yet casework is basic in the treatment of problem children. So it is in the treatment of problem adults—those willful, aggressive, disturbed, irresponsible, and almost always immature members of society who find themselves in conflict with its laws. To use authority wisely is of course essential."[40] The issue, however, is by no means as clearly resolved as Meeker suggests; and there is ample evidence that when psychotherapeutic measures are imposed in an involuntary relationship, the resistance and hostility engendered may far outweigh any positive effects.

[39] Quoted in Klockars, "A Theory of Probation Supervison," p. 551.
[40] Ben Meeker, "Probation Is Casework," *Federal Probation* 12 (1958), p. 53.

Third, and perhaps most important, it can be questioned whether the theory that underlies the view of the probation or parole officer as a therapeutic agent—that mental illness is the cause of crime—is generally warranted. Some offenders undoubtedly suffer from psychological disturbances that give rise to violations of the law, and many of them can possibly benefit from psychotherapy administered in the free community. Given what we know about criminal behavior, however, the bulk of criminal activity with which society attempts to deal can probably *not* be viewed in this light. The argument that the social role of the probation and parole officer is best patterned on that of the medical practitioner—who diagnoses and cures a specific illness with scientific techniques—is based on little more than wishful thinking—as is the claim that authority is an aid because lawbreakers are "immature."

As a means of devising a varied social policy that can help steer the offender onto the path of law-abiding behavior, the attempt to dress probation and parole work in the garb of psychiatry is likely to do more harm than good.[41]

Do Probation and Parole Reduce Crime?

The superiority of probation and parole to imprisonment in reducing crime is a basic tenet of the majority of people working in the field of corrections. "Correctional authorities strongly recommend that an offender be given probation whenever possible," notes Hazel Kerper. "If he can serve his time in the community, he can continue to take care of his family. He doesn't lose his job, nor suffer the many harmful effects of incarceration. The Model Penal Code and the American Bar Association *Standards Relating to Sentencing Alternatives and Procedures* both make probation the preferred form of disposition after conviction, thus requiring an affirmative showing to justify incarceration."[42] The belief in the desirability of parole is no less strong, for it is argued that to release men and women from prison under the supervision of the state is far preferable to setting the offender free to manage as best he can, with no effort made to forestall his slipping back into a life of crime.

Many probation and parole officers bring to their work a dedication

[41] The need for a variety of approaches in probation work provided the basis for such experimental programs as the Community Treatment Project carried out by the California Youth Authority and the National Institute of Mental Health in Sacramento, Stockton-Modesto, and San Francisco. See Stevens H. Clarke, "Juvenile Offender Programs and Delinquency Prevention," Seymour L. Halleck et al., eds., *The Aldine Crime and Justice Annual 1974* (Chicago: Aldine, 1975), pp. 393–94.

[42] Hazel B. Kerper, *Introduction to the Criminal Justice System* (St. Paul, Minn.: West, 1972), p. 345.

and an enthusiasm that are remarkable in light of the limited resources at their disposal and the frequent lack of public appreciation.[43] They are convinced that whatever the worth of imprisonment as a deterrent and as a symbol of society's condemnation of criminal behavior, an enlightened policy of leading convicted offenders to conformity must rely primarily on probation or parole officers. It is in their work, they argue, that society can find the best hope for reducing recidivism. This is a declaration of faith, however, rather than an established fact. The evidence that probation and parole can be effective in the control of crime is not as clear as official support might suggest. It is true that offenders placed on probation show lower recidivism rates than offenders who have been imprisoned. It is also true that many offenders who are released from prison before the expiration of their sentences refrain from crime while they are under the supervision of the state. The difficulty lies in interpreting these findings and using them as the basis for a rational penal policy.

The Reluctance to Experiment

The major stumbling block to an understanding of the meaning of the statistics showing the relative superiority of probation is that offenders placed on probation and offenders sent to prison are not strictly comparable. Judges and probation officers (who prepare the presentence reports and the recommendations, which are accepted by judges almost without exception) are well aware that supervision in the free community must be reserved for those offenders who are least likely to commit new crimes. The community, after all, is hardly willing to accept the random release of convicted criminals in the name of scientific experimentation. Thus it is extremely difficult to determine whether the lower rates of recidivism among probationers are the result of the method of treatment itself or of the characteristics of the probationers that led to their selection. A similar problem presents itself with regard to parole. That inmates released for supervision in the community before the expiration of their sentences exhibit lower recidivism rates than inmates required to serve their full terms does not necessarily mean that parole has aided rehabilitation. It may be that only those most likely to refrain from crime are released on parole and that the experience of parole itself is irrelevant.

Systems of parole and probation, in short, may commit two kinds of errors: they may set free offenders who will commit new crimes and who should be kept confined; and they may confine offenders who will not commit new crimes and who should be released. The courts and the governmental agencies responsible for placing convicted offenders in the community are understandably anxious to avoid the first error, which is

[43] See, for example, Claude T. Mangrum, "The Humanity of Probation Officers," *Federal Probation* 36 (June 1972), pp. 47–50.

readily detected and arouses a public outcry. The second error can be more easily ignored, since keeping people uselessly confined fails to plague the public conscience. But granting probation and parole only to those offenders likely to conform to the law violates accepted research procedures, and, as a result, little is known about the actual effects of supervision in the community as compared to confinement.[44] What is known, in a crude fashion, is which offenders are most likely to commit offenses again, regardless of the treatment they may receive.

The first effort to create tables of expected rates of parole violations, based on an empirical study of the characteristics of convicted offenders, was the work of social scientists at the University of Chicago.[45] In subsequent years, Sheldon and Eleanor Glueck, Daniel Glaser, Lloyd Ohlin, and a number of other social scientists, united in the hope that society's treatment of the criminal could be improved by the application of scientific research, continued to build predictive scales linking various factors in the offender's background and violations of the law while on parole.[46] Costs would be reduced as well, as one writer pointed out. "Any correctional agency not using a prediction procedure to study the effectiveness of its decisions and operations is perpetrating a crime against the taxpayer," asserted J. Douglas Grant. "This is no longer a theoretical argument."[47]

Predicting Recidivism

Some of the major relationships found between the background of the offender and the likelihood that he or she will commit new crimes while on parole or probation can be summarized as follows:

The younger the offender, the greater the likelihood that he will violate probation or parole.

The earlier the onset of delinquency or criminality, the greater the likelihood that the probationer or parolee will commit new offenses.

The lower the age at which the offender left home, the more likely he will be to pursue a criminal career.

Women are less likely than men to violate parole or probation.

The offender who is married and living with his spouse is less likely

[44] The unwillingness to experiment does not simply represent society's distaste for scientific research in the formation of public policy, or a fear of taking a chance with convicted offenders. There is also the problem of legal obligations to maintain equality in the handling of convicted criminals with the same characteristics, and a moral question about experimenting with modes of corrections involving different degrees of punishment. See Gresham M. Sykes, "Feeling Our Way: A Report on a Conference on Ethical Issues in the Social Sciences," *American Behavioral Scientist* 10 (June 1967), pp. 8–11.

[45] See Dressler, *Practice and Theory of Probation and Parole*, p. 147.

[46] Ibid., Chapter 8.

[47] It's Time to Start Counting," *Crime and Delinquency* 8 (July 1962), pp. 259–64.

to commit new crimes than is the single, separated, divorced, or widowed offender.

The offender with a long record of offenses is a less favorable risk
than a first offender.

Blacks exhibit higher rates of probation and parole violation than do
whites.

The person who has been regularly employed and has a job while on
parole or probation is a better risk than the one who has a history of
unemployment and does not have a job at the beginning of probation
or parole.

Persons convicted of crimes against property are more likely to commit new offenses than are those convicted of crimes of violence. Offenses that do not involve the individual's vocation are apt to show the
lowest rates of subsequent crime.[48]

Administrators of correctional systems have shown little interest in
using the prediction scales so carefully devised by the sociologists, according to Dressler.[49] A survey in the 1960s indicated that of the forty-
eight states responding to the questionnaire, only Illinois, Ohio, California, and Minnesota used statistical prediction methods for parole selection.[50] Judges are probably even less inclined to use such techniques.
This is not because those responsible for releasing convicted criminals
into the community are skeptical of the generalizations presented
above—indeed, the substance of those correlations represents little more
than the codified experience contained in current practices of probation
and parole selection. Rather, it would appear that the reluctance to use
prediction scales is the result of a suspicion of attempts to quantify the
causes of human behavior and of an unwillingness to adhere to static
formulas in a changing world. The decision to place an offender on probation or parole may take statistics into account—but it is likely to be
made without according them a dominant, fixed, or explicit role in the
decision-making process.

**Are Some
Approaches
Better Than
Others?**
Innovative Programs Activities carried out in the name of probation and
parole vary greatly in time and place. The size of caseloads, the training
and objectives of probation and parole officers, the extent and availabil-

---

[48] See David Dressler, *Practice and Theory of Probation and Parole*, pp. 150–58. It might be
noted that these characteristics—with the exception of the offender's job status—are
beyond the control of anything the probation or parole officer might do.

[49] Ibid., pp. 146–47.

[50] See Victor H. Evjen, "Current Thinking on Parole Prediction Tables," *Crime and Delinquency* 8 (July 1962), pp. 215–38.

ity of community resources, the degree of supervision expected and practiced—all these elements and others differ from one jurisdiction to another, as well as within particular probation or parole agencies. While these variations may have an impact, many of the reports on programs presented in the correctional literature do not include sufficient information to provide for a judgment of their effectiveness. Thus, for example, the Royal Oak program, developed in the municipal court at Royal Oak, Michigan, attempts to reduce the caseload assigned to each probation officer and to provide expert care in counseling by a heavy reliance on a volunteer staff. The program is described with great enthusiasm and the clear expectation that it can reduce crime—but there are few data to indicate what effect, if any, the additional manpower has had on recidivism.[51] If the superiority of particular programs is to be demonstrated, the following criteria are essential: (1) a comparison between a treatment group and either a randomly selected control group or a group demonstrably equivalent to the treatment group; (2) an objective measure of delinquent or criminal behavior; and (3) a clear description of the treatment or service accorded both the treatment group and the control group.[52] In examining programs that do meet these criteria, the differences among measurable effects appear to be slight.

In a review of innovative programs designed to prevent delinquency, Stevens Clarke found that guided group interaction, intensive supervision, treatment "contracts" undertaken in the name of transactional analysis, and placement in a foster home made little difference in the recidivism rate. After examining eight well-known projects often cited as offering hope for an enlightened penology (the Silverlake experimental program; Youth Center Research Project; Achievement Place; Community Treatment Project carried out in Sacramento, Stockton-Modesto, and San Francisco; Los Angeles Community Delinquency Control Project; Streetcorner Research Project; Seattle Atlantic Street Center; and Neighborhood Youth Corps Program in Cincinnati), Clarke concluded that "the studies reviewed present little evidence that the juvenile offender treatment programs succeeded in reducing delinquency and much evidence that they failed. Only three of the eight programs (Youth Center Research Project, Streetcorner Research Project, and Achievement Place) showed any evidence of success, and there is a strong possibility that their apparent success is an artifact of evaluation, since the methodologies of the three are the weakest of the eight."[53]

[51] Keith J. Leenhouts "Royal Oak's Experience with Professionals and Volunteers in Probation," *Federal Probation* 34 (December 1970), pp. 45–51.
[52] See Stevens H. Clarke, "Juvenile Offender Programs and Delinquency Prevention," p. 386.
[53] Ibid., p. 399.

Robert Martinson—whose work was discussed in Chapter 13—reached much the same judgment with regard to various innovative probation and parole programs, both for juveniles and for adults. In the widely reported Warren studies, for example, a project developed by the California Youth Authority, a control group of young people was assigned to regular detention for eight to nine months and then released to regular supervision. The experimental group received much more elaborate treatment, with offenders placed in twelve-man caseloads in the community and given a form of therapy designed to fit previously determined "interpersonal maturity level." The data indicate that the members of the treatment group committed more offenses than did members of the control group.[54] In sum, Martinson argues, we simply cannot say that these innovative methods of treating the criminal have much effect on offender behavior, even when the treatment takes place in the community and employs the techniques of a rational correctional philosophy. But, he notes, there is "one encouraging set of findings that emerges from these studies. . . . From many of them there flows the strong suggestion that even if we can't 'treat' offenders so as to make them do better, a great many of the programs designed to rehabilitate them at least did not make them do *worse*. And if these programs did not show the advantages of actually rehabilitating, some of them did have the advantage of being less onerous to the offender himself without seeming to pose increased danger to the community. And some of these programs—especially those involving less restrictive custody, minimal supervision, and early release—simply cost fewer dollars to administer."[55]

Evaluation Research The effort to evaluate the effectiveness of various forms of probation and parole services—foreshadowed by the parole prediction studies in the decades prior to World War II—greatly increased in the 1950s and 1960s. The growing influence of quantitative research methods in the social sciences, coupled with the increasing cost of corrections, helped create a widespread demand for objective data. In the mid-1960s, according to Stuart Adams, "correctional self-assessment received a new impetus, this time from the planning-programming-budgeting movement (PPB). PPB made its appearance in the Department of Defense, spread quickly to other federal agencies. . . . By 1968, discussions of cost-benefit analysis began to be heard at the major correctional conferences."[56]

The evaluation movement in community corrections has been viewed

---

[54] Robert Martinson, "What Works?—Questions and Answers About Prison Reform," in Halleck et al., *The Aldine Crime and Justice Annual 1974*, pp. 352–84.

[55] Ibid., p. 378.

[56] *Evaluating Research in Corrections—A Practical Guide* (Washington, D.C.: National Institute of Law Enforcement and Criminal Justice, 1975), p. 4.

with a good deal of ambivalence by correctional personnel, and administrative officials in correctional agencies have frequently shown a reluctance to face the implications of the research findings. "One or more researchers in almost every one of the half-dozen correctional systems which conduct the most extensive evaluative research," says Daniel Glaser, "have, at one time or another in recent years, informed me of the suppression of their research reports. In some state correctional systems, it is quite evident that research units have been largely co-opted into service of the *status quo*, for they have abandoned longitudinal evaluative statistics compilation in favor of 'head counts' only."[57]

The reasons for the lack of enthusiasm for evaluative research are obvious, Glaser maintains. "Correctional officials procure financial appropriations for their agency by convincing the legislature that their programs protect society, either by incapacitating criminals or by changing them into noncriminals. When research confirms these claims, the officials are happy to promulgate the findings. Frequently, however, research has indicated that added appropriations to make treatment more effective, by reducing caseloads, hiring more psychiatrists, etc., have made no difference in post-treatment criminality or may even have increased it."[58]

Yet if correctional officials have often proven to be somewhat skittish about coming to grips with the objective analysis of the effectiveness of probation and parole programs, the evaluation studies undertaken in recent years have contributed to a major shift in the viewpoint of many criminologists who now take a position of agnosticism concerning the community treatment of criminals. The superiority of any particular form of probation and parole, it is argued, including such long-cherished aspects as small caseloads and intensive counseling, has not been clearly demonstrated. Nor has it been established that probation and parole—whatever may be their advantage with regard to cost or humanitarian concerns—are superior to imprisonment in terms of their influence on the offender's subsequent criminality.[59] In the last thirty years or so,

---

[57] Daniel Glaser, "Correctional Research: An Elusive Paradise," in Leon Radzinowicz and Marvin E. Wolfgang, eds., *Crime and Justice*, vol. III (New York: Basic Books, 1971), p. 183.

[58] Ibid., p. 183. Martinson's experience, discussed in Chapter 12, is pertinent here. For an excellent account of the difficulties encountered in trying to adapt social science research to correctional practice, see Edward Katkin, "Psychological Consultation in a Maximum Security Prison: A Case History and Some Comments," in Stuart E. Golann and Carl Eisdorfer, eds., *Handbook of Community Mental Health* (New York: Appleton-Century-Crofts, 1972), pp. 641–58.

[59] For a collection of readings presenting this changed perspective, see the anthology edited by Radzinowicz and Wolfgang, *Crime and Justice*, vol. III. Of particular note are the following: Walter C. Bailey, "An Evaluation of One Hundred Reports," pp. 187–95; David A. Ward, "Some Implications of Negative Findings," pp. 195–201; R. F. Sparks, "The Effectiveness of Probation," pp. 211–18; Dean V. Babst and John W. Mannering, "Probation versus Imprisonment," pp. 224–31; Frank R. Scarpiti and Richard M. Stephenson, "Results of Probation," pp. 231–42.

many criminologists have moved from a rather uncritical attachment to "enlightened" community programs for the rehabilitation of the criminal offender to a mood of some confusion and doubt. If the United States in the 1970s showed, in general, a sharpened sense of limits—including limits on what could be done in the quest for human perfectibility—much of the assessment of probation and parole in the literature of criminology exhibited a similar pattern.

The Therapeutic State

The argument that probation and parole should be viewed as a form of psychiatry is based on the implicit assumption that crime is a medical issue rather than a matter of morals or sociocultural determinants. The lawbreaker is suffering from a disease, he or she is to be cured, and the treatment is to be determined according to the expertise of modern science.

That criminal behavior results from sickness rather than from sin or society is not universally accepted, but the increasing tendency to equate crime with illness disturbs many social scientists.[60] Modern society, it is argued, is moving inexorably in the direction of becoming the therapeutic state, in which all manner of deviant behavior is labeled ill health and, in the name of the public welfare, subject to supervision and control. Those categorized as mentally ill, mentally defective, epileptics, alcoholics, drug addicts, juvenile delinquents, and psychopaths have all been swept into the ambit of state control, and now the state threatens to extend its compass to include adult criminals, the alienated, and the dissident as well.[61]

The fear of the benevolent state has a long history. In 1835 Alexis de Tocqueville pointed out that the emergence of despotism and tyranny in democratic societies might bear little resemblance to earlier forms of oppression. Instead, argued de Tocqueville, it was likely to be both gentler and more extensive. The power of the state would be absolute, detailed, regular, provident, and mild; the will of the people would not be shattered but softened. In this new form of rule, the state does not destroy, but it compresses, enervates, extinguishes, and stupifies a people, until the nation is reduced to a flock of timid animals, with the government as the shepherd.[62] It is de Tocqueville's benevolent despotism

[60] For an analysis of the "sick role" and a comparison of illness and crime, see Eliot Freidson, *Profession of Medicine* (New York: Harper & Row, 1970), pp. 227–43.

[61] See Kittrie, *The Right to Be Different;* see also Robert Martinson, "The Age of Treatment: Some Implications of the Custody-Treatment Dimension," *Issues in Criminology* 2 (Fall 1966), pp. 275–93.

[62] See Alexis de Tocqueville, *Democracy in America* (New York: New American Library, 1956), pp. 302–04.

come of age that is now seen by a number of sociologists as a threat to individual liberties no less serious than the harsh repression of Nazi or Soviet totalitarianism. Indeed, some observers view all forms of the modern bureaucratic state as dangerous, inclined to seize those defined as "troublesome," "difficult," or "out-of-step" and to lead them back to the ways of conformity by one means or another.

According to Kittrie, the therapeutic state made its appearance in the latter part of the nineteenth century as science replaced religious faith and the government assumed new responsibilities for the protection of the public welfare.[63] Many persons previously subject to the traditional criminal law—such as the mentally incompetent and youthful offenders—began to be handled with allegedly enlightened procedures aimed not at punishment but at cure. Kittrie is willing to grant that the original impulse may have been a sympathetic concern, producing "a humanizing climate of new social expectations and aims."[64] It soon became evident, he argues, that the therapeutic state poses dangers far outweighing the possible benefits. First, the standards determining the need for treatment are vague, lack an adequate basis in tested theory, and are shot through with value judgments, despite all the claims to scientific status. Second, these standards are used in an arbitrary and uncertain manner without the safeguards of due process of law, even though long periods of involuntary confinement may be the result no less than in the case of a criminal trial. For example, Kittrie notes, a California physician justified an individual's involuntary commitment to a mental asylum on the grounds that the individual had "paranoid feelings of persecution" and might seek redress for his persecution—and the physician "had no assurance that such redress would be of an orderly or lawful type." In Georgia, a young woman was similarly confined on the basis of evidence that she had joined the Jehovah's Witnesses, spent many hours away from home, knocking on strange doors, and "taken to sitting by the roadside at night."[65]

A particularly striking example is to be found in the case of Frederick Lynch, charged in the District of Columbia Municipal Court with passing bad checks.[66] In spite of his declaration that he was mentally responsible at the time the crime was committed, he was found not guilty on the grounds of insanity and confined to a mental hospital. By its nature, the appellate court argued, a jail sentence is for a specified period of

[63] Kittrie, *The Right to Be Different,* Chapter 8; see also Philip Rieff, "The Triumph of the Therapeutic," in F. James Short and Richard Stivers, eds., *The Collective Definition of Deviance* (New York: The Free Press, 1975), pp. 392–410.
[64] *The Right to Be Different,* p. 396.
[65] Ibid., p. 363.
[66] Ibid., p. 43.

time; hospitalization, to be effective, must be initially for an indeterminate period, since hospitalization is remedial and its limits are determined by the condition to be treated. The United States Supreme Court finally reversed the decision of the lower court, but on the narrow grounds that a person found not guilty by reason of insanity but who refused to plead this defense may not be automatically committed to a mental hospital; rather, a civil procedure is required. "Frederick Lynch," notes Kittrie, "on his bad check charge, could have been sentenced to a maximum of 12 months in jail. The more likely probability would have been probation. His commitment to a mental institution, on the other hand, was for an indeterminate period of time. Harassed, branded, and tired, Lynch committed suicide."[67]

Criticisms of state-imposed therapy have increased sharply in the last several decades, most notably in the area of mental health. "During the decade of the sixties," says Alan Stone, "it became apparent that the legal status of the mentally ill had taken on a new and political dimension. It had been transformed into a civil rights and civil liberties issue of the first order. Liberal progressives over the past century had urged that the courts treat the mentally ill as patients rather than as criminals. That overriding principle translated into law led to an expansion of medical power over decision making affecting the lives of more and more categories of persons designated mentally ill.[68]

The flaws in this system of involuntary confinement were largely ignored for several generations, Stone points out, as the mentally ill, the aged, the young, the sexually dangerous, and the mentally retarded were warehoused in "mega-institutions" under execrable conditions. A number of critics began to suggest that the entire mental health enterprise was ideologically corrupt, mental illness was a myth, the mental health professions were the new inquisition, and the mentally ill were the scapegoats of society. Three things are now obvious, Stone argues: the mega-institutions presided over by the mental health professions are an acknowledged disaster; community mental health centers have not proved to be the panacea promised by their zealous proponents; and people are increasingly distrustful of the coercive use of psychiatry in dealing with "troublesome" members of society. "Five years into the decade of the seventies there is enough evidence to suggest that the United States is engaged in an all-out legal war over the fate of the mentally ill."[69]

[67] Ibid., p. 44.
[68] Alan A. Stone, *Mental Health and Law: A System in Transition* (Rockville, Md.: National Institute of Mental Health, Center for Studies of Crime and Delinquency, 1975), p. 1.
[69] Ibid., pp. 1–2.

In the last decade or so, the criticisms of state-imposed therapy began to increase in volume in criminology. It was not only those declared mentally ill who were seen as oppressed in the name of treatment; criminal offenders were also beginning to be perceived as threatened by the benevolent state playing its role of *parens patriae.*

By the end of the 1960s, as we have seen, the number of people who still believed in conventional means of rehabilitating the criminal in a custodial setting had diminished sharply. The possibility of rehabilitating the lawbreaker by means of probation or parole was viewed more favorably, but doubts were emerging in this area as well. Probation and parole placed less of a burden on the taxpayer and avoided the punishing aspects of imprisonment; and if they were no more effective than imprisonment in reducing crime, they were still preferable on those grounds alone. Nevertheless, they were no longer so easily accepted as the answer to the problem of corrections.

At this moment in history, however, American society had just witnessed almost a decade's growth in the crime rate, the fear of crime had become a major public issue, and lawlessness was beginning to take on overtones of revolutionary disorder for a large number of people. In prisons, the control of violent, aggressive inmates who had no prospects of being rehabilitated was said to be threatening the entire correctional system. There appeared to be an acute need, in short, for more effective means of bringing the lawbreaker back to the ranks of the law-abiding— a need that became especially pressing, in the minds of many, just when faith in the conventional means of rehabilitation was waning. It was in this situation that a number of new techniques for the modification of behavior—such as operant conditioning, psychosurgery, drug therapy, and aversion therapy—began to rise into prominence in the field of corrections.

Potent means of altering human behavior—such as certain kinds of brain surgery—had been known for some time in the field of psychiatry. In 1890 a Swiss psychiatrist by the name of Burkhardt discovered that removing portions of his patients' brains greatly modified the disturbed behavior they exhibited—although he was forced to discontinue his experiments because of objections from his colleagues.[70] In 1936, in the United States, Walter Freeman and James Watts introduced prefrontal lobotomy, an operation that consists of severing the connection between the frontal lobes of the brain and the midbrain. Irritable, uncooperative, unclean, and helpless schizophrenics became quiet, clean, and cooperative.[71] Insulin-shock therapy and electroconvulsive therapy were also

[70] Kittrie, *The Right to Be Different,* p. 305.
[71] Ibid., p. 305. During the 1940s, some 50,000 patients were lobotomized in the United States. "Freeman, a lobotomy zealot," says one writer, "calculated he had personally per-

brought to America in the 1930s and were thought to be particularly useful in the treatment of manic-depressive psychoses. There were frequent unfortunate side effects, however (the destruction of the capacity to think abstractly and a loss of ambition, conscience, and planning abilities in the case of lobotomies, and severe convulsions and occasional heart failures in the case of shock treatment), and the use of such therapies declined, particularly after the introduction of tranquilizing drugs provided hospitals with other means of reducing the custodial burden of the staff.[72]

The use of drugs and psychosurgery to control the behavior of those declared mentally ill was supplemented in the 1960s by what has come to be known as *behavior modification*. Building on the research of Skinner, Lindsley, Ferster, and DeMyer, experimenters developed a body of principles for the control of behavior based on the systematic manipulation of rewards and punishments.[73] The use of token economies (a system under which patients purchase tokens to be exchanged for certain privileges), desensitization, and aversive conditioning, involving what the psychologists and the psychiatrists call negative and positive reinforcements, proved to be effective in modifying the behavior patterns of adult psychotics, autistic children, and persons said to be suffering from neurotic fears.[74] Within a short time, the application of such techniques had proliferated, and behavior modification had become an important—if highly controversial—part of treatment programs for "maladaptive behavior."[75]

---

formed over 4000 operations, using a gold-plated ice pick, which he carried with him in a velvet-lined case. After the local application of a mild pain killer, Freeman would plunge the ice pick through the thin bone of the upper inner angle of the eye socket, severing the frontal nerve connections to the thalamus. No elaborate preparations or precautions preceded this grisly operation, which often took place in the patient's home" (Richard Restack, "The Promise and Peril of Psychosurgery," *Saturday Review* [September 25, 1973], p. 56).

[72] Kittrie, *The Right to Be Different*, pp. 306–07. According to another writer, "Studies of hospitalized schizophrenic patients clearly indicate that the major tranquilizers, particularly of the phenothiazine group, have made a substantial contribution to therapeutic effectiveness. . . . It should be noted that the early successes of the major tranquilizers helped to transform the social environment of mental hospitals. Patients were viewed more optimistically and with less fear. This in turn improved the interpersonal climates and encouraged other therapeutic approaches" (David A. Hamburg, ed., *Psychiatry as a Behavioral Science* [Englewood Cliffs, N.J.: Prentice-Hall, 1970], p. 49).

[73] See Bertram S. Brown, Louis A. Wienckowski, and Stephanie B. Stolz, "Behavior Modification: Perspective on a Current Issue," Department of Health, Education, and Welfare Publication No. (ADM) 75–202, 1975.

[74] See Theodore Ayllon, "Behavior Modification in Institutional Settings," *Arizona Law Review* 17 (1975), pp. 3–19.

[75] The growth in the use of these techniques reported in the social science literature is particularly marked after 1969.

The use of drugs to control behavior and the techniques of behavior modification drew the attention of correctional officials. Such methods offered the promise of efficacy wrapped in the mantle of therapy at a time when the hope of rehabilitating criminals had been seriously undermined and demands for "doing something about crime" had reached a clamorous pitch.

The extent to which behavior-control techniques have been adopted by correctional systems in the United States is impossible to state with any precision. There is no national clearinghouse for such information, and there is, in fact, much disagreement about what should be included in the category of behavior modification.[76] Furthermore, many correctional systems that do use such techniques are hesitant to say so, for reasons that we will examine in a moment. It is clear, in any case, that by the beginning of the 1970s a large number of prison officials, using techniques that bore little resemblance to the methods employed for the purpose of rehabilitation in the past, were involved in efforts to modify or control the behavior of individuals convicted of breaking the criminal law.

In the prison system of Iowa, for example, in a program of so-called aversion therapy, inmates who broke institutional rules by refusing to get out of bed, eating with a group other than the one assigned, giving cigarettes to other inmates, swearing, or lying were defined as suffering from a "severe behavior problem" and were forced to take apomorphine, a drug that induces vomiting for up to an hour, accompanied by sweating, cramps, and fluctuations in blood pressure and heartbeat.[77] In a number of states, electric shock treatments were introduced in programs designed to alter the behavior of sex offenders, particularly child molesters; the idea was to focus their attention on more "suitable" subjects— that is, adult women.[78] The use of Prolixin, a powerful tranquilizer (often producing dangerous and irreversible side effects), was reported at a number of custodial institutions throughout the United States; and in California experiments were conducted using anectine as a means of controlling unruly prisoners. Anectine, a derivative of curare that is used

[76] See H. M. and M. T. Parsons, "A Glossary of Behavioral Terms in Behavioral Modification" (Silver Spring, Md.: Institute for Behavioral Research, June 1975). The managing attorney of the Mental Health Law Project, in Washington, D.C., prefers the term applied behavior analysis and uses it to refer to the work of those who try to change human behavior by the use of operationally defined and experimentally manipulated variables, emphasizing the effect of environment stimulation and using a model of social reinforcement based on a learning theory of behavior rather than a medical or disease theory. See Paul R. Friedman, "Legal Regulation of Applied Behavior Analysis in Mental Institutions and Prisons," *Arizona Law Review*, 17 (1975), pp. 39–104. The definitional issue, however, is far from resolved.

[77] See *Des Moines Sunday Register* (February 10, 1974).

[78] See *The New York Times* (February 15, 1974).

Electronic Rehabilitation

The treatment of the institutionalized offender in the community . . . presents the problems of a potential escape and increased risk to the community. One approach to this problem has been the development, in prototype form, of small personally worn transmitters that permit the continual monitoring of the geographical location of parolees. This system, which also involves the use of intensive treatment and the help of volunteers in the community, is known as an electronic rehabilitation system . . .

The impetus for the use of electronic intervention in the treatment of offenders emerges from several sources. There has been a rapid increase in the use of telemetry for medical purposes and a shift in the budget allocations of the electronic industry from defense research and development projects to feasibility studies in the public sector. In addition, there has been a marked increase in the research and development of law enforcement technology. Some of this research has been aimed at facilitating surveillance through the use of specially equipped helicopters, computerized information retrieval systems, and infrared sensors.

Considerable effort is also being devoted to the development of systems for the rapid, electronic location of objects in an urban setting. Many of these systems are being developed primarily for monitoring the location of motor vehicles such as buses or police cars. One presently operative system provides the location of a vehicle every 5 seconds within a limited urban area with an accuracy of approximately one block. The Institute of Public Administration has indicated the feasibility of developing a broadscale vehicle locator service within 2 years. In a report prepared for the Office of Urban Transportation of the U.S. Department of Housing and Urban Development, the organization notes, "Another, secretive, law enforcement use of AVM [Automatic Vehicle Monitor] systems would be in 'bugging' suspect vehicles, valuable shipments, etc.; movement could be traced through the city without a conspicuous 'tail.' Future refinement of the craft may make it possible to implant a transponder on a subject's person—in his shoe, for instance." . . .

. . . Many components of potentially effective monitoring and intervention systems usable with offenders have been developed in various laboratories but have not yet been often integrated into operable systems. For example, devices have been developed for measuring penile erection during the therapeutic treatment of sexual deviates or for the objective measurement of sexual preferences. These devices have generally recorded changes either by using a plethysmograph or a strain gauge. Transducers have been designed that provide an electrical output suitable for the continuous monitoring and recording of penile changes. The linkage of these transducers to a portable transmitter rather than to a recorder would not be difficult and could, when included within an electronic locator system, provide the capability of precisely monitoring sex offenders within the community.

From Ralph K. Schwitzgebel, *Development and Legal Regulation of Coercive Behavior Modification Techniques with Offenders* (Rockville, Md.: National Institute of Mental Health, Center for Studies of Crime and Delinquency, 1971), pp. 17–21.

medically in small doses as a muscle relaxant, was administered in massive doses, causing inmates to lose all control of voluntary muscles, including those used for breathing. Jessica Mitford's account of this project states that the underlying idea of the experiment, as reported by the researchers involved, "was to develop a strong association between any violent or acting-out behavior and the drug Anectine and its frightful consequences," including "cessation of respiration for a period of approximately two minutes duration." As the subject experienced feelings of terror, he was scolded for his misdeeds and warned that he must conform in the future. Inmates were selected for the program on the grounds that their institutional behavior had been marked by "frequent fights, verbal threatening, deviant sexual behavior, stealing, and unresponsiveness to the group therapy program."[79]

Project START (Special Treatment and Rehabilitative Training) at the Medical Center for Federal Prisoners at Springfield, Missouri, is one of the most ambitious programs based on behavior modification and social reinforcement, drawing on the experience of correctional treatment programs in New Jersey and West Virginia.[80] The program is designed for those confined offenders who are said to be most intractable, verbally and physically assaultive, deceitful, and manipulative within the prison walls. Prisoners of this type, claim the project directors, form only a small proportion of the inmate population, but they are an extremely disturbing element within the institution; and their obvious indifference to demands for conformity means they will pose a threat to the community when they are released. The solution, according to Project START, is to isolate such prisoners in a single, well-guarded cellblock—a prison within a prison—where they are reduced to a minimum level of existence. They are then allowed to work their way up through a series of stages marked by a growing number of privileges if they conform to a specified set of rules established by the staff. The inmate's conforming behavior, carefully monitored by his captors, is suitably reinforced, in the expectation that the inmate will learn new habits according to the principles established by studies of operant conditioning. "The START program is not viewed as a panacea," says Albert Scheckenbach. "Rather, it is a treatment alternative when repeated efforts with other types of aproaches have not had any beneficial reults. . . . START is an alternative to the 'treatment-by-transfer' cycle and a positive effort to provide an alternative to long term segregation for offenders who are chronic management problems."[81]

[79] See Jessica Mitford, *Kind and Usual Punishment* (New York: Alfred A. Knopf, 1973), pp. 127–28.

[80] Albert F. Scheckenbach, "START: Special Treatment and Rehabilitation Training." Paper presented at Conference on Behavior Control in Total Institutions, New York (December 1973), sponsored by the Institute of Society, Ethics, and the Life Sciences.

[81] Ibid., p. 9.

Much of the money to support projects of this type has been supplied by
the Law Enforcement Assistance administration as part of the federal
government's anticrime program, and in 1973 $13 million in LEAA fund-
ing was sought for the establishment of a federal center for correctional
research at Butner, North Carolina. Here, it was expected, a well-staffed
research organization with ample resources could at last find ways to
control criminal behavior, not with programs of education, job training,
and the like that had proven so ineffective in the past, but by the techniques of drug therapy and behavior modification. But to the surprise of
the social scientists and prison administrators supporting this endeavor,
attempts to find new methods of controlling criminal behavior had
reached something of a turning point. An outburst of newspaper stories,
magazine articles, public speeches, legislative proposals before Congress, and lobbying efforts by private organizations revealed that a sizable portion of the public strenuously objected to "applied behavior
analysis" and intended to see it curbed. "The Government today banned
any further use of Federal anti-crime money for behavior modification,"
The New York Times announced, "calling a halt to the programs it has
funded for the systematic manipulation of the behavior of inmates, juvenile offenders, and alcoholics."[82] The Law Enforcement Assistance Administration declared that to the best of its knowledge the agency had
not funded psychosurgery, but programs involving drugs and behavior
modification would be halted. The National Institute of Mental Health—
which was supporting a $1 million research project in psychosurgery—
said the project would be stopped, and the federal center for correctional
research at Butner curtailed its plans.[83] The American Psychological Association declared that the termination of such programs was an injustice
to the public and to prison inmates and would tend "to stifle the development of humane forms of treatment that provide the offender the opportunity to fully realize his or her potential as a contributing member of
society."[84] B. F. Skinner, whose book *Beyond Freedom and Dignity* had
helped to bring the arguments for the control of behavior to the attention
of the public, wrote a letter to *The New York Times* asserting that it was a
mistake to place behavior modification in the same category as the use of
drugs, shock therapy, and psychosurgery.[85] For the moment, though, the
public outcry against "brainwashing" and "behavior control" had much
reduced the momentum of the movement to find more effective means of
rehabilitating criminal offenders.[86]

[82] February 15, 1974.
[83] *Human Events* (June 15, 1974).
[84] See Brown, Wienckowski, and Stolz, "Behavior Modification," p. 17.
[85] *The New York Times* (February 26, 1974).
[86] For a more favorable view of the new behavior-control techniques, see Ralph K.
Schwitzgebel, *Development and Legal Regulation of Coercive Behavior Modification with Of-*

Apprehension over the new forms of treatment had actually been growing for some time among lawyers, psychologists, psychiatrists, sociologists, and others, as was pointed out earlier, even though the debate broke into a wider public consciousness only on occasion. "For more than a decade," Seymour Halleck noted, "the practice of involuntary and indeterminate commitment of the mentally ill has been rigorously criticized by those who fear that psychiatrists are too arbitrary in depriving people of liberty. More recently, the use of treatments such as lobotomy, behavior therapy, and drug therapy has been questioned on the grounds that such treatment deprives the patient of the right to choose his own course of action. The new critiques go beyond questioning the imposition of treatment upon involuntary patients. Some treatments offered to voluntary patients are also being attacked as repressive and dehumanizing. A few critics even fear that the psychiatric profession has involved itself in a gigantic conspiracy to control the behavior of citizens who deviate from social norms."[87]

At the heart of the growing controversy was the status of psychiatry as a medical specialty. Were the definition, diagnosis, and treatment of mental illness based on objective scientific knowledge, with treatment determined by the patient's best interests and, whenever possible, dependent on informed consent? Or were the definition and diagnosis of mental illness heavily influenced by disguised value judgments, with treatment little more than the incantations of a witch doctor or a modern version of Bedlam's involuntary restraints? The suspicion that the latter was closer to the mark fueled the professional debates, which then began to move into the courtroom. And when law enforcement officials attempted to place "troublesome" inmates, "persistent" offenders, and other vaguely defined types of convicted criminals in the category of those needing psychiatric help, to be subjected to the new techniques of behavior modification, the issue emerged with special force, with the added element of political contention. If those charged with the care of the mentally ill were willing to sacrifice the well-being of their patients for institutional tranquility, was it not also likely that those charged with the maintenance of law and order would use their power to suppress every challenge to state authority—including the suppression of political dissent?[88]

The use of psychiatry as a means of controlling dissent is not to be dis-

fenders (Rockville, Md.: National Institute of Mental Health, Center for Studies of Crime and Delinquency, 1971).

[87] Seymour L. Halleck, "Legal and Ethical Aspects of Behavior Control," *American Journal of Psychiatry* 131 (April 1974), pp. 381–85.

[88] See Robert Martinson, "The Age of Treatment," *Issues in Criminology* (Fall 1966), pp. 275–93.

missed lightly, warned Kenneth Keniston in a story about a future that may come to pass. A speaker at the Eighth Annual Meeting of the Community Health Organization congratulates his colleagues on the progress that has been made in combating urban unrest. "Pre-critical intervention" and "preventive rehabilitation" have done much to ensure law and order, he tells his audience, once it was realized that "inner-city violence is a product of profound personal and social pathology. It requires treatment, rather than punishment, rehabilitation rather than imprisonment." Using local citizens as "pathology detectors," Community Health teams have made masive efforts to detect all groups or individuals prone to violence or to advocating violence. Relying on a classic study entitled—Keniston tells us, with more than a touch of malice—"Relapse Rates in Seven Saturation Projects: A Multi-Variate Analysis," Congress has come to realize that short-term therapy is not enough and has passed the Remote Therapy Center Act. The construction of 247 centers, largely in the Rocky Mountain region and each with a capacity of one thousand patients, has provided a "prolonged reacculturative experience in a psychologically healthy community" that has done much to maintain domestic tranquilty. In addition, mobile treatment teams ("Motreat") are available on a stand-by basis, and on numerous occasions have been able to calm agitated populations with psychopharmacological sprays and gases; to pinpoint antisocial leaders for therapy; and to lay the basis for society's prompt return to healthy functioning. The speaker tells his audience that recent research and legislation enable the United States to focus on other groups, such as college students and intellectuals, who possess a potential for pathological behavior. We are now nearing the goal, he concludes triumphantly, of being able to insist upon total mental health from the womb to the grave. The audience bursts into applause.[89]

Four Criticisms The dangers seen by Keniston and like-minded critics fall into four main categories. First, it is argued that the new methods of treatment are often little more than crude trial-and-error procedures based on flimsy knowledge but presented with a deceptively confident air. Indeed, says one psychiatrist, we may well be the victims of a reign of error, for attempts to impose therapy in the interest of crime control are too often founded on faulty diagnosis and unproven techniques reflecting the bias of those who administer therapy rather than the findings of science.[90] Behavior modification, in particular, is frequently questioned on the grounds that in many instances it is nothing more than a set of rewards and punish-

[89] Kenneth Keniston, "How Community Mental Health Stamped Out the Riots (1968–1978), *Transaction* (July–August 1968), pp. 21–29.

[90] See Lee S. Coleman, "Perspectives on the Medical Research of Violence," *American Journal of Orthopsychiatry* 44 (1974), pp. 675–87.

ments overlaid with scientific terminology in order to avoid criticism. Behavior modification in institutions is often a fraud and a sham, argues Edward Opton. "A principal modus operandi of institutional behavior modification is mystification—disguising basically simple ideas in esoteric jargon. The primary tactic by which the institutional behavior modification movement seeks to grasp power to insulate itself from the checks and balances of a democratic society is through a bogus wrapping of itself in the ceremonial robes of science in general and medicine in particular. To believe oneself privy to putative mysteries, to keep those mysteries within one's fraternity, and to convince others that there is a secret is the essence of wizardry and the key to its prerogatives and powers."[91] As an example, Opton cites part of the findings of one well-known institutional behavior modification program involving psychotics: "That the contingency structure was highly influential in regulating the behavior of the group is further shown by the fact that all but one of the patients changed their work assignments immediately when reinforcement was shifted from preferred to non-preferred jobs."[92] So stated, says Opton, the results sound impressive, "until one realizes that, translated into plain English, the sentence says only that the inmates were unwilling to work at one menial hospital job for nothing when they were offered pay for doing another. Crazy they may have been, but not that crazy."[93]

Second, the new techniques of rehabilitation are often criticized as forms of punishment disguised as therapy. So-called aversion therapy, for example, may be little more than the imposition of painful or frightening circumstances on inmates who have angered institutional officials. The "hole"—those cells in which prison inmates are kept in solitary confinement under conditions of extreme deprivation—may be relabeled the Adjustment Center, but its function is still punishment rather than rehabilitation. Similarly, in programs such as START, aggressive prison inmates may be selected for behavior modification and stripped of all privileges on the grounds that the restoration of privileges can be used to induce conformity—just as animals in learning experiments may be underfed to make them more attentive to the food pellets serving as rewards. The fact remains, however, that inmates made to take part in these programs are subjected to the most punishing conditions of imprisonment in the name of treatment.

Third, it has seemed to a number of observers that efforts to modify the behavior of criminals are aimed not at rehabilitating the offender but

[91] Edward M. Opton, Jr., "Institutional Behavioral Modification as a Fraud and Sham," *Arizona Law Review* 17 (1975), pp. 20–28.
[92] Ibid., p. 25.
[93] Ibid.

at producing the docility of the slave. The word *rehabilitation* is usually used to mean the reorientation of the criminal's values and internalized norms so that the individual will by preference conform to the standards of the law-abiding. Programs of behavior modification, drug therapy, and the like, however, often appear to have as their primary goal the achievement of conformity to all institutional regulations without protest, regardless of the prisoner's convictions or sentiments. The convenience of the custodial officials is the goal, not the transformation of the offender's character.[94] "The treatment philosophy and programs not only have been a waste of time and money," argues one psychiatrist, "but also a boon to those who seek ever greater power over the prisoner's life. Since it is this *unchecked power* which is the basis of the psychological brutality of modern prison life, we can only acknowledge that every new psychiatrist, every new treatment unit . . . every group therapy session, merely strengthens the grip of a system which offers freedom in exchange for one's pride, one's dignity and one's identity. The treatment model has provided an incredibly powerful tool for the perpetuation and growth of the techniques of prisoner manipulation and coercion available to prison officials."[95]

Fourth, and perhaps somewhat inconsistent with the first three criticisms, the new techniques of treatment have been criticized on the grounds that they threaten to destroy the individual's existing personality and insert another in its place. Rather than being examples of sham science, conventional methods of social control in new dress, or mere punishment, the new techniques are seen as potent methods of psychic alteration. The essential qualities that make each human being unique are transformed. The new individual neither resists nor accepts—most fearful of all, he is a different person, brought into being by today's Doctor Frankensteins. Capital punishment is no longer the ultimate punishment that can be inflicted by the state; in its place, according to these critics, is the death of identity imposed in the name of therapy. An earlier, more religious age might have spoken of the death of the soul.

Some of the criticism directed against the new modes of rehabilitation may be overly harsh. The social scientists and correctional officials engaged in such efforts have been neither knaves nor fools, and the systematic and widespread use of psychiatry to suppress political dissent is still an Orwellian vision of the future rather than a prevailing reality. The ability of behavior modification to bring about persistent, important changes in the personality is limited and is certainly outstripped by the ingenious methods of mind control described in such fictional accounts

---

[94] See Aryeh Neier, letter to *The New York Review of Books* (March 7, 1974).
[95] Coleman, "Perspectives on the Medical Research of Violence," p. 14.

as *A Clockwork Orange.* Nonetheless, advocates of the new techniques frequently show little awareness of how these methods can be misused or how they can infringe upon inmates' legal rights, nor do they seem to see the political and ethical implications of the new procedures. "I believe that the day has come," claims one psychologist, "when we can combine sensory deprivation with drugs, hypnosis, and astute manipulation of rewards and punishment to gain almost complete control over an individual's behavior. It should be possible then to achieve a very rapid and highly effective type of brainwashing that would allow us to make dramatic changes in a person's behavior and personality. I foresee the day when we could convert the worst criminal into a decent, respectable citizen in a matter of a few months—or perhaps even less time than that."[96]

Statements such as these must be viewed with some skepticism, for they often represent simply the puffery of academic disciplines. But if the claims for psychosurgery, and drug therapy, and behavior modification are exaggerated, the potential power of these techniques is not to be taken lightly. In the decades ahead, these fields may show significant development, and their ability to influence behavior may be greatly increased. It is possible, for example—to return to a science-fiction scenario of the future—that a drug could be found that will accelerate the aging process. Since age is highly correlated with criminal behavior, a penal program of sudden, premature aging might be introduced, with the convicted offender sentenced not to twenty years in prison but to twenty years of instant aging. In what might be called a Rip van Winkle Program of crime control, the youthful offender could be returned to society in a few months as a middle-aged man, his criminal proclivities markedly diminished. Such a notion can be dismissed as speculative, perhaps. What cannot be dismissed is the probability that new techniques of modifying criminal behavior will confront society in coming years with profoundly disturbing legal and ethical issues.

Conclusions

The history of a social idea sometimes takes on the appearance of a parabolic curve; a small, uncertain beginning is followed by increasing acceptance and regard. A peak of public enthusiasm is reached, and then the idea traces a declining path, falling in public esteem until it is generally viewed as a vast mistake.

The idea of using custodial institutions for the reformation of criminals

[96] James V. McConnell, "Criminals Can Be Brainwashed—Now," *Psychology Today* (April 1970), p. 74.

would appear to follow such a trajectory, at least in a crude fashion. Starting with the reforming efforts of such men and women as Jean Jacques Philippe Vilain, Elizabeth Fry, and John Howard, the concept of the prison as a place for the rehabilitation of the criminal took official form in England with the Penitentiary Act of 1799. The character of the criminal, it was argued, could be transformed by penitence in the disciplined and monastic atmosphere of the custodial institution. The faith in penitence was soon replaced by a faith in the redeeming qualities of hard labor, but the enthusiasm for the prison as an agency for rehabilitating the offender—rather than simply as a means of punishment or deterrence—continued to move upward for almost one hundred years, reaching a peak that can be marked with the Declaration of Principles of the Cincinatti Prison Congress in 1870 and the establishment of the Reformatory Movement. Shortly thereafter, belief in the efficacy of the custodial institutions as an instrument of rehabilitation began to falter. The penitentiary and the reformatory gradually came to be viewed not as valued social inventions, to be shown with pride to European visitors, but as a harsh necessity where efforts at rehabilitation might be made but few accomplishments could be expected. In the last twenty years or so the idea of imprisonment as a means of reform has declined rapidly, and after the riot at Attica Prison in 1971 the drop has been precipitous. In the space of two hundred years, the custodial institution emerged as a humanitarian innovation (compared to the earlier brutal treatment of convicted criminals), gained widespread acceptance, and then came to be regarded with increasing anger as a symbol of man's inhumanity to man.

Even as the enthusiasm for the custodial institution was reaching a pinnacle, however, the idea of treatment in the community was beginning to make its appearance—in the form of American developments in probation—and starting on its ascending course. As the hope of reformation by means of imprisonment declined, faith in community corrections seems to have increased; and at some point (the data are inadequate to pinpoint it precisely) the number of convicted criminals under supervision in the community became larger than the number of convicted criminals held in custodial institutions. It is still too early to say if the idea of community corrections, in turn, has reached its peak and started on a downward path, although the growing skepticism being expressed about the efficacy of probation and parole does suggest that the concept of community corrections may be losing strength. It is clear, however, that Americans are deeply disturbed by the inability of society to curb crime and are showing some inclination to consider new ways of dealing with the problem that go beyond conventional forms of treatment both in custodial institutions and in the community. The stage may be set for the emergence of a new philosophy of corrections, new modes of treatment or control—and operant conditioning, the use of drug therapy, and psychosurgery may be the first, uncertain signs of a trend in the making.

It is this possibility that alarms the critics of the therapeutic state. The alliance of a deterministic view of man and the state acting in the name of the public good has greatly enlarged its sphere of influence in the last several decades, it is argued, and criminals along with other "troublesome" people are now subjected to arbitrary and punishing procedures that cannot be justified. In the future, the therapeutic state is likely to become still more powerful, expanding its control over the offensive as well as the dangerous. "Under a future therapeutic ideal," Kittrie warns us, "police and criminal process might be abandoned. The environment would be manipulated and controlled. Preventive measures would be taken to render any antisocial action impossible. . . . When one demonstrated antisocial tendencies, he would not be subject to a criminal trial but rather would be medically diagnosed and treated so that the behavior would not recur. Complete histories of individuals would be kept from birth to death, to generate the statistical knowledge necessary to sound diagnosis and to provide the necessary feedback to measure the efficacy of treatment. Secrets would be taboo, privacy unheard of, resistance to the new controls pathological."[97]

This is speculation, of course, for the empirically grounded theory that can lay bare the course of future developments does not yet exist. Nonetheless, American reactions to criminal behavior appear to be in a period of transition. In the concluding chapter we will examine efforts to curb crime in which the rehabilitation of the criminal has been abandoned and society appears to be moving off in other directions.

Recommended Readings

For an excellent, comprehensive view of probation and parole, the reader should see David Dressler, *Practice and Theory of Probation and Parole* (New York: Columbia University Press, 1969) and David T. Stanley, *Prisoners Among Us* (Washington, D.C.: Brookings Institution, 1976). *Federal Probation,* a journal published since 1937, is geared to practitioners as well as those with an academic interest in the area. Nicholas N. Kittrie, *The Right to Be Different: Deviance and Enforced Therapy* (Baltimore: Penguin Books, 1973) raises many of the issues now plaguing the rehabilitative ideal. Some of the new techniques for the treatment of the criminal receive a sympathetic discussion in Ralph K. Schwitzgebel, *Development and Legal Regulation of Coercive Behavior Modification Techniques with Offenders* (Rockville, Md.: National Institute of Mental Health,

[97] Kittrie, *The Right to Be Different,* p. 350.

Center for Studies of Crime and Delinquency, 1971). For a more critical viewpoint, see Jessica Mitford, *Kind and Usual Punishment* (New York: Alfred A. Knopf, 1973) and Seymour L. Halleck, "Legal and Ethical Aspects of Behavior Control," *American Journal of Psychiatry* 131 (April 1974), pp. 381–85.

Chapter 15
Reducing Crime:
Current Trends

"Criminal justice is a major American industry," says Daniel Glaser. "It supports millions of people, directly or indirectly, and consumes much public and private wealth. Yet few are very satisfied with the justice system as a whole, and each of its major parts—police, courts, corrections, and prevention—evokes many complaints."[1]

The complaints fall into two main categories. First, the justice system is ineffective, it is argued, in that the great majority of people who commit crimes are not detected, apprehended, tried, convicted, and punished. If more criminals were caught and punished, the crime rate presumably would be lower. Second, the justice system—despite its name—is in fact unjust, for it fails to provide equal treatment for all and live up to its own standards for a fair, rational determination of guilt and assignment of penalties.

"The legal system is bankrupt," declares Robert Lefcourt in a wide-ranging criticism of the capitalist structure of American society, "and cannot resolve the contradictions which, like air pollution, have grown visibly more threatening to society but whose resolution still is not given high priority."[2]

Attacks such as these do not come only from those intent on establishing a radical critique of the American social order or who have suffered at the hands of the police or the courts; complaints about contemporary administration of justice come from every segment of society. "Much bitterness and dissatisfaction stem from the widespread conviction that American criminal codes are unfair, unequitable, and—in a word—unjust," asserts the report of a group of influential business and professional leaders. "The sense of justice is a basic human need. Any society rests upon insecure foundations if it contains major elements that

[1]*Strategic Criminal Justice Planning* (Rockville, Md.: National Institute of Mental Health, Center for Studies of Crime and Delinquency, 1975), p. 3.

[2]"Law Against the People," in Richard Quinney, ed., *Criminal Justice in America* (Boston: Little, Brown, 1974), p. 253.

believe its laws and the manner of their administration are unjust. Yet, injustice does exist; there is discriminatory enforcement of unpopular laws, police corruption, inordinate court delay, and brutality in the prisons. Our institutions are defective."[3]

The crescendo of criticism of the administration of justice in the 1960s and 1970s was echoed by the growing discussion of possible solutions—but this was a time, as we saw in Chapter 14, when faith in conventional techniques of rehabilitation as a solution to the crime problem was much diminished and new techniques such as drug therapy or operant conditioning were viewed as scientifically dubious or politically unacceptable. If a just and effective way of reducing crime was to be found, a reliance on the reformation of the offender did not—for the moment, at least—appear to be promising.

Some people, it is true, maintain a degree of optimism about the possibility of rehabilitation. Prison officials, with careers tied to existing institutional arrangements, show an understandable reluctance to proclaim that prisons not only do not work but cannot work.[4] There are many suggestions for shoring up the existing system of community corrections, such as providing halfway houses, reducing caseloads for probation and parole officers, and reforming sentencing procedures. In general, however, arguments about the best way to control crime have moved away from the model in which criminals are caught, reformed, and released. Planning for the administration of criminal justice based on such a model is simply more of the same and has proven ineffective, argues Leslie Wilkins, and could well mean the total breakdown of the system by the year 2000.[5] Something different is needed.

Recent proposals for something different have taken three major forms. First, it is argued that a much stricter system of enforcement is needed, with the emphasis on policing, punishment, and deterrence. This is not regression, it is said, but a realistic acceptance of society's inability to rehabilitate criminals; if penalties are fair, quick, and certain, deterrence will prove to be effective after all. Second, it is argued that the criminal law should reduce the scope of its activities. By involving itself with a vast number of deviants whose behavior should be of no concern to anyone but themselves, the justice system has become so overloaded that it can be neither fair nor effective. The solution lies in adopting a rational

---

[3] *Reducing Crime and Assuring Justice* (New York: Committee for Economic Development, 1972), p. 12.

[4] One survey of the nation's prison officials showed that 63 percent believed some rehabilitation programs can change inmate behavior for the better. Another 14 percent agreed with the statement that there was not enough evidence to justify scrapping the idea of rehabilitation. See *Corrections Magazine* 1 (May–June 1975), p. 5.

[5] See Leslie T. Wilkins, "Crime and Criminal Justice at the Turn of the Century," *The Annals of the American Academy of Political and Social Science* 408 (July 1973), pp. 13–29.

policy of nonintervention. Third, it is claimed that the best way to control crime is to prevent it. Instead of waiting until a crime has been committed and then bringing the cumbersome machinery of law enforcement into play, attention should be devoted to making it difficult—or impossible—for crimes to occur in the first place—such as improving locking devices or doing away with the need of carrying cash.

These ideas do not represent an abrupt break with past thinking. Instead, they appear to be an additional step in a long line of theorizing about the sources of human behavior that has gradually shifted attention from man's internal self—whether it be biological or psychological—to his external environment. New discoveries may draw attention once again to the soma and the psyche; and it is true that the concern with therapy has focused attention on changing the individual rather than the social environment. Nonetheless, the emphasis on the manipulation of external circumstances for the betterment of society is part of an important body of theory in the social sciences. The use of this approach, in the effort to find better ways of dealing with crime, is thus in line with much current thought.[6]

Cracking Down on Crime

When people speak of the need for stricter law enforcement, they are generally referring to more arrests of suspected offenders, a higher rate of prosecutions and convictions (with cases moving through the courts at a faster pace), and harsher sentences—that is, longer periods of imprisonment and the use of imprisonment rather than probation. Achieving these objectives, of course, often requires more police, more resources for prosecuting attorneys, more judges and courtroom facilities, and more correctional institutions. Communities have found that developing and sustaining a program of strict law enforcement is apt to be an expensive business, and the relationship between additional resources and outcome is often unclear.

A national survey in 1972 indicated that 81 percent of the people interviewed believed that the police "should be tougher in dealing with crime and lawlessness."[7] In recent years, after the Supreme Court declared that existing death-penalty provisions were unconstitutional because they

---

[6]In 1970, a national survey indicated that almost 60 percent of those interviewed assigned the blame for crime and lawlessness to society, rather than the individual, with younger persons and persons of higher socioeconomic status being the most inclined to take this viewpoint. See *Sourcebook of Criminal Justice Statistics—1974* (Washington, D.C.: Government Printing Office, 1975), p. 177.

[7]See Michael J. Hindelang, *Public Opinion Regarding Crime* (Washington, D.C.: Government Printing Office, 1975), p. 11.

led to discriminatory and erratic enforcement, thirty-five states have passed new capital-punishment statutes. Twelve states have replaced judicial discretion in sentencing with fixed-term, mandatory penalties for such crimes as selling heroin, robbery, kidnapping, and arson; and other states are considering similar legislation. Fourteen states have adopted measures that require the criminal to compensate the victim. In many jurisdictions the proportion of convicted felons who are imprisoned is increasing, and in a number of states prison sentences appear to be lengthening.[8] In Detroit, in the summer of 1976, a curfew was imposed, and 450 policemen (laid off in an economy drive) were recalled when marauding teenage gangs began roaming through the downtown business area.[9] In the same year, seventeen major cities obtained federal funds to aid in the prosecution of "career criminals," or offenders with long records of previous convictions—although in Franklin County, Ohio, the public defender applied for and received a federal grant to aid in the defense of such offenders, arguing that he was being outgunned by the enlarged staff of the prosecutor's office.[10]

Assessing the impact of such measures is no less difficult than assessing efforts at rehabilitation, and for the same reasons: control groups are often inadequate or lacking altogether, and official figures give a poor picture of the incidence of crime. The available evidence does suggest that increasing the manpower and resources of the criminal justice system does not have the dramatic effect on the crime rate that is sometimes predicted by enthusiastic advocates of a get-tough policy.

A study conducted by the New York Police Department in 1954 in the 25th precinct in Manhattan (East Harlem) involved a doubling of the officers assigned to the area. After four months it was found that the number of serious crimes reported to the police decreased and that the reduction was greatest for street crimes; muggings, for example, fell from sixty-nine to seven. These gratifying results were used to support police demands for increased manpower for the department as a whole, which grew by 54 percent over the next twenty years while the population remained approximately the same. But crime rates increased even more rapidly than the number of police.[11]

In the early 1960s felonies (particularly robberies) committed in the New York subway system began to increase at an alarming rate, and in 1965 the police patrols in the subway were more than doubled. At first

[8] See Timothy D. Schellhardt, "Law and Order," *The Wall Street Journal* (June 24, 1976).

[9] See Charles Mohr, "Police Chief Pressed as Detroit Seeks to Halt Gang Terrorism," *The New York Times* (August 19, 1976).

[10] See Timothy D. Schellhardt, "Cracking Down: Experimental Program Musters Legal Forces Against Repeat Offenders to Boost Convictions," *The Wall Street Journal* (August 19, 1976).

[11] See James Q. Wilson, *Thinking About Crime* (New York: Basic Books, 1975), Chapter 5.

the number of crimes declined—and then, within a year or so, the robberies again increased at a rapid rate and continued to do so during the following years.[12]

In 1972 the Police Department of Kansas City, Missouri (which has approximately 1300 officers in a city of just over half a million), undertook one of the most comprehensive experiments ever conducted to study the effect of different types of police work. Fifteen police beats were randomly divided into three groups. In the first group, routine patrols were eliminated and officers were instructed to respond only to calls for service; in the second group, routine patrols were maintained at the customary level of one car for each beat; and in the third group, patrols were increased to two or three times their usual level. The Police Department and the Police Foundation, which funded the project, agreed that the study would continue for one year if reported crime did not reach "unacceptable" limits. As things turned out, rates of reported crime were unaffected by the experimental variation in types of police patrols. In fact, carefully collected data based on surveys, participant observation, and officially reported crime indicated that "decreasing and increasing routine preventive patrol within the range tested . . . had no effect on crime, citizen fear of crime, community attitudes toward the police on the delivery of police services, police response time, or traffic accidents."[13] After examining the studies in New York, Kansas City, and elsewhere, Wilson concluded that massive increases in the number of police in small areas probably leads to a decrease in some crimes, such as muggings and auto thefts, although the crimes may simply be displaced to other areas and may increase again after a short period, as criminals become familiar with the new policing procedures.

Other forms of increased police activity—such as more detective work—also appear disappointing. A study by the Rand Corporation, for example, focusing on the effectiveness of investigative work in law enforcement agencies in the United States, found that differences in investigative training, staffing, workloads, and procedures have no appreciable effect on crime, arrest, or clearance rates. The most important factor determining whether a case will be solved is the amount of information the victim can supply the police. If the victim cannot provide helpful clues, the police are not likely to discover or apprehend the culprit.[14]

[12] Ibid., pp. 86–87.

[13] See George L. Kelling, Tony Pate, Duane Dieckman, and Charles E. Brown, "The Kansas City Preventive Patrol Experiment," in Seymour Halleck, ed., *The Aldine Crime and Justice Annal 1974* (Chicago: Aldine, 1975), p. 208.

[14] See Peter Greenwood and Joan Petersilia, *The Criminal Investigation Process,* vol. I. (Santa Monica, Calif.: Rand Corporation, 1975), pp. vi–ix.

As for attempts to secure harsher sentences, the evidence is fragmentary, but it too suggests that cracking down on criminals is not a simple matter. In New York State, for example, the so-called Rockefeller laws, which reclassified many drug offenses from misdemeanors to felonies, restricted plea bargaining, and mandated severe penalties for those convicted, took effect in 1973. In 1976 a study revealed that there were actually fewer convictions and sentences than under the old laws. "The risk of punishment facing offenders did not increase noticeably," it was reported. "The number of drug offenders sentenced to prison declined, and the speed with which cases were processed did not improve." The restrictions on plea bargaining resulted in a greater demand for trials and greater delay, and judges and juries become more reluctant to reach a guilty verdict.[15]

Even if the courts do become stricter in the granting of probation and do impose longer sentences, there is serious doubt whether punishment is thus made more certain for the general run of criminals—and this question is often the basis for the argument in favor of a crackdown on crime. As Richard Moran has pointed out, only a small proportion of persons who commit crimes are caught, tried, and convicted, and they do not form a representative sample of the criminal population. By making sentences more severe, society further discriminates against the poor and members of minority groups but does little to increase the certainty of punishment for the great mass of offenders.[16] Certainty of punishment as a means of deterrence can be obtained not by punishing more harshly the few criminals who are caught, but by catching more criminals and making sure they are punished. Imposing stiffer penalties on the few who fall into the hands of the law may give the appearance of a tougher policy, may have an influence on chronic offenders, and may be emotionally satisfying to a portion of the public; but it fails to provide the substance of stricter law enforcement.

A policy of cracking down on crime, then, raises two distinct questions. First, do the steps taken by law enforcement agencies actually produce more arrests, more convictions, and harsher penalties? And second, do more arrests, more convictions, and harsher penalties reduce crime? We have examined the difficulties in establishing the link between punishment and crime; the advocates of a strict law enforcement policy sometimes brush these difficulties aside with the assertion that common sense *must* lead to a belief in the efficacy of punishment. But the evidence suggests that an expanded police force does not necessarily

[15] See "Drug Law Effectiveness Questioned in U.S. Study," *The New York Times* (September 5, 1976).
[16] See Richard Moran, review of *Thinking About Crime*, by James Q. Wilson, in *Contemporary Sociology* 5 (July 1976), pp. 413–14.

mean that more criminals will be apprehended. Increased prosecution facilities do not necessarily guarantee either the certainty or the speed of punishment. And while it may be true that capturing criminals and punishing them quickly does check some crime, the details remain unknown.

Even if we assume that a get-tough policy does lead to more arrests, more convictions, and severer sentences, and these in turn result in the reduction of certain types of crime, the question still remains whether the benefits justify the expense. This calculation is seldom attempted in any explicit fashion. Those who urge an expanded program of law enforcement apparently assume a lowering of the crime rate is so desirable that little or no justification of the cost is required. A price must be placed on decreasing the number of muggings, assaults, burglaries, and other crimes, however, if community resources are to be allocated on a rational basis—and it is possible that the public has somehow decided that the expenditure necessary for a significant impact on the crime rate is simply not warranted. In any event, fulminating about the problem of crime and making token gestures often seem to be preferred to increasing taxes or reallocating funds from programs such as aid to education, unemployment insurance, and old-age benefits.

In addition to economic considerations, efforts at more vigorous law enforcement are apt to touch off heated political debates. For some, a get-tough policy raises Orwellian visions of a police state which keeps citizens under constant surveillance and represses all dissent. The demand for more effective law enforcement leads easily to such excesses as the widespread use of paid informants, it is argued, and these in turn are likely to become *agents provocateurs*. [17] For others, doubts about the increased activity of law enforcement agencies may be rooted in more conservative views, such as a fear of "federal control of local affairs" or an aversion to "bureaucratic red tape." [18]

Cracking down on crime, in short, involves numerous issues that resist easy analysis. Social scientists are sometimes quick to characterize a call for stricter law enforcement as little more than a clamor for brutality. This is almost certainly an error. The public is often much more aware of the moral and political dilemmas and of the need for at least a rough accounting of costs and benefits than the student of crime is likely to acknowledge. Nevertheless, the current trend toward more police, greater

[17] See Gary T. Marx, "Thoughts on a Neglected Category of Social Movement Participant: The Agent Provocateur and the Informant," *American Journal of Sociology* 80 (September 1974), pp. 402–42.

[18] See, for example, the editorial "Crime and Empire Building," *The Wall Street Journal* (September 1, 1976), in which the Law Enforcement Assistance Administration is criticized for "meddling in local police policies."

resources, and harsher sentences as a means of dealing with crime is best viewed warily, for it enters an area in which little is known and the abuse of power is easy.[19]

Nonintervention

A number of analysts believe that cracking down on crime is a move in precisely the wrong direction. In trying to solve the problem of illegal behavior, it is argued, American society should do not more but less. Edwin Schur, for example, analyzing the problem of juvenile delinquency, has suggested that the legal definition of *juvenile delinquent* is much too broad, since it includes, in addition to young people who have committed what would be considered crimes if committed by an adult, such categories as "habitual truants" and "children in need of supervison." Moreover, the existing theories of causation are seriously flawed, Schur argues, and the procedures of the juvenile court are both unfair and ineffective. Instead of reducing delinquency, the system contributes to it by stigmatizing the child. Thus, Schur has claimed, the basic rule of public policy should be to leave children alone wherever possible.[20] "Basically, radical non-intervention implies policies that accommodate society to the widest possible diversity of behavior and attitudes," says Schur, "rather than forcing as many individuals as possible to 'adjust' to supposedly common societal standards. This does not mean that anything goes, that all behavior is socially acceptable. But traditional delinquency policy has proscribed youthful behavior well beyond what is required to maintain a smooth-running society or to protect others from youthful depredations."[21]

Schur's thesis concerning juvenile delinquency—growing from the earlier work of such social scientists as Edwin Lemert, who had pressed for "judicious nonintervention"—is part of a general reconsideration of the role of the criminal law, for both juveniles and adults.[22] As was pointed out in Chapter 2, the modern state is seen as intruding in a great variety of areas in which it does not belong. The criminal law, in particular, is

[19] See Jack P. Gibbs, *Crime, Punishment, and Deterrence* (New York: Elsevier, 1975) and Franklin E. Zimring and Gordon J. Hawkin, *Deterrence: The Legal Threat in Crime Control* (Chicago: University of Chicago Press, 1973).

[20] See Edwin M. Schur, *Radical Non-Intervention: Rethinking the Delinquency Problem* (Englewood Cliffs, N.J.: Prentice-Hall, 1973), pp. 153–73.

[21] Ibid., p. 154.

[22] See Edwin M. Lemert, "The Juvenile Court—Quest and Realities," in President's Commission on Law Enforcement and Administration of Justice, *Task Force Report: Juvenile Delinquency and Youth Crime* (Washington, D.C.: Government Printing Office, 1967), pp. 96–97.

frequently misused—with disastrous results, according to many critics—and in a number of areas may well be causing more crime than it prevents. In the 1950s the Wolfenden Committee, appointed by the British Parliament to study prostitution and homosexuality, stated in its report that the proper purpose of the criminal law is "to preserve public order and decency, to protect the citizen from what is offensive or injurious, and to provide sufficient safeguards against exploitation and corruption of others, particularly those who are especially vulnerable because they are young, weak in body or mind, inexperienced, or in a state of special physical, official or economic dependence."[23] Prostitution and homosexuality involving consenting adults were not viewed as falling within these proscriptions. "Unless a deliberate attempt is to be made by society," said the report, "acting through the agency of the law, to equate the sphere of crime with the sphere of sin, there must remain a realm of private morality and immorality which is, in brief and crude terms, not the law's business."[24]

In the following decade, American social scientists pointed to other forms of behavior that were "not the law's business." Gambling, public drunkenness, the use of drugs like marijuana, abortion—all had been mistakenly defined as crimes and all should be decriminalized. Nonintervention should take the form of ceasing to declare such behavior crimes.[25]

Decriminalization   In general, there are five main arguments in support of decriminalization for certain acts. First, the behavior is not considered a serious or important wrong by most people, or, if so considered, the behavior results in no serious, tangible harm. Second, the use of criminal sanctions does not in fact deter people from engaging in the behavior; and if the behavior is to be controlled, other means should be found. Third, labeling the behavior criminal tends to encourage the formation of deviant subcultures in which the behavior is reinforced rather than diminished. Fourth, using the criminal law to control such behavior corrupts the process of law enforcement, fosters organized crime, and breeds disrespect for the legal system. Finally, these minor offenses or nonoffenses consume a large portion of the resources available for law enforcement that could

[23] Great Britain. Committee on Homosexual Offences and Prostitution, *Report,* Command No. 247 (1957), p. 23.
[24] Ibid., p. 48.
[25] See, for example, Sanford H. Kadish, "The Crisis of Overcriminalization," *The Annals of the American Academy of Political and Social Science* 374 (November 1967), pp. 157–70; H. L. A. Hart, *Law, Liberty, and Morality* (Stanford, Calif.: Stanford University Press, 1963); and Herbert L. Packer, *The Limits of the Criminal Sanction* (Stanford, Calif.: Stanford University Press, 1968). Decriminalization, of course, does not mean that the government has no interest in controlling the behavior in question, but that if the behavior is controlled, something other than the criminal law will be used.

better be devoted to more serious crimes. On pragmatic grounds alone, the law should cease trying to enforce disputed moral standards of minor importance.

In earlier portions of this book, we have examined the themes of "victimless" crimes, deterrence, deviant subcultures, the corruption of law enforcement, and the effect of overloading on the legal system. Here we see that these elements are part of a general problem in the United States today: the overextension of the criminal law. "The plain sense that the criminal law is a highly specialized tool of social control," said Sanford Kadish, "useful for certain purposes but not for others; that when improperly used is capable of producing more evil than good; that the decision to criminalize any particular behavior must follow only after an assessment and balancing of gains and losses—this obvious injunction of rationality has been noted widely for over 250 years, from Jeremy Bentham to the National Crime Commission, and by the moralistic philosophers as well as the utilitarian ones."[26] A rational public policy for dealing with crime, according to this argument, should focus on a sharp limitation of the scope of the criminal law—a policy of "radical non-intervention," in Schur's words, or, as Lemert phrased it, "judicious nonintervention."

Decriminalization involves the long, complicated procedures of formal legal change. New statutes must be written and guided through the legislative process. The public must accept the idea that removing the stigma of illegality from behavior is not the same as conferring approval upon it. The procedure is difficult and uncertain, and it is not surprising that law enforcement agencies have sometimes tried to accomplish the same end by means of an informal process that is labeled diversion.

"The *diversion* of persons from the criminal justice system has long been **Diversion** practiced in the United States," it has been pointed out, "largely because the system allows—in fact, requires—considerable discretion on the part of the police, with regard to decisions to arrest or dismiss and court referral or informal disposition, and on the part of the prosecuter or intake worker, with regard to official or unofficial processing. Diversion from the justice system may occur, of course, at any stage of the judicial processing; but concern over the tremendous burden placed on the courts and the injustices associated with the inability of the courts to handle the volume of cases, compounded by evidence that criminal processing often does more harm than good, has resulted in a focus on diversion of certain groups of offenders before court processing."[27] The criminal law is selectively enforced, that is to say, by law enforcement

[26] Kadish, "The Crisis of Overcriminalization," pp. 169–70.
[27] Elinor Harlow, *Diversion From the Criminal Justice System* (Washington, D.C.: Government Printing Office, 1973), p. 1.

agencies, in the interest both of justice and of administration. Decriminalization is accomplished not by legislation but by the day-to-day decisions of prosecutor and police. The drunk who is picked up, brushed off, and sent home; the brawling husband and wife who are separated and cajoled or threatened into harmony; the teenager whose trial on a marijuana charge is postponed indefinitely on a promise of good behavior—are all "diverted" from the machinery of the law in an informal process in which discretion rather than rules guide official action.[28]

In recent years, attention has been devoted to the possibility of systematizing the process of diversion and enlarging its scope. "There is an increasing awareness that the criminal process is only one of a number of society's methods of dealing with antisocial conduct," says one law professor, "and that in many cases it may not be in the best interests of either society or the accused to pursue that process under the particular circumstances. . . . An example of this increasing awareness is reflected by the fact that communities in the United States are currently working toward establishing pretrial diversion programs in their criminal justice systems."[29] Rather than being left to the unregulated judgment of individual officials, diversion is becoming an explicit alternative to the usual sanctions of the legal system, with an articulated rationale, standards of selection, and so on.[30]

The justification of diversion is not usually based on administrative convenience or a reduction of costs, although it seems likely that the growing burden of the criminal justice system has prompted increased interest in this area. Rather, it is argued that diversion serves the needs of society and the offender. By freeing the police and the courts of unnecessary work, diversion allows them to function more effectively in "serious" matters and thereby establishes greater respect for the law. Diversion benefits the offender by shielding him from such hardships as the stigma of a criminal trial and conviction and the cruelty of imprisonment.[31] There is a general assumption, then—usually remaining implicit, with little or no effort at justification—that many of the offenses coming to the attention of the law are insignificant and that punishment in such cases is unwarranted or useless. The question of who should have the power to make such judgments—and to translate them into policy by deciding not to enforce the criminal law—remains largely ignored.

[28] See Frank W. Miller, *Prosecution: The Decision to Charge a Suspect With a Crime* (Boston: Little, Brown, 1969).

[29] See John W. Palmer, "Pre-Arrest Diversion: Victim Confrontation," *Federal Probation Quarterly* 38 (September 1974), pp. 12–18.

[30] See Robert M. Carter, "The Diversion of Offenders," *Federal Probation* 36 (December 1972), pp. 31–36.

[31] See, for example, National Advisory Commission on Criminal Justice Standards and Goals, *A National Strategy to Reduce Crime* (New York: Avon, 1975), pp. 468–71.

At the present time, there are numerous programs of diversion, involving both misdemeanors and felonies and adults as well as juveniles.[32] (The juvenile court, of course, was viewed by its early proponents as a diversion of youthful offenders from the formal procedures of the criminal court and the punitive sanctions of the criminal law.) The Night Prosecutor's Program in Columbus, Ohio, supported by a grant from the Law Enforcement Assistance Administration, illustrates many of the features of such efforts. Focusing on "primarily interpersonal disputes in which there is a continuing relationship"—that is, family fights and neighborhood squabbles—the program encourages the prosecutor to exercise discretionary power and use an administrative hearing rather than a criminal trial. The complainant and the accused are instructed to appear at a hearing in approximately one week, at which time the matter is discussed and the parties to the quarrel are urged to resolve their differences. When cases of this sort are funneled through the criminal court, notes John Palmer, the law school professor who helped design the project, "the waste of economic assets and manpower resulting from such a procedure is evidenced by the estimated cost of $200 every time a warrant is served, an arrest occurs, and an initial appearance is made before a judge. The cost of bond money, the arrest record, the family breakdowns, and other social costs cannot be estimated, but it is enormous."[33] The use of administrative hearings saves an estimated $798,400 a year, the imposition of criminal sentences are avoided, and—presumably—the conflicts are resolved just as effectively as they would be by the use of criminal proceedings, if not more so. "Hearings are free flowing, without regard to rules of evidence, burdens of proof, or other legalities," says Palmer. "Emotional outbursts are common with the responsibility of the hearing officer to insure that they do not get out of control. . . . It is this writer's firm conviction that without the opportunity for the controlled display of emotionalism, shouting, and other forms of confrontation, the basic issues often do not come to the surface."[34]

Similar results are claimed for programs in California, Illinois, New York, Washington, D.C., Colorado, Connecticut, and Missouri that handle such offenses as public drunkenness, drug offenses, and many forms of juvenile delinquency, as well as family and neighborhood disputes.[35] By means of informal administrative hearings and, if necessary, informal sanctions (such as the threat of invoking the criminal process), disputes are resolved, juveniles are assigned "useful community work" to be car-

[32] Ibid., pp. 471–78.
[33] See John W. Palmer, "Pre-Arrest Diversion: Victim Confrontation," p. 28.
[34] Ibid., p. 472.
[35] See A National Strategy to Reduce Crime, pp. 475–78.

ried out under supervision, alcoholics are placed in detoxification centers. The clumsy moralism of the criminal law is thus avoided, it is argued, and the numerous petty violations of the law are handled with considerably less time and trouble.

Diversion may appear to be an obviously preferable course for many offenders. Such a practice, it has been pointed out, "gives society the opportunity to consider the possibility of reallocating the existing resources to programs that promise greater success in bringing about correctional reform and social restoration of offenders. Given the choice between expanding the capacities of police, courts, and institutions to the point where they could accommodate the present and projected rates of criminal activity and the opportunity to establish diversion programs with public funds, the economics of the matter clearly favor a social policy of diversion."[36]

But diversion poses a number of difficulties, as even its advocates are aware. That those accused of crime are saved from the stigma of a trial and subsequent punishment also means that suspected offenders are pushed into alternative forms of treatment without the protection of due process of law. There is the question of who is to make the decision to divert offenders from criminal proceedings, as was suggested above, and this involves the questions of which offenses are to be judged "minor" and which individuals deserve to be steered away from the criminal court. Such decisions should not be imposed by government officials— no matter how good their intentions—without public scrutiny and approval, for the door is thus opened for an arbitrary or dicriminatory enforcement of the law. Furthermore, diversion has been described correctly as an opportunity, not a solution. If administrative proceedings have the advantage of economy and dispatch but do little or nothing to change the offender's behavior, diversion is simply a disguise for inaction—a form of hypocrisy presumably not intended by the proponents of nonintervention. There is also the danger that, in lieu of punishment, offenders may be pressured into conforming to standards of behavior deemed desirable by law enforcement officials but which have nothing to do with reforming criminal behavior. (The diversion movement, like probation and parole, is apt to use such vacuous phrases as "satisfactory participation" and "demonstrated self-improvement.")

Finally, the impact of diversion on the crime rate remains largely unknown. It can be argued that diversion avoids the self-fulfillng prophecy of labeling lawbreakers, the counterproductive effects of imprisonment, and the sense of resentment and alienation that produces more crime rather than less. But proof is lacking. For example, a careful evaluation of

---

[36] Ibid., p. 470.

the Manhattan Court Employment Project to divert criminal defendants failed to substantiate early claims of a considerable difference in recidivism rates between those exposed to the normal processes of the criminal justice system and those placed in a diversion program of group therapy and employment counseling. The data indicated that when defendants are channeled into an alternative path, they do neither better nor worse than those who pass through the ordinary procedures of the police, the courts, and the correctional systems in New York City. This finding in itself "could be regarded as a sufficient mandate for a program that seeks to inject humanity into a system that is not known for either excessive humaneness or demonstrated effectiveness," notes Franklin Zimring, but he adds that diversion programs have been oversold and widely misconceived.[37]

In less populous industrial societies, diversion may be used in cases of delinquency, which can be disposed of by a fine in lieu of prosecution. Vilhelm Aubert, in describing the Norwegian experience, says, "This option, called 'forlegg,' amounts to a bargain between the offender and the police. Strictly speaking, the offender need not plead guilty in order to be dealt with in this informal, discreet, and quick way. It suffices that he declares himself willing to accept a writ issued by the police and imposing a fine. Thus, the basis of the penalty and the termination of the conflict between the offender and his society assume a form strongly reminiscent of a private contract."[38] This avoidance of the criminal law and its time-consuming procedures in the case of delinquencies is part of a larger movement in which the legal system has come to be used less and less for the resolution of conflicts of many kinds. Hearings replace trials; administrative boards replace the courts; and mediators replace lawyers in an industrial society in which legal procedures often appear clumsy, inefficient, or uncertain.[39]

The pressure to divert criminal cases in the United States exists in no small measure because the legal system is marked by a fundamental structural defect. A great variety of acts declared criminal by the law are viewed, both by the legal system and by society, as minor or petty offenses, deserving no more than minor or petty punishments. Such punishments, however, are too slight to act as an effective deterrent, even if they were administered quickly and surely, which they are not. As a consequence, the volume of petty-crime cases is large, further diminish-

---

[37] See Franklin F. Zimring, "Measuring the Impact of Pre-trial Diversion from the Criminal Justice System," *University of Chicago Law Review* 41 (Winter 1974), pp. 224–41.

[38] Vilhelm Aubert, "Law as a Way of Resolving Conflict: The Case of a Small Industrialized Society," in Laura Nader, ed., *Law in Culture and Society* (Chicago: Aldine, 1969), p. 297.

[39] Ibid., p. 286.

ing the quick and certain assignment of penalties for minor offenses and absorbing resources needed to combat other forms of crime.[40]

Despite the many problems connected with developing methods of diversion that are both just and effective, such efforts will undoubtedly continue. As Isidore Silver has pointed out, six recent national commissions dealing with crime or social disorder have come to much the same conclusion: American society has overused the criminal law and the criminal justice system.[41] The campaign to translate this conclusion into a public policy of nonintervention is not likely to abate, although diversion may proceed at a faster pace than decriminalization.

Reducing Criminal Opportunity

"Of all the things a citizen or a community can do to reduce crime," declares the National Advisory Commission on Criminal Justice Standards and Goals, "the most immediate and most direct approach is to eliminate obvious opportunities for criminals. Locked cars, well-lighted streets, alarm systems, and properly designed and secure housing make crime, particularly acquisitive crimes such as larceny, burglary, auto theft, and robbery, more difficult to commit."[42]

Criminal opportunity can be reduced in three main ways. First, physical security can be improved. Replacing the face-to-face exchange between bank tellers and customers with the use of phones and television screens; providing more effective locking devices for cars, houses, and offices; surrounding residential areas with walls or high fences; rewriting building codes to require more secure windows and doors—all involve what has been called a "hardening of the target." It has been argued that such measures may simply move the commission of crime from one area to another and that criminals—particularly property offenders—will search for an easy victim until they find one. While there may be some truth to this assertion, many crimes are the work of casual thieves and burglars, and locking cars and windows may well frustrate such offenders. Furthermore, it is argued, "criminals are not infinitely mobile;

[40] See Hugh B. Price, "A Proposal for Handling of Petty Misdemeanor Offenses," *Connecticut Bar Journal* 42 (March 1968), pp. 55–75.

[41] See "Introduction," *A National Strategy to Reduce Crime*, p. xiii. The commissions cited by Silver are the President's Commission on Law Enforcement and Administration of Justice (1967); the National Advisory Committee on Civil Disorders (1968); the National Commission on the Causes and Prevention of Violence (1969); the President's Commission on Campus Unrest (1970); the National Commission on Obscenity and Pornography (1970); and the United States Commission on Marijuana and Drug Abuse (1972).

[42] *A National Strategy to Reduce Crime*, p. 146. See also T. A. Repetto, *Residential Crime* (Cambridge, Mass.: Ballinger, 1974).

their area of operations can extend just so far before robberies, thefts, and burglaries become less profitable and not worth the trouble or risk."[43]

Second, the likelihood of detecting the commission of a crime can be increased. Thus, for example, sensors for detecting illegal entry; elaborate alarm systems linked to police headquarters (frequently triggered by mistake, it should be pointed out); and antishoplifting "tags" that can be identified by scanning devices—all may contribute to the quicker, more efficient apprehension of offenders.

Third, surveillance can be made more effective. Methods include improved street lighting, television scanners in shopping areas and banks, electronic listening devices (often of dubious legality), and the employment of private police. The last has become a $12 billion industry in the United States; and the claim has been made that private guards "may soon become the major resource in United States crime prevention. . . . Various local studies indicate private guards already outnumber public police officers and the gap is growing."[44] Reliance on the protection offered by private police has a number of drawbacks, though. Such employees are often badly trained and inexperienced, carrying weapons that are a danger both to themselves and to others. In effecting a citizen's arrest—which they are legally entitled to do—they are under no obligation to inform suspects of their legal rights embodied in the *Miranda* warning (discussed in Chapter 9). Most important, however, according to Oscar Newman, the use of private police involves a serious self-deception. "When people begin to protect themselves as individuals and not as a community," he argues, "the battle against crime is effectively lost. The indifferent crowd witnessing a violent crime is by now an American cliché. The move of middle- and upper-class population into protective high-rises and other structures of isolation—as well guarded and as carefully differentiated from the surrounding human landscape as a military post—is just as clearly a retreat into indifference."[45] The solution, Newman maintains, is not to rely on paid protectors but to create a community in which each citizen feels responsible for aiding in the policing of the *polis*.

An essential element in the creation of such a community is an appropriate architectural design. "Today barbarism has taken over many city

[43] *A National Strategy to Reduce Crime*, p. 150.

[44] Clark Whelton, "In Guards We Trust," *The New York Times Magazine* (September 19, 1976). See also Milton Lipson, On Guard—The Business of Private Security (New York: Quadrangle/The New York Times Book Company, 1975); and James S. Kakalik and Sorrel Wildhorn, *Private Police in the United States* (Santa Monica, Calif.: Rand Corporation, 1971).

[45] *Defensible Space* (New York: Collier Books, 1973), p. 3; and *Design Guidelines for Creating Defensible Space* (Washington, D.C.: National Institute of Law Enforcement and Criminal Justice, 1976).

Selling Security

How to Safeguard Your Building Against the World's Craftiest Criminals.

A report to executives from Johnson Controls

Today's building is like a small city. To function economically it must allow free access to thousands of people, total strangers included.

Then how do you keep undesirables from coming in, how do you keep the world's craftiest criminals out?

Up 'til Now, a Losing Battle

Your building security man has a tough job. With crime up 17% last year, his job is getting tougher.

He has hundreds of thousands of square feet to defend. He must defend it at all hours against all comers. And chances are he's trying to do it with antiquated key locks, a few door buzzers, and a handful of $3-an-hour security guards.

What is he defending against? A mixed bag of muggers, junkies, rapists, firebugs, bombers, vandals, pilferers, petty thieves, *and* the mastermind looking for the big score. And it's no contest. In most of today's buildings, the security system is just no match for the world's craftiest criminal.

How Do You Stop Him?

Antiquated security systems treat buildings like walled fortresses. This perimeter defense may catch a few nightprowlers. But it cannot control the throngs of people, including every type of criminal, that enter your building during the day. Your security system must keep these people from roaming freely about. No guard force can do this. The Johnson Controls JC/80 computerized security system can.

How to "Button up" the Free Access Building

Each building employee and tenant gets an access card impregnated with an indelible, in-

From an advertisement that appeared in *The Wall Street Journal* (April 30, 1975). Reprinted by permission of Johnson Controls, Inc.

visible code. Instead of metal locks, the doors (and sometimes the elevators) of your building are equipped with unpickable access card *readers*. When a card is slipped into the card reader slot, the JC/80 *acts*.

It may open a door. Or it may deny access. It sounds an alarm if it comes across a card reported lost or stolen. It also notes and records members card identity, time, and place of entry. It can be programmed to tell you instantly who's *in* and who's *out*.

Sensors That Protect Our Missile Bases

But it is foolhardy to think that even the most sophisticated access control can forever thwart the master criminal. He may rent space in your building and batter his way through the floor. Well, we'll be waiting for him with the same esoteric, on-the-spot detection devices we've installed on missile bases, in banks, in art museums. To name a few:

■ A device that fills a room or passageway with a pool of silent energy. If a man "wades into" this invisible pool, an alarm goes off.

■ A stress alarm that measures the "sag" in a one-foot-thick concrete floor if a man so much as creeps across it.

■ A detector that sounds off if a criminal so much as reaches out to touch a safe, file cabinet, or an electric junction box.

■ A "scream alarm" that goes off when a victim cries out.

And there's more, devices that sniff, and listen, and watch, and instantly report to the computer anything out of the ordinary.

Clever Crook vs. Computer

Now suppose that in spite of everything, the world's craftiest criminal has penetrated the heart of your JC/80 protected building. His hand reaches out for a bracelet or valuable document. A sensor notes this movement. It signals the JC/80 computer. You'd expect an alarm to sound. But what happens is much, much more.

The JC/80 explodes into action! It drops the building maintenance schedule it has been dictating, flashes a light, and rings a bell to alarm the guard on duty. It immediately projects a floor plan of the penetrated area onto an illuminated screen, tells the guard what's happened and where. At the same time, from dozens of contingency plans stored in its memory, the JC/80 produces the one right plan to deal with the situation at hand.

It may turn on lights in the penetrated area, lock all doors to prevent escape, zoom in on the intruder with closed circuit TV. It may call the police automatically. It may send elevators to the ground floor for security guard use. It may broadcast prerecorded orders to all building and security personnel, telling them what's happened, where to go, what to do, what to watch out for. If the criminal makes a break for it, they won't even have to hunt him down. The computer will "track" his flight through the building and type out a running report of the action.

streets," says Jane Jacobs, "or people fear it has, which comes to much the same thing in the end."[46] Some people will never feel safe, she admits, no matter what the objective circumstances, but that is a different matter from the fear experienced by "normally prudent, tolerant, and cheerful people who show nothing more than common sense in refusing to venture after dark—or in a few places, by day—into streets where they may well be assaulted, unseen or unrescued until too late."[47] The first thing to understand about cities, Jacobs says, is that peace in public places is maintained only in part by the police. Of much greater importance is the intricate, almost unconscious, network of voluntary controls and standards enforced by the people themselves. Enforcement by the people of the community arises only under certain conditions, however—and in many cities these conditions are lacking. If city streets are to be safe, they must have a clear demarcation between public and private space, and they must be thronged with people who provide the necessary watchful eyes. If streets are deserted, they become a stage for crimes that none will see or hear.

As Jacobs points out, however, one can't make people use streets when they have no reason to do so. "The safety of the street works best, most casually, and with least frequent taint of hostility or suspicion," she argues, "precisely where people are using and most enjoying the city streets voluntarily and are least conscious, normally, that they are policing."[48] The best way to achieve this is to have a substantial quantity of shops and public places sprinkled along the sidewalks of a district, particularly places that will be used in the evening and at night, such as stores, bars, and restaurants. The North End of Boston is an outstanding example, for there—in a relatively poor, crowded area—the streets are constantly used by a great variety of people who have come to shop or to stroll, and the crime rate is extremely low. Watchfulness arises spontaneously from the flow of community activities and serves as an effective curb on criminal behavior.

Oscar Newman has applied much the same argument to the analysis of urban housing. In many cities, says Newman, families are trapped in high-rise buildings, and criminals find it easy to roam the elevators, fire stairs, hallways, and roofs. Going from the street to one's apartment is equivalent to running the gauntlet. Attempts to provide security by means of a guard or doorman restrict entry to a single location, thus removing thousands of feet of street from all forms of social and visual contact. "The fear and uncertainty generated by living in such an envi-

---

[46] *The Death and Life of Great American Cities* (New York: Random House, 1961), p. 30.
[47] Ibid., pp. 30–31.
[48] Ibid., p. 36.

ronment can slowly eat away and eventually destroy the security and sanctity of the apartment unit itself."[49]

Residential environments need to provide defensible space, Newman argues, "which inhibits crime by creating the physical expression of a social fabric that defends itself."[50] The way to achieve this is through better architectural design that will influence the nature of the social relationships to be found in the community. "By grouping dwelling units to reinforce associations of mutual benefit; by delineating paths of movement; by defining areas of activity for particular users through their juxtaposition with internal living areas; and by providing for natural opportunities for visual surveillance, architects can create a clear understanding of the function of a space, and who its users are and ought to be. This, in turn, can lead residents of all income levels to adopt extremely potent territorial attitudes and policing measures, which act as strong deterrents to potential criminals."[51]

Clear demarcation of the area belonging to the residents, a smaller number of families sharing a building and an entry so that they can more easily learn to recognize one another, shared outside play and sitting areas to decrease social isolation, the design of lobbies, halls, elevators, and fire stairs so that intruders can be readily detected—all of these can encourage the creation of a self-regulating community rather than an anonymous mass that places the task of policing in the hands of others. "For one group to be able to set the norms of behavior and the nature of activity possible within a particular place," Newman points out, "it is necessary that it have clear, unquestionable control over what can occur there. Design can make it possible for both inhabitant and stranger to perceive that an area is under the undisputed influence of a particular group, that they dictate the activity taking place within it, and who its users are to be. This can be made so clearly evident that residents will not only feel confident, but that it is incumbent upon them to question the comings and goings of the people to insure the continued safety of the defined areas. Any intruder will be made to anticipate that his presence will be under question and open to challenge; so much so that a criminal can be deterred from even contemplating entry."[52]

An indifference to such principles in the construction of high-rise, elevator-serviced, double-loaded corridor apartment buildings for the use of low-income families has proven disastrous. An example is the Pruitt-Igoe housing development in St. Louis, Missouri, built in 1955, with 2764 apartments in thirty-three buildings eleven stories tall, set in

[49] Newman, *Defensible Space*, p. 3.
[50] Ibid., p. 3.
[51] Ibid., pp. 3–4.
[52] Ibid., pp. 2–3.

The first thing to understand about cities, Jane Jacobs says, is that peace in public places is maintained only in part by the police. Of much greater importance is the intricate, almost unconscious network of voluntary controls enforced by the people themselves. Such enforcement, however, arises only under certain conditions. City streets must have a clear demarcation between public and private space, and they must be thronged with people who provide the necessary watchful eyes. Deserted areas become a stage for crimes that none will see or hear.

dangerous isolation. Constant vandalism, a vacancy rate of 70 percent, and high crime rates produced a growing disenchantment with the project. Pruitt-Igoe, built at a cost of $26 million, was demolished in 1973.[53]

The emphasis on physical aspects of the urban environment as a major factor in the prevention of crime represents a significant shift in public policy. Instead of seeking to modify the internal characteristics of the criminal or potential criminal, this approach puts the stress on changing external, objective conditions. This philosophical shift can be found in other areas as well. Efforts to lower the automobile accident rate, for example, have begun to concentrate on the redesign of automobiles and highways rather than programs to improve the driver's habits and skills. Attempts to protect the consumer from exploitative contracts have increasingly involved a concern with details of the Commercial Code and the standardization of contract forms, with less attention paid to making the consumer more knowledgeable. A growing awareness of how difficult it is to change people's attitudes, beliefs, and motives has undoubtedly contributed to this change in the focus of concern, both in these areas and in the area of criminal behavior.[54]

Future Trends

What will be the future course of crime in the United States? Social scientists—including criminologists—have paid little attention to this issue.[55] Futurism has its critics, of course, and it is true that the year 2000 and beyond remains a fan-like array of possibilities—in the words of the futurologist Bertrand de Jouvenel—rather than a predictable sequence of events.[56] Exploring these possibilities is a worthwhile enterprise, nonetheless, for it allows us to see some of the implications of various social

[53] See Lee Rainwater, "Fear and the House-as-Haven in the Lower Class," *Journal of the American Institute of Planners* 32 (January 1966), pp. 23–37.

[54] See, for example, Amitai Etzioni, "Human Beings Are Not Very Easy to Change After All," *Saturday Review* (June 3, 1972).

[55] See, however, Joseph F. Coates, "The Future of Crime in the United States from Now to the Year 2000," *Policy Sciences* 3 (March 1972), pp. 27–45; Leslie T. Wilkins, "Crime and Criminal Justice at the Turn of the Century," *The Annals of the American Academy of Political and Social Science* 408 (July 1973), pp. 13–29; Sheldon L. Messinger, "The Year 2000 and the Problem of Criminal Justice." Paper delivered at Conference on Criminal Justice sponsored by the Center for the Study of Democratic Institutions and the Center for Studies in Criminal Justice, Chicago (June 24, 1973); Gresham M. Sykes, "The Future of Criminality," *American Behavioral Scientist* 15 (January–February 1972), pp. 403–19; and Laurin A. Wollan, Jr., "Coping with Crime in Tomorrow's Society," *The Futurist* 10 (June 1976), pp. 124–34.

[56] See Robert A. Nisbet, "The Year 2000 and All That," *Commentary* (June 1968), pp. 60–66; see also Dennis H. Wrong, "On Thinking About the Future," *The American Sociologist* 9 (February 1974), pp. 26–31.

policies, and it may reveal some of the early warning signs of impending changes. Present approaches to the problem of crime may persist into the future—with the advocates of different policies more or less maintaining their present relative strength. On the whole, however, this appears highly unlikely, for both the problem of crime and its perceived solution are almost certain to change in years ahead. In previous chapters we have seen again and again that crime and reactions to crime are largely a product of the structure of society—and there are few social commentators who can foresee anything other than accelerating change in that structure between now and the year 2000 and beyond.

The crime rate showed some signs of decline in 1976 and 1977, but social forces likely to produce crime, such as social alienation and anomie, may increase in the next several decades, and crime rates may continue their upward climb. A resurgence of social turmoil, for example, triggered by a decline in economic growth and an increasingly bitter conflict over a shrinking stock of material rewards, is envisioned by a number of analysts as an ominous possibility.[57] The loss of public control over government agencies such as the FBI and the CIA, adumbrated by the events of the Watergate break-in and subsequent disclosures, may become even more extensive, leading to a level of governmental lawlessness far more threatening than the street crime that now occupies much of the public's attention. Individuals may increasingly engage in crime as a form of sport, breaking the law "for fun" or for the sake of adventure in a world that has grown ever more routinized and bureaucratized.[58] American society may witness a large increase in what can be called "urban piracy," with poverty-stricken slum dwellers raiding the affluent suburbs and then returning to the refuge of the central city.

On the other hand, a change in the age structure is likely to reduce the crime rate. "Age cohort patterns are a most important factor in the unfolding patterns of crime," noted Joseph Coates in 1972. "It is generally recognized that the age group 16-to-24 is the most crime-prone in the United States: In 1968 there were 2,800,000 serious crimes committed by people under age 24, whereas those between 25 and 44 committed only 1,800,000 crimes. Now the nation is virtually at the peak of the post-World War II baby boom's move to young manhood. The veterans returning in 1946 and marrying and starting their families produced a bulge in the population distribution which year-by-year moves through the population age distribution. That observation, when coupled with the fact that birth rates are now lower than at any time since the Great

[57] See, for example, Robert L. Heilbroner, *An Inquiry into the Human Prospect* (New York: W. W. Norton, 1975).
[58] See Alvin Toffler, *Future Shock* (New York: Random House, 1970), pp. 255–57; see also Sykes, "The Future of Criminality."

Depression, suggests that over the next 25 years there will be a great diminution in the percent of population in this crime-prone age and, consequently, a real downturn in serious crime."[59]

Equally important, internal migration in the United States may continue at a high level in the next thirty years but show a marked change in character. In the past, a large share of migration has consisted of rural to urban moves in which uneducated and unskilled agricultural workers have been pushed off the land by mechanization and drawn to the city by occupational opportunities. In many instances the structure of the migrants' lives has collapsed under the strain of social change and poverty-stricken urban living conditions, with high crime rates a frequent result. With the great majority of the population now urbanized, much of the migration in the future may consist of city-to-city migration by families accustomed to urban living and with occupational skills suited to an industrial economy. The result may be a marked decrease in the influence of urbanization on crime rates, although the relationship between migration and crime awaits further examination.[60]

Changes in the major institutional areas of society are likely to have the most far-reaching influence on crime, however, and include changes in the structure of the community, the family, the educational system, the production and distribution of goods and services, the socioeconomic stratification system, and the system of political power. While sociological theory is still far from being able to make even the crudest predictions with regard to such matters (or, indeed, to find commonly accepted operational definitions of the variables involved), it still may be possible to come to a better understanding of the ways in which the major institutions of society change over time and how such changes are likely to affect the crime rate.

At least one important feature of community structure—namely, the spatial distribution of the population—is almost certain to be affected in the years ahead by the problem of finding adequate energy supplies. Efforts to reduce one of the most common forms of energy consumption—the use of automobiles to get to and from work—may involve not only new modes of transportation but also a shift in residence from the suburbs back to the city or an accelerating shift in offices, stores, and facto-

[59] See Joseph F. Coates, "The Future of Crime in the United States from Now to the Year 2000," p. 31. See also Bureau of the Census, *Current Population Reports*, Series P-25, No. 601, "Projections of the Population of the United States: 1975 to 2050" (Washington, D.C.: Government Printing Office, 1975).

[60] Illegal immigration to the United States, particularly from Mexico and the Caribbean, is seen by a number of writers as posing acute problems in coming decades. See John D. Huss and Melanie J. Wirken, "Illegal Immigration: The Hidden Population Bomb," *The Futurist* 11 (April 1977), pp. 114–24; and Department of Justice, Domestic Council Committee on Illegal Aliens, *Preliminary Report*, December 1976 (mimeographed).

ries from the metropolis to the suburbs. Whether society centralizes or decentralizes, it seems likely that crime rates would be affected, as new patterns of urban densities, social interaction among different social classes, and demands on city services are established.

In recent years, patterns of authority within the family, the definition of appropriate sex roles, and the economic status of women have all changed—and markedly, in some cases—and these changes are likely to continue. Although the proportion of women in the labor force may not keep climbing at the same rate, the proportion is likely to continue to increase, as are divorce rates, the level of schooling of women, the number of small families, and the number of the aged. Such changes suggest that both the form and content of socialization in the family may shift in the next several decades, particularly with regard to how children identify with parental figures, a process that has long been viewed as a key element in the inculcation of social norms. This is not to say that the process of socialization will be impaired—the evidence concerning caring for children outside the home, for example, indicates that it neither harms nor helps.[61] The process of socialization is likely to be modified, nevertheless, and the possible impact on various forms of behavior, crime included, warrants study.

Of the many current debates concerning schooling in America, the arguments about the proper link between education and jobs may be most relevant to the incidence of criminal behavior. Many criminologists are willing to argue that while the causal connections between employment and crime are far from clear, it is difficult to imagine a successful program for the reduction of crime that does not take into account the need for jobs to provide a decent level of economic security and psychological satisfaction.[62] The ability of the educational system to provide the appropriate training for available jobs and to insure equality of educational opportunity appears to be a major factor in the future direction of the crime rate, particularly among juveniles.

Changes in the production and distribution of goods and services—and in the class system—will undoubtedly be of prime importance. If the scramble for material rewards in American society is intensified, as Heilbronner and others have claimed is likely, and class antagonisms as well as racial conflicts are sharpened rather than reduced, the crime attribut-

[61] See "Good Day Care: Does It Affect Children?" *Carnegie Quarterly* 24 (Summer 1976), p. 3.

[62] See, for example, Harvey Brenner, *Paper No. 5. Estimating the Social Costs of National Economic Policy: Implications for Mental and Physical Health, and Criminal Aggression.* A Study Prepared for the Use of the Joint Economic Committee, Congress of the United States (Washington, D. C.: Government Printing Office, 1976). The contention about the lack of any clear relationship between crime and economic conditions, long accepted in criminology (see pp. 252–53), is apparently due for an extensive, systematic reexamination.

able to alienation and anomie can be expected to increase. And beyond this—which is, after all, a struggle for a larger share of the pie within a framework of a more-or-less accepted socioeconomic system—we may see a rise in the level of discontent with the system itself and in pressures to abolish all forms of second-class citizenship. Whether demands for a more egalitarian society would result in more or less crime is problematical—as is the nature of society's response to such demands. What is likely, however, is that to an increasing extent in the years ahead the inequalities of American society will be used to justify a variety of crimes and that changes in the class structure will be reflected in a rise or fall of the crime rate. If, for example, an increasingly technological society finds it ever more difficult to use and reward unskilled individuals with little education, the result may be a sharply divided society with a lumpen proletariat that finds crime a welcome alternative to a world without hope.[63] A permanent criminal class may arise to prey on the well-to-do, who can be envied but never joined. A similar problem may be posed by the promise—or threat—of automation for workers on the higher ranges of the occupational ladder who will find bored affluence an easy road to deviance. (The idea that the Devil finds work for idle hands has a singular persistence—perhaps in part because the experience of each generation seems to verify it anew.)

At least two opposing possibilities are evident with regard to the organization of state power. The system of government in the United States might become more democratic, with greater participation at the local level in a variety of voluntary associations, neighborhood organizations, and the like; or power might become more centralized in the hands of an entrenched oligarchy. While the centralization of political power may be linked to the extent of criminality, there has been little explicit theorizing to join the two—unless one assumes that a more democratic society entails a movement toward socialism and that Bonger's views are applicable (see Chapter 7). The extent to which political power is concentrated in the hands of a few does seem to be related to *reactions* to crime, however, if not to the causes of crime. The legal rights of criminal defendants are apt to be whittled away, it can be hypothesized, as a strong, centralized government authority enlarges the scope of police activity in the suppression of dissident thought as well as the control of deviant action.

For some commentators, the development of an oppressive police state in the American capitalist social order is seen as assured.[64] These argu-

---

[63] See Sidney M. Wilhelm, *Who Needs the Negro?* (Cambridge, Mass.: Schenkman, 1970).

[64] See, for example, Stanley Aronowitz, "Law, The Breakdown of Order, and Revolution," in Richard Quinney, ed., *Criminal Justice in America* (Boston: Little, Brown, 1974), pp. 394–414; and Barry Krisberg, *Crime and Privilege: Toward a New Criminology* (Englewood Cliffs, N.J.: Prentice-Hall, 1975).

ments, part of a larger debate about the nature of American society and its probable future, carry us beyond the scope of the present work. (In general, American social science, including criminology, has been reluctant to accept the idea of inevitable lines of social development.) Nevertheless, the possibility that a changed political structure might use a war against crime as a disguise for ensuring political control is likely to serve as a major focus of concern in coming decades.

Conclusions

The extent to which criminology should aid in the development of more effective means of reducing crime is a matter of some dispute. Some criminologists take the position that such efforts are simply one more tactic of oppression by a capitalist social order. The field of criminology, says Barry Krisberg, "has prostituted itself in serving law enforcement and criminal justice agencies. Criminological theory has fostered and disseminated the hegemonic concepts of the ruling class, and empirical criminological studies have often supplied the technology of social control that has been employed in both domestic and foreign spheres."[65] Criminology, it is argued, must work for far more radical change, for nothing less can cure society's ills.[66]

Other writers, working within a framework of more conventional criminology, view such accusations as a gross distortion. Crime, they point out, is a very real threat (particularly for the poor and members of minority groups), and criminology should aid in the task of restraining it within the democratic structure of American society. The idea that law enforcement is an act of political repression is nonsense.

The argument has been strident on occasion and the issues have been presented in exaggerated terms, but this does not mean that the debate is pointless. The use of the social sciences by the government poses complex ethical problems, and these problems become particularly acute in the area of crime. It seems likely, however, that the majority of scholars working in the field of criminology believe that their discipline is capable of producing knowledge that can help to make the control of crime both humane and effective. By insisting that the content of the criminal law and its relationship to society be continually reexamined, criminol-

[65] *Crime and Privilege*, p. 16. Krisberg cites the work of Morris Janowitz, *The Social Control of Escalated Riots* (Chicago: University of Chicago Press, 1968) and Ralph Schwitzgebel, *Development and Legal Regulation of Coercive Behavior Modification Techniques with Offenders* (Rockville, Md.: National Institute of Mental Health Service Publication No. 2067, 1971).
[66] See, for example, Aronowitz, "Law, The Breakdown of Order, and Revolution, pp. 394–414.

ogy can aid in the attempt to distinguish dangerous behavior from deviant activity that can safely be tolerated. By analyzing the intricate causes of crime at both the social and the individual level, criminology can help to lay bare the prejudices and easy assumptions that frequently convert the label "criminal" into a misleading term. By showing how the police and the courts function, criminology can contribute to a clearer understanding of the contradictions and difficulties of existing methods of law enforcement. And by examining current trends in attempts to reduce crime, criminology can help to underscore the constant problem of finding ways to reduce crime that stay within a framework of justice.

Criminology, in short, is more than a scientific study of behavior characterized as crime by the law. It also involves a critical review of the categories established by the law, a close attention to the values underlying social behavior, and an on-going debate about the discrepancy between what society does do and what it should do. It is in this sense that criminology can be seen as caught in an endless conflict between the goal of scientific objectivity and a passion for justice. The conflict is not to be resolved, for it is the tension between these elements that provides criminology with a promise of continuing vitality.

Recommended Readings

A cogent—and controversial—presentation of many of the issues now being discussed in the handling of the criminal is found in James Q. Wilson, *Thinking About Crime* (New York: Basic Books, 1975). For the argument that society might do less rather than more in reacting to the delinquent, the reader should see Edwin M. Schur, *Radical Non-Intervention: Rethinking the Delinquency Problem* (Englewood Cliffs, N.J.: Prentice-Hall, 1973) and Herbert L. Packer, *The Limits of the Criminal Sanction* (Stanford, Calif.: Stanford University Press, 1968). An important discussion of how society, using improved community design rather than techniques for rehabilitating the offender, might deal with so-called predatory crime is found in Oscar Newman, *Defensible Space* (New York: Collier Books, 1973). For an attempt to glimpse the future of crime, the reader should see Joseph F. Coates, "The Future of Crime in the United States from Now to the Year 2000," *Policy Sciences* 3 (March 1972), pp. 27–45.

Copyrights and Acknowledgments

Picture Credits

p. 2, Joan Sydlow/Editorial Photocolor Archives

p. 24, top, United Press International; bottom, Martin Dain/Magnum

p. 25, top left, Leonard Freed/Magnum; top right, Mary Ellen Mark; bottom, Cornell Capa/Magnum

p. 52, The Bettmann Archive

p. 53, top, Brown Brothers; bottom, Ellis Herwig/Stock, Boston

p. 82, Ian Berry/Magnum

p. 110, Leonard Freed/Magnum

p. 111, top and bottom, Ken Karp

p. 146, Burt Glinn/Magnum

p. 147, top, John Blair/Black Star; bottom, Neal Boenzi/The New York Times

p. 182, top, George Silk/Life Magazine © Time Inc.; bottom, Brown Brothers

p. 183, top, Museum of Modern Art/Film Stills Archive

p. 218, Claus Meyer/Black Star

p. 219, top, Will McBride/Black Star; bottom, Dennis Brack/Black Star

p. 234, Charles Gatewood

p. 276, Danny Lyon/Magnum

p. 277, top, Michael Abramson; bottom, Jean-Pierre Laffont

p. 300, The Bettmann Archive

p. 301, top, Bob Adelman/Magnum; bottom, Charles Moore/Black Star

p. 322, Bob Adelman/Magnum

pp. 346 and 347, Mary Ellen Mark/Magnum

p. 374, top, Charles Gatewood; bottom, Martin Dain/Magnum

p. 375, top left, Los Angeles County Sheriff's Department; top right, Sepp Seitz/Magnum; middle, David Moore/Black Star; bottom, Charles Gatewood

pp. 422 and 423, Museum of Modern Art/Film Stills Archive

p. 452, Museum of Modern Art/Film Stills Archive

p. 478, Brown Brothers

p. 479, top and bottom left, Brown Brothers; bottom right, Vernon Merritt/Black Star

p. 506, top, Charles Harbutt/Magnum; middle and bottom, Danny Lyon/Magnum

p. 507, top, George L. Walker/Black Star; middle, Los Angeles County Sheriff's Department; bottom, R. Benyas/Black Star

pp. 558 and 559, Gilles Peress/Magnum

p. 606, top, Lida Moser/Black Star; bottom, Ken Karp

p. 607, top left and right, Ken Karp; bottom, Judy Swulius/Black Star

616

Name Index

Newman, Donald J., 73n, 352n, 354n, 359n, 360, 362n
Newman, Oscar, 601, 604, 614
Newton, Huey, 501
Niederhoffer, Arthur, 370, 379n, 384, 389n, 392n, 403
Nisbet, Robert A., 128n, 172n, 181n, 185n, 217n, 293, 608n
Nolde, Hans C., 36n
Normandeau, A., 74n

O'Donnell, John A., 176
O'Dwyer, William, 193n
Oelsner, Lesley, 359n
Ohlin, Lloyd, 244n, 283, 500n, 555n, 563
O'Meara, Joseph, 363
O'Neill, Gerard K., 540n
Opton, Edward M., Jr., 579
Orwell, George, 22n
Osborne, Thomas Mott, 516
O'Toole, Richard, 293n
Owens, Maurice E. B., III, 77n

Packer, Herbert L., 345n, 493, 594n, 614
Pallas, John, 537
Palmer, John W., 596n, 597
Palmer, Ted, 514n
Paolucci, Henry, 9n, 40
Pappenfort, Donald M., 555n
Park, Robert E., 79
Parks, Evelyn, 400n
Parsons, H. M., 573n
Parsons, James B., 102
Parsons, M. T., 573n
Parsons, Talcott, 244n, 257, 310n, 518n
Pate, Tony, 590n
Paulsen, Monrad G., 448n
Pearson, Geoff, 16n
Peel, Sir Robert, 68, 369
Penick, Betty K. Eidson, 77n
Perkins, Rollin M., 63n, 65, 131n, 132n, 171n
Perkus, Cathy, 225n, 229
Persow, Charles, 531n
Petersilia, Joan, 590n
Peterson, David M., 502n, 524n
Peterson, Virgil W., 190
Piliavin, Irving, 292n, 302–03
Pincoffs, Edmund L., 481n
Pittman, David J., 187
Piven, Herman, 555n
Platt, Anthony M., 15, 55, 230, 340n, 400n, 401n, 403, 445, 451

Ploscowe, Morris, 189, 191
Plucknett, Theodore F. T., 44n
Polanski, N. A., 516n
Polanyi, Karl, 248
Pollner, Melvin, 306n
Pomeroy, Wardell B., 172n
Porterfield, Austen, 148
Pound, Roscoe, 121
Powers, Sanger B., 336n
Prat, Thomas Brian, 311n
Prendergast, William B., 212n
President's Commission on Law Enforcement and Administration of Justice, 23n, 26n, 104, 105, 114n, 115n, 120n, 126, 144, 164, 171, 186n, 190, 201, 368n, 472n, 503n, 504n
Price, Hugh B., 600n
Pringle, Patrick, 368n
Proal, Louis, 220
Puttkammer, Ernest W., 354n

Queen, Stuart, 250n
Quennel, Peter, 112n
Quinney, Richard, 18n, 29n, 40, 51, 100, 208n, 212n, 215, 216, 217, 220n, 221n, 231, 233, 399–400, 402, 445n, 586n, 612n

Raab, Selwyn, 477n
Radcliffe-Brown, A. R., 461n
Radin, Max, 32, 461n
Radzinowicz, Leon, 465n, 119n, 252n, 440n, 451, 460n, 465n, 540n, 567n
Rainwater, Lee, 253, 608n
Rankin, Anne, 338n, 339n
Ransford, H. Edward, 158n
Ranulf, Svend, 482, 483
Ray, Isaac, 11
Reasons, Charles E., 17n, 441n
Reckless, Walter C, 311, 312n
Reich, Charles A., 121, 123, 388n
Reid, John F., 349, 350, 351n
Reik, Theodor, 191
Reimer, Hans, 499
Reiss, Albert J., 18n, 76n, 97, 278, 292n, 311, 330n, 379n, 385
Remington, Frank J., 334
Renfrew, Charles B., 102
Repetto, T. A., 600n
Restack, Richard, 572n
Retsky, Harold G., 518n
Reuss-Ianni, Elizabeth, 206
Rhead, Clifton, 380n
Rhodes, Albert Lewis, 278

Rice, Kent, 253n
Richards, T. W., 295
Rieff, Philip, 569n
Riesman, David, 34n, 87n
Robinson, James, 513
Robinson, James O., 490n
Robinson, William S., 97
Robson, L. L., 466n
Rodell, Fred, 168
Roebuck, Julian, 529
Rogers, A. J., III, 27n
Rogers, Joseph W., 307n, 308n, 311n
Rolf, C. H., 485n
Romilly, Sir Samuel, 10
Rose, Arnold, 55n
Rosen, Lawrence, 255n
Rosenberg, Bernard, 241n
Rosenberg, Maurice, 412n
Rosett, Arthur, 27n, 358n, 364
Ross, Edward Alsworth, 87, 129, 290
Ross, H. Laurence, 122, 123n, 487n
Rossi, Peter H., 74n
Rothman, David J., 8n, 10n, 243n, 468, 469, 496, 549, 550
Rottenberg, Simon, 282n
Rowan, Charles, 377
Rubin, Jerry, 437
Rubington, Earl, 30, 311n
Rubinstein, Jonathan, 331, 376n, 380n, 388, 397n, 398n
Rudoff, Alvin, 512
Rudwick, Elliott, 155n
Rusche, Georg, 463, 464n, 466n, 470, 496
Rush, Benjamin, 541
Russell, Sir William, 211
Rustin, Bayard, 159n
Ruth, Henry S., Jr., 197
Ryan, William, 299n
Rycroft, Charles, 290n

Sage, Wayne, 425
Samenow, Stanton E., 38n
Savitz, Leonard D., 91
Scarpiti, Frank R., 567n
Schafer, Roy, 290n
Schafer, Stephen, 210, 220, 233
Scheckenbach, Albert F., 575
Schell, Jonathan, 224, 225
Schellhardt, Timothy D., 102n, 589n
Schelling, Thomas C., 194n
Schepses, Erwin, 91
Schmid, C. F., 252n

Subject Index

Individualistic theory of crime causation, 16
Individual violence. *See* Violence, individual
Industrialization, 248–50; and police, 367–69; and prison labor, 470
Information, 354–56
Infringement of patent rights, 97–98
Inmate code, 500–01, 527–30
Inmate cohesion, 500–01
Inmate militancy, effect of, 535–39
Inmate self-government, 516–17
Inmate social structure, 500–02, 526–30, 530–35; effect of ethnic militancy on, 535–39
Inmate solidarity, 529–30
Inmate wages, 508
Innovation, 266–67
Inquisitorial system, 407
Insanity, plea of, 68–71
Instructions to jury, 429–30
Insulin shock therapy, 571–72
Intelligence and crime, 13
"Intent-to-do-serious-bodily-harm murder," 132
"Intent-to-kill murder," 132
Interaction between criminal and victim as causal factor in crime, 93–94
Internalized norms and crime, 245–46
Interrogation, police, 345, 348–52
Irresistible impulse, 69

Jail, 335–36
Japanese-Americans and crime rates, 253
Judeo-Christian system of morals, 79
Judge, role of, 410–13
Judicial discretion, 338–39, 438, 440–41
Judicial reprieve, 547
Jury: composition of, 424–26; deliberations of, 431–33; effectiveness of, 428–29; as "jury of one's peers," 424; research on, 432–33; selection of, 421, 424–26
Just deserts, 481–82
Justice Department, 400
Juvenile court. *See* Court, juvenile
Juvenile delinquency, 67–68, 445–46
Juvenile rights, 446–49

Kefauver committee, 195–96
Kindred, 461–62
King, Martin Luther, Jr., 154
Knowledge and criminal intent, 61
Kulturkampf, 420

Labeling: and crime causation, 30, 247; and critical criminology, 16; and organizational demands, 304–05; and personal bias, 302–04; and secondary deviance, 297–99; theoretical criticisms of, 305–07
Larceny, 78, 86, 88–91; number known to police, 131
Law: administrative, 46; characteristics of, 43–44; civil, 46–48; forms of, 44–46; ignorance of, 63; in state and federal constitutions, 45–46; statutory, 45. *See also* Criminal law
Law and Society Association, 35
Law Enforcement Assistance Administration (LEAA), 26–27, 576
Law schools, 33
Lawyers: defense, 415–20; intellectual style of, 34–35
"Legalism," 230–32
Legal self-help, 49
Lex talionis, 461, 481–82
Lobotomy, 571
Lombroso, Cesare, 11–12
Lotteries, 190
Lower criminal court, 408

Machismo, 279–80
Mafia, 195–201, 203, 280
Mai Lai massacre, 66
Malloy *v.* Hogan, 348
Manhattan Bail Project, 339
Manslaughter, 132–33
Mapp *v.* Ohio, 342–43
Marijuana, 20, 178–80, 184–85, 292–93
Marx, Karl, 33, 50
Mass media, 22–23, 28
McCone Commission, 158
Medical model of crime, 568, 577
Mens rea, 47, 57–62, 70–71
Mental abnormality and crime, 13, 36–39, 68–71, 241–42
Migration and crime, 249–50, 610
Milieu therapy, 512–13
Miranda *v.* Arizona, 348–52
Misdemeanors, 71–75, 352

Misrepresentation in advertising, 97–98
Mistake of fact, 63–64
M'Naghten Rules, 68–69
Model Penal Code, 45, 489, 561
Modernization and crime, 257–58, 261
Monopolies, 100–01, 103
Morissette *v.* United States, 58
Motivation of public officials dealing with crime, 16–17
Moynihan Report, 253
Murder, 78, 131–35

Napoleonic Code, 44
Narcotics. *See* Drugs, opiate
National Advisory Commission on Civil Disorders, 154–55, 158
National Commission on Civil Disorders, 154–55, 400
National Commission on the Causes and Prevention of Violence, 154–55, 157, 400
National Crime Information Center, 91
National Opinion Research Center (NORC), victim survey of, 76
Nazi Germany, 483
Negligence, 61
Negotiated outcomes, 302–05
Negotiated plea. *See* Plea bargaining
Neighborhood approach to control of police, 394–95
Neutralization, techniques of, 307–11
New York City: police department, 366; riots in, 369
New York State, drug laws of, 591
Nineteenth century, criminology in, 10–12
Nixon administration, 224–25, 356–57
Nolo contendere, 358
Nonconforming behavior, 216–17
Nonintervention, 593–600
Norman Conquest, 44, 167, 368, 421, 462
Northeastern states, crimes against the person in, 149
Norway, and experience with diversion, 599
Numbers game, 191–93
Nuremburg trials of war criminals, 66

Rationalization of motives, 105, 307–11
Ray, Isaac, 11
Reasonable doubt, 47, 64, 430
Reasonable man, 63–64
Rebellion, 266–67
Receiving stolen goods, 120
Recidivism, 477, 511–14, 561–68; prediction of, 563–64
Recklessness, 61
Recognizance, 547
Reducing criminal opportunity, 600–01, 604–05, 608
Reformation. *See* Rehabilitation
Reformatory movement, 470–72
Regional traditions as causes of crime, 148
Rehabilitation, 454–55, 493–95; ideal of, 459–60; new techniques of, 571–73, 575–81; in prison, 509–14
Religious oaths as form of trial, 406
Restraint of trade, 97–98, 103
Retreatism, 266–67
Retribution, 458–59, 481–82
Riots, 129, 154–55, 158–59
Ritualism, 266–67
Robbery, 78, 86, 88, 94–96; number known to police, 131
"Rockefeller laws" on drugs, 591
Romilly, Sir Samuel, 10
Rorschach test, 170
Russell Sage Foundation, 35

San Francisco police department, 392–93
Scientific ethos, 34
Searches, 340–45
Sedition, 210–11
Self-concept, 311–13
Self-defense, 64–65
Self-incrimination, 345, 348–52
Senate Crime Investigating Committee, 195–96
Senate Subcommittee on Criminal Laws and Procedures, 40
Sentences: inconsistency of, 440–41; indeterminate, 442–43, 471; mandatory, 438
Sentencing, 438, 440–43
Sexual norms, 167–69
Sexual offenses, 165, 167–74
Sexual psychopath laws, 170
Sheriffs, 368
Shoplifting, 89–90, 103–04
Simon, Theodor, 13

Sixth Amendment, 348, 356
Social activism, 35–36
Social class. *See* Social stratification
Social contract, 20
Social disorganization and crime, 248–57
Socialism and crime, 259–60
Socialization, 249–50
Social mobility and organized crime, 203
Social norms and crime, 245–46
Social-psychological theories of crime causation, 318–32
Social psychology, 38, 285
Social sciences and jury selection, 425–26
Social stratification, 18–19; and crime, 96–99, 159–61, 229–30, 252, 254, 256–57, 611–12. *See also* Criminal law
Social structure: and crime, 244–45, 257–68; and punishment, 461–74, 476–80, 482–84. *See also* Prisons, inmate social structure of
Social work in probation and parole, 556–57, 560–61
Sociological perspective on causes of crime, 13, 28–31, 36–39, 236–37, 243–48, 281–83
Sociologists, intellectual style of, 34
Sociology, criticisms of, 14–16
Solidarity of inmates, 500–01
Southern states, crimes against the person in, 149
Soviet bloc, police of, 401
Specific deterrence. *See* Deterrence, specific
Specificity of law, 43
Stability of law, 43
Stare decisis, 45
Status quo, maintenance of, 18–20
Statutory rape, 138
Strict liability, 61–62
Structure of courts, 409–10
Subculture: delinquent, 271–74, 278, 294; of violence, 278–81
Suicide, 154
Suspicion, and occupational personality of police, 380–81, 384
Symbolic interactionism, 285–87, 290–97

Tarde, Gabriel, 11
Techniques of neutralization, 307–11
Theft. *See* Larceny

Thematic Apperception Test, 170
Therapeutic state, 546–47, 568–70
Thief subculture, 529
"Third degree," 349
Ticket-of-leave system, 549
Tithings, 368
Tocqueville, Alexis de, 128, 411, 469, 568–69
Torts, 46–48
Torture, 9
Touchiness, and occupational personality of police, 385–86
Traffic accidents, 154
Transferred intent, 61
Transportation of criminals, 466–67, 549
Treason, 72, 210–11, 464
Treatment in the community, 474, 476
Trial, criminal, 420–21, 424–30; cross-examination in, 426–27; and evidence, hearsay, 427; and evidence, presentation of, 426–29; and "jury of one's peers," 424; and jury selection, 421–26; as *Kulturkampf*, 420; privileged communication in, 427; and *voir dire*, 421, 424–26
Trial, political, 435–37
Trial by battle, 406
Trial calendar, 411–12
Trials: accusatory system of, 406–07; adversarial system of, 406–09; inquisitorial system of, 407
True bill, 355
Twentieth century, criminology in, 13–14, 16–22
Twin studies in genetic theory of crime, 241

Unemployment: and crime, 253–56; and prison commitment rate, 443
Uniform Crime Reports, 18, 75–79, 145
U.S. Constitution, 45–46; Eighteenth Amendment to, 185, 201–02, 204, 341; Eighth Amendment to, 187, 336, 341; Fifth Amendment to, 345, 348–52, 427, 433; Fourteenth Amendment to, 187, 448; Fourth Amendment to, 341; Sixth Amendment to, 348, 356
U.S. Supreme Court, 213–14, 325, 328, 345, 348–52